Labouring the Canadian Millennium

Writings on Work and Workers, History and Historiography

Bryan D. Palmer

Editor

Canadian Committee on Labour History
St. John's, Newfoundland

The Canadian Committee on Labour History and the editor gratefully acknowledge the generous support of the Faculty of Arts of the Memorial University of Newfoundland. / Le Comité canadien sur l'histoire du travail et l'éditeur remercient chaleureusement la Faculté des Arts de la Memorial University de Terre-Neuve de leur généreuse contribution.

Canadian Committee on Labour History
Arts Publications, FM2005
Memorial University of Newfoundland
St. John's, NF A1C 5S7 CANADA

Manuscript was prepared for the printer by the staff of the Canadian Committee on Labour History.

Cover Illustration: "Approaching the Millennium," by Ellison Robertson
Cover Design: Helen Houston

Printed and bound in Canada

Canadian Cataloguing in Publication Data

Main entry under title:
    Labouring the Canadian millennium: writings on work and workers, history and historiography

ISBN 1-894000-04-8

1. Labor—Canada—History. 2. Labor movement—Canada—History. 3. Working class—Canada—History. 4. Labor—Canada—Historiography. 5. Labor movement—Canada—Historiography. 6. Working class—Canada—Historiography. I. Palmer, Bryan D., 1951-. II. Canadian Committee on Labour History.

HD8106.5.L34 2000   331'.0971   C00-901586-8

The National Question

Cultures

Abstracts / Résumés / 471

CONTENTS

CONTRIBUTORS / COLLABORATEURS

Cynthia Comacchio teaches at Wilfrid Laurier University and is currently working on a sociocultural history of adolescence in English Canada during the first half of the 20th century.

David Frank teaches Canadian history at the University of New Brunswick, where he is also editor of *Acadiensis*. His teaching includes a course entitled Canadian History on Film. He recently published *J.B. McLachlan: A Biography*.

Judy Fudge teaches employment and labour law at Osgoode Hall Law School. With Eric Tucker, she has recently completed *Labour Before the Law: Workers' Collective Action and the State in Canada, 1900 to 1948*. She is especially interested in the legal regulation of women's work.

Anthony Giles teaches industrial relations at Université Laval. Besides an abiding interest in IR theory and comparative and international IR, his current obsession is with globalization, work reorganization and the management of work in transnational corporations.

Ralph P. Güntzel teaches history and Canadian Studies at Franklin College of Indiana and is working on a book on Québec labour and sovereigntism.

Michiel Horn is professor of history at Glendon College of York University. A former president of the York University Faculty Association and the Ontario Confederation of University Faculty Associations, his most recent books are *Becoming Canadian: Memoirs of an Invisible Immigrant* and *Academic Freedom in Canada: A History*.

Ian McKay teaches history at Queen's University, Kingston.

Desmond Morton graduated from the Royal Military College (B.A., 1959), Oxford (B.A. Hon., 1961, M.A., 1966), and the London School of Economics, (Ph.D., 1968). In July 1994 he became founding director of the McGill Institute for the Study of Canada. Morton is the author of 36 books on Canadian political, military and industrial relations history, including *Working People: An Illustrated History of the Canadian Labour Movement*.

Becki L. Ross is jointly appointed in Women's Studies and Sociology at the University of British Columbia. Recent publications include articles in *The Journal of the History of Sexuality, Atlantis: A Women's Studies Journal,* and *Society and Space,* and a chapter in *Painting the Maple: Essays in Race, Gender, and the Construction of Canada.* She was named a "queer hero" in the June 29, 2000 edition of *Xtra-West* magazine. Her ongoing research into Vancouver's history of erotic entertainment was recently deemed internationally newsworthy.

Jacques Rouillard est professeur au département d'histoire de l'Université de Montréal. Spécialisé en histoire des travailleurs, il a publié de nombreux ouvrages dont une histoire du syndicalisme québécois.

Joan Sangster teaches history and is Director of the Frost Centre for graduate work in Canadian Studies and Native Studies at Trent University, Peterborough. Her latest book was *Earning Respect: the Lives of Working Women in Small-town Ontario, 1920-60,* and she is currently writing about girls and women in conflict with the law.

Murray E.G. Smith is Associate Professor of Sociology at Brock University, St. Catharines, Ontario. He is the author of *Invisible Leviathan: The Marxist Critique of Market Despotism beyond Postmodernism* and the editor of *Early Modern Social Theory: Selected Interpretive Readings.*

Eric Tucker teaches law at York University and writes in the areas of occupational health and safety regulation and labour law. He is the co-author, with Judy Fudge, of a forthcoming book, *Labour Before the Law: Workers' Collective Action and the Canadian State, 1900-1948.*

INTRODUCTION

Labour Confronts the Millennium

Bryan D. Palmer

WE TAKE OUR THEME and our title for this special collection of essays from Ellison Robertson's painting, which adorns our cover. "Labouring the Millennium," pre-pared by Robertson in July 2000 at the request of *Labour/Le Travail*, offers an artistic representation of the possibilities present as the working-class and its movements enter a new historical period. It also illustrates some of the constraints that will loom, threatening and large, as labour struggles to have its varied voices heard and its complexly diverse agendas recognized into the 21st century.

Labour/Le Travail wanted to mark the millennium in some way. We have opted to present a collection of commissioned essays that are purposively eclectic, but that address themes of importance in understanding labour's significance and history over the course of the last century, as well as suggesting how labour will inevitably face changing circumstances. It was critical to have statements from varied quarters, and to continue our longstanding project of both continuing to address *traditional* themes of union organizing and the politics of labour, as well as striking out in bold *innovative* efforts to rechart and reconceptualize the meanings of work in our society. We felt it was our responsibility to provide historiographic summary as well as generate controversy, to address specific staples in the Canadian working-class experience, such as influential strikes, and to attempt to delineate new ways of seeing class as it has been lived on the ground and constructed by social commentators.

As a consequence we offer wide-ranging synthetic statements on working-class families and the critically important, but tension-ridden, relations of women, work, and union organization. But we present, as well, new views of particular sectors, such as one area of sex-trade labour, that intersect with this gender-based appreciation of labouring life. The potential present to represent workers and the dimensions of their formative cultural, political, and socio-economic being seems, with the technologies of the twenty-first century, to be prodigious. Film and video are demonstrable examples. But the freedom to express new visions is also clouded by constraints to intellectual openness, and the academic freedom of those who both support labour and work to have its causes appreciated and extended is not to be taken lightly given the history of limitation so evident over the last century.

To enter a new millennium is to appreciate that nothing is sacred. Socialism as a project and a centerpiece of working-class radicalism can never be an icon, but demands a vigilant interrogation as well as a staunch defence of its basic principles. Historiographic controversies central to the birth of this journal deserve rethinking in light of subsequent developments. Pivotal events, such as the Asbestos strike of 1949, benefit from fresh analysis, just as themes of ongoing relevance — from industrial relations and employment law to Quebec labour and the independence project — must never be allowed to grow stale because they are seemingly overexposed in the mundane mainstream culture of electronic and print reporting.

The following essays are presented in this spirit, a gift in the endeavour to create a more thinking millennium. Hopefully, it will be one less laboured in the ways of its predecessor, where exploitation and oppression often seemed to override the art of work, presented all too briefly here in an evocative photoessay on the memorabilia of labour and the left.

This journal was conceived more than twenty-five years ago in the spirit of recognizing and reversing the class inequalities and the blindspots of our age and of many previous historical epochs. Want and need always stalked the men, women, and children of the working class, while abundance and indulgence marked the privileged lives of those who owned and lived off a large piece of their varied productions. At some point in the next millennium, surely, this state of bedrock difference can be overcome. Our successors can then commission another Robertson-like representation, "Freeing the Millennium."

INTRODUCTION

Labour Confronts the Millennium

Bryan D. Palmer

Nous avons pris le thème et le titre de cette collection spéciale d'articles du tableau de Ellison Robertson dont la photo est en couverture. *Labouring the Millennium/Le Travail au prochain millénaire*, peint par Robertson en juillet 2000 à la demande de *Labour/Le Travail*, offre une représentation artistique des possibilités à mesure que la classe ouvrière et ses mouvements entrent dans une nouvelle période historique, ainsi que certaines des contraintes qui se dresseront menaçantes, à mesure que la classe ouvrière luttera pour se faire entendre et faire reconnaître ses programmes divers et complexes.

Labour/Le Travail a voulu marquer le millénaire d'une façon précise. Nous avons choisi de présenter une collection d'articles rédigés sur commande qui sont intentionnellement éclectiques, mais qui se basent sur des thèmes importants relatifs à l'histoire de la classe ouvrière au cours du dernier siècle et qui exposent en détail la façon dont la classe ouvrière devra faire face aux circonstances changeantes. Il était important de solliciter les opinions de tout le monde et de continuer notre projet à long terme : traiter les thèmes *traditionnels* de l'organisation syndicale et des politiques du travail, ainsi que faire de grands efforts *innovateurs* afin d'examiner et de reconceptualiser les significations du travail dans notre société. Nous avons pensé que c'était notre responsabilité de fournir un résumé historiographique ainsi que de provoquer les controverses, traiter les questions précises sur l'expérience de la classe ouvrière au Canada telles que les grèves importantes et d'essayer de trouver les moyens de montrer la vie de la classe ouvrière telle qu'elle est vue par les commentateurs de notre société.

En conséquence, nous offrons une gamme variée d'énoncés synthétiques sur les familles de la classe ouvrière et les relations importantes et intenses entre les femmes, le travail et l'organisation syndicale. Cependant, nous présentons également de nouveaux points de vue des secteurs particuliers tels que les travailleurs de l'industrie du sexe. La possibilité de représenter les travailleurs et travailleuses et les dimensions de leurs anté cé dents culturels, politiques, sociaux et économiques, semble sans limite grâce à la technologie avancée du vingt et unième siècle. Les films et les vidéos en sont de bons exemples. Toutefois, la liberté d'exprimer de nouvelles idées est embrouillée par les contraintes de l'ouverture d'esprit et celles de la liberté académique des défenseurs de la classe ouvrière qui aimeraient être appréciés contrairement à ce qui leur est arrivé au cours du dernier siècle.

Entrer dans un nouveau millénaire c'est apprécier que rien n'est sacré. Le socialisme en tant que projet et pièce de résistance du radicalisme de la classe ouvrière ne peut jamais être un icône, mais demande une interrogation vigilante ainsi qu' une défense féroce de ses principes de base. Les controverses historiographiques essentielles à la publication de ce journal méritent d'être prises en considération à la lumière des développements subséquents. Les événements importants, tels que la grève de l'amiante de 1949, bénéficieront d'une nouvelle analyse, comme les thèmes toujours pertinents — allant des relations industrielles et lois sur les normes d'emploi à la classe ouvrière et au projet de l'indépendance du Québec — ne doivent jamais être ignorés simplement parce qu'ils sont surutilisés dans les médias imprimés et électroniques de la culture du courant dominant.

Les articles contenus dans ce journal ont été rédigés dans cet esprit, visant à créer un nouveau millénaire de réflexion. Nous espérons qu'ils pourront souligner l'art du travail et non pas les thèmes de l'exploitation et de l'oppression si présents dans le passé.

Ce journal a été conçu il y a plus de vingt-cinq ans dans l'esprit de reconnaître et de renverser les inégalités des classes et les angles morts de notre génération et de nombreuses périodes historiques précédentes. Le désir et le besoin préoccupaient les hommes, les femmes et les enfants de la classe ouvrière, tandis que l'abondance et l'indulgence ont marqué la vie privilégiée des propriétaires qui vivaient de leurs roduits. À une certaine époque du prochain millénaire, nous en sommes certains, cette barrière peu naturelle pourra être surmontée. Nos successeurs pourront ensuite demander une autre représentation artistique comme celle de Robertson mais intitulée, « *Freeing the Millennium/La libération au prochain millénaire* ».

INSTITUTIONS & IDEAS

Some Millennial Reflections on the State of Canadian Labour History

Desmond Morton

AT INTERVALS, someone invites me to comment on the state of labour history. Once it was the Institut d'histoire de l'Amérique francaise; later it was Noah Meltz and Gérard Hébert, armed with a grant to describe the state of industrial relations research.[1] And last May it was Bryan Palmer, inviting prompt submission of twenty-five pages, if possible by the end of June. Bryan has been no great fan of the illustrated Canadian labour history Terry Copp and I produced in 1980 and which recently struggled into a fourth edition.[2] I was suitably flattered and beguiled. I admire the journal he, Greg Kealey and James Thwaites, Andrée Lévesque, and Jacques Rouillard and how many others have kept going. To contribute to *Labour/le Travail (L/LT)* is an honour and a responsibility. Moreover, quick turn-arounds are my specialty. And so, to the dismay of my staff, I cut back on my current work and got busy.

[1]See Desmond Morton, "E.P. Thompson dans les arpents de neige: les historiens Canadiens-Anglais et la classe ouvrière," *Revue d'Histoire de l'Amérique française*, 37 (septembre 1983), and "Labour and Industrial Relations History in English-speaking Canada," in Gérard Hébert, Hem C. Jain, and Noah M. Meltz, *The State of the Art in Industrial Relations* (Kingston and Toronto 1988), 241-260 (also translated as *Histoire du travail et des relations industrielles au Canada* (Montréal 1988), 295-317, on which much of this article has been based.

[2]See Bryan D. Palmer, *Working-Class Experience: Rethinking the History of Canadian Labour, 1800-1991* (Toronto 1992), 418, where the book is described, probably reasonably, as "of uneven quality."

Desmond Morton, "Some Millennial Reflections on the State of Canadian Labour History," *Labour/Le Travail*, 46 (Fall 2000), 11-36.

Admittedly, what I dropped is so remote from the interests and values of *L/LT* and its loyal guardians that they may well question Bryan's judgement. After seven years of academic administration and corporate fundraising at the University of Toronto's Mississauga campus, I became the major beneficiary of Charles R. Bronfman's $10 million gift to McGill University to improve the Study of Canada in an old anglophone institution. Since mid-1994, I have earned my wages by trying to provide McGill and its community with rather more teaching, seminars and conferences about Canada than it might otherwise enjoy. My misspent youth with the NDP, under the roof of the United Packinghouse Workers, sometimes seems very far off.

Admittedly, in alternate years at McGill, I teach an upper-year course on industrial relations history. Back in the days of the late H.D. Woods, Jacob Finkelman, and Shirley Goldenberg, this was a field of some significance at McGill. Now the Faculty of Management treats it as a detour for those ill-fitted for business, while Arts spares industrial relations students the full rigours of Economics. Few of my students come from either program. Most encountered unions as they grew up in Ontario or British Columbia or had to join during a summer job. Some had parents who voted NDP; this year, one had been a Tory candidate in British Columbia in 1997. He proved to be more knowledgeable and more pro-union than most of his fellow students. I still do speaking stints for old friends in the Steelworkers, the Firefighters, and even the Public Service Alliance, but frankly, like David Bercuson and Terry Copp, I am better known these days for my historical and political advice to Canada's much-battered military.

So what do I now know about the state of labour history? Less than I should. I read what I can, much of it rationed out by the editorial board of *L/LT*. Should I, aware of my scholarly limits, phone Bryan and beg off? Then came the May issue of the *Literary Review of Canada*. There, in a Palmer review of Russell Jacoby's new book, I had my answer.[3] It might not be what he or Jacoby intended, but if I cared, I should write. Eric Hobsbawm's plea that we should be "concerned with changing the world as well as interpreting it" was not restricted to revolutionaries.[4] More than most intellectual fields, the study of the working class is *engagé*. Its goal is not winning a teaching job, tenure, or promotion; it aims to change consciousness and conduct. Jacoby's message, Palmer seemed to suggest, is that those of us who still believe that knowledge and ideas should have practical outcomes should quit hiding behind the academic bric-a-brac and risk getting our hands and reputations dirty.

[3]Bryan D. Palmer, "Pluralism Popped," *Literary Review of Canada*, 8 (May 2000), 9-12, a review of Russell Jacoby, *The End of Utopia: Politics and Culture in an Age of Apathy* (New York 1999).
[4]. E.J. Hobsbawm, "Labour History and Ideology," *Journal of Social History*, 7 (Summer 1974), 380, cited by G.S. Kealey and Peter Warrian, eds., *Essays in Canadian Working-Class History* (Toronto 1976), 12.

The changes I seek are not necessarily monolithic or even dramatic. I don't happen to share Palmer's (or Hobsbawm's or Jacoby's) enthusiasm for a revolutionary transformation of society. Georg Lukacs' commitment to "annihilate capitalism" seems premature, given the fate of his alternative. Small victories are better than massive defeat. Those who preferred the Common Sense Revolution to Bob Rae now have to live with Mike Harris and boil their drinking water. Espousing unreal objectives and ignoring awkward realities are among the ways intellectuals evade responsibility. During World War I, the government was largely indifferent to the slightly fey Anglo-Saxon radicals of the Socialist Party of Canada. The Social Democratic Party seemed much more dangerous — not just because it had more "foreigners" but because it was also politically more realistic. In 1945, Liberals found the Communist Party a useful tool to help eviscerate the CCF, a party that had appeared to be dangerously close to power.

***

At McGill and, earlier, at the University of Toronto, I have been inclined to bill myself an "industrial relations historian," and I do so here, not because I scorn working-class history but because I have not been very successful in finding the evidence I need.[5] Instead it is a way of trying to be useful in a field which has changed working-class lives for the better and, in its current manifestation as "human relations," seems bent on changing most of those lives for the worse. History is also a reminder of both continuity and change. Transformations of skill, resources and technology are unprecedented only to those who are wilfully ignorant of history. Confronted by Mergenthaler's 1884 invention of the Linotype, typesetters could have fought the machine to their own collective extinction. By co-opting the machine and adapting the "art preservative" to its potential, an honourable but obsolete craft transformed itself and lasted another few generations until photo-offset technology was too much for it.[6]

[5]I have been hunting for the voices of the working-class women who were wives or mothers of CEF soldiers in World War I and who depended on the paternalistic and often chilly benevolence of the Patriotic Fund. See Desmond Morton and Cheryl Smith, "Fuel for the Home Fires: The Patriotic Fund, 1914-1918," *The Beaver*, 75 (August-September 1995), 12-19; and Morton, "Entente Cordiale? La Section Montréalaise du Fonds patriotique canadien, 1914-1923: le Bénévolat de guerre à Montréal," *Revue d'histoire de l'Amérique française*, 53 (automne 1999).

[6]On printers, see Wayne Roberts, "The Last Artisans: Toronto Printers, 1876-1914," in Kealey and Warrian, *Essays*, 125-142; Desmond Morton, "The Mergenthaler Challenge: Typographers and the Response to Technological Change (unpublished paper, 1986) or, for a better documented and more modern experience, see Joel Novak, "Grain Terminal Automation: A Case Study in the Control of Control," *Labour/Le Travail (L/LT)*, 22 (Fall 1988), 163-180. For an apocalyptic but suggestive view of current industrial relations, see Leo Panitch and Donald Swartz, "Towards Permanent Exceptionalism: Coercion and Consent in Canadian Industrial Relations," *L/LT*, 13 (Spring 1984), 133-157.

Of course, history also serves as John Donne's shroud: a reminder of the mortality of humanity, institutions, and conventional wisdom. The industrial relations system which Canadians accepted in the 1940s may conceivably have been an accident of circumstances, an "exception" whose time, by the 1990s, had already passed. Apparently not many labour historians were watching. Whatever we know or profess about "the nature of employment relations in an industrial society" must be based on past experience, accurately and systematically interpreted.[7] Even our prophecies about the labour market or technological change depend on projections from the past. History has much to offer that is directly relevant to the understanding of industrial relations, not to mention working-class politics and popular culture. Where else can we look to learn about the "actors" and the "environment."[8] Weary negotiators may wish that memories of past practices and remote grievances could be erased, but they would be the last to wish amnesia on themselves. Experience is our most painfully acquired human attribute, and history is its synonym.

Of course, workplace relations are not the whole of labour history or even, necessarily, its biggest end. Historians who directed their research at the working class — and their numbers grew substantially since the 1960s — have largely ignored the modern era of regulated collective bargaining.[9] "Fordism," the auto magnate's belief that high wages were sufficient compensation for autocratic management, had little appeal to academic radicals, whatever the attraction to workers.[10]

Fifteen years ago, I noted the absence of a comprehensive history of industrial relations in Canada. Unlike many of my concerns, this one is as good as new. Canadian business historians have seldom concerned themselves with the structure and functioning of corporate management as employer nor with its approach to

[7]Morley Gunderson and Allen Ponak, "The Canadian Industrial Relations System," in Gunderson and Ponak, *Union Management Relations in Canada* (Don Mills 1982), 2-3.

[8]Alton Craig, "Model for the Analysis of Industrial Relations," in Hem Chand Jain, ed., *Canadian Labour and Industrial Relations: Public and Private Sectors* (Toronto 1974), 2-12.

[9]State of the art reviews of Canadian labour history flourished in the late 1970s and early 1980s. See Gregory S. Kealey, "Labour and Working-Class History in Canada: Prospects in the 1980s," *L/LT*, 7 (Spring 1981), 67-94; D.J. Bercuson, "Through the Looking-Glass of Culture: An Essay on the New Labour History and Working-Class Culture in Recent Canadian Historical Writing", *L/LT*, 7 (Spring 1981), 95-112; and "Recent Publications in Canadian Labour History," *History and Social Science Teacher*, 14 (Spring 1979); K.W. McNaught, "E.P. Thompson vs. Harold Logan: Writing About Labour and the Left in the 1970s," *Canadian Historical Review* (*CHR*), 63 (June 1981), 141-168.

[10]See for example Charlotte A.B. Yates, *From Plant to Politics: The Autoworkers Union in Postwar Canada* (Philadelphia 1993). In the 1970s, of 47 articles in *L/LT* susceptible to periodization, only two dealt with the period after 1940. Of 113 articles published in the 1980s, there were 19 in the post-1940 period, many of them dealing with politics. (See Appendix A-1 and A-2).

negotiating with employees. Labour historians have been equally loath to poke through business records. Given the bilateral, adversarial assumptions of industrial relations, the one-sided approach is undoubtedly congenial, but each side loses the opportunity to know its adversary as other than a caricature.[11]

As an enthusiastic new deputy minister of labour, William Lyon Mackenzie King tried to persuade Adam Shortt of Queen's University to become the Canadian version of John R. Commons and create systematic industrial relations history. He failed.[12] For most of the ensuing half-century, Canadian labour and its fragile organizations were mysteries shared with students by departments of economics or political economy. A historical approach focused on the succession of frail and conflictual central labour bodies which had represented Canada's organized workers to the public. This approach, pioneered in 1928 by Professor Harold Logan of the University of Toronto, persisted through successive editions of his text.[13] Labour history was a family tree in which the TTA begat the CLU, the TTLC fostered the TLC, which ejected the ACCL, and so on to merciful sleep.

Though Mackenzie King failed to establish a "Wisconsin School" in Canada, his new Department of Labour provided the basis for the kind of scholarship he needed for his approach to labour peace: the collection and distribution of factual, statistical information. For all the limitations of its local correspondents, its statistical methods and its ideology, the *Labour Gazette* remains an indispensable chronicle of Canadian labour and industrial relations history from 1900 at least until its popularization in the 1960s. A succession of Labour Department librarians gathered every imaginable printed source relating to labour. When national and provincial archives would not give house room to John Moffatt's collection of Provincial Workmen's Association papers in 1926, Margaret Mackintosh eagerly took them in.[14] Her tidy, energetic mind encouraged her to share with Logan the lonely experience of being Canada's pioneering trade union historian.[15]

[11]Unlike Québec, where state *concertation* draws on deep strains of a shared nationalism, not even professed socialism interferes with an adversarial perspective. When Bob Rae shared his province's fiscal plight with Bob White, he got simple advice; "Why can't Ontario just do like the Reichmanns and declare bankruptcy, maybe pay 50 or 60 cents on the dollar?" See Bob Rae, *From Protest to Power: Personal Reflections on a Life in Politics* (Toronto 1996), 207. A rare example of a book-length case study was G.F. MacDowell, *The Brandon Packers' Strike: A Tragedy of Errors* (Toronto 1971).

[12]Jay Atherton, "The Department of Labour and Industrial Relations, 1900-1914," MA thesis, Carleton University 1972, 99.

[13]Harold Logan, *The History of Trade Union Organization in Canada* (Toronto 1928); and *Trade Unions in Canada* (Toronto 1948).

[14]See Atherton, "Department of Labour," and Nancy Stunden, "Labour Records and Archives: The Struggle for a Heritage," *Archivaria*, 4 (Summer 1977), 73-91. See also Russell G. Hann and Gregory S. Kealey, "Documenting Working-Class History: North American Traditions and New Approaches" *Archivaria*, 4 (Summer 1997),92-114.

[15]M. Mackintosh, *An Outline of Trade Union History in Great Britain, the United States and Canada* (Ottawa 1938), among other publications.

Like other people, unions and their members ultimately felt the need to record their ancestry and to gain the respectability which a genealogy allegedly confers. From James McArthur Conner, self-appointed historian and guardian of the records of the Toronto Trades and Labour Council, to Leslie Wismer, Jack Williams, and Morden Lazarus, veterans of the labour movement struggled to create history as they understood it: factual, uncritical.[16] In the more affluent and confident 1960s, unions and labour federations began commissioning histories, from Paul Phillips's discreet account of the British Columbia Federation of Labor to Terry Copp's sponsored but more critical account of the International Union of Electrical Workers in Canada. Union mergers and fold-ins, and the growth of public sector unions, expanded the market for institutional history.[17]

No commissioned project was more ambitious or longer in gestation than the Canadian Labour Congress's plan to celebrate the centennial of Canada's Confederation with a comprehensive history of Canadian labour, written by Eugene Forsey. The table officers of the CLC reckoned without the extraordinary perseverance and commitment to detail of their former research director, and they certainly underestimated the difficulties of their task. Forsey sent young researchers to scour the country for records, sometimes in vain. At Saint John and Moncton, Richard Rice arrived only days after valuable collections had been destroyed. From a mass of material assembled from damp basements and tinder-dry attics, from local public libraries and private homes, researchers provided Forsey with the means to do for

[16]For example, J.M. Conner, "Trade Unions in Toronto," in Jesse Middleton, ed., *The Municipality of Toronto: A History, Volume II* (Toronto 1923). Without exhausting the range one can cite: Morden Lazarus, *Years of Hard Labour* (Don Mills 1974), and *Up From the Ranks: Trade Union V.I.Ps. Past and Present* (Toronto 1977); Jack Williams, *The Story of Unions in Canada* (Toronto 1974); Leslie E. Wismer, *Proceedings of the Canadian Labour Union Congress* (Ottawa 1951); Tom McEwen, *The Forge Glows Red: From Blacksmith to Revolutionary* (Toronto 1974); and Eileen Sufrin, *The Eaton Drive, 1948-1952* (Toronto 1982).

[17]Paul Phillips, *No Power Greater: A Century of Labour in B.C.* (Vancouver 1967); J.T. Copp, *The I.U.E. in Canada* (Elora 1980). See also, for example, Warren Carragata, *Alberta Labour: A Heritage Untold* (Toronto 1979); Elaine Bernard, *The Long Distance Feeling: A History of the Telecommunications Workers Union* (Vancouver 1982). More recent examples now include public-sector unions: Wayne Roberts, *Don't Call Me Servant: Government Work and Unions in Ontario, 1911-1984* (North York 1994); Doug Smith, Jock Bates, Esyllt Jones, *Lives in the Public Service: A History of the Manitoba Government Employees' Union* (Winnipeg 1993). In Quebec, Jacques Rouillard's work on the textile workers of Valleyfield led him to major work on the Confédération des syndicats nationaux and finally to a comprehensive provincial labour history. See Rouillard, *Les Syndicats Nationaux au Québec de 1900 - 1930* (Québec 1979); *Histoire de la CSN* (Montréal 1981); and *Histoire du syndicalisme au Québec: des origines à nos jours* (Montréal 1989). Fortunately the larger central body, the FTQ, and one of its most durable leaders, now have book-length studies: Louis Fournier, *Histoire de la FTQ, 1965-1992: La plus grande centrale syndicale au Québec* (Montréal 1994); *Louis Laberge: Le syndicalisme c'est ma vie* (Montréal 1992).

Canada what Commons had done for the United States and the Webbs for Great Britain 70 years before. Even in the lifespan of Forsey's work, publishers, readers, and historical fashion had changed. But by the time the book was published in 1982, it had survived three successive publishers and much painful editing.[18]

Institutional labour history can only be a foundation. As such, of course, it is indispensable. Even the historians most critical of Forsey's traditional approach were active in urging publication of his massive book.[19] Simply put, a later generation could not build securely without a foundation. Yet there was much that was sterile and a little that was absurd in the historians' preoccupation with the mergers and splits, quarrels and reconciliations, that shaped the complex family tree of Canadian unionism.

For much of the 20th century, what little of Canadian labour history was published focused primarily on local unions and central labour bodies. Doris French's misleadingly titled biography of Daniel O'Donoghue was almost unique among authored monographs: its tiny size and production quality bespeak the publisher's nervous investment.[20]

From Mackintosh to Senator Forsey, organizational and ideological links with the United States provided labour history's unifying theme. If the uniquely North American institutions of the "international union" linked much of Canadian labour with the "pure and simpledom" of the American Federation of Labor, the stubborn survival of confessional, national and revolutionary unionism provided a welcome Canadian distinction.[21] Because those distinctions were also underlined in the rhetoric of union rivalry, underlying similarities were sometimes overlooked. Both its Catholic sponsors and its Trades and Labor Congress critics insisted on the peace-loving nature of the Confédération des Travailleurs Catholiques du Canada: did anyone notice that the CTCC led some of the biggest strikes in Canada during the 1920s, thirty years before the Asbestos or the Dupuis Frères strikes made it one of several precursors of the Quiet Revolution?[22]

[18]E.A. Forsey, *Trade Unions in Canada, 1812-1902* (Toronto 1982). See Stunden, "Labour Records," 74-5.

[19]Among many acknowledgements, see G.S. Kealey, *Toronto Workers Respond to Industrial Capitalism, 1867-1892* (Toronto 1980), xiv.

[20]Doris French, *Faith, Sweat and Politics: The Early Union Years in Canada* (Toronto 1962).

[21] For example, Alan B. Latham, *The Catholic and National Labour Unions of Canada* (Toronto 1930). No such attention has yet been directed at the dominant labour organization, the Trades and Labor Congress. It would now be a labour of considerable difficulty to reconstruct much of its history. Latham is now largely superseded by the work of Jacques Rouillard (see footnote 17).

[22]Jacques Rouillard, *Histoire de la C.S.N* (Montréal 1981); Jacques Rouillard, *Les Syndicats Nationaux au Québec de 1900 - 1930* (Québec 1979); Evelyn Dumas, *The Bitter Thirties in Quebec* (Montréal 1975).

However much labour conflict filled headlines and editorial columns, it seldom attracted academic attention. An exception was Stuart Jamieson, a British Columbia scholar whose short text on industrial relations in Canada, first published in 1957, illuminated the importance of history in shaping industrial conflict.[23] One of several valuable research contributions of the Woods Task Force to the understanding of the Canadian labour relations system emerged from its contract with Jamieson to study strike activity since 1900. *Times of Trouble* often supplanted Logan and also Charles Lipton's egregiously flawed *Trade Union Movement of Canada* as the textbook of choice in the labour history courses that blossomed in Canadian universities during the early 1970s.[24]

***

Until the university explosion in the 1960s, Canadian history departments showed little interest in labour and the working class. John Irwin Cooper's article on Québec ship labourers and Clare Pentland's article on the Lachine strike of 1843 were lonely exceptions.[25] Radical thought by working men seems to have interested only a professor of English at the University of Toronto, Frank Watt.[26] Most Canadian intellectuals were preoccupied by nation-building; only a wry dig by F.R. Scott reminded his fellow poet, Ned Pratt, that labourers, not Sir John A. Macdonald or Sir Donald Smith, had driven every spike in the CPR but the last.[27] Donald Creighton treated working men much as his hero, Macdonald, did when he used the "navvies" as foils for a political trick on the Opposition during the Toronto printers' strike of 1872. Not until Forsey did a historian notice that the Macdonald government's Trade Unions Act was a practical nullity since no union bothered to register.[28]

---

[23]Stuart Jamieson, *Industrial Relations in Canada* (Toronto 1957), and later editions.

[24]Stuart Jamieson, *Times of Trouble: Labour Unrest and Industrial Conflict in Canada, 1900-1966* (Ottawa 1968); Charles Lipton, The *Trade Union Movement of Canada, 1827-1959* (Montréal 1959).

[25]John I. Cooper, "The Quebec Ship Labourers Benevolent Society," *CHR*, 30 (December 1949), 336-343; H.C. Pentland, "The Lachine Strike of 1843," *CHR*, 29 (September 1948), 255-277.

[26]F.W. Watt, "The National Policy, the Workingman and the Proletarian Idea in Victorian Canada," *CHR,* 41 (March 1959), 1-26; and "Literature of Protest," in Carl Klinck, *Literary History of Canada* (Toronto 1965), 457-473.

[27]F.R. Scott, "All the Spikes but the Last," *Selected Poems* (Toronto 1966), 64.

[28]D.G. Creighton, "George Brown, Sir John A. Macdonald and the Workingmen," *CHR*, 24 (December 1943), 362-375. See also Bernard Ostry, "Conservatives, Liberals and Labour in the 1870s", *CHR*, 41 (June 1960), 93-127. (I am indebted to the late Senator Forsey for pointing out the limits of the 1872 Trade Unions Act.) See Desmond Morton, *Working People: An Illustrated History of the Canadian Labour Movement* (Montreal 4th ed. 1999), 27.

Admittedly, when labour activity intersected with politics, as it did in 1872 and in the Winnipeg General Strike of 1919, historians would sometimes take note. The first serious study of the Winnipeg strike emerged as a by-product of a major interdisciplinary exploration of the roots of Social Credit in Alberta.[29] Fascination with the CCF and its founding president, J.S. Woodsworth, led Kenneth McNaught to a further look at the Winnipeg strike, as well as such varied topics as the "labour churches" and Vancouver's militant dockside unions.[30] The CLC's decision to help create the New Democratic Party coincided with a burst of university expansion. New scholars and old, with liberal or social-democratic sympathies, were attracted to the roots of labour radicalism, the failure of the CCF, and the evolution of a union commitment to partisan politics.[31] Most such students came from political science: Irving Abella was an exception — a historian who explored the considerable role of Communists in building CIO and CCL industrial unions in the 1940s, and their eventual defeat at the hands of CCFers allied to more conservative unionists.[32]

The dramatic growth of Canadian universities through the 1960s helped guarantee that the old staples of Canadian historiography, politics, religion, external policy, and biography, would not satisfy the flood of new graduate students. However exciting Creighton's "Laurentian" perspective might be to unreflecting nationalists, it did not fit most Canadian realities beyond the English-speaking élites of Toronto and Montréal, and how many times could the same straw be threshed? Maurice Careless's alternative thesis of "limited identities" of region, culture, and class came closer to fitting the familiar facts of the period; it also invited whole new ranges of research. Looking at the local and the specific was no longer seen as an implicit confession of limited talent or energy.[33]

[29]D.C. Masters, *The Winnipeg General Strike* (Toronto 1950). On the historiography of the strike, see Kenneth McNaught and D.J. Bercuson, *The Winnipeg Strike, 1919* (Toronto 1974), 99-123; and G.S. Kealey, "1919: The Canadian Labour Revolt," *L/LT*, 13 (Spring 1983), 11-44.

[30]Kenneth McNaught, *A Prophet in Politics: A Biography of J.S. Woodsworth* (Toronto 1959). Another political enthusiast, writing on the margins of labour and reform, was Richard Allen, *The Social Passion: Religion and Social Reform in Canada, 1914-1928* (Toronto 1971).

[31]See Martin Robin, *Radical Politics and Canadian Labour, 1880-1930* (Kingston 1968); Gad Horowitz, *Canadian Labour in Politics* (Toronto 1968); Leo Zakuta, *A Protest Movement Becalmed: A Study of Change in the CCF* (Toronto 1964); and, in some contrast, David Kwavnick, *Organized Labour and Pressure Group Politics: The Labour Congress, 1956-1968* (Montréal 1972). A CBC radio documentary series led to P.W. Fox's "Early Socialism in Canada," included in a book of essays, *The Political Process in Canada* (Toronto 1963), edited by the first leader of the Nova Scotia NDP, Professor James Aitchison.

[32]Published as: *Nationalism, Communism and Canadian Labour* (Toronto 1973).

[33]Gregory S. Kealey, "The Working Class in Recent Canadian Historical Writing," *Acadiensis*, 7 (Spring 1978), 116-7; J.M.S. Careless, "Limited Identities in Canada", *CHR*, 50

The result, claimed Carl Berger, was a "golden age" of Canadian history. Among those who turned in the 1960s to the history of labour, working people and related themes were Terry Copp, who used the pioneering work of Herbert Ames to study the working poor of Montréal in the early decades of the 20th century; Ross McCormack, who analyzed the prewar labour politics of Winnipeg and the West; and Donald Avery, whose *Dangerous Foreigners* finally gave a sympathetic account of "Sifton's sheepskins," the central European immigrants who had been the uncertain chorus of the radical movements of central and eastern Canada for the first third of the century.

Perhaps the ablest of the generation was David J. Bercuson, whose work on the Winnipeg General Strike provided a new model for industrial relations history in Canada.[34] Ignoring a rich and romantic mythology of 1919 and an even more durable effort to make the general strike serve its appointed role in Marxist historiography, Bercuson treated the strike as a Winnipeg event. He reconstructed personalities and circumstances with a harsh objectivity that might have given pleasure to the well-rounded ghost of William Lyon Mackenzie King. Bercuson's second book, on the One Big Union, was virtually a sequel. It underlined his earlier argument: the OBU may have been trapped between the fantasies of its leaders and the cold hostility of employers but, like any North American union, its challenge was to improve the material circumstances of its members and it failed.[35] It was a proposition that later radical unions, from the Workers' Unity League to the Canadian Union of Postal Workers, could ignore at their peril.

***

By no means all of Bercuson's contemporaries accepted his analysis or his conclusions. In a 1979 retrospective on a decade of remarkable achievements by his generation of labour historians, Bryan Palmer distinguished between a "first generation" of scholars such as Bercuson, and a "second generation" to which he,

(March 1969), 1-10. Another influential article, if largely as a goad to his colleagues, was S.R. Mealing, "The Concept of Social Class in the Interpretation of Canadian History," *CHR*, 46, (September 1965), 201-216.

[34] J.T. Copp, *The Anatomy of Poverty: The Condition of the Working Class in Montreal, 1897-1929* (Toronto 1974); Donald Avery, *"Dangerous Foreigners": European Immigrant Workers and Labour Radicalism in Canada, 1896-1932* (Toronto 1979); Ross McCormick, *Reformers, Rebels and Revolutionaries: The Western Canadian Radical Movement, 1899-1919* (Toronto 1979); and D.J. Bercuson, *Confrontation at Winnipeg: Labour, Industrial Relations and the General Strike* (Montréal and Kingston 1974).

[35] D.J. Bercuson, *Fools and Wise Men: The Rise and Fall of the One Big Union* (Toronto 1978). For different views of Bercuson's work, see McNaught, "Thompson vs. Logan", 152-3, and Bryan Palmer, "Working-Class Canada: Recent Historical Writing," *Queen's Quarterly*, 86 (Winter 1979-80), 595-6.

Gregory Kealey, Craig Heron, Peter Warrian, Ian Mckay and others belonged.[36] Behind those who were committed to "objective" evidence-based scholarship as their mentors understood it, came a larger wave who had gravitated to labour and working-class history by way of student activism, New Left Marxism, and the contemporary belief that the academy might well become the hotbed of the revolution. Their radicalism was reinforced by an academic job market which had easily absorbed their predecessors but which, by the early 1970s, had fewer tenure-stream posts to offer. Excluded from easy access to the professorate, the *Wissenschaften* of the "new" labour historians became, perforce, a *Gemeineschaften* struggling for positions as well as principles.[37] Talent, energy, organization, and solidarity might not deliver a revolution but it could produce one of the most homogeneous and influential groups in the disparate crowd of Canadian historians.

The field expanded dramatically. The first Canadian Historical Association *Register of Dissertations* reported nine theses in labour and working-class history, four at the doctoral level. By 1976, there were 89, 23 of them leading to a PhD.[38] In 1971, the Committee on Canadian Labour History was formed to launch first a regular *Bulletin* and then, in 1976, an increasingly self-confident and influential journal, *Labour/Le Travailleur*. Almost simultaneously, a Regroupement de Chercheurs en Histoire des Travailleurs québécois began its separate existence and launched its own publication, *Histoire des Travailleurs québécois*. Both committees sponsored a remarkable amount of work, surveying archives, collecting records, compiling impressive bibliographies and, above all, publishing articles, notes, research reports and reviews.[39] By the mid 1970s, no one could claim that

[36]Most clearly in Palmer, "Working Class Canada", 601-608. Bercuson's personal conclusions persuaded him that military history would be a more congenial area of research. Bercuson's recent work includes *True Patriot: The Life of Brooke Claxton, 1889-1960* (Toronto 1993), and *Blood on the Hills: The Canadian Army in Korea* (Montréal and Kingston 1999). Terry Copp took a similar direction, studying the Normandy Campaign in detail and writing (with W.J. McAndrew), *Battle Exhaustion: Soldiers and Psychiatrists in the Canadian Army, 1939-1945* (Montréal and Kingston 1990). The same could be said of me, though in fact I cheerfully detoured through the industrial relations field from the study of political-military relations as a way of gaining further insights on leadership and conflict.
[37]Morton, "Arpents de neige," 172-3 and n.25.
[38]See Appendix A. Based on the Canadian Historical Association, *Register of Dissertations*, (Michael Swift, ed.) 1 (1966), 9,(1976). Coding is by the author, beyond category of "Social History."
[39]Russell Hann, G.S. Kealey, Linda Kealey, and Peter Warrian, *Primary Sources in Canadian Working-Class History* (Kitchener 1972); G. Douglas Vaisey, *The Labor Companion: A Bibliography of Canadian Labour History Based on Material Printed from 1950 to 1975* (Kitchener 1976) and in bibliographical articles in the Canadian Committee on Labour History's annual *Bulletin* and with Marcel Leduc, in *L/LT* 8-9 to 1982 (Autumn 1979). See also G.S. Kealey, "An Index to the Publications of the Committee on Canadian Labour History, 1972-1981," *L/LT*, 8-9 (Autumn-Spring 1981-2), 433-461. The academic

the history of Canadian working people and their organizations was stifled for lack of sources. Nor could there be any illusion of even-handed objectivity. Second generation labour history was vigorously committed to radical social and economic change. Other approaches were received politely, occasionally published in *Labour/ Le Travail*, as the journal was soon renamed, and robustly denounced.[40]

"First generation" historians were, on the whole, respectfully treated by their younger critics but, from the first, the enterprise was managed by the newer generation. It was they who travelled abroad, to Warwick, Rochester, and Binghamton, to meet their American and British mentors. They read the old and new world classics of working-class history by Herbert Gutman, Eugene Genovese, Raymond Williams, Eric Hobsbawm, and, above all, E.P. Thompson. They returned determined to transform the field from being merely "a category of political economy, a problem of industrial relations, a canon of saintly working-class leaders, a chronicle of union locals, or a chronology of militant strike actions."[41]

Not since Bishop Stubbs or Sir Frederick Maitland has a British historian had more influence on Canadian historical scholarship than Thompson. His "culturalist" approach to class angered other European Marxists but it opened up immense possibilities in North America.[42] Thompson had discovered a self-conscious working class in 18th century England: Kealey, Palmer, and the "new" school would find a Canadian working-class culture in Ontario a century later. Thanks to Clare Pentland, whose doctoral dissertation had located Canadian industrialization far earlier than Harold Innis and other Canadian economic historians, the 1880s could become the high point for both industrial change and class conflict.[43] In southern Ontario and Québec, newly smoking factory chimneys were growing behind the

publishing boom of the 1960-70 period directly assisted the expansion of labour and working-class history. Particularly noteworthy was the expansion of the University of Toronto Press's Social History reprint series. Among the titles brought back to circulation were Mackenzie King's *Industry and Humanity*, Herbert Ames's *The City Below the Hill* and *Canada Investigates Industrialism*, an abridged version of the report and testimony before the Royal Commission on the Relations of Labour and Capital, 1889, introduced by Greg Kealey.

[40]With the 13th issue, the unconscious bias in the French title was rectified and the name was changed. See *L/LT*, 13 (Spring, 1984), 5.

[41]Kealey and Warrian, "Introduction," *Essays*, 8. On influences, see Hann *et al.*, *Primary Sources*, 12 *ff*; Bryan D. Palmer, "Most Uncommon Common Men: Craft and Culture in Historical Perspective," *L/LT*, 1 (1976), 5-31.

[42]E.P. Thompson, *The Making of the English Working Class* (London 1963). On its significance, see Russell Hann and G.S. Kealey, "Documenting Working-Class History: North American Traditions and New Approaches," *Archivaria*, 4 (Summer 1977), 98; Kealey, "Labour and Working Class History," 80-8. For a retrospective assessment, see Royden Harrison, "The Last Ten Years in British Labour Historiography," Canadian Historical Association, *Historical Papers* (1980), 212-227.

[43]H.C. Pentland, *Capital and Labour in Canada, 1650-1860* (Toronto 1981).

tariff walls of Macdonald's National Policy. Tens of thousands of men and women found surplus on family farms, were seeking work amidst the heat, clangor, and menace of new machinery.

On both sides of the border, the 1880s was the decade of the Knights of Labor, the extraordinary working-class organization whose records Kealey had been able to study at Rochester. Skeptics have called it the "seek and ye shall find" principle, but Kealey had discovered in the documents evidence of a working class "in which divisions of ethnicity, skill, religion and even sex were recognized, debated and, for a few years in the 1880s at least, were overcome."[44] In neighbouring Hamilton, Palmer reported that skilled workers "in light of their workplace power and organizational strength, as well as their history of cultural involvement," served as "the cutting edge of the working-class movement as a whole."[45]

While the "second generation" condemned the "presentism" as much as the "liberal realism" of their more conventional colleagues, they were not inhibited from offering the example of the Knights of Labor to modern workers and their potential mentors. In a textbook widely promoted for university labour history courses, Bryan Palmer concluded: "Such a rich and varied movement culture of resistance and alternatives, premised on a wide-ranging solidarity, is precisely what is lacking in Canadian labour's response to the crisis of the 1980s."[46]

In the usual way of academic controversy, some of the Kealey-Palmer claims for their "new" history were challenged. While colleagues welcomed innovative research and a willingness to explore unfamiliar topics, ideology is not always an adequate substitute for evidence. Skilled workers in Hamilton, Bercuson argues, proved to be as exclusive, conservative, and indifferent to the fate of the unskilled as were other skilled workers across North America.[47] While the Knights of Labor certainly fostered a rhetoric of working-class solidarity, Stanley Ryerson argued, the Order was also devoutly committed to labour-employer harmony and industrial peace.[48] The Knights' ideals were not as big a problem as the difficulty of imbuing them in the thousands of recruits they acquired in 1885 and 1886, before the new members took strike action or were sacked by hostile employers. If, as Kealey insisted, Toronto's working class achieved unity across ethnic and sectarian barri-

[44]Kealey, "Labour and Working Class History," 89. On the Knights, see Gregory S. Kealey and Bryan D. Palmer, *"Dreaming of What Might Be": The Knights of Labor in Ontario, 1880-1902* (Cambridge, Massachusetts 1982).

[45]Bryan D. Palmer, *A Culture in Conflict: Skilled Workers and Industrial Capitalism in Hamilton, Ontario, 1860-1914* (Montréal 1979), xii. See also Craig Heron, "The Working Class in Hamilton, 1890-1913," PhD thesis, Dalhousie University, 1980.

[46]Bryan D. Palmer, *Working-Class Experience: The Rise and Reconstitution of Canadian Labour, 1800-1980* (Toronto 1983), 297. For a denunciation of presentism, see page 1.

[47]David J. Bercuson, "Through the Looking Glass of Culture," 97-9, 101.

[48]Stanley B. Ryerson, "A propos de *Les Syndicats nationaux ...de Jacques Rouillard*," *Revue d'histoire de l'Amérique française* 35 (décembre 1981), 401.

ers, it must have been for the briefest of moments in the city contemporaries sometimes called "the Belfast of North America."[49] Palmer's research into the "rich associational life" of Hamilton artisans was undoubtedly exhaustive, but it also revealed that many of the associations were shared with the city's middle class. Even the relatively proletarian volunteer fire brigades drew upward of a third of their members from the non-artisan classes.[50]

It is easier to *wish* to write labour history from "the bottom up" than to be able to do so. Working-class newspapers and songsheets, lodge reports, and union resolutions were written, then as now, by a somewhat atypical labour élite. Describing intellectuals as "brainworkers" did not make them part of the labouring classes.[51] Charles McKiernan, the proprietor of Joe Beef's Tavern in Montréal, brilliantly brought to life by Peter De Lottinville, was no more a common man than was Frank Smith, the Irish cattle drover who rose to ownership of the Toronto Street Railway and a seat in the Canadian Senate.[52]

Once the exaggerations, the ritual references to respected mentors, and the polemics are set aside, the "new" history bears a considerable reference to the old. "For all the citations of E.P. Thompson and Raymond Williams," wrote Christopher Armstrong of Palmer's *A Culture in Conflict*, "the bulk of Palmer's book is a solid examination of the experience of skilled workers in Hamilton in attempting to organize themselves to secure and protect their rights."[53] Whether these workers also formed a cutting edge or a rearguard is rather a matter of rhetoric or perspective than of fact. The late Kenneth McNaught, initially a sympathiser and supporter, concluded that the radicals had failed: "The cannonading from the left has served principally to achieve those goals which the captains of artillery most vigorously rejected at the beginning of the campaign." Instead of establishing fresh interpre-

[49]Bercuson, "Looking Glass," 102. The first edition of Kealey's book on Toronto workers featured a riot scene. The second edition was modified to show the inside of a workshop. For views of Toronto's sectarian experience, see G.S. Kealey, "The Orange Order in Toronto: Religious Riot and the Working Class," in Kealey and Warrian, *Essays*, 13-34; Desmond Morton, *Mayor Howland: The Citizen's Candidate* (Toronto 1973), 77-82; Mark McGowan, *The Waning of the Green: Catholics, the Irish, and Identity in Toronto, 1887-1922* (Montréal 1999).
[50]Bercuson, "Through the Looking Glass," 99. Palmer, *Culture in Conflict*, 46-9, does not confirm his criticism.
[51]Russell Hann, "Brainworkers and the Knights of Labor: E.E. Sheppard, Phillips Thompson and the Toronto *News*, 1885-1887," in Kealey and Warrian, *Essays*, 35-57.
[52]Peter de Lottinville, "Joe Beef of Montreal: Working Class Culture and the Tavern", *L/LT*, 8-9 (Autumn-Spring 1981-2), 9-40. An earlier interpretation of working-class culture is Bryan Palmer's "Discordant Music: Charivaris and Whitecapping in Nineteenth Century North America," *L/LT*, 3 (1978), 5-62. On Smith, see Morton, *Howland*, 44; *Dictionary of Canadian Biography*, XIII, 965-968.
[53]Christopher Armstrong's review, *Ontario History,* 72 (June 1981), 125.

tations of the role of the "left," the "State" or the labour movement, concluded Ken McNaught:

... most of the recent writing strengthens older notions: the most effective workers' response to the ever-tightening industrial discipline was unionization; that the slow evolution of effective unionization reflected differences of region, culture and industrial context; that while gross inequalities and exploitation produced the fears and goals of the workers, the forms and policies were determined by the leaders — a great many of whom became "collaborators"; that violence has been provoked and employed more often by the state than by the workers; that despite clear evidence of various perceptions of class membership and class conflict, the dominant expressions of such perceptions have been the non-revolutionary strike and efforts to influence government policy through pressuring the major parties and/or supporting a democratic socialist party.[54]

***

McNaught could not, of course, inveigle his younger, more radical colleagues back to the conventional "liberal realism," nor would they easily accept his "older notions." Those who tire of intellectual disputation should accept the obverse of McNaught's text: the "new" labour history delivered much of solid value. Its practitioners were better equipped than most for the other waves of change in the study of the past, most notably feminism, which emerged as an intellectual force in the late 1960s. Radical slogans, vehement denunciations, and role models like Thompson, Gutman, and Stanley Ryerson, who had been marginalized by their contemporaries, were necessary morale builders for young scholars embarking on a pioneering venture. The work was long, arduous, and uncharted; missionary zeal and solidarity were prerequisites. By their teaching and publications, Kealey, Palmer, Heron, Hann and others brought the focus of labour history back from superstructure, politics, and the exceptionalism of Western Canada to regions that had been largely neglected by their predecessors: Ontario and the Maritimes.[55] Québec, on the whole, was left to the enthusiastic efforts of the *Regroupement*.[56] Like most of their Québec counterparts, the "second generation" historians seem to have accepted Québec's departure as virtually inevitable. The title of their journal

[54]McNaught, "Thompson vs Logan," 167-8.
[55]Because Memorial University of Newfoundland could offer appointments to both Linda and Greg Kealey, St. John's became home to *L/LT* and to the group's undoubted inspirational leader. By the early 1980s, an impressive flow of innovative labour history was evident. The 1980-1 issue of *Industrial Relations Research in Canada* reported Allen Seager's "Alberta Coal Miners"; J.H. Tuck's "Canadian Railway Workers and the Wartime Crisis, 1914-1921"; Ian McKay's "Cumberland Coal Fields"; Ian Radforth's "History of the Working Class in Ontario"; D.W. McGillivray's "Independent Workers of Cape Breton"; and Joan Sangster's "Women in Radical Politics and Labour". The list is far from exhaustive. Canadians, of course, were about to elect their most pro-business government since 1930.
[56]See Hann *et al.*, *Primary Sources*, 13.

and an occasional article in French was sufficient reflection of both a transitional reality and of a major phenomenon in the Canadian labour scene.[57] By focussing heavily on the 19th century and, for a time on the Knights of Labor, the "second generation" risked being dismissed as antiquarians, but history's relevance is surely not limited to the day before yesterday.

Far from ignoring the issues, as opposed to the ideology, of industrial relations, the "new" historians and their journal have been significant contributors. From Wayne Roberts's 1975 essay on the Toronto printers to Alberta sociologist Graham Lowe's work on the feminization of the Canadian office, "second generation" history has heeded many of the concerns of industrial relations without the neutral style.[58] More than half the articles in the first dozen issues of *Labour/Le Travail* dealt with the familiar topics of organization, industrialization, labour conflict, and the processes of production.[59] Indeed, the journal focussed some overdue attention on the nature of work itself. The influence of American mentors, David Montgomery and Harry Braverman, directed attention to the continuing workplace issues of technology, skill transformation, and informal job control, though with little of the optimism of conventional American business historians.[60] On occasion, as in a Palmer-Heron omnibus article on early 20th century labour conflict in Ontario, they have even reached out to include managerial approaches.[61] "Second generation" labour historians have been almost unique in Canada as a conscious, though highly dispersed, intellectual "collective," sharing ideas, enthusiasms, and any available job opportunities.

In return, much that was written about Canada's past since the 1970s has been influenced by issues and arguments that Kealey and his colleagues have raised and disseminated. A.A. den Otter's excellent business history of the Galts and western coal mining devotes notably more attention to both labour and technique than most such works of an earlier vintage would have allowed.[62] Similarly, Margaret E.

[57]In 44 issues of *L/LT* published between 1976 and 1999, 23 of 220 articles were published in French, six of them in the last fifteen issues. As Palmer argues, this is certainly better than the *Canadian Historical Review*. As is true with the *CHR*, francophone scholars prefer to appear in the national and international francophone journals their colleagues normally read. (Letter, Bryan Palmer to author, 12 June 2000).

[58]Roberts, "Last Artisans"; Graham Lowe, "Class, Jobs and Gender in the Canadian Office," *L/LT*, 10 (Autumn 1982), 11-38; and "The Feminization of Clerical Occupations in Canada, 1901-1931," *Canadian Journal of Sociology*, 5 (December 1980), 363-384.

[59]Thirty-three out of fifty-nine articles in L/LT issues 1-12 related to strikes, union formation, industrial relations legislation and practice. Of 115 articles published by the end of 1990, 59 related to industrial relations issues, though only 38 of 107 articles published during the 1990s. (Author's coding) See Appendix B.

[60]Palmer, *Working-Class Canada*, 601.

[61]Craig Heron and Bryan D. Palmer, "Through the Prism of the Strike: Industrial Conflict in Southern Ontario, 1901-1914," *CHR*, 58 (December 1977), 423-458.

[62]A.A. den Otter, *Civilizing the West: The Galts and the Development of Western Canada* (Edmonton 1982).

McCallum's study of Ganong's Chocolates, a small New Brunswick chocolate factory, was originally inspired by a desire to discover the impact of tariffs and government regulations on an actual business, but she rapidly incorporated the workforce as a factor. Hadn't one of the proprietors, ignoring family feelings, married a "dipper"?[63] Donald MacLeod's study of the technology of Nova Scotia gold and coal mining raised a conundrum of occupational safety that is still with us: did the miners' union's hard-won fight to appoint its own safety inspectors cost lives because officials chosen from the ranks of miners lacked comprehensive technical training?[64] A generation earlier, only a rare historian might have raised the question.[65]

The flood of research generated by Kealey, Palmer, Hann and their colleagues could enrich anyone with the wits to use it. The "new" history has jogged companionably with work inspired by older themes of labour history: union organization, nationalism, and politics. The left-nationalist tradition which had produced Lipton's *Trade Union Movement* renewed itself a generation later with Robert Laxer's *Canada's Unions*.[66] While overt nationalism was condemned by Hann and Kealey as "neo-Creightonism," the "new" historians welcomed Robert Babcock, an American historian who argued that the outcome of the 1902 TLC convention at Berlin was firmly guided by Sam Gompers and the American Federation of Labor.[67] *Gompers in Canada* was a beneficial example of what may be learned about Canada from American sources. Perhaps an equal interest in Canadian sources might have told Babcock that Canadian unionists believed that by deposing a Liberal MP as TLC president and a clutch of aging former Knights of Labor from the leadership of their organization, they were pursuing their own best interests.[68] Sally Zerker's history of the Toronto Typographical Union became

[63]Margaret McCallum, "Family, Factory and Community: A Social History of Ganong Brothers ... 1873-1946," PhD, University of Toronto, 1987; and her "Separate Spheres: The organization of Work in a Confectionery Factory: Ganong Brothers, St. Stephen, New Brunswick," *L/LT*, 24 (Fall 1989), 69-90.

[64]Donald E. MacLeod, "Colliers, Collier Safety, and Workplace Control: The Nova Scotian Experience, 1873 to 1910," *Historical Papers* (1983), 226-253. See also MacLeod's "Mining Men, Miners and Mining Reform: Changing the Technology of Nova Scotia Gold Miners and Colliers, 1858-1910," PhD thesis, University of Toronto 1981.

[65]The improved quality of even "unprofessional" labour history may also reflect the "new" generation. A fine example was Lynne Bowen's *"Boss Whistle": The Coal Miners of Vancouver Island Remember* (Lantzville 1982).

[66]Robert Laxer, *Canada's Unions* (Toronto 1976).

[67]Robert Babcock, *Gompers in Canada: A Study of American Continentalism Before the First World War* (Toronto 1975). Even Senator Forsey praised Babcock although, as often, it was his own detailed research which helped fuel the Canadian refutation. See Forsey, *Trade Unions*, ch. XVII.

[68]Hann *et al.*, *Primary Sources*, 11.

another Creightonesque assault on the evils of international unionism and its alleged Canadian dupes.[69]

Not all Marx-inspired labour history passed through a "culturalist" prism. The issues that Harry Ferns and Bernard Ostry treated as an aspect of politics in their savage biography of the young Mackenzie King became central in William Baker's study of the 1906 Lethbridge miners' strike.[70] The legislative legacy of that strike, the Industrial Disputes Investigations Act, and its influential creator, became the core of one of the few books to qualify unequivocally as Canadian industrial relations history, Paul Craven's *An Impartial Umpire*.[71] Craven claimed ideological inspiration from my own mentor, the late Ralph Miliband, and his *State and Capitalist Society*; he also gave overdue recognition to the benefits unions, their members, and Canadian society gained from the IDI Act and from Mackenzie King. After all, as the author insists, "an industrial relations policy based on making the trains run on time makes a capitalist economy work better."[72]

For labour historians, perhaps even most historians, the neutrality of industrial relations is usually uncongenial. Human nature as well as the scholastic device of the thesis leads us to choose sides. For all its value in setting the legislative scene and in defining the Mackenzie King world view, even Craven's book does little to make employers or even workers fully dimensioned participants. Few Canadian business historians devote much space to labour relations: all are loyal to their side, even William Kilbourn's lively history of his father's firm, the Steel Company of Canada.[73] *A Living Profit*, Michael Bliss's study of entrepreneurial attitudes at the turn of the century, includes a fascinating chapter on labour — as yet another of the headaches that separated business men from a satisfying life. The hero of his biography of Sir Joseph Flavelle apparently paid as little attention to the labour problems of his businesses as he did to the immense male and female workforce of the Imperial Munitions Board of 1916-1918.[74]

---

[69]Sally F. Zerker, *The Rise and Fall of the Toronto Typographical Union, 1832-1972: A Case Study of Foreign Domination* (Toronto 1982).

[70]William Baker, "The Miners and the Mediator: The 1906 Lethbridge Strike and Mackenzie King," *L/LT*, 11 (Spring 1983), 89-117; H.S. Ferns and Bernard Ostry, *The Age of Mackenzie King: The Rise of the Leader* (Toronto 1975, original 1955).

[71]Paul Craven, *"An Impartial Umpire": Industrial Relations and the Canadian State, 1900-1911* (Toronto 1980).

[72]Craven, *"An Impartial Umpire,"* 307; Ralph Miliband, *The State in Capitalist Society* (London rev ed. 1972).

[73]William Kilbourn, *The Elements Combined: A History of the Steel Company of Canada* (Toronto 1960).

[74]J.M. Bliss, *A Living Profit: Studies in the Social History of Canadian Business, 1883-1911* (Toronto 1974), 74-94; Bliss, *A Canadian Millionaire: The Life and Business Times of Sir Joseph Flavelle, Bart., 1857-1939* (Toronto 1978). In Bliss's massive history of Canadian business, *Northern Enterprize, Five Centuries of Canadian Business* (Toronto 1987), brief references to labour or unions appear on only 15 of its 640 pages.

***

Among historians, those who trespass too closely on their contemporary world may be accused of the sin of "presentism." This is less because of a decent jurisdictional concern for the rights of their fellow social scientists than because historians fear that the truth will be obscured by incomplete evidence and contemporary bias. Would Ferns and Ostry have savaged the memory of the young Mackenzie King so enthusiastically if trashing the dominant Canadian politician of their young lives was not a satisfying form of rebellion? What if they had shared Paul Craven's access to the King diaries? How far has the great dream of the Soviet Union as a workers' paradise survived post-1989 revelations — or how far does the equal and opposite myth of benevolent liberal capitalism survive the dreadful Yeltsin years in Russia?

Yet the present remains, both as a working environment and as a challenge, particularly for those who relate their scholarship to the issues and struggles of the present world. What is the point of history research that is largely out of touch with the contemporary reality of working-class life and crises? When British Columbia's Social Credit government assaulted the rights and expectations of working people, they merely conformed to left-wing rhetoric about right-wing regimes. Were left-wing warnings vindicated? "We are witnessing today the end of the era of free collective bargaining in Canada," proclaimed Leo Panitch and Donald Swartz. Coercion, they insisted would once again be the means by which State and capital would secure the workers' subordination. Who could mourn the death of a liberal myth? Bryan Palmer anticipated that established union leaders would, as in 1983, sell out their more militant comrades. And, well aware of labour's unpopularity and the rotten alternatives, they did.[75]

In the early 1990s, the counter-attack on workers' incomes and acquired rights resumed across much of Canada. Governments and private employers both responded to the challenges of shrinking revenues, global competition, and the worst recession since the 1930s. Hundreds of thousands of hitherto secure, well-paid and unionized public-sector and manufacturing jobs vanished. Re-employment, when it happened, came largely through minimum-wage service occupations or "McDonaldization." Unions which had fought wage restraint in the 1970s and "give-backs" in the early 1980s, checked with their bankers and their members and, this time, frequently offered concessions. All too often, they were whatever the employer chose to offer. Global corporations and their imitators could ignore local, even national, indignation.

Days lost due to strikes, a measure of union militancy, were already low in the late 1980s; they fell even lower in the new decade. 'What was the point,' workers

[75]Panitch and Swartz, "Towards Permanent Exceptionalism," 133. See also Leo Panitch and Donald Swartz, *From Consent to Coercion: The Assault on Trade Union Freedoms* (Toronto 1985). See also Bryan D. Palmer, "The Rise and Fall of British Columbia's Solidarity," in Bryan D. Palmer, ed., *Essays in Canadian Working-Class History: The Character of Class Struggle* (Toronto 1986), 176-200.

lamented? And what was the use of political alternatives when NDP governments, in power in three provinces including Ontario, seemed as resistant to workers' demands as their pro-business rivals?[76]

Did labour historians have pertinent answers for working people adrift in the worst economic storm in their lifetime? Was a romanticized recollection of working-class history or Wobbly heroism relevant to workers whose jobs had apparently departed to a Mexican border town? Threatened with desperate financial choices, anxious to avoid massive public-sector layoffs, Bob Rae offered Ontario union leaders a new version of the historic deal TLC and CCL leaders had accepted in 1944: an enhanced collective bargaining role in return for income constraints. They promptly turned him down, largely unaware of the history he had described and, frankly, less worried by layoffs than by the precedent of broken contracts.[77] Had the avoidance of "presentism" become escapism? Were collective agreements more important than the lives affected by layoff? How many (or how few) labour historians had given any attention to the advent of Canada's first durable industrial relations regime?[78]

Second generation labour historians deserve enormous credit for creating an impressive body of historical material on 19th- and early 20th-century working-class history. Is that enough? No one would have expected conventional, purportedly value-free historians to choose topics or analysis to promote social justice. As self-conscious role-players in the labour struggle, the "new" historian must share some responsibility for their choice of agenda. Of 96 articles in the first nineteen issues of *Labour/Le Travail* that could be categorized by period, only 22 touched on the forty-year period between 1940 and 1980.[79] Many of these refought battles

[76]Morton, *Working People*, 336-353. See also Jamie Swift, *Wheel of Fortune: Work and Life in the Age of Falling Expectations* (Toronto 1995).

[77] When Bob Rae introduced his Social Contract in his Sefton Lecture at the University of Toronto's Woodsworth College, his analogy was historical: the wartime trade-off of labour peace in return for enduring collective bargaining legislation. The speech brought a standing ovation and widespread incomprehension among the labour leaders in the front row. As another member of the audience observed to me, it was soon apparent that this history was not part of their baggage. See Rae, *From Protest to Power*, 206.

[78]The list is not long. Here are the leading sources: L.S. MacDowell, *I Remember Kirkland Lake": The Gold Miners' Strike of 1941-42* (Toronto 1983); "The Formation of the Canadian Industrial Relations System During World War Two," *L/LT*, 3 (1978), 175-6; "The 1943 Steel Strike Against Wartime Wage Control", *L/LT*, 10 (1982), 65-85; also Jeremy Webber, "The Malaise of Compulsory Conciliation: Strike Prevention in Canada During World War II," *L/LT*, 15 (1985), 57-88. See also J.T. Copp, ed., *Industrial Unions in Kitchener, 1937-1947* (Elora 1976); and "The Experience of Industrial Unionism in Four Ontario Towns, 1937-1947," *Bulletin of Canadian Committee of Labour History*, 6 (Autumn 1978) 4-11.

[79]Based on a survey of articles in *L/LT* issues 1-19. Almost half the more modern articles appeared since 1984, an evident reorientation of interest. For an analysis of the magazine's content, from its origins in 1976 to the end of 1999, see Appendix A.

of the early Cold War or pursued similar traditional themes. Only a few used historical methods to enliven contemporary issues with relevant experience. J.A. Frank's comparative study of four violent and relatively recent Ontario strikes stood out for relevance.[80] So did articles on the Canadian Union of Postal Workers, and on the effect of automation on the role of grain handlers.[81] Beyond the journal, William Kaplan's study of the seamen's unions and the Hal Banks interlude brought a lawyer's evaluation of conflicting evidence to a problem more often obscured by polemics.[82] Rosemary Speirs' unpublished thesis on the railway unions and technological change after 1945 is a rare but valuable example of work that badly needs doing, not for the sake of locomotive firemen but for all of us who face fundamental changes in the way we work.[83] And who doesn't?

One area in which "new" history was hospitable was its recognition of the re-emergence of women as a force in Canadian labour and in its history. The expansion and transformation of bargaining issues by women generated a rich flow of books and articles, much of it generated by women determined to set the record straight. Feminist labour historiography has been summarized by Bettina Bradbury and presented in a series of monographs and collected essays.[84] Women historians also took a lead in recognizing the reluctant evolution of the state in the face of the real and perceived needs of working women.[85]

The recent past presents labour historians with problems as well as opportunities. Since the 1950s, industrial relations specialists were forced to reckon with the

[80]J.A. Frank, "The 'Ingredients' in Violent Labour Conflict: Patterns in Four Case Studies," *L/LT*, 13 (1983), 87-112.

[81]Don Wells, "The Impact of the Postwar Compromise on Canada's Unions: The Formation of an Auto Worker Local in the 1950s," *L/LT*, 36 (1995), 147-174; See also Novek, "Grain Terminal Automation.".

[82]William Kaplan, *Everything That Floats: Pat Sullivan, Hal Banks and the Seamens' Unions of Canada* (Toronto 1987).

[83]Rosemary Speirs, "Technological Change and the Railway Unions, 1945-72," PhD thesis, University of Toronto, 1974. See also Ian Radforth, "Pulpwood Logging Industry in Northern Ontario, 1950-1970," *Historical Papers* (1982), 71-102.

[84]Bettina Bradbury, "Women's History and Working-Class History," *L/LT*, 19 (1987), 23-44. See also Linda Briskin and Lynda Yantz, eds., *Union Sisters: Women in the Labour Movement* (Toronto 1983). A pioneering book, evidence of the energy of the new movement, was Janice Acton, Penny Goldsmith, Bonnie Shepard, eds., *Women at Work: Ontario, 1850-1930* (Toronto 1974).

[85]See, for example, Ruth Roach Pierson, "Gender and the Unemployment Insurance Debates in Canada, 1934-1940," *L/LT*, 25 (Spring 1990), 77-104; Ann Porter, "Women and Income Security in the Post-War Period: The Case of Unemployment Insurance, 1945-1962," *L/LT*, 31 (1993), 111-144; Joan Sangster, "Women Workers, Employment Policy and the State: The Establishment of the Ontario Women's Bureau, 1963-1970," *L/LT*, 36 (1995), 119-146; as well as James Struthers, *The Limits of Affluence: Welfare in Ontario, 1920-1970* (Toronto 1994).

phenomenon of government-employee unionism but historians seldom echoed their interest.[86] There is much that is old and familiar to historians in the struggle to organize both ill-paid service employers and the better-paid but vulnerable employees of the so-called knowledge industries, but there is much that is new too — and some things, such as payment in stock options, which will strike some of us as analogous to company scrip.

***

Almost fifteen years ago, when I last reviewed the state of labour and industrial relations history, I reproduced the weary academic cliché that there was much more to be done. At the time, it occurred to me that historians who were fearful of "presentism" might feel safe in the 1920s, a decade of brilliant hopes and blighted achievements. There was also more to do in the 1930s than the Depression and Third Parties. Jim Struthers' book on the roots of unemployment insurance filled only one of many gaps in the social and industrial relations landscape.[87] For example, the revival of manufacturing with a much higher degree of mechanization was a foretaste of the aftermath of the 1990s recession. In both situations, layoffs led employers to seek either cheaper labour or more capital-intensive production. By 2000, we can see both processes at work.

If reform was less generally despised by radical historians, its processes might be better understood and, therefore, defended or improved. Why did ideas rigidly defended in the dreary 1930s seemingly dissolve without argument after *Blitzkrieg* in 1940. And what was the process through which capitalism survived its apparent rout in the war years. In the 1990s, as in the 1930s, historical hindsight might have been helpful.

The major advances in labour and working-class history during the 1980s and 1990s have come through the expansion of women's history. In an earlier article, I suggested that Ruth Pierson's significant work on World War II needed to be pursued in both directions, before 1939 and from 1945. Pierson herself has helped meet that request.[88] In the 1990s alone, Joy Parr published her study of gender and work in Paris and Hanover, Ontario; Denyse Baillargeon explored the impact of

[86]The standard work is Jacob Finkelman and Shirley Goldenberg, *Collective Bargaining in the Public Service: The Federal Experience in Canada* (Montréal 1983), the first book-length analysis, though it lacks significant historical perspective. More valuable is Mark Thompson and Gene Swimmer, eds., *Conflict or Compromise: The Future of the Public Sector in Industrial Relations* (Montréal 1984), a collection of articles, many of them with an historical approach.

[87]James Struthers, *"'No Fault of Their Own': Unemployment and the Canadian Welfare State, 1914-1941* (Toronto 1983).

[88]Ruth Roach Pierson, *"They're Still Women After All": The Second World War and Canadian Womanhood* (Toronto 1986); Pierson, "Gender and Unemployment Insurance."

the Depression on Montreal housewives, Suzanne Morton looked at life in a post-Explosion Halifax housing development, and Andrée Lévesque explored the social controls a conservative Catholic society devised for single women.[89] Ruth Frager looked at men, women, and work in Toronto's pre-1939 Jewish community, Franca Iacovetta broke old assumptions with her account of Toronto's Italian immigrant working class in the 1950s, and Joan Sangster brought a feminist and radical perspective to the lives of working women in small factory towns in Ontario in ways that at least one of them, my mother-in-law, found quite fascinating.[90] Closer to traditional industrial relations, Sylvie Murphy gave us a feminist view of a women's auxiliary in a local of the International Association of Machinists; Michele Martin brought together a major study of women's role in delivering telephone service; and Pamela Sugiman looked at gender politics in the Canadian district of the United Autoworkers.[91] And those are merely samples from a three-page summary of recent labour books and articles by women. In no journal have they been more densely represented than in *Labour/Le Travail*. If women have found an overdue voice in scholarly discourse as in real life, what about their children and adolescents? We know what adults thought of them but can we ever find their voices?[92]

In the 1980s, a few labour historians anticipated that the forty years after the war were exceptional and, from a radical standpoint, not even very valuable. The notion that the revolution would settle for allowing most workers a home, a car, a

[89]Joy Parr, *The Gender of Breadwinners; Women, Men and Change in Two Industrial Towns, 1880-1950* (Toronto 1990); Denyse Baillargeon, *Ménagères au temps de la Crise* (Montréal 1991; Suzanne Morton, *Ideal Surroundings: Domestic Life in a Working-Class Suburb in the 1920s* (Toronto 1994); Andrée Lévesque, *Making and Breaking the Rules: Women in Quebec, 1919-1939* (Toronto 1994).

[90]Ruth A. Frager, *Sweatshop Strife, Class, Ethnicity and Gender in the Jewish Labour Movement of Toronto, 1900-1939* (Toronto 1992); Franca Iacovetta, *Such Hardworking People: Italian Immigrants in Postwar Toronto* (Montréal 1992); Joan Sangster, *Earning Respect: The lives of Working Women in Small Town Ontario, 1920-1960* (Toronto 1995).

[91]Michele Martin, *"Hello Central": Gender, Technologies and Culture in the Formation of Telephone Systems* (Kingston and Montréal 1991); Sylvie Murray, *A la jonction du mouvement ouvrier et du mouvement des femmes: la ligue auxiliaire de l'Association des machinistes, Canada, 1903-1980* (Montréal 1990); Pamela Sugiman, *Labour's Dilemma: The Gender Politics of Auto Workers in Canada, 1937-1979* (Toronto 1994).

[92]Joy Parr's *Labouring Children: British Immigrant Apprentices to Canada* (London and Montreal 1980) and Neil Sutherland, *Children in English-Canadian Society: Framing the Twentieth Century Consensus* (Toronto 1976) inevitably reflected the largely adult perspective of their evidence. Another contributor, cut off by his tragically early death was John Bullen. See his "Hidden Workers: Child Labour and the Family Economy in Late Nineteenth Century Urban Ontario," *L/LT*, 18 (1986), 163-188. See, more recently, Richard Marquardt, *Enter At Your Own Risk: Canadian Youth and the Labour Market* (Toronto 1998).

[93]See Appendix B.

cottage, free medical care, and old age security in return for eight hours of boring labour was hard to swallow. It would have looked good in the 19th century and it may fade fast in the 21st. And it may indeed have been exceptional. The stagnation of American labour organizations and their decline since the 1950s was delayed in Canada by legislation, declining general income levels since 1978, and the acceptance by both major Canadian parties of growing levels of public debt between 1974 and 1994. Historians may be content to leave economists, sociologists, and political scientists to wrestle with the conundra of the present and the future, taking comfort from the fact that none of them anticipated the collapse of most Communist regimes at the end of the 1980s or, for that matter, the Asian economic crisis of the late 1990s.

Some historians bridle at being invited to anticipate futures. It is ironic that those who are professionally indoctrinated to look backward should have anything useful to say about where we are going. Yet few of us turn down the chance, partly because it may be our only opportunity to be heard, and chiefly because we believe that futures are not inevitable but chosen, and because those who write of workers, their families and their conditions, make conscious choices about the futures we seek. Experience is our most useful guide, and history is its analytical version.

"Second generation" historians of Canada's working class and labour movement must expect a third generation that may live in a very different and rather less optimistic society than those of us who shared or even slightly pre-dated the so-called "Big Generation" of the 1960s. Proportionately, there will probably be fewer of them. Certainly the number of doctoral theses on industrial relations and working-class history is significantly smaller, while military history, a more conservative and usually less popular specialty in the "Peaceable Kingdom" has actually outpaced the field in the 1990s.[93] Having made their major contribution some decades ago, labour historians must wonder whether they will find successors as Canadian universities face the most substantial changing of the professorial guard since the 1960s.

***

If we are both fortunate and deserving, the new "new" historians will inherit our virtues and our ideals and they will surpass our experience. They will speak to their age as we have spoken to ours. And they will see more clearly for being spared grand and illusory ideologies. We may not like them very much but we will do what our unloved mentors did to endure them and to make them better than they might otherwise be. Life will go on, but we know that it can be worse — or better.

Appendix A

An Analysis of *Labour/Le Travail*, Issues 1-44, 1976-1999

1. Principal Themes

Period	Ind. Rel.	Strikes	Unions	Working Lives	Gender	Ethnic Issues	Politics
1970s	11	6	1	11	2	2	7
1980s	17	10	10	22	12	5	17
1990s	18	7	18	12	26	3	21

	Politics	Class	Ideas	Historiography	Agriculture and Fisheries
1970s	7	—	7	2	—
1980s	17	10	6	10	5
1990s	21	6	5	6	6

2. Periodization

	1800-1850	1850-1900	1900-1920	1920-1930	1930-1940	1940-1950	1950-1970	1970-1990	None
1970s	1	11	22	6	5	2	—	—	6
1980s	5	17	35	21	16	12	7	—	23
1990s	9	17	17	18	18	16	31	4	18

3. Location

Period	British Columbia	West	Ontario	Quebec	Atlantic	Canada	United States
1970s	2	7	13	6	4	10	2
1980s	6	13	12	14	13	21	8
1990s	7	8	23	10	10	31	—

4. Language

Issues	Articles in English	Articles in French	Total Articles
1-10	47	4	51
11-20	42	3	45
21-30	42	6	48
31-40	55	2	57
41-50	20	1	21
Total	206	16	222

Note: Articles and, in the early years, Critiques, have been counted. Articles treating more than one of the chosen themes or covering more than one period or location have been counted more than once.

Appendex B
Topics of Graduate Theses in Progress, on Canadian Topics as
Reported to The Canadian Historical Association

The CHA's Register of Dissertations began in 1966 under the editorship of Michael
Swift, with the intention of including MA and PhD theses covering all aspects of
Canada's past as well as history theses on other fields written by Canadians. Theses
were categorized by era, by region, and by type, with cross-referencing to theses
already categorized by region. My initial intention was to compare statistics for
each ensuing decade. However, the Register grew much larger the second year as
more universities reported. In 1986, as an economy measure, MA dissertations in
progress were dropped but reinstated in 1987, though perhaps imperfectly. By 1996,
the Register had grown substantially and categorization was by era and region. In all
the years consulted, clerical errors were common, with theses mis-categorized, US
topics included in Canadian categories, and titles sometimes repeated.

1. PhDs and MAs in Progress as Reported in the Register of Dissertations

Year	Canadian History		Social History		Labour History		Military History	
	PhD	MA	PhD	MA	PhD	MA	PhD	MA
1966	149	167	3	2	4	5	3	11
1967	230	374	2	4	5	11	7	6
1976	468	604	33	38	23	66	13	20
1986	339	*	42	*	28	*	14	*
1987	429	455	80	71	29	38	14	17
1996	581	615	106	138	25	11	33	37
1998	548	558	92	78	19	18	34	28

2. Labour and Military History Theses as a Percentage of Theses in Canadian History

Year		1966	1967	1976	1986	1987	1996	1998
Labour	PhD	3.7	2.2	5.0	8.3	6.8	4.3	3.4
History	MA	3.0	2.9	10.9	*	8.4	1.8	3.2
Military	PhD	2.0	3.1	2.9	4.1	3.3	5.6	6.2
History	MA	6.5	1.6	3.3	*	3.7	6.0	5.0

* No report of MA theses in progress was made in 1986.
# In 1986, 18 of 28 doctoral theses were related to Industrial Relations and its actors and 10
related to working-class life.
In 1996, the balance was 12 for industrial relations and 13 for working-class life.
Source, *Register of Post-Graduate Dissertations in Progress in History and Related Subjects*
1 (1966), 1 (1967), 11 (1976), 20 (1986), 21 (1987), 30 (1996) and 32 (1998).

Industrial Relations at the Millennium: Beyond Employment?

Anthony Giles

"from a materialist perspective ... the task ... is not to re-interpret but to transcend the very idea of industrial relations."[1]

AS THE NEW MILLENNIUM approaches, Industrial Relations (or IR[2]), *qua* field of study, is barely a century old. Conventionally dated from the publication of the Webbs' *Industrial Democracy* in 1897 in the UK and the work of John R. Commons in the United States in the early years of the 20th century,[3] the field of IR began to take root in universities during the inter-war years and then grew rapidly in the context of the postwar settlement and the ensuing 30-year economic boom. When, from the mid-1970s onwards, that boom petered out and the settlement began to unravel, IR too began to slide into a crisis, one from which it has yet to emerge. Indeed, for reasons to be explored below, IR in its present form is unlikely to survive for another one hundred years, and it may even be extinct much sooner than that.

In the first part of this essay, I take a brief backward glance at how IR emerged out of the general concern with the "labour question" to form a distinct field of study and research. In the second part, I take stock of the crisis of relevance that the field has been experiencing in the 1980s and 1990s and examine how that crisis is provoking a transformation of IR into "Employment Relations." In the third part of the essay, I assess this strategy of renewal and find it wanting in a number of respects. In its place, I argue that IR should be recast as the study of *work relations*.

[1]Richard Hyman, *The Political Economy of Industrial Relations* (London 1989), xi
[2]To avoid any ambiguity between the notion of industrial relations as a field of study and as a field of social reality or practice, the former meaning will be rendered here by its acronym,"IR," whereas the latter will be written out in full.
[3]Sidney and Beatrice Webb, *Industrial Democracy* (London 1897); John R. Commons, "American Shoemakers, 1648-1895," *Quarterly Journal of Economics*, 24, 1 (November 1909), 39-84.

Anthony Giles, "Industrial Relations at the Millennium: Beyond Employment?," *Labour/Le Travail*, 46 (Fall 2000), 37-67.

From the Labour Question to Industrial Relations

"industrial relations are in the nature of relations between human beings, arising in connection with the parties to, the terms of, and the working-out of, an agreement, expressed or implied, between Capital, Labor, Management, and the Community ... to unite in the work of production."[4]

Although the objects it studies are found around the world, IR as an institutionally distinct field of teaching and research was largely an Anglo-American invention. In most continental European countries, for example, research into the various aspects of industrial relations was long conducted by social scientists belonging to disciplines like law, sociology, and business administration, with little contact between them.[5] Thus, although there are nearly 40 national associations affiliated to the International Industrial Relations Association (IIRA),[6] and while there have been efforts recently in some countries to carve out a distinct identity for those interested in IR,[7] the field remains very much an Anglo-American phenomenon.

In the Anglo-American countries, IR originated as a response to two problems[8]: the intellectual dissatisfaction with the way neo-classical economics treated wage

[4]W. L. Mackenzie King, *Industry and Humanity* (Toronto 1918), 534.

[5]See Richard Hyman, "Industrial Relations in Europe: Theory and Practice," *European Journal of Industrial Relations*, 1, 1(1995), 17-46. Hyman detects something of a "loosening of disciplinary compartmentalization" in Europe and the emergence of a distinctly European "intellectual synthesis"; however promising these developments are, it is clear that they are embryonic. For an earlier assessment of the European tradition that draws similar conclusions, see Peter B. Doeringer, "Industrial Relations Research in International Perspective," in Peter B. Doeringer, with Peter Gourevitch, Peter Lange and Andrew Martin, eds., *Industrial Relations in International Perspective* (New York 1981), 1-21.

[6]Most of the 37 national associations listed by the IIRA outside the Anglo-American countries are obviously marginal since their membership is rarely more than a few hundred. In terms of individual members of the IIRA, in only five countries — the US, Australia, Canada, Sweden and the UK — were there more than 40 members; and in the great majority of the 86 countries with individual members there were fewer than 10. International Industrial Relations Association, *Membership Directory*, 4th edition (Geneva 1997).

[7]German scholars, for example, launched the journal *Industrielle Beziehungen* (subtitled —in English — "the German Industrial Relations Journal") in 1994.

[8]There are only a handful of historical treatments of the development of IR. At an international level, the two best synopses are Roy Adams, " 'All Aspects of People at Work': Unity and Division in the Study of Labor and Labor Management," in Roy J. Adams and Noah M. Meltz, eds., *Industrial Relations Theory: Its Nature, Scope, and Pedagogy* (Metuchen 1993), 119-160 and Hyman, "Industrial Relations in Europe." For Canada, see Anthony Giles and Gregor Murray, "Towards an Historical Understanding of Industrial Relations Theory in Canada," *Relations industrielles*, 43, 4 (1988), 780-810. For the US, the most thorough treatment is Bruce E. Kaufman, *The Origins & Evolution of the Field of Industrial Relations* (Ithaca 1993). British treatments include George Sayers Bain and H. A. Clegg, "A Strategy for Industrial Relations Research in Great Britain," *British Journal of*

determination, trade unionism, collective bargaining, and social legislation; and the "labour problem" itself, that is, the stirrings of working-class action and the threat it was thought to pose, particularly in its radical forms, to the established social order. In particular, IR was born of a desire to create a middle ground between the conservative implications of neo-classical economics and the radicalism of Marxism on the intellectual terrain, and between repression and revolution on the politico-industrial terrain. Like all species of reformism, then, IR has always faced the delicate task of reconciling what Richard Hyman has called its two faces — the problem of social welfare and the exigencies of social control.[9]

Although the roots of IR can be traced back to the wider concerns over the labour question, the field itself only began to take shape when employers and the state were faced with problems of industrial and political unrest during and immediately after World War I. Indeed, the first official use of the term "industrial relations" is usually cited as the US Congress' 1914 Commission on Industrial Relations — a term that was quickly imported into Canada when the federal government appointed its own Royal Commission on Industrial Relations in 1919.[10] Comparing the 1919 Commission with its 19th century predecessor, the Royal Commission on the Relations of Labor and Capital, Kealey comments that the

very titles of the two Royal Commissions convey much about the transformation that had taken place in Canadian industrial capitalist society in the approximately thirty intervening years. The rather quaint, Victorian "Relations between Labour and Capital" with its echo of classical political economy gives way to the modern sounding "Industrial Relations," hinting now not at conflicting classes but at a system of mutual interests.[11]

That this was more than a hint was confirmed by two treatises published in Canada around the same time: Mackenzie King's *Industry and Humanity* and R.M. MacIver's *Labor in a Changing World*.[12] Both of these works sit at the transition point between the "labour question" and IR. Although still couched generally in terms of social classes, the focus in both was not so much on the conditions of the labouring classes as on the problems of modern, large-scale industry. More particularly,

Industrial Relations, 12 , 1 (March 1974), 91-113. The discussion in this section draws liberally on all of these sources.

[9]Hyman, *The Political Economy of Industrial Relations*, ch. 1.

[10]Gregory S. Kealey, "1919: The Canadian Labour Revolt," *Labour/Le Travail*, 13 (Spring 1984), 10. The British government too appointed a commission to study similar matters in 1917 (the Whitley Committee on Industrial Conciliation), although the first official use of the term industrial relations came later.

[11]Kealey, "1919," 10-11.

[12]King, *Industry and Humanity*; R. M. MacIver, *Labor in a Changing World* (Toronto 1919). The following analysis draws on Giles and Murray, "Towards an Historical Understanding," 787-90.

alongside labour and capital, management entered the picture as an actor in its own right, one whose authority rested not so much on the justifications of property, but on technical and intellectual grounds. Thus, while both King and MacIver urged that labour be brought into "partnership" with management and capital, and advocated a more pronounced role for the state in this regard, the overriding concern was to quell industrial conflict and integrate workers into the social relations of large-scale industry through the creation of mechanisms of worker representation and labour-management dialogue — though not necessarily independent unions and collective bargaining.

Over the following two decades, these themes slowly began to find expression in academe. Courses in "labour problems" and similar subjects had been offered at universities for some time, but the 1920s and 1930s saw the first academic appointments in IR and the creation of the first academic units specifically devoted to the subject. In the UK, the first chairs in IR, endowed by the industrialist Montague Burton, were established in the 1920s.[13] In the US, the Rockefellers underwrote the creation of an "Industrial Relations Section" in the Economics Department at Princeton in 1922, an initiative that was soon replicated, with the financial assistance of other industrialists, at Michigan, Stanford, MIT, and the California Institute of Technology.[14] In Canada, Queen's University also benefited from the largesse of the Rockefellers, supplemented by the support of a number of prominent Canadian companies, when it opened an Industrial Relations Section in its business school in 1937, later to become the Queen's Industrial Relations Centre. Like its American forerunners, the section at Queen's was devoted primarily to hosting conferences, training managers, disseminating information and conducting research on topics of contemporary concern.[15]

The role of business benefactors in promoting and supporting these early centres and appointments was a conscious effort to mould the treatment of labour issues in universities. Clarence J. Hicks, an industrial relations manager who suggested the establishment of the Princeton IR Section and secured the funding for it, acted out of a concern that existing teaching about labour problems was too slanted:

There has been an almost universal stress in the universities on the importance and value of collective bargaining through labor unionism. This is a subject that deserves adequate treatment in any labor course, but it is hardly fair to the student, to the employer, or to the public to send a graduate out with an idea that militant collective bargaining is universally needed and is the only remedy for alleged unfair conditions. The graduate is surprised to find that in the majority of companies such unfair conditions do not exist, and that the average

[13]Bain and Clegg, "A Strategy for Industrial Relations Research," 98.
[14]Kaufman, *Origins and Evolution*, 45-46.
[15]See Laurence Kelly, *Industrial Relations at Queen's: The First Fifty Years* (Kingston 1987).

employee is being fairly treated, not because of collective bargaining, but because of the fairness and friendliness and good business sense of his employer.[16]

Besides wishing to correct the bias of university professors towards the trade union movement, business also wanted a wider and more practical approach that would include the coverage of issues that were of concern to management, particularly those touching on the personnel function.

Yet despite these efforts to shape the new field, writing on labour and industrial relations continued to be predominantly reformist in character. And an important characteristic of this tradition was its cross-disciplinary flavour. Indeed, the founders of IR in the US, Canada, and the UK were for the most part economists or sociologists whose interest in labour issues led them to favour an historically and sociologically oriented mode of research and thinking that was known as institutional labour economics. Thus, besides laying the foundations of IR, they also pioneered the field of labour history.[17] In the UK, the Webbs published *The History of Trade Unionism* before going on to write *Industrial Democracy*. In the US, Commons and his associates at the University of Wisconsin produced *The History of Labor in the United States*. In Canada, one of the few scholars whose work falls into this tradition, H.A. Logan, is regarded as having been not only a pioneer in the development of labour history, but also a leading authority in labour economics.[18] Straddling sociology, labour economics and labour history, this institutionalist approach naturally led the founders of the field to give considerable attention to wider social and policy issues, and thus the role of the state in the field of labour relations and the wider area of social legislation was a common theme in the interwar years.[19]

Despite this emergent synthesis, the labour economists-cum-labour historians were not the only academics to develop an interest in labour issues. The interwar years also saw the growth of a number of fields and disciplines that were guided by more managerial concerns with behaviour at work and its links to issues like productivity and motivation. These fields — industrial psychology, personnel studies and the human relations tradition in sociology — focused less on institutions and more on individual workers and small groups at the level of the shop or the firm, thus creating a stream of research that expressed the social control face of IR in contrast to the reformist orientation of the institutional labour economists.

[16]Clarence J. Hicks, *My Life in Industrial Relations* (New York 1941), 144.

[17]See David Brody, "Labor History, Industrial Relations, and the Crisis of American Labor," *Industrial and Labor Relations Review*, 43, 1 (October 1989), 7-18.

[18]H. A. Logan, *A History of Trade Union Organization in Canada* (Chicago 1928). For a brief appreciation of Logan's contributions, see Mark Inman, "In Memoriam: Harold Amos Logan, 1889-1979," *Canadian Journal of Economics*, 13, 1 (February 1980), 123-24.

[19]For example, W. Milne-Bailey, *Trade Unions and the State* (London 1934); John R. Commons, *Legal Foundations of Capitalism* (1924; Madison 1957).

From the late 1930s onwards, in the context of the spread of industrial unionism
in North America, war-time political and industrial tensions, and the struggle to
establish collective bargaining, the field of IR spread rapidly. In the UK, more
academic positions in IR were created from the late 1940s onwards. In the US, no
fewer than twelve IR centres or institutes were created in 1945-1950 alone. In
Canada, Queen's was not left long without competition. The University of Toronto,
for example, established an Institute of Industrial Relations in 1943, although it
seems to have had more of a sociological bent than one of IR.[20] The first full-fledged
department in the field was created at Laval University within its Faculty of Social
Sciences in 1944, and the University of Montreal followed closely on its heels in
1945.[21] McGill University joined in this rush when it opened an Industrial Relations
Centre in the late 1940s. More generally, scholars who identified with the emerging
field began to be appointed to positions in economics or business in other universities, like Stuart Jamieson at the University of British Columbia; and the field of
labour law began to expand in tandem with the emergence of a distinct field of
collective bargaining and arbitration law and jurisprudence.

These were also the years during which the broader institutional apparatus of
a field of study was fashioned. The first academic journal in the field, *Relations
industrielles/Industrial Relations* (as it eventually came to be called[22]), was
launched by Laval University in 1945, followed in 1947 by the *Industrial and Labor
Relations Review* in the US, in 1959 by the Australian *The Journal of Industrial
Relations*, and in 1964 by the *British Journal of Industrial Relations*. Academic
associations were also created in these years: in the United States, the Industrial

[20]The institute's first director, the economist V. W. Bladen, who found himself "thrown into
the muddy field of industrial relations," developed an interest in Elton Mayo's Hawthorne
studies and "came under the spell of Chicago" and that school's concern with "what men
do" at work and its tradition of detailed "in-plant studies." V. W. Bladen, "Economics and
Human Relations," *Canadian Journal of Economic and Political Science*, 14, 3 (August
1948), 301-02. The current Centre for Industrial Relations at Toronto was founded in 1965,
apparently as an unconnected development.
[21]On Laval, see Gérard Dion, "Les relations industrielles à l'Université Laval," in Georges-
Henri Lévesque, Guy Rocher, Jacques Henripin, Richard Salisbury, Marc-Adélard Tremblay, Denis Szabo, Jean-Pierre Wallot, Paul Bernard and Claire-Emmanuèle Depocas, eds.,
Continuité et rupture: les sciences sociales au Québec (Montréal 1984), 65-85 and James
Thwaites, "Évolution et développement (1943-1987)," in Albert Faucher, ed., *Cinquante
ans de sciences sociales à l'Université Laval* (Sainte-Foy 1988), 183-217. On Montréal, see
Émile Bouvier, "Les transformations des sciences sociales à l'Université de Montréal," in
Lévesque *et al.*, *Continuité et rupture*, 135-39.
[22]Originally entitled the *Bulletin des relations industrielles de Laval/Laval Induustrial
Relations Bulletin* and published on a monthly basis, it became the quarterly *Relations
industrielles/ Industrial Relations* five years later.

Relations Research Association (IRRA) was founded in 1947[23]; in Britain, the British Universities Industrial Relations Association (BUIRA) was founded in 1950[24]; in Canada, the Canadian Industrial Relations Research Institute (renamed the Canadian Industrial Relations Association (CIRA) in 1978) came into being in 1964; and, internationally, the IIRA was founded in 1966.

In short, IR flourished in the postwar era, although in retrospect three tensions revolving around the identity of the field can be identified. First, was it a distinct, self-contained field of study or a multidisciplinary umbrella? Second, was it primarily a pragmatic and practical field geared to intervention or was it an academic area in which scientific goals would predominate? And, third, where did it stand in relation to the ideological issues that are inevitably bound up with class and labour-management conflict?

On the first issue, the dominant — or at least official — view in the early postwar years was that IR was a multidisciplinary meeting ground for scholars from any discipline who were interested in labour and employment issues. Thus, the IRRA's constitution stressed that the new association would encourage research "in all aspects of the field of labor — social, political, economic, legal and psychological — including employer and employee organization, labor relations, personnel administration, social security, and labor legislation."[25] BUIRA, for its part, merely stipulated that members should have "a primary interest in industrial relations."[26] And CIRA even more generously opened its doors to "all persons who have an academic or professional interest in the field of industrial relations in Canada."[27] However, although this loose conception of the field was sustained in the early postwar years, a period during which contributions to the field were made by economists, labour historians, labour lawyers, sociologists, political scientists and others, a second, narrower conception of IR eventually began to displace the multidisciplinary vision. Increasingly, those associated with the new IR centres and departments, as well as those teaching in business schools (where IR tended to be located in most universities), began to focus on the functioning and malfunctioning of the core institutions of union-management relations: unions themselves, the collective bargaining process, strikes, grievances, and public policy in labour-

[23]William H. McPherson and Milton Derber, "The Formation and Development of the IRRA," in Milton Derber, ed., *Proceedings of the First Annual Meeting of the Industrial Relations Research Association* (Champaign 1949), 2-4.
[24]BUIRA was originally called the Inter-University Study Group in Industrial Relations. See John Berridge and John Goodman, "The British Universities Industrial Relations Association: The First 35 Years," *British Journal of Industrial Relations*, 26, 2 (July 1988), 155-177.
[25]IRRA Constitution and Bylaws, in Derber, ed., *Proceedings of the First Annual Meeting*, 236.
[26]Berridge and Goodman, "The British Universities Industrial Relations Association," 158.
[27]Canadian Industrial Relations Research Institute, *Constitution*, article 3, cited in *Relations industrielles*, 19, 4 (October 1964), 519.

management relations. Theoretically, this narrowing was expressed in attempts to develop theories of industrial relations, notably by John Dunlop and Allan Flanders,[28] both of which essentially specified collective bargaining institutions and the outcomes of collective bargaining as the heart of IR.

The effect of this focus, in retrospect, was two-fold. First, it helped to entrench IR as a distinct academic speciality. Second, however, it weakened IR's claim to being a broad church that could bring together specialists from the full range of fields and disciplines that were concerned with the larger set of problems arising from work and employment. Thus, scholars who, despite an avid interest in labour issues, saw their professional identities and careers tied to one of the more traditional disciplines, began to drift away. As David Brody points out in his analysis of how labour history came to separate from IR in the 1950s and early 1960s, the movement affected a number of disciplines:

There was, at once, a retreat from the interdisciplinary scope and the methodological eclecticism that had for so long characterized labor scholarship. Sociologists, political scientists, and anthropologists lost interest in labor topics, while labor economics took up neoclassical analysis with a vengeance, applying it first to the study of human capital, then to whatever else could be subject to deductive, individual-level microanalysis.[29]

To Brody's list we need to add another important group: increasingly, those associated with the fields of personnel and organizational behaviour also felt that the dominant IR approach excluded their concerns, and they too joined the exodus. The result, as Bruce Kaufman has stressed, was a "hollowing out" of IR.[30]

A second tension that eventually emerged in the postwar years concerned the field's practical edge. Although the tradition of involvement in the practical aspects of IR continued, the distinctly reformist tradition of the founders of IR weakened as the new collective bargaining system engineered in the 1930s and 1940s now seemed to call for mechanics and administrators, a role that IR academics were happy to play. Indeed, many of the key figures in the postwar field fashioned careers bridging academia, practical involvement in the field as mediators and arbitrators, and consulting with (or even working in) government. This view of IR as both an academic and a practical sphere was reflected in the fact that both CIRA and the IRRA welcomed practitioners into their ranks (although BUIRA did not). And in the area of teaching, instructional programs were designed as much to train industrial relations specialists as they were to foster research. Even in Québec, where the two industrial relations departments were housed in social science faculties, they were

[28] John T. Dunlop, *Industrial Relations Systems* (New York 1958); Allan Flanders, *Industrial Relations: What is Wrong With the System?* (London 1965).
[29] Brody, "Labor History, Industrial Relations, and the Crisis of American Labor," 9.
[30] Kaufman, *Origins and Evolution*, ch. 6; see also Adams, "All Aspects of People at Work," 128-31.

self-consciously practical in vocation, seeking to train, inform, and educate those involved in the field of industrial relations in modern techniques and thinking.[31]

This practical involvement in the field did not prevent the early postwar generation from developing a rich body of research. In Canada, for example, the two key figures of postwar academic IR, Gérard Dion and H.D. Woods, somehow found time not only for direct involvement in union-management relations as arbitrators, chairs of labour-management committees, and counsellors to government, but also to research and write about the evolving industrial relations system. Their style of research, inherited from institutional labour economics, was heavily descriptive and case-based, oriented chiefly to the formal institutions of IR, and frequently aimed, directly or indirectly, at the pressing policy issues of the time. However, as time passed, IR research gradually began to move away from this tradition and towards a superficially more scientific approach, one which stressed quantitative methods, deductive reasoning, and a focus on the individual rather than the institution.[32] The result of this shift was a dulling of the practical, policy-oriented edge of IR.

The third tension within postwar IR was the longstanding rivalry between its two faces, social welfare and social control. Here, IR tried hard to achieve a "balance." Institutionally, the new centres and associations went to great lengths to hold themselves above — although not aloof from — the labour-management fray. The IRRA, for example, actually included in its constitution the statement that, "The Association will take no partisan attitude on questions of policy in the field of labor"; and BUIRA took a similar line.[33] However, neutrality did not mean that the field lacked an ideological slant. Indeed, while it was possible to be neutral with regard to particular issues or disputes, this could not be extended to the more fundamental question of collective representation and bargaining. Almost to a person, the field was shot through with a profound commitment to the social value — indeed, the inevitability — of union representation and collective bargaining. Thus, where these core values came under attack — as they did in Québec under the Duplessis regime — the new field of IR distinguished itself through its consistent defence of the rights of workers to organize, as in the case of the long and unflinching struggle waged by Laval's Industrial Relations Department in the face of government hostility.

But the conviction that collective representation was desirable did not prevent a drift toward a preoccupation with the exigencies of social control. Although there were some differences between national traditions, postwar IR was dominated by

[31]Dion, "Les relations industrielles à l'Université Laval"; Bouvier, "Les transformations des sciences sociales."
[32]On this shift in research patterns, see Peter Cappelli, "Theory Construction in IR and Some Implications for Research," *Industrial Relations*, 24, 1 (Winter 1985), 90-112.
[33]IRRA Constitution and Bylaws, 236; Berridge and Goodman, "The British Universities Industrial Relations Association," 172.

an approach that has been termed "pluralist-institutional."[34] This entailed an acceptance of the inevitability of a divergence of interest between labour and management, though not of a thoroughgoing division. Thus, the underlying contention of most IR scholars was that unionization brought with it a rough equalization in the power balance between employees and management, a view that at one and the same time provided a justification for state intervention aimed at facilitating union organizing and requiring employers to negotiate with unions, as well as the potential for industrial disruption. During the 1950s and 1960s in particular, the first issue — providing the mechanisms that would allow organization — seemed fairly well settled. True, there were problem areas, for not all employers meekly submitted to the dominant consensus; but on the whole, this part of what increasingly came to be called the "industrial relations system" seemed to be functioning well.

Thus it was the potential for industrial disruption that served as the guiding thread for IR in the postwar years. And here the task of IR was to contribute to the muting of this conflict, particularly through the analysis of the institutions of industrial relations and the way in which those institutions and the procedures they embodied could be shaped in a way that would promote the peaceful and mature handling of disputes. Hyman's comment on IR in the UK also applies to North America:

New disciplines are unlikely to gain admittance to Academe unless they display modesty and deference in the face of established subject areas, and due respect for conventional demarcations. In the case of industrial relations, the entry fee appears to have involved the abandonment of the broad social and political concerns of the pioneer studies. The problem of welfare was relegated to the periphery, while the preoccupation with job regulation brought the problem of control to the centre of the agenda.[35]

Despite these various tensions, the years of the postwar boom were nevertheless good ones for IR. Working from the handful of academic beachheads established in the 1930s and 1940s, as well as within the expanding business schools of the 1950s and 1960s (and the odd economics department or law faculty), IR scholars began to build up a body of knowledge and research about labour-management relations such that, by the end of the 1960s and the early 1970s, IR had become a solidly established field of study. Housed for the most part in business schools or in cross-disciplinary teaching or research centres, self-consciously neutral as to the partisan battles between the labour and management communities which it saw as its clientele, blending scientific ambitions with a continuing, if somewhat weakened devotion to pragmatic intervention, and proclaiming itself as an interdisciplinary

[34]Doeringer, "Industrial Relations Research," 10. Doeringer contrasts this Anglo-Saxon approach, which was oriented toward economics, with the continental European "class approach," which drew more heavily on sociology, law, and history.
[35]Hyman, The Political Economy of Industrial Relations, 8.

meeting ground for all those who were interested in work, IR seemed to have come of age.

The high water mark in this tradition in Canada was almost certainly the Prime Minister's Task Force on Industrial Relations and the large research programme it sponsored.[36] The Report itself was a classic statement of the liberal-pluralist credo and a masterful attempt to calm the growing uneasiness of politicians about Canada's strike record and the apparent growing turbulence in industrial relations. With the advantage of hindsight, however, the call put out to IR academics to help decipher the first rumblings of what was to become, in Eric Hobsbawm's[37] evocative phrase, the "landslide" of the last quarter of the 20th century, also marked the beginning of what was to become a far gloomier period for IR.

From Industrial Relations to Employment Relations

Short of an unexpected resurgence of union victories academic IR will have to make major adjustments. Otherwise it may follow the example of the Cigarmakers and the Sleeping Car Porters, both leaders in their time.[38]

The world of work, employment, and labour relations has undergone dramatic and far-reaching change since the mid-1970s. Whether interpreted as a transition from Fordism to Post-Fordism,[39] a second industrial revolution,[40] the advent of a "new economy" or a "network society,"[41] a B-phase of a Kondratieff long wave,[42] or in some other way, it is abundantly clear that the combined weight of globalization, capitalist restructuring, technological change, neo-liberalism, new social movements, and a host of other forces too numerous to list here, has undermined the seemingly stable IR "systems" that provided a focus and *raison d'être* for the field of IR in the postwar era.

Given these wrenching changes that have swept through IR's claimed territory, the world of employment, one might have supposed that the field would have been prodded into a thoroughgoing reexamination of its theoretical underpinnings; that

[36]Task Force on Labour Relations, *Canadian Industrial Relations* (Ottawa 1968). See Appendix J for a list of the research studies commissioned by the Task Force.

[37]Eric Hobsbawm, *Age of Extremes: The Short Twentieth Century 1914–1991* (London 1994), Part 3.

[38]George Strauss, "Industrial Relations as an Academic Field: What's Wrong with It?" in Jack Barbash and Kate Barbash, eds., *Theories and Concepts in Comparative Industrial Relations* (Columbia 1989), 257.

[39]David Harvey, *The Condition of Postmodernity* (Oxford 1990), Part II.

[40]Michael J. Piore and Charles Sabel, *The Second Industrial Divide: Possibilities for Prosperity* (New York 1984).

[41]Manuel Castells, *The Rise of the Network Society*, vol. 1 of *The Information Age: Economy, Society and Culture* (Oxford 1996).

[42]Terence K. Hopkins and Immanuel Wallerstein, eds., *The Age of Transition* (London 1996).

it would have provided a site for a lively, interdisciplinary exploration of the transformation of work; that it would have served as a magnet for students thirsting for an understanding of the topsy-turvy labour market; that it would have continued its tradition of pragmatism by guiding IR professionals and policy makers through the maze of changes that confront them. Unhappily, this has not been IR's fate.

Although the field continued to expand into the 1970s, by the 1980s and 1990s IR scholars were beginning to wonder openly about the continued viability of their field. Like other fields of academic endeavour, IR has of course lived through a number of episodes of intellectual soul-searching and internal battles over the orientation of the field.[43] However, the last twenty years have been characterised by a far deeper introspection and fretfulness about the future of the field. Joel Cutcher-Gershenfeld, for example, argues that the "field of industrial relations is at a crossroads regarding its substantive focus."[44] Mark Thompson suggests that "…we are at a turning point in our profession or to use the popular academic phrase, 'a paradigm shift.' Our continued concentration on the institutions and issues of the traditional industrial relations system puts us at risk of being marginalized in the broader communities of the academy and policy makers."[45] Thomas Kochan is blunter still: "the field of industrial relations is in a profound state of crisis."[46] Although not everyone in the field shares this pessimism and worry,[47] it is remarkably broadly shared.

One of the obvious signs of trouble is the decline of IR within the university setting, which has taken two principal forms. First, in the US in particular, there has

[43]An early example was the famous exchange between John Dunlop and Willliam Foote Whyte, "Framework for the Analysis of Industrial Relations: Two Views," *Industrial and Labor Relations Review*, 3, 3 (April 1950), 383-401; another was the debate on pluralism in the UK: H. A. Clegg, "Pluralism in Industrial Relations," *British Journal of Industrial Relations*, 13, 3 (November 1975), 309-316 and Richard Hyman, "Pluralism, Procedural Consensus and Collective Bargaining," *British Journal of Industrial Relations*, 16, 1 (March 1978), 16-40.

[44]Joel Cutcher-Gershenfeld, "The Future of Industrial Relations as an Academic Field: A Strategic Planning Approach," in Harry C. Katz, ed., *The Future of Industrial Relations* (Ithaca 1991), 152.

[45]Mark Thompson, "Industrial Relations: The Mother of All Disciplines," 1997 H.D. Woods Memorial Lecture, in *The Changing Nature of Work, Employment and Workplace Relations: Selected Papers from the 34th Annual CIRA Conference*, edited by Paul-André Lapointe, Anthony E. Smith and Diane Veilleux (Québec 1998), 5.

[46]Thomas A. Kochan, "What Is Distinctive about Industrial Relations Research?" in Keith Whitfield and George Strauss, eds., *Researching the World of Work: Strategies and Methods in Studying Industrial Relations* (Ithaca 1998), 31.

[47]The editor of the *British Journal of Industrial Relations*, for example, in his millennium editorial was stubbornly upbeat, claiming that "Industrial relations remains a vibrant inter-disciplinary field with a strong policy orientation." Stephen Wood, "The *BJIR* and Industrial Relations in the New Millennium," *British Journal of Industrial Relations*, 38, 1 (March 2000), 1.

been an attrition in the number of independent IR institutes and degree programmes, either through abandonment or by being renamed Human Resource Management or Employment Relations.[48] Second, and more broadly, there has been a marked shift in the centre of gravity within business and management programs away from IR and towards HRM. In Canada, for example, although the 1980s saw the creation of the first English-language PhD program in IR (at the University of Toronto), a general decline in the standing of IR in business schools — both in terms of IR courses and academic positions —began in the mid-1970s and has continued through the 1980s and 1990s.[49] Where IR continues to exist, questions are raised about its relevance. Mark Thompson's students at UBC "wonder why they should be taking an industrial relations course at all" and "about a curriculum that requires an exotic and seemingly archaic course."[50] Even at Laval University, the home of the largest free-standing academic IR unit in Canada, the department has been grumpily discussing a possible change in the name of its undergraduate degree program from *Relations industrielles* to *Relations industrielles et gestion des ressources humaines*.

A second sign of difficulty has been the stagnant or falling membership in the major academic associations, especially in North America. In the United States, for example, the IRRA lost almost one thousand members between 1987 and 1998.[51] In Canada, CIRA has been experiencing similar difficulties. Although it has always been a relatively small academic association, its membership has shrunk from over 400 at the beginning of the 1990s to less than 300 by the end of the decade. In addition, although it occasionally succeeds in attracting scholars from other disciplines to its annual meetings, it has suffered from the decisions of the Administrative Sciences Association of Canada and the Canadian Economics Association to hold their own free-standing conferences separate from the Learneds, making it more difficult to promote CIRA as a multidisciplinary meeting ground. Finally, in contrast to the IRRA in the US, declining membership and waning relevance do not seem to have sparked any effort within the association to stimulate a serious dialogue about the future of the field in Canada.[52]

[48]Kaufman, *Origins and Evolution*, 143-48.

[49]Anthony Giles, "Does Industrial Relations Belong in the Business School?" in Allan Ponak, ed., *Teaching and Research in Industrial Relations*, Proceedings of the 27th Annual Conference of the Canadian Industrial Relations Association (Québec 1991), 69-79.

[50]Thompson, "Industrial Relations: The Mother of All Disciplines," 4.

[51]The difficulties of the IRRA are discussed in Kaufman, *Origins and Evolution*; Cutcher-Gershenfeld, "The Future of Industrial Relations"; and F. Donal O'Brien, "The State of the IRRA," in Paula B. Voos, ed., *Proceedings of the 51st Annual Meeting of the IRRA*, vol. 1 (Madison 1999), 1-17.

[52]Outside North America, the picture hasn't been so bleak. The IIRA, for example, expanded strongly in the 1980s, though membership has been stagnant in the 1990s.

Third, there is a widespread feeling that IR has lost its audience. As noted above, IR has long prided itself on what Kochan calls its "problem-centred orientation" and its tradition of active involvement in public policy debates, participation in public agencies and links to practitioners. Managers, however, appear to have lost interest in promoting "good labour relations" and have become preoccupied instead with circumventing or avoiding altogether the model of industrial relations long favoured by academic IR. Similarly, the attention of state officials and politicians has been focused not on issues of industrial justice or conflict management, but on the challenges of competitiveness, productivity, and the fostering of workplace innovation. Thus, while IR scholars are still called upon from time to time — as witnessed, for example, by the Sims report or the Canadian Work Research Network supported by Human Resources Development Canada (the name of which speaks volumes in itself) — it is clear that their traditional perspective has much less resonance in management and policy-making circles than it once did.

The fourth sign of difficulty is IR's increasing isolation from other disciplines. Roy Adams, for example, writes that "Industrial relations has not been successful in unifying inquiry into labor and labor management. Instead of achieving recognition as the central institutional vehicle for bringing together those who probe into some or 'all aspects of people at work,' industrial relations has been challenged by the emergence of other interdisciplinary fields the most notable of which are human resources management (personnel) and organizational behavior."[53] This isolation is evident in the scarcity of contributions from outside the field to IR journals, to conferences and to the membership ranks of the academic associations. Indeed, John Godard contends that IR is unable anymore to serve as a meeting ground for those interested in work and is "collapsing in on itself."[54] As he notes, there is a considerable amount of IR-related research being conducted in fields like labour studies, sociology, and political studies, but most of it has not penetrated through the curtain surrounding IR.

Fifth, and perhaps even more fundamentally, there is a sense that IR theory has been unable to come to grips with the profound changes that have occurred since the 1970s. This problem can be traced back to the social and industrial turbulence of the late 1960s, which, as Hyman notes, "left industrial relations academics strangely unmoved. Across Europe, and in more muted form in North America, established institutions of class compromise were under challenge; yet academic industrial relations seemed caught in the time-warp of the transatlantic conservatism of the 1950s."[55] Having constructed a theoretical approach that was rooted in

[53]Adams, "All Aspects of People at Work," 120.
[54]John Godard, "IR After the Transformation Thesis—A Return to Institutionalism?" 1998 H. D. Woods Memorial Lecture, in Paul-André Lapointe, Renaud Paquet, Diane Veilleux and Terry H. Wagar, eds., *Institutional Transformations in the Regulation of Work Relations: Selected Papers from the 35th Annual CIRA Conference* (Québec 1999), 4.
[55]Hyman, *The Political Economy of Industrial Relations*, ix.

the material context of the postwar boom, IR was unable to comprehend the magnitude of the changes. Indeed, the most widely cited theoretical contribution of the last two decades — *The Transformation of American Industrial Relations* [56] — was merely an attempt to graft a "strategic decision making" component onto the older systems theory of industrial relations. [57] Thus, in addition to its other woes, IR is facing a crisis of theory: systems theory has been virtually abandoned because its material foundations have disappeared, with the result that "today ... theoretical disorientation seems even more apparent than when Dunlop wrote." [58]

The reasons for this angst about the future of the field are not difficult to fathom. The most obvious and frequently cited problem that IR has faced is the seeming decline in the salience of its traditional core objects of study — the formal institutions of collective labour-management relations. Chief amongst these, of course, is the institution of unionism. This is most clearly the case in the United States, where the union movement has been devastated since the mid-1970s, but, with a few exceptions, it is a world-wide phenomena. [59] Even in Canada, where IR scholars are fond of pointing to the relative stability of union density rates and are quick to rankle at any suggestion that it is the strong public sector union density that is propping up the union movement, there should perhaps be more disquiet than there is over the fact that in the private sector union density has declined to less than 20 per cent. [60]

But the decline of unionism — and with it the subsiding of manifest industrial conflict — is only the proximate cause of IR's loss of relevance. Instead, as many in the field have observed, the real source of the difficulties lies in the sweeping changes that have occurred in the political economy of capitalism. To begin with, economic and labour market restructuring has changed the familiar setting of industrial relations in a number of important ways: the structure of employment has continued to shift away from those industries in which unions were traditionally strongly entrenched; rising levels of domestic and international competition have created pressures on firms, unions and governments; the decline of the Fordist model of mass production and the increased importance of smaller and dispersed

[56] Thomas A. Kochan, Harry C. Katz and Robert B. McKersie, *The Transformation of American Industrial Relations* (New York 1986).

[57] See Anthony Giles and Gregor Murray, "Trajectoires et paradigmes dans l'étude des relations industrielles en Amérique du Nord," in Gregor Murray, Marie-Laure Morin and Isabel da Costa, eds., *L'état des relations professionnelles: traditions et perspectives de recherche* (Québec and Paris 1996), 74-76.

[58] Richard Hyman, "Theory and Industrial Relations," *British Journal of Industrial Relations*, 32, 2 (June 1994), 166.

[59] See International Labour Office, *World Labour Report 1997-98: Industrial Relations, Democracy and Social Stablity* (Geneva 1997), especially chapter 1.

[60] Gregor Murray, "Unions: Membership, Structures, Actions, and Challenges," in Morley Gunderson, Allen Ponak and Daphne Gottlieb Taras, eds., *Union-Management Relations in Canada* 4th edition (Toronto 2000), Table 4.5.

production units and networks of production among small and medium-sized firms have combined to alter the face of industry; and a host of new technologies are changing the way work is conceived and executed across a wide range of occupations. In this context, employer-labour relations and employment strategies have changed: employers are more willing to challenge openly the legitimacy of unions and the traditional models of labour-management relations, to bypass unions through direct communication with workers through a range of mechanisms designed to enhance loyalty and promote involvement, and to adopt any of a range of non-standard forms of employment that undercut the traditional patterns of worker mobilization, solidarity and identity formation. Mark Thompson sums up the implications for IR in the following terms:

The sectors where most of us have done our research are diminishing in importance as sources of employment and wealth. In some cases, they are shrinking in size absolutely. The events on which our discipline has lavished so much attention and analysis are less frequent and important. The institutions we study and support politically are not significant in the growing sectors of the economy. As a profession, we have very little to say to employees in those sectors whose working conditions are frequently precarious.[61]

These economic and market changes have been accompanied by changes in the political sphere, changes that amount to a political disavowal of some of the cherished assumptions of IR. The rise of neo-liberal ideology and its concomittant policy choices — the obsessive focus on inflation and deficit-cutting, privatization, deregulation, and "individual responsibility" have pushed the traditional concerns of IR to the back burner. More insidiously, perhaps, the focus on international competitiveness as a key overarching state policy objective has put IR on the defensive. In Canada, for example, although outright attacks on unionism and collective bargaining have been largely confined to the public sector, the shift to competitiveness as a policy paradigm has been used to justify a range of regressive steps in labour legislation at the provincial level, as well as a reorientation of labour policy toward the promotion of changes that fits comfortably into the competitiveness strategy: workplace innovation, "partnerships," productivity growth, and stemming the brain drain have replaced wages and working conditions, employee representation, and strikes as the key considerations.

It is hardly surprising, then, that IR appears to be melting down. But despite all the doom and gloom, the field has not stood still, content merely to look back wistfully at the golden age of stable collective bargaining as its contemporary relevance crumbles. Instead, an examination of the literature reveals that there have been changes of three kinds: in the focus of IR research; in the conceptual models brought to bear on these subjects; and in the conception of the field itself. In the

[61]Thompson, "Industrial Relations: The Mother of All Disciplines," 10.

remainder of this part I examine these changes, the first two briefly and the third in more detail.[62]

Milton Derber once criticized IR scholars for their tendency to "follow the headlines,"[63] a trait that has been in ample evidence over the last twenty years or so. First, spurred by the resurgence of managerial opposition to unions and the perception that the initiative in industrial relations had shifted from unions and government to management, IR researchers in the 1980s and 1990s began to pay more attention to the role of corporate strategy and the factors influencing the industrial relations policies of firms. From here it was only a short step to another sphere that IR had long ignored — the workplace, and especially the issues of flexibility, employee involvement, and the propagation of new, "high performance" workplace models.[64] Although other aspects of the changing face of work and employment have also received considerable attention — including the various forms of non-standard or peripheral employment, work in the services sector, and globalization — it is the belated rediscovery of management and the workplace (or, perhaps, the management *of* the workplace) that has increasingly become the *leitmotif* of modern IR research. In fact, Kochan goes so far as to speculate that the wave of workplace-based research in the 1980s and 1990s "may serve as the contemporary equivalent of the Webbs and Commons in documenting both the problems and the promising features of the practices they observed at work-places."[65]

Hyperbole aside, it is clear that in terms of the choice of research topics, IR has certainly not been treading water. However, there is more to the change than a simple enlargement, for associated with the shift in attention to the management of the workplace is a conceptual change of no little significance. In particular, the firm is replacing the "industrial relations system" as the key framework for research and debate in IR. This shift can be traced to Kochan, Katz, and McKersie's reformulation of Dunlop's systems approach. A central feature of their approach was the elaboration of a multi-level strategic choice model which identified three key tiers of industrial relations activity, all three of which — long-term strategy and policy making, collective bargaining and personnel policy, and the workplace — were

[62]Two caveats concerning the following discussion are necessary. First, the intention is to identify a selected number of key trends in IR in recent years, and not to engage in a full-blown literature review. Second, the discussion focuses on mainstream IR and therefore ignores — for the moment — more critical approaches.

[63]Milton Derber, "Divergent Tendencies in Industrial Relations Research," *Industrial and Labor Relations Review*, 17, 4 (July 1964), 605.

[64]A leading example of this research is Casey Ichniowski, David I. Levine, Craig Olsen, and George Strauss, eds., *The American Workplace: Skills, Compensation and Employee Involvement* (Cambridge 2000). For an inspired critique, see John Godard and John T. Delaney, "Reflections on the 'High Performance' Paradigm's Implications for Industrial Relations as a Field," *Industrial and Labor Relations Review*, 53, 3 (April 2000), 482-502.

[65]Kochan, "What is Distinctive About Industrial Relations Research?" 40.

situated within firms.[66] On empirical grounds, there is little difficulty with such a focus, particularly in the US where the decentralization of industrial relations processes and the extraordinary latitude enjoyed by management is more pronounced than anywhere else. However, the effect of the conceptual focus on the workplace and the firm as the key sites of industrial relations has been to shift the thinking of IR toward micro issues, not only in the US, but in Anglo-American IR more generally.

Associated with the shift in focus is a subtle reconceptualization of the firm. In the older models of industrial relations, like systems theory, little distinction was made between the firm and its management: they were treated, together, as one of the "actors" or "parties" to industrial relations alongside workers and their organizations and the state. In contemporary IR research on issues like the high performance workplace, however, the firm is typically portrayed as a neutral site, its identity separated from that of its management. Thus, while there is still scope for a conflict of interest between managers and workers, this conflict occurs within the context of a firm to which all belong and whose survival and performance is not associated with one of those parties, but with all. The effect of this conceptual sleight of hand has been to elevate the goals of the firm to the status of neutral constraints which are imposed from the outside by the exigencies of, for example, global competition. And that external context has made one particular exigency paramount to mainstream IR scholars: how to foster and sustain workplace innovation, thereby shifting IR's conceptual focus away from the fashioning of the "web of rules" or the "institutions of job regulation" and towards the process of organizational change.

In turn, this has shifted concern more fully toward the promotion of co-operation, both in the workplace and at the bargaining table. This empties the employment relationship of even latent conflict, rendering it as a "problem" to be solved. Legitimate conflict remains, but it is now displaced to other fields: the conflict between work and family, between men and women, between the majority and minorities.

Finally, these changes have reinforced the methodolgical trends noted earlier. On the basis of a study of the contents of the leading IR journals in the US, Canada, the UK, and Australia, Whitfield and Strauss conclude that, beginning in the 1960s but more particularly since the 1970s, "There has undoubtedly been a shift away from research that is classed as primarily inductive, qualitative and directly concerned with policy problems and towards research that is quantitative, deductive and concerned primarily with theory building and testing (discipline-oriented)."[67] Despite some variations among countries, the overall trend, they argue, "seems to be toward making IR research methods resemble those of neighbouring fields, such

---

[66]Kochan, Katz, and McKersie, *Transformation*, 15-18.

[67]Keith Whitfield and George Strauss, "Methods Matter: Changes in Industrial Relations Research and their Implications," *British Journal of Industrial Relations*, 38, 1 (March 2000), 145.

as labour economics and much American organizational behaviour research. The specific emphases may differ, but the approach to research probably will not. America may be the leader here, but Britain is moving in a similar direction."[68]

At the same time that research topics, concepts and methodologies have been changing, there has been a shift at a still more general level — the definition and name of the field itself have come under some scrutiny. In particular, reflecting the above trends, but also as a more direct response to the perceived isolation and fading attractions of IR, there is a developing consensus around the proposition that IR as traditionally conceived is too closely associated with a narrow concern with unions and collective bargaining and that a more modern and wider appellation is needed. The leading candidate appears to be "employment relations."[69]

Although the academic associations and existing journals have so far stoutly resisted efforts to get them to abandon their traditional names, a number of scholars in the field have advocated the replacement of Industrial Relations with Employment Relations.[70] In addition, books and articles that would have been styled IR only a few years ago are now being given the new label.[71] Finally, several recently launched journals in (or close to) the field have opted for titles using "employment."[72] However, beneath this seeming consensus, a considerable degree of ambiguity over the exact nature of this redefinition and its implications remains. Indeed, it is possible to discern at least three competing conceptions of ER, and thus, three different strategies for reinventing IR.

The first is a simple name change and a broadening of the field so as to include the study of phenomena that have typically been the preserve of Personnel/HRM. In this conception, the new Employment Relations would entail, as Joel Cutcher-Gershenfeld puts its, the reassertion of IR "as a core source of new ideas (though not the only source) regarding theory, practice and policy on all aspects of the employ-

[68]Whitfield and Strauss, "Methods Matter," 148.

[69]The term "employment relations" is hardly new. The IRRA itself, for example, published a research volume in 1960 entitled *Employment Relations Research: A Summary and Appraisal*, with chapters on the labour force and labour markets, selection and placement, compensation, public policy and dispute settlement, the history and theory of the labour movement and technological change and industrial relations.

[70]Kaufman, *Origins and Evolution*, 167; Thompson, "Industrial Relations: The Mother of All Disciplines," 10; Cutcher-Gershenfeld, "The Future of Industrial Relations," 154.

[71]Richard Locke, Thomas Kochan and Michael Piore, *Employment Relations in a Changing World Economy* (Cambridge, Mass. 1995); Greg J. Bamber and Russell Lansbury, *International and Comparative Employment Relations* 3rd edition (London 1998) (the older editions of which were entitled *International and Comparative Industrial Relations*); Harry C. Katz and Owen Darbishire, *Converging Divergences: Worldwide Changes in Employment Systems* (Ithaca 2000).

[72] *New Technology, Work and Employment, Employee Relations*, and the *International Journal of Employment Studies*. Bucking the trend, however, is the *European Journal of Industrial Relations*.

ment relationship."[73] Similarly, Mark Thompson endorses the idea of adopting ER, but cautions against trying to include "all of the topics traditionally within human resources management. It would focus on relations, not management, in keeping with the pluralistic tradition of our field."[74] In essence, then, this strategy — one favoured by the liberal-pluralist wing of IR — is to continue to differentiate IR from its main rivals while at the same time attempting to occupy some of their territory, chiefly that of HRM.

The second conception of ER uses the term as a new appellation for the broad conception of IR that prevailed in the early postwar years, implying a strategy of reconstituting a multidisciplinary alliance of researchers who are interested in problems springing from the employment relationship. As a president of the IRRA recently pleaded:

All of those who study the many aspects of work should be part of this association. Our tent is large enough to cover not just those with degrees in industrial relations, but also the psychologists, sociologists, economists, and lawyers who study the nature of work, the organization of work, the motivation of workers, and the resolution of disputes about work.[75]

Although usually expressed as an appeal to the many disciplines that touch on the world of work, this strategy essentially represents something of a peace treaty between IR and HRM. Thus, within this rebuilt broad church, IR would continue to exercise a considerable degree of autonomy, though its distinctiveness would no longer rest on a specialization in unions and collective bargaining, but on institutions and collective action more broadly.[76]

A third, much more ambitious meaning attached to the notion of Employment Relations is that of a unified IR/HRM paradigm rather than a multidisciplinary alliance. This strategy tends to be implied rather than articulated coherently. For example, Katz and Darbishire's comparative analysis of employment systems offers only a minimal definition — systems of employment relations, they write, govern "such matters as the rights of workers, unions, and managers; the nature work practices; and the structure and mechanisms of union representation"[77] — and their analytical framework focuses on "workplace practices," including management authority structures, the role of work teams, compensation systems, career structures and relations with unions. For their part, Locke, Kochan and Piore focus on four elements of employment relations: employment and staffing practices, compensation, skill formation, and work organization. In both of these cases, the

---

[73]Cutcher-Gershenfeld, "The Future of Industrial Relations," 152-53.

[74]Thompson, "Industrial Relations: The Mother of All Disciplines," 10.

[75]Donal, "The State of the IRRA," 5.

[76]See, for example, Kaufman, *Origins and Evolution*, ch. 8; and Cutcher-Gershenfeld, "The Future of Industrial Relations."

[77]Katz and Darbishire, *Converging Divergences*, 2.

conception of employment relations clearly is built on a synthesis of IR and HRM, although no effort is made to justify or defend the particular components.[78]

The differences between these three approaches to ER have important implications for the future of the field, since each represents not only a distinct intellectual direction, but a particular strategy in relation to other fields and disciplines. For our purposes, however, what is important is the wider consensus around the need for a new definition of the field. Indeed, at all three levels, IR's crisis of relevance has provoked a shift away from industrial relations and towards a broader notion of employment relations: in its substantive focus, the field is more than ever willing to explore the firm and the workplace, the unorganized sector, and employment relationships that fall outside the dominant postwar model; in terms of the concepts and methodologies that it mobilizes in this task, there is an emergent focus on the organization and the individuals that work in these organizations; and in terms of self-definitions, there are attempts to redefine the field so that it covers all aspects of employment.

From Employment Relations to Work Relations?

"Employment is simply one form of work."[79]

Is "employment relations" the right path to follow? The first thing that must be said is that "employment relations" is certainly preferable to "industrial relations." The widening of the field to include all forms of employment relations, as well as its new found interest in management and the workplace, are potentially welcome developments. On the one hand, it treats the non-union workplace as an arena in which, despite the lack of formal representation, employers and workers interact and manage to fashion arrangements for regulating work and determining the outcomes. On the other hand, the broader notion of employment relations also brings onto the research agenda dimensions of employer-employee relations that were almost wholly ignored in traditional IR research, notably the production strategies and practices of firms and managers and their impact on the capacity of workers to mobilize collectively. Finally, employment relations is vastly preferable to the execrable "human resource management," redolent as it is with the notion that the worker is little more than an *instrumentum vocale*, or "speaking tool," as slaves were regarded in Roman legal theory.[80]

[78]One exception to this implicit mode of paradigm building is Stephen Hill's elaborate construction of an employment relations approach that seeks to frame the issue in terms of a variety of human resource issues. See Stephen M. Hills, *Employment Relations and the Social Sciences* (Columbia 1995).

[79]R.E. Pahl, "Editor's Introduction: Historical Aspects of Work, Employment, Unemployment and the Sexual Division of Labour," in R.E. Pahl, ed., *On Work: Historical, Comparative and Theoretical Approaches* (Oxford 1988), 12.

[80]Perry Anderson, *Passages from Antiquity to Feudalism* (London 1978), 24-25.

There are, however, three broad reasons for doubting that salvation can be found by converting IR to "ER." First, as currently conceived, ER is in very real danger of becoming a managerial science only slightly more liberal than HRM, thereby having the opposite effect than that sought by those who wish to preserve a distinctive approach. Second, the rush to abandon some of the key analytical principles of IR overlooks the distinct possibility that the current era of transformation may well be followed by a resurgence of some of the old-fashioned tensions, problems and conflicts that were at centre stage in the "old IR," leaving the field as analytically ill-prepared as it was when the postwar settlement crumbled. Third, there are grounds for doubting that the concept of "employment" is much of an improvement over "industrial relations" as the conceptual touchstone of a field of study. After looking at each of these problems, I will argue that a better strategy is to go beyond employment and recast the field as the study of "work relations."

As should be clear from the discussion in the preceding section, the first problem is that ER, at least in its North American form, is rapidly becoming a more overtly managerial science, veering even more sharply than postwar IR to the social control face of the field's tradition. In fact, as John Godard has argued, the "new consensus" around the promotion of the high performance workplace bears an uncanny resemblance to the old human relations tradition.[81] He cites three aspects of this drift toward managerialism: an overemphasis on the economic effects of new work systems and their impact on competitiveness, with a corresponding lack of attention to their impact on workers and the wider economy; a heightened risk that ER will simply be absorbed into HRM; and the fact that ER all but ignores the underlying conflictual dynamic of the employment relationship.

It is important to stress that these problems do not arise from ER's focus on the workplace or the firm. No one would suggest, for example, that labour process researchers or the new labour historians of the 1970s and 1980s adopted a managerial orientation by virtue of the fact that they sought to explore, *inter alia*, variations in managerial strategies for controlling work and workers. In other words, there is nothing inherently wrong — and much that is commendable — in studying management and its practices. However, when the study of the workplace and firm-level employment practices begins to adopt managerial perspectives and problem definitions as the fundamental point of departure in research, the risk becomes real that the wider issues of equity and social justice will fade away to the status of pious afterthoughts. Moreover, when the focus shifts to the firm, the connections between production, firms and the wider system of social relations in which they are embedded become hazy.

This is more than a mere risk in the dominant vision of North American IR/ER. Synoptically, this interpretation holds that globalization and technological change have conjoined to create a "challenge of competitiveness" that requires firms to

---

[81]Godard, "IR After the Transformation Thesis"; Godard and Delaney, "Reflections on the High Performance Paradigm's Implications."

take one of two paths. The first of these paths (the "low road") entails competition through cost-cutting, with a particular focus on labour costs, achieved through a mixture of work intensification, wage cuts, and opposition to unions. The second path (the "high road") is more progressive. As Batt recently summarized it:

The argument is that work organized under the logic of mass production to minimize costs alone is no longer compatible with current markets, which demand competitiveness on the basis of quality, cost, innovation, and customization .... High involvement systems, by contrast, produce better quality and efficiency because work is designed to use a higher-skilled work force with broader discretion in operational decision-making; human resource ... practices such as training, performance-based pay, and employment security provide complementary incentives for workers to continuously learn and innovate....[82]

Admittedly, IR researchers are virtually all lined up behind the high road option, and much recent research in IR is a thinly disguised attempt to convince employers, unions and governments that this path is more profitable and socially beneficial than the low road. Yet despite this liberal tinge, the underlying message is clear: the *sine qua non* of the high performance workplace is the results for *employers*; and the way to achieve this is for workers and their unions to adjust to the new reality. The task of researchers is, first, to identify the factors that will lead to the successful implantation of new work systems and the conditions under which they can be sustained over time, and, second, to demonstrate (primarily to managers) that this option is more profitable, at least in the long term. The dynamic here is not one of give and take, of struggle around the modalities of new patterns of work, but rather one of abandoning the blinkered defence of old ways and joining management in the search for prosperity and survival.

The second problem is with the assumption that the last quarter century represents a sharp and absolute break with the past that has seen a fundamental change in the nature of the employment relationship. On this view, the changes have been so profound that the world of work has irrevocably altered: gone are the days of "adversarialism," "inflexible collective agreements," and workplace rigidities. Unions may survive, but they will have to become partners with management in the relentless quest for higher productivity if they want to be able to offer anything to their members. Strikes will become oddities, registering a failure of communication.

Against this interpretation, it might be proposed that the events of the last quarter century, although obviously bringing about significant and, in some cases irreversible changes, represents as much a long-term cycle in the social relations of production. Disciples of Kondratieff will need no convincing of this alternative view, but even those who are more skeptical might admit of the possibility that history is replete with examples of extended periods during which class conflict

---

[82]Rosemary Batt, "Work Organization, Technology, and Performance in Customer Service and Sales," *Industrial and Labor Relations Review*, 52, 4 (July 1999), 539-40.

has seemingly been quelled, management has exercised a relatively unrestrained hand, the state has ceased to pretend to be interested in the plight of workers, and conditions of misery were said to be rapidly becoming a thing of the past. As John Kelly argues, the literature advocating social partnerships between labour and management is characterized by "an absence of any historical analysis of patterns of labour-management relations. Union cooperation with employers has been promoted repeatedly throughout the history of capitalism, and defended on the now-familiar grounds that union militancy is anachronistic and destructive .... Yet the persistence of industrial conflict and the regular outbreak of strike waves over the past century ought to have cast at least some doubt on the validity of these latter claims."[83] The problem, then, is the not inconsiderable risk that transforming IR into ER will leave the field unprepared to analyze the resurgence of conflict.

But there is a third, and wider problem entailed by the notion of employment, the fact that employment is not the only, nor indeed even the main social form through which productive work is organized. Thus, replacing IR with ER leaves the field with the same problem: a core definition that is linked to a geographically and historically bounded phenomenon.

To begin with, in historical terms the use of employment as a social mechanism for organizing work is relatively recent. Although there is no shortage of examples of paid labour in the pre-industrial, pre-capitalist age, it is widely recognized that the modern employment relationship emerged in intimate connection with the spread of capitalist social relations of production. Indeed, in some ways the distinction between work performed for remuneration and work performed in the context of, say, the home or the family farm, only took on importance at a late stage. "The notion that one should obtain most, if not all, of one's material wants as a consumer by spending the money gained through employment emerged for the first time in the nineteenth century."[84]

To be sure, employment became the dominant form of organizing labour in the 19th and 20th centuries in the advanced capitalist political economies; and, although we might quibble over the details, in the industrialized communist countries as well. Yet, at the end of the 20th century, the majority of the world's working population still falls outside what the World Bank calls the "modern employment sector."

Of the 2.5 billion people working in productive activities worldwide, over 1.4 billion live in poor countries .... In poor countries 61 percent of the labor force works in agriculture, mainly tending family farms, while 22 percent work in the rural nonfarm and urban informal sectors, and 15 percent have wage contracts, mainly in urban industrial and service employment.[85]

[83]John Kelly, *Rethinking Industrial Relations: Mobilization, Collectivism and Long Waves* (London 1998), 14-15.

[84]Pahl, "Editor's Introduction," 12.

[85]World Bank, *World Development Report 1995: Workers in an Integrating World* (Oxford 1995), 2.

Even in the middle-income economies, the proportion of workers in formal paid employment in industry and services is only 46 per cent.[86] Thus, outside the 24 high-income countries, the notion of employment is inapplicable for the majority of workers, or takes on such a different social meaning as to be fundamentally altered.

Furthermore, even in those countries where employment is the dominant social mechanism for organizing work, the last twenty-odd years have seen a pronounced shift away from the standard model of employment that informs much of traditional IR thinking. We certainly don't need to subscribe to the more fantastical versions of the end-of-employment thesis to appreciate that this trend is of key importance in understanding how work is organized. Although there is considerable debate over how to define standard as opposed to nonstandard employment, and despite a number of variations from country to country, it is clear that employment relationships have become, as Lowe, Schellenberg, and Davidman put it, "more diverse, individualized, implicit, deregulated, decentralized, and generally more tenuous and transitory."[87]

Last, even if the concept of employment was loosened sufficiently to allow the various nonstandard forms (including some types of self-employment) to be included, it would still exclude unpaid work, that is, work that is necessary or socially useful but that is carried on outside the domain of the market — whether in the household, the volunteer sector or even in the workplace itself. As Anne Forrest has convincingly argued, the dominant theoretical traditions in IR have served to exclude unpaid work from the field.[88]

In sum, then, although the drift towards "employment relations" as an alternative to IR is potentially positive, three problems raise doubts about its viability as a strategy of renewal. First, the current pattern of research suggests that the field might simply be subsumed under the umbrella of HRM and converted into an even more managerial science than it currently is. Second, the downgrading of conflict within the approach runs the risk of leaving it shorn of the capacity to analyse conflict in the future. Third, and more fundamentally, employment, for the reasons spelled out above, is an inherently constrictive concept that, although widening the

[86]It might be argued that work in the urban informal sector should be included in the notion of employment, and even paid employment; but its unofficial, clandestine or illegal nature serves to exclude it from the commonly understood definition of employment current in IR/ER.

[87]Graham Lowe, Grant Schellenberg and Katie Davidman, "Re-Thinking Employment Relationships," Canadian Policy Research Networks, Discussion Paper No. W/05. (Ottawa 1999), 4.

[88]Anne Forrest, "The Industrial Relations Significance of Unpaid Work," *Labour/Le Travail*, 42 (Fall 1998), 199-225. For a thorough review of the problem of excluding unpaid work in various forms from national labour force and production statistics, see Lourdes Benería, "Le travail non rémunéré: le débat n'est pas clos," *Revue international du Travail*, 138, 3 (1999), 317-342.

boundaries of the field beyond its traditional obsession with formal labour-management relations, remains tied to an historically and geographically defined phenomenon. If IR is to survive for any length of time as a distinct field, then, it needs to go beyond employment. In the remainder to this section, I offer some thoughts on how this might be accomplished.

The obvious candidate to replace employment is *work*. Whereas employment is a geographically and historically specific social arrangement through which productive activity is organized, the activity of work is universal. To be sure, the cultural and social significance of work, and even its very distinctiveness as an activity separate from other aspects of life, has evolved over time and continues to vary across societies.[89] Nevertheless, it is the genus of which employment is a species and therefore provides a more secure foundation for the reinvention of IR.

Indeed, in some respects, it is not even necessary to redefine IR, for one of the most frequently cited definitions of the field — "an interdisciplinary field that encompasses the study of all aspects of people at work"[90] — already does so. More generally, just as "employment" has crept into the vocabulary of IR over the last decade or so, it is possible to detect a growing use of the term "work," either alone or in conjunction with employment. A particularly telling example is the title of the IRRA's recently launched magazine, *Perspectives on Work*, the editorial introduction to which actually contained more references to "work and employment" than to "industrial relations."[91]

However, it is also clear that these references are not really meant to extend the purview of IR to all forms of work. As a number of commentators have observed, "work" is often used, within IR and more generally, as virtually synonymous with paid employment.[92] Thus, while its growing use hints at a willingness to broaden the field so as to cover a wider range of contemporary remunerated activities, it still falls well short of the radical redefinition that is required to provide a foundation for a more general field.

This is not to argue that the widest possible meaning of work should be adopted. Raymond Williams, for example, notes that the general meaning of work — the sense of "doing something," "something done" or "activity and effort or achievement"[93] — encompasses a range of activities that are more properly regarded as leisure or recreation. Instead, what is needed is an intermediate sense, one that is

[89]See, for example, G.M. Kelly, "L'emploi et l'idée de travail dans la nouvelle économie mondiale," *Revue internationale du Travail*, 139, 1 (2000), 5-35.
[90]Thomas A. Kochan, *Collective Bargaining and Industrial Relations* (Homewood 1980), 1.
[91]"Work and Employment Relations for the 21st Century," *Perspectives on Work*, 1, 1 (1997), 2-5.
[92]See Forrest, "The Industrial Relations Significance of Unpaid Work"; Peter Nolan, "Work," in William Outhwaite and Tom Bottomore, eds., *The Blackwell Dictionary of Twentieth-Century Social Thought* (Oxford 1994), 715-17.
[93]Raymond Williams, *Keywords* (London 1976), 281.

wider than paid employment or remunerated activity on the one hand, yet is narrower than simply the expenditure of effort. One such definition is offered by Claus Offe and Rolf Heinz, who seek to draw a line between "useful activities" and "work" by reference to largely subjective criteria: "with all due credit to the many utility creating activities outside the sphere of gainful employment, an activity can only be described as 'work' if it is directed towards an objective that is both *premeditated* and also *regarded as useful not only by the worker but also by others*, and accomplished with a reasonable degree of efficiency and technical productivity."[94] On these grounds, they exclude from the realm of work purely leisure activities (like hobbies), "relationship work," participation in voluntary associations, and so on. A wider definition is offered by Henrietta Moore who includes unwaged productive work, domestic work, welfare work, emotional work, and human capital work.[95] A third approach is to focus on the transformational character of work, as does Robert Cox:

Work can be defined as action toward the transformation of nature for the purpose of satisfying human needs and desires. The direct satisfaction of human needs and desires is not work, e.g., eating, conviviality, sexual activity, and sleep. Work is what is done to make these direct satisfactions possible — producing the food, building the physical structures within which actions to satisfy human needs take place, creating symbols that evoke such activity, and building the social institutions and moral codes that channel and regulate this activity.[96]

Although these various approaches to the question are hardly identical, they have three characteristics in common: all seek to situate paid employment as just one type of a range of social arrangements through which people produce the material and symbolic conditions of human existence; all stress the social embeddedness of work[97]; and all focus not on work in the abstract, but on the pattern of relations between individuals, groups and organizations that spring from the way work is organized. This latter point is crucial, for it indicates that Kochan's definition — the study of "all aspects of people at work" — is in fact too wide. IR has never contemplated such a focus; instead, the traditional objective, although

[94]Claus Offe and Rolf G. Heinze, *Beyond Employment: Time, Work and the Informal Economy*, translated by Alan Braley (Philadelphia 1992), 67.

[95]Henrietta L. Moore, "The Future of Work," *British Journal of Industrial Relations*, 33, 4 (December 1995), 657-678.

[96]Robert W. Cox, *Production, Power, and World Order: Social Forces in the Making of History* (New York 1987), 13.

[97]As Pahl puts it, using the classic example of childcare provided by mothers in the home compared to that provided by paid caregivers, "clearly it is not the nature of the task that matters most in determining whether or not it is to be financially rewarded and whether it is to count as 'work', but rather the social relations in which the task is embedded." "Editor's Introduction," 12.

too often narrowly interpreted, has been the patterns of social relations connected to work — in short, *work relations*. It is this focus on the social relations of work that can and should be extended outside of the walls of the standard employment relationship, outside the boundaries of the market and into the household and other sites of productive work, outside the borders of the small group of rich nations where IR has always been concentrated, and outside the limits of the specific historical epoch in which paid employment has held sway.

Although the intellectual advantages of such a redefinition seem obvious, what possible relevance would such a strategy have for the *field* of IR? Would a focus on work relations be any more promising than the current drift towards employment relations? In fact, it is possible to identify three clear advantages, each of which could contribute to a genuine revitalization of IR.

First, a focus on work relations would help overcome the limits of ethnocentrism that have long constrained the reach and appeal of IR. As we saw earlier, IR has traditionally been centred in the Anglo-American world, partly because of academic traditions and partly because its central concepts do not easily apply outside a relatively small set of countries. A focus on work relations, however, would have a wider resonance. On the one hand, it would lay the basis for a richer cross-fertilization with European traditions of social analysis, one of the characteristics of which has been to situate industrial relations phenomena within their wider socio-political setting. On the other hand, opening the field to the study of patterns of work relations outside the formal employment sector would open the door to its application to the vast regions of the world in which structured employment relationships are overshadowed by other modes of social relations of production.

Second, the study of work relations would loosen the influence of HRM and labour economics on the field and provide the basis for a more genuinely multi- or even interdisciplinary alliance of the kind that IR claims to want to foster. Although it would be naive to expect that a name change alone would have sociologists, political scientists, historians or labour lawyers beating at IR's doors, it is at least as likely to spark some genuine cross-disciplinary interest as is the current obsession with productivity in the "high performance workplace." Moreover, in a number of closely connected fields and disciplines, there are some signs of a parallel rethinking process that might lead to more openness to the fostering of the study of work relations from a number of different disciplinary perspectives. One natural ally is the field of labour studies, itself a cross-disciplinary effort to promote a wider understanding of labour. Indeed, in many respects, labour studies has assumed the mantle that IR used to wear, particularly in its orientation to the social welfare lens and its more rounded attempt to integrate the full range of social science disciplines. Moreover, as a precarious, even peripheral component of academic life, it too would presumably benefit from a wider alliance.

As for IR's ex-allies, at least some scholars in the fields of labour history, labour law, and even HRM have begun to consider ways of redrawing the conceptual maps of their analytical territories in ways that are not dissimilar to that proposed above for IR. For example, labour history underwent a transformation some time ago that saw a widening of its scope beyond the traditional labour institutions and incorporating a wider conception of work; and Christopher Tomlins has recently argued for the need to reconsider "the temporal and substantive bounds of American labor history" and has advocated an "approach that treats the social relations that structure production and reproduction as the subject for labor-historical inquiry and concentrates that inquiry in particular on the nature and character of the means by which human agents seek actively and continuously to characterize, construct and reconstruct those social relations, and thereby achieve degrees of influence and control over the social processes they structure."[98] In the field of labour law, there has been a shift underway for some time from the notion of "labour law" to "employment law"[99]; and some are working to stretch the notion of labour law even further, to include a range of work arrangements traditionally ignored by their discipline.[100] Even in the field of HRM, there are those who have expressed disquiet over the state of their field.[101] Moreover, there is a developing "radical" approach to HRM that takes it as an object to study and critique rather than as a practice to expound and ameliorate.[102] In the UK, for example, the analysis of HRM often breaks with the pro-managerial, prescriptive style of much North American writing; and even in

[98]Christopher Tomlins, "Why Wait for Industrialism? Work, Legal Culture and the Example of Early America—An Historiographical Argument," *Labor History*, 40, 1 (1999), 6, 12. See also the replies by David Montgomery, Daniel Nelson, and Howard Rock, as well as Tomlins' rejoinder.

[99]In 1986, the authors of the leading casebook in the field widened the coverage beyond collective labour relations law to include "all three legal regimes (common law, statutory regulation, and collective bargaining) governing *work relations*" (The Labour Law Casebook Group, *Labour Law*, 4th ed. (Kingston 1986), vii, emphasis added.) By the 1998 edition, the title had changed to *Labour and Employment Law*. A similar evolution has occurred in Québec, where *le droit de l'emploi* has begun to replace *le droit du travail*. See, for example, Fernand Morin and Jean-Yves Brière, *Le droit de l'emploi au Québec* (Montréal 1998).

[100]See, for example, Harry Arthurs, "Landscape and Memory: Labour Law, Legal Pluralism and Globalization," in Ton Wilthagen, ed., *Advancing Theory in Labour Law and Industrial Relations in a Global Context* (North-Holland 1998), 21-34; Guylaine Vallée, "Pluralité des statuts de travail et protection des droits de la personne: Quel rôle pour le droit du travail?" *Relations industrielles*, 54, 2 (1999), 277-312; Alain Supiot, "Les nouveaux visages de la subordination," *Droit social*, 2 (février 1999), 131-145.

[101]See, for example, Jeffrey Pfeffer, "Incorporating Social Context: Towards a Broader View of Organizations and HRM," in Paula B. Voos, ed., *Proceedings of the Fiftieth Annual Meeting of the IRRA*, vol. 1 (Madison 1998), 228-235

[102]For example, Barbara Townley, *Reframing Human Resource Management: Power, Ethics and the Subject of Work* (London 1994).

the US there are already some forums that seek to promote a more critical view, like the Critical Management Studies Workshop.[103]

Third, recasting IR as the study of work relations would provide a stimulus to more serious theoretical reflection. Just as the shift from industrial to employment relations has led at least some scholars to explore the *terra incognito* of the non-unionized workplace and company unions (rather than simply dismissing them as irrelevant or the property of HRM), a broader shift to work relations would force IR scholars to engage in a more thoroughgoing rethinking of their key analytical categories.

Although this is hardly the place to engage in such an exercise, it is worth noting that a number of unconventional approaches that have so far remained marginal in IR (at least in the English-speaking countries) offer some intriguing analytical possibilities. For example, as Gregor Murray, Christian Lévesque, and Guylaine Vallée have recently argued, a core concept that bridges a variety of mainstream and critical analyses in IR is "labour regulation."[104] Although they apply it only to advanced capitalist societies, the notion of labour regulation might easily be extended to other regimes of work relations, for, as Karl Renner once wrote, "No society has yet existed without a regulation of labour peculiar to it, the regulation of labour being as essential for every society as the digestive tract for the animal organism."[105] Another potentially generalizable framework would be John Kelly's recent argument in favour of a focus on "collective mobilization."[106] Like the concept of labour regulation, collective mobilization, at least if it is understood as encompassing a wide range of forms of collective action, is applicable outside the narrow confines of employment-based systems. A final example of a potential framework for the study of work relations would be Robert Cox's effort to redefine IR in terms of the social relations of production — defined in terms of "the power relations governing production, the technical and human organization of the production process, and the distributive consequences"[107] — which can be applied to a wide variety of work settings:

... production relations govern every kind of work. Production relations exist in subsistence agriculture and in domestic housework, as well as in the large modern factory. Production relations govern the itinerant peddler in India, the shoeshine boy in Mexico City, the pimps and prostitutes of Taipei, the advertising executives Madison Avenue, the stockbrokers of

[103] Visit http://www.aom.pace.edu/cms/manifesto.html

[104]Gregor Murray, Christian Lévesque and Guylaine Vallée, "The Re-regulation of Labour in a Global Context: Conceptual Vignettes from Canada," *Journal of Industrial Relations*, 42, 2 (June 2000), 234-257.

[105]Karl Renner, "The Development of Capitalist Property and the Legal Institutions Complementary to the Property Norm," in Vilhelm Aubert, ed., *Sociology of Law* (Baltimore 1969), 37.

[106]Kelly, *Rethinking Industrial Relations*, ch. 3 and 4.

[107]Cox, *Production, Power, and World Order*, 17.

Wall Street, the bank employees of Zurich, and the police, soldiers, and civil servants of all countries.[108]

In sum, then, a focus on work relations is a promising avenue through which to develop a less ethnocentric, more multidisciplinary, and more theoretically provocative approach than would be the case if IR simply stays on its present path towards Employment Relations.

Conclusion

It will be recalled that the original purpose of the IRRA was "the encouragement of research in all aspects of the field of labor — social, political, economic, legal, and psychological — including employer and employee organization, labor relations, personnel administration, social security, and labor legislation." In the mid-1990s, the association appointed a committee to re-examine that statement, and it proposed the following revision:

the encouragement of research on all aspects of work and the workplace, including employer and employee organization, employment and labor relations, employment and labor law, human resources, labor markets, income security, and other fields, including the international and comparative dimensions of the fields, in all pertinent disciplines — history, economics, psychology, sociology, law, management, and others.[109]

Besides reflecting the changes that have been discussed above — note, for example, the replacement of "personnel" with "human resources management," the addition of "employment" relations and law, and the inclusion of "management" as a "pertinent discipline" — this new statement of purpose, focusing as it does on "work and the workplace," is entirely consistent with the central argument of this essay: that IR, if it can be broadened sufficiently and reopened to influences from all of the social sciences, still has a potentially vital role to play in encouraging an understanding of the social relations within which work and production are organized, modified, and transformed. However, if it continues to drift towards a managerial version of employment relations, the lofty ambitions expressed in the IRRA's new statement of purpose will go unrealized. In short, if IR is to be rescued, it needs to go beyond employment.

Although he bears no responsibility for the analysis and arguments set out in this essay, I would be remiss if I were to fail to acknowledge the profound influence that my friend and colleague Gregor Murray has had on my thinking about these issues over the years.

[108]Cox, *Production, Power, and World Order*, 13.
[109]IRRA, *Newsletter*, 38, 3 (September 1996).

WORKING FOR WAGES:
THE ROOTS OF INSURGENCY

by Martin Glaberman and Seymour Faber

"This book is designed to fill a gap in studies of the American working class — to examine the sources of insurgency.... We try to seek out those elements of work in capitalist society that induce resistance to the society in one form or another."

188 pages, paper, $20US, postage free, from Bewick Editions, P.O. Box 14140, Detroit, MI 48214, USA

For a New Kind of History:
A Reconnaissance of 100 Years of
Canadian Socialism

Ian McKay

THE CENTENNIAL OF CANADIAN socialism is upon us — in 2001 if one focuses on
the creation of the first free-standing pan-Canadian socialist organization, in 2005
if one selects the formation of the first party to attract the support and the votes of
thousands of supporters.[1] It is symptomatic of the problem of socialist memory in
Canada that this centennial will probably be pretty much forgotten. Some of the
reasons for this oblivion relate to the hegemonic neo-liberalism of the late 20th

[1]There were many socialist parties, including Canadian branches of the US-based Socialist
Labor Party, and a wide range of socialist intellectuals, in late-Victorian Canada; but in terms
of continuing free-standing Canada-wide institutions, the clearest time and place of birth is
Toronto and Montréal, June-October 1901, culminating in a Thanksgiving weekend conference in Toronto launching the pan-Canadian career of the Canadian Socialist League,
founded as an Ontario body two years earlier. The formation of the Socialist Party of Canada,
founded in British Columbia in 1905, marked the start of the first electorally successful
Canada-wide socialist party. Providing Canadian socialism with this birth certificate is a
way of marking a general distinction between, on the one hand, socialist ideas articulated in
larger bodies devoted to other issues, or in strictly local or provincial terms, or as "echoes"
of a political movement decisively centred outside the country, and on the other hand, a
socialist political movement principally focused on the socialist transformation of capitalist
realities, working on a "Canadian" as well as a local, provincial, or international level, and
adapting and reintegrating international socialist ideas to the peculiarities of the Canadian
social landscape. For this early institutional history, see especially Gene Homel, "James
Simpson and the Origins of Canadian Social Democracy," PhD thesis, University of
Toronto, 1978, which contains much fascinating food for reflection on this period; and
Martin Robin, *Radical Politics and Canadian Labour, 1880-1930* (Kingston 1968) —
which, despite its age, has not been superseded on many points of detail.

Ian McKay, "For a New Kind of History: A Reconnaissance of 100 Years of Canadian
Socialism," *Labour/Le Travail*, 46 (Fall 2000), 69-125.

century, which has transformed "socialism" into an epithet. But others of them relate to the strange and inadequate way the Canadian socialist past has customarily been constructed by socialists themselves for use in the present.

Some General Reflections on Methodology and Historiography

What has been most sorely lacking in the writing of our socialist history is an adequate theorization of that project of liberal order that goes under the heading "Canada." No history of Canadian socialism is minimally adequate unless it understands the force of qualification the adjective "Canadian" exerts over the noun "socialism." "Canada" denotes a project of liberal rule in a territory secured by force of British arms and modeled primarily on British and American precedents, a project which became hegemonic in northern North America from the third quarter of the 19th century. Grasping that Canada is a project of *deep liberalism* is key to a new critical history of Canadian socialism. The innovation is to treat Canadian socialism(s) as a series of relatively autonomous experimental attempts to escape the liberal labyrinth. Before the 1940s, socialists were positioned as the liberal project's most serious and rigorous *external* critics, who contested its defining characteristics: the epistemological and ontological primacy of the individual, the structuring influence of private property, and the political subordination of the state to its functions of capitalist accumulation and bourgeois legitimation. The real reason for the anomaly of a relatively influential Canadian socialist movement in a continent otherwise quite hostile to a formal socialist politics lies not in the ideological convolutions traceable back to some supposed Tory tinge,[2] but rather to the conjunctural specifics of a new liberal "passive revolution"[3] in the

[2]An earlier tradition tried to explain this "Canadian exceptionalism" in North America by looking at 18th-and early 19th-century Toryism. The *locus classicus* of this discussion can be found in Gad Horowitz, *Canadian Labour in Politics* (Toronto 1968). A more promising avenue to explore is that of the markedly radical nature of the Canadian liberal order, a program that was imposed from the centre with Jacobin zeal and ruthlessness, with a much weaker republican opposition than found in the United States, over a subcontinent containing a multitude of aliberal positionalities, which explains both its conceptual rigidity (well beyond the 1940s), its necessary compromises (most notably with religious and ethnic communitarianism in Québec), and its characteristic political debates (classical liberal federalism countered by pragmatic "functional politics"). For further reflections on the liberal-order reconnaissance of Canadian history, see Ian McKay, "The Liberal Order Framework: A Prospectus for a Reconnaissance of Canadian History," *Canadian Historical Review*, forthcoming.

[3]On Gramsci's concept of the passive revolution, see the editors' helpful comments in Gramsci, *Selections from the Prison Notebooks* ed. and trans. by Quintin Hoare and Geoffrey Nowell-Smith (London 1971), 46; Christine Bucci-Glucksmann, "State, transition and passive revolution," in Chantal Mouffe, ed., *Gramsci and Marxist Theory* (London 1979), 207-236. There remains to be written a major study of the "Canadian passive revolution" of the 1940s, but for interesting work on new liberalism, see Robert Campbell, *Grand*

1940s, whereby a threatened liberal order transformed both itself (into a "new democracy" answerable to its "citizens") and many of its socialist adversaries (into "new democrats" comfortable with Fordism at home and American globalism abroad) in response to an apprehended social insurrection. What arguably set the Canadian experience apart from the American was the coincidence of socialist leftism with the first powerful "independentist" articulation of Canadian nationalism: socialists in Canada became, thanks to the passive revolution, "internal" to the Canadian project. Elements of socialism became central to the myth-symbol complex that legitimates both the existence of the Canadian state-nation and the Québec state-within-a-state that, at least for the time being, it encompasses.

As Stuart Hall reminds us, hegemonic ideological formation, such as the liberal order in Canada, formulates its own objects of knowledge, its own subjects, is driven by its own logic, establishes its own regime of truth; it evolves its "space of formation" and constantly interrupts, displaces and rearranges its opponents. Relations of power are not, then, monopolized by the state, but affect the entire social body. Yet an ideology's transition to hegemony within the state is decisive, because it allows for the naturalization of particular readings of the social world. In the case of Canadian liberalism, the "liberal revolution" of the mid-19th century would gradually acquire precisely this self-perpetuating character, through a myriad of laws, an array of cultural institutions, and an implied philosophy of "individualism," applied not just to abstract thought but also to such seemingly unconnected realms as religious faith and material life. Liberalism involved not just a "political ideology" in the narrow sense but an entire approach to political economy and daily life. By reason of its holism and ambition, because from its inception it was based upon historic compromises with aliberal forces (such as the Catholic Church in Québec), and because of its deep involvement in conflictual capitalist social relations, liberal order was never finally or perfectly "sealed": in the interstices of its commonsense have emerged a multitude of oppositional ideological formations, from various forms of nationalism to contemporary feminism. The most historically significant of these challengers to date, in terms of its impact on the state, has been "socialism," understood positively in this essay, following the lead of Margaret Cole, as a three-fold doctrine: "(1)the belief that any society founded on large-scale private ownership is unjust; (2)the conviction that a more equitable form of society can be established, one that will contribute to the moral and material improvement of humankind; and (3)the idea that social revolution is imperative" (with significant debate regarding whether such revolution necessarily entails violence).[4]

Illusions: The Politics of the Keynesian Experience in Canada 1945-1975 (Peterborough 1987); Barry Ferguson, *Remaking Liberalism: The Intellectual Legacy of Adam Shortt, O.D. Skelton, W.C. Clark, and W.A. Mackintosh, 1890-1925* (Montréal and Kingston 1993).
[4]Cited in Harry Ritter, ed., *Dictionary of Concepts in History* (New York 1986): 418. I have found consistently helpful Michael Luntley, *The Meaning of Socialism* (London 1989), especially for its discussion of the socialism/liberalism distinction (9-12).

The very etymology of "socialism" suggests its profoundly adversarial rela-tionship to liberal order.[5] To be a socialist in Canada means to seek to 'de-link' the liberal concept of individuality from the socialist concept of species-being, to articulate new conceptions of the sociality of human beings, and to think of ways in which their "metabolism" with the natural world could be placed on a "rational basis." In less abstract terms, there has never been a historically significant Canadian socialism that was not preoccupied with establishing a relationship with the tradition of a (variously construed) "Marx," whose words have been read in Canada since the 1870s, but with very different emphases depending on the time, place, and access to appropriate texts. These various "Marxes" have all agreed that a full program of human freedom entails conscious, rational control over economic and social forces. "The main enemies of such freedom were the 'blind forces' of the market; freedom would only be realized by rational planning, by liberating people from objective dependence on things and alienated social forces." Socialism aims to establish a society in which production is subject to the associated control of the producers, "not left to the mercy of the spontaneous decisions of millions of consumers and the calculations of thousands of capitalists."[6]

What would happen if we started to take these international definitions seriously in the writing of Canadian socialist history? For one thing, we would change the subject(s) of the history of Canadian socialism, to encompass a far greater diversity of people — those of religious and cultural figures, the First Nations and visible minorities, feminists and environmentalists, Québec national-ists and so on — whose words and deeds can be linked directly to the post-liberal counter-logic of socialism. This would entail decentering the formal parties as *the* core of the "history of Canadian socialism." The parties are significant, but their significance lies in their being partial experiments in making socialism a thing of this world. Second, certain narrative conventions would be re-opened for scrutiny. Every socialist movement in Canada and every socialist has, by not realizing their full ambitions, compromised to some extent with the liberal order. Canadians are "liberals by default": it is what they become when their socialist powers of resistance are worn down. Quite apart from its coercive apparatus, which is never

[5]The word "socialism" evidently first appeared in Italy in 1765, in Ferdinando Facchinei's commentary on Beccaria's *On Crime and Punishment*; twenty years later, it appeared in the writings of Appiano Buonafede to underline the idea that sociability is a natural human condition. See G. de Bertier de Sauvigny, "Liberalism, Nationalism, and Socialism: The Birth of Three Words," *The Review of Politics,* 32 (1970), 147-66; Arthur E. Bestor, "The Evolution of the Socialist Vocabulary," *Journal of the History of Ideas,* 9 (1948), 259-302. The *Oxford English Dictionary* (1989) suggests a somewhat different early history of the word.

[6]I draw here from Andrzej Walicki, *Marxism and the Leap to the Kingdom of Freedom* (Stanford 1995), quotations at 6, 14, 17, 38, without endorsing his tendentious equation of Marxism and totalitarianism; the last quotation comes from Donald Sassoon, *One Hundred Years of Socialism: The West European Left in the Twentieth Century* (London 1997), xxii.

to be overlooked, the liberal historic bloc has persistently penetrated, fractured and fragmented the territory of the dominated classes and groups, making it difficult — but never impossible — to conceptualize alternative counter-hegemonic practices and discourses.

The existing historiography on Canadian socialism is extensive, varied and often superbly researched and written. Research tools, such as bibliographical aids and published primary documents, are easily accessible.[7] Collections of essays abound.[8] Collected writings and reprints of books from some prominent socialists have also appeared.[9] The major parties — the Socialist Party of Canada,[10] the various Labour (and Farmer-Labour) parties,[11] the Communists,[12] the Co-operative

---

[7]A useful general research tool is Peter Weinrich, *Social Protest from the Left in Canada, 1870-1970: A Bibliography* (Toronto 1982). For the important manifestos of the CCF-NDP, see Michael Cross, ed., *The Decline and Fall of a Good Idea: CCF-NDP Manifestoes, 1932 to 1969* (Toronto 1974); for NDP policy statements, see Cliff Scotton, ed., *New Democratic Policies 1961-1976* (Ottawa 1977).

[8]A useful collection for left nationalism is David Godfrey and Melville Watkins, eds. *Gordon to Watkins to You: A Documentary: the Battle for Control of Our Economy* (Toronto 1970). See also Leo Heaps, ed. *Our Canada* (Toronto 1991); Laurier LaPierre *et al.*, eds., *Essays on the Left: Essays in Honour of T.C. Douglas* (Toronto and Montréal 1971).

[9]See, for some of these collections, Larry Hannant, ed., *The Politics of Passion: Norman Bethune's Writing and Art* (Toronto 1998); L.D. Lovick, ed., *Till Power is Brought to Pooling: Tommy Douglas Speaks* (Lantzville, B.C. 1979); Edith Fowke, ed., *Towards Socialism: Selections from the Writings of J.S. Woodsworth* (Toronto 1948). Among the reprints of "socialist classics," see William Irvine, *The Farmers in Politics* (Toronto 1976 [1920]); League for Social Reconstruction, *Social Planning for Canada* (Toronto 1975 [1935]); J.S.Woodsworth, *Strangers Within Our Gates, or Coming Canadians* (Toronto 1972 [1909]); *My Neighbor: A Study of City Conditions* (Toronto, 1972 [1911]); League for Social Reconstruction, *Social Planning for Canada* (Toronto 1975 [1935]).

[10]On the S.P.C., see particularly Peter Campbell, "'Making Socialists': Bill Pritchard, the Socialist Party of Canada and the Third International," *Labour/Le Travail*, 30 (Fall 1992); David Frank and Nolan Reilly, "The Emergence of the Socialist Movement in the Maritimes, 1899-1916," *Labour/Le Travailleur*, 4 (Fall 1979), 85-113.

[11]Local labour parties emerged across Canada in the first decade of the 20th century; in the second, they attained a limited national presence. The most substantial monograph is James Naylor, *The New Democracy: Challenging the Social Order in Industrial Ontario, 1914-25* (Toronto 1991).

[12]On the Communists, see especially Ian Angus, *Canadian Bolsheviks* (Montréal 1981); Robert Comeau et Bernard Dionne, *Le droit de se taire: Histoire des communistes au Québec, de la Première Guerre mondiale à la Révolution tranquille* (Montréal 1989); M. Fournier, *Communisme et anticommunisme au Québec 1920-1950* (Montréal 1986); John Manley, "Does the International Labour Movement need Salvaging? Communism, Labourism and the Canadian Trade Unions, 1921-1928," *Labour/Le Travail*, 41 (Spring 1998); Manley, "'Starve, Be Damned!': Communists and Canada's Urban Unemployed, 1929-1939," *Canadian Historical Review*, 79, 3 (September 1998); Norman Penner, *Canadian*

Commonwealth Federation[13], and the New Democratic Party[14] have attracted serious scholarly attention. Much less studied, it would seem, have been the New Leftists of the 1960s in Canada,[15] and the Marxist-Leninist vanguard parties of the 1960s-1980s.[16] Even scarcer have been attempts to describe and theorize the history of these left movements taken together.[17] The co-operative movement has generated a large literature, some of which has focused on the often complex relationship

Communism: The Stalin Years and Beyond (Toronto 1988); William Rodney, Soldiers of the International: A History of the Communist Party of Canada, 1919-1929 (Toronto 1968); Merrily Weisbord, The Strangest Dream: Canadian Communists, the Spy Trials and the Cold War (Toronto 1983). For a glimpse of Communist Party cultural activities, see Ruth McKenzie, ed., Eight Men Speak and Other Communist Plays of the 1930's (Toronto 1976), and for the experience of a Communist education in Québec, see G.A. Cohen, If You're An Egalitarian, How Come You're So Rich? (Cambridge, Mass. 2000). A vivid sense of the research possibilities still open to historians of Communism in Canada is provided by George Bolotenko, "The National Archives and Left-Wing Sources from Russia: Records of the Mackenzie-Papineau Battalion, the Communist Party of Canada and Left-Wing Internationals," Labour/Le Travail,37 (Spring 1996), 179-203.

[13]The literature on the CCF is immense. The most significant titles include Gerald Caplan, The Dilemma of Canadian Socialism: The CCF in Ontario (Toronto 1973); Seymour Martin Lipset, Agrarian Socialism: The Cooperative Commonwealth Federation in Saskatchewan, a Study in Political Sociology (Berkeley 1968); D. McHenry, The Third Force in Canada: The Cooperative Commonwealth Federation 1932-1948 (Berkeley 1950); Walter Young, The Anatomy of a Party: The National CCF 1932-1961 (Toronto 1969); Leo Zakuta, A Protest Movement Becalmed (Toronto 1964).

[14]Out of an immense literature, one might especially mention Dan Azoulay, Keeping the Dream Alive: The Survival of the Ontario CCF/NDP, 1950-1963 (Montréal and Kingston 1997); Desmond Morton, NDP: The Dream of Power (Toronto 1974); Norman Wiseman, Social Democracy in Manitoba (Winnipeg 1983).

[15]For accounts contemporaneous with the New Left, see Dimitri Roussopolous, ed., The New Left in Canada (Montréal 1970), and his edited collection Canada and Radical Social Change (Montréal 1973), and T. Reid and J. Reid, eds., Student Power and the Canadian Campus (Toronto 1969). Cyril Levitt, Children of Privilege: Student Revolt in the Sixties (Toronto 1984), is a comparative sociological study. There are some interesting reflections in Norman Penner, The Canadian Left: A Critical Analysis (Scarborough 1977), ch.7.

[16]See, however, the interesting Bourdieuvian (and acerbic) reflections of Pierre Milot, Le paradigme rouge: L'avant-garde politico-littéraire des années 70 (Montréal 1992), especially Ch.2 and 3; and Roger O'Toole, The Precipitous Path: Studies in Political Sects (Toronto 1977), which attempts to apply insights derived from the sociology of religion to the Toronto left of 1968-69. Bryan D. Palmer, ed., A Communist Life: Jack Scott and the Canadian Workers Movement, 1927-1985 (St. John's, 1988) has interesting materials on Canadian Maoism.

[17]But see Penner, The Canadian Left: A Critical Analysis and his "The Socialist Idea in Canadian Political Thought," PhD Thesis, University of Toronto, 1975.

between business-oriented pragmatism and socialist ideology.[18] Socialism in Québec during the 1960s and 1970s, especially insofar as it touched upon the rise of nationalism and the history of the Communist Party among francophones, has generated an extensive library.[19] Political scientists have analyzed voting patterns and speculated on the more distant ideological forces contributing to Canadian socialism.[20] General thematic studies — particularly on the questions of religious radicalism,[21] ethnic minorities,[22] feminism,[23] socialist leadership in the trade union movement[24] and the impact of the Cold War[25] — have become much more significant in the past ten years. A recent, welcome trend has been to focus on the

[18]See especially Ian MacPherson, *Each for All: A History of the Co-operative Movement in English Speaking Canada, 1900-1945* (Toronto 1979) and Rusty Neal, *Brotherhood Economics: Women and Co-operatives in Nova Scotia* (Sydney 1998).

[19]Andrée Lévesque, *Virage à gauche interdit. Les communistes, les socialistes et leurs ennemis au Québec, 1929-1939* (Montréal, 1984); Robert Comeau et Bernard Dionne, *Le droit de se taire: Histoire des communistes au Québec, de la Première Guerre mondiale à la Révolution tranquille* (Montréal 1989); Pierre Jalbert, *De la social-démocratie européen au Parti Québéecois* (Montréal 1982).

[20]By far the most important title in this vein, and a fresh look at the history of social democracy, is Alan Whitehorn, *Canadian Socialism: Essays on the CCF-NDP* (Toronto 1992).

[21]The major title here on the Protestant side is still Richard Allen's rich and fascinating *The Social Passion: Religion and Social Reform in Canada 1914-1928* (Toronto 1973); for the Catholics and the left, see Gregory Baum, *Catholics and Canadian Socialism: Political Thought in the Thirties and Forties* (Toronto 1980). The post-1960 Christian/Marxist dialogue is largely unstudied; see Donald Evans, *Communist Faith and Christian Faith: A Report of the Committee on Christian Faith, The United Church of Canada* (Toronto 1964) for an interesting contemporary document.

[22]See Peter Krawchuk, *The Ukrainian Socialist Movement in Canada, 1907-1918* (Toronto 1979); Varpu Lindström-Best, *Defiant Sisters: A Social History of the Finnish Immigrant Women in Canada, 1890-1930* (Toronto 1988).

[23]See especially Linda Kealey, *Enlisting Women for the Cause: Women, Labour, and the Left in Canada, 1890-1920* (Toronto 1998); Linda Kealey and Joan Sangster, eds. *Beyond the Vote: Canadian Women and Politics* (Toronto 1989); Janice Newton, *The Feminist Challenge to the Canadian Left, 1900-1918* (Montréal and Kingston 1995); Joan Sangster, *Dreams of Equality: Women on the Canadian Left, 1920-1950* (Toronto 1989).

[24]The most important recent title here is Craig Heron, ed., *The Canadian Labour Revolt* (Toronto 1998). The classic account of CP/CCF rivalry in the labour movement is still Irving Abella, *Nationalism, Communism, and Canadian Labour: The CIO, the Communist Party, and the Canadian Congress of Labour, 1935-1956* (Toronto 1973). A study of the most significant free-standing Canadian radical socialist labour movement can be found in David Bercuson, *Fools and Wise Men: The Rise and Fall of the One Big Union* (Toronto 1978).

[25]Gregory S. Kealey, "The RCMP, the Special Branch and the Early Days of the Communist Party of Canada," *Labour/Le Travail*, 30 (Fall 1992), 169-204; Reginald Whitaker and Gary Marcuse, *Cold War Canada: The Making of a National Insecurity State, 1945-1957* (Toronto 1994).

history of socialist ideas.[26] Biographies of leading Canadian socialists have been especially significant: the best of them are suggestive meditations on structure, agency and subjectivity in the context of one person's life-history.[27] The memoirs of many leading participants are also available, and many of them attain a high standard.[28] Although this is a field numerically dominated by partisans of the NDP, both Communists and, more recently, "independent Marxists" have also contributed major studies, which have sought to highlight the contributions of rank-and-file socialists and local groups in the manner of "history from below."[29]

The core deficiency of this literature is theoretical. It generally does not yield, beyond the "case studies" and "biographies" that are its preferred sites, much in the way of general (and politically useful) insights. By and large, these titles usher us into fondly recollected past worlds. Before 1975, this literature of exemplary figures and forward movements might have functioned well as inspiration. Now it seems a melancholy monument to old abandoned hopes, a vast resource for recrimination. It is not a literature that often asks, or demands that we ask ourselves, hard questions. Much of it is written with the conviction that empiricist induction, warm-hearted humanism and base-and-superstructure reductionism are all that

[26]M. Horn, *The League for Social Reconstruction: Intellectual Origins of the Democratic Left in Canada 1930-1942* (Toronto 1980). There are some interesting reflections on proto-socialist ideology in 19th-century Canada in G.S. Kealey and B.D. Palmer, *Dreaming of What Might Be: The Knights of Labor in Ontario, 1880-1900.* (New York 1982). See also David Laycock, *Populist and Democratic Thought in the Canadian Prairies 1910 to 1945* (Toronto 1990); Alan Mills, *Fool for Christ: The Political Thought of J.S. Woodsworth* (Toronto 1991). Peter Campbell, *Canadian Marxists and the Search for a Third Way* (Montréal and Kingston 1999) represents a particularly significant step forward in the intellectual reconstitution of early Canadian socialism.
[27]Of the scores of titles one might mention Larry Hannant, *The Politics of Passion: Norman Bethune's Writing and Art* (Toronto 1998); Nicholas Fillmore, *Maritime Radical: The Life and Times of Roscoe Fillmore* (Toronto 1992); Gérard Fortin with Boyce Richardson, *Life of the Party* (Montréal 1984); D. Francis, *Frank H. Underhill: Intellectual Provocateur* (Toronto 1986); Claude Larivière, *Albert Saint-Martin. Militant d'avant-garde* (Montréal 1979); Joseph Levitt, *Fighting Back for Jobs and Justice: Ed Broadbent in Parliament* (Ottawa 1996), Kenneth McNaught, *A Prophet in Politics: A Biography of J.S. Woodsworth* (Toronto, 1959); and Cameron Smith, *Unfinished Journey: The Lewis Family* (Toronto 1989). A new standard for socialist biography is set by David Frank, *J.B.McLachlan: A Biography* (Toronto 1999).
[28]The outstanding title out of this collection of memoirs is David Lewis, *The Good Fight: Political Memoirs 1909-1958* (Toronto 1981). Also noteworthy: William Beeching and Phyllis Clarke, eds., *Yours in the Struggle: Reminiscences of Tim Buck* (Toronto 1977); Thérèse Casgrain, *A Woman in a Man's World* (Toronto 1972); Eugene Forsey, *A Life on the Fringe: The Memoirs of Eugene Forsey* (Toronto 1990); Donald MacDonald, *The Happy Warrior: Political Memoirs* (Markham, Ont. 1988).
[29]See especially O. Melnyk, *No Bankers in Heaven* (Toronto 1989), an invaluable collection of oral biographies.

sound socialist scholarship requires. Much of this literature should be critiqued not because it is *present-minded* (what else could a politically useful socialist history be?), but because it is *presentist*, because it abolishes the *alterity* of the past. Particularly among Marxists, but by no means confined to them, there has also been a related tendency to a form of teleological class reductionism, which sees "socialism" as a necessary outcome of "proletarianization" — a belief that stands in an awkward relationship with the fact of the deep and tenacious roots of liberalism in the working class itself. And it is often also mechanical and simplistic: it reduces the dynamic grammar of hegemony to the passive and predictable reflection of underlying class interests. Many of these patterns can be related to "socialist triumphalism," a narrative pattern in which those at the end-point of socialism's necessary evolution could fortify themselves with the conviction that, as the first of the "true socialists," they were better positioned than anyone before them (or beside them) to "achieve socialism."

The more concrete failings of this literature flow from these underlying theoretical problems. It should hardly need saying that a fundamental fact of Canadian political and cultural life is the existence within the territory claimed by the Canadian state of two predominant linguistic communities or nations. But only the most diligent and focused reader of this literature would ever think that this fact was of much importance for socialists. Strange, but true — there is not, in this vast library of titles, one major study of French/English relations on the Canadian left.[30] Does "our Canada" include "Québec"? It does so fitfully, awkwardly, and marginally — either by lumping Québec and "French Canada" into "Canada as a whole," or by following the fashion in the (re-) writing of Canadian history, of simply regarding "English Canada" (read Ontario, and often just southern urban Ontario)

[30]The figures of Stanley Ryerson and Charles Taylor stand out as the most important socialist participants in an "anglophone/francophone" dialogue within Canadian socialism. See Gregory S. Kealey, "Stanley Bréhaut Ryerson: historien marxiste," in *Le droit de se taire: Histoire des communistes au Québec, de la Première Guerre mondiale à la Révolution tranquille* (Outremont 1989), 242-272, which may also be read, in English, in Gregory S. Kealey, "Stanley Bréhaut Ryerson: Canadian Revolutionary and Marxist Historian," *Workers and Canadian History* (Montréal and Kingston 1995): 48-100. For a contextualization of the "national question" and debates over the "nationalist deviation" in the Communist Party in the 1940s-1960s, see Penner, *Canadian Communism*, 177-181, 227-229, 256-259. Charles Taylor's work is generally pitched at a higher level of abstraction than that of Ryerson, but the Québec case has clearly strongly influenced his social-democratic advocacy of a "politics of recognition." Important texts to which subsequent scholars might refer are *The Pattern of Politics* (Toronto and Montréal 1970), and *Reconciling the Solitudes: Essays on Canadian Federalism and Nationalism* (Montréal and Kingston 1993). There is also a literature on the vexed relations of the early NDP with francophones: see, for instance, André Lamoureux, *Le NPD et le Québec 1958-1985* (Montréal1985); David H. Sherwood, "The N.D.P. and French Canada, 1961-1965," MA Internal Research Project, No.5, Report No.12, Division III, McGill University, 1966.

as the essence of the country as a whole, or by following the parallel fashion in Québec of projecting back into the past an independence from Canada that many aspire to see in the future.[31] This is poor history, but worse politics, because it will leave the coming cohort of radicals profoundly uninformed about a fundamental defining fact of the Canadian socialist experience, and subtly anesthetize them to the ambiguity and the danger of the intertwined "nation-building" projects to which both francophone and anglophone socialists have subscribed. And if the "Canadian" in the phrase "Canadian socialism" is radically undertheorized, so is the "socialism." We find a recurrent partisan pattern of treating one part as the whole. This is particularly the case with histories which take the NDP (which itself is generally and problematically presented as a necessary organic outgrowth of the CCF) as *the* only (or only worthy) exponent of socialism in Canada. What remains profoundly unexplored, on either side of the phrase "Canadian socialism," are relations with the hegemonic liberal order, without which "Canada" itself is inexplicable and the challenges facing its successive schools of socialists difficult to conceptualize. How many times have we told the story of radicals who betrayed the (transcendental) "true values" of the movement, as measured by a "revolutionary yardstick"? Or cynical and calculating governments which "skimmed off" the best of the socialists' demands? Of youthful high hopes replaced by middle-aged disillusionment? Of sell-outs to the bourgeoisie? Of the "failure" of this or that "socialist program" (often juxtaposed to the implied — generally undemonstrable — path to success had the counterfactual "correct path" been followed)? Both in left polemics and 'high-brow' historical literature, these narratives work through a kind of symbolic violence to establish the credentials of the narrator as the person-who-knows. But from the standpoint of the critique of liberal order, not to mention at a time when such socialist epistemological certainty has at best an antiquarian charm, these narratives are not only stale and self-serving, but naïve. All Canadian socialisms have failed, insofar as every one of them has failed to transcend the liberal order that is socialism's ground, context, and antithesis; and every Canadian socialist has necessarily made compromises with hegemonic liberalism, whether in daily life, in political tactics, or in cultural formation. This is at least a century-old recurrent pattern, which has affected tendencies, movements and individuals, both "opportunistic scoundrels" and "proletarian fighters." And yet, in another way, all Canadian socialisms have succeeded, at least to the extent of creating spaces of resistance, some of them extremely complex and durable, from which projections of an alternative humanity have attained reality-status. They have emerged, sometimes with dazzling speed, and attracted a mass following; and many have lastingly changed the terms of the project of liberal order itself. Whatever short-term polemical mileage can be derived from narratives of the "revolution

[31]In this essay, I use the word "Canada" to denote a process of liberal order, not a "nation" or "nation-state." The term "Canadian socialism" means "socialism found on the territory claimed by the Canadian project."

betrayed" or the "pragmatic education of the idealists" or the "inevitable matura-tion" of the young hotheads, the sense of inevitability they create is profoundly *defeatist*. A less teleological and judgmental approach would reconstruct a variety of Canadian socialisms — i.e., politico-discursive formations specifying distinctive problem-sets and solutions — as plausible (or at least explainable) responses to the specific challenges posed by liberal order. Each socialism was, in a sense, a kind of experiment in post-liberalism. One is asked to give up the "bogus certainties" about history's final destination; one is put to work exploring the "conjunctural specifics," probing each socialism for its rational core, its "answers" to the recurrent problems liberal order generates for anyone who wants to live otherwise. The unilinear narratives, and perhaps especially those driven by Marxism-Leninism, can only lead to a stark choice between faith and empirical evidence. Post-orthodox, non-determinist narratives, on the other hand, may lead to a more optimistic conclusion. Like many Canadians before us, we daily encounter aspects of the liberal order that are irrational, unjust, and alienating — aspects of social reality that cannot be definitively "sealed" by the ideological formation in which we are obliged to live. These fissures are open to alternative post-liberal interpretations. We socialists have everything to gain from a sympathetic and detailed under-standing of all such interpretations, both internationally and in Canada.

An alternative approach to the "vertical bias" of socialist historiography would entail trying to work back from demonstrably significant texts — texts that historical evidence suggests were read by many people — to their conditions of construction. Socialists, often inspired by specific important trends or events, share, at a minimum, a common perception that liberal order is unjust and its replacement by a different system is possible and desirable. In archetypal forums — program-matic texts and manifestoes, party congresses and public meetings — socialists try to "reverse the discourse" on liberalism, to turn its language back on itself, to hold it to account against its own principles. There is, moreover, a dominant aspect of liberal order — a "core problem" or "problems", or a "matrix-event" — which above all others calls out for socialist analysis and activism. A "cohort" of such socialists can be defined by their preoccupation with this problem and by sharing significant common understandings of the ways in which it should be understood (if not necessarily how it ought to be resolved). The combination of "matrix-event," "cohort," "paradigm," and the specific parties and groups associated with them — and usually an extensive cultural penumbra of institutes, schools, summer camps, concerts, books and so on — can be termed a "political formation." I see four such formations in Canadian socialist history, with a fifth under construction today: the first, shaped pivotally by the transition from competitive to monopoly capitalism and by the rise of the theory of evolution, which flourished from c.1900 to c.1920, and which emphasized above all socialist education in the light of evolution's political message; a second, shaped pivotally by the Russian Revolution, which theorized the need for a socialist revolution guided by a proletarian vanguard party, which flourished from c.1917 to c.1935; a third, whose matrix-event was the Great Depression, which insistently advocated the national management of the economy, which flourished from c.1932 to c.1960; a fourth, whose matrix-events were the perceived collapse of American civilization and the Cold War disorganization of the "older lefts," which highlighted the overcoming of alienation through direct democracy by direct action, and which flourished from c.1960 to c.1975.; and a fifth, shaped decisively by neoliberalism and the rise of feminism and other new social movements, which is unfolding today.

The origins of such formations can be tied down, loosely, to particular periods — yet doing so involves risks. There is the danger of simply repeating the older tropes of necessary progress, and the more subtle peril of forgetting that older paradigms of socialism are frequently (and often effectively) re-activated in subsequent periods. A formation shaped by a particular cohort and a particular matrix-event often persists beyond the two decades normally allotted a generation. An additional requirement of any theorization of socialism in Canada is that of confronting regional and national plurality: a pattern found in one nation or region cannot be casually generalized, without incurring the risk of oversimplification, beyond its borders. We need "horizontal" analyses that seek to re-create the complex networks which bound socialists — and their parties, journals, social and intellectual networks — in formations of alliance and antagonism unevenly developed across the Canadian sub-continent. The analytical outcome of a more "horizontal" approach to analysis would be a more inclusive narrative — written in terms of major and minor figures, parties, currents, texts, and debates — that seeks to track the socialist ideal in all its complex diversity. This would be a kind of history that makes it possible to imagine a socialist tradition that is both discontinuous and continuous: discontinuous in that it undoubtedly features "breaks" and "differences in focus" separating one formation from another, continuous in that it nonetheless persists in theorizing a "Canadian socialism" as an exit from a persisting liberal order. Each formation, then, was distinct; a socialist of the 1940s shared with fellow socialists, even those with whom he or she differed politically, a hierarchy of key problems and a language in which to discuss them, distinct from those which had predominated twenty years earlier. Yet, because all were concerned to chart a path out of capitalist social relations and liberal order in northern North America, all can be made, at least in our unapologetically present-mided historical imaginations, "alternative voices" in a continuing socialist conversation. Socialism as "Evolutionary Science," Socialism as "Revolutionary Praxis," Socialism as "National State Management," and Socialism as "Revolutionary Humanism and National Liberation," discussed through works of William Irvine, Maurice Spector, F.R.Scott/David Lewis, and Pierre Vallières[32], are descriptive names I have applied to these formations.

[32]I have selected the titles I go on to discuss in this essay because they are ones that I know, but also because they were of known contemporary importance. So far as I am aware, no

The First Socialism: Evolutionary Science

The first Canadian socialist formation (c.1900 to c.1920) was dominated by those we can describe as "scientific evolutionists," and took shape under the shadow of two related developments: the rise of monopoly capitalism and of evolutionary theory. A tone of patronage suffuses discussions of this formation. In the 1920s, Maurice Spector, the most accomplished revolutionary writer of a new formation, looked back on the people he aimed to displace:

Although we live in an epoch of the collapse of Capitalism and the social revolution, it is not enough to proclaim the principles of proletarian dictatorship and workers' power if we hope to succeed in rallying the masses to fight for these principles. We must beware of turning these principles into abstract formulae. The Socialist parties on this continent have not in the past carried on consistent political activity. The S. P. of C. [Socialist Party of Canada] has mistaken a study circle for a political party and courses of lectures on Marx's Capital for revolutionary activity. The S.P. of A. [Socialist Party of America] and the I.L.P. [Independent Labour Party] have aped bourgeois respectability and considered electioneering as the highest form of political action. The Workers' Party wants neither the village chapel atmosphere of the S.P. of C. nor the 'democratic' conceptions of the S.P. of A. The Workers' Party will strive to be a party of action — a party of the masses. Revolutionary political activity to us means disciplined work in the labor unions, agitation in election campaigns, agitation from the floor of Parliament, mass demonstrations, organizations of the unemployed, and participation in the everyday struggles of the working class. For we realize that only through their mass experiences with the Capitalist dictatorship in the everyday struggle will the working class be rallied by its vanguard to the struggle for proletarian dictatorship. The struggle for power will inevitably grow out of the struggle for bread.[33]

Spector's caricature was vengeful, one-sided, and perceptive. Versions of it have proved extremely durable. In particular, many historians have described a passage from the village-chapel "Christian Socialism" of the early 20th century to more secular, often Marxist, socialism of the 1920s.

---

one has ever compiled a list of the "most influential fifty writings" in the Canadian socialist tradition. Irvine's work was highly influential in Alberta, and subsequently strongly influenced C.B.Macpherson's path-breaking analysis of *Democracy in Alberta;* Spector's journalism in *The Worker* was widely read across the working-class movement, although it never was published in book form (and surely should be); *Make This Your Canada* was a bestselling book in the 1940s; and *Nègres blancs d'Amérique,* first published in Montréal by Éditions Parti pris in 1966, and co-published in Montréal and Paris by Éditions Parti pris and Éditions François Maspero in 1968, was then published in New York, Italy, Germany, and Mexico: one hazards the guess that it is the most widely-read socialist book written by a Canadian citizen.

[33]"Closing Address of Maurice Spector at Workers' Party Convention," *The Worker*, 15 March 1922.

How, other than as a crude first draft, can the first formation be distinguished from the radicalism of the 19th century[34] or the revolutionary socialist *praxis* of the 1920s? The key, I believe, lies in the paramount status first-wave socialists accorded a theory of social evolution. First-cohort socialists ultimately felt themselves to be underwritten by the "inscrutable power" of Evolution, that great massive social and natural force that was simultaneously the *process* of change, the *explanation* of change, and the *politico-ethical* practices logically required by that change. The key idea was the inevitable adaptation of society to its environment. Herbert Spencer's "organic analogy" — that is, that organic and social bodies shared the four fundamental qualities of naturally growing in mass, becoming increasingly complex, acquiring an ever-greater mutual interdependence of parts, and outliving as aggregatives the life-span of any individual — unified this formation.[35] This socialism attained a certain "fixity" in certain small formal institutions —the Canadian Socialist League (fd. 1901); the Social Democratic Party (fd. 1911); and especially the Socialist Party of Canada (fd. 1905), whose ideological rigour, modest membership figures, petit-bourgeois or "labour-aristocratic" personnel and distance from positions of power in both the labour movement and Canadian politics more broadly have led some scholars to dismiss its legacy as "impossibi-list".[36]

Such evaluations seem limited in two respects. First, they underestimate the degree to which this first cohort of socialists, to a degree approached again only in the 1930s, focused on cultural struggle — on the changing of minds, on building alternative sources of authority, and on connecting socialist insights into the economy with an ethical critique of capitalism. Measuring first-wave socialism strictly by the yardsticks of electoral success or trade-union influence downgrades this cultural struggle, which diffused socialist ideas through wide-ranging labour

[34]That such a turn-of-the-century break was evident to contemporaries — e.g., Phillips Thompson — can be gleaned from Gene Homel, "Fading Beams of the Nineteenth Century: Radicalism and Early Socialism in Canada's 1890s," *Labour/Le Travail*, 5 (1980), 7-32.

[35]See Mark Pitinger, *American Socialists and Evolutionary Thought* (Madison 1993) for a superb guide to this moment in the history of North American socialism. In Laurence Gronlund's *The Co-operative Commonwealth* — the book which, perhaps more than any other, put Spencerian Marxism on the North American map, and whose title was to echo loudly in Canadian party politics — Spencer was likened to the hen "that had adopted and tended an orphaned duckling, and that afterwards flapped her wings and cackled horror-stricken when her *protégé* persisted in going into the water. He has nobly vindicated the organic character of society; but now, when it is simply obeying the law of evolution, he is thoroughly convinced that it is going astray." Laurence Gronlund, *The Co-operative Commonwealth: An Exposition of Socialism* (Boston 1890 [1884]), 97.

[36]The classic statement is Ross McCormack, *Reformers, Rebels, and Revolutionaries: The Western Canadian Radical Movement, 1899-1919* (Toronto 1977); a subtler but no-less-critical evaluation can be found in Mark Leier, *Red Flags and Red Tape: The Making of a Labour Bureaucracy* (Toronto 1995).

media . It also misses what was "first formationist" about much of the cultural work outside the parties — in, for example, the Industrial Workers of the World, the Western Federation of Miners, and others. This was a pre-1914 ferment in Canada whose intellectual challenge to liberalism worried some of its stalwarts a good deal. Even O.D. Skelton, an academic far from the fray, felt he had to respond urgently to the claims of socialism.[37] Second, the role of evolutionary theory has been seriously misconstrued. There was no automatic connection between espousing a theory of social evolution and an enthusiasm for "evolutionary" (i.e. strictly parliamentary) socialism as it subsequently came to be understood. For many in this cohort, evolutionary sociological theory mandated a revolutionary social vision: radical socialists could pull from Spencer — selectively read and filtered through Marx — the message that to change capitalism one had to understand its laws, and that without social science, there could be no effective social revolution. The world of political economy analyzed in Marx's *Capital*, Vol. I, could then appear as a "case study" of a more general process of evolution in the social world. One could, and many did, arrive at "revolutionary" political conclusions via a journey through "evolutionary theory."

The applied sciences of the first-wave socialists were most often based on Marx, *Capital*, Vol. I, Frederick Engels, *Socialism: Utopian and Scientific*, Herbert Spencer (especially *The Study of Sociology*), and the many authors published by the Charles H. Kerr and Company, of whom Karl Kautsky and Arthur M. Lewis (the author of *Evolution Social and Organic*) were among the most significant. In economics, the first-wave socialists focused on the labour theory of value, which proved the exploitiveness of capitalism and the increasing gap between rich and poor. Some were also attending to new economic historians, who demonstrated, to Canadian socialists' satisfaction, that world capitalism had impoverished workers, expropriated primary producers, and led civilization repeatedly to the brink of war. In general these socialists evinced slight interest in Canadian history as such. In anthropology, they were deeply impressed by Morgan's writings (often as they encountered them indirectly through Engels). First-wave Canadian socialists based their political hopes and dreams on the prospects of a socialist ascent to power — which a surprising number of them described as a "revolution" led by the "working class" — but most of them were then forced to confront the dilemma that the working class was a small proportion of the Canadian population. Socialism would come about primarily through a widespread process of working-class education and by "making socialists" through persuasion.

[37]O.D.Skelton, *Socialism: A Critical Analysis* (Boston and New York 1911). Skelton's work — the first major book-length treatment of the topic in Canada — achieved international renown for its refutation of socialist economics; it confidently predicted the movement would come to nothing in a country such as Canada.

At the same time, first-wave socialism was characterized by interesting and symptomatic absences. In general, "Canada" as a category of analysis was, to our eyes, virtually absent: this cohort was fully immersed in a North Atlantic world of socialist discourse, and only a few spared a thought for the "peculiarities of the Canadians" or the "specific nature of the Canadian state." What we would today take to be a defining position for Canadian social democrats — viz., a belief in the state's necessarily comprehensive involvement in planning and providing social services and economic development — was noteworthy by its absence. It is in fact something of an oversimplification to see these first-wave Canadian socialists as working in "Canada" at all. They derived their theoretical sustenance from continental theory and their political strategies from both the United States and Britain, from whence many had recently come.

One could reference here the work of Colin McKay, who with George Wrigley could be called the co-founder of the Canadian Socialist League, and who drew explicitly on Spencer's *Social Statics* and from works of American Spencerian sociology to fashion a durable and sophisticated critique of the Canadian liberal order.[38] Or E. E. Winch, W. A. Pritchard, Arthur Mould, and R. B. Russell, whose "Marxism of the Third Way," expressed in such diverse institutions as the SPC, the One Big Union, the Communist Party, and the CCF, combined a belief in education with a drive to educate the working class to live up to its historical responsibilities.[39] Or A.E. Smith, whose transition from Methodism to Communism does not seem to have entailed a disruption of the "biological standpoint" from which he interpreted history and his own political activism.[40] But, arguably, *the* most influential and widely-read text from this first formation came from William Irvine (1885-1962), the Methodist-turned-Unitarian whose writings capture the flavour of the United Farmers of Alberta and "Radical Calgary".[41] Irvine's 1920 *The Farmers in*

[38]Note in this connection Ian McKay, ed., *For a Working-Class Culture: A Selection of Colin McKay's Writings on Sociology and Political Economy, 1897-1939* (St. John's, 1996); "Changing the Subject(s) of the 'History of Canadian Sociology': The Missing Spencerian Marxists, 1890-1940," *Canadian Journal of Sociology*, 23, 4 (1998), 389-426; "A Third Kind of Marxism: Colin McKay, Socialist Political Economy and the Great Depression," *Studies in Political Economy*, 55 (Spring 1998), 127-154; "Of Karl Marx and the Bluenose: Colin Campbell McKay and the Legacy of Maritime Socialism," *Acadiensis*, 27, 2 (Spring 1998), 3-25.
[39]See Campbell, *Canadian Marxists and the Search for a Third Way.*
[40]Tom Mitchell, "From the Social Gospel to 'the Plain Bread of Leninism': A.E. Smith's Journey to the Left in the Epoch of Reaction After World War I," *Labour/Le Travail*, 33 (1994), 125-151.
[41]For Irvine's interest in Spencer, see Anthony Mardiros, *William Irvine: The Life of a Prairie Radical* (Toronto 1979), 98-99; and for an excellent contextual introduction to his thought, see Reginald Whitaker, "Introduction" to Irvine, *The Farmers in Politics.* (My only reservation would be that I would tend to substitute the word "Spencerian" for "Hobbesian" in Whitaker's characterizations of Irvine's politico-ethical universe.) For a general account

Politics[42] brought the Spencerian socialist[43] tradition into direct and fruitful contact with the largest mass movement of its time. Irvine's thought suggests the limitations of simply dismissing first-wave socialism for its supposed "vulgarity," "impossibilism," or "reformism," terms which are not so much erroneous as beside the point. At the core of Irvine's socialism was the conviction that radicals could scientifically interpret society in ways which accelerated the evolutionary progress of equality.

His work can be seen as an exploration of four great Spencerian themes. There is, first and fundamentally, the announcement of an epistemological break: a leap forward to a new scientific understanding of society. Just as in natural evolution, where "the higher an organism develops, the more complex its parts become," so it was in human society.

The human organism has developed from a simple splotch of protoplasm. Included in that organism are many parts, hands, feet, stomach, heart, eyes, ears, and brains, etc. All have special functions to perform. No one would think of arguing that the development of these various organs meant anarchy, that the hands would carry off the lungs, or the feet walk off with the nerves; on the contrary, it is well-known that in the pursuit of the purpose of the intelligence, every organ becomes of service, acting in co-operation for the well-being of the organism. Society is like the human body. Once it was a social plasm, the simple form. As it evolved, it developed many parts and functions, in the performance of which groups of people act as units. It would be insane, if it were possible, to throw a man into a chemical solution that would reduce him into his original protoplasm for the sake of sameness and primitive unity. For surely the unity of parts acting in harmony is higher and more admirable than the original bit of jelly.[44]

Second, Irvine, in company with some neo-Hegelian liberals, believed that the evolution of industrial society had attenuated the epistemological and ontological coherence of the individual as the primary unit of social and political analysis. Only if "the individual" were conceptualized as the specification of a function or group would a more equitable social order be conceivable. As one might expect, this fundamental change would come about organically: "society will embrace the new social order without any cataclysmic upheaval. We are gradually growing towards it. The old cells are dropping off one by one, and new cells are being formed. The stability of society while in the process of reconstruction has already given confidence to the diffident, and paved the way for further progress. The fear of

---

of Irvine, see J.E. Hart, "William Irvine and Radical Politics in Canada," PhD thesis, University of Guelph, 1972.

[42] William Irvine, *The Farmers in Politics* (Toronto 1976 [1920]).

[43] It was not yet a "Spencerian Marxist" position: Irvine expressed criticisms of what he took to be some of the political implications of Marxist thought, while endorsing the substance of "Marxist materialism." His later work — e.g., *Is Socialism The Answer? The Intelligent Man's Guide to Basic Democracy* (Winnipeg 1945) — is much more clearly "Marxist."

[44] *The Farmers in Politics*, 184-185.

destruction has been allayed, and conservatism in itself has ceased to be a virtue."[45] Third, the group, united on the basis of its specific material needs, will replace "the individual" as the molecule of the new post-liberal political order. In contrast to Spencer, in whose sociology class played no functional role, Spencerian socialists thought class was decisive. They believed (on structural-functionalist, organicist grounds) that only the subaltern classes — specifically the working class for the SPCers, the farmers for Irvine and many other Prairie radicals — could *functionally* usher in the new social order. And fourth, for all its "telescopic" distancing effect, Irvine's cosmic socialism used natural-scientific discourse as an ethical critique. In particular, the evolutionary concepts of "degeneration" and "atavism" were brought to bear on the questions of the hour.[46] Contrary to Spector, Irvine was not so much confusing the party with a study-group as he was opposing the hypothesis that the party itself could functionally create the cultural preconditions of a new society.

For Irvine, democratic citizenship could be given an entirely new, post-liberal meaning, as the "socialization of responsibility."[47] With the collapse of the bankrupt two-party system, one was opened up to the possibility of the direct democracy of producers' groups, to a post-patronage, post-corruption political universe in which honest political debate and dialogue is possible. Irvine glimpsed, in "group government" — a democracy in which government was answerable to producers' groups organized according to occupation, in an Canadian adaptation of the British concept of "guild socialism" — a way of transcending the politics of liberal order. In this version of socialism, the language of liberal rights was turned against itself: against the merely formal rights of citizenship and party, one championed the real rights and responsibilities that would follow from function.

In his brief précis of the "socialism we have (thankfully) lost," Maurice Spector elegantly distilled what later generations would find rather "abstract" or "idealist" about first-wave socialism. Its "cosmic" evolutionary perspective did not easily combine with, and might even distract from, any *strategic* politics of socialist transformation. Concrete interventions in the present day were difficult to link to so general an evolutionary vision. But for self-proclaimed revolutionaries like McKay and gradualist Fabians like W.F. Hatheway, eclectics like Irvine and "hard Marxists" like the DeLeonites, the theory of evolution was definitional. Evolution, which taught scientific as well as moral lessons, would vindicate them. Few attempts were made to adjust the ideology to the conditions of Canadian society; and there was a yawning void where later cohorts would expect to find a detailed strategic conception of how the party, the decisive place of integration where

---

[45]*The Farmers in Politics*, 86-87.

[46]On the "moral degeneration" or "moral degeneracy" of the party system, see *The Farmers in Politics*, 55, 64, and 76. On atavism (and weeding) see: "The socially atavistic are being weeded out; atavism is a continually rarer phenomenon. Yesterday is passed, to-morrow is not yet; this is the twilight of the gods." (24)

[47]*The Farmers in Politics*, 45.

narrow corporate interests are translated into a disciplined class politics, would interact with its social base. Spector's brisk treatment of his predecessors alerts us to the ways in which they inhabited a very different ethical and political formation than the one he worked to bring into being.

From a 21st century perspective, however, Spector's disparagement seems less interesting than the first formation's often overlooked contributions. Many of Irvine's arguments have a contemporary feel, at a time when radical energies are once again being poured into the re-activation of the concept of citizenship.[48] Irvine was characteristic of the best thinkers of his formation in stressing the possibility that working people themselves could become their own educators. His "Spencerian" connections between seemingly disparate phenomena — such as capitalism and environmental degradation — have retained their interest. Most significant and valuable was Irvine's construction of a well-theorized and grounded counter-hegemonic challenge to liberalism at the level of *political theory*, in his deceptively simple call for *group government* — an ingenious "Canadianization" of a British atttempt to think through Marxist political theory in a non-Fabian, non-statist direction. This entailed a profoundly subversive "defamiliarization" of liberalism's claims to the mantle of "democracy." Irvine's subsequent political itinerary — into the Ginger Group, CCF, and ultimately into the role of CP fellow traveler[49] — would reveal the staying power of his post-liberal politics.

The Second Socialism: Revolutionary Praxis

Revolution is the keyword of the second socialist formation, dominated by a cohort which rose to prominence from 1917 to 1935 during a period in which the liberal order was challenged by the century's most severe crisis of capitalism. The Communists are certainly the most famous of the forces within the revolutionary formation which organized in this period; but it is a mistake to reduce this second socialism to them. The One Big Union, perhaps Canada's most original and intelligent counter-model to American business unionism, and its leader, R.B. Russell, considered themselves to be as entitled as the Communists to the mantle of vanguard revolutionaries; there was also a rival francophone attempt to organize a section of the Communist International in Québec. Before the "solidification" of the party there were scores of revolutionary groups which have faded from the historians' view as the CPC has come to monopolize attention. Still, there is a certain merit to this focus on the CPC. The most lasting and memorable monuments to the period came from the Communists and especially from *The Worker*, the party's

[48]See Chantal Mouffe, ed., *Dimensions of Radical Democracy: Pluralism, Citizenship, Community* (London 1992).
[49]His analysis of "Premier Stalin" as a proponent of "human resources development" suggests how one could combine first-wave Spencerianism with third-wave state-building: with lamentable effects, as we now know. See Irvine, *Is Socialism The Answer?* (Winnipeg1945), 14.

newspaper, wherein a discourse of heroic revolutionary *praxis* was richly developed. And, gradually, there came to be, around the Communists, a cohort of people who might dispute many of the CPC's specific policies, but shared much of its worldview. Such people exercised an influence well beyond their numbers, especially in the labour movement. In the interwar period especially, revolutionary analyses suddenly had a plausibility and an audience they had earlier lacked. The pivotal matrix-event was the Russian Revolution; closer to home, general strikes and "apprehended insurrections" from Vancouver Island to Cape Breton demonstrated the power of the working class. State violence and repression, exemplified by armed occupations of the coalfields and the imprisonment of radicals, as well as the development of a security apparatus, suggested the extremes which defenders of liberal order would countenance. There is a rich and abundant literature on what is perhaps the most researched period in the history of Canadian leftism.

But there has been little reflection on the implicit philosophy and sociology, the historical analysis, the cultural networks, and the shared language — in a problematic word, "the paradigm" — which influenced this second formation. Any such reflection here must be taken as preliminary. One is struck particularly by five new developments. First, for *both* the communist and non-communist left, the party as a disciplined and "professional" institution assumed a reality-status in this period it had earlier lacked. Second, the status of "revolution" also changed, from a word denoting a general "speeding-up" of social evolution, conceived in a very general or "cosmic" sense, to one that pertained to immediate political phenomena in actual countries, orchestrated by professional revolutionaries guided by specific theories.[50] (And after the revolution, a "dictatorship of the proletariat" — the phrase did not originate in this period,[51] but it unquestionably achieved a new prominence in it — would work to transform social life as a kind of "collective social scientist.") Third, there was, at the same time, a heightened socialist awareness of the relativity of any position. Even those who had studied a question minutely, and had a sound training in socialist theory, might disagree in their diagnoses. And since the new paradigm involved a far tighter interconnection between theory and practice, an intensified sense that "socialism" was not a "cosmic" tendency but an objectively definable future immanent in the present, an awareness of political "relativity" led

[50]Maurice Spector would write in 1923 that in five years, the revolution had ceased to be a "myth" and had become the "inspiring reality of a proletarian state." "Delegate To Comintern Reports to Convention. Maurice Spector Sums Up Work of Fourth Congress," *The Worker*, 15 March 1923.

[51]It originated, of course, with Marx, although he applied it to the Paris Commune, a politically heterogeneous body in which his own supporters were in the minority. For important books on the subject, see Etienne Balibar, *On the Dictatorship of the Proletariat*, trans. Graham Lock (London 1977); and John Molyneux, *Marxism and the Party* (London 1978).

not to "relativism" but to an intensified search for objectively "true readings."[52]
Fourth, a sharpened dialectical sensibility made socialist discourse less all-embracing and speculative and more empirical and historically specific; and "Canada"
itself, with all of its internal contradictions, became, perhaps for the first time in
socialist thought, something which was *necessarily* an important category. And
fifth and finally, class analysis underwent a subtle shift. The *historic bloc* many
socialists had theorized as necessary for the success of their movement (most
commonly, the industrial working class) was now elevated to the status of the prime
mover of the social world.

One field in which the distinction between the first and second formations was
clear was the labour movement. Here a core text, whose lessons were not confined
to Communists, was Lenin's *Left-Wing Communism: An Infantile Disorder*, which
was read in Canada as an injunction to Communists to struggle within the labour
movement, no matter how reactionary its leadership, and to take the leading role in
"united fronts."[53] Although Lenin is nowadays almost as unfashionable a figure as
Spencer, a full reconnaissance of Canadian socialist history would need to revisit
his work carefully — and especially to note the selective way it was appropriated
and interpreted to address specific Canadian circumstances.[54] The major thinkers
who influenced Communists — Lenin above all, Trotsky, Bukharin, Luxemburg
— were all serious revolutionaries; many non-communists were reading John
Strachey,[55] H.G. Wells, and G.D.H. Cole, all of whom could also be seen as
professional, "credentialled" socialists. From the classical tradition of Marxism one

[52]Of course, for Communists there was the additional challenge of interpreting, correctly,
the sometimes delphic pronouncements on North American questions of the Communist
International. For an illuminating international guide to the policies of the International, see
Fernando Claudin, *The Communist Movement: From Comintern to Cominform* (Harmondsworth 1975).

[53]John Manley's articles on the CP in the 1920s contain the most interesting reflections on
the "united front" tactic; see "Does the International Labour Movement Need Salvaging?
Communism, Labourism, and the Canadian Trade Unions, 1921-1928," *Labour/Le Travail*,
41 (Spring 1998), 149-50, on the difficulties in "concretizing" the Comintern's changing
advice on the united front tactic. See also Penner, *Canadian Communism.*

[54]For useful reflections, see Mark A. Gabbert, "Socialist History and Socialism's Future,"
Labour/Le Travail, 29 (Spring 1992), 247-8, who after conceding the partial truth of the
conventional charges against Lenin, adds: "There is the legacy of Lenin's political combat-
iveness, his internationalism, his clear-headed understanding of the essential barbarism of
capitalist civilization, and his recognition that the transition to socialism would involve a
political crisis of major proportions."

[55]John Strachey is reported to have told David Lewis in 1946 of his close affiliation with
the Communists in the 1930s. Cameron, *Unfinished Journey*, 178. For a skeptical appraisal
of him, see David Caute, *The Fellow Travellers: A Postscript to the Enlightenment* (London
1977). Strachey's *The Coming Struggle for Power* was one of the "mandatory" books
Canadian leftists were expected to have read in the 1930s. A similarly positioned figure was
Harold Laski.

retained *The Communist Manifesto* and *Anti-Duhring*, which was popularized under the revealing title of *Socialism: Utopian and Scientific* — but both texts could be read in ways which suggested an unbridgeable chasm dividing the "new left" c.1925 from the "old left" c.1910.[56]

Any search for the matrix of assumptions uniting a second formation of socialists runs the risk of distortion — of re-inventing a happy family of the left, when the evidence suggests precisely the opposite: parties locked in a bitter struggle for power and influence. The theses put forward by Leninism were, intentionally, not ones on which a middle ground could easily be found. "Vanguardism," the combined tactics of democratic centralism within and united front without, and the Communist emphasis on revolutionary mass terror, both before and after the inauguration of the dictatorship of the proletariat, were not subjects conducive to the achievement of a bland consensus. Communists themselves came to be deeply divided about them. The Canadian party was one of the last in the world to adhere to Stalin's leadership; by the early 1930s, among Marxist-Leninists, there were stark divisions between those who had accepted and those who had refused the party's transition to the new "ultra-left" line of 1928. Among non-Leninist Marxists, one also finds a plethora of perspectives.

So there is no point in looking for homogeneity. But is there then any plausibility to "horizontal" analysis? What defines a formation is not agreement on how to conduct politics, but rather a shared focus on a similar problem (in this case, the evident collapse of the capitalist world order), similar solutions (as suggested by the Soviet example, which drew enthusiastic support from most socialists), and a number of shared debates (in this case, most fundamentally, the question of how best to organize and run the party). The sheer energy the state poured into repression of the Communists, most notoriously under Section 98 and (in Québec) the Padlock Laws, greatly enhanced the Communists' status as the left's true fighters. Their efforts to influence the labour movement made them, no matter how small their numbers, an inescapable presence on the left, especially in the largest cities and resource towns. That the CCF issued a "Regina Manifesto" resounding, at least in its opening and concluding passages, with words of "eradicating capitalism," suggested the impact of second-formation socialists (especially strong in British Columbia) on the party. That its leadership purged Ontario dissidents with a thoroughness that recalled "democratic centralism" at its most energetic, suggested the extent to which, bittterly divided as it was, the second formation also shared certain party-centred and "objectivist" insights into how to wage socialist politics. That J.S. Woodsworth, revered leader of the Ginger Group and subsequently of the CCF, published regularly in the Communist Maurice Spector's *The Worker*, and that he, William Irvine, and many others shared a high opinion of the Soviet Union, is

[56]And Spencer was more or less retired as a serious influence on socialism, although favourable references to him were retained in Socialist Labor Party materials published in the 1940s, and reprinted as late as the 1970s.

also suggestive; so, of course, is the blunt critique Spector eventually published of Woodsworth's "misleading middle-class language."[57]

Without making any claim that he was typical, I think the writings of Maurice Spector captured many of the changes, both stark and subtle, that divided the second from the first cohort.[58] In the 53 articles signed by him in *The Worker* from 1922 to 1928 — which is undoubtedly only a fraction of his contributions — a new socialism announces itself. In them the word "revolution" occurs no fewer than 119 times. It was a time, for Spector, when it was imperative for revolutionaries to seize the moment, and transform the consciousness of the workers. Held back by "Social-Democrats" and "Labour Leaders," the workers of the world, shortly after the Treaty of Versailles, had been lulled with "pipe-dreams of Reconstruction" and the routine and inertia of the Second International. "The objective conditions for revolution were ideal. But the subjective factor — the will of the masses — was lacking. The opportunists, not the Communists, dominated the masses. There was the lesson of that crisis for us. If we had had strong Communist parties then, there would have been a different story to tell. That is true, because having a strong Communist Party means that already the masses are giving their allegiance to Communism — are coming under Communist influence."[59] What was bracing about this new discourse was its cold-water realism, its grasp on the present moment, its "non-telescopic" sense of political immediacy, its new kind of inter-nationalism, and its explicit theorization of the need for revolutionaries to overcome the "subject/object" distinction. The Soviet Revolution, the Congresses of the International, the defeat of the revolution in Germany: these were experienced as events in *our* movement. And, for the first time in Canada, there was in this

[57]Maurice Spector, "A Criticism of the Bourgeois Element in Mr. Woodsworth," *The Worker*, 17 July 1926.

[58]For one title on Spector, see Gary O'Brien, "Maurice Spector and the Origins of Canadian Trotskyism," MA thesis, Carleton University, 1974. The relative neglect of Spector is symptomatic of the theoretical weakness of left historiography in Canada. Because he was on the "wrong side" in 1927-8, the ascendant Tim Buck faction had no reason to honour his memory; neither did the CCF-NDP tradition. In consequence, some of the most energetic, insightful and well-crafted Marxist writings in our history have been generally neglected. Spector, who remained politically active as a Trotskyist down to the 1950s, deserves a major biography. For brief comments on Spector's career, see James P. Cannon, *The History of American Trotskyism: Report of a Participant* (New York 1944), 49-50, 63; and Maurice Isserman, *If I Had a Hammer: The Death of the Old Left and the Birth of the New Left* (Urbana and Chicago 1993), 72-3, 75, wherein he is glimpsed at the time of negotiations between the Shachtmanites and the Socialist Party. Angus, *Canadian Bolsheviks,* is an attempt to rehabilitate the reputation of the Spector-MacDonald leadership.

[59]"Delegate To Comintern Reports to Convention. Maurice Spector Sums Up Work of Fourth Congress," *The Worker*, 15 March 1923.

socialism a sustained emphasis on anti-colonialism.[60] At a time when the world was polarizing, between forces of revolution and forces of reaction, there was no room for compromise. It was time to choose sides, and there were really only two: revolution or reaction. At the time of the death of Ebert, leader of the German social democrats, Spector wrote a bitter obituary under the headline "Ebert Dies and Cheats Gallows," which revisited his role as a "notorious social traitor" who had assassinated Rosa Luxemburg and Karl Liebknecht. It was evidence not only of the new "language of politics" but also of Spector's whole-hearted internationalist attachment to the German Revolution,[61] which he thought had dramatic lessons to teach Canadians.[62] The fate of the "ultra lefts" in the Fisher-Maslow group within the KPD, who had seized control of the party in the wake of the failed revolution of 1922, and whose cardinal error had been to "neglect Lenin's teaching that 'the actual struggle for power can begin only when the Communists have won over to their side a majority of at least the decisive sections of the working class'," was also instructive.[63]

Like the first-wave socialists, those of the second formation believed it was possible and necessary to integrate first-order apprehensions of the social world with much more abstract concepts. The difference between the two formations lay, in part, in rival constructions of "evolution." What for the first formation was a direct relationship between the evolution of the cosmos and the ultimate victory of the cause, was transformed by second-wave socialists into a relationship mediated by revolutionary activism, which, if it was undertaken correctly, would advance the pace of history." This was the logic of their unflinching support for the Soviet Revolution. For them, the social-democrats could never have mustered the wit and strength to fight the counter-revolution. Only the "heroism and vision of the Communist Party" could have defied "blockade, intervention and starvation." And with the conclusion of the period of civil war, when "military and political

[60]Maurice Spector, "Maurice Spector Sums up Work of 4th Congress," *The Worker*, 2 April 1923. Note, however, Peter Campbell, "East Meets Left: South Asian Militants and the Socialist Party of Canada in British Columbia, 1904-1914," *International Journal of Canadian Studies*, 20 (Fall 1999), 35-65 for a fascinating glimpse of variegated first-wave attempts to come to grips with colonialism. For a fascinating account of how a debate over anti-colonial struggle intersected with SPC/CP struggles in Vancouver, see David Akers, "Rebel or Revolutionary? Jack Kavanagh and the Early Years of the Communist Movement in Vancouver, 1920-1925," *Labour/Le Travail* 30, (1992), 9-44.
[61]M.S. [Maurice Spector], "Ebert Dies and Cheats Gallows," *The Worker*, 14 March 1925.
[62]An unresolved dilemma in the historiography of Canadian socialism is how much emphasis to place on "external influences" and how much on "homegrown ideas": this is particularly marked in the case of the Communist Party, where a full-fledged debate on the role of the Comintern has not yet taken place. In general, historians have been swift to note international influences, but less attentive to the ways in which they may have been "put to work" in the specific Canadian environment.
[63]Maurice Spector, "E.C.C.I. Letter to German Party," *The Worker*, 14 November 1925.

expediency had to take precedence over economic rationality," "the transition to Communism can be undertaken scientifically."[64] Irvine had written in *The Farmers in Politics* about the "Copernican Revolution" effected by Spencer's and Darwin's Theory of Evolution. Those who were fully integrated into the second formation believed, however, that the political 'Copernican Revolution' had happened in Russia, and the role of Copernicus had been filled by Lenin.

Second-formation language constructed, in essence, a bi-polar universe. Dichotomizing categories (scientific socialism vs. utopian socialism, revolution vs. reform, proletariat vs. bourgeoisie, realism vs. sentimentalism) were given a new intensity. What was generally new in the second formation was its application of objectivizing categories to immediate political and economic circumstances. In the implied epistemology of *The Worker*, it was possible to determine, with a reasonable degree of certainty, the objective truth, and to apply this knowledge to day-to-day politics. When Spector spoke of the "working class" and its "interests," he did so from a position of epistemological security: it was possible for true Communists to define the interests of workers quite apart from the workers' own experience. Yet this vanguard sensibility should not be stereotyped. At its most subtle (certainly in Gramsci's thought, and at moments in Spector's) the "vanguard" could only be such if its relationship with its followers was fully dialectical, if its leadership functioned not as something "imposed from without" but rather as a kind of long-term proletarian memory bank and steering mechanism.

One of the most interesting distinctions of the second socialism was the construction of "Canada" as an important category of analysis. That there is more reflection on "national questions" in a paper of 1925 than in, say, one from 1910 was in part a reflection of the rise of Canadian nationalism in the 1920s; but it was also the paradoxical outcome of the second formation's internationalism.[65] Communists especially were required to adopt a non-Canadian "subject-position" — to see themselves as part of a movement of revolutionaries throughout the world. Yet this very removal in the imagination required them to highlight Canada's specific position in that world. The Communist International demanded that they think in such terms; and, of course, Lenin's text on *Imperialism* provided a model of how such analysis should be undertaken. One was hence required to theorize the "peculiarities of the Canadians" by virtue of one's enrollment in the world working-class movement. For all its universalism, the new formation tended to advocate Canadian independence, carefully distinguished from the merely bourgeois inde-

[64]Maurice Spector, "Maurice Spector Sums up Work of 4th Congress," *The Worker*, 2 April 1923.

[65]First-wave Canadian socialists were internationalists, but in ways which rarely transcended the boundaries of the British Empire; and their newspapers eagerly devoured news of socialism's upward ascent across the globe, from New Zealand to Germany, but with special emphasis on developments in Great Britain, from which many first-wave socialists came, and to which they often looked for inspiration.

pendence advocated by Mackenzie King. And, even more ironically, their demographic situation required them to work out, in however early and contentious a way, and often very reluctantly, a politics which created more space for organized ethnic minorities than had hitherto existed in the Canadian socialist imagination.[66]

It is customary to explain the waning influence of this revolutionary cohort in terms of Stalinization, the Cold War and state repression, divisions between language minorities and the majority: all these and other explanations have their plausibility. From the perspective of the critique of liberal order, however, one might highlight other features of the situation as well. The politics of "industrial concentration" followed by the second cohort, and its focus on the trade-union movement, qualified its chance of an effective alliance with other subaltern groups and classes. In many parts of the country, Irvine's "universal class" of farmers was still predominant. There were of course places — Toronto's Spadina, 'The Main' in Montréal, North-End Winnipeg, east-end Vancouver, industrial Cape Breton — where the revolutionary subject-position constructed by the discourse "touched down" to interpellate living human beings. The "red bases" were real, and their cultural legacy merits much closer study on the part of people today who would like to multiply "zones of resistance" — but they were also fragile, demographically precarious, and widely separated from each other in a far-flung archipelago.

The counter-hegemonic strategy of building a "united front" of labour against capital sat uneasily with a classic Leninist strategy of "speaking truth to the erring" and ruthlessly exposing "middle-class language" and values wherever one encountered them. And if, until our own time, every Canadian socialism has been gender-specific, one might venture to say that there was a heightened masculinism in the tough-minded military language characteristic of the second formation. A rhetoric justifying armed force against the revolution's enemies probably convinced some workers, familiar themselves with the day-to-day violence of the capitalist workplace or the use of the military to repress strikes. Yet it must also have raised ethical qualms. The strategy of armed violence could also be, and was, critiqued for being fundamentally adventurist and unrealistic. The Communist discourse of *realpolitik* was to that extent self-refuting, given the gap between any "hard-boiled" assessment of the situation and the likelihood of a violent overthrow of the Canadian political system.

Perhaps most damagingly, the claim to have mastered an objective science of revolution was compromised by the eventual appearance of diametrically opposed readings emanating from the same science. There were very few empirical controls built into the party-centred model of knowledge; and little sense of experimental openness about the ways in which Marxist-Leninist formulae might be adapted and

[66]For one fascinating and heartbreaking case study, see Henry Srebrnik, "Red Star Over Birobidzhan: Canadian Jewish Communists and the 'Jewish Autonomous Region' in the Soviet Union," *Labour/Le Travail*, 44 (Fall 1999), 129-147.

applied in a Canadian setting.[67] The new paradigm's very insistence on the "before-and-after" chasm separating the serious from the frivolous, the "real" from the "abstract" socialist, imposed a barrier to its successful recapture of enduringly powerful aspects of the first cohort's work. The second formation deliberately de-emphasized aspects of antecedent socialists, who were often dismissed as mere "social democrats" unworthy of serious examination. Paradoxically, this avoidance of the past de-Marxified the second formation's political economy, which in *The Worker* was subordinated to the class struggle. The ironic consequence was that, when capitalism actually did seemingly start to crumble, Marxist-Leninists were not easily distinguished from "new liberals" in their underconsumptionism, nor from mere bourgeois journalists in their sensationalist muckraking. And the overall contours of the "bourgeois state," or the "socialist state" which might replace it, were as radically undertheorized within this formation as they had been by the first. These were fundamental *political*, as well as theoretical, problems.

The Third Socialism: National State Management

A third formation, whose matrix-events were the Great Depression and the rise of fascism, gradually emerged from 1932 to 1935 and attained hegemony on the left in the 1940s, when it was swept up in the new liberal "passive revolution" that gave rise to the welfare state. If the contrasts between the first two formations seem relatively obvious, that between the second and third is almost counter-intuitive. The argument is that — notwithstanding a fair degree of continuity in party structures and personnel, a continuing interwar "crisis of capitalism," and leadership disavowals of any discontinuity — this formation marked a significant and enduring change in the language of Canadian socialism.

There is, of course, generally accepted evidence of discontinuity. There were many new political institutions that were either founded after 1932 or which changed their function and much of their language. No one disputes that a line can be drawn from post-war Farmer-Labour through the Ginger Group through to the CCF (fd. 1932/3): but here the argument would be that, nonetheless, the CCF of 1939 was in many respects radically *unlike* the Ginger Group of 1929, in its *actual* leadership, ideology and tactics. Similarly, no one would dispute that a vertical line of descent can be drawn from the post-war Workers Party of Canada through the Communist Party of Canada to the Labour-Progressive Party (fd. 1943): but here the argument would be that, nonetheless, the Labour Progressives of 1944, who had internalized the new Popular Front strategy enunciated by the Comintern in 1935, were also in many respects radically *unlike* the Communists of 1927. And,

[67]The most striking example, of many, was perhaps the tragic fate of Spector himself. The same Spector one encountered in *The Worker* in 1925 as an authoritative guide to international revolutionary politics was scientifically "proved" to be an unreliable element and a shallow Marxist, at least by the official party decree in 1928. See "The Communist Party of Canada Maintains Leninist Ideological Clarity," *The Worker,* 24 November 1928.

to go even further, the argument would be that both the CCF and Communists had changed in roughly the same ways: that a certain convergence within a common formation had occurred. For both parties, the question of the *socialist state* had become paramount — a "convergence" in outlook that ironically inspired the left's most divisive internal struggle.

How should this "third language of socialism" be distinguished? By the rise of "state" and "nation" as paramount concepts. It was a period marked by the emergence of a galaxy of major new socialist stars: for instance, David Lewis, F.R. Scott, T.C. Douglas, King Gordon, among the CCFers, and Tim Buck, Stanley Ryerson, Tom McEwen, Norman Bethune, among the Communists. And certain events in this period have been generally marked: the CCF's near victory in Ontario in 1943 and its triumph in Saskatchewan in 1944, to form the first socialist government in North America; and the Communist Party's switch to a Common Front strategy in 1935, in line with a general Comintern pattern, its dramatic success in organizing the Mackenzie-Papineau Battalion in its fight for Republican Spain, its electoral victory under the name of the Labour-Progressives in 1943 in a constituency in Montréal, followed swiftly by its débâcle in the Gouzenko Spy Affair of 1945. The CCF has in particular been analyzed at length in both historical and social scientific writing, which has probed its seemingly anomalous existence on a continent where socialism of any sort has rarely been powerful. The pitched battles between CCFers and Communists in the labour movement are also well-documented, as are the federal government's efforts to use industrial legality to "edit out" radicals from the trade unions. Depending on who is telling the story, this is the time in which Canadian socialism actually began — under the auspices of the CCF, which overcame the negative, divisive (and — one sometimes reads between the lines — foreign) influence of the Communists to eventually become the New Democratic Party in 1961, "the party that changed Canada"; or, conversely, it is the time in which Canadian socialism began to die — as the Communists were ground down by the bourgeois state, aided and abetted by the unreliable social democrats, who consistently rejected calls for proletarian unity and in whose hands the socialist vision was travestied to one of merely contesting elections.

These are well-ordered historiographical rail lines, serviceable and much-travelled, and it would be folly to blow them up. The "separate socialist spheres" they describe must have existed to some degree. Yet, from the perspective of the critique of liberal order, neither the partisan perspectives of the warring parties nor the histories which rehash their point of view ask all the questions that need to be asked. The more interesting questions, from this perspective, lie elsewhere.

The charismatic aura which surrounds the great stars, especially the CCFers, suggests that they now figure in a nationalist myth-symbol complex, that they have become "national figures" and not mere leftists.[68] And this is deeply suggestive.

[68] One indication: T.C.Douglas, who regularly figures on popular lists of Canadian heroes, enjoys a respect in Canada as one of the founders of "medicare" which is not reducible to his role as the country's first socialist premier.

Perhaps the domination of nationalist party-mindedness explains why critical examinations of socialism in the period have been so slow to come. One has the impression of a period overcrowded with scholars, when in fact there are many significant questions about it that are left to be resolved. For example, why did class and class struggle recede in socialist thought and analysis? Why did the nation loom so large? What was the general 'left reception' of Keynes? Did a language of painfree modernity replace the earlier emphasis on dialectic and struggle? If so, why? Were the Labour Progressives just another name for the Communists — or did the strategy of "Labour Progressivism" position its partisans in a different realm, somewhere between the CCF and the Liberals, with whom they were to some extent and in some places allied?[69] These questions of detail lead to a more general question of theory: how did the two major socialist parties relate to a general transformation of liberalism, the Fordist "passive revolution" which reshaped the Canadian political order in the 1940s and 1950s?

A provisional answer to this last question opens a path to a more complex understanding of this formation. Both parties could be re-interpreted as elements in this new liberal passive revolution — simultaneously resisting and promoting a newly conceptualized managerial liberalism that had overtly learned from Keynes, and covertly from Marx, about the requirements of preserving power; and which had, in the Soviet Union, a countermodel drawing the support from many of Canada's sober-minded citizens. This was the epoch, precisely the one in which Stalin's terror reached its full fury, in which the third edition of Sidney and Beatrice Webb's *Soviet Communism: A New Civilization*? ditched its hesitating question-mark. The conventional dichotomizing strategy pitting Communists against CCFers — the "revolutionaries" against the "democratic left," if one prefers — misses some important things that a more horizontal, cohort-specific view opens up. In some respects, the CP unintentionally instructed the CCFers in the arts of party-building, political-economic analysis, and strategy.[70]

One can read "irony" but also a profound historical logic into the fact that, out of the fierce competition among political tendencies in the 1920s and 1930s, there did emerge a party of quasi-professional socialists who followed a strategy of "industrial concentration," with a strongly hierarchical leadership convinced of its superior ability to read the historical situation and act decisively in it. That party was the ostensibly anti-Leninist CCF, as shaped especially by David Lewis, the ardent Labour Bundist whose "parliamentary Marxism" was not as far removed

---

[69]The Communist/Liberal alliance is too often subjected to a kind of scandal-mongering critique, when in fact it is a problem calling out for more sensitive and subtle treatment. Perhaps the most interesting treatment of how the LPP/Liberal alliance felt on the ground can be found in Weisbord, *The Strangest Dream: Canadian Communists, the Spy Trials and the Cold War*.

[70]For interesting reflections on ties between the CCF and CP, see Penner, *The Canadian Left: A Critical Analysis*, 258 and *passim*.

from the perspective of the CP as he would later make it out to be.[71] The CCF, ostensibly the CP's "democratic antithesis," actually incarnated (at least after 1936 or so) certain important features of the vanguard party — a canon of official, must-read literature, study cells, a hierarchical top-down national leadership, strict party discipline, and so on; one might even say it did so with more Leninist discipline than the Communists, who in their LPP heyday in the 1940s had attracted a substantial middle-class membership and were virtually allied with the Liberal Party. There were of course major differences between Spector's "vanguard revolutionary party" guided by Leninist theory, capable of disciplined mobilization, and so deeply integrated into the world revolutionary movement that it might be considered one of its battalions, and the "mass party" constructed principally by David Lewis out of the more decentralized and federal "coalition" framework of the CCF. But it is interesting to note certain symptomatic "horizontal" similarities.

Both the CCF and the CP, and many of the intellectuals and other figures active in this moment, marginalized an older language of class struggle and emphasized a new language of national management and consolidation. And this had the effect of taking both parties into new conceptual terrain, and making them *both* highly vulnerable to the new liberal politics of *passive revolution*. In a sense, they were both called upon to *govern*, at least in their imaginations, and — for the Saskatchewan CCF at any rate — ultimately in reality. In this period, and in marked contrast to anything before or after it, it was easy to get the impression that a weakened and discredited liberal order was being encircled by a world-changing matrix of socialist ideas and initiatives. And this was a period in which the charge of positivism habitually and often misleadingly brought to bear against all older traditions of Canadian socialist thought has a certain validity. Value-free science and state planning were esteemed as fundamental aspects of modernity: "science" could be organized "for the people." After the first socialism's belief in a truth imminent in a cosmic evolutionism, and the second's that the truth was revolutionary and dialectical, the third formation developed a new "positive" emphasis that the truth was "out there," empirically accessible to professional social scientists and economists.

It was the third formation, then, that wrestled most urgently and directly with the logic of the conventional liberal order, as encirclement, as temptation — and as that which had to be defended against the more radical liberal despotism of fascism. The logic of this moment was complex and defies a unilinear reading. Yet, precisely because it is so bound up with the formation of the modern Canadian project, it has been systematically misrepresented. Often writers on the NDP have equated the CCF's socialism with the liberal Keynesian welfare state that the NDP (founded after the Canadian Labor Congress' 1956 revealing appeal to all "liberally

---

[71]Obviously, one would need to correlate Lewis's caution here with the Cold War. For an excellent discussion of David Lewis's Marxism, see Smith, *Unfinished Journey*, 285-7 and *passim*.

minded" Canadians) has doggedly supported since the 1960s. One can readily understand why so many people, perhaps especially on the left of the party, have invested in this emphasis on seamless continuity. For some of today's mainstream New Democrats, it not only frees them from any guilt-by-association with Communists, but it also allows them to narrate their party's history as a tale of martyrdom in the interests of the nation: the CCF's proposals in the 1940s, short-sightedly opposed by a well-orchestrated cabal of fanatics, were really just reforms that led to the widely-accepted welfare state consensus. For their Marxist critics, the same thesis of continuity has often given them the soft-headed social-democratic "Other" from which their genuinely revolutionary project can be distinguished.

From the liberal-order perspective, neither reading captures what is most interesting about the 1940s. The most compelling statement of the third socialist formation can be found in *Make This Your Canada* (1943), authored by David Lewis and Frank Scott, which sold 25,000 copies in less than a year[72] — making it one of the most widely-read socialist texts in Canadian history. Given Frank Scott's subsequent closeness to Pierre Trudeau and his eventual stature as an authority on the constitution, and David Lewis's leadership of the federal New Democratic Party from 1971 to 1975, one might expect this book to be a quintessential "social-democratic" expression of moderation, a call for a humane welfare state to redress some of the more problematic features of capitalism. It certainly emerges, not from the left wing, but from the powerful centre of the party, from two of its most respected and influential figures. In retrospect, both its authors, although awkward about the book, attempted to place it in welfare-state narratives.[73] What a fresh reading of *Make This Your Canada* surprisingly suggests is that it was, for all intents and purposes, a Marxist text — albeit a Marxism shaped by the imperatives of the national management formation. True, there is an emphasis on the continuity of the outlook of the CCF with pre-1914 "democratic socialist analysis," in the text's one, somewhat dismissive reference to the record of "the tradition" on Canadian soil.[74] But the key point is that *Make This Your*

---

[72] Alan Whitehorn, *Canadian Socialism: Essays on the CCF-NDP* (Toronto 1992), 159. *Un Canada Nouveau: Vue d'ensemble de l'historique et de la politique du mouvement C.C.F.* (Montréal 1944) appeared one year later.

[73] It is odd how books devoted to the authors skate around the issues raised by *Make This Your Canada* itself. Sandra Djwa's immensely stimulating *The Politics of the Imagination: A Life of F.R. Scott* (Toronto, 1987) devotes a mere 287 words to the book, and 84 of these, oddly enough, focus on J.S.Woodsworth. David Lewis, *The Good Fight* barely refers to the book, except to congratulate F.R.Scott for his "democratic socialist's political thesis" (221-2) and to complain about the hostile reception given the book by the media (309, 313, 314, 316). For a discussion of the book, which ably brings out its "Marxist side," see Smith, *Unfinished Journey*, Appendix J, 508-510.

[74] "At the time," the authors write of the pre-1914 socialists, "... they had few listeners and even fewer adherents," *Make This Your Canada,* 113-114. Of course, this positive reference back to the correctness of the views of the adherents of the Socialist Party of Canada and

Canada looks forward to a country in which capitalist ownership has been *replaced* by social ownership, and "the rapacious system of monopoly capitalism" *replaced* by a "democratic socialist society."[75] True, there is a *small* opening for the private ownership of small, non-monopolistic companies, and the door is left slightly ajar to the market as an indicator of consumer demand.[76] But these are qualifications in a pattern of a comprehensive socialization of the economy, as systematic a replacement of capitalist by socialist social relations of production as would be found in, say, some Eastern European countries after 1945.[77] *Make This Your Canada* does not even attempt to conceal its obvious indebtedness to the "the mountainous labors of Karl Marx," thanks to whom, according to the authors, socialism obtained a "positive programme for political action by the working classes for the purpose of supplanting capitalism by a new economic order."[78] This is no mere rhetorical flourish. The implied ontology and epistemology of *Make This Your Canada* were clearly drawn from Marx's base-and-superstructure model. The text represents the "forces of production" as the chief agents in breaking down whole economic systems (such as 18th century mercantilism), in passages which obviously echo Marx's 1859 *Preface*.[79] A "relentless logic" of events proceeds from the material base to the superstructure. History teaches that political revolutions follow swiftly on economic revolutions. We learn, when we read of the consequences of "technological revolution," that "nothing could stop the process of change, and states that did not adapt themselves more gradually, like England, were changed swiftly and violently, like France."[80] This was "technological determinism" of the first order.

---

the Social Democratic Party of Canada did accommodate both Marxist parties in the "democratic socialist" tradition.

[75]*Make This Your Canada*, 197.

[76]*Make This Your Canada*, 162-3, 172.

[77]David Lewis would later convey the impression that the extent of nationalization advocated in *Make This Your Canada* had been greatly exaggerated by fear-mongers. One finds more compelling the analysis of this book by Cameron Smith. With regard to the question of the extent of nationalization, Smith points out that the book never actually defines monopoly capital. "To escape nationalization, *Make This YOUR Canada* said companies had to (1)be in no position to exploit the public, (2)show no signs of becoming a socially dangerous vested interest, (3)be operated with reasonable efficiency under decent working conditions, and (4)be ready loyally to play their part in the fulfillment of the national plan." The book "set down criteria for deciding which industries would be nationalized. That approach assumed everything would be nationalized except those industries exempted." This reversed the earlier approach of the CCF's other "bible," *Social Planning for Canada*, which stressed "that nothing would be nationalized except those industries that fit the criteria for nationalization." Smith, *Unfinished Voyage*, 510.

[78]*Make This Your Canada*, 84.

[79]*Make This Your Canada*, 41.

[80]*Make This Your Canada*, 42. A no-less-relentless "logic of events" would bring more and more Canadians to support the policies and objectives of the CCF. *Make This Your Canada*, 145.

No less than second-wave socialists did Scott and Lewis believe it was possible to be objectively correct about the way the world was going. Herein lay the appeal of the CCF, which had understood that its "imaginative political programme" needs must be based on "a correct social philosophy" and a "fearless economic analysis."[81]

As one would expect, classes exist in the Marxist world of *Make This Your Canada*, but they are not the same entities one finds in Spector's *The Worker*. They are objective functions, not potentially revolutionary agents. The book's implicit sociology of trade unionism suggests a pliable movement whose quest for "labour unity", challenged by divisions of race, language, religion and "geographical isolation," called out for state assistance.[82] Similarly, there is an implicit critique of capitalist autocracy and the commodification of labour, but this is developed not *via* an in-depth critique of capitalism, but rather by way of noting "the undemocratic habits of big business."[83] The working class, although existing objectively within this text and endowed with its own interests, becomes a sociological category among many others: it was one of the "four major classes of modern industrial society" (the others were the white collar and professional workers, the farmers, "and, finally, the few who own and control the industrial and financial resources of the country.")[84] There is "contradiction" within capitalism in *Make This Your Canada* — but it is not the contradiction described by *The Communist Manifesto*. Decisive is not the struggle between classes, or between the forces and relations of production, but rather the *moral* and *historical* contradiction between a profit-oriented economy and the "objectives of a progressive society."[85] Similarly, "monopoly" and "monopoly capitalism" operate in the text, but — as is generally the case with both Second and Third Wave Socialisms — they are not rigorously constructed in terms of Marx's "mountainous labours" on the question of value. In short, this is a very Webbian Marx.

When *Make This Your Canada* comes to explain its own place in history, it does so in a way which erases prior knowledges, especially those developed by earlier autodidacts. Explicitly, the text invites readers to take up the subject-position of the frustrated "socially-minded production men," who are "offended by a system which frequently interferes with their production job."[86] It is striking that there is no parallel attempt to put the reader into the shoes of the frustrated worker on the

[81]*Make This Your Canada*, 122.
[82]*Make This Your Canada*, 78.
[83]*Make This Your Canada*, 17.
[84]*Make This Your Canada*, 91. This Mackenzie-King-like quadrilateral formation subsequently reduces to one closer to populism, involving two primary classes, "monopolies" and "us," members of "the 99%."
[85]*Make This Your Canada*, 101.
[86]*Make This Your Canada*, 53.

assembly line.[87] In the "Canada" constructed by *Make This Your Canada*, there would be ample room for university-trained experts. Of course, formally, full sovereignty in the "new Canada" will rest with the people. On this point, Prime Minister-elect M.J. Coldwell's imagined "victory speech" upon the CCF's electoral triumph, which is presented to us as the text's moment of concrete utopianism, is clear. "It is not the C.C.F. as a party, but you as a people who have won power to-day. Because it is not physically possible for each one of you to be a member of the government, some of us are privileged to be the trustees of your power. But we in the Cabinet shall not forget, and you in the country must always remember, that in the New Canada which was born to-day, the government is the Board of Trustees for all the people — that and no more."[88] These trustees of the "New Canada" will be closely advised by the National Planning Commission — a "small group of economists, engineers and statisticians assisted by an appropriate technical staff." Lest this appear to be a government by bureaucrats, the text immediately adds: "Keeping the responsibility for planning in the hands of a democratic government is the guarantee that we shall have no totalitarian state nor a society dominated by 'experts'."[89]

Yet in two respects *Make This Your Canada* is self-subverting in its position on the role of the expert in the New Canada. Again and again, it is the Soviet Union that shimmers before the reader as capitalism's Other. No other country or model comes close.[90] It is in the Soviet Union that "we" find proof of a post-capitalist society's ability to mobilize its population to meet a great purpose. "The Soviet Union is an example of a whole economy being run successfully on new lines."[91] It is in the "Russian" people that we can see a vast population embarked "upon a colossal plan of organized social revolution," which has already given them "a powerful new system capable of withstanding the onslaught of the world's mightiest armies."[92] There is almost a hushed reverential tone when *Make This Your Canada* describes "all the energies of a united people and the techniques of planning

[87]And, needless to say, not the woman who works in the home. There is not a shadow of "socialist feminism" in the text: in this respect one can trace a marked retreat from the proto-feminism in *The Farmers in Politics* and many other works from the "first cohort," which were at least conscious of the women's question.
[88]"Prime Minister Coldwell" speaking in *Make This Your Canada*, 147.
[89]*Make This Your Canada*, 150-1.
[90]Oddly enough, given the NDP's subsequent adulation of the Scandinavian experiments in social democracy, there was no sustained discussion of Swedish successes in combating the Great Depression, and only glancing references to Australasia.
[91]*Make This Your Canada*, 87.
[92]*Make This Your Canada*, 187. The text was, of course, constructed in the depths of World War II, when all eyes were turned to the Nazi invasion of the Soviet Union. But attempts to "explain away" the text's pro-Sovietism by referencing "Stalingrad fever" surely trivialize the depth, scope and persistence of CCF fascination with the Soviet Union as a working planned economy.

and production," turned to the one purpose of defeating the Nazis.[93] These energies could be so mobilized because, the text implied, "successive national plans," based on the interests of "all her people," had brought the Soviet Union's techniques of planning and production to bear on the one overriding purpose of defeating the Nazi enemy. Such was the socially unifying effect of the Soviet system: "the people" felt the country belonged to them. They were right to think so. Given the number and the fervour of these pro-Soviet declarations, and the text's eloquent and symptomatic silences (no gulag, show trials, or cults of personality shadow its imagined Soviet Union) the reader could well imagine the New Canada would be something like the new Soviet Union, with the added plus of parliamentary government. The "democratic caveat" — "We must recognize the truth of all this, and apply its lesson, at the same time that we remain determined to pursue our own democratic course and never to allow dictatorship of any kind to rule our country"[94] — qualified but hardly undermined this Webb-like enthusiasm for a Soviet regime that had undertaken such feats of national state management.[95]

The text's attempted rebuttal of the imagined charge of "expert domination" and "regimentation" subverts itself in a second way. The reader is advised again and again that Canada's Depression miseries had receded precisely because a wartime government, acting under the force of circumstances, had had to implement planning policies it had once dismissed as utopian. Wartime planning had shown Canadians what to keep and what to remove in order to achieve justice and equality.[96] Since the text constructs as "models" both the Soviet Union *and* war-time Canada, its symptomatic silences on the question of how CCF planning was to be qualitatively different from that undertaken by Soviet planners or by the Liberal government's Ottawa Men are eloquent. There was merely the *formal* guarantee of "parliamentary sovereignty." The text walks the razor's edge, between an overtly post-liberal politics and capitulation to the managerial ethos of the liberal passive revolution.

Make This Your Canada is a celebration of a specific kind of socialist state: one in which a democracy is supplemented by comprehensive and systematic state planning, similar to (at least in general terms) the type of planning seen in both the Soviet Union and wartime Canada. In contrast to either first-wave or second-wave

[93] *Make This Your Canada*, 24. That Stalin concluded a pact with Hitler and that the Soviet government was not prepared for the Nazi invasion, having recently liquidated a good portion of the Red Army, are facts unworthy of inclusion.

[94] *Make This Your Canada*, 25.

[95] David Lewis would remark in "Canada Swings Left," *The Nation*, 158 (10 June 1944), 673: "The press and the air are filled with the warning: 'The C.C.F. will take away your homes, confiscate your savings and your insurance policies, grab our farm, and regiment your life in a bureaucratic strait-jacket.' (American New Dealers will recognize the formula.) Because the Soviet Union is deservedly popular with the masses of the people, the old epithet 'Communist' has been replaced by 'National Socialist'."

[96] *Make This Your Canada*, 3.

socialism, this expression of a third-wave socialism works with a construction of the social order that recognizes class only in a very general way: any sense of "the workers" taking control of the means of production and seizing the surplus value generated by their labour is missing. If the "master-thinkers" of the first wave were Kautsky and Spencer, and of the second wave Lenin and Trotsky, those of the third were Saint-Simon, Keynes, the Webbs, and (a certain Canadianized version of) Josef Stalin, who could all in various ways be seen as the architects of new and effectively managed states, the most successful of which was the Soviet Union.[97]

There is, in addition, something else that is new about third-wave Canadian socialist discourse as epitomized by this text: its emphatic and unabashed Canadian nationalism. It was in the very title: *Make This Your Canada*. "Nation" more than "class" is the key to its architecture. The "despair and irony of modern history"[98] described in this text was not the failure of the international proletarian revolution — but the inability of Canadians to achieve any national purpose: "Canada, by her neglect of her unemployed, her depressed areas and her youth during the 1930s, provides a striking example of a state that was not a national community."[99] *Make This Your Canada* draws deeply from the language of national patriotism.[100] When he assumes the reins of office, the authors imagine, Prime Minister Coldwell will remind all Canadians that Members of Parliament are merely the trustees of the people; and the election of the CCF will mark the people's "final victory." Against the people are the people's enemies, the "claims and power of special privilege," "monopoly," the forces of cynicism and withdrawal. Indeed, anyone who disagrees with strengthening democracy is a reactionary "who denies the very cause for which we are fighting."[101] "The people" as constructed in this discourse and articulated to a more traditional socialist critique of capitalism is a category that treats as one the entire population inhabiting the territory claimed by the Canadian state. This is a call to construct a national-popular general will.[102] Maritime and western dispari-

[97]No history of Canadian socialism will measure up which does not acknowledge the extent to which the Soviet Union was held up as the fulfillment of socialist hopes, both inside and outside the CP. For an impressive theorization of this problem, see Mark Kristmanson, "Plateaus of Freedom: Nationality, Culture and State Security in Canada," PhD Thesis,, Concordia University, 1999. For a parallel suggestive discussion with regard to the status of women, see Joan Sangster, "The Communist Party and the Woman Question, 1922-1929," *Labour/Le Travail*, 15 (Spring 1985), 25-56.

[98]*Make This Your Canada*, 29.

[99]*Make This Your Canada*, 192.

[100]The hold of "the interests" over the state is blamed for the frustration of the "national will" (37), and the book vividly denounces "the unpatriotic strike of capital for higher profits" at the start of the war. (28) A text that has virtually nothing to say about the working class has a great deal to say about "the people": the "people's needs" (9-10), the "common people," even the "democratic concept and organization of a people's citizen army fighting a people's war." *Make This Your Canada*, 60, 103.

[101]*Make This Your Canada*, 108, 15, 16, 22, 91 ("monopoly"), 61.

[102]Cf. Antonio Gramsci, *Prison Notebooks*, 131.

ties are explained in terms of technological determinism[103] and to dwell upon them is to insist on differences that are less fundamental than others.[104] Differences of "race" and language pose graver difficulties. Writing the book in North Hatley, in the Eastern Townships, Lewis and Scott, both English-speaking Quebeckers, acknowledged that there were "genuine differences of language, culture, tradition and religion " at play in Canada in the 1940s. Yet, clearly, these differences could not be allowed to disrupt the formation of a Canadian national subject-position. The language of self-determination had already been pre-empted by the text's prior commitment to a "Canadian" nationalism with parliament in Ottawa as its sovereign voice. The text becomes elusive and even incoherent at this point. And when translated into French, it did not say the same thing as it did in English.[105]

[103] *Make This Your* Canada, 105. Lewis will later advance a vintage "culture of poverty" explanation for the alleged political passivity of the Maritime Region. See Lewis, *The Good Fight*, 158.

[104] Within "the people," as imagined by this text, one finds the co-operators, building on the heroism of the 19th-century Rochdale pioneers (75), and Canada's Catholics, who were members of the country's largest single denomination (and who could be described via an aggressive reading of the papal encyclicals *Rerum Novarum* (1891) and *Quadragesimo Anno* (1931) as incipiently socialist (85)). For discussion, see Baum, *Catholics and Canadian Socialism*.

[105] *Make This Your Canada* enigmatically finds French-Canadian nationalism offensive, without being able to be explicit about the offense entailed: "The small anti-democratic forces in Quebec encourage the unfortunate mistake made by the Quebec people, feed on it and built it into a false theory which threatens the welfare both of the French-Canadian people themselves and of Canada as a whole." (107) This is an arresting, rich and ambiguous passage: what, precisely, is this "unfortunate mistake"? how can entire people make such a "mistake"? what is the "theory" and wherein lies its falsity? What is the immediate danger to the French-Canadian people? The reader guesses: (1) French-Canadian nationalism and/or separatism; (2) by being manipulated by self-interested bigots and demagogues; (3) who propound a 'theory' of integral nationalism *à la* Charles Maurras or, closer to home, a Laurentian nationalism along the lines of Abbé Groulx; (4) thereby opening up French Canadians to the ultimate risk of a Fascist victory. In the French-language edition, the passage undergoes a metamorphosis: "D'une part, un petit groupe de Canadiens de langue anglaise, intolérants et bigots, a toujours cherché à priver le Canada français de ses droits. D'autre part, un petit groupe de Canadiens de langue française, également bigots, s'est servi des griefs réels des Canadians français pour favoriser le développement d'un provincialisme étroit et antisocial." David Lewis and Frank Scott, *Un Canada Nouveau: Vue d'ensemble de l'historique et de la politique du mouvement C.C.F.* (Montréal 1944), 139. This French-language version does more than clarify the English-language text: it transforms it, because "the mistake" — i.e., resistance to the transcendent cause of Canadian National Unity — is now shared out equally between the two language groups, both of whom harboured the intolerant, the bigoted, the narrow (but, seemingly, only in the French-Canadian case, the "provincial"). One can trace in *Make This Your Canada* the shape of the contradiction that would shape left nationalism in Canada ever since: why, if it is right for "us" to be nationalist,

Because the CCF speaks for Canada, it has a claim to speak for Canadian sovereignty — even to extend the effective sovereignty of a social democratic Canadian state into the "Canadian northland," this "last great North American frontier" which it will save, in a kind of Socialist Manifest Destiny, *from* the "robber barons" and *for* "the new era of democratic social planning"[106] It is nationalism, not socialism, which serves as the Other of capitalism. Leaving to one side the Conservatives and Liberals, whose ties to the capitalist class disqualified them from this task of national salvation at the outset, the obvious challenger to this left nationalism was the Communist Party. Lewis and Scott predictably scorn the CP as a party which had made no attempt to become a mass organization, bound as it was to a mechanistic and inherently divisive philosophy. Yet nowhere is the CP denounced for its Marxism, for its atheism, for its slavish pro-Sovietism, for its class militancy. These silences suggest a certain delicacy for the CCF. To undermine completely the legitimacy of the Communists' Marxist perspective could call into question the CCF's own privileged access, via Marxist theory, to what was essentially "Canadian."

The conventional account of the Canadian left's civil war tells half the story. The CCF, and many of its members, were both drawn to and repulsed by the Communist Party. *Make This Your Canada* is only superficially an anti-communist, and not at all an anti-Marxist, text.[107] Later CCF/NDP works, influenced especially by the Cold War, would absolutize the distinction between "social democracy" and "communism" — but this, revealingly, is not a binary opposition set to work in *Make This Your Canada*. Subsequent historians sought to give the CCF-NDP an immaculate conception, and protect themselves from the Canadian equivalents of Joseph McCarthy; it followed that they would dwell lovingly on the anti-CCF rhetorical excesses of the Communists' "third period," and build up the Social Gospel into the primary motivation of the CCF (and no influence whatever on the CP). Those more sympathetic to the CP, or at least to the ideal of working-class revolution, have often repeated the same binary, simply reversing the "plus" and "minus" signs. But re-reading *Make This Your Canada* with some liberal-order questions helps destabilize these habitual responses. The priority announced in this text in 1943 was not the construction of a liberal-democratic welfare state. It was, rather, the construction of a sleek, efficient, modernized, centrally-planned socialist

---

i.e., to set about to construct "our own" national project in northern North America on the grounds of a universal ideology (i.e., socialism), is it so wrong for "them," the French Canadians/Québécois, to be nationalist? Because, of course, the first nationalism claims to "speak for" and assumes epistemological and political primacy over the second.

[106] *Make This Your Canada*, 157.

[107] An indication of what might be loosely called its 'proto-communist cultural sensibility' can be seen in the tone of revolutionary asceticism which pervades it, as seen in its selection of an illustrative example of capitalism's irrationality (entrepreneurs making costume jewelry when children cried out for shoes) and in its denunciation of the wartime production of luxury automobiles. *Make This Your Canada*, 23, 15.

state, in which planning for social welfare was just one, not particularly crucial, aspect of the socialist program. In fact, the very idea of elevating partial welfare schemes into overall strategies for social change is *explicitly critiqued and rejected* in this text.[108]

Nevertheless, this welfare-state addendum gradually came to be remembered as the whole program. In highly selective CCF-NDP invented traditions the entire rationale of the party is, and always has been, and always will be, the same: the provision to Canadians of compassionate and effective social programs through a liberal democratic regime. But, clearly, as we have seen, the paradigm of national management was never so narrowly bound. In its earliest, most radical expressions, it proposed an integral socialist state. One might argue that, even as their actual policies, in power and out, came to resemble less and less the sweeping plans outlined in *Make This Your Canada*, many of the newly-baptized "social democrats" remained (and some still do remain) within its conceptual universe. They champion an attenuated but still powerful post-liberal ideal of the Canadian state as a "national manager," an exalted conception of citizenship and equity, and an all-inclusive "democratic Canadianism." When they do this, they have recourse to a language of socialism that has otherwise been subordinated in their thinking and by their party to the hegemonic authority of post-1960 new liberalism.

The socialism articulated in *Make This Your Canada*, socialism as national management, would endure in various forms long after the 1940s, and well beyond the CCF. In many respects, and obviously with allowance for the need of the "vanguard party" to present itself as superior to social democrats and as unfailingly orthodox, it might be argued that the post-1935 Communist Party came to develop a parallel socialist discourse, in which nationalism, the management of the economy, and the restoration of harmony to the international order were seen as paramount. In this new style of Communist discourse, the Soviet Union was now represented, not as the exemplar of revolutionary working-class *praxis*, but rather as a fully rational, well-managed state, the true homeland of a scientific "modernization theory" (and a model for Ottawa to follow.) Similarly, as the CCF transformed into the NDP, it was perhaps less a matter of a movement succumbing to the

[108]As the text advises us, schemes for social security cannot be "an adequate national objective." (32) More vividly: "...social insurance schemes are umbrellas and not homes. Umbrellas are necessary as additional protection but they are no substitute for a home." *Make This Your Canada*, 34. Obviously, all modern economies were "developing in the direction of central control and regulation," and "New Canadians" would hardly want to resist this trend. But the CCF's priority was the socialization of the capitalist economy, not providing for its victims. In the six-part specification of "what is to be done," we find: "(1)Full employment, (2)Continuous production unbroken by recurring crises, (3)Democratic participation by the people in the control of the economy, (4)An expanding national income, (5)An equitable distribution to all the people of the goods and services produced by all the people, (6)A comprehensive system of social security." *Make This Your Canada*, 35.

iron law of party oligarchy, and rather more one of a "socialist model of national management" undergoing "realist" amendments. If Keynesian economic formulae and Swedish social welfare schemes allowed for "socialism" without the trauma of large-scale socialization, then what need of revolution, parliamentary or otherwise? Yet Lewis's continuing (if increasingly closeted) "evolutionary Marxism," his profoundly shrewd grasp of power within the trade-union movement as the nucleus of hegemony within the postwar left, his genius for making base-and-superstructure arguments politically and culturally acceptable, even under Cold War conditions — all of these meant that positions that bore more than a passing resemblance to those of "Eurocommunism" would still surface in the NDP as late as the 1970s, inside and outside the Waffle,[109] and as late as the early 1980s within the Parti Québécois, which named a different "people," "state" and "nation", but in ways that would have been recognizable to the authors of *Make This Your Canada*[110]

It was thanks to this cohort of state-building socialists, inside or outside the two main leftist parties, that "socialism" came to be written — although not in indelible ink — into the myth-symbol complex of the Canadian state-nation. Saskatchewan's brave government stood as an exemplar of Canadianism, not just of "prairie radicalism." There came to be a profound identification of social democrats with the project of *renovating* the Canadian liberal order, focusing especially on Ottawa as the proper carrier of socialist hopes and dreams. In sharp contrast to their marginalized comrades in the United States, third-formation socialists could honestly tell themselves that they were shaping a new Canadian state for a new Canadian people. And many of them commenced a long march through the federal and provincial institutions, a march which changed the marchers — into new liberals and bureaucrats — as much as it changed the institutions.

It would be hard to fix a "death date" for this third formation. Certainly, by the 1970s, when the CP was largely peripheral, no one was expecting that the election of an NDP government would transform the fundamentals of Canadian capitalism. The obvious "external pressure" was the Cold War and Canada's vulnerability to American ideological and military influences. But there also were three major internal contradictions. First, the marginalization of the First Socialism's project of "socialist education" and of Second Socialism's "class warfare" in socialist think-ing, and especially the reliance on a professionalized labour bureaucracy as the way to secure the support (and the money) of rank-and-file workers, carried with it the risk of a profound alienation from working people. It was easy to succumb to the

[109]Some evidence of a residual Marxism was to be found in the hard-hitting "corporate welfare bums" campaign of the 1972 election. See David Lewis, *Louder Voices: The Corporate Welfare Bums* (Toronto 1972).

[110]For an analysis of "social democracy" within the PQ, see Leon Dion, *Quebec: The Unfinished Revolution* (Montréal and London 1976), Ch.5. Dion discerned that what had been a marked "social democratic" tendency within the PQ was being weakened by a convergence with the Liberals, accelerated by the party's own technocratic bias.

liberal-utilitarian temptation of substituting the "passive party" allegiance for the "active cultural struggle"envisaged by the earlier cohorts: the "political check-off" was one of the most powerful of the forces that changed the prospects of Canadian socialists. Second, as the grey and bureaucratic "socialism of administration" gradually came to resemble more and more the liberal order that contained it — necessarily so, perhaps, at the level of subordinate provincial governments — those who had once questioned liberal order were increasingly disposed to defend it. And third, and perhaps most crucially, by so fervently embracing the Canadian nationalist agenda, bedecking their pamphlets with maple leaves and their rhetoric with "the people," all with a discernibly centralist bias, the third-wave socialists were to find themselves unable to address the "other nationalism," that would arise in Québec.

The Fourth Socialism: Revolutionary Humanism and National Liberation

These contradictions of conventional leftism, both social democratic and Communist, would be relentlessly exposed by a fourth formation, wherein a new paradigm of socialism evolved in the 1960s and 1970s. The matrix-event here was the Cold War, which simultaneously disorganized and discredited the older socialist forms and made the struggle against nuclear war seem a matter of human survival. Internationally, this "break" often announced itself without subtlety: an "obsolete communism" and a "sold-out social democracy" were overtaken by a New Left proclaiming a new emancipatory politics, a "socialism" of self-management, anti-imperialism, decolonization, and direct democracy. This and other aspects of the New Left were strongly influenced by American precedents, which influenced these leftists of the 1960s as strongly as British and Soviet models had moved their predecessors in the 1930s.

To simplify, New Leftism could be seen as a critique of, and alternative to, the first three formations. Against the Spencerian evolutionists' "necessary progress" was counterposed the need to individually resist a looming nuclear disaster and the image of individuals heroically struggling against it. Against the Leninist "dictatorship of the proletariat" as a necessary phase of working-class revolution, this cohort drew from "actually existing socialisms" the conclusion that, unless the oppressed truly empowered themselves, a formal shift in the ownership of the means of production did not an emancipatory social revolution make. And against quasi-Keynesian strategies of socializing investment and managing the national economy, this cohort, often repulsed by consumerism and the "culture industries," would contrast the humanist critique of alienation made by the young Marx with the economism of his distant descendants, the state planners.[111] All three earlier

[111] In terms of "implicit" (and in an increasingly academic environment, often "explicit") theorization, the fourth socialism favoured the young Marx — whose works had not been widely read (or even translated) before the 1960s — over the old, the Lenin of *State and Revolution* over the Lenin of *Left-Wing Communism*, and often Mao and Che Guevara over

socialisms were brought before the bar and asked: How does your project address what is really wrong with modern life — the profound sense so many people have of being alienated from themselves, from their own products, from their own societies? How does your politics speak to the problem of spiritual suffocation in an oppressive, meaningless and ugly world? Or counter both superpowers' drive to exterminate humanity in a nuclear war? New Leftists — only some of them happy to call themselves "socialist" — identified new objectives, and marginalized old ones. Their goal was a future of de-alienated men and women realizing their full human nature. And if, for some working in this new paradigm, old theoretical concepts — e.g., the decisive revolutionary working-class party as *the* instrument of socialist transformation — remained in place, they were nonetheless often functioning in a different way: as *anticipatory forms* of a humanistic, emancipated society more than as *functional requirements* of systemic change.[112] For many others, oppressed Third World nations, ethnic groups, and (especially in the 1970s) women and sexual minorities came to play as central a role in strategies for socialist revolution as class. Freud became as significant as Marx.

If, for some, existing parties could integrate at least part of the new paradigm — this was a major time of growth and ideological change for the NDP, which embraced New Left ideas to a surprising extent[113] — for many others in the fourth wave the conventional Canadian left parties, and perhaps *no* parties, could do so. Rather than investing energies in political parties, one could turn to the Company of Young Canadians, the Student Union for Peace Action, the Student Christian Movement, or a host of community groups. This was a cohort attracted by a plethora of ideologies, from anarcho-syndicalism to left nationalism, whose basis of unity lay only in a humanistic critique of capitalism and the liberal order — "the system" — and an impatient sense that radical action could bring about its downfall. It was, finally, a formation that demarcated itself generationally, to an extent not really seen before in Canadian socialist history. The leading anglophone theoretical

---

both. But this is perhaps to give too "Marxist" a reading of the fourth wave, which also drew from all manner of non-Marxist sources — Freud, Lévi-Strauss, Sorel, Bakunin — and which was characteristically disinclined to invest too much time in reading the Marxian economic theory that the first cohort would have considered the *sine qua non* of genuine socialism.

[112]For a most influential title, see André Gorz, *Strategy for Labor: A Radical Proposal*, trans. by Martin Nicolaus and Victoria Ortix (Boston 1967).

[113]New Left themes resounded throughout the history of the Waffle movement within the NDP, and can also be traced in *Canadian Dimension,* the Winnipeg-based magazine that has most clearly reflected left-wing thought in or near the party from the 1970s on. In Edward Broadbent, *The Liberal Rip-off: Trudeauism vs. the Politics of Equality* (Toronto 1970) one finds a marked break with the world of *Make This Your Canada*: Yugoslavia has replaced the Soviet Union as an exemplary model, by virtue of its programs for worker self-management.

journal of this youth-oriented socialism was a Montréal publication called *Our Generation.*[114]

In some respects the history of Canadian socialism could be written with only glancing attention to the New Left. By and large Canadian New Leftists were sympathetic bystanders to movements organized by other people in other places. They were against the bomb and the Vietnam War. They were for the American Civil Rights and later the Black Power movements. They cheered on African and Latin American national liberation struggles, and occupied university campuses with "non-negotiable demands" familiar across North America and Europe. Yet, in another way, the impact of this cohort, in one specific respect, was massive, and reshaped the entire field of Canadian politics. This was because New Leftism and left nationalism coincided to contribute to a profound crisis of Canada itself. In anglophone Canada, left nationalism, whose socialist forms were evident in the emergent mass universities and in the left-nationalist "Waffle" movement within the NDP, integrated conventional nationalist themes carried forward from the days of *Make This Your Canada* with contemporary discourses of anti-imperialism, participatory democracy, and feminism.[115] But the place where the fourth formation became genuinely dominant within socialism was francophone Québec.

Historians of Canadian socialism have conveyed a sense of francophone Québec as being generally marginal to the organized socialist movement before the 1960s.[116] But after 1960, francophone Québec, and more particularly Montréal,

[114]For a brief but interesting discussion of "youth radicalism in the sixties," see Doug Owram, *Born at the Right Time: A History of the Baby-Boom Generation* (Toronto 1996), chapter 9, which draws to some extent on the archives of the Student Union for Peace Action.

[115]For core texts, see Kari Levitt, *Silent Surrender: The Multinational Corporation in Canada* (Toronto 1970); James Laxer, *The Energy Poker Game: The Politics of the Continental Resources Deal* (Toronto 1970).

[116]Whether Québec's marginal position in the historiography relating to the first three formations is a matter of the bias of historical investigation and a product of the mechanical application of dated categories, or whether it reflects a radical contrast that any interpretive framework would have to contend with, is a question that awaits a more thorough investigation. Certainly there was enough of a francophone radical tradition in Montréal for the fourth cohort to remember: see Lévesque, *Virage à gauche interdit* on the interwar period. A first impression is that francophones were consistently patronized, their national issues reduced to marginal status (certainly in both of the "main parties"), and their quest for cultural survival subordinated within paradigms which stressed political economy. An awkward cross-cultural socialism can be occasionally glimpsed. Alfred Charpentier remembered, in his reflection on the turn-of-the-century socialist movement in Montréal, that his father had been visited in 1904 by two socialists (one of whom was Dick Kerrigan, who was the next year to attend the founding convention of the IWW): the book they brought with them, in translation, was Robert Blatchford's *Merrie England.* Alfred Charpentier, "Le Mouvement Politique Ouvrier de Montréal (1882-1929)," in Fernand Harvey, ed., *Aspects historiques du mouvement ouvrier au Québec* (Montréal 1973), 151.

was the storm-centre of New Left politics in Canada. And herein lay, of course, a paradox. The New Leftism of Montréal unfolded on what was still formally Canadian territory, but in a post-Canadian, Québécois "imagined space." It was constructed, in part, as a formation that rejected the active centralizing federal state imagined by *Make This Your Canada*.[117] Québec became far more a *nation* than a province, and the Québécois as a "new people" embraced left-wing programs with a speed that outrivalled the parallel "Canadian" upheaval of the 1940s. In part because of the "economic determinism" of the first wave and the "class reduction-ism" of the second, third-wave Canadian socialism rarely confronted the "national question" explicitly.[118] In the 1960s, faced with the matrix-event of Québec's unquiet revolution, with its markedly socialist overtones, the bill for this long neglect came due — with compound interest. It was impossible for English-Canadian leftists to reject socialist upheaval in Canada's largest province and city. Yet it was difficult to articulate — to the community imagined by socialists in the 1940s — a project within which the Canadian state was part of a "colonizing power" that had to be resisted and dismantled. For third-wave socialists who had wrapped themselves in maple leaves and identified whole-heartedly with the project of national state management, the Québec Revolution posed a wrenching and multi-faceted problem, because it inherently called into question the "Canadian subject position" with which Canadian socialists, both Communist and CCF, had identified since the late 1930s. The "falsely generic" Canadian, who just happened to speak English, was discursively represented as an arrogant colonizer against which the national liberation movement needed to assert itself. This unflattering description suggested that an anglophone third-wave socialist should liquidate a nation- and state-building subject-position for which sacrifices had been made for three decades. "Canada" had become, in part through the socialists' own activism and in large part through the passive revolution designed to contain it, a qualified kind of state-nation, unified not by ethnicity or a common culture, but by the activities of a shared federal state espousing a "new liberal" doctrine. And, practically speaking, to step outside this pan-Canadian political common sense was to court electoral disaster among anglophones, as both the Conservatives and New Democrats would discover with "Two-Nations" formulations in the 1960s. There seemed no easy "parliamentary road" to reconciliation. Yet to *refuse* any attempt to see onself as the "Other's other" was equally impossible. It meant writing off Montréal, rejecting the data documenting francophone economic and social oppression, and — more dangerously — distancing and withdrawing oneself from "fellow Canadians,"

[117]One might add to the sense of irony by noting that Frank Scott, notwithstanding his status as a civil libertarian, approved of the very application of the War Measures Act under which Pierre Vallières was arrested. David Lewis, for his part, was opposed to it.

[118]The exception was the purge of the Québec CP in the 1940s, to remove elements perceived by the leadership to be too inclined to French-Canadian nationalism. For an interesting account, see Robert Comeau and Bernard Dionne, *Les communistes au Québec 1936-1956: Sur le Parti communiste du Canada/Parti ouvrier-progressiste* (Montréal 1980), 32-70.

thereby acknowledging the very difference of identities that one had initially been determined not to recognize.

To the conventional "factors" cited in Quiet Revolution historiography, a historian of Canadian socialism would want to consider additional elements: the political and conceptual *lacunae* of the earlier paradigms when it came to nationalism, the new openness of Québec to the French left, the reception of the French Revolution of May 1968, and the relative weakness in Québec of the partisans of the first three socialisms, who arguably might have diverted New Leftism into other channels (as was perhaps the case with the NDP in much of anglophone Canada). Arguably no other North American political jurisdiction came as close to a New Left *political* revolution, an actual crisis of the ruling political order, as did Québec in the late 1960s and early 1970s. It is in this specific Québec-centred sense that one could say that New Leftism, far from being marginal to the history of Canadian socialism, has on the contrary defined many of its postwar patterns.

The "red decades" opened in the early 1960s in Montréal and wound down in the early 1980s. These were years in which a new Québécois nationalism gained tremendous strength, culminating in the election of a social democratic Parti Québécois (PQ) government in 1976 and the holding of the first sovereignty-association referendum in 1980. They were also years in which socialism and nationalism were forcefully conjugated together. To some extent this occurred within the major sovereignist political parties — the Rassemblement pour l'Indépendance National (RIN) and later the PQ, both of which touched on the discourses of socialism when they spoke of a general "projet social." To a greater extent, it was more closely associated with a diversity of extra-parliamentary "New Left" phenomena and scores of revolutionary groups and publications (such as *La Revue socialiste, Parti Pris, Québec Libre, Résistance, Révolution québécoise,* and *Socialisme québécois*). In the wake of the October Crisis of 1970, this vast network of activists tended to be retrospectively reduced to the Front de Libération du Québec, founded in February 1963 by three RIN (and Réseau de Résistance) activists, and purportedly a shadowy, unrepresentative groupuscule lacking deep roots in society. But this is surely misleading. There were scores of groups, and hundreds of revolutionaries, in the Montreal of the 1960s. There was a sea of revolutionary socialist activism in which the urban guerrillas could swim. Nor was the FLQ's newspaper *La Cognée*[119] (fd. October 1963), which functioned as an informal nerve centre of the *gauchistes,* an isolated phenomenon. Not just a thriving left-wing press, but also a mass media alive to marxisant and independentist ideas, testified to a socialist cultural ferment

---

[119]The revolutionary publication, much hounded by the police, appeared in 1965 thanks to the federal government, which unwittingly supplied paper and prepaid envelopes. For interesting extracts from it, along with other contemporary documents, see R. Comeau, D. Cooper and P. Vallières, eds., *FLQ: un projet révolutionnaire (1963-1982)* (Montréal 1990).

whose only close parallel in Canadian history was the radical labour upsurge of 1917-1922.

Not all the movements in play were new — there were Communists, Trotskyists, and NDPers, at least on the margins, and some activists had had previous experience, especially with the Parti socialiste du Québec (which had spun away from its parent NDP on the 'national question')[120] or with the Communist Party. And not all were unequivocally socialist. Nonetheless, new socialist accents, and very young activists, were a hallmark of Montréal's red decades. *Gauchistes* were generally determined to combine international insights (derived from such books as Frantz Fanon, *Les Damnés de la Terre,* Albert Memmi, *Le Portrait du Colonisé,* and Régis Debray, *La Revolution dans la Revolution*) with the particularities of the Québec struggle: to make Che's slogan 'two, three, many Vietnams' the lived experience of a North American society. This fourth-wave socialist formation had a protean, dynamic quality, flowing out of avant-garde cafés, quickly mobilizing popular-cultural forms for the purposes of resistance, and uniting mainstream cultural producers with political radicals into a politico-literary avant-garde.

Québec New Leftism was easily misread as a merely updated version of Québec nationalism, when in fact solidarity with, even a prior allegiance to, the world revolutionary socialist movement was a common attribute of this cohort.[121] If the second and third socialist formations had looked for inspiration in Russia, this francophone cohort was inspired above all by Cuba, where a new "revolutionary marxist humanism" was exemplified by Che Guevara. The Guevarist belief that armed struggles centred in *foco* of liberation could spark the mass sympathy of the oppressed and accelerate the development of revolutionary conditions had a particular resonance in Québec.[122] For those who identified Québec with the Third World, the Tricontinental Congress held in Havana in January 1966 sounded the tocsin of revolutionary activism worldwide.[123] This was not a paradigm peculiar to the FLQ's *La Cognée* nor to Québec: it was the common property of the fourth formation. Its development with nationalism in Québec produced what was both literally and symbolically a different "language of socialism" than anything heard before on Canadian territory.[124]

[120]The Parti socialiste du Québec, once the wing of the NDP/NPD, merged with the MLP in March 1966 at a "left unity" congress.

[121]From its very first manifesto in 1963, the FLQ proclaimed its allegiance to "oppressed people of the world" who had been "breaking their chains and winning the liberty which is their right." The FLQ's first flag was based, not on the colours of 1837, but on an Algerian design in Cuban colours.

[122]See Che Guevara, *Guerrilla Warfare* (Harmondsworth 1969).

[123]Maspero, the French publisher which published the French translation of the Havana Tricontinental Conference, also distributed *Révolution québécois.*

[124]The details in this paragraph are drawn from Louis Fournier, *F.L.Q.: The Anatomy of an Underground Movement,* trans. Edward Baxter (Toronto 1984).

By far the most famous text from this period was Pierre Vallières's *Nègres blancs d'Amérique: Autobiographie précoce d'un 'terroriste' québécois*, translated into English under the title *White Niggers of America*. Materially abused, enduring a shantytown childhood and an adolescence and young manhood spent passing from one demeaning job to the next, and subsisting on manual labour during a six-month sojourn in France, Vallières knew that capitalism was a cruel fraud perpetrated on the basis of exploitation and exclusion. His spiritual odyssey — from an impassioned Catholicism, within the Franciscan order, then into liberal Catholic personalism, then into existentialism and phenomenology — was no less typical of his time. Vallières's individual path to a *praxis*-oriented Marxism was one followed by many of his generation across Europe and North America.

For Vallières in 1965, the FLQ embodied the activist vision of the young Marx — whose works on alienation, hitherto known only to select scholars, were now achieving a worldwide renown. It was possible to *will* new patterns in history, to *will* the transcendence of the split between subject and object: why could this not happen in Québec? All that was missing was a movement with a broader vision and a longer-range strategy. For this, Vallières would turn, like most within his formation — and not just in Québec — *away* from any models available in "Canada," a tainted project, and *towards* the wider world. In his case, he turned towards the Black Power movement in the United States. In fact, it was the prospect of linking up with other North American revolutionaries, especially Black activists, that led Vallières and his comrade-in arms Charles Gagnon (who shared with him a working-class background, an interest in sociological ideas, and the political experiences acquired at *Révolution québécoise,* which the two men had founded in 1964) to New York in 1966. And it was on the advice of Paul Sweezy, editor of the independent Marxist *Monthly Review,* that Vallières and Gagnon took their case to the doorstep of the United Nations, where in September they announced a 30-day hunger strike to bring attention to "political prisoners" attached to the FLQ being held in Canadian prisons. Arrested on 27 September 1966, the two would spend nearly four months in "The Tombs," and on their release on 13 January 1967, they would promptly be apprehended by US Immigration officials, taken illegally to Canada, and arrested on arrival by the RCMP. Gagnon would spend 41 months in jail, and Vallières 44, before they were both acquitted in 1973.

Nègres blancs, written in a New York jail cell, and perhaps the most internationally acclaimed book ever written by a socialist active on Canadian territory — one has to pick one's words carefully here — is customarily read into the narrative of the Quiet Revolution, where it is overshadowed by the 1970 assassination of Pierre Laporte. Perhaps in 2001 this text can be more interestingly read as a document of a New Left sensibility, and as a reflection on the possibilities of "being socialist" under conditions of late capitalism.[125] One could even question how

---

[125] For Vallières's later critiques of the liberal order, see especially *Le devoir de résistance* (Montréal 1994) and *La Liberté en Friche* (Montréal 1979). An interesting pattern of

"nationalist" the text of *Nègres blancs* actually is, at least if we mean by this an acceptance of the "myth-symbol complex" internalized by many Québécois (or French Canadians — to use the term often used in the book), given the ruthlessly critical view taken by *Nègres blancs* of "provincial peculiarities" and the "really existing nationalism" of the book's intended audience. Viewed from the vantage-point of Paris, Vallières would remember, Québec looked like a small provincial society whose inhabitants had mythologized their own past. In the 1960s, in fact, were there any *national* problems? Vietnam, Latin America, the re-birth of neo-Nazism, the patterns of development and underdevelopment explored by André Gunder Frank: none of these were *national* in scope, but *international*. To declare the independence of Québec would be a meaningless gesture — it would pose no real danger to Washington, the real master of North America, on whose behalf the Canadian state merely acted. Notwithstanding some reversions in the text to more traditional tropes of French-Canadian nationalism,[126] its predominant bias was towards connecting *local* with *international* struggles: the "local" context was a secondary consideration. One might even go so far as to suggest that Québec itself was somewhat marginalized in the text. Vallières's socialist intellectual itinerary, down to the Fall of 1963, had consisted very largely of international figures and forces: he worked through Lenin (who did not really impress him), Rosa Luxemburg, Mao Tse-tung, Castro, and Che Guevara, before turning, for the first time in his life, to the social history of Québec.[127] The somewhat sketchy "history of Québec" presented by *Nègres blancs* was not that far removed from the narratives of Pierre Elliott Trudeau, who juxtaposed the "Duplessist" Québec to the land enlightened by liberals such as himself after 1960.[128] Before the Quiet Revolution,

---

obituaries of Vallières in the mainstream Montréal media was the consistent attempt to make him a post- or even an anti-socialist, a marked misrepresentation and oversimplification of his position. See Jean Dion, "Pierre Vallières (1938-1998): 'Je défends la liberté'," *Le Devoir*, 23 December 1998.

[126]Vallières at one point would even refer to the "Anglo-Saxons" with their acute sense of their own interests: "Déjà en 1840, les Anglo-Saxons, qui possèdent un sens aigu de leurs intérêts, avaient profité du climat d'hystérie provoqué par la rébellion canadienne-française pour proclamer provisoirement l'Union des deux Canadas (Ontario et Québec)...." Pierrre Vallières, *Nègres blancs d'Amérique* (Montréal 1994 [1968]), 76. References to the French text are to this edition. Even to this day, however, this is a somewhat conventional usage in French. This interpretation of the 1837 rebellion, which functioned as a "myth of origin" for the *felquistes,* erased from its record English-speaking supporters in Lower Canada, and the points of common interest between rebels in Lower and Upper Canada.

[127] *Nègres blancs*, 264-5.

[128] *Nègres blancs*, 99-107, n.2. The approach to Québec's history is even more dichotomized in Vallières, *La Liberté en Friche.* For subtler characterizations of the Duplessist régime, see Gilles Bourque, Jules Duchastel, and Jacques Beauchemin, *La société libérale duplessiste. 1944-1960* (Montréal 1994); and for a stimulating discussion of the historiographical trends which indirectly affected Vallières, see Ronald Rudin, *Making History in Twentieth-Century Quebec* (Toronto 1997).

Vallières argued, a monolithic ideology had strangled dissent; after it, all the institutions of Québec were suddenly called into question, by the combined forces of secularism, separatism, and Marxism.[129] The Church in particular draws Vallières's furious fire, with an anticlerical passion rarely heard on the left since the 1920s. Vallières's historicization of his politics was only Québec-centred in a certain limited sense: the "history of Québec" he constructed in his text contained many victims and moments of repression, but few national heroes, working models or valuably persisting traditions. In fact, the very title of the book — which alone did so much to ensure its notoriety — came to Vallières's mind *in English* and emerged as a way of making an otherwise indifferent *American* audience take notice of events in Québec.[130]

The "nationalism" of *Nègres blancs* thus typified an ambiguity that ran through much fourth-wave socialist thought about the possibilities open to radicals in northern North America. *Nègres blancs* can be seen as performing a series of dramatic refusals of "older socialisms." In the book's spontaneist, often anarchistic politics, "socialism" might be as much a pejorative word to designate the obsolete paradigm of an older generation, as it was the name to give to a future open to humanity's full development. The Communists were warmly praised in the text, but as heroic figures from a distant age.[131] Marxist political economy was bleakly evoked in a description of experts with libraries crammed with statistical tables. As for the USSR itself, it was merely one of the largest state-capitalist trusts in the world. The very text of Lenin — *Left-Wing Communism: An Infantile Disorder* — which had inspired so much of Spector's Marxism and theoretically "grounded" the CP of the 1920s and 1930s in the realities of Canadian trade unionism and labour politics, was now seen as a device used by complacently self-satisfied old leftists to curb the militancy of the young.[132] The CCF-NDP tradition was briefly noted, but mainly

[129]*Nègres blancs*, 90.

[130]After describing the "wall of indifference" towards Québec issues he encountered in New York, Vallières remarked in his 1979 preface: "C'est en voulant percer ce mur d'indifférence et de mépris que j'inventai, pour désigner les Québécois, le concept des nègres blancs d'Amérique. C'est d'ailleurs en anglais que ce concept se formula spontanément dans ma tête. White Niggers of America. Les Noirs américains furent les premiers, et pour cause, àsaisir ce que pouvait être, sur les rives du Saint-Laurent, la condition particulière des Québécois francophones" (31). And one should note that the shock tactic of using the word "Nigger" in titles was also in evidence in one of the most widely-circulated underground classics of its time, widely read in the 1960s: Jerry Farber's "Student as Nigger." According to Owram, *Born at the Right Time,* 238, this text was even read into *Hansard.*

[131]*Nègres blancs*, 143.

[132]*Nègres blancs*, 322; and also these reflections on his father's leftist sympathies: "On discutait des réformes opérées par le CCF en Saskatchewan mais le CCF ignorait que des milliers de travailleurs québécois auraient aimé entendre ses *leaders* leur dire en français [sic] que leur parti était prêt à leur donner un coup de main, à eux aussi. Les gars étaient suls. Ils votaient obligatoirement pour Duplessis, comme ils allaient à la messe...." (150) This

to underline the weakness and tendency to compromise of social democracy; besides, the CCF had been unable to communicate with the masses of French-Canadian workers, and Vallières had felt like a maladroit delinquent in its middle-class Outremont outposts.[133] Many of these political specifics were Québécois, but much of the New Left paradigm brought to these specifics would have been familiar to radicals throughout the western world. Yet the book was "socialist" in the sense we have given to this word. Vallières, no less than Irvine, Spector, Scott and Lewis, identified his goal as the ultimate creation of a new egalitarian society, in which money would no longer serve as the cement of the social order, and science would be put at the collective service of a free humanity.

What was most Québécois about *Nègres blancs* was its first-person memoir of growing up in a downtrodden working-class suburb of Montréal. It would be difficult to think of another left-wing book in either francophone or anglophone Canada in which the author takes such pains to present an "unvarnished" and "completely candid" account of himself — his bitter relationship with his mother, his embrace and subsequent rejection of Catholic mysticism, his sexual relation-ships with women, his personal relationships with comrades, and the "adventure of ideas" which had held him spellbound since adolescence. The "Pierre Vallières" we meet in *Nègres blancs* — tortured by a sense of inferiority, twice on the brink of suicide, without secure anchorage in a world which seems "bestranged" and hostile, his words coming to us from the Manhattan House of Detention for Men — is a tragic figure drawn from Dostoyevsky's *Notes From Underground*. Under the rubric of the "precocious" and the "autobiographical," the self-confessional Vallières seemingly delivers himself up to the reader. The veils of self-presentation are lifted one by one. It is a kind of New Left truth-telling characteristic of the 1960s and North America, and atypical of socialist discourse at any earlier time, at least in Canada. The "personal as political" was enacted as a kind of ethical imperative. Laurier LaPierre was quick to note the parallels of this text with *Soul on Ice* by Eldridge Cleaver and *The Autobiography of Malcolm X*.[134] The truth of radical humanism, the possibilities of an emancipatory release of the human essence, was most vibrantly conveyed by the details of one person's autobiography, in this case the author's unflinchingly honest exploration of his own attempts to understand himself, his outcries of impatience and burning anger, and his salvation in marxist *praxis*. For Vallières, a Marxism adequate to the task of "de-alienating" the masses had to be prepared to organize a victorious popular revolution, "a successful

was, characteristically of the New Left, a too-easy handling of the question of working-class conservatism and the popular base for non-leftist politics.

[133]*Nègres blancs*, 266. Vallières voted for the NDP in 1962, which set him apart from many of his friends, who voted Créditiste.

[134]Laurier LaPierre, "Canada's Eldridge Cleaver and Malcolm X," *New York Times Book Review*, 11 April 1971, Section 7, 1, 10, 12.

collective psychoanalysis," which was only the first step to the transformation of life from top to bottom.[135]

Although Vallières makes no explicit mention of Sorel, a theme of "redemptive violence" runs through the text, as it would through many of the New Left.[136] Vallières argues that those who attempt to slow down the turn to violence, are themselves practising a form of terror by delaying the working class from realizing its inherent and inescapable vocation: that of the class-conscious destroyer of capitalism.[137] Vallieres's socialist revolution will be total: nothing will remain the same. Marx appears here, not so much as a political economist, but as the philosopher of praxis, whose writings had rescued Vallières from his long "proletarian's pilgrimage" transversing the works of Gide, Malraux, Camus, Proust, Mauriac, Dostoyesvky, Heidegger, and Husserl, as well as Sartre. Vallières's Marx was a revolutionary humanist, an exponent of the possibilities of a humanity free from the bondage of bourgeois civilization and culture.

An earlier Canadian reading of Marx — such as the one made by *Make This Your Canada* — might have suggested a very different, less voluntarist relationship between the means and ends of socialist struggle, one that placed a question mark over the thesis of redemptive "proletarian violence." A subsequent contemporary feminist reading of this text might underline the extent to which women are marginalized within it — and not just in the easily critiqued "personal" memoirs, with their dated sexual politics, but also in the patrilineal genealogy Vallières constructs for his intended proletarian movement. Apart from Thérèse Casgrain, dismissed in one line, no woman appears in the text as a significant political figure. The passage with which the text ends, which begins by summoning comrades and drinking buddies to take up the work of proletarian revolution — "Hé! Georges, qu'est-ce que tu attends pour te décider? Et vous autres, Arthur, Louis, Jules, Ernest? Debout, les gars, et tous ensemble: au travail!..."[138] — are energetic and

---

[135]"Toute psychanalyse (individuelle ou collective) fait peur. Et c'est un réflexe normal. Car une psychanalyse honnête propose rapidement des actes à poser, des actes qui contredisent radicalement nos vieilles habitudes d'agir et de penser. Plus un acte à poser provoque chez le patient (individu ou collectivité) de la résistance et de l'angoisse, plus cet acte, comme l'a démontré Freud, est nécessaire. Se désaliener n'est pas une entreprise romantique... Seuls les démagogues malhonnêtes peuvent promettre le bonheur aux masses comme le père Noël, chez Eaton, promet des jouets aux enfants." *Nègres blancs*, 390.

[136]In a sense, Jean-Paul Sartre is an obscure and powerfully shaping presence in this text. *Les Temps modernes* had been a model for Vallières's early journalism, and Sartre's interest in Fanon as an expositor of Engels's theory of violence as the "midwife of history" was influential, not just for Vallières but for the New Left in general. And one can hear more than an echo of Sartre in the text's critique of the "vast emptiness" characteristic of lives in capitalist societies. *Nègres blancs*, 96, 388-89.

[137]*Nègres blancs*, 351.

[138]*Nègres blancs*, 351.

eloquent. Still, one misses — and Vallières himself would later reach this conclusion about his earlier positions — any words for Esther, Marie, or Danielle.

Vallières's voluntarist Marxism was, in a sense, an applied politico-ethical vision, which condemned capitalism for its inhumanity, injustice, and "abnormality." A strong *moral* critique of the liberal order and the culture of consumption pervades *Nègres blancs*. Bourgeois ideology pacified working-class people, bathing them in irrationality and "sexual perversion." It also taught them to despise worldly existence, to accept the "survival of the fittest" as an ideology, and to forget about the chances of making effective political choices. Vallières gives no explicit sign of having read the Frankfurt School, but his condemnation of the "culture industries" echoes this body of socialist thought. A genuinely proletarian revolution, total and liberating, required a transformation not just of the workers' economic lives but also of their culture, ethnicity, traditions, customs, needs and tastes. At the limit of his utopianism, and echoing the Marx of *The German Ideology* and the *Economic and Philosophical Manuscripts of 1844,* Vallières called for the *disappearance* of commodity categories — of calculation in terms of value, of money, and of the financial and credit systems. Here Vallières's text was at one with much New Left cultural criticism, from the *Port Huron Statement* of the SDS to the new Hegelianism of Herbert Marcuse, which depicted the "one-dimensional lives" of people trapped in capitalist culture.[139]

Nègres blancs was considered so incendiary a book that elaborate steps were taken to prevent the Québec people from reading it; and it itself became a text in the long-running state trials of its author.[140] There is good empirical evidence, then, for the view that contemporaries thought it conveyed its point of view powerfully. Vallières was able to "speak for a generation" of the 60s, and not only francophones, because he dared to name problems that, on the left, had long been repressed. The core problem he identified was the national oppression of the Québécois at the heart of a "Canadian" liberal order; he was able to integrate the empirical and personal details of this history with his own sense of a revolutionary world afire. No Canadian book from the epoch of the New Left captures its spirit so well.

Yet how was it that Vallières, former seminarian, student of philosophy and isolated theoretician, could identify without hesitation the ways in which a future working-class struggle should evolve and the all-embracing goals it should pursue? Kindred questions would haunt much New Left discourse. On whose behalf was one speaking? Was it even legitimate to "speak on someone's behalf"? As was the case with earlier socialist formations, the politics of the form precluded the

[139]Isserman, *If I Had a Hammer* (Urbana and Chicago 1993) makes a highly original contribution in linking these archetypal "New Left" concerns to "Old Left" perceptions of the culture industries.

[140]As Vallières would marvel in 1994, "Le zèle politique de la police étant ce qu'il est, même l'exemplaire du livre obligatoirement déposé à la Bibliothèque nationale par l'éditeur fut saisi, sans doute par souci scrupuleux de 'nettoyage intellectuel'." *Nègres Blancs,* 9.

possibility of an extended, open-ended dialogue with contrary evidence. The enthusiastic, premeditated celebration of political violence seems out of keeping with any realistic sense of what such violence was expected to accomplish and the politico-ethical costs it would entail for both its architects and objects. As both Gagnon and Vallières would later conclude, although in different ways,[141] the turn to armed violence, at this time and in this form, was a mistake. Around the world, many former New Left activists would draw the same conclusion.

Nothing mounted by the New Left in the United States carried the focused disruptive potential of the October Crisis, which brought the entire Canadian state into question; and it is too easily forgotten that the revolutionary-socialist FLQ Manifesto, issued after the kidnapping of British diplomat James Cross, aroused a surprising degree of popular support, especially in working-class Montréal, but also including that of much of the English-speaking Canadian left. Then the Chénier cell executed Pierre Laporte, and such support rapidly eroded. It is important to locate this "error in judgment" or "accident" within the context of a political form which placed almost no controls over the activities of particular cells, and which tended to exalt redemptive, "therapeutic" violence. In the struggle for hegemony on the Québec left which ensued, the ambiguously social-democratic Parti Québécois would win the allegiance of most of the cohort of 1968.[142]

It is hard, at the beginning of a very different century, fully to re-experience the politics of *Nègres blancs*. There is, in Canadian socialism, no text more demandingly utopian and apocalyptic than this one, the polar opposite of the "sane and sensible" language beloved of the CCF. A measure of the changing times was the transformation of the book, from "banned substance" to "required undergraduate reading," and of its author, from "outlaw" to "celebrity." Vallières himself found these transformations bittersweet. Mixed in with the success of his text reaching many thousands of people was the realization that he himself had been transformed into a kind of commodity, a celebrity in the culture of consumption he so despised. He became, like many superstars of the 60s, a person closely watched for signs of "accommodation" and "betrayal." Meanwhile, the *serious* discussion of his ideas went nowhere. It was the signature contradiction of New Leftism that it itself exemplified the trends to fragmentation, ultra-liberalism, and commodification that it also brilliantly critiqued.

Second, it is difficult to know what to make of the *felquiste* contribution overall to an exploration of the Canadian liberal labyrinth. Vallières's politics was Québécois, and not Canadian; and including *Nègres blancs* — a text in which

---

[141]Whereas Vallières turned to the Parti Québécois and then to non-affiliated radicalism, Gagnon rallied to Marxism-Leninism.

[142]For contemporary accounts of subsequent Québec leftism, see Marc Ferland and Yves Vaillancourt, *Socialisme et Indépendance au Québec: Pistes pour le mouvement ouvrier et populaire* (Montréal and Sainte-Foy 1981); for a right-wing journalistic account of left politics in Québec in the 1970s, see Jacques Benoît, *L'extreme gauche* (Montréal 1977).

"Canadians" are Others against which a Fanonist campaign of decolonizing violence is fully warranted — will strike many federalists and sovereignists alike, on
opposite grounds, as absurd and offensive. Tough luck. The exclusion of this book
and of the moment of possibility it epitomized from any balanced consideration of
socialism on 20th-century Canadian territory would be historically irresponsible,
as would be any avoidance of the cultural and political divisions it highlighted.

Since the 1960s, many politically active people in Québec have been active
in extra-parliamentary, Maoist, Trotskyist, socialist, and social-democratic directions, most of them at the same time supporting sovereignty in a polity starkly
divided between federalist and sovereignty camps. Many of these people remain
"Canadian socialists" — that is, they are socialists on soil the world recognizes as
belonging to a state called "Canada" — and yet do not feel themselves to be in
league with leftists elsewhere in the country. Outside Québec, interest in the
territory's self-determination or sovereignty has waned on the left. In the thirty
years crisis over the constitution which has dominated and, to an extent, immobi-
lized Canadian politics, an influential socialist framework for constitutional debate
has not emerged. Socialists have generally been conscripted into the rival camps,
where they have only temporarily and to a small extent inserted even the slightest
indications of a socialist counter-logic. Vallières's refusal to "see" any socialist
history in anglophone Canada is paralleled by the disinterest in the Québec question
on the part of the majority of anglophone socialists. Such dualism has rewards. And
it is, in a sense, the political counterpart of the New Left's phenomenological
moment. If the "constitution" and "French/English relations" and the details of
Canadian history are outside my personal frame of reference, why should I integrate
them into my politics? It was the achievement of the fourth formation, especially
as it rose to prominence in Québec, to raise the "national questions" which Canadian
socialists had hitherto repressed — but they still remain unanswered.

A Fifth Socialism?

Vallières's subsequent development after *Nègres blancs* — into feminism, environmental activism and gay liberation[143] — exemplifies that followed by many of
his cohort. Once the revolutionary moment receded, many of the "personalist"
aspects of New Leftism remained. Many of his generation followed something like
his path. They took up employment within the state apparatus (in the universities
or, like him, became social workers in the state bureaucracy). Many transferred
their hopes to the international level — to El Salvador and Nicaragua, to Africa, to
the Balkans (Vallières himself would embrace the cause of Bosnia). They became
much less convinced, over time, that the working class would lead the revolution.
They came to take the oppression of women and of homosexuals, and the degrada-

---

[143]See Pierre Vallières, *Homosexualité et subversion* (Montréal 1994).

tion of the environment, as seriously — and, over time, more seriously — than class exploitation.

There is a conventional way of closing this discussion of the century of socialism — with a few cautionary tales about the inevitable disappointment of youthful hopes, or (if one is a follower of the neo-liberal party line of the daily newspapers) the inherent corruption and totalitarianism of any and all socialist attempts to escape the neo-liberal labyrinth such organs daily celebrate. Socialism is merely the term to denote the "illusion of an epoch." The "history of socialism" in Canada would thus have a beginning, a middle, and an end: all that remains, on the occasion of its hundredth anniversary, is to write the obituaries. And, in certain hands, these will not be flattering. The four formations we have discussed, it will be said, were all fatally compromised by their simple-minded orthodox Marxism, that master-narrative whose day is done. The "socialisms" we have reconstructed via certain texts were all abject failures, and their emancipatory ambitions came to nothing. Throughout we find deluded provincials, struggling to "read into" Canadian circumstances an international significance they would never have. The children — of October, of the 1940s, of 1968 — have grown older and wiser, and the world has gone on. If any elements can be salvaged from this "building site in ruins" — and a true sceptic would doubt even this — they would be the ideals of "pluralism," "radical democracy" and "citizenship."[144] Everything else from the history of socialism is debris slated for the dust-heap of history.

Nothing could be further, of course, from the "liberal-order" reading I am proposing. Socialism happens in Canada because liberalism is deficient. Neo-liberalism (liberalism without an expanding welfare state) is doubly so. Over time, again and again, capitalism and the liberal order create armies of critics and activists. It is happening again. They do not yet call themselves "socialists," but they likely will.

In contrast with the earlier socialisms, women will not in the future be subordinated to party-lines and intellectual formations dominated almost completely by men. Within the historiography on Canadian socialism, the most dynamic and critical recent work has highlighted the uphill battles fought by women for respect and equity within the socialist movement. It has measured the glaring gap between socialists' proclaimed ideals of gender equality and their mixed record.[145] It is not accidental that the four works I have considered as archetypal were written by men. In ways both coarse and subtle, all four past formations were male-dominated. The outstanding question debated among historians is not whether socialist formations marginalized women, which they all did, but whether they all did so uniformly. Similarly, not even the most sympathetic reconstruction can produce a

[144]See Chantal Mouffe, *Dimensions of Radical Democracy: Pluralism, Citizenship, Community* (London 1992).

[145]See especially Janice Newton's aptly titled *The Feminist Challenge to the Canadian Left, 1900-1918.*

"history of Canadian socialism" that overlooks the full collusion of all earlier formations in the oppression of gays and lesbians, who were characteristically interpreted as symptoms of the degeneracy of capitalism rather than as people entitled to solidarity and respect.[146] And such an effort cannot produce a "Canadian socialist formation" that had really grasped the central significance, to any socialist project on Canadian soil, of First Nations issues, which were never allowed (for instance) to cloud the exuberant "manifest northern destiny" of *Make This Your Canada*.

Such gestures of demarcation are commonly made by those creating a new socialist formation. A new formation first makes its presence known by declaring itself unlike all previous socialist traditions. Brought into being by neo-liberal globalization, centred on a cohort of activists drawn from the new social movements, the universities, and (to some extent) the church, a cohort is working out a new paradigm of radical politics — one that combines feminism, environmentalism, and communitarianism. It may very well eschew the name "socialist," which carries so much baggage and which does not intuitively answer to many contemporary ideals. But so far as it seeks bases of unity from which to launch a post-liberal politics, so far as it continues a dialogue with Marx and expresses serious interest in economic and social equality, so far as it tries to transmit a general collective sensibility, it is working within the socialist tradition.

If the history of Canadian socialism has two major lessons to teach, it is that Canadians will often respond to calls for a radical egalitarianism, and that opportunities to reach large numbers of them can emerge swiftly, to reward the cohort which has best shaped the language and practice of its formation to articulate the subjective and objective needs of fellow citizens. To an extent never paralleled before in Canadian history, we now have a substantial socialist intelligentsia, with magazines, journals, lobbies and networks; we have a far more nuanced and sophisticated understanding of 'Marxist theory' in all its permutations; we have a well-established "socialist political economy"; and we have proto-socialist cadres drawn from the new social movements with "impossibilist" demands that cannot be easily accommodated by a second liberal "passive revolution." And we have the most radical stimulus of all: a totalitarian neo-liberalism violently imposing market logic on every human relationship, no matter the danger to living human beings and the communities that sustain them. What is primarily lacking is a powerful

[146]For David Lewis's views on homosexuality — "I know that to normal people this practice is an odious one...." — see Gary Kinsman, *The Regulation of Desire: Sexuality in Canada* (Montréal and New York 1987), 169. Interesting materials can also be found in Peter Dickinson, *Here is Queer: Nationalisms, Sexuality and the Literatures of Canada* (Toronto 1999), ch. 3, on homophobic attacks launched against the poet Patrick Anderson, editor of the Labour Progressive Party's *En Masse* magazine in Montréal. It should also not be forgotten that the FLQ Manifesto itself spares time to insult Pierre Trudeau's allegedly deviant sexuality.

political party that wholeheartedly believes in a post-liberal egalitarian order. Yet, nonetheless, the NDP, even given its origins in the new liberal passive revolution of the 1940s and 1950s, finds itself inhibited from venturing too far into neo-liberalism, partly because of the socialism in its history, and partly because of the non-negotiability of much of the identity-politics flourishing in its constituencies. Whether it can do something new with the old question of the socialist party-form, whether it can reconcile Marxist political economy with the new social movements, whether it can say something persuasive and emancipating to Canadians about the national question — these are key issues to be confronted before the fifth formation encounters its moment of opportunity.

At the beginning of a new formation, it is customary to engage in the exercise of judging the antecedent formations highly defective. But the historic risk, for each formation, has been that of being condemned to perpetually re-invent the wheel — of jettisoning insights earlier formations had achieved, and of misrecognizing the lessons they had to teach. And an equal risk has been that of imposing on Canadian realities successive models drawn from outside Canada, without due regard for the historical experiences of past Canadian socialists, wrestling as they did with the challenges cast up by a persisting liberal order. Perhaps one break with the past that fifth-formation activists could consider would be a refusal of past patterns of refusal. Finding an exit from the capitalist liberal labyrinth will not become easier by disregarding all previous attempts to do so. A less sweeping and hubristic approach would concede that all conceptual frameworks constructed to interpret and solve human problems are subject to revision — as a "fifth socialism" is bound to be. "Nothing has worked" in one limited sense, then — the "revolution" hoped for by Communists and CCFers did not happen, and the "New Jerusalem" is a distant destination — and yet, in another way, "everything worked." A "socialist good sense," which neoliberals quite rightly see as a formidable obstacle, did attain and still retains a fair measure of popular acceptance in Canada. In taking sober measure of the reinvigorated right, and the obvious sense of disorientation that prevails on the left, our "pessimism of the intelligence" should not be so exaggerated that it obscures the resources at our disposal, many of them the neglected legacies of a past century of socialist thought and struggle.

My thanks to members of the audience at the "Historians and their Audiences" conference at York University, April 2000, for their interest and comments and to Labour/Le Travail's anonymous readers, Peter Campbell and Gerald Friesen for their critiques.

Industrial & Labor Relations Review

January and March 2001   Vol. 54, Nos. 2 & 3

January 2001:

The Development of the Neoclassical Tradition in Labor Economics
George R. Boyer and Robert S. Smith

The Use of Flexible Staffing Arrangements in Core Production Jobs
Cynthia L. Gramm and John F. Schnell

Immigration Reform and the Earnings of Latino Workers: Do Employer Sanctions Cause Discrimination? Cynthia Bansak and Steven Raphael

Gender and Promotion in the Economics Profession
John M. McDowell, Larry D. Singell, Jr., and James P. Ziliak

Prevailing Wage Laws and Construction Labor Markets
Daniel P. Kessler and Lawrence F. Katz

Also: four papers from a Cornell-Princeton symposium on
unions and labor markets.

March 2001: *Special symposium issue**

Studies of WAGE INEQUALITY within industries:

Retail Banking   (Larry W. Hunter, Annette Bernhardt, Katherine L. Hughes, and Eva Skuratowicz)
Telecommunications   (Rose Batt)
Semiconductor Manufacturing   (Clair Brown and Ben Campbell)
Steel   (Patricia Beeson, Lara Shore-Sheppard, and Kathryn Shaw)
Grocery Stores (John Budd and Brian McCall)
Trucking   (Dale L. Belman and Kristen A. Monaco)
Steel, Apparel, & Medical Electronics & Imaging Industries
  (Thomas Bailey, Peter Berg, and Carola Sandy)

Subscription orders received by March 1, 2001 will include this special
issue as a **FREE BONUS.**

Annual rates (four issues), U.S.: $26 individual; $43 institution.
Foreign: $34 individual, $50 institution.

ILR REVIEW
201 ILR Research Bldg.
Cornell University
Ithaca, NY 14853-3901 U.S.A.

Tel. (607) 255-3295   Fax
(607) 255-8016   E-mail
ILRR@cornell.edu

GENDER, FAMILY & SEX

Feminism and the Making of Canadian Working-Class History: Exploring the Past, Present and Future

Joan Sangster

AS WE ENTER the 21st century, working people have reason to be pessimistic about their fate in the new millennium. Despite technological advances, a communications revolution, and a globalized economy, labour remains alienating for many workers, hazardous, and lacks the remuneration necessary for a decent standard of living. In "post-Fordist" North America, even the better paid, if routinized work in industry has been replaced by lower-paid service work in multiple jobs, with far less job security. Moreover, age-old patterns of capital accumulation and women's exploitation seem to be irrepressible. At the turn of the century, many immigrant women toiled in their homes, doing sweated labour, providing piece work for the competitive garment industry. In 1999, an exposé of sweated labour in Toronto uncovered a similar contracting out system, exploiting Asian women who were paid below the minimum wage, unable, due to family responsibilities, to work outside the home, fearful of being deported if they protested their conditions of work.

Pessimism about the "state of work" at this juncture might be tempered by our recognition, as historians, of the ever-present possibilities of change over time, in both predictable and unpredictable ways, and of the prospect of resistance to the

Joan Sangster, "Feminism and the Making of Canadian Working-Class History: Exploring the Past, Present and Future," *Labour/Le Travail*, 46 (Fall 2000), 127-65.

current order. Yet, the prevailing political moment does not look auspicious in this regard. Union membership has not increased dramatically in the last decade, and the shift to a "Mcjobs" economy, along with the globalized downgrading of labour, militates against unionization. Many governments within Canada have been eroding union and workers' rights, and organized workers, who one would expect to be the strongest opponents, have not been able to mobilize to reverse these trends.[1]

Moreover, despite indications that women, after years of feminist organizing, have made some important gains in areas such as reproductive rights, other signs of progress represent a double-edged sword. The slightly narrowing wage gap between particular male and female workers, some contend, has emerged in part because men's wages are decreasing overall. Moreover, as the example of the Asian garment workers indicates, patterns of sexual and racial subordination remain firmly fixed within the social organization of work. The repercussions for women extend far beyond the workplace, affecting their psyches and physical health, their ability to construct lives of sexual and familial safety and pleasure, their hopes, or lack of them, for their childrens' future.

Behind this rather bleak backdrop lurks the suspicion that this *is* a turn for the worse, and that other possibilities may have existed. In a more optimistic political climate, thirty years ago, feminist activists, including academics, harboured hopes for a reinvigorated working-class movement, transformed by feminism and committed to a broadly based politic of liberation for oppressed peoples. An intellectual and political space was created, which, though never dominant in the academy and the community, fostered new critiques of history and society and thus also hope for a different future. Out of this climate emerged the first attempts to create a Canadian feminist working-class history.

Certainly, past research and praxis were never unproblematic; there were weaknesses we saw at the time, and those we recognized in retrospect. Class and gender analyses sometimes chafed uneasily against each other; race and colonialism were inadequately addressed. Working-class and women's history, two allies with potentially different interests at heart, experienced very real tensions, just as women activists in the labour movement and on the Left found masculinist barriers circumscribing their political work.

Our pasts, both written and lived, however, must be assessed for their insights and advances, as well as their limits and failures. As we face a new century, it is a propitious time to re-examine past attempts to create a thoroughly gendered analysis of Canadian working-class history since the "renaissance" in women's and labour history in the 1970s.[2] We need to explore the ways in which class and gender

[1]Leo Panitch and Donald Swartz, *The Assault on Trade Union Freedoms: From Wage Controls to the Social Contract* (Toronto 1993).

[2]While recognizing that labour and working-class history sometimes mean different things, I have used the terms interchangeably. I am concentrating on feminism and working-class history, as lack of space prevents me from addressing whether a class analysis permeated women's history, but the latter *is* a question needing critical inquiry.

were problematized, how interpretive strategies changed over time, and were ultimately complicated by theoretical challenges such as critical race and post-structuralist theory. Is it fair, now, to echo the claims of academics in other nations that working-class history, and especially its "unhappy marriage" with feminism,[3] is in crisis, if not a state of decline?

This attempt to re-examine our histories/historical writing must be related to the course of feminist and working-class politics within Canadian society, to the political and intellectual evolution of the historical profession, and to changing trends in social theory within the wider academy. Nor were these three factors separate; they were closely intertwined. As E.H. Carr argued many years ago, history is inevitably influenced by the historian and her social and political context, by the way in which culture and society are reacted to, and lived out through the historian's outlook and writing.[4] While this might also be characterized in Fou-cauldian terms as a "history of the present," an exploration of the construction of history within the prevailing political discourses, I am influenced less by a relativist claim that history is a discursive — and ultimately unknowable — construct, more by an attempt to both locate my own and other histories in their social context, analyzing those systems of thought which have masked, or offered emancipatory potential to the working-class and women.

Problematic Possibilities

Labour and women's history did not originate, but were rejuvenated in the 1970s. This renaissance was encouraged by political and social movements of the time, as well as by the opening up of previously élite universities to a new cohort of youth, including more women, who had high ideals, and were quick to cast a critical eye on their elders.[5] The New Left and student radicalism, a resurgence of interest in social history and Marxist writing (long shunned in Canadian academe), Québec's Quiet Revolution and the civil rights and anti-war movements all fostered new interest in the history of workers, radical, and socialist movements. At the same time, a revitalization of feminist writing and organizing sparked new attention to women's history. Attempting to understand our current place in society aroused a keen interest in the past; like other oppressed groups, women sought out a history which did not denigrate them by omission, stereotyping or trivialization. Nor were

[3]On the earlier "unhappy marriage" between feminism and marxism debates see Lydia Sargent, *Women and Revolution* (Boston 1981).
[4]E.H.Carr, *What is History?* (London 1961), chap 2. Carr actually referred to the historian as "he," not a surprising reference in that period.
[5]Douglas Owram, *Born at the Right Time: a history of the baby boom generation* (Toronto, 1996); Patricia Jasen, "In Pursuit of Human Values (or Laugh when you say that): The Student Critique of the Arts Curriculum in the 1960s," in Paul Axelrod, John Reid, ed., *Youth, Universities and Canadian Society: Essays in the Social History of Higher Education* (Montréal 1989), 247-74.

these two political incentives always separate. Schooled in the women's movement, but sympathetic to the Left, one early practitioner of Canadian women's labour history remembers embracing this project because it allowed her to "combine activism and research."[6]

Labour history in English Canada already had a history. In previous decades, a few lonely materialists like Clare Pentland and social democrats like Harold Logan had preserved the study of class relations and the labour movement. But very few authors had combined an interest in women and labour, save for writers located outside of academe.[7] Unlike the American and British scenes, where scholars Alice Henry, Ivy Pinchbeck and Alice Clark had produced historical or social science investigations of labouring women, this field was open territory in Canada.

What came to be called the new labour history emerged in the 1970s, combining the established focus of the so-called old labour history (very recently reinvigorated in the late 1960s)[8] in the study of trade unions and labourist/CCF politics with novel interest in the social, intellectual and cultural dimensions of working-class experience, and in radicalism located outside social democratic politics. Influenced by historians E.P. Thompson and Herbert Gutman, by neo-Marxist and socialist-humanist writings, by a desire to study class relations as they were lived out in daily life, the new labour history changed the terrain of Canadian historical writing.[9] In French Canada, where an old labour history was less evident, the landscape was different again. Two schools of research emerged (and persisted), one exploring the conditions of working-class life, the other, labour institutions and radicalism.

[6]Linda Kealey, personal communication to author, 9 August 1999.
[7]One early scholarly exception was Jean Scott, "The Conditions of Female labour in Ontario," *Toronto University Studies in Political Science,* 1 (1892), 84-113. Articles on women workers did appear in the Left and progressive press; for example, Irene Biss Spry, Irene Forsey and others wrote for the *Canadian Forum.* Labour historian Joanne Burgess has recalled the influence of Spry on her own intellectual path towards working-class history. Joanne Burgess to author, 31 August 1999.
[8]Gregory S. Kealey suggested two overlapping cohorts of the 1960s and 1970s: the first doing more "institutional" but certainly novel topics, and a second cohort, more interested in 19th century class formation, class, culture and marxism. See Gregory S. Kealey, *Workers and Canadian History* (Montréal 1995), 125. Earlier in the 1960s, two historians made tentative suggestions about integrating class into historical scholarship. See S. Mealing, "The Concept of Class and the Interpretation of Canadian History," *Canadian Historical Review,* 46 (1965), 201-18; J.M.S. Careless, "Limited Identities in Canada," *Canadian Historical Review,* 50 (1969), 1-10. It is important to note that the latter article discussed region, class and ethnicity, but not women.
[9]Carl Berger, *The Writing of Canadian History: Aspects of English-Canadian Historical Writing since 1900* (Toronto 1986), chap. 11.

Moreover, Québec historians, unlike English ones, were centrally concerned with the relationship of the working class to the nation and nationalism.[10]

The designation of working class history as either "old" or "new," with the new primarily concerned with working-class culture, always oversimplified what was actually written. The "old" supposedly concentrated on the formal institutions of labour, but in English Canada, the "new" also wrote about the state, trade unions, political campaigns, and so on. An emphasis on culture did not reign supreme in the new labour history, even if some of its advocates urged the study of class relations *through* the lens of culture. Nonetheless, defensive critiques of the work of the new labour history quickly surfaced within English-Canadian academe; opponents charged these writers had a "idolatorous" fascination with esoteric aspects of working-class life; they "dreamed of" resistance and class struggle when there was none; they "glorified Communism,"[11] and unfairly neglected the 20th century. Interestingly, some recent feminist critiques of the new labour history repeat similar affirmations about the overemphasis on class resistance found in this writing, perhaps indicating the dangers of historiographical reification and over-generalization.[12]

Critics of the new working-class history generally had little use for utopian ideals and "foreign" theories from abroad, supposedly tainting solid Canadian traditions of pure empiricism and polite reformism. Yet, such antagonistic responses were themselves ideological and sometimes rested precariously on vast

[10]For a comparison of English and French labour history see Joanne Burgess, "Exploring the Limited Identities of Canadian Labour: Recent Trends in English-Canada and Québec," *International Journal of Canadian Studies*, 1-2 (Spring-Fall 1990),149-67. By the 1970s there had emerged a number of sociological and historical works on Québec labour. Jean Hamelin and Yves Roby, *Histoire economique du Québec, 1851-90* (Montréal 1971); Andrew LeBlanc and James D. Thwaites, ed., *Le Monde Ouvriere au Québec; bibliographie retrospective* (Montréal 1973); Noel Belanger, *et al.*, ed., *Les Travailleurs Québéçois, 1851-96* (Montréal 1975); Fernand Harvey, *Le mouvement ouvrier au Québec* (Montréal 1980). Many of these Québec historians, along with Jacques Rouillard and Joanne Burgess, connected with English colleagues through the new journals like *Labour/Le Travail*.

[11]Terry Morley, "Canada's Romantic Left," *Queen's Quarterly*, 86 (1979), 110-19.

[12]Karen Dubinsky, *et al.*, "Introduction," in Franca Iacovetta and Mariana Valverde, eds., *Gender Conflicts: New Essays in Women's History* (Toronto 1992), xvii. The only text cited is Bryan Palmer, *A Culture in Conflict: Skilled Workers and Industrial Capitalism in Canada* (Montréal 1979). Who gets cited (or omitted) creates its own powerful rendition of historiography. This lends some credence to the postmodern claim that the construction of historiography is just that: a construction. See Keith Jenkins, "Introduction," to Keith Jenkins, ed., *The Postmodern History Reader* (London 1997), 19. The claim that resistance was an important theme in early labour history (as it was in Black history, or more recently, gay history) has a ring of truth, but it need not be totalized or assumed to reside in one Marxist text. For example, if you want to criticize a preoccupation with resistance, why not cite Irving Abella, ed., *On Strike: Six Key Labour Struggles in Canada, 1919-49* (Toronto 1974).

generalizations about a range of politics and writings.[13] Ultimately, critics probably objected less to the study of culture (cultural topics are currently popular, and we hear few complaints), far more to the Marxist assumptions of class conflict underlying this work. Broader political lessons were at stake, between established social democratic ideas and tactics and New Left challenges to the labour and academic establishment.

It is true that new works in labour history drew consciously on international theoretical debates (yet references to *au courant* theory — certainly not Marxism — are taken for granted today), and having cut their teeth on student and anti-war protests, some authors were not immune to issuing declarations about the superior virtue of their quest for holistic views of "society, culture, work" rather than the older, narrower emphasis on unions and "institutions."[14] What is especially note-worthy is that these contentious debates centred very little — if at all — on gender. The issue of gender made its way into this contest when it was introduced as evidence that class, or at least class consciousness, did not really exist. Since the working-class was fractured by different experiences based on gender, ethnicity, religion, and region, David Bercuson argued, class was obscured and a unitary class consciousness lacking.[15] If all working-class Canadians were not "one for all" like the Musketeers, then class was all for nought. This was certainly not what some of us intended as the message of our work on women that Bercuson cited, nor did Marxists generally explore class as singularly unified and/or imbued with revolu-tionary consciousness. The earlier call to explore the "limited identities" in Cana-dian history was thus used to suggest that class consciousness was a fabrication of Marxist minds — though an essentialized gender experience was not. Some echoes of this critique are still heard; a recent study of Calgary labour similarly searches for a "single" working-class consciousness, uncomplicated by gender and ethnic differences, and, not surprisingly, finds it did not exist.[16]

---

[13]Kenneth McNaught "E.P. Thompson vs Harold Logan: Writing about Labour and the Left in the 1970s," *Canadian Historical Review*, 62, 2 (1981),141-68. McNaught discredited the works of some of the "new" labour historians, then promptly lauded the work of his own students like David Bercuson. A few critiques of so-called culturalism also came from within the new labour history. See Ian McKay, "The Three Faces of Canadian Labour History," *History Workshop Journal*, (1987), 172-9, and his "Historians, Anthropology, and the Concept of Culture," *Labour/Le Travail*, 8/9 (1981-2), 185-241.

[14]Russell Hann, G. Kealey, L. Kealey, P. Warrian, *Primary Sources in Working Class History* (Kitchener 1973), Introduction, 9-21. See also Bryan Palmer (response to Morley), "Working-Class Canada: Recent Historical Writing," *Queen's Quarterly*, 86 (1979), 594-616.

[15] David Bercuson, "Through the Looking Glass of Culture," *Labour/Le Travailleur*, 7 (1981), 95-112.

[16]David Bright, *The Limits of Labour: Class Formation and the Labour Movement in Calgary, 1883-1929* (Vancouver 1998), 41.

Where did these debates about class leave women's labour history and feminism? It is revealing that it is difficult *not* to write about working-class and women's history as if they were "two separate tribes," to use an American interpretation of their relationship.[17] There were initially some fundamental differences between the two, for women's history, by its very definition, assumed gender to be the central defining category of historical analysis, while for labour history, class was the definitive analytic framework. Trying to create a gendered working-class history, or a women's history centrally informed by class and race, have proven to be far more difficult than we imagined. However, I think it is significant that, early on, few feminist historians championed the Bercusonian critique. Instead, we re-doubled our efforts to explore working-class history as women lived it, altering the concentration on male realms of work and politics.

Neither the study of class formation, or the term "working-class history" need be ethnocentric, masculinist endeavours. But for the first decade, even longer, these adjectives have been pertinent to Canadian labour history. One of the first major collections of the new labour history contained not one article on women.[18] Reinterpretations of the Winnipeg General Strike, labour radicals, and the founding of the Canadian CIO, all published in the early 1970s, generally ignored women.[19] Two seminal studies followed by Gregory Kealey and Bryan Palmer. Though differently positioned politically, they examined workers' responses to 19th century industrialization, with a proclivity to centre on skilled male workers and their actions in the public sphere.[20]

Many of the dominant themes and paradigms in both the old and new labour history cast men in leading roles. Industrialization, proletarianization, and unionization were often explored, with forms of production employing male workers taken as the norm, or at least perceived to be the most important focus of study. Under the influence of Harry Braverman and David Montgomery, the workplace, the labour process, and managerial attempts to de-skill the (male) worker also took centre stage, though women were subsequently added to the discussion, particularly

[17]Richard Oestreicher, "Separate Tribes? Working-Class and Women's History," *Reviews in American History*, 19 (1991), 228-9.

[18]Gregory S. Kealey and Peter Warrian, eds., *Essays in Canadian Working-Class History* (Toronto 1976). This should be contrasted to the first book on women's history in the same series, which did have articles on working-class women. See Alison Prentice and Susan Mann Trofimenkoff, eds., *The Neglected Majority* (Toronto 1977).

[19]David Bercuson, *Confrontation at Winnipeg* (Montréal 1974); Ross McCormack, *Reformers, Rebels and Revolutionaries: The Western Canadian Radical Movement, 1899-1919* (Toronto 1977); Irving Abella, *Nationalism, Communism and Canadian Labour: The CIO, the Communist Party and the Canadian Congress of Labour, 1935-56* (Toronto, 1973).

[20]Bryan D. Palmer, *A Culture in Conflict: Skilled Workers and Industrial Capitalism in Hamilton, Ontario, 1860-1914* (Montréal 1979); Gregory S. Kealey, *Toronto Workers Respond to Industrial Capitalism, 1867-92* (Toronto 1980).

in later Canadian collections.[21] As Sonya Rose has argued, a long-standing ideological investment in "separate spheres," a remnant of 19th century ideology, but incorporated into Marxism and the social sciences, lingered on in 20th century analysis. The public world of production tended to be associated with men, politics and work; the private world of family, nurturing, and unpaid work, with women.[22] Nor were these two equal in importance. Even socialists and communists throughout much of the 20th century saw women's true liberation coming when they *entered* the world of social production and joined the working-class struggle, leaving behind the private realm.

But all this has been said before. Indeed, twenty years ago, a critical article by Joan Kelly called for a feminist theory of "double vision," integrating, rather than separating, the spheres of production, sexual and social life.[23] Subsequent critiques of Braverman by feminist labour historians suggested that labour process theory rested on the experiences of male, not female workers. Acute analyses of labour historians' accent on the male artisan, the shop floor and industrial work, on unions dominated by men, began to figure in reviews of Anglo-American working-class history. Even the very periodization of working-class history, as Susan Porter Benson argued, utilized a time frame based on the impact of capital on male, rather than female, workers.[24]

Yet, the tendency to feature male not female versions of work continued through the 1980s as important Canadian studies were done of metalworkers, bushworkers, steel workers, sailors, and miners — and more![25] Given the prevailing

[21]By the time a Canadian book was published on the labour process, critiques of Braverman, including feminist ones, were taken into account. Essays on paid and unpaid women workers were found in Craig Heron and Robert Storey, eds., *On the Job: Confronting the Labour Process in Canada* (Montréal 1986).

[22]Sonya Rose, "Gender and Labour History: The nineteenth-century legacy," *International Review of Social History*, 38 (1993), Supplement, 145-62.

[23]Joan Kelly, *Women, History and Theory: The Essays of Joan Kelly* (Chicago 1984), chap. 3.

[24]For feminists critiques of Braverman see Veronica Beechy, "The Sexual Division of Labour and the Labour Process: a Critical Assessment of Braverman," in S. Wood, ed., *Degradation of Work? Skill, Deskilling and the Labour Process* (London 1982), 54-73. Note, as well, Susan Porter Benson, "Response," to David Montgomery in *International Labor and Working-Class History*, 32 (Fall 1987), 31-8.

[25]Ian Radforth, *Bushworkers and Bosses: Logging in Northern Ontario, 1900-80* (Toronto 1987); Laurel Sefton McDowell, *Remember Kirkland Lake: The History and Effects of the Kirkland Lake Gold Miners Strike, 1941-2* (Toronto 1983); Craig Heron, *Working in Steel: The Early Years in Canada, 1883-35* (Toronto 1988); Eric Sager, *Seafaring Labour: The Merchant Marine of Atlantic Canada, 1820-1914* (Montréal 1989); Al Seager, "Socialists and Workers: The Western Canadian Coal Miners," *Labour/Le Travail*, 16 (1985), 23-60; For metalworkers, loggers and rail workers all together, see *Labour/Le Travail*, 6 (1980). A review essay in 1987 noted the three faces of labour history to be: the labour process, institutions, and working-class culture, with gender even not mentioned as a theme. Ian Mackay, "The Three Faces of Canadian Labour History."

silence in Canadian history on the working class, these were significant studies, and by the late 1980s some gestured at gender, noting how the masculinity of workers, or family relations were important. However, the prevailing prototypes of labour history persisted, in some cases even into the 1990s.[26]

Despite these masculinist inclinations in labour history there were openings and possibilities for meaningful alliances with feminism, and perhaps more so in Canada than in the US for Canadian political traditions encompassed stronger democratic socialist traditions, and a more concerted socialist influence on the reborn women's movement of the 1970s.[27] Nor were Canadian activists troubled by the split in the American women's movement, still apparent in the 1970s, over one of the most crucial issues for labour: the contest between protective labour legislation and the Equal Rights Amendment.[28]

As well as these broader political influences, women's and working-class historians shared overlapping occupational experiences, challenging the main-stream of the historical profession, not only with ideas, but with the prospect of opening up a men's club to women and people from more plebian backgrounds. A few female faculty members (there were few then) first introduced women's history courses in the early 1970s, and by 1975, a new professional grouping, the Canadian Committee on Women's History reflected the changing persona of the profession.[29] The Canadian Committee on Labour History, its fraternal partner, had been established four years earlier, though only it, as far as we know, was infiltrated by the RCMP searching for radicals.[30]

Second, women's and working-class historians were often engaged in research probing common questions and themes, such as the effects of industrialization and urbanization on society, the creation of consciousness and ideology, the unfolding of resistance. And both groups included historians who linked their research to political commitments they felt no need to hide under false declarations of objec-

[26]In his 1998 study of the nascent Calgary labour movement, David Bright, *The Limits of Labour* concentrates on the traditional (male) spheres of productive and public work, unions and politics. However, one might make an argument that it is still acceptable to write about male workers, and to focus on the formal institutions of labour.

[27]On the weakness of socialism in the US movement at this time, Ellen Ross, "Women's History in the U.S.," in Raphael Samuel, ed., *People's History and Socialist Theory* (London 1981), 182-8. On the Canadian movement, Linda Adamson, Linda Briskin, Magaret Macphail, *Feminists Organizing for Change: The Contemporary Women's Movement in Canada* (Toronto 1988).

[28]Dennis Deslippe, *Rights not Roses: Unions and the Rise of Working-Class Feminism, 1945-80* (Urbana: University of Illinois 2000), chap.5.

[29]If Marxists were men unwelcome in the profession because of their ideas, women had been just plain unwelcome. On earlier attitudes towards female faculty (and Marxists) see Michiel Horn, *Academic Freedom in Canada* (Toronto 1999), 215-6, 259-60.

[30]Steve Hewitt, "Intelligence at the Learneds: The RCMP, The Learneds and the Canadian Historical Association," *Journal of the Canadian Historical Association*, 8 (1998), 267-86.

tivity. As Deborah Gorham and others remember, it was the women's movement, events like the Berkshire Conference, or books like *Sexual Politics*, that stimulated their feminist commitment to women's history.[31] Like some working-class historians, they were interested in international theoretical debates, and in deconstructing (never a word used then) the unstated political assumptions about what was even deemed "worthy" of study in Canadian history. "Whose history" and "whose nation" they asked, does mainstream history represent —and possibly defend?[32] History was to make radical connections to the present. "From the beginning," remembered Susan Mann, "women's history has harboured the premise that oppression ... is the common lot of the female half of humanity. Once documented, that oppression would become an intellectual and political weapon, first to change the past then to change the future."[33]

Third, the new working-class history provided an important opening for feminist research, by rejecting — a least in rhetoric — the emphasis on formal institutions, and calling for studies of the family, community, and leisure, even if this approach was stronger in English than in French Canada. Culture, as Bryan Palmer notes, was never the simple "object of inquiry." The broader point was to open up "the way that class mattered in Canadian society ... [and] the actual activities of men and women as they lived out their lives" beyond the workplace and conventional politics.[34] The goal of linking working-class and women's history was thus placed more squarely at the centre than at the margins, since women always were more likely to be found in back yards, dance halls or in fleeting, unskilled employment, rather than in trade union offices.

Canadian women's history in these early years has been somewhat (mis)characterized as concentrating on "articulate, white middle-class"women, primarily social reformers.[35] Understandably, in the midst of a re-birth of feminism, some

[31]Deborah Gorham, "Women's History: Founding a New Field," in Beverly Boutilier and Alison Prentice, eds., *Creating Historical Memory: English Canadian Women and the Work of History* (Vancouver 1997), 273-97.
[32]L. Kealey, R. Pierson, J. Sangster and V. Strong-Boag, "Teaching Canadian History in the 1990's: Whose 'National' History Are We Lamenting?" *Journal of Canadian Studies*, (Summer 1992), 129-31.
[33]Susan Mann [Trofimenkoff], quoted in Marlene Shore, "Remember the Future: The Canadian Historical Review and the Discipline of History, 1920-95," *Canadian Historical Review*, 76, 3 (September 1995), 449.
[34]Bryan Palmer, *Working-Class Experience: Rethinking the History of Canadian Labour, 1800-1991* (Toronto,1992), 13.
[35]K. Dubinsky *et al.*, in Iacovetta and Valverde, eds., "Introduction," *Gender Conflicts*, xiv. I made a similar statement in piece written much earlier on working-class women's history and should have known better because the existing research on working-class women allowed me to write the article. Joan Sangster, "Canadian Working Women," in W.J.C. Cherwinski and Greg Kealey, eds., *Lectures in Canadian Working-Class History* (St. John's 1985), 59-78. A recent version of this overgeneralization is: "many historians of Canadian

researchers were fascinated by a previous generation of reformers and suffragists. And before being disparaging, we should recall that these were days long before Nellie McClung graced the Heritage Minutes on our TVs. Moreover, middle-class reformers never comprised the singular concern of feminist historians. Another current of women's history, exemplified by the "non-professional" collective which produced *Women at Work* in 1974, was centrally concerned with working-class women,[36] as were some Québécoise historians.[37] Given further focus by Wayne Roberts' *Honest Womanhood*, this brand of women's history promoted working-class women as the subject, and Marxist and feminist theory as the practice.[38] Moreover, even in the early writing on women reformers, class was not totally absent, perhaps because of the parallel influence of Marxist thought in working-class history. Carol Bacchi's suffragists, for example, were defined very much by their class interests, while the agenda of Barbara Robert's immigration reformers was shaped by their class and "Anglo" or "white" identity. Wayne Roberts and Alice Klein were critical of the manner in which the working girl was constructed as a problem by her middle-class "betters" — a theme taken up again in work in the 1990s.[39]

Fourth, and very significantly, the emergence of both women's history and labour history occurred in the midst of a reawakening of the Canadian Left, in various configurations from the left caucus of the NDP to ultra-left Trotskyist and Maoist groups. Though small, they had a significance beyond their numbers, and this had repercussions for academic thought and endeavours. Political and academic life were never symbiotic in any simplistic sense, and relations between the

women have given lavish attention to the winning of female suffrage between 1916 and 1919 as the critical watershed in the construction of modern feminism." This neither describes the range of research in women's history, or the dominant interpretations of suffrage. Nancy Christie and Michael Gavreau, *A Full-Orbed Christianity: The Protestant Churches and Social Welfare in Canada, 1900-40* (Montréal 1996), 116.

[36] Janice Acton, *et al*, *Women at Work: Ontario, 1880-1930* (Toronto 1974). See also early collections from BC such as Barbara Latham and Poberta Pazdro, eds., *Not Just Pin Money: Selected Essays on the History of Women's Work in British Columbia* (Victoria 1984).

[37] For example, one book produced in the early 1980s was literally divided into works on working-class women and feminists. Marie Lavigne and Yolande Pinard, eds., *Travailleuses et feministes* (Montréal 1983).

[38] Wayne Roberts, *Honest Womanhood: Feminism, Femininity and Class Consciousness Among Toronto Working Women, 1893-1914* (Toronto 1976).

[39] Carol Bacchi, *Liberation Deferred? The Ideas of the English Canadian Suffragists, 1877-1918* (Toronto 1982); Barbara Roberts, "A Work of Empire: Canadian Reformers and British Female Immigration," in Linda Kealey, ed., *A Not Unreasonable Claim: Women and Reform in Canada, 1880s-1920s* (Toronto 1979), 185-201; Alice Klein and Wayne Roberts, "Besieged Innocence: the 'Problem' and Problems of Working Women - Toronto, 1896-1914," in Janice Acton *et al.*, *Women at Work*, 211-60. The latter theme is taken up by Carolyn Strange, *Toronto's Girl Problem: The Perils and Pleasures of the City* (Toronto 1995).

women's movement and feminist scholars were sometimes difficult and strained. Nonetheless, this political climate did have an important effect on the questions explored by historians.

Indeed, both political organizing and academic writing fostered theoretical innovations producing a new hybrid, "Marxist-feminist" theory. There were innovative attempts to join feminism and socialism analytically, transforming the Anglo-American Left, for some time stymied in its analysis of "the woman question." Heidi Hartmann's dual systems theory kicked off a debate on the relationship between capitalism and patriarchy, as two mutually reinforcing, but distinct systems of exploitation and oppression.[40] Critiques followed, often working towards a more integrated analysis of these systems, until a distinctly socialist-feminist theoretical stance came to argue strongly that we should search for a "historically specific analysis of capitalist patriarchy ... looking at the multiplicity of relations of power based on class, race, ethnicity and gender."[41]

Inspired by these debates, works explored the role of patriarchy and capital in shaping the sexual division of labour, the relationship between the realms of reproduction and production, especially *vis à vis* women's domestic labour, and the interplay of economic structure and ideology in shaping class and gender relations. Both Marxist structuralism and socialist-humanism were used as guideposts — and foils — against which to probe women's oppression. This theoretical agenda also preoccupied Canadian political economists and sociologists such as Pat Armstrong, Hugh Armstrong, and Patricia Connelly, whose pathbreaking work was utilized by historians in an academic milieu increasingly characterized by a vibrant interdisciplinarity.[42]

Historians embarking on these new paths were thus never alone. Class formation, working women and trade unions were seen as important research areas *and* a crucial field of political action by a much larger group of academic/activists. Books like *Union Sisters* and *Hard Earned Wages*, appealing to a broadly-based

[40]There are many early works in this genre. See, for example, Zillah Eisenstein, ed., *Capitalist Patriarchy and the Case for Socialist Feminism* (New York 1979); Michèle Barrett, *Women's Oppression Today: Problems in Marxist Feminist Analysis* (London 1980); Shelia Rowbotham, *Women, Resistance and Revolution* (London 1973). Some early Canadian interventions were Charnie Guettel, *Marxism and Feminism* (Toronto 1974); Dorothy Smith, *Feminism and Marxism* (Vancouver 1977).
[41]Linda Briskin, "Identity Politics and the Hierarchy of Oppression," *Feminist Review*, 35 (1990), 103-4.
[42]For examples of early work, Pat Armstrong and Hugh Armstrong, *The Double Ghetto* (Toronto 1978); Pat Armstrong and Hugh Armstrong, "Beyond Sexless Class and Classless Sex: Towards a Feminist Marxism," *Studies in Political Economy*, 10 (1983), 7-43; Pat Connolly, *Last Hired, First Fired* (Toronto 1979); Meg Luxton, *More than a Labour of Love: Three Generations of Women's Work in the Home* (Toronto 1980). On early feminist political economy see Heather Jon Maroney and Meg Luxton, eds., *Feminism and Political Economy* (Toronto 1987).

audience, explored contemporary women's struggles in the labour movement and in non-traditional work, while a text such as *Feminists Organizing for Change*, advocated a socialist-feminist praxis for the women's movement. Both were legacies of this period.[43] And it is no accident that some of us writing working-class women's history were spending our spare hours organizing strike support committees; we felt no need to hide the fact that an interest in socialist and feminist theory and praxis informed the questions we asked of the past.

For making similar declarations, Marxists had been vehemently denounced as romantics and ideologues. Though parallel fears were voiced by conservative thinkers that feminist scholarship would be biased, ideological and partial, women's history was never immersed in the same intense political debates as working-class history. Perhaps it was difficult to construct a critique of women's history when we were only making the entirely reasonable claim that 50 per cent of the population deserved some historical attention. Perhaps too, women were such outsiders, and in such short supply in academe that we felt more inclined to stress sisterhood and commonality, rather than explore our intellectual differences — a particularly Canadian tendency which may have later inhibited constructive criticism and debate.

It is important to recall how this political and theoretical context framed the first decade, and more, of writing on labour and women's history. The labour movement was not yet cowed by neo-liberalism, and a number of key struggles involving women workers, from the Fleck strike in Ontario to SORWUC organizing in BC, highlighted their increased participation in the working-class movement.[44] Both an academic and activist Left were intent on bringing to light women's and labour's buried past.

Expanding and Complicating Possibilities

These fortuitous conditions, however, did not necessarily immediately transform our analysis of class formation. The history of women as workers, paid and unpaid, and a gendered history of class formation, not to mention the question of race, were only partially integrated into working-class history. In fact, I have asked myself if I am nostalgically ignoring a macho culture within working-class history that continued to marginalize women. Did we face a hard-drinking, cigar chomping group of men intent on playing Big Bill Haywood and stubbornly defending the masculine boundaries of the discipline? I don't think so. Labour history generally welcomed feminist research exploring gender and class. Though *some* (usually, but

[43] Linda Briskin and Lynda Yanz, eds., *Union Sisters* (Toronto 1983); Jennifer Penney, ed., *Hard Earned Wages* (Toronto 1983); Adamson, Briskin and Macphail, *Feminist Organizing for Change*.

[44] Heather Jon Maroney, "Feminism at Work," *New Left Review*, 141 (1983), 51-71; Bank Book Collective, *An Account to Settle: The Story of the United Bank Workers (SORWUC)* (Vancouver 1979).

not always male) practitioners saw class as definitive, gender a crucial additive, they were always willing to contest this issue with those of us who disagreed. If tensions were there, between class and gender, feminism and socialism, debating "who was on top," in which theory, and why, they were not necessarily negative: they could be productive. Moreover, within History Departments, some of us doing women's history were profoundly isolated to a degree that a new generation of feminists can hardly imagine. I found intellectual encouragement from labour historians, and from political friends and colleagues from other disciplines who were interested in Marxist and feminist theory.[45]

Perhaps, I also wondered, the integration of feminism into working-class history encountered few denunciations from more conservative critics such as David Bercuson because we were an inconsequential "fraction" that never even got gender on the negotiating table. It is true that, even after a decade, as Bettina Bradbury charged in a retrospective in 1987, our attempts to integrate women into working-class history were still circumscribed. Using household and family as examples, she argued that more substantive attention to gender was essential if we were to achieve that holistic picture of working-class life that the new labour historians had always acclaimed.[46]

Bradbury's own work on the family economy, however, had already contributed immensely to a recasting of working-class history.[47] Indeed, two distinct patterns were emerging in research and critique. On the one hand, women were being integrated into existing themes in labour history, and, on the other hand, some reflective assessments of the field began to argue for shifting the paradigms of working-class history, using new perspectives and creating syntheses that moved

[45]While I recognize that some feminist graduate students still feel isolated, I think there is a far more accepting atmosphere for feminist work and female colleagues in many institutions, the product of twenty years of feminist activism. I never had one female professor in all my years in university; I encountered no other students doing women's history; I experienced instances of dismissal from fellow students; and there were not yet any jobs advertised in women's history. There were no email networks like the CCWH one to remind me I was not alone. I had a supportive, respectful PhD thesis supervisor, Richard Allen, a true blessing in those times. Graduate students in sociology and political science, with longer traditions of Marxist debate, were more likely to be politically and intellectually interested in women's history.

[46]Bettina Bradbury, "Women's History and Working-Class History," *Labour/Le Travail*, 19 (1987), 23-44. Joanne Burgess argues that this goal remained even more remote in Québec, given the lack of *rapprochement* and integration of the existing two "schools" of labour history. See Burgess, "Exploring the Limited Identities."

[47]For example, Bettina Bradbury, "The Family Economy and Work in an Industrializing City: Montréal 1871," *CHAR* (1979), 71-96; "The Fragmented Family; Family Strategies in the Face of Death, Illness and Poverty, Montreal, 1860-85," in Joy Parr, ed., *Childhood and Family in Canadian History* (Toronto 1982), 109-28; "Pigs, Cows, Boarders: Non-Wage Forms of Survival Among Montreal Families, 1861-91," *Labour/Le Travail*, 14 (1984), 9-46.

away from the conceptual subordination of gender to class. Alice Kessler-Harris' call to see gender, like class, as a "historical process", and to emphasize the "reciprocal and changing relationships" of work, household and community was symptomatic of this shift.[48]

By the early 1990s, a feminist labour history had substantially elaborated on the earlier masculinist story of work. Using sources including government documents, the census, union collections, accounts of strikes, company records, reformers' archives and oral history, and drawing very decidedly on wider Anglo-American debates and research, new territory was explored. Certain female jobs and workplaces were analyzed, as was the creation and tenacity of a sexual division of labour. Given the desire of the renewed women's movement to challenge the "female wage ghetto," this accent on uncovering the basis of the gendered division of labour understandable. The interaction between gender and technology was explored less, though later works in labour studies, influenced by the information revolution and globalization, did begin to analyze technology, gender, and class.[49]

[48] Alice Kessler-Harris, "A New Agenda for American Labor History: A Gendered Analysis and the Question of Class," in J. Carroll Moody and Alice Kessler-Harris, *Perspectives on American Labor History: The Problems of Synthesis* (DeKalb 1989), 217-34. See also her later, "Treating the Male as the 'Other': Redefining the Parameters of Labor History," (from a paper given in 1991) *Labor History*, 34, 2-3 (Spring-Summer 1993), 190-204. Calls for new syntheses of labour history were heard more often in the US than in Canada, perhaps because Canadians, sensitive to Québec and regional interests, knew the difficulties of attempting such "centralizing" initiatives.

[49] The following lists denote examples only. The literature is vast enough that I have not attempted to cite all of relevant works in this section of the paper. On female occupations and the sexual division of labour, see Graham Lowe, "Class, Job and Gender in the Canadian Office," *Labour/Le Travail*, 10 (1982), 11-37; Margaret McCallum, "Separate Spheres: The Organization of Work in a Confectionary Factory, Ganong Bros.," *Labour/Le Travail*, 24 (1989), 9-90; Marilyn Porter, "She was skipper of the shore crew: Notes on the sexual division of labour in Newfoundland," *Labour/Le Travail*, 15 (1985), 105-23; Andrée Lévesque, "Le Bordel: Milieu de Travail Contrôle," *Labour/Le Travail*, 20 (1987), 13-31; Gail Cuthbert Brandt, "Weaving it Together: Life Cycle and the Industrial Experience of Female Cotton Workers in Quebec, 1910-50," *Labour/Le Travail*, 7 (1981), 113-26; Shirley Tillotson. "We may all soon be 'first-class men': Gender and Skill in Canada's early twentieth century urban telegraph industry," *Labour/Le Travail*, 27 (1991), 97-125; Jacques Ferland, "In Search of the Unbound Prometheia: A Comparative View of Women's Activism in Two Quebec Industries," *Labour/Le Travail*, 24 (1989), 11-44; Jacques Ferland, "Syndicalisme 'parcellaire' et syndicalism 'collectif': une intérpretation socio-technique des conflits ouvrièrs dans deux industries québécoises, 1880-1914," *Labour/Le Travail*, 19 (1987), 49-88; Mercedes Steedman, "Skill and Gender in the Canadian Clothing Industry," in *On the Job*; Joy Parr, "Disaggregating the Sexual Division of Labour — a Transatlantic Case Study," *Comparative Studies in Society and History*, 30, 3 (1988), 511-33; Michelle Martin, *"Hello Central?" Gender, Technology and Culture in the Formation of Telephone Systems*

Women's work was necessarily defined differently than men's, with studies of servants, domestic work, and feminized occupations taking a central place. The latter were especially strong in Québec, undoubtedly because of the simultaneous interest of feminist historians with the effect of the Catholic Church on women's lives.[50] The relationship of women and the labour movement to the law and social policy, especially with regards to protective legislation and welfare state provision, was also explored, often by political economists and sociologists as well as historians.[51] Building on the most basic wisdom of second-wave feminist writing,

(Montréal 1991); Heather Menzies, "Technology in the Craft of Cheesemaking: Women in Oxford County, 1860," *Ontario History*, 87, 3 (1995), 292-304, and *Women and the Chip: Case Studies of the Effects of Informatics on Employment in Canada* (Montréal 1981).

[50]Marta Danylewycz, Beth Light and Alison Prentice, "The Evolution of the Sexual Division of Labour in Teaching: A Nineteenth Century Ontario and Quebec Case Study," *Histoire Sociale/Social History*, 16, 31 (May 1983), 81-109; Judi Cobourn, "I See and am Silent: A Short History of Nursing," in *Women at Work: Ontario*, 127-63; Marie Lavigne and Yolande Pinard, *Les femmes dans la société québécoise: aspects historiques* (Montréal 1977); Yoland Cohen and Michele Dagenais, "Le métier d'infirmière: savours Feminins et reconnaissance professionnelle," *RHAF*, 41, 2 (1987), 155-77.

[51]Linda Kealey "Women and Labour during World War I: Women Workers and the Minimum Wage in Manitoba," in Mary Kinnear, ed., *First Days, Fighting Days: Women in Manitoba History* (Regina 1987), 76-99; Margaret McCallum, "Keeping Women in Their Place: The Minimum Wage in Canada, 1910-25," *Labour/Le Travail*, 17 (1986), 29-56; Ruth Roach Pierson's *They're Still Women after All: The Second World War and Canadian Womanhood* (Toronto 1986); Ruth Roach Pierson, "Gender and the Unemployment Insurance Debates in Canada, 1934-40," *Labour/Le Travail*, 25 (1990), 77-104; Margaret Hobbs and Ruth Roach Pierson, "A Kitchen That Wastes no Steps...: Gender, Class and the Home Improvement Plan, 1936-40," *Historie Sociale/Social History*, XXI (1988), 9-37; Jane Ursel, *Private Lives, Public Policy: 100 Years of State Intervention in the Family* (Toronto 1992); Jane Haddad and Stephen Milton, "The Construction of Gender Roles in Social Policy: Mothers Allowances and Day Care in Ontario Before World War II," *Canadian Womens Studies*, 7, 4 (1986), 68-70; Susan Prentice, "Workers, Mothers, Reds: Toronto's Postwar Daycare Fight," *Studies in Political Economy*, 30 (1989), 115-41; Brigette Kitchen, "The Family and Social Policy," in Maureen Baker, ed., *The Family: Changing Trends in Canada* (Toronto 1984); Margaret Little, "Claiming a Unique Place: The Introduction of Mothers' Pensions in BC," *B.C. Studies*, 106 (1995), 80-102. Those working on the history of crime and the law also contributed to our knowledge of working-class women's lives. For example, see Constance Backhouse, "Desperate Women and Compassionate Courts: Infanticide in Nineteenth Century Canada," *University of Toronto Law Journal*, 34 (1984), 447-78 and "Nineteenth Century Prostitution Law: Reflection of a Discriminatory Society," *Histoire Sociale/Social History*, XVIII, 36 (1985), 387-423; Judith Fingard, *The Dark Side of Life in Victorian Halifax* (Porters Lake, NS 1989); Indiana Matters, "Sinners or Sinned Against? Historical Aspects of Juvenile Delinquency in British Columbia," in *Not Just Pin Money*; Andrée Lévesque, *Making and Breaking the Rules: Women in Quebec, 1919-39* (Toronto 1994); Dorothy Chunn, *From Punishment to Doing Good: Family Courts and Socialized Justice in Ontario, 1880-1940* (Toronto 1992).

that gender was socially and historically constituted, writers also explored the ethnic, class and cultural forces shaping the experiences of working-class women, indicating their distinct differences from middle-class women of different backgrounds.[52]

Biographies of female labour leaders were seldom written, but collective pictures of the activities and ideas of women involved in union work, labour politics and the Left were attempted, with some attention not only to women wage earners, but also to women who organized as auxiliary members, consumers and supporters of other radical causes.[53] Another body of work probed the family economy as it

[52] Marie Lavigne, Yolande Pinard and Jennifer Stoddart, "The Fédération Nationale Saint-Jean-Baptiste and the Women's Movement in Québec," in Linda Kealey, ed., *A Not Unreasonable Claim*, 71-87; Wendy Mitchinson, "The YWCA and Reform in the 19th century," *Historire Sociale/Social History*, 24 (1979), 368-84; Helen Lenskyj, "A Servant Problem, or a Servant Mistress Problem? Domestic Service in Canada, 1890-1930," *Atlantis*, 7, 1 (1981), 3-11. On ethnicity and race see Jean Burnet, ed., *Looking into My Sister's Eyes: an Exploration in Women's History* (Toronto 1986); Tamara Adilman, "A Preliminary Sketch of Chinese Women and Work in British Columbia," in Latham and Padro, eds., *Not Just Pin Money*; Joan Sangster, "Finnish Women in Ontario, 1890-1930," *Polyphony: The Bulletin of the Multicultural History Society of Ontario* 3, 2 (Fall 1981), 46-54; Ruth Frager, "Politicized Housewives in the Jewish Communist Movement of Toronto," in Linda Kealey and Joan Sangster, eds., *Beyond the Vote: Canadian Women and Politics* (Toronto 1989), 258-75. Much of the work on ethnicity was tied to immigration history and politics. Sociologists and political scientists made important contributions. For example, see Agnes Calliste, "Canada's Immigration Policy and Domestics from the Caribbean," in Jessie Vorst, ed., *Race, Class and Gender: Bonds and Barriers* (Toronto 1989), 133-65; Helen Ralston, "Race, Class, Gender and Work Experience of South Asian Immigrant Women in Atlantic Canada," *Canadian Ethnic Studies*, 33, 2 (1991), 129-39; Roxanna Ng, "The Social Construction of Immigrant Women in Canada," in Roberta Hamilton and Michèle Barrett, eds., *The Politics of Diversity: Feminism, Marxism and Nationalism* (Montréal 1986), 269-86. For an exploration of the differences between First Nations and white women see Sylvia Van Kirk, *Many Tender Ties: Women in Fur Trade Society, 1670-1870* (Winnipeg 1980).

[53] Two exceptions are Susan Crean, *Grace Hartman: a woman for her time* (Vancouver 1995) and the recent Andrée Lévesque, *Scènes de la Vie en Rouge: L'époque de Jeanne Corbin, 1906-1944* (Montréal 1999). There were more biographies of male labour leaders, simply because there were more. There were a few earlier hagiographic accounts of radical women, such as Louise Watson, *She Never Was Afraid: the Life of Annie Buller* (Toronto 1976) and some articles, such as Joan Sangster, "The Making of a Socialist-Feminist: The Early Career of Beatrice Brigden," *Atlantis*, 13, 1 (1987), 13-28; Susan Walsh, "The Peacock and the Guinea Hen: Political Profiles of Dorothy Gretchen Steeve and Grace MacInnis," in *Not Just Pin Money*, 365-79. For some examples of women in union and left politics, see also Janice Newton, *The Feminist Challenge to the Canadian Left 1900-1918* (Montréal 1995); Linda Kealey, *Enlisting Women for the Cause: Women, Labour and the Left in Canada, 1890-1920* (Toronto 1998); Sylvie Murray, *A la Junction du mouvement ouvrier et du mouvement des femmes: La Ligue Auxiliaire de l'Association Internationale des*

altered over time, showing how both children's work and that of married women were consistently important to family subsistence, even if they did not take the form of waged labour.[54] The idea of "separate spheres" was also examined, not as a reality determining women's lives, but as an ideology, and often a contradictory one, obscuring the overlapping relations of women's private and public lives.[55]

Exploring militancy, resistance and struggle were arguably well-worn motifs in the new labour history, and feminist historians were not immune to adopting them.[56] While granting the limitations in focusing on resistance, early studies were interested in more than creating one-dimensional "working-class victims" — or heroines.[57] They wrestled, however imperfectly, with the role of economic struc-

Machinistes, Canada, 1903-80 (Montréal, 1990); Joan Sangster, *Dreams of Equality: Women on the Canadian Left 1920-60* (Toronto 1989); Ruth Frager, "No Proper Deal: Women Workers and the Canadian Labour Movement," in Linda Briskin and Lynda Yanz, eds.,*Union Sisters*, 44-64; Pamela Sugiman, *Labour's Dilemma: The Gender Politics of Auto Workers in Canada, 1937-79* (Toronto 1994); Mona-Josée Gagnon, "Les Femmes dans le mouvement syndical Québécois," in Marie Lavigne and Yoland Pinard, *Les Femmes dans La Société Québécoise* (Montréal 1977), 145-68; Nadia Fahmy-Eid and Lucie Piche, *Si le travail m'etait conte...autrement. Les travailleuses de la CTCC-CSN: quelques fragments d'historie, 1921-76* (Montreal 1987).

[54]Joy Parr, ed. *Childhood and Family in Canadian History* (Toronto 1982); Parr, *Labouring Children: British Immigrant Apprentices to Canada, 1869-1924* (Toronto 1994); John Bullen, "Hidden Workers: Child Labour and the Family Economy in Late Nineteenth Century Urban Ontario," *Labour/Le Travail*, 18 (1986), 163-88; Jane Synge, "The Transition from School to Work: Growing up Working Class in Early 20th Century Hamilton," in K. Ishwaren, ed., *Childhood and Adolescence in Canada* (Toronto 1979); Bettina Bradbury, *Working Families: Age, Gender, and Daily Survival in Industrialization Montréal* (Toronto 1993), and some of the essays in her edited collection, *Canadian Family History: Selected Readings* (Toronto 1992); Lorna McLean, "Single Again: Widows's Work in the Urban Family Economy, Ottawa, 1871," *Ontario History*, 83, 2 (1991),127-50; Veronica Strong-Boag, "Discovering the Home: the Last 150 Years of Domestic Work in Canada," in Paula Bourne, ed., *Women's Paid and Unpaid Work: Historical and Contemporary Perspectives* (Toronto 1985); Meg Luxton, *More than a Labour of Love: Three Generations of Women's Work in the Home* (Toronto 1980).

[55]Jennifer Stoddart and Marie Lavigne, "Les travailleuses montrealaises entre les deux guerres," *Labour/Le Travailleur*, 2 (1977), 170-83; Ruth Frager, "No Proper Deal," in *Union Sisters*; Janet Guildford and Suzanne Morton, eds., *Separate Spheres: Women's Worlds in the 19th Century Maritimes* (Fredericton 1994).

[56]Certainly an exception is Susan Mann Trofimenkoff, "A Hundred and One Muffled Voices: Canada's Industrial Women of the 1880s," *Atlantis*, 3, 1 (Fall 1977), 66-83, as it did not stress resistance. A number of early articles did examine points of conflict, such as strikes, including Joan Sangster, "The Bell Telephone Strike of 1907: Organizing Women Workers," *Labour/Le Travailleur*, 3 (1978), 109-30; Mary Horodyski, "Women and the Winnipeg General Strike," *Manitoba History*, 11 (Spring 1986), 28-37.

[57]Dubinsky *et al.*, "Introduction," *Gender Conflicts*, xvii. Another author argued that we (primarily I) created oppositional ideologies such as feminism where they did not exist. See

tures and both dominant and alternative ideologies in the creation of women's consciousness, though we often failed to address, until recently, the simultaneous process of accommodation.[58] French-Canadian feminists also had to counter the claim that they had overemphasized the patriarchal "victimization" of working women, supposedly obscuring other stories, including the economic improvement in women's lives over the early 20th century.[59] The emphasis on resistance in all working-class history, claims a recent American critique, was a shortcoming that reveals a hopelessly "teleological" emancipatory narrative in which a classless society is the utopian end.[60] But is this really such a horrible thought? Sounding vaguely like earlier conservatives, this criticism would surely not be levelled against writings on the history of slavery.

Pushed and buoyed by feminist theory and organizing, the new labour history was increasingly more likely to take women into account than had the "old". This is not to say that this writing is unassailable, simply that feminist complaints were being heard. In synthetic overviews, gender assumed increased prominence, more so if the focus was on working-class experience rather than the labour movement.[61] Similarly, overviews of women's history incorporated more material on working-

---

Dan Azoulay, "Winning Women for Socialism: The Ontario CCF and Women, 1947-61," *Labour/Le Travail*, 36 (1995), 59-90. Ruth Frager also offers a critique which I find far more balanced. As she points out, by focussing on women on the Left interested *in* the woman question, the outlook of those women with stronger class and ethnic loyalties tend to be obscured.

[58]For later discussion of accommodation, see Joan Sangster, *Earning Respect: The Lives of Working Women in Small-Town Ontario, 1920-60* (Toronto 1995) and on both resistance and the creation of consent, Mercedes Steedman, *Angels of the Workplace: Women and the Construction of Gender Relations in the Canadian Clothing Industry, 1890-1940* (Toronto 1998).

[59]This is only one part of the critique in Fernand Ouellet, "La question sociale au Québec, 1880-1930: la condition feminine et le mouvement des femmes dans l'historiographie," *Histoire Sociale/Social History*, XXI 42 (1988), 319-45. For a strong reply see Micheline Dumont, "Historie des femmes," *Histoire Sociale/Social History*, XXIII 45 (May 1990), 117-28.

[60]Laura Frader, "Dissent over Discourse: Labor History, Gender and the Linguistic Turn," *History and Theory*, 34 (1995), 214. Before being too disparaging about the conventions of past writing, we should perhaps take a closer look at current codes: the requisite references to Foucault, the claims that all is "contested, fluid, and constructed," etc.

[61]The second edition of *Working-Class Experience*, for example, integrated new research on gender and women, though it was criticized for not going far enough on this account, reflecting higher expectations placed on the treatment of working-class experience than examinations of the labour movement, such as Craig Heron, *The Canadian Labour Movement: A Short History* (Toronto 1989 and 1996). I based this on eleven book reviews. 50 per cent of the ones for Palmer felt he did not include enough on women; none of the reviews of Heron mentioned this issue.

class women, though these were seldom judged by their class analysis.[62] Finally, *Labour/Le Travail*, a bell-wether of sorts, began to reflect more gender sensitivity, on its editorial board, and in its content, as the proverbial metal workers were now joined by candy makers and office employees.[63] Feminist political economy was also flourishing, while sociologists were using historical research on women, work, and unions to offer theoretically informed contributions to a feminist working-class history.[64]

Still, there were silences, lacuna and problems with these attempts to integrate a gender and class analysis. While recent work has concentrated on the differences defined by race and ethnicity, we should not forget that the divide of two solitudes — English Canada and Québec — also complicates attempts to explain class formation in feminist terms. One of the benefits of new feminist and labour academic groupings like the CCWH and CCLH was their role in linking historians from two nations in scholarly dialogue. Yet, with a few exceptions, most explorations of Canadian women's labour history stick to one side of the border or the other. The decline of a Left preoccupation with the "Québec question" may only accentuate this division, discouraging attempts at comparative histories of women from both cultures.

Undoubtedly, working-class women in Québec shared experiences with their English Canadian sisters; whether it was union wives organizing into auxiliaries, the sexual division of labour in garment factories, or the regulation of teachers, historians have noted these commonalities. However, language and culture, not to mention political alienation and the equation of language *with* class divisions, have created a distinct understanding of class in Québec. Also, as Andrée Lévesque argues, the ideological influence of the Church created different sets of domestic, familial, and sexual expectations for working-class women in Québec to negotiate. The importance of Catholic unions, strong state involvement in labour issues (ranging from Duplessis' intense anti-unionism to Parti Québécois sympathies),

---

[62]Even works which took gender as their primary interpretive guide and category of "difference", such as Veronica Strong-Boag, *The New Day Recalled: The Lives of Girls and Women in English Canada, 1919-39* (Toronto 1988) were not inattentive to class. Still, none of the book reviews I located for Alison Prentice, *Canadian Women: A History* (Toronto 1988) mentioned the book's analysis of class. I think there is an important question here for another inquiry: if we judge labour historians guilty of slighting gender, we should also ask if gender historians have slighted class.

[63]Of course, working-class and women's history was published elsewhere as well. However, *Labour/Le Travail* provides one measure of attitudes towards gender. The Board was initially male dominated with one or two women only of about 11 members. By 1987-90, it was at least 40 - 50 per cent women, a conscious political choice.

[64]See, for example, the articles by Gillian Creese, Alicia Muszynski, and Jim Conley in Gregory S. Kealey, ed., *Class, Gender and Region: Essays in Canadian Historical Sociology* (St. John's 1988).

different patterns of public sector union mobilization — to name only a few examples — have resulted in a distinct history of class formation for Québec women and men.

The strategy of blending women into existing historical concerns has also been criticized, sometimes referred to as "adding women and stirring," implying that research on women was grafted onto masculine moulds inattentive to the complexities of gender. To some extent, this was true. Women were integrated into themes such as unionization, strikes, the workplace, political parties and so on. A perennial dilemma was how to fully integrate analyses of domestic labour and paid work, informal and formal labour, fleeting as well as life long work, for women's work lives encompassed these more complex combinations of work, in contrast to men's. Fewer Canadian studies innovated with integrated analyses of work, encompassing domestic and paid work, community and culture, family and workplace, as did some American works, though by the 1990s, some community-based studies, with tightly-defined temporal and geographical foci, were emerging. Such studies followed in the footsteps of the new labour history, with its search for deep description of working-class life, though by the 1990s they faced less criticism from the historical mainstream for their concentration on the local and particular, in lieu of the national and synthetic.[65]

While considerable attention was focused on the cooperative family economy, the dark side of family life, namely "patriarchy," conflict and violence, was less often explored, until a few studies on wife battering opened discussion of the underside of working-class life.[66] And the links between sexuality and work, as well as explorations of working-class sexuality remained underdeveloped until feminist, gay, and lesbian studies sparked new interest in this area by the 1990s, producing works surveying gay sex in working-class communities and the sexuali-

[65]For a good example of a community study see Suzanne Morton, *Ideal Surroundings: Domestic Life in a Working-Class Suburb in the 1920s* (Toronto 1995). Undoubtedly, the positive embrace of such studies reflected the postmodern emphasis on the local and particular, which has had taken root in the profession. One exception to this embrace is Michael Bliss, "Privatizing the Mind: The Sundering of Canadian History, the Sundering of Canada," *Journal of Canadian Studies*, 26 (Winter 1991-1992), 5-17.

[66]By the 1990s, this was changing. Kathryn Harvey, "To Love, Honour and Obey: Wife Battering in Working Class Montreal," *Urban History Review*,19, 2 (October 1990), 130-40; Judith Fingard, "The Prevention of Cruelty, Marriage Breakdown and the Rights of Wives in Nova Scotia, 1880-1990," *Acadiensis*, 22,2 (1993), 84-101; Terry Chapman, "Till Death Do Us Part: Wife Beating in Alberta, 1905-20," *Alberta History*, 36,4 (1988), 13-22. The manner of exploring this topic remains contentious. For example, a review of *Working-Class Experience* criticized the author for integrating "too much" material (only a few paragraphs) on family violence into the text, reflecting "an almost sordid preoccupation" with it. For this peculiar charge, see Craig Heron, "Towards a Synthesis in Canadian Working-Class History: Reflections on Bryan Palmer's Rethinking," *Left History*, 1, 1 (1993), 117.

zation of women's work.[67] Lacking a language of discourse analysis, earlier studies also overlooked opportunities to explore the gendered iconography of radical and left politics.[68]

Yet, surveying the current scene, I am tempted to argue that we still need more "add women and stir" studies. Save for Pamela Sugiman's important study of the UAW, we have few book-length studies of the CIO which take women and gender seriously.[69] Given the immense influence of transnational (especially American) migration, ideas, and organizing in Canadian history, the legacy of the AFL/CIO especially should be interrogated with reference to its impact on gender and labour.[70] We also need to develop an understanding of the emergence of retail and service work, while agricultural and domestic workers are often ignored in the period between 1920 to 1970.[71] And the latter would offer more attention to ethnic and racial differences as women of colour often found that domestic service was the only job open to them in these years. Indeed, the tendency in labour history to focus on industrial work reinforced an emphasis on white workers.[72] Women's experience of events like the Depression, the transformations in white collar work and unions like CUPE in the post 1960s period, women's long-standing role in the underground economy, the racialization of female occupations with changing immigration policy: all these, and more, need exploration.

[67]For recent exceptions, see Kathryn Macpherson's excellent chapter on sexuality in *Bedside Matters: The Transformation of Canadian Nursing, 1900-90* (Toronto 1996), 164-204. On gay history, Steven Maynard, "Horrible Temptations: Sex, Men, and Working Class Male Youth in Urban Ontario, 1890-1935," *Canadian Historical Review*, 78, 2 (1997), 191-235; Line Chamberland, "Remembering Lesbian Bars: Montreal, 1955-75," in Veronica Strong-Boag and Anita Clair Fellman, eds., *Re-thinking Canada: The Promise of Women's History* (Toronto 1997), 402-23.

[68] Sangster, *Dreams of Equality*.

[69] Sugiman, *Labour's Dilemma*. See also Eileen Suffrin, *The Eaton Drive: The Campaign to Organize Canada's Largest Department Store, 1948-52* (Toronto 1982); Julie Guard, "Fair Play or Fair Pay? Gender Relations, Class Consciousness and Union Solidarity in the Canadian UE," *Labour/Le Travail*, 37 (Spring 1997), 149-77.

[70]Marcel van der Linden, "Transnationalizing American Labor History," *Journal of American History*, 86, 3 (1999), 1078-92.

[71]Examples covering the earlier period include Marilyn Barber, "The Women Ontario Welcomed: Immigrant Domestics for Ontario Homes, 1870-1930, *Ontario History*, 72, 3 (1980), 148-72; Magda Fahrni, "'Ruffled' Mistresses and 'Discontented' Maids: Respectability and the Case of Domestic Service,1880-1914," *Labour/Le Travail*, 39 (1996), 69-98. On the later period, Sedef Arat-Koc, *et al.*, eds., *Maid in the Market: Women's Paid Domestic Labour* (Halifax 1994).

[72]Similar critiques were made in the US, though American women of colour were more significant in terms of numbers in the earlier period, and shared a different relationship to wage work. Lois Rita Helmbold and Ann Schofield, "Women's Labor History, 1790-1945," *Reviews in American History*, 17 (September 1989), 501-2.

By the 1980s, as well, the limitations of concentrating on gender and class, to the detriment of race and ethnicity, were starkly apparent. Some early studies had explored the intersection of ethnicity, work, and radicalism, while others were attentive to French-Canadian working-class culture.[73] However, more attention to the integration of class, gender and ethnicity awaited later works by Lindstrom-Best, Frager, Iacovetta, and others. Their analyses, often drawing on analogous international research,[74] consciously avoided the stereotype of the oppressed immigrant woman, exploring women's coping strategies, agency, and resistance. They also suggested that ideologies promoted by a dominant Anglo-Celtic culture, such as the middle-class idealization of domesticity, were not necessarily shared by working-class immigrants (indeed, as Roberts and Klein hinted earlier, they may not have been shared by many working-class women) who developed their own ideals of working-class "femininity."

Arguably, both ethnicity and race need to be more fully integrated into our analyses of Canadian class formation. Important investigations, such as those by Dionne Brand, Agnes Calliste, and Alicia Muszynski, looking at Afro-Canadian and Caribbean workers, and Native and Asian fisheries employees, and early works emanating from British Columbia, have broken this mould.[75] Moreover, given the

[73]Robert Harney's work is notable: one example was "Montreal's King of Italian Labour: A Case Study of Padronism," *Labour/Le Travail*, 4 (1979), 57-84. See also Ruth Bleasdale, "Class Conflict on the Canals of Upper Canada in the 1840s," *Labour/Le Travail*, 7 (1981), 9-40; Donald Avery, *'Dangerous Foreigners': European Immigrant Workers and Radicalism in Canada, 1896-1832* (Toronto 1979); Bruno Ramirez, *On the Move: French Canadian and Italian Migrants in the North Atlantic Economy, 1860-1914* (Toronto 1990). Ethnicity was also interwoven into works on male workers, See Radforth, *Bushworkers and Bosses*; Al Seager, "Miners' Struggles in Western Canada," in Deian Hopkin and Gregory S. Kealey, eds., *Class, Community and the Labour Movement: Wales and Canada, 1850-1930* (St. John's 1989), 160-98.

[74]Varpu Linstrom Best, *Defiant Sisters: A Social History of Finnish Immigrant Women in Canada, 1890-1930* (Toronto 1988); Ruth Frager, *Sweatshop Strife: Class, Ethnicity, and Gender in the Jewish Labour Movement of Toronto, 1900-39* (Toronto 1992); Franca Iacovetta, *Such Hardworking People: Italian Immigrants in Postwar Toronto* (Montréal 1992).

[75]Dionne Brand, *No Burden to Carry: The Lives of Black Working Women in Ontario, 1920s to 1950s* (Toronto 1991); Agnes Calliste, "Canada's Immigration Policy on Domestics from the Caribbean: The Second Domestic Scheme," and "Women of 'Exceptional Merit': Immigration of Caribbean Nurses to Canada," *Canadian Journal of Women and the Law.* 6, 1 (1993), 85-102; Alicia Muszynski, "Race and Gender: structural determinants in the formation of British Columbia's salmon fishery," *Canadian Journal of Sociology*,13, 1-2 (Winter-Spring 1988), 103-20, and *Cheap Wage Labour: Race and Gender in the fisheries of British Columbia* (Montréal 1996). Collections from BC indicated a regional proclivity to take race more seriously in the 1980s. See Latham and Padro, eds., *Not Just Pin Money* and David Cobourn and Rennie Warburton, eds., *Workers, Capital and the State in British Columbia* (Vancouver 1988); Veronica Strong-Boag and Gillian Creese, eds., *B.C. Reconsidered: Essays in Women's History* (Vancouver 1992).

political preeminence of First Nations organizing in Canada, it is not surprising that sophisticated analyses of the impact of colonialism on First Nations women's work (though often centred on the 18th and 19th centuries) have been produced.[76] But more sustained research and critique are needed, with the kind of careful attention that Gillian Creese gives to race relations in the BC labour movement. Never relying on simplistic depictions of all workers as consistently racist, or of race as either structurally *or* ideologically determined, she shows under what conditions the labour movement opposed Asian immigration, but also why, on occasion, it embraced cross-race class solidarity.[77]

Trying to work out the "simultaneity" of race, gender and class relations remains one of the more difficult tasks facing labour historians.[78] Just as American historian David Roediger has made race and the privilege of "whiteness" a central focus — while still maintaining class as a crucial analytic category — we need to re-examine the way in which race has shaped Canadian class formation. Even if much-quoted American theories of race (such as Roediger's) are useful as intellectual stimulants to this work, close empirical attention to the historical specificity of race and colonialism in Canada is crucial, for the relationship of race to labour worked itself out in fundamentally different ways in Canada.[79]

Finally, gender became both a complicating and enriching factor in the pursuit of a feminist working-class history. In its first flushes, women's historians noted that their task inevitably involved the study of gender relations between men and women, and that their goal was, ultimately, a more holistic "history of society" even if their focus was on the understudied: women.[80] However, by the 1990s, the notion that gender analysis was a more theoretically sophisticated approach was embraced

[76]One of the first examinations of Native women's work was Sylvia Van Kirk, *Many Tender Ties: Women in Fur-Trade Society, 1670-1870* (Winnipeg 1980). Later discussions include Jo-Anne Fiske, "Colonization and the Decline of Women's Status: The Tsimshian Case," *Feminist Studies*, 17, 3 (1991), 509-35, and her "Fishing is a Woman's Business: The Changing Economic Roles of Carrier Women and Men," in Bruce Cox, ed., *Native Peoples, Native Lands: Canadian Indian, Innuit and Metis* (Ottawa 1988), 186-90; Ron Bougeault, "The Indians, the Metis and the Fur Trade: Class, Sexism and Racism in the Transition from Communism to Capitalism," *Studies in Political Economy*, 12 (1983), 45-80; John Lutz, "After the Fur Trade: the Aboriginal labouring class of British Columbia, 1849-90," *Journal of the Canadian Historical Association*, 3 (1992), 69-94.
[77]Gillian Creese, "Exclusion or Solidarity?: Vancouver Workers Confront the Oriental Problem," *B.C. Studies*, 80 (1988-89), 24-51.
[78]Roediger is using a term coined by Terra Hunter. See his "Race and the Working-Class Past in the United States: Multiple Identities and the Future of Labor History," *International Review of Social History*, 38 (1993), 127-43.
[79] David Roediger, *The Wages of Whiteness: race and the making of the American working class* (New York 1991).
[80]Kelly, *Women, History and Theory*; Ruth Roach Pierson and Alison Prentice, "Feminism and the Writing and Teaching of History," *Atlantis*, 7, 2 (1982), 37-46.

by some historians who believed that asking questions about "women alone" inevitably presupposed the answers, isolating "women from social relationships" and "presuming she existed in certain ways "[81] Perhaps influenced by the men's movement and by feminists' urgings that men interrogate their own actions and ideas, there was also increasing academic interest in exploring the gendering of men and masculinity — though why asking questions about men and "masculinity" did not hold the same risk of "presupposing" the answers, has not been adequately addressed.

The shift seemed slightly ironic. Just after some of us had retreated from a male-dominated Left, manliness was now the topic of choice! After all those years of reading endlessly about metal workers, we thought a concentration on telephone operators and candy makers *was* important, only to be told our time was up! The positive results of talking gender, of course, are apparent in some of the research produced. A focus on gender enriches the study of class formation, by exposing men's work, leisure, family lives, and sexuality to a feminist analysis, sensitive to the social constitution of gender, the creation of masculinity and heterosexuality. Its beneficial results are already apparent in Joy Parr's analysis of the polar worlds of mens and women's work in small town Ontario, in Rosenfeld's study of family lives of railway workers, and in Cecilia Danysk's evocative reconstruction of the masculinity of hired hands in the prairie west.[82] Gillian Creese's recent study of office workers also connects race and masculinity, showing how both company and union preferences for the white, male breadwinners created a "technical job hierarchy" structured by race and gender.[83]

Applied along with feminist insights about power, with historical sensibility, and without an air of determined superiority, a focus on gender history will enhance our search for a feminist working-class history. In working-class history, in which women have for so long been struggling for equal time, though, I believe it is unwise to create an academic hierarchy, with women's history relegated to the partial,

[81]Joy Parr, "Gender History and Historical Practice," *Canadian Historical Review*, 79, 3 (1995), 362. For the earlier debate, Joan Sangster, "Beyond Dichotomies: Reassessing Gender History and Women's History in Canada," *left history*, 3, 1 (1995): 109-21, and replies from Franca Iacovetta and Linda Kealey, Karen Dubinsky, and Lynn Marks, and my response in *left history*, 3, 2 and 4, 1 (1996), 205-48.

[82]Joy Parr, *The Gender of Breadwinners: Women, Men and Change in Two Industrial Towns, 1880-1950* (Toronto 1990); Mark Rosenfeld,"It was a Hard Life: Class and Gender in the Work and Family Rhythms of a Railway Town, 1920-50," Canadian Historical Association, *Historical Papers* (1988), 237-79; Cecilia Danysk, *Hired Hands: Labour and the Development of Prairie Agriculture, 1880-1920* (Toronto 1995). For some earlier works on the gendering of men see Susan Mann Trofimenkoff, "Henri Bourassa and the Woman Question," in *The Neglected Majority*, 104-115; Trofimenkoff, "Les femmes dans l'oevre de Groulx," *Revue d'histoire de l'Amerique francaise*, 32, 3 (1978), 385-98.

[83]Gillian Creese, *Contracting Masculinity: Gender, Class, and Race in a White-Collar Union, 1944-94* (Toronto 1999), 205.

inadequate and less theoretical; ideally, gender should complement, not replace a focus on women.[84]

Overlapping with debates about gender history, were other post-structuralist winds of change sweeping through academe. Although the period up until the late 1980s was one of immense possibility, there were also portents of serious problems looming. Just as feminist explorations of labour were flourishing, labour and the left were foundering. Politically, the non-NDP Left was now in disarray and depression. The Canadian women's movement, which had developed a strong social-democratic and labour focus, sometimes even a socialist-feminist one, was markedly different in this respect from the US one, where liberal and radical feminism dominated. But the federal election women's debate of 1987 marked a high point of public visibility, and in subsequent years the movement struggled to confront inequalities within its midst, at the same time that an aggressive campaign of capital, often aided by governments, ate away, both ideologically and materially, at social welfare provision, notions of equity, not to mention the "privilege" of having work. Despite the production of sophisticated books focusing on feminism and the need to democratize unions, such as *Women Challenging Unions*, the locus of scholarship was shifting.[85] Soon, performativity, not class formation, would assume the centre of academic debate. Notions of social transformation seemed to be assuming new, dare I say, "culturalist" forms. Shopping, consumerism and lipstick, once the focus of a socialist-feminist critique, were being "celebrated," as Dawn Currie recently notes, as "subversive" forms of pleasure.[86] The postmodern had certainly arrived.[87]

[84]For the arguments that gender went beyond the narrower vision of women's history see Lykke de la Cour, Cecilia Morgan and Mariana Valverde, "Gender Regulation and State Formation in Nineteenth-Century Canada," in Allan Greer and Ian Radforth, eds., *Colonial Leviathan: State Formation in mid-nineteenth century Canada* (Toronto 1992), 163-91; Mariana Valverde, *The Age of Light Soap and Water: Moral Reform in English Canada, 1885-1925* (Toronto 1991) and her "Comment," *Journal of Women's History*, 5, 1 (1993), 121-5; Karen Dubinsky, *et al.*, "Introduction," *Gender Conflicts*; Joy Parr, "Gender History and Historical Practice."

[85]Linda Briskin and Patricia McDermott, eds., *Women Challenging Unions: Feminism, Democracy and Militancy* (Toronto 1993).

[86]Dawn Currie, *Girl Talk: Adolescent Magazines and Their Readers* (Toronto 1999), 5-6.

[87]I am not arguing that studying working-class consumption and popular culture leads to the demise of class, unless class becomes a vague discursive construction in these studies. Though frankly, if only the liberating effects of popular culture are claimed for working-class women, one does have cause to be critical. Moreover, some recent works fail to acknowledge their overlap with "older" writing on this topic, or that their interpretations of working women's "subjectivities," shaped by new theoretical/political suppositions, may be partial, as were older interpretations of women's "ideologies." For all its strengths, this seems true of Nan Enstad, *Ladies of Labor, Girls of Adventure: Working Women, Popular Culture and Labor Politics at the Turn of the Twentieth Century* (New York 1999).

The Demise of Class?

The challenge of these new theoretical and political currents to the foundations of working-class history should not be underestimated. In assessing them, one has to try to ward off excessive defensiveness and welcome critiques, even if they strike at the core of our understandings of history and politics. In writing this article, I tried to interrogate my own inclination to construct a narrative around "the rise and decline of working-class history." Is it possible that class has permeated historical analysis more generally, and that working-class history has simply merged into other projects, such as women's, ethnic, or regional history? Certainly, working-class history always had the potential to encompass many areas of the social, even political past, to advocate a broader, synthetic class analysis of Canadian society.

Some recent women's history, such as Karen Dubinsky's exploration of sexual violence, integrate class as an important variable in their analysis.[88] Working-class history gets considerable press in syntheses of Canadian history, and works like *No Burden to Carry*, focusing on Afro-Canadian women, simultaneously enhance our knowledge of working women.[89] Perhaps, turning to other topics, such as crime and punishment (to which I plead guilty), does not mean abandoning a larger project of understanding the racialized and gendered nature of class formation.[90] Perhaps, we are simply witnessing a profound redefinition of the field, as it responds to a new political context, social theory and critiques of our past practice. Academic fields are always in epistemological flux, and to imply such shifts are crises suggests a hierarchy, with certain theories and topics more "important" than others.[91]

I consulted friends in the field, read recent journals, thought about my teaching experience, looked at theses in progress, and surveyed the literature. I pictured the small number of middle-aged academics nominating each other for positions at recent CCLH meetings, then the larger crowd of historians, including feminists, at other meetings. And I could not completely shrug off the notion that working-class history, and the partnership of labour and feminist history is in trouble; both the "traditional" topics of working-class women's history *and* class analysis are

[88]Karen Dubinsky, *Improper Advances: Rape and Heterosexual Conflict in Ontario, 1880-1929* (Chicago 1993).

[89]Dionne Brand, *No Burden to Carry* and also Peggy Bristow, *et al.*, eds., *We're Rooted Here and They Can't Pull Us Up: Essays in African Canadian Women's History* (Toronto 1994). For a synthesis which integrates social history and labour see Margaret Conrad and Alvin Finkel, *History of the Canadian Peoples*, vol. 2 (Toronto 1993).

[90]Joan Sangster, "Girls in Conflict with the Law: Exploring the Construction of Female Delinquency in Ontario, 1940-60," *Canadian Journal of Women and the Law*, 12, 1 (2000), 1-31.

[91]It would be disingenuous to suggest that we can avoid prioritizing for "history always involves the power of exclusion, for any history is always someone's history, told by that someone from a partial point of view." Joyce Appleby, Lynn Hunt, Margaret Jacob, "Telling the truth about history," in Keith Jenkins, ed., *The Post Modern History Reader*, 217.

decidedly beleaguered. This does not appear to be true in other disciplines such as political economy. And part of the problem is the very "smallness" of Canadian academe; the critical mass of feminist historians writing about labour was always modest, so that any deflation of the field is keenly felt here. Since women's and gender history appear to be healthier enterprises, offered some well-deserved recognition by the historical profession, I am still obliged to ask why class has fallen on hard times.

Neither the political or theoretical context in recent years has been propitious for either class or materialist analyses. The academic retreat from class and the decline of the political and intellectual left were intimately connected.[92] In the wake of the collapse of socialist alternatives and the rise of neo-conservatism and neo-liberalism, a profound pessimism overtook many radicals. The labour movement has been substantially weakened, more so in the US than Canada, and in the face of sustained assaults from the state and business, and without an internal Left, it has also tended to close ranks defensively, rejecting radical perspectives. Although more women are found in trade union offices, and separate and autonomous organizing have increased the visibility of gender, race, and sexual orientation issues, labour militancy is not necessarily the order of the day. Contradictions abound: while women's needs are more visible, unions have been inclined, as Linda Briskin notes, to accept issues of gender "representation," but avoid more threatening "transformative demands coming from the rank and file."[93]

But it was not simply hard times or the triumphant logic of capitalism that led to a erasure of class and disillusion with labour. The intellectual Left (which increasingly became an *academic* left) hurried class to an untimely demise as theoretical and political interests and loyalties shifted from marxism to post-structuralism. Class "slipped off the charts of radical social theory," abandoned as critics pronounced it deconstructed. It was deemed both politically inadequate and intellectually deficient, both as marxist structuralism on the one hand, and socialist humanist "historicism" on the other.[94] Moreover, in the broader historical profession, changes in social theory engendered an aversion to the very notion of structure in history, to the grounding of texts in historical contexts, to "modernist empiricist" strategies of recovery, and certainly to marxist "interventions of dissent" lodged

[92]Ellen Meiksins Wood, "A Chronology of the New Left and its Successors, or 'Who's Old Fashioned Now?'" in R. Miliband and L. Pantich, eds., *Socialist Register, 1995* (London 1995), 22-49.

[93]Linda Briskin, "Autonomy, Diversity and Integration: Union Women's Separate Organizing in North America and Western Europe in the Context of Restructuring and Globalization," forthcoming, *Women's Studies International Forum*, 22, 5. My thanks to Linda for offering me a pre-publication copy of this paper.

[94]John Hall, "Introduction: The Reworking of Class," to John Hall, ed., *Reworking Class* (Ithaca 1997), 9. For views from the other side see Ellen M. Wood, *The Retreat from Class: A New 'True' Socialism* (London 1990); Ralph Miliband, Leo Panitch, John Saville, ed., *The Retreat of the Intellectuals: Socialist Register, 1990* (London 1990).

against mainstream history.[95] Recent popular polemics claiming that Marxism helped to kill Canadian history are thus out of touch with academic reality, endowing marxism with mythical influence beyond its due.[96]

Canadian academe has always been deeply enveloped in international scholarly debates and politics, and internationally "radical pluralism" was embraced in political theory and practice. The working class was increasingly seen as ephemeral, if not an impediment to social change; instead, an array of new social movements (some of which were not opposed to capitalism) captured the political imagination of many radicals. Identity politics, with its egalitarian emphasis on exposing multiple oppressions, has a strong appeal for feminists, but there is inevitable friction with marxist analyses of class, as the latter are seen as falsely imposing a "social totality, a phoney universalism,"[97] a hierarchy of analytic, and therefore political, importance.

The political pessimism about class is echoed in recent Anglo-American feminist critiques of working-class history which portray a *fin-de-siècle* scene, to my mind, worse than it actually is! Sonya Rose recently lamented that the "dominant paradigms in labour history continue to be reproduced as though neither women or gender were particularly relevant." Likewise, Laura Frader claims that the new labour historians (like the old) retained a "universalist, unitary notion of class," and still see "men as workers, women as wives, mothers and daughters."[98] Such sweeping claims are far more bleak than mine, unless I am going to plead "Canadian exceptionalism" to these trends.[99]

It is perhaps inevitable that each generation of scholars finds fault with the previous one, and urges the embrace of its own persuasions. Calling for more Foucault, less Marx, one British historian grumbles that the older generation is unfairly "patrolling the boundaries" of labour history as they cling to passé

[95]Elizabeth Fox-Genovese, "Literary Criticism and the Politics of the New Historicism," in H.A. Veeser, ed., *The New Historicism* (New York 1989), 87. For the second quote, see Alun Munslow, *Deconstructing History* (London 1997) 9,23.

[96]Jack Granatstein, *Who Killed Canadian History?* (Toronto 1998).

[97]Alex Callinicos, *Theories and Narratives: Reflections on the Philosophy of History* (Durham, North Carolina 1995), 120.

[98]Sonya Rose, "Gender and Labour History," 147. Laura Frader, "Dissent Over Discourse: Labor History, Gender and the Linguistic Turn," *History and Theory*, 34 (1995), 217, 225. For a more comprehensive critique, which is less absolute, see Ava Baron, "Introduction," in Ava Baron, ed., *Work Engendered: Toward a New History of American Labor* (Ithaca 1991).

[99]For example, Frader's argument in "Dissent over Discourse" that the "old" and "new" labour historians shared a common view of "the unity and inclusiveness of class membership" and a "teleological" focus on socialism simply does not apply to Canada. As a small academic community we benefit from engagement with international scholarship, but there remains the need to interrogate these works in relation to our own experience.

paradigms such as "human agency."[100] While similar claims are not so expansively made in Canada, they have been incrementally suggested. Recent critiques have understandably called for the inclusion within working-class history of topics previously ignored, such as sexuality, religion, consumerism, and popular culture.[101] At a deeper level, some are also challenging marxist perspectives, the apparent privileging of class over other identities, and urging new approaches embracing post-structuralism.

Almost echoing Bercuson's earlier critiques, one theorist argues that previous labour historians mechanistically "equated all working-class agency with resistance."[102] Early feminist research, other critics claim, "agreed that the common (if never universal) physical experience of being born 'female' constituted the possibility for shared gender identity across class, racial and ethnic divisions." This suggestion of implicit "essentialism" may itself oversimplify, since many earlier marxist authors, as we saw, stressed class differences among women.[103] While recognizing the need for openness to new topics and overall critique, we should also guard against the tendency to set up strawpersons, often of the Marxist variety,[104] rather than really engaging with past writings. The question is: do emerging critiques really advance the prospect of a feminist labour history, and if so, how? Certainly, invocations for more attention to gender, ethnicity and race as tools of analysis, and as conceptual constructions themselves, are central to their rhetoric. But what happens to gender, class and race in practice?

[100]John Vernon, "Whose Afraid of the Linguistic Turn?: the politics of social history and its discontents," *Social History*, 19 (1994), 81-98.

[101]Lynn Marks, "The Knights of Labour and the Salvation Army: Religion and Working-Class Culture in Ontario, 1882-90," *Labour/Le Travail*, 28 (1991), 89-128 and Steven Maynard, "Rough Work and Rugged Men: The Social Construction of Masculinity in Working-Class History," *Labour/Le Travail*, 23 (1989), 159-69," and "Queer Musings on Masculinity and History," *Labour/Le Travail*, 42 (1998), 183-97.

[102]Labour historians "assumed that the exercise of agency on the part of oppressed groups is always evidence of resistance." Mariana Valverde, "As if Subjects Existed: Analyzing Social Discourses," *Canadian Review of Sociology and Anthropology*, 18,2 (1991), 183. Note also David Bright's claim that previous historians "explained away" class divisions in *The Limits of Labour*.

[103]The authors do not cite any examples. See Kathryn McPherson, Cecilia Morgan and Nancy Forestell, eds., *Gendered Pasts: Historical Essays in Femininity and Masculinity in Canada* (Toronto 1998), 3.

[104]To cite one small example: in a book which offers an insightful and important reading of gender and 19th labour, Christina Burr states that previous historians did not consider cartoons and literature to constitute "real" sources. While recent theorizing has undoubtedly encouraged fuller explorations of representation, this is a curious characterization of historians previously labelled "culturalists!" Christina Burr, *Spreading the Light: Work and Labour Reform in Late-Nineteenth-Century Ontario* (Toronto 1999), 7. For other examples of the simplification of past work in women's and labour history see Nancy Christie and Michael Gavreau, *A Full Orbed Christianity*, 114, 116-7, 122.

Their pessimism with the failure of working-class history to take gender seriously, claim some feminist historians, led to their embrace of the linguistic turn. Claims that gender is now on the agenda of working-class history because of the confluence of "literary theory, feminism and post-structuralism" myopically overlook the earlier influence of socialist-feminist theory.[105] More fundamental is the question of whether we are simply replacing working-class history's failings concerning gender, with a linguistic approach that obscures class.[106] A few Canadian examples, notably Carolyn Strange's work, reveal the possibilities of using discourse analysis, informed by post-structuralist theory, in working-class history. Strange deftly uncovers the meanings assigned to working-class women's work and pleasure in the industrializing city by experts and reformers, though, as she admits, her method privileges discourses "from above" and discourages deducing conclusions about women's actual experiences. Other works explore the discursive meanings of working-class masculinity and femininity and the gendered meanings attached to social policy and the law.[107] Studies by Joy Parr, Shirley Tillotson, Mercedes Steedman, and Gillian Creese have also deconstructed the notion of skill, showing how both skill and occupation could be unstable categories, assigned gendered and racialized meanings, which might alter over time. Even if a rhetoric of deconstruction is employed, however, materialist conceptions of work and the economy are still in evidence, unlike the more radical, anti-materialist claims for deconstruction offered up by international scholars like Joan Scott.

Indeed, when such international writers suggest that the economy is simply "constructed as material"[108] (I'm sure the unemployed feel differently!), a more fundamental boundary is violated. It seems inescapable that core post-structuralist ideas will pull the rug out from many of the traditional concepts underpinning working-class history. By rejecting class as a taken-for-granted "foundational" category and deriding "grand theory," they question a basic starting point for past analyses. By belittling "liberals and Marxists'" so-called fascination with "just the

---

[105] Sonya Rose, "Gender and Labour History: The nineteenth-century legacy," *International Review of Social History*, 38 (1993), 160. Some authors also lament the fact that, save for Joan Scott (often simply equated with feminist post-structuralist history), linguistic explorations ignore women and gender.

[106] Class is being completely "occluded from the lexicon of radical terms on the basis of its pernicious [supposedly economistic] history." Stanley Aronowitz quoted in Alex Callinicos, *Theories and Narratives: Reflections on the Philosophy of History* (Durham, North Carolina 1995), 202.

[107] Burr, *Spreading the Light*; Steven Penfold, "Have You No Manhood in You?: Gender and Class in the Cape Breton Coal Towns, 1920-6," *Acadiensis*, 23, 2 (1994), 21-44; Margaret Hobbs, "Equality or Difference? Feminism and the Defence of Women Workers During the Great Depression," *Labour/Le Travail*, 32 (1993), 210-23.

[108] William Sewell, "Towards a Post-Materialist Rhetoric for Labor History," in L. Berlanstein, ed., *Rethinking Labor History: Essays on Discourse and Class Analysis* (Urbana 1993), 15-38.

facts," they question the intensive emphasis on empirical research integral to both the old *and* new labour histories.[109] By suggesting that everything — skill, wages, class, even the economy itself[110] — is socially constructed in the discursive realm, they reject some rudimentary tools of materialist analysis. And as Mariana Valverde argues, there *is* a certain logic carrying one from the (more generally accepted) deconstruction of notions of "male/female" skill to a complete deconstruction of class.[111] Whether post-structuralists see this as liberating, or Marxists as debilitating, I think both would agree the challenge to a feminist working-class history as it has been conceived is quite fundamental.

New social theory and pluralist politics have also challenged experience, the subject, and human agency, all earlier ingredients of working-class history. Questioning the "unity of the subject," as Mariana Valverde notes, is a *sine qua non* of post-structuralist history. The "fragmented, unstable subject is not regarded as a rational autonomous unit producing meanings and values," but rather is constituted by the ebb and flow of conflicting meanings generated by various discourses. Instead of "ready-made historical agents," "women" and "workers" are "signifers in the process of being defined by competing discourses." The inverted comma around woman and worker projects her/them into the realm of the "constructed" and "unknowable" rather than a real, grounded, physical being, capable of reflection, suffering, exploitation, and conscious revolt — all the latter notions being part of the "new," but now older, labour history. Indeed, they were integral to earlier women's history too — witness Susan Mann's declaration about the intent of feminist history to name and counter women's oppression.[112]

The post-structuralist subject thus stands in direct contrast to the Thompsonian subject whose consciousness emerged from the interplay of human agency with social, cultural and economic formations and ideologies. Indeed, resistance based on "conscious, reflective agency" and an understanding of "differential access to power," (not the automatic "reflex" resistance of Foucauldian theory) is largely absent from the post-structuralist equation. Even though subjectivity is unconscious, ambiguous and fragmented, some materialist feminists counter, it may still spawn discourses and practices calling for emancipation from the experiences of

[109]M. Valverde, "PostStructuralist Gender Historians: Are We Those Names?" *Labour/Le Travail*, 25 (1990), 227. We might consider the different interpretations of 'empiricism.' Valverde may be using it in a negative sense as pure positivism; however, some historians would use the word to denote the extensive use of research, the weighing of evidence and sources in creating a historical interpretation. The former denotes an ideology, an empiricism; the latter describes a research idiom, the empirical.

[110]William Sewell in Berlanstein, ed., *Rethinking Labor History*, 19-25.

[111]M. Valverde, "Deconstructive Marxism," *Labour/Le Travail*, 36 (1995), 331.

[112] See also the earlier statement that "changes happen in the minds of women." Elaine Silverman, "Writing Canadian Women's History: 1970-82," *Canadian Historical Review*, 63, 4 (1982), 533.

domination,[113] a claim rather close to that old Marxist maxim that "people make their own history though not in conditions of their own choosing."

Like ideas concerning human agency, the recovery of womens' and workers' experiences and voices was also central to the reconstructed labour and women's history of past decades. Yet, this is also questioned, in part by those employing a critical race analysis to show very effectively how white race privilege was too often built into homogeneous renditions of women's or workers' experience.[114] But a more fundamental challenge came from post-structuralist writers who see all such projects as unfeasible, for one can never separate the layers of meaning in order to uncover any "true" experience; rather, the latter is a linguistic process of meaning creation, not a recoverable reality. Portraits of experience, as Joy Parr argues, drawing partially on these ideas, are "rendered in the style of their time ... they were interpretations, reclamations of sensations which first had been organized, then claimed as experience."[115]

Such arguments have fostered new understandings of the power of language and narrative structure in our reconstructions of women's experience, reinforcing a healthy skepticism concerning our strategies of historical recovery. And attempts to de-centre the "unitary" subject have encouraged exploration of the many axes of identity, including sexual orientation, race, ethnicity, age, and culture shaping the working-class subject. The question is: how do the multiple identities fracturing the subject of postmodern history differ from the multiple identities characterizing Bercuson's construction of the working-class subject? He assumed experience did exist, but working-class consciousness and culture were not a part of it. Post structuralist-informed histories assume experience can't be located, and again, class and class consciousness are not in sight. Do they both, ultimately, come to a similar ideological resting point? Moreover, does the emphasis on the "*un*limited identities" of the subject lead us into a cul-de-sac of interpretative and political immobility, merely "hymning the virtues of schizophrenia?"[116]

The sense that class has been too "fundamental" and "privileged"[117] a category in previous research has also been forwarded by Canadian authors. Lynn Marks' foray into new and important topics — religion and leisure — is posited as a corrective to earlier Marxist works which she sees as over-emphasizing working-

---

[113]Linda Alcoff, "Feminist Politics and Foucault: The Limits to Collaboration," in Arleen Dallery, *et al.*, eds., *Crises in Continental Philosophy* (New York 1990), 74,76.

[114]Some African-American writers, however, still use the concept of experience, sometimes drawing on "standpoint" theory and critique post-structuralist thought for "decentring" the voices of the marginalized. Patricia Hill Collins, *Black Feminist Thought: knowledge, consciousness and the politics of empowerment* (Boston 1990); Barbara Christian, "The Race for Theory," *Feminist Studies*, 14, 1 (1988), 67-79.

[115]Joy Parr, "Gender History and Historical Practice," 364.

[116]Terry Eagleton, *Ideology*, (London 1991), 198.

[117]Lynn Marks, *Revivals and Roller Rinks: Religion, Leisure and Identity in Small-Town Ontario* (Toronto 1996), 7.

class resistance and ignoring, not only gender, but also the role of religion in working-class life. Better to start from the principle of multiple, shifting identities based on age, religion, culture, class, and gender, searching for the "integrated" picture, she argues, in concert with other post-structuralist critiques. Claiming that earlier Marxist interpretations saw fraternal orders as "bastions" of working-class consciousness, for example, she counters this with a characterization of them as "bastions of masculinity."[118] Instead of such polarities, perhaps a gender and race analysis of fraternal orders might have complimented earlier marxist works, which, though they stressed patterns of working-class solidarity also alluded to the cross class and accommodationist aspects of such orders.[119]

As Gail Brandt argued, aspects of postmodernism, including the emphasis on difference, culture and representation have struck a responsive chord with feminist historians.[120] But this is perhaps less clearly so for feminist *labour* historians in North America, whose responses have ranged widely, from enthusiasm to strong criticism. Indeed, confusion and contradiction may actually characterize current attempts to address these theoretical issues in relation to working-class history. While marxism is often dismissed as reductionist and economistic,[121] materialist suppositions still underpin much of the writing of labour history. While an under-lying political pessimism with class politics is apparent, historians are still genu-flecting to the trilogy of race, class and gender. While fundamental tensions exist between post-structuralism and materialism, we are still often borrowing some post-structuralist concepts, or searching for a pluralist accommodation of both.[122]

[118]Marks cites Palmer, *A Culture in Conflict* which does not use the term a "bastion" of working-class culture, nor does Gregory S. Kealey's work on the Orange Order, which is not cited. These earlier works explored somewhat different topics: the mobilization of the labour movement in large cities, not small towns.

[119]Palmer, *A Culture in Conflict*, 43.

[120]Gail C. Brandt, "Postmodern Patchwork: Some Recent Trends in the Writing of Women's History," *Canadian Historical Review*, 72,4 (1991), 441-70.

[121]Dismissing the "new" labour history as "mechanistic" marxism conflates diverse tradi-tions of materialism, and ignores the attempts of this work *to* de-centre "mechanistic" models by exploring agency, culture, language and the social. Neville Kirk, "History, language, ideas and postmodernism: a materialist view," in Keith Jenkins, ed., *The Postmodern History Reader*. It is revealing that Marxists are portrayed as "angry," and "dogmatic" but liberals less so. As feminists should we not be wary of caricatures in which radicals are denigrated in this way — something we have often encountered as well?

[122]I admit to limited "borrowing." See Joan Sangster, "Girls in Conflict with the Law." For an example of the second tendency, see Burr, *Spreading the Light*, 7. She notes she draws on Marks' "deconstructionist cultural-materialist" analysis. For the view that we have moved beyond the "polarized" debate, see Frader, "Dissent over Discourse"; Franca Iacovetta and Wendy Mitchinson, eds., "Introduction," *On the Case: Explorations in Social History* (Toronto 1998), 12, and for a critical view of efforts to eclipse very real theoretical tensions, see Bryan D. Palmer, "On the Case: A Roundtable Discussion," *Canadian Historical Review*, 81,2 (2000), 281-7.

Perhaps, easy accommodation, resting comfortably under one umbrella, is not possible.

Although they may pay more attention to culture or language, recent works have rarely fully embraced all the tenets of post-structuralist theory or abandoned the practice of "methodological empiricism."[123] A number of good studies continue to explore "age old" questions in labour history, such as the persisting sexual division of labour and feminized occupations, state regulation of women, the participation of women in socialist politics, and the creation of political consumer activism from the daily domestic labour of housewives.[124] New research on Native women's work draws on debates concerning colonialism, gender and race, and it is often scaffolded on frameworks of productive and reproductive relations.[125]

Often, we find ourselves wrestling with ongoing interpretive dilemmas, even if linguistic conventions have changed the tenor of our conversations. What was the relationship, we asked earlier, between the economic/social structures and ideologies framing the lives of women workers, and the ways women understood their world? How were dominant ideologies and relations of ruling negotiated or internalized? How could alternative ones develop? Yet, the puzzles of subjectivity are not completely different: how do various discourses shape subjectivity, how do contradictory impulses and ideas within subjectivity, of accommodation and resistance, of radicalism and religiosity, work themselves out? Neither is the problem of 'resistance' completely extinct, even if authors are more likely to explore its everyday subtle, veiled, and mundane manifestations, or the "subjugated knowledges" working against the grain of dominant discourses.

Nor have we yet jettisoned "experience." If we were to fundamentally destabilize the subject and reject the notions of experience, then some of the basic premises of works of the 1990s, like *Such Hard Working People*, or *No Burden to Carry*, would need reappraisal. Along with other intersections of ethnic and African-Canadian history, and very much like recent Native history, they take as their goal the recovery of the experiences and voices of marginalized ethnic and racialized working peoples, previously silenced by social, economic and cultural

[123]McLennan quoted in Keith Jenkins, "Introduction," *A Postmodern History Reader*, 10. He is referring to the extensive use of observation based on research, including archival, documentary and human sources, and the weighing and interpreting of such evidence.

[124]Steedman, *Angels of the Workplace*; McPherson, *Bedside Matters*; Linda Kealey, *Enlisting Women for the Cause*; Margaret Little, *No Car, No Radio, No Liquor Permit: The moral regulation of single mothers in Ontario, 1920-70* (Toronto 1998); Nancy Forestall, "The Miners Wife: Working-Class Femininity in a Masculine Context, 1920-50," in McPherson, C.Morgan, N. Forestall, eds., *Gendered Pasts: Historical Essays in Femininity and Masculinity in Canada* (Toronto 1999), 139-57; Julie Guard, "Women Worth Watching: Radical Housewives in Cold War Canada," in G. Kinsman, D. Buse, and M. Steedman, eds., *Whose National Security: Canadian State Surveillance and the Creation of Enemies* (Toronto).

[125]Alicia Muszynski, *Cheap Wage Labour*; John Lutz, "Gender and Work in Lekwammen Families, 1843-1970," in K. McPherson *et al.*, *Gendered Pasts*, 80-105.

relations of power. Though we are sometimes urged to deconstruct the identities of white male workers, do we similarly want to question the voices of ethnic, racialized women workers? Or, are some identities more "authentic" than others — a hierarchical view surely incompatible with post-structuralist tenets. I can't quite imagine (and hope I don't see) a review of Ruth Frager's *Sweatshop Strife*, for example, which suggests that the author's conclusions about the nature of Jewish garment workers' strong class and ethnic consciousness were misguided because (a) we have "deconstructed class," and (b) anyway, this "consciousness" is more a figment of Frager's meaning making than true experience.

But these are, ultimately, the logical ends of some current social theory, especially the incessant calls to deconstruct class and destabilize all group identities. The challenge for feminist and working-class historians may be to refrain from what one American critic sees as a liberal, pluralist multiculturalism — invoked in ritualized invocations of the value of "inclusion" and "difference" — as the end in itself, thus avoiding questions about the relationship of "difference" to class and economic inequality.[126] For Canadians, this is not a new issue, as they have long been aware, for example, that the state's interest in promoting multicultural history does not come without ideological baggage.[127]

Conclusion

In this paper, I have attempted to sort through the changing goals, suppositions, and political contexts framing the writing of Canadian women's labour history over the last thirty years. My aim was to ask whether the story of class formation has become thoroughly gendered, whether a feminist spirit has suffused the study of working-class experience, without ever disguising my own proclivity to favour a *rapprochement* of materialism and feminism, both in politics and scholarship. From the perspective of postmodernism, this review could be dismissed for assuming "its object of inquiry", surmising the importance of exploring class, rather than deconstructing it from the start, and I concede to writing from within, rather than rejecting these basic assumptions.

There is no doubt that, over a quarter century ago, nascent scholarship on the Canadian working class was limited in its horizons, concentrating initially on male-defined production and the public sphere, failing to make good on its initial promise to open up the totality of working-class life for historical reappraisal. However, prompted by a political climate of feminist challenge and socialist discussion in both society and in interdisciplinary scholarship, these limitations were immediately the focus of feminist revisionism. Both women's history and

[126]Russell Jacoby, *The End of Utopia: Politics and Culture in an Age of Apathy* (New York 1999), 29-67.
[127]Gregory S. Kealey, *Workers and Canadian History*, 147; Bruno Ramirez, "Les rapport entre les etudes ethniques et le multiculturalisme au Canada: évers de nouvelles perspectives," *International Journal of Canadian Studies*, 3 (1991), 170-9.

labour history, feminism and socialism, existed in tandem, sometimes in tension, sometimes in productive debate, sometimes in alliance. In fact, one could argue that, in both French and English Canada, gender, ethnicity and race revitalized the study of class, stretching out its boundaries, in terms of sources, themes and interpretative possibility.

By the 1990s, the professional, political, and theoretical context had fundamentally changed. Other topics, including culture, took centre stage for historians, and other movements of emancipation — such as gay rights or First Nations self determination — emerged, broadening our definitions of oppression and political activism. Nor do such shifts *necessarily* nullify the development of a more sophisticated class analysis in Canadian history, or a complementary concern with labour.[128] Also, feminist history is no longer positioned on the margins of academe; recognition of the importance of the "limited identities" — now very much including gender — in Canadian history is now standard fare.

However, the left's disintegration and the post-structuralist intellectual moment also altered the picture. With historical materialism in retreat, class relations and labour issues no longer command significant, sustained, and energetic attention. A more generalized radical pluralism in which class is not an objective reality, in which identities are fluctuating, unstable, indeterminate, and power always "de-centred," has had a destabilizing effect on feminist working-class history, for the latter has rested, implicitly, on materialist concepts concerning production and reproduction, social structures and the creation of social life, and of the importance of human activity in shaping subsistence and consciousness. Obviously, my sympathies lie with those historians who argue against a "replacement of class with language and culture as the central category of analysis....[and] divorcing the study of work entirely from any notion of an economy."[129]

Some would argue that the new historical skepticism will produce more introspective, open-ended, detached, "ironic"[130] ways of viewing the past, less likely to privilege class. Certainly, post-structuralist theory has offered useful critiques of the way in which historians themselves created a masculinist version of class. It has encouraged debates about the relationship of the discursive to the non-discursive, guarded us against the temptations of essentialism and, usefully unsettled any "innocent" notion that we can "grasp the scheme of things entire."[131]

Yet, as Marlene Shore points out, long before post-structuralism, historians skeptically interrogated the intellectual paradigms shaping the texts they produced,

[128]One exception indicating continuing academic interest in labour is the participation of some academics in the Workers Arts and Heritage Centre, Hamilton, Ontario.
[129]Richard Price, "The Historical Meanings of Work," *International Journal of Social History*, 34 (1989), 327-32.
[130]Mariana Valverde,"'Post Structuralist Gender Historians," 236. For a critique of the "ironic" gaze, see Alex Callinicos, *Theories and Narratives*, 208-10.
[131]Elizabeth Fox-Genovese, "Literary Criticism and the politics of the new historicism," 87.

and suggested knowledge was partial and partisan.[132] Moreover, skepticism is a doubled-edged sword which may also cut so deep it paralyses judgements about causality, priority, and political importance. It can also become a self-generating intellectual universe or "ideology", while denying that role. Both feminists and materialists alike have objected to the failure of some post-structuralist theories to allow the veracity of any "truth claims" — thus calling into question feminist and socialist emancipatory projects.[133]

Moreover, however difficult it is to create "hyphenated" political projects, linking feminism, socialism, and anti-racism, we can't leave out a crucial ingredient, without spoiling the whole mix. In part, the complaints lodged against class reflect basic political disinterest in such issues, but we are not simply bystanders to a political context: we are a part of it. We need to redouble our efforts to understand how class, race and gender differ over history, as well as how to put them together. They may all encompass "lived experiences"[134] of oppression but — even granting social constructionism — gender and race *appear* more visible markers of difference, take on different material and ideological forms, and may also have some potential to be coopted by liberal pluralism. In transnational theoretical debates, American feminists have rather ardently embraced French feminist theory of a postmodern bent, but perhaps Canadians should carve out an alternative project — drawing on our different political history — by exploring theory dedicated to redefining materialism, production, reproduction, and sexuality.[135]

Surely, as globalized capitalism and the deconstruction of the welfare state become more menacing forces, even a "totalizing logic" for working peoples, some of the traditional topics of labour history, including wage work, the sexual division of labour, consumer organizing, and socialist politics, should seem more, not less prescient. This is especially true for women, who have dramatically increased their participation in wage work since the 1960s, yet who face persisting, and new, barriers, alienations, and injustices in their work lives — as the opening example of garment workers indicates.

[132]Marlene Shore, "'Remember the Future': The *Canadian Historical Review* and the Discipline of History, 1920-1995," *Canadian Historical Review*, 76 (September 1995), 435-55. For a spirited polemic arguing that the "new" in much post-structuralist history is hardly "new" or "radical" and that the only difference is that "there is a self-conscious drive to make representation the only legitimate field of study," see Raphael Samuel, "Reading the Signs," *History Workshop Journal*, 32 (Autumn 1991), 92-102.

[133]Linda Alcoff, "Feminist Politics and Foucault," 70.

[134]Mark Leier, "W[h]ither Labour History: Regionalism, Class and the Writing of B.C. History," *B.C. Studies* 111 (1996), 61-75 and responses by Veronica Strong-Boag, Bryan Palmer, and Robert McDonald.

[135]On the American attraction to the former and neglect of French materialist-feminism, see Lisa Adkins and Diana Leonard, "Reconstructing French Feminism: Commodification, Materialism and Sex," in L. Adkins and D. Leonard, eds., *Sex in Question: French materialist feminism* (London 1996), 8.

Utopian visions, as social critics lament, are currently seen as misguided at best, sinister at worst; we embrace limited, partial integrations into, and accommodations to the social order, rather than imagining its demise. If the denigration of class and the derision of emancipatory projects has not permeated our efforts to create a feminist labour history, they do hang, like dense a fog of indifference and scepticism, over our present efforts. Without some political renewal, theoretical shifts, and new utopias, our project of creating a feminist working-class history may languish, and all that we will be left with are the complex accommodations of our negotiated postmodern, "post-feminist" age.

I want to thank Leah Vosko and anonymous reviewers for commenting on this paper, and the editors of Atlantis *for encouraging me to publish this longer version of my work.*

THE AMERICAN REVIEW ⬚⬚⬚ OF CANADIAN STUDIES

THE ASSOCIATION FOR CANADIAN STUDIES IN THE UNITED STATES

Published by the Association for Canadian Studies in the United States (ACSUS), *The American Review of Canadian Studies* seeks to examine Canada and the Canadian point of view from a decidedly American perspective. Its analysis—both interdisciplinary and disciplinary—strives to define Canada's arts, culture, economics, politics, history, and society from without, breaking away from the insularity of the Canadian academy, recognizing Canada's objective position in the world. Recent theme issues include: "The Arnold E. Davidson Festschrift" and "The Second Thomas O. Enders Issue on the State of the Canada-United States Relationship." Also published regularly are general issues featuring essays, review essays, and book reviews from a wide variety of disciplines.

DIRECT SUBMISSIONS AND EDITORIAL ENQUIRIES TO:

Robert Thacker, Editor

The American Review of Canadian Studies

Canadian Studies Program

St. Lawrence University
Canton, New York
13617

Phone:
(315) 229-5970

Fax:
(315) 229-5802

E-mail:
arcs@stlawu.edu

RECENT AND FORTHCOMING ESSAYS

"Searching Bluebeard's Chambers: Grimm, Gothic, and Bible Mysteries in Alice Munro's 'Love of a Good Woman'"

"Writing the Present in Nicole Brossard's *Baroque d'aube*"

"Continuity Strategies among Political Challengers: The Case of Social Credit"

"'An unprecedented influx': Nativism and Irish Famine Immigration to Canada"

For subscription and membership information, contact:

The Association for Canadian Studies in the United States

1317 F Street NW, Suite 920
Washington, DC 20004-1105

(202) 393-2580   Fax: (202) 393-2582

E-mail: info@acsus.org
http://www.acsus.org

"The History of Us": Social Science, History, and the Relations of Family in Canada

Cynthia Comacchio

JUST AS THE 20TH CENTURY gasped its last, Canada's purported national newspaper pledged an "unprecedented editorial commitment" to "get inside the institution that matters the most to Canadians: the bricks themselves, our children, our families." Judging by the stories emanating weekly from "real families" in Toronto, Calgary and Montréal, commitment to "the bricks" remains strong despite unremitting bleak prophecies about the family's decline. There is much concern, however, that their mortar is disintegrating. At the dawn of a new millennium, Canadians worry about such abiding issues as the decision to have children, their number and timing; finding decent, affordable shelter; whether both parents will work for wages and how child care will be managed [and paid for] if they do; how domestic labour will be apportioned; what single parents must do to get by; and — most pressing of all — how to master the wizardry that might reconcile the often-conflicting pressures of getting a living with those of family.[1]

These "family matters" strike certain transhistorical chords. If we have more options than did our forebears of a hundred or even fifty years ago, most of us still have to take into account the available material support before we can make the

---

[1]"Family Matters: A Year in the Life of the Canadian Family," *The Globe and Mail*, 11 September 1999. The criteria used to decide the representativeness of the families is not discussed; the title suggests there was no editorial compunction about the existence of "the Canadian family." The seer of the "end of history" also contends that "unstable families" contributed greatly to the discordances marking the 20th century; see F. Fukuyama, *The Great Disruption* (New York 1999). My title is owed to a quip by the inimitable E.P.Thompson; see "Happy Families: Review of Lawrence Stone, *The Family, Sex and Marriage in England, 1500-1800*," *New Society*, 8 September 1977, 499-501.

Cynthia Comacchio, "'The History of Us': Canadian Families and Socioeconomic Change," *Labour/Le Travail*, 46 (Fall 2000), 167-220.

major life decisions signified in family formation. Unromantic though these deliberations may be, they are fundamental.

For the vast majority throughout history, family relations have been intermeshed with the structures of work. The family has historically constituted the principal site of production. Even in the "advanced" western world, until as recently as a century ago, few could subsist outside some form of family setting. The welfare of most families, in its every sense, was the measure of its members' mutual assistance as constituted in labour, thus individual and collective contributions to the family economy. The labour of families is connected even more directly to capitalist development when we consider that the production of family farms allowed for the local surplus accumulation that, along with the importation of foreign capital, supported the transition to industry. Industrialization did not destroy this historic relationship of work and family, but gradually reconfigured it to accord with the new relations of production.

Nearly twenty years ago, in a path-breaking effort to unlock marxist theory to gender issues, sociologist Dorothy Smith conceptualized home and family as "integral parts of, and moments in, a mode of production." Family relations do not stand apart from, but are organized by and within capitalist economic and political relations, the most significant of which are class relations. By recognizing these relations to be mutually necessary and supportive, we:

can begin to see the social organization of class in a new way. We discover the family or forms of family work and living, as integral to the active process of constructing and reconstructing class relations, particularly as the dominant class responds to changes in the forms of property relations and changes in the organization of the capitalist enterprise and capitalist social relations.[2]

The working class, I would add, finds its own means and methods of adaptation through a domestic reorganization characterized by selectivity; that is to say, it accepts some bourgeois practices and standards of family life, rejects others, and creates still others that reflect the cultural heritage, community, and individual needs of individual families.

Smith, among others who have engaged in this integration of family into models of capitalist relations, effectively proposed a refinement of the 19th century views of Marx and Engels. Both were convinced of "the dissolution of family ties" that industry bred, while equally convinced that the survival of the working-class family meant the very survival of the working class. Marx never developed a comprehensive theory of the reproduction of labour power, all the while conceding its importance for any theory of capitalist production: "the maintenance and reproduction of the working class is, and must ever be, a necessary condition to the

[2]D. Smith, "Women, Class and Family," in V. Burstyn, D. Smith, eds., *Women, Class, Family and the State* (Toronto 1985), 6-7.

reproduction of capital."[3] The connection between work and family is critical to capitalist production, but equally important is the relationship between identity and family. Social identities are learned and internalized in the family setting, a process of interpellation crucial to the formation of self-identities: our families are where we are first introduced to, and absorb the meaning of, the differential status conferred by class, gender, race, and age. Families replicate, reproduce and perpetuate the interwoven relations of patriarchy and capitalism. Moreover, the family's often-contradictory internal relations are mirrored in the contradictions between the "earthly family" in its material basis and the "holy family" as it is configured in ideal terms, to borrow Marx's evocative imagery.[4]

If work has defined family for many, it has not defined it in the same way for all families, nor for all family members. For the bourgeoisie, production was gradually distanced from domestic life — though not as quickly and definitely as was initially postulated in theories about the "sundering" of work and home. Bourgeois family strategies became less a matter of subsistence, more a matter of the maintenance of certain living standards, "respectability," and children's prospects rather than their day-to-day contributions to the family economy. For the working class, the change was essentially a difference in source of subsistence rather than a departure from traditional interdependence, as the family economy became a family wage economy. In both instances, the roles of women and children were altered not so much in substance as in conceptualization. Much work, both productive and reproductive, and in varying degrees depending upon the family's material circumstances, remained in the home which was women's domain; children also continued to work in different ways, not necessarily "waged" in the customary sense. Through the course of the 20th century, however, work and family became increasingly disassociated in the public imagination as in state policy. Work was redefined as the wage labour of men functioning as primary breadwinners. This remaking of the history of the family — more a recasting, looking too selectively backwards — has had repercussions that continue to affect us as historians and as 21st-century citizens. If we obscure and confuse the historic relations of work and family, we not only limit our understanding of much of our socioeconomic development since colonial times, we all too often allow the recurrent "family values" debates of our own times to hinge on the ahistoric concept of "the family" and the scapegoat figure of the "working mother."

Families, then, pose as much a "problem" for historians as for social commentators. It is evident that "the family" is not only integral to a larger process, but is itself continually in process, undergoing palingenesis in a series of successive rebirths and regenerations. While conceding that "the family" is imaginary, and that actual families are eminently mutable, family historians have identified the

[3]F. Engels, *The Condition of the Working Class in England* (1845; Stanford, Ca. 1968), 145, 160-1, 225; K. Marx, *Capital* (Moscow 1971), 1, 460.
[4]Marx, in Marx, Engels, *Collected Works* (New York 1975), 5, 4.

major influences at work on domestic relations over the past two centuries: economic changes, particularly the shift from domestic to factory production; demographic changes sparked by the decline in family size; changes in the socio-economic status of women; and the changing relations between the private sphere, represented by "the family," and the public interest increasingly represented by the state.[5] Structural and familial change are so entwined, however, that it is difficult to trace causation, to establish which initiates and which responds in any given moment.

What follows is a selective overview of the Canadian historiography on family. The roots of family history not only extend backwards much further than the "new social history" born of the tumultuous 1960s; they are buried deep in several other disciplines, most notably sociology, anthropology, and demography, whose practitioners were concerned as much with the historical process of family change as with the state of families contemporary to their times. I begin in pre-history, so to speak, to consider how pioneering social scientists, by grappling with the family's relationship to structural change, historicized early 20th century family studies and offered up many of the questions, concepts, theories, and methods that continue to inform scholarship on families in the past. Turning to the body of historical publications that followed in the wake of, and were often inspired by, the "new social history," I highlight the monograph studies that, in my judgement, served as signposts in the field's development, especially for what they have revealed about the critical nexus of family, work and class. The historiography mirrors the family's history: "family" consists of so many intricately plaited strands that separating them out is frustrating and often futile. I have attempted to classify this material both topically and chronologically within broad categories, but the boundaries blur so that most of these works could fit as comfortably in several others. Many of them, in fact, will be recognized as important contributions to fields such as labour, ethnic, women's, or gender history rather than as works of family history *per se*. Like much of family life, family history is a messy prospect; family reaches into virtually every corner of human existence.

I. *Foundations: The Social Sciences and the Archaeology of Families*

To locate public interest in families in the just-past century belies a certain inadequacy of historical memory. From the beginnings of European attention to the "New World," families were crucial to plans for cultural and economic supremacy formulated in imperial centres of power. The *Jesuit Relations* (1632 - 1673) of New France transcribed the earliest-known commentaries on family life. While the great

[5]In a recent attempt to make sense of changes/continuities in Canadian family history, I adopted an interpretive framework based on the idea of punctuated equilibrium, a biological concept employed figuratively to suggest how families persist through sharp points of disruption that are eventually met by adaptation and restabilization: C.R. Comacchio, *The Infinite Bonds of Family: Domesticity in Canada, 1850-1940* (Toronto 1999), 3-11; 149-56.

fur-trading enterprises that dominated the 18th century comprised "companies of [male] adventurers," their registers expose the domestic arrangements underpinning vast networks of commerce. By the second half of the 19th century, a consciously "scientific" approach to families was already making its way to British North America under the auspices of a developing European social science, influenced particularly by the ideas of Frédéric LePlay (1806-82).[6]

For LePlay, the family was not only the foundation but the determining element of all social organization. While conducting the first empirical investigations of European working-class and peasant families, he developed a typology in which a series of family forms each corresponded to a particular stage of social development: the patriarchal family, the stem family, and what came to be known as the "nuclear" family, described in his terms as "individualist" or "particularist." In the LePlayian hierarchy, the stem family (famille-souche) was correlated to the highest degree of social stability. A modification of the extended patriarchal family, it was characterized by its inheritance pattern, in which one offspring, usually the youngest son, continued to live with the family until he inherited the estate.

With the blessing of LePlay's Société d'Economie Sociale de Paris, the Baron Charles Gauldrée-Boilleau, French consul at Québec, inaugurated the study of Canadian families in 1861. At the farm of Isidore Gauthier in the parish of Saint-Irenée on the Lower St. Lawrence, the Baron applied LePlay's methods of observation and classification to conclude that the hard-working nine-member Gauthier household exemplified the stem family. The Consul's experiment was followed by a more methodical undertaking by Léon Gérin (1863-1951) in 1898. The first Canadian-born social scientist, Gérin's brief sojourn at LePlay's Ecole de Science Sociale in Paris shaped his life's direction as well as that of early Canadian sociology. In the parish of Saint-Justin, he confirmed Gauldrée-Boilleau's findings about the economic basis of family relations and the signal importance of the stem family within that matrix. He had to concede, nonetheless, that "l'analogie est loin d'être parfaite:" geography and history had made Quebec's rural families more nuclear in structure, less territorially-stable, less communal, than the French peasant families against which they were measured.[7]

[6]E.M. Nett, Canadian Families: Past and Present (Toronto 1993), 5-10; see S.R. Mealing, ed., The Jesuit Relations and Allied Documents: A Selection (Ottawa 1990); and the seminal works by S. Van Kirk, Many Tender Ties: Women in Fur-Trade Society in Western Canada, 1670-1870 (Winnipeg 1980), and J. Brown, Strangers in Blood: Fur Trade Company Families in Indian Country (Vancouver 1980). On LePlay's ideas, see R. L. Howard, A Social History of American Family Sociology, 1865-1940 (Westport, Conn. 1981), 75-7.
[7]Léon Gérin, "L'habitant de Saint-Justin," in Gérin, Le Type économique et social des canadiens: milieux agricoles de tradition française (Montréal 1937), 17-18, 20-22, 86, 174. This study was originally published in the Proceedings of the Royal Society of Canada (1899). The Baron's conclusions can be found in C. Gauldrée-Boilleau, "Paysans de Saint-Irenée de Charlevoix en 1861 et 1862," in P. Savard, ed., Paysans et ouvriers québécois d'autrefois (Québec 1968). Gérin spent six months in Paris, late 1885 to spring 1886, and

When Gérin actually retraced the Baron's path to the Gauthier doorstep in 1920, some sixty years after the original visit, he was dismayed to find the family gone, the land sold, the house taken down.[8] Intrigued by the wider sociohistoric implications of this family's story, he followed its tracks to the Saguenay valley, where, a mere five or six years after the Baron's visit, "le fameux centre traditionnel" of the Gauthier family of Saint-Irenée had transplanted itself — in the manner of so many others — to pursue better economic prospects. In the new setting as before, traditional class-based habits of solidarity, manifested in shared labour, economic self-sufficiency, and mutual dependence, remained fundamental to the Gauthier family's security.

Committed to his view that the stem family constituted "l'axe directeur, le pivot central, le centre de gravité" of Québec's socioeconomic life, Gérin was perturbed by the "complications sociales" he saw unfolding around him. Studying rural families on the south bank of the St. Lawrence as they coped with an industrializing environment, he found mixed results: some had benefited from the economic changes, adapting to the new conditions "dans l'ordre materiel et dans l'ordre moral," thus able to sustain themselves as families. Others were losing their self-sufficiency, and, unable to withstand "l'attraction puissante du grand atelier," were in danger of "degenerating." He surmised — regretfully — that the new order appeared to favour families of the "particularist" or nuclear form, in which individual initiative was valued more than the collective, familial good. Those that failed to make this transition were shaken, uprooted, and sliding into instability.[9]

Gérin's observations were echoed in contemporary studies of urban neighbourhoods, where industry was taking a visible toll on working-class families. In these communities, family study imitated some social science techniques — observation, interview, the gathering of quantitative data — following upon the famous Booth and Rowntree surveys of London's slums. But Canadian investigators were also inspired by the muckraking journalism of American Progressives. Montréal businessman, reformer and politician Herbert Brown Ames published his famous survey of the impoverished working-class families of west-end Montréal first in the *Montreal Star*, and then in a book, *The City Below the Hill* (1897), whose title signified the world of the urban underclass both literally and figuratively. Similar explorations by various reform-minded citizens' groups drew attention to urban

---

attended lectures by the LePlayian social scientists, the Abbé Henri de Tourville and Edmond Demolins. The latter's interest in rural families, and his active encouragement that Gérin undertake a Canadian study, motivated Gérin's work. See J.C. Falardeau, "Notes Biographiques," in Falardeau, P. Garigue, eds., *Léon Gérin et l'habitant de Saint-Justin* (Montréal 1968).

[8]Gérin, "L' habitant," 17.

[9]Gérin, "L'émigrant déraciné, en bordure à la zone vallonneuse du sud", in Gérin, *Le type économique et social*, 155, 183; originally published as "Deux familles rurales de la rive sud du Saint-Laurent: les débuts de la complication sociale dans un milieu canadien-français," *Proceedings of the Royal Society of Canada* (1908).

pathologies as a clarion call for state intervention.[10] By the interwar years, the confluence of a rising academic social science and public preoccupation with a modernity both enticing and terrifying, saw social scientists adopt a taxonomy of "social problems" in which families served as barometers to gauge the nature of structural change, its impact on the collectivity, and what was in store for the future. The state also became increasingly involved in family-watching, establishing the Canadian Council on Child and Family Welfare (later the National Welfare Council) in 1920 to act as a clearing-house for family study and related policy initiatives. The latter were primarily directed at parents, especially maternal, education in the interests of healthier, happier families for a more productive, "efficient" modern Canada.[11]

It was at this moment that Canadian sociology took on a more definite professional form, though much of the leadership would come from the United States. At the University of Chicago, Robert Parks and Ernest Burgess were concentrating on the interaction and adjustment of various institutions in the context of modernization. Influenced by LePlay's ideas, they devised a dynamic, historicized notion of family as process, positing a dialectic between family and society that allowed for a range of stable family types, each relating in different ways to the larger society. The local culture constituted a specific "ecology" which encouraged the success of certain family types while making others obsolete. Accordingly, as had Gérin, they found the isolated nuclear family best-suited to industrial urban settings that demanded continual adaptation.[12]

The interactionist approach, as Marlene Shore has indicated, was imported to Canada by the Chicago-trained Carl Addington Dawson, who was instrumental in establishing sociology at McGill University. With Warner Gettys, Dawson pro-

[10]Herbert Brown Ames, *The City Below the Hill: A Sociological Study of a Portion of the City of Montreal, Canada* (Montréal 1887; reprinted, Toronto 1972); see T. Copp's classic *The Anatomy of Poverty: The Condition of the Working Class in Montreal, 1897-1929* (Toronto 1974) on the Ames survey, especially 15-29. C. Strange, *Toronto's Girl Problem: The Perils and Pleasures of the City, 1880-1930* (Toronto 1995), 106-10, discusses the role of the city's Social Survey Commission and its 1915 report. See also S. Burke, *Seeking the Highest Good: Social Service and Gender at the University of Toronto, 1888-1937* (Toronto 1997) on the role of the settlement houses in social surveys.

[11]I discuss the Council's role in Comacchio, *Nations Are Built of Babies: Saving Ontario's Mothers and Children* (Montréal/Kingston 1993); also *The Infinite Bonds*, 90, 96-7, 120, 139.

[12]Parks and Burgess's *Introduction to the Science of Sociology* was first published in 1921. The American Sociological Society, which included Canadian social scientists, established a section on family sociology in 1924; see Howard, *A Social History of American Family Sociology*, xi, 65-8. On early Canadian sociology, see R. J. Brym, with B. Fox, *From Culture to Power: The Sociology of English Canada* (Toronto 1989), 15-18; and M. Shore, *The Science of Social Redemption: McGill, the Chicago School, and the Origins of Social Research in Canada* (Toronto 1987).

duced a widely-used textbook, *An Introduction to Sociology* (1929), which classified the family as a "crescive institution." As such, its form and function correspond
to historic conditions, so that "any fundamental changes going on in the latter are
reflected in the family units." Also like their Chicago mentors, Dawson and Gettys
inventoried modernization's harmful effects, yet concluded optimistically that the
family was exhibiting "remarkable tenacity," holding its own by means of "modifications and readjustments to a changing social order."[13]

Established during the Depression to examine the relations of industry and
community, McGill's Social Science Research Project could not overlook the place
of family within this complex of interactions. As Gérin's studies had intimated, its
participants' immediate community was the perfect laboratory for testing the
modernization hypothesis. Produced by the Chicago-trained Everett C. Hughes, the
first English language analysis of the Québec situation stressed how the "rural folk
society" of the town he named "Cantonville" was disrupted by industrial capitalism.
In his ominously-titled *French Canada in Transition*, Hughes reiterated the Baron's
findings of nearly a century before — that rural society was established on the
relationship of family and land — but he regarded this relationship as a "core
vulnerability" rather than the foundation of community stability.[14] Meanwhile, in
an ethnographic study of the agricultural community of Saint Denis de Kam-
ouraska, Hughes' student surpassed him in highlighting Quebec's "folk society"
and its "rural lifeways". Searching out "the factors responsible for culture change
in the direction of urbanization and anglicization," Horace Miner concluded that
families behaved "as units in all matters," their internal synchrony essential to their
own material survival and to a local economy based on "the family system ... which
was brought over from France in the 17th century and has remained unchanged."[15]
Mentor and student alike overplayed the precipitous nature of modernization,
neglecting to consider that the Quebec countryside had been drawn into industry's
orbit, gradually but inexorably, over the course of a half-century — that, in fact,
Gérin's preliminary visit to Saint-Justin in 1898 had given him some cause to worry
about the changes already materializing. When they paid their respective visits,

[13]Shore, *The Science of Social Redemption*, xvi, 118; C.A. Dawson, W. Gettys, *An Introduction to Sociology* (New York 1929), 61, 77-9. Gettys was Professor of Sociology at the
University of Texas. Honours programs in sociology were established at McGill in 1926
and at the University of Toronto in 1932.

[14]Hughes began the study, with the assistance of his Canadian-born, Chicago-trained wife
Helen MacGill, before leaving McGill for Chicago in 1938; see E.C. Hughes, *French
Canada in Transition* (Chicago 1943), 8-9. Shore, *Science*, 270, notes that LePlay's theories
about family "found expression" in Hughes' work because of their influence on his mentor
Park. Hughes himself acknowledges his debt to Gérin in Ch. 2, "The Rural Society," *French
Canada in Transition*. Shore, 227-30, discusses some of the studies undertaken by McGill
students under the aegis of the Social Science Research Project.

[15]H. Miner, *St. Denis, A French Canadian Parish* (Chicago 1939), ix, 63-70. Miner was in
St. Denis from July 1936 to June 1937.

their subject communities had already moved well away from being isolated, family-based, self-sufficient peasant enclaves.

By World War II, the francophone social sciences were finding new energy, much of it directed to the study of Québec families and their place in the modern socioeconomic order. It was on the very basis of their "mistaken historical judgement" that Université de Montréal sociologist Philippe Garigue disputed the findings of Hughes and Miner, among others, both anglophone and francophone, who supported "folk society" theories about "traditional" Quebec families. Garigue maintained that such theories derived from a "conscious or unconscious" exaggeration of the French origin of Québec institutions. Few French institutions were exported directly to New France; even those so transferred were greatly modified by their new environment. The "uniquely French-Canadian" family, he asserted, actually resembled that of New England more than that of France: "il est donc possible de dire que la famille canadienne-française est nord-américaine." Folk society proponents ignored the "cultural homogeneity" that extenuated urban-rural differences in families. More important, they assumed that change resulted directly from "Anglo-Saxon" importations, thereby dismissing the "inherent dynamism" of French-Canadian culture.[16] Garigue's own landmark analysis, begun in 1953 and published nearly a decade later, stressed the historic identification of religious values of duty and sacrifice with familial values that sustained family-oriented, rather than sentimental and individualist, ideas about love and marriage. This relatively stable value system had endured despite structural changes and the family's functional adaptations, facilitating cultural transmission across generations and ensuring the survival of French Canada.[17]

With our privileged hindsight, we can see the irony in Garigue's conclusions. Even as his findings were coming to light in publication, many of those traditional values were being challenged as Québec entered its Quiet Revolution amidst a larger sociocultural revolution that would once again shake the equilibrium of

[16]P. Garigue, *La vie familiale des canadiens français* (Montréal 1962), 19-26; see also Garigue, "The French Canadian Family," in M. Wade, ed., *Canadian Dualism* (Toronto 1960), 181-200. Garique argued that francophone social scientists were skewing their findings on urban families by looking too hard for "une difference majeure" between these and rural families, as in the work of M. Lamontagne, J.C. Falardeau," The Life Cycle of French Canadian Urban Families," *Canadian Journal of Economics and Political Science,* 13, 2 (May 1947), 233-470. During the 1940s, Father Georges-Henri Lévesque was a leading force in establishing a secularized sociology at Laval University; see D. Whyte, "Sociology and the Nationalist Challenge in Canada," *Journal of Canadian Studies,* 19, 4 (1984-85),115-28. Shore, *Science,* 270, indicates that E.C. Hughes was a tremendous influence on Lévesque.

[17]Garigue, *La vie familiale* , 12, 24, 91-2; see also J.C. Falardeau, "The Changing Social Structures," in Falardeau, ed., *Essais sur le Québec contemporain* (Québec 1953), 104, 120.

modern families throughout the western world.[18] As in other moments of social turbulence, fears about "family crisis" inspired the need, or at least a public perception of the need, for concerted research on family life. The result was the first federal-government sponsored Canadian Conference on the Family, leading to the 1965 creation of the Vanier Institute of the Family, the nation's central agency for family research. By the 1960s as well, the functionalist paradigm steadily advanced by Chicago's Talcott Parsons since the 1940s was firmly in place as the cornerstone of modern family sociology, affirming the LePlayian heritage that made the family the primary element of social order, and reinforcing structural explanations for its historic changes. Not surprisingly, Frederick Elkin's *The Family in Canada*, the first "state of the art" survey of Canadian family sociology, followed the prevalent structural-functionalist line. Elkin reassured Canadians that "the family does not disappear, rather it changes and adapts and develops new patterns," all the while maintaining crucial socializing functions for its members. He also observed that the country's distinctive geography and history, class, religious, ethnic, occupational "and other groupings" made it "much too heterogeneous" to have "one or ten or twenty distinctive family types."[19] For all Elkin's seeming sensitivity to diversity, functionalist sociology encouraged understandings of families, past and present, as socioeconomic entities acting in common, united in uncontested — and uncontestable — familial objectives. The model paid scant attention to the differential effects of gender, age, class, geography, and so on, and even less to any family form other than the one decreed to represent the modern ideal: the self-enclosed male-breadwinner nuclear family. Only recently challenged for its assumptions of universality and its normative premises, it left a lasting imprint on public discourses about family, on social work practices and government policies, some remnants of which persist even as the 21st century commences.

[18]Other sociological inquiries of the time reveal foreboding about the acclaimed 1950s nuclear family despite its iconographic status; for example, J. Seeley, A. Sim, E. Loosley, *Crestwood Heights* (Toronto 1956), sparked a flurry of media and public attention. Examining a well-to-do Forest Hills neighbourhood in Toronto, its authors argued that affluence was making upward mobility a new pressure for families, and that materialism appeared to be overriding all "traditional" values. Although their sample was hardly representative, the study cast a dark light on postwar urban/suburban families and their inward-looking detachment from the wider community, both supporting the modernization thesis and challenging the theory of familial malleability. On the study, see V. Strong-Boag, "Their Side of the Story: Women's Voices from Ontario Suburbs," in J. Parr, ed., *A Diversity of Women: Ontario, 1945-80* (Toronto 1996), 42-3.
[19]F. Elkin, *The Family in Canada* (Ottawa 1964), 8, 31-2. Elkin, a University of Montréal sociologist, dismissed many of the studies on French-Canadian families as "moralistic ... commentaries on history," but his own views that "a pervasive familism" sustained the links between "survival, the family and the rural world" differed little from those of Hughes and Miner. On Parsons' influence, see D.H.J. Morgan, *Social Theory and the Family* (London 1975).

Although it preceded the initial stirrings of "the new social history" in Canada by some thirty years, it is tempting to identify an interdisciplinary bridge of sorts between Canadian sociology and social history in Samuel D. Clark's 1942 monograph, *The Social Development of Canada*. Infused with Innisian staples theory, Clark's synthesis of historical writing on Canadian society focused on the interplay of frontier development and social formation. He found that the age and gender composition of frontier communities, which favoured single young men, greatly affected social stability. Because of their dependence on the family unit, groups historically responsible for regulation and welfare either failed to become established or could not sustain themselves in its absence. As a result, many of the "normal controls of society" were also missing or ineffectual, as were the family mores and the religious and communal institutions traditionally upheld by the efforts of women — along with "most of the niceties and refinements of social relationships depending upon companionship within the family group."[20] Familial stability was itself contingent upon the specific frontier environment and the nature of production. Since timber production was closely tied to agriculture, timber communities saw the most stable family/social organization. Male-dominant mining communities, located within access of urban centres and all their purchaseable depravities, contained the least stable families. More emphatically than that of the family sociologists with their universalized modernization schema, Clark's work drew out the links between family, class, and the nature of production in specific historic and geographic settings. He also implicitly connected women with families, and both with stabilizing or "civilizing" trends.

Clark's provocative notions were not taken up with any unseemly haste by his colleagues in history. While Canadian historians of the time ascribed much importance to familial networks as key sources of colonial governance, trade and economic development, and were tremendously interested in settlement and nation-building, families did not signify in their work. Their scholarly objectives could not help but reflect prevailing notions about the subject hierarchy that historians should rightfully pursue. But it does seem curious that so little was made of the familial when so much pointed to it. In the classic works of Innis, Creighton, and Lower, there are no families knitting together the crucial Native-European trading networks; no families clearing land, homesteading, populating and reproducing imperial values in frontier territory; no families using family capital to invest in and extend the commercial empire of the St. Lawrence. It is as though "families are

[20]S.D. Clark, *The Social Development of Canada* (Toronto 1942), 1-5, 8-10. Clark completed his Master's degree at McGill in 1935, but found the ecological approach unappealing; see Shore, *Science*, 180; on Clark, see C. Berger, *The Writing of Canadian History: Aspects of English Canadian Historical Writing, 1900-1970* (Toronto 1976), 163; H.H. Hiller, *S.D. Clark and the Development of Canadian Sociology* (Toronto 1982).

everywhere but families are nowhere," an "absent presence" that is a powerful motive force despite its seeming invisibility.[21]

In 1958, a harbinger of sorts appeared in the form of Arthur Lower's *Canadians in the Making: A Social History of Canada*, proclaimed by its publishers to be "the first book of its kind in Canada" and "a landmark in Canada's national growth." The author himself declared the book "experimental, and, as far as I know, a pioneering effort."[22] Lower's political framework and "great man" narrative must have comforted those apprehensive about any radical reconfiguration of the field that this "experiment" might augur. Yet it *is* "pioneering," in that he attempted to chronicle, insofar as the extant literature allowed, some of the sociocultural activity that went on within, around, at times even beneath history's exalted echelons. He even touched lightly on gender and family relations, arriving at interpretations necessarily coloured by the ideas and values of his own time. Conceding that "white blood must have begun to pass into the wigwams from the first," he contended that "this does not argue a return current; interbreeding was confined to the Indian mother's side," except for those (apparently) few white men who were "anchored by an Indian wife." (11) He proffers the usual stereotypes about "sturdy yeomen" with large families, French-Canadian habitants with even larger families, poor-but-ambitious "immigrant stocks" with the largest families of all, and a few "local family compacts" boasting remarkable patriarchs and their equally-remarkable scions. Women take the form of "eternal Eves" or their mirror opposites, the "tractable daughters and obedient wives" who qualified to be "the flower of Canadian womanhood." The historian's personal longing is palpable in his depiction of a Victorian tableau of "dignity and gravity," an imagined 19th century ritual in which "every respectable citizen walked to church on Sunday morning in plug hat and cut-away coat, followed by his numerous family, and decorously returned to eat his Sunday dinner of roast beef." (321) Here was the high point of a social harmony embodied in the mythic family, well-mannered, well-dressed and well-fed, captained by the middle-class, white, probably Protestant, likely urban *pater-familias*. Lower did not question the universality of this family experience, nor did

[21]For example, H.A. Innis, *The Fur Trade in Canada* (New Haven 1930, 2nd edition Toronto 1956), 66-7, cites a memorandum, November 1681, M. Du Chesneau, "Irregular Trade in Canada," which opens with "The King, having been informed that all the families in Canada were engaged with the coureurs de bois ...," but there is nothing about this relationship in his classic study; in his conclusion, 392, he notes without comment that "the existence of small and isolated sections of French half-breeds throughout Canada is another interesting survival of this contact." Even the innovative work of H. Clare Pentland, *Labour and Capital in Canada, 1650-1860* (Toronto 1981) says nothing about the role of families in capital accumulation and industrial production. On families as an "absent presence," see L. Davidoff, M. Doolittle, J. Fink, K. Holden, *The Family Story: Blood, Contract and Intimacy, 1830-1960* (London 1999), 52-3.
[22]A. Lower, *Canadians in the Making: A Social History of Canada* (Toronto 1958), xv. The publishers' comments were on the original cover jacket.

he probe the roots of its patriarch's authority in the historic relations of class, gender, race and family. We can only assume that he believed it to represent the rightful order of things, the family to live by, if not with.

II. Transitions: From Family Sociology to the History of Families

i. Demography and Family Reconstitution: Accounting for Families

Not long after Lower's experiment, a fresh wave of scholarly interest in ordinary lives brought about a self-consciously "new social history" that made class both central subject and means of analysis. In recovering the experiences of common people, those dedicated to emerging sub-fields of working-class, women's, ethnic, and Black history invariably hit upon the bedrock of family, so imbricated are all other social relations in those of domesticity. Initially, the surest way across the threshold of private homes appeared to be quantitative. The first generation of family historians took advantage of the methodological groundwork already put in place by social scientists, assisted by the timely technology embodied in the first generation of computers, to develop "cliometrics."[23]

   The big questions of early family history thus tended to be those that lent themselves to numerical answers, and were posed with a view to understanding the impact of structural change — specifically industrialization — on families. Historians examined such quantifiable matters as residence, household size, organizational structure, developmental cycles, inheritance systems, and migration. Necessarily community-based, these studies were detailed collective biographies of a manageable number of families inhabiting a shared, designated geographic space. Where data were available for more than one such "snapshot", it was possible to conduct longitudinal studies to trace the motion — or lack of motion — of a number of families over a certain period. The data's own limitations meant that time and space were fairly circumscribed, as were any generalizations that could be made about "the family."[24]

[23]Most demographic studies of the time were not focused specifically on the family, but on the population *en masse*. Prominent among Canadian demographers were Nathan Keyfitz, who studied population trends and birth rates, and Jacques Henripin, who produced important historical studies on the patterns of population growth and fertility in Québec and demographic variations in English and French Canada; see J. Henripin, "From Acceptance of Nature to Control: the Demography of the French Canadians Since the Seventeenth Century," *Canadian Journal of Economics and Political Science*, 23 (February 1957), 10-19; Henripin, *La population canadienne au début du xviiie siècle; Nuptialité-fecondité-mortalité infantile* (Paris 1954), and *Trends and Factors of Fertility in Canada* (Ottawa 1972). See also N. Keyfitz, "Some Demographic Aspects of French-English Relations in Canada", in M. Wade, ed., *Canadian Dualism*, 66-95.

[24]In England, the Cambridge Group for the History of Population and Social Structure, established in 1964 under the direction of Peter Laslett, used these tools to demonstrate that "the great family of Western nostalgia" — the three-generation household — had never

In Canada, this new wave of historical demography was exemplified by Louise Dechêne's *Habitants et marchands de Montréal au XVIIe siècle* (1974). Although Dechêne's specific purpose was to examine the trade relations girding the colonial economy, her careful reading of notarial records revealed that these economic ties were often ties of family. The two institutions "closest to the people" were those of family and parish, twin pillars of the colony's social structure. The nuclear family structure predominated, and the availability of land made partible inheritance common practice. As Gérin had observed in the late 19th century, it was not so much land that bound family members as a reciprocity characterized by a generationally defined sense of duty. Also significant was public acknowledgement of the family's importance as the colony's "only effective and truly compelling instrument of social control."[25] Dechêne's masterful study, and subsequent Québec-based population analyses, corrected earlier LePlayian views respecting transplanted French peasant families by establishing what was distinctly North American about their domestic arrangements, all the while confirming the centrality of the family as a unit of production.

Beginning where Dechêne's story closed, and in many ways a complementary study, Allan Greer's reconstitution of the socioeconomic history of three parishes [Sorel, St Ours, St Denis] in the Lower Richelieu Valley from the mid-18th to the mid-19th centuries (1985) also focused on the lives of the settler-peasants or habitants. Close examination of similar notarial and parish records supports Greer's contention that Quebec rural society was comprised of feudal social relations upheld, and in turn upholding, pre-capitalist values. In the first two chapters, which treat the peasant household and family reproduction, he draws out clues from estate inventories to compensate for the absence of personal papers, diaries and letters.

constituted more than a tiny minority in Western Europe since the 16th century, and that the nuclear or conjugal unit had actually preceded industrialization. The early 1970s marked the publication of the immensely influential *Household and Family in Past Times*, edited by Laslett and R. Wall (Cambridge, England 1972), and T.K. Rabb, R.I. Rotberg, eds., *The Family in History: Interdisciplinary Essays.* (New York 1973). The flagship *Journal of Family History* began publication in 1976.

[25]L. Dechêne, *Habitants et marchands de Montréal au XVIIe siècle* (Paris 1974); translated by L. Vardi as *Habitants and Merchants in 17th Century Montreal* (Montréal/Kingston 1992). Dechêne notes, 237, that Gérin had "discovered in the Quebec countryside the stem family so dear to his teachers in France." As discussed, Gérin may have been convinced that this was the ideal, but he was not convinced about its predominance, having found three family types in the Maskinonge district that he studied; see Gérin, "L'habitant de Saint Justin," 215; also Garigue, *La vie familiale*, 24. The abundance of parish records has seen quantitative history flourish in Québec: see also H. Charbonneau, A. Guillemette, J. Legare, B. Desjardins, Y. Landry, F. Nault, *Naissance d'une population: les français établis au Canada au xviie siècle* (Montréal 1987). See I. Caccia, L.Y. Dillon, "A Current Bibliography on the History of Canadian Population and Historical Demography in Canada, 1994-98," *Histoire sociale/Social History*, 32 (Fall 1999), 73-85.

He is thus able to piece together a remarkably detailed account of household composition, material culture, production and consumption, marriage practices, sexual behaviour, and the community's larger demographic patterns. Greer concludes that their shared feudal subordination made the situation of individual peasants and their families much like that of their European counterparts; as did Dechêne's, however, his micro-historical approach also uncovers what is North American in both the smaller lives of, and the larger demographic patterns, affecting these families.

Although very influential in Europe, the proto-industrialization model of family change has had limited influence on Canadian research. Canadian historians acknowledge the continuation of domestic production through the early stages of industrial development, and note the ways in which farm families typically did not rely on agricultural production alone, most engaging also in some form of seasonal wage labour. But the primary focus has tended to be the rural family or the industrial family. David Gagan's study of Peel County (1981) used census reports, assessment rolls, wills, and mortgages to get at the adjustments that farm families had to make during a time when population growth was exceeding land availability. His analysis revealed how such correlates as land ownership, family size, inheritance prospects, and economic status determined the family's ability to sustain and reproduce itself. One of the preferred responses was out-migration, placing entire families in the position of "hopeful travellers" on the move to improve their situations while maintaining their integrity as family units.[26] Adding a cultural dimension, Chad Gaffield's work (1987) on Eastern Ontario's predominantly francophone Prescott County also uncovered evolving family strategies that combined traditional ideals of land ownership and cultivation with newer notions about later marriage, family limitation, and investment in children's education. Integral to the group's family strategies was the preservation of its Franco-Ontarian identity.[27] Bruce Elliott's examination of 775 Irish-Protestant families who left North Tipperary for the Ottawa and London areas between 1818 and 1855 also demonstrated how land and cultural identity underpinned family solidarity among the largest non-francophone ethnic minority group in 19th century Canada.[28] Gerard Bouchard's comprehensive

[26]D. Gagan, *Hopeful Travellers: Families, Land and Social Change in Mid-Victorian Peel County, Canada West* (Toronto 1981).
[27]C. Gaffield, *Language, Schooling and Cultural Conflict: The Origins of the French Language Controversy in Ontario* (Montréal/Kingston 1987). For a comparative view, see C. Gaffield and G. Bouchard, "Literacy, Schooling and Family Reproduction in Rural Ontario and Quebec," *Historical Studies in Education*, 1, 2 (Fall 1989), 201-18.
[28]B. Elliott, *Irish Migrants in the Canadas: A New Approach* (Montréal/Kingston 1988). See also J.I. Little, *Crofters and Habitants: Settler Society, Economy and Culture in a Quebec Township, 1848-81* (Montréal/Kingston 1991); F. Noel, *The Christie Seigneuries: Estate Management and Settlement in the Upper Richelieu Valley, 1760-1854* (Montréal/Kingston 1992); C.A. Wilson, *A New Lease on Life: Landlords, Tenants, and Immigrants in Ireland and Canada* (Montréal/Kingston 1994); M. Conrad, ed., *Intimate*

Quelques arpents d'Amérique (1996), the outcome of some twenty years of research, reconstituted virtually the entire population of the Saguenay region. Bouchard made the rural family the key determinant of economic development, positioning it at the centre of structural change rather than as a mere receptor, often an unwilling and unwitting one at that. Most important, Bouchard's findings call into question much conventional wisdom concerning the "inherent" conservatism of rural families, especially francophone Catholic families. The Saguenay's demographic patterns were not merely local, culturally specific variants, but intrinsic to a larger North American process wherein rural families were meeting structural changes creatively, often with a view to avoiding the "all or nothing" choice that industry seemed to present.[29]

Taken from the other (urban-industrial) side, Michael Katz's seminal analysis of industrializing Hamilton, Canada West (1974) was the first Canadian project to make extensive use of the (then) new computerized data-processing systems. Katz's micro-study of the 1851 and 1861 censuses emphasized the structural inequality that characterized the city of 12,000: 60 per cent of resources were controlled by an élite of the richest 10 per cent, while the poorest sector (two-fifths of the population) held 6 per cent. The "intensive transiency" of a population in flux ensured the continuation of such inequality. On the level of families, Katz confirmed their nuclear structure, but found households to be malleable, in that many contained the boarders whose presence signified both the importance of surrogate families to those (largely single men) on their own, and the contributions of extra-familial members to fragile working-class family economies. Using similar statistical testing, subsequent studies of property ownership mapped these patterns of inequality in other settings; in Toronto, in 1871, for example, half of all adult men owned a house, but a substantial segment of the male labouring population was nonetheless impoverished.[30]

Relations: Family and Community in Planter Nova Scotia, 1759-1800 (Fredericton, N.B. 1995).

[29]G. Bouchard, *Quelques arpents d'Amérique: Population, économie, famille au Saguenay, 1838-1971* (Montréal 1996). Bouchard's research, published regularly in scholarly journals, was conducted over 25 years through the Institut universitaire de recherches sur les populations, at Université de Québec (Chicoutimi). On the larger question of rural families and change, see the review essay by R.W. Sandwell, "Rural Reconstruction: Towards a New Synthesis in Canadian History," *Histoire Sociale/Social History*, 27, 53 (May 1994), 1-32.

[30] M. Katz, *The People of Hamilton, Canada West: Family and Class in a Mid-Nineteenth Century City* (Cambridge 1975). See G. Darroch and L. Soltow, *Property and Inequality in Victorian Ontario: Structural Patterns and Cultural Communities in the 1871 Census* (Toronto 1994); they used a sample of 5,699 individuals, composed of adult male and female heads of households [313 were women], and males over 20. See also D.G. Burley, *A Particular Condition in Life: Self-Employment and Social Mobility in Mid-Victorian Brantford, Ontario* (Montréal/Kingston 1994).

Peter Gossage's recent work (1999) demonstrates the methodological and analytical gains made in the two decades since the watershed Katz study. Gossage comes so much closer to revealing how family relations are articulated to the new relations of production, in fluctuating rhythms of give-and-take, initiate-and-respond, as he explores these in the context of industrializing Saint-Hyacinthe, Québec, in the late 19th century. Reconstituting the family histories of several hundred couples through parish records, his main concern is to understand how marriage, household composition, and fertility were affected by the transition, especially the class basis of evolving demographic patterns. The latter revealed that the middle class was increasingly delaying marriage and restricting family size. Changes in these areas reflected a domestic reorganization related to the town's particular economic reorganization. The new patterns suggest the widening gap between the bourgeoisie and the struggling working class. Like Bouchard, Gossage contends that the demographic response of urban, francophone Catholic families fit the overall North American trend. While culturally prescribed, subjective, individualized motivations underlie such personal decisions as those involving marriage and family formation, equally important are the "boundaries set by constantly changing sets of material constraints, opportunities and circumstances."[31]

The interdisciplinary, University of Victoria-based Canadian Family History Project, a long-term collaborative effort focusing on the 1901 census, promises to further our understanding of the material basis and work relations of early 20th century families. Its first monograph, Unwilling Idlers (1998), coauthored by Peter Baskerville and Eric Sager, compares 1891 and 1901 census data for six cities. Reading the census as a text that encodes a three-way relationship between the government, the enumerators, and the enumerated, the authors found that recurrent joblessness affected more than 1 in 3 families. More telling, however, is the fact that low average wages were a constant drag on household income and standards of living for most of the working class. Ultimately, the market could not sustain many of these urban families, the state would assist them only minimally and in keeping with perceived economic truths, and the family itself was the last shelter against destitution — a historic function that was becoming increasingly difficult to fulfil, but one whose importance for vulnerable working-class families was arguably greater than ever.[32]

[31]P. Gossage, Families in Transition: Industry and Population in Nineteenth-Century Saint-Hyacinthe (Montréal/Kingston 1999), 180.

[32]P. Baskerville, E. Sager, Unwilling Idlers: The Urban Unemployed and Their Families in Late Victorian Canada (Toronto 1998). The cities are Victoria, Vancouver, Winnipeg, Hamilton, Montreal and Halifax. On the project, see E. Sager, "Research Note: the Canadian Families Project," The History of the Family: An International Quarterly, 3, 1 (1998), 117-23. Funded by the Social Sciences and Humanities Research Council of Canada, it is supported by its host institution and four other participating universities, and consists of 11 scholars from the disciplines of history, sociology, geography and historical demography.

Even a cursory glance at thirty years' worth of demographic studies indicates that this approach to families in history has retained its validity, becoming methodologically more sophisticated, consequently more adept, in uncovering the symbiosis of family and work relations, familial and structural change. Demography has been particularly useful in showing how, somewhere "between the level of classes and that of isolated individuals," families occupy a critical position in the socioeconomic order.[33] Historians working within these quantitative frameworks encouraged awareness of the ambiguities, complexities, and ongoing mutations that typify domesticity, past and present. Most significant among their findings was the fact that both the fertility decline and the nuclear family structure preceded industrialization, rather than being its chief demographic results. But the demographers' spotlight on the family unit ultimately imparts very little about the internal power dynamics of families and the interactions of their individual members, with each other and outside the family. How did families decide on their collective approach to needs that arose and conditions that were changing, or promising to change? How were priorities chosen and paths charted for individual members? How did individual family members — people of different ages, different sexes, unequal prospects, probably harbouring unique hopes — live within their defining parameters, staking their claims as family members and as autonomous individuals? Answers to such questions clearly cannot be inferred from numerical data, prompting family historians to turn their attention to specific life stages, both on their own and within the broader context of the life course. Even the shifts in method and approach, however, did not move attention far from the perennial question of how families adapted to modernizing forces.

ii. *Life Stages: Childhood, Youth, Marriage, Parenting, Sex (and Foucault)*

Although Philippe Ariès' work has been criticized for inferring broad historical trends from a narrow upper-class source base, his *Centuries of Childhood* (1962), which located an overall shift in societal perceptions of children in 17th century Europe, inspired an international scholarly interest in the most enigmatic of all historical subjects.[34] Once it was recognized that children have a history — that childhood is specific to time and place — age joined the identifying categories of class, gender and race, taking its place in the "trinity of oppressions" that historians

On the role of statistical information in state formation, on reading statistics, see G. Emery, *Facts of Life: The Social Construction of Vital Statistics, Ontario, 1869-1952* (Montréal/Kingston 1993).

[33]Davidoff, *et. al.*, *The Family Story*, 7; T. Harevan, "The History of the Family and the Complexity of Social Change," *American Historical Review*, 96, 1 (February 1991), 1-3; K.A. Lynch, "Old and New Research in Historical Patterns of Social Mobility," *Historical Methods*, 31, 3 (Summer 1998), 95.

[34]P. Ariès, *Centuries of Childhood: A Social History of Family Life* (New York 1962); originally published in 1960. For a critique of the Ariès thesis, see D. Archard, *Children: Rights and Childhood* (London 1993).

could no longer overlook in their forays into past societies. The distinguishing feature of the "modern" childhood, that dependent, insulated life-stage before the assumption of adult responsibilities, is the absence of labour. Although we still lack a history of child labour, most of those that consider children support the view that, until very recently, children in the majority of households were expected to work in some capacity, as befitting their age, ability, gender, and the family's needs. The childhood that we recognize as such, along with the prolonged dependency that has come to characterize modern adolescence, were not so much biologically as economically determined, first enjoyed in families that could afford them in the material sense.

Historians of education must be credited with opening the field of Canadian childhood history. Influenced by American historiographical trends of the 1960s and 1970s, especially the revisionist work of Michael Katz during his tenure at the Ontario Institute for Studies in Education, they broke through the "institutional" walls of traditional education history to cast a critical eye on the relationships of socioeconomic and educational change, public schooling and state formation. Their work exposed the double edge of 19th century school reform, as it democratized access to education through public funding and compulsory attendance laws, expanding state control over working-class families just as parents' control over their children's participation in the family economy declined. The new education history also underscored the connections between school reform and the period's fundamentally class-based social anxieties.[35] "Nation-building," with its often fiercely-racist and eugenic motivations, was as much behind the "new education" as were pedagogical developments, emerging ideas about childhood, and the Protestant middle-class reformist notions encapsulated in the Social Gospel.

These themes were taken up by Neil Sutherland in his inaugural *Children in English Canadian Society, 1880-1920* (1976). In detailing how childhood was reconceptualized and institutionalized through reform campaigns and related state initiatives, demonstrating the growth of public support for a "modernized" child-

---

[35] M. Katz, *The Irony of Early School Reform* (New York 1968), inspired much of the Canadian revisionism. See A. Prentice and S. Houston, *Schooling and Scholars in Nineteenth-Century Ontario* (Toronto 1988); also A. Prentice, *The School Promoters: Education and Social Class in Mid-Nineteenth Century Upper Canada* (Toronto 1977). More recently, Bruce Curtis, *Building the Educational State: Canada West, 1836-1871* (London, Ontario 1988), 14-15, argues that "educational practice was centrally concerned with political self-making, subjectification and subordination." On the evolution of Canadian education history, see H. Graff, "Towards 2000: Poverty and Progress in the History of Education," *Historical Studies in Education,* 3, 2 (Fall 1991), 203-5; J. D. Wilson, "From Social Control to Family Strategies: Some Observations on Recent Trends in Canadian Educational History," *History of Education Review,* 13, 1 (1984), 1-13; C. Gaffield, "Back to School: Towards a New Agenda for the History of Education," *Acadiensis,* 15 (1986); N. Sutherland, "Does Lawrence Cremin Belong in the Canon?," *Historical Studies in Education,* 10, 1-2 (Spring/Fall 1998), 205-11.

hood as the nation's best way forward, Sutherland crafted an influential interpretive framework.[36] He pieced together the overlapping concerns of contemporary social reformers to reveal children through the anxious eyes of their middle-class parents and would-be protectors. But we also saw how fearful these adult observers were about the contaminant effects of their neighbours' children, many of whom could not aspire to a family life that conformed to the ideal family reflected back to them in their parlour mirrors. The childhood experience was contingent; the family's socioeconomic position was key to its nature; and it was, in fact, fear of the repercussions of an impoverished childhood for the future citizenry that galvanized the child welfare movement.

Much of the post-Sutherland historiography also approached children through the "child-saving" or family-centred reform campaigns of the late 19th -early 20th centuries. P.T. Rooke and R.L. Schnell (1987) discussed the conjoining of childhood and citizenship through legal and political structures, as the "right to childhood" rallied reformers. Within a framework of "rescue and restraint," with public schooling at the forefront, various new institutions created "total environments" in which to implement the middle-class design of modern childhood; the post-World War II welfare state was the "final element in the creation of childhood as an ideology in modern industrial societies." Theresa Richardson (1989) was probably the first childhood historian to use Foucauldian concepts in her comparative analysis of Canadian and American "mental hygiene" campaigns. Richardson considered how medicine, social science, and the pseudo-science of eugenics operated as "the childhood gaze," recasting childhood as a medical "psychobiological" phenomenon. Child welfare policies devised in accordance were largely responsible for the creation of the "social phenomenon of the maladjusted and mentally disordered child," who was also most likely to belong to a working-class, immigrant or "non-white" family.

My own work (1993) explored early 20th century attempts to improve infant and maternal welfare by means of "scientific motherhood," which constituted a medical regulation of maternity increasingly underwritten by the state. I used elements of social reproduction theory to situate their joint campaign within a

---

[36]N. Sutherland, *Children in English Canadian Society, 1880-1920: Framing the Twentieth-Century Consensus* (Toronto 1976); reissued by Wilfrid Laurier University Press, 2000. See also N. Sutherland, "Children and Families Enter History's Mainstream," and the articles in the Special Issue on Childhood and Family in the Twentieth Century, *Canadian Historical Review,* 78, 3 (September 1997). Among the early essay collections are J. Parr, ed., *Childhood and Family in Canada* (Toronto 1982); R. Smandych, G. Dodds, A. Esau, eds., *Dimensions of Childhood: Essays in the History of Childhood and Youth in Canada* (Winnipeg 1991); B. Bradbury, ed., *Canadian Family History* (Toronto 1993). The most recent collection is E.A. Montigny, L. Chambers, eds., *Family Matters: Papers in Post-Confederation Canadian Family History* (Toronto 1998). For a comparative study of English/French Canadian approaches, see A. Turmel, "Historiography of Childhood in Canada," *Paedagogica Historica,* 33, 2 (1997), 509-20.

perceived crisis in the family that entwined these health issues with middle-class anxieties about rapid socioeconomic change, related urban pathologies, "racial" degeneration, and declining industrial productivity. Medical/state intervention in working-class families was critical to the success of "national efficiency" projects. As Katherine Arnup (1994) discovered in pursuing similar themes, traditional gender ideals, racist assumptions, and class suspicion — all bolstered by contemporary science — imbued medical and psychological theories that singled out "maternal ignorance" to explain why mothers and babies were dying, and why the state should uphold a very limited, primarily "educational" intervention.[37] Despite their interest in modern scientific methods, women were constrained in their childrearing choices by their material circumstances — the conditions of family life that their educators refused to consider as they persistently denied the class basis of these "social problems." Although neither of us dealt with the question of a widening gap between middle-and working-class families in terms of quality of life, our shared conclusions suggest that this was the case in early 20th century Canada.

A broad notion of "education" — with a profoundly regulatory purpose — became the panacea for a vast litany of "problems" stemming from economic conditions that were leaving a substantial number of Canadian families struggling to get by. It also justified increasing state intervention in the traditionally sacrosanct private domain. But it was not only the fragmenting, physically and morally-undermined urban working-class family that was seen to require such "education," as Jeffery Taylor reveals in *Fashioning Farmers* (1994). Taylor uses an Althusserian variant of post-structuralist theory to explain attempts by the state, through its educational institutions (specifically by means of public schooling, sociology, scientific management and home economics) to shape the family's role in reproducing the values of modern industrial capitalism. In early 20th century Manitoba, capitalist production and exchange values permeated rural life right through to the farm household. Traditional patterns of shared labour were to be up-dated by attempts to organize the farm family economy along factory lines, to make it "not so much a cooperative family unit but a miniature corporation, with the wife as

[37]P.T. Rooke, R.L. Schnell, *Discarding the Asylum: From Child Rescue to the Welfare State in English Canada, 1800-1950* (Llanham, Maryland 1983); T.R. Richardson, *The Century of the Child: The Mental Hygiene Movement and Social Policy in the United States and Canada* (Albany, New York 1989); C.R. Comacchio, *Nations Are Built of Babies*; K. Arnup, *Education for Motherhood: Advice for Mothers in 20th Century Canada* (Toronto 1994). See the essays in K. Arnup, R. Pierson, A. Lévesque, eds., *Delivering Motherhood: Maternal Ideologies and Practices in the 19th and 20th Centuries* (London 1990). On working-class motherhood, the classic study is Ellen Ross, *Love and Toil: Motherhood in Outcast London, 1870-1919* (London 1993); on race and families, see J. Jones, *Labor of Love, Labor of Sorrow: Black Women, Work, and the Family from Slavery to the Present* (New York 1985). See also J. Modell, D. Ross, eds., *Children in Time and Place: Developmental and Historical Insights* (Cambridge 1993).

purchasing agent." Also integral to the cause were a more pronounced gendered division of labour, "practical" education for farm children, and such reinforcing extracurricular activities as Boys and Girls Clubs.[38]

Nor was the profound faith in education diminished by war and depression. The mid-20th century witnessed a resurgence of the cult of domesticity in their aftermath, its gender and family prescripts drawing new impetus from an economic affluence that was placing more Canadians in a position to achieve the long-standing male-breadwinner-family ideal. Mona Gleason's recent study (1999) concentrates on how psychologists constructed, perhaps consecrated, the "norm" that upheld 1950s domesticity amidst a public clamouring for "normalcy" that manifested in nostalgia for the "traditional" family. Drawing on Michel Foucault's theories about the "technologies of the self," Gleason's conceptual framework is structured around the "technologies of normalcy" — comparing, differentiating, hierarchizing, homogenizing, and excluding — as promoted through school and public health systems, child guidance clinics, advice manuals, and popular media. By deconstructing the period's own "myth of the modern family," she shows how efforts to "normalize" the ideal aimed to entrench and reproduce the gender and family values of the dominant class, thereby "limiting what was truly acceptable to the confines of psychology's discursive construction of normalcy," and also, needless to say, limiting what was realistically attainable by many Canadian families.

Much of what we know about family life in the past, as these studies suggest, is conveyed through the eyes of middle-class observers, many of them professionals self-classified as "family experts," who alternated between exaltation and condemnation of what they saw or believed to exist in Canadian homes. While confining us to the fairly recent past, oral testimony offers some hope of getting through these obscuring filters, permitting a gateway to the day-to-day business of family that might not otherwise materialize, especially in regard to the working-class and immigrant families who left few written records in their own voices.[39] In her

[38]J. Taylor, *Fashioning Farmers: Ideology, Agricultural Knowledge and the Manitoba Farm Movement, 1890-1925* (Regina 1994).

[39] In these millennial times, historians are becoming more accepting of the role and value of memory as a viable approach to private lives; see J.A. Robinson, "Autobiographical Memory: A Historical Prologue," in D.C. Rubin, ed., *Autobiographical Memory* (Cambridge 1986), 19-23. The classic on imagination and historical representation is H. White, *Metahistory* (Baltimore 1973). See also J. Sangster, "Telling Our Stories: Feminist Debates and the Use of Oral History," *Women's History Review*, 3, 1 (1994), 5-28; J. Jeffrey and G. Edwall, eds., *Memory and History: Essays on Recalling and Interpreting Experience* (Lanham, Maryland 1994). Among family stories recounted through memory, see D. Chong, *The Concubine's Children: Portrait of a Family Divided* (Toronto 1996);C.M. Blackstock, *All the Journey Through* (Toronto 1997); J. Kulyk Keefer, *Honey and Ashes: A Story of Family* (Toronto 1998); W. Choy, *Paper Shadows: A Chinatown Childhood* (Toronto 1999); W. Johnston, *Baltimore's Mansion* (Toronto 1999).

examination of domestic life during the Great Depression, Denyse Baillargeon features the personal recollections of thirty francophone, Catholic, Montréal women. Their memories of everyday routines and rituals underscore how the structures of class, gender and custom brace domesticity, as the Depression context throws traditional family strategies — so often the coping strategies of women — into bold relief. Commitment to their familial roles, and all the ingenuity and resourcefulness expected of housewives of their class and time, gave these women the skills to "make do" and "get by." Even during long stretches of joblessness, men rarely took on "women's duties" in the home, the corollary being that mothers rarely worked outside the home, otherwise doing everything possible to keep families fed, clothed and sheltered. These families were accustomed to periodic unemployment, as Sager and Baskerville have shown; along with their historic, class-based experience of "stretching," even in good times, such expectations served as directions for domestic management and family relations.[40] But, as Joan Sangster reveals in her case study of wage-earning women in Peterborough, Ontario, while conventional role ascriptions offered women networks of support in their dual worlds of work and family, they also perpetuated their subordination and dependency in both settings. Taking a critical stance on memory that acknowledges how it is neither entirely "unmediated" nor entirely discursively-constructed, Sangster allows her oral histories (91 women, 10 men) to show how gendered understandings of "respectability" infused working-class self-identity, class identification, family life, and workplace culture. The women's stories emphasize the distinctly "feminine" consciousness that made them define themselves in specific reference to family, despite their roles as wage labourers.[41]

Personal memories corroborate historic trends, placing human beings and real lives into the statisticians' reports. They are also important because they disclose inlaid images, archetypes, and narrative threads that reveal much about past lives through collective storying. Neil Sutherland employs memory as just such an activating instrument in his second major childhood study, *Growing Up* (1997). Sutherland collected the childhood memories of people born between 1910 and 1950 in two Vancouver neighbourhoods, and in the rural, north-central British Columbia community of Evelyn, along with the oral testimonies, autobiographies, and personal records of others across English Canada. Multifaceted and free-ranging, these memories constitute "the central scripts of childhood," displaying common patterns and enough common structure to permit the weaving together of

---

[40] D. Baillargeon, *Ménagères au temps de la Crise* (Montréal 1991); translated by Y. Klein, *Making Do: Women, Family and Home in Montreal During the Great Depression* (Waterloo 1999).

[41] J. Sangster, *Earning Respect: The Lives of Working Women in Small-Town Ontario, 1920-1960* (Toronto 1995).

individual life stories across social class and geographic region.[42] At the same time that he emphasizes the material, class-delineated boundaries of childhood, Sutherland reasserts what is eternal about it: growing up has always been a complex process defying easy generalization, and even the best-laid attempts to reconfigure childhood — to make it a uniform "middle-class" experience — have not had even, predictable, "progressive" results. These collected memories also confirm the persistence of traditional family economies, consequently historic patterns of family/work relations. However much compulsory schooling, mass culture, consumerism, and family-centred leisure may have eroded distinctive elements of working-class culture, the continued importance of mutual assistance among kin, children's contributions of wages or services, and the domestic production entailed in sewing, canning, vegetable and fruit growing and small animal husbandry, is notable even past the mid-point of the 20th century. Despite increasing income and leisure, the historic relations of work and family were often preserved, whether by choice or necessity.

Much of the literature on courtship, marriage, and sexuality in the past, in Canada as elsewhere, is concerned more with public expectations or social constructions than actual practices. This is largely attributable to the specific challenges involved in locating sources — especially behavioural evidence — about the most intimate of all intimate relations. Of the early work in this area, Peter Ward's *Courtship, Love and Marriage in Nineteenth-Century English Canada* (1990) and Serge Gagnon's *Mariage et famille au temps de Papineau* (1993) are the closest Canadian examples of the so-called "sentiments" or "emotions" approach to family history. Incorporating some quantitative data with the highly individualized material of journals and personal correspondence, Ward points to the intersections of the private (romantic, emotional or sentimental) with the public, or 'civic' aspects, of marriage (duty and responsibility). He insists on the "ordinariness" of the views emanating from his sources, and contends that "the courtship and marriage rites of English Canadians cut across social boundaries." The sources' decidedly anglophone, Protestant, middle-class provenance suggests otherwise, but they do effectively demonstrate how a period's romantic images, gender ideals, and class-based social conventions are encoded in private, reflective discourses. Focusing on francophone Catholic families, Gagnon's study addresses the value system encompassing marriage and family in Québec during the late 18th and early 19th centuries. Like Ward's anglo-Québec couples, the francophone couples most likely to accept the stringent requirements placed before them by Church and state were of the middle class, those of better or worse means either less compliant in the face of

[42]N. Sutherland, *Growing Up: Childhood in English Canada from the Great War to the Age of Television* (Toronto 1997). Sutherland explains this "schematic" model and its application to his own work, 7-12.

these prescriptions, or perhaps more willing to contest them.[43] From opposite sides of the cultural divide, these histories are remarkable in that they are not particularly divergent. What we need are further explorations of how class and what can broadly be called "culture" — ethnicity, region, language, religion — fashion courtship and marriage practices, and what this entails for gender, sexual, and family relations.[44]

In addition to the problematic source base, emerging analytical trends have pointed the historical study of sexuality in the direction of discourse rather than practice or behaviour. It is in addressing such evasive historical subjects as sex that post-structuralist concepts and tools of analysis, notably Derridian deconstructive reading, Lacanian psychoanalysis, and Foucault's emphasis on the material body and the discourses of power, have proven most valuable. Foucault's influence — already noted in several instances — dominated the 1990's historiography. By placing power at the centre of private relations, he turned attention to the formidable "heterosexual matrix" of class, race, gender and sexuality that upholds what is normative through its compulsory, disciplinary and exclusionary elements. Foucauldian discourse analysis has encouraged interrogation of "timeless" concepts too long presumed to be universal, definitive, unproblematic. Moreover, as an explanatory concept, "regulation" is more fluid and relational than earlier "social control" approaches that tended to assign an omniscient power to the regulators.[45]

[43]P. Ward, *Courtship, Love and Marriage in Nineteenth-Century English Canada* (Montréal/Kingston 1990); S. Gagnon, *Mariage et famille au temps de Papineau* (Sainte-Foy, Québec 1993). See also A. Gagnon, "The Courtship of Franco-Albertan Women, 1890-1940," in E.A. Montigny, L. Chambers, eds., *Family Matters.*

[44] Family biographies have filled in some of the details for some individuals, but they tend to be concerned with "special" middle-class families for whom both public and private records exist; see K.M.J. McKenna, *A Life of Propriety: Anne Murray Powell and Her Family, 1755-1849* (Montreal/Kingston 1994), and J.I. Little, *The Child Letters: Public and Private Life in a Canadian Merchant -Politician's Family, 1841-1845* (Montréal/Kingston 1995).These gender prescriptions and their outcome for public roles and private relations are the subject of Cecilia Morgan's *Public Men and Virtuous Women: the Gendered Languages of Religion and Politics in Upper Canada, 1791-1850* (Toronto 1996), which delves into the ideals conveyed through the language of politics and religion in the public discourses of Upper Canada. The cult of domesticity and its "separate spheres" ideology were grafted uneasily onto a frontier society, but nonetheless took root in the public imagination, at least insofar as the latter can be "read" through public discourses. Yet there was clearly a tension between the negative implications of family among reformers who challenged the patronage and nepotism that characterized colonial politics, and the profound social importance ascribed to domesticity, a theme that needs further exploration.

[45]M. Foucault, *The History of Sexuality, 1, An Introduction* (New York 1984); *The Order of Things: An Archaeology of the Human Sciences* (London 1989); Foucault, "The Order of Discourse," in R. Young, ed., *Untying the Text: A Post-Structuralist Reader* (London 1987), 48-78. See J. Weeks, "Foucault for Historians," *History Workshop Journal,* 14 (August 1982), 165-78; C. Waters, "Legacies of Foucault: New Writing on the History of Sexuality," *Gender and History,* 2, 2 (1990), 218-22; J.D. Wrathall, "Provenance as Text: Reading the

I won't enter into the debate, often circular, concerning post-structuralist threats to class analysis, whereby the very concept of class as a meaningful category of personal experience/historical understanding is deconstructed into absurdity. It is sufficient to note that, insofar as Canadian historians have embraced elements of post-structuralist method, none to date has lost sight of the material world containing discourses; all acknowledge the real class, gender, and racial dimensions of power relations and avoid arguing that reality is accessible only through representation, or the "from-things-to-words move" as Michele Barrett succinctly defined it.[46]

In an early synthesis of the disparate bits of historical analysis on sexuality in Canada, sociologist Gary Kinsman introduced many history students to social construction as a means of understanding that identifying categories are actively "made" by dominant social groups employing moral regulation to sustain hegemony. Thus sexuality comprises a set of historically and culturally specific social relations, whose shifting [and plural] definitions correspond to parallel shifts in other social relations. Approaches such as Kinsman's also decentred Victorian sexual repression by revealing that the Victorians discussed and regulated sexuality in very public ways. Contemporary medical, psychological, and social-scientific theories, often premised on Darwinian or pseudo-Darwinian ideas, made classification a promising new tool of social analysis and suggested the necessary forms of regulation, as demonstrated in Mariana Valverde's influential study of the discourses of social/moral reform, principally those of the social purity movement.[47]

Within this context of moral/social regulation, Serge Gagnon's *Plaisir d'amour et crainte de Dieu* (1990) examines the regulation of sexuality in rural,

---

Silences Around Sexuality in Manuscript Collections," *Journal of American History,* 79, 1 (1992); J. Kucich, "Heterosexuality Obscured," *Victorian Studies* 40, 3 (Spring 1997). See also J. Weeks, *Against Nature: Essays on History, Sexuality and Identity* (Concord, Mass.: 1991), and R. Porter, L. Hall, *The Facts of Life: The Creation of Sexual Knowledge in Britain, 1650-1950* (New Haven, Conn. 1995).

[46]The classic deconstruction of deconstruction is, of course, B.D. Palmer, *Descent into Discourse: The Reification of Language and the Writing of Social History* (Philadelphia, Penn. 1990). See also M. Barrett, "Words and Things: Materialism and Method in Contemporary Feminist Analysis," in M. Barrett and A. Phillips, eds., *Destabilizing Theory: Contemporary Feminist Debates* (Stanford, California 1992), 203-4. Theorists and practitioners discuss its applications in K. Jenkins, ed. *The Postmodern History Reader* (London 1997).

[47]G. Kinsman, *The Regulation of Desire: Sexuality in Canada (*Montréal 1987; 2nd edition, Montréal 1996*)*; M. Valverde, *The Age of Light, Soap and Water: Moral Reform in English Canada, 1885-1925 (*Toronto 1991). Although not Foucauldian, Jay Cassels, *The Secret Plague: Venereal Disease in Canada, 1838-1939* (Toronto 1987) discusses these public discourses, increasingly dominated by a medical profession keen to extend its social authority with the assistance of the state.

colonial, French-Catholic Lower Canada as documented in the correspondence between parish priests and their bishops. What is astonishing, in light of the Church's strict prohibitions, is the relative rarity of sexual infractions. Though this may well be a matter of "getting away with it," rates of illegitimacy were exceedingly low by comparison to those of contemporary Europe and North America. It is here that the significance of religion, culture, and community comes into play, and the primacy of family over that of self-individuation is made visible in a time and place where collective familial welfare may have preempted even the most fundamental of human urges. A sense of a "sexual geography," with a slightly higher number of indiscretions in more recently settled areas than in the old parishes, and in parishes closer to anglophone, Protestant communities, also points to the entwining of class, community, and cultural heritage where sexual mores and sexual behaviour are concerned.[48]

Engaging this concept of sexual geography with respect to youth, gender and class are two complementary studies, Karen Dubinsky's *Improper Advances* (1993) and Carolyn Strange's *Toronto's Girl Problem* (1993). Both are essentially discourse analyses informed by Foucault's theories of power, discipline, and regulation. Both make the fundamental point that sex is a gendered experience, but also one that is class-bound. They explore the coalescence of social constructions about gender and sex with laws regulating the sexual conduct of women and men, though largely the former, who were paradoxically made out to be victims and predators at once. Also evident in Dubinsky's rural and northern communities and Strange's big-city Toronto are inchoate middle-class fears about gender inversion, with all its implied familial and social dangers, that fostered a veritable "moral panic" about youthful lower-class female sexuality, and a range of regulatory, at times punitive, measures to contain it.[49] In their respective settings, Dubinsky and Strange chart the spatial dimensions of sexuality, pointing out that public outcry about the "dangers" of public spaces, whether backroads or city amusements, diverted attention from the violence against women that was so often perpetrated in the "safety of home." The connections drawn between economic independence and

---

[48]S. Gagnon, *Plaisir d'amour et crainte de Dieu: Sexualité et Confession au Bas-Canada* (Québec 1990). On these themes, see the essays in J. Weeks and J. Holland, eds., *Sexual Cultures: Communities, Values and Intimacy* (London/New York 1996).

[49]K. Dubinsky, *Improper Advances: Rape and Heterosexual Conflict in Ontario, 1880-1929* (Chicago 1993); Strange, *Toronto's Girl Problem.* See also A. McLaren, "Policing Pregnancies: Sexuality and the Family, 1900-1940," *Transactions of the Royal Society of Canada*, 3 (1992), 17-23; J. Sangster, "'Incarcerating "Bad Girls': The Regulation of Sexuality Through the Female Refuges Act in Ontario, 1920-1945," *Journal of the History of Sexuality*, 7, 2 (1996), 239-75; T. Myers, "Qui t'a débauchée?: Family Adolescent Sexuality and the Juvenile Delinquents Court in Early-Twentieth-Century Montreal," in Montigny, Chambers, eds., *Family Matters.* See the synthesis offered by T. Loo and C. Strange, *Making Good: Law and Moral Regulation in Canada, 1867-1939* (Toronto 1997).

sexual behaviour are important. If most young women could not afford to leave the parental home, however, we might wonder whether the new sexual expressiveness so feared by middle-class observers was truly limited to public spaces, therefore limited on all counts. Dubinsky's *The Second Greatest Disappontment* (1999) further explores these evasive relations of gender, class, race, sexuality and "space" through the Foucault-inspired concept of "the tourist gaze." She considers the mutability of sexuality, specifically heterosexuality, in relation to changing gender and marital ideals, wryly packaged within a deconstruction of the "cultural code" imprinted in the popular association of Niagara Falls ("the greatest theme park of heterosexuality") with honeymoons. Dubinsky also links early 20th-century changes in "the public culture of heterosexuality" with the identification of honeymoons as rituals signifying an "adult citizenship" premised on the twin achievements of sexual maturity/marriage. Consequently, the 19th century's upper-class "bridal tour" became a heterosexual "coming out" for the middle-class young marrieds of the 1920s, making its way into working-class practices after World War II.[50]

If the 20th century saw the emergence of a distinctive life-stage between childhood and adulthood, we need to know how this development variously reflected new ideas about childhood and youth, a changing economy that restricted work opportunities for young people while calling for more schooling, and the related changes in family models that increasingly emphasized affective relations over the historic concept of the family as a unit of mutual, often material, assistance and shared labour. While we still lack a history of adolescence, the post World War II era, currently hot in historical circles, has inspired several recent publications that consider that liminal stage against the backdrop of the Baby Boom and the youth-centred "revolutions" of the 1960s. Doug Owram's *Born at the Right Time* (1996) is our first generational history, chronicling the up-bringing and coming-of-age of the century's epoch-making birth cohort, the notorious Boomers. Owram outlines post-war economic and demographic trends and their far-reaching sociocultural repercussions, as well as the role of the media and popular culture in disseminating certain "family values." His examination of the converging student, sexual, and women's liberation movements confirms how age is not only a component of self-identity, but is salient to collective identity and the dialectics of power.[51] The middle-classness of his subjects does not lend itself to examination of this point, but it is evident that the newly-protracted life-stage between childhood and adult independence, while more and more common across class, race, and

[50]K. Dubinsky, *The Second Greatest Disappointment: Honeymooning and Tourism at Niagara Falls* (Toronto 1999). Dubinsky uses Foucault, both directly and through British sociologist John Urry's Foucauldian concept of "the tourist gaze," which denotes the invention and organization of the tourist experience.

[51]D. Owram, *Born at the Right Time: A History of the Baby Boom Generation* (Toronto 1996).

regional boundaries, was still dependent on the family's economic standing. A broader affluence made teenagers' wages less important to the working-class family economy, while, as Sangster shows, a new postwar trend was replacing teenagers with mothers as secondary breadwinners, as a growing proportion of women reentered the workforce after having children. Teen labour increasingly took the form of part-time work, and the primary occupation of youth became high school. Once again, however, class differentials remained. Attendance increased for all classes and ethnic groups across the nation, but high-school graduation was still predominantly confined to the "Canadian" middle class.

Mary Louise Adams (1997) relies on Foucault, primarily his notion of surveillance, to explain how the dominant discourses captured in the popular media, educational literature, film, and government reports of the 1950s were explicitly meant to affirm traditional understandings of masculinity, femininity and "normal" heterosexuality. As did Dubinsky's second study, Adams' examination of the construction of the normative reveals much about how its opposite — homosexuality — was demonized in Cold War Canada. In *L'amour en patience* (1997) Gaston Desjardins tackles the same topic, same period, for Québec. His approach is also Foucault-inspired, his method, discourse analysis; his sources cover a range of popular, religious, medical, and psychological literature, and the government publications and educational films at the basis of sex education in the schools. Even in supposedly repressive Catholic Québec, the emphasis on the negative aspects of sexuality — sex as sin — and Church authority in all sexual matters, gave way to recognition of the importance of physical intimacy (within heterosexual marriage, of course) and the expertise of doctors and psychiatrists. With Owram, Adams and Desjardins stress the turning-point nature of the 1950s, during which adolescence became both a recognized life-stage, and, in Adams' words, "one of the distinctive markers of the postwar world." Yet there are signs that a distinctive "youth culture" was making its presence felt by the 1920s, in the wake of structural, cultural, and technological changes intensified by World War I. Like Owram as well, they note the middle-class basis of their subject group without examining the class elements to any degree. Was youth culture a largely "constructed" menace to middle-class respectability and domesticity? Was it a "homogenizing" instrument where working-class and immigrant families were concerned? The problem, as usual, is situated between words, images, and their assimilation, on the one hand, and the material limits of participation, on the other.[52]

[52] M.L. Adams, *The Trouble With Normal: Postwar Youth and the Making of Heterosexuality* (Toronto 1997); G. Desjardins, *L'amour en patience: La sexualité adolescente au Québec, 1940-1960* (Québec 1997). On 1920s youth culture, see P. Fass, *The Damned and the Beautiful: American Youth in the 1920's* (New York 1977). The classics on adolescence include J. Kett, *Rites of Passage: Adolescence in America 1790 to the Present* (New York 1977); J. Modell, *Into One's Own: From Youth to Adulthood in the United States, 1920-1975* (Berkeley, Calif. 1989);G. Palladino, *Teenagers: An American History* (New York 1997).

My sketch of some of the historical writing on life stages and their keynote experiences underscores the basic point that multifarious sociocultural elements are at work in their definition, timing, and how they are lived out within different social groups. Class and culture, as well as biology and often to greater effect, establish particular points of entry and passage. Moreover, just as life stages are fluid and contingent, individuals are not frozen in them, do not necessarily move consecutively through them, may experience several simultaneously, and may, of course, skip some in large part or even altogether. Childhood, adolescence, sexual relations, marriage, and parenthood are no more universal than they are historically unchanging. Much depends on the when, where, and how of family life.

iii. *Family Dynamics: Life Course, Gender Roles, Family Strategies and Family Economies*

The life-course framework is often used in association with life-stage analysis, with the intention of stressing the fluidity and mutability of life stages and family life. Life-course historians attend to the ways in which family members follow their own paths, but these individual life-histories are examined as they converge with larger histories: those of the family itself, as well as those of generations, communities, regions, nations. By getting a sense of how the phases of the life course have changed over time, historians can identify such developments as the increasing systematization of the life course itself over the 20th century. The challenge lies in avoiding a mechanistic model that, while ordering life-stages logically, might not leave room for divergences, making life decisions appear inevitable and masking the personal, idiosyncratic, or perhaps just-plain-foolish choices that must have been as common in the past as they are in our own family circles.[53]

Life-course analysis has been applied most productively in studies on women and gender. Without conflating the history of women and the history of families, historians working in these areas share many questions, as they look to understand how these ties came about, why they persist, and how they have changed, in order to appreciate how family operates as the principal site for the manufacture of gender identity, and why this is also a class issue. There is simply no denying the elemental

There is no Canadian history of adolescence yet see my take on it, C.R. Comacchio, "Dancing to Perdition: Adolescence and Leisure in Interwar English Canada," *Journal of Canadian Studies*, 32, 3 (1997), 5-35; also C. Sethna, "Wait Till Your Father Gets Home: Absent Fathers, Working Mothers and Delinquent Daughters in Ontario during World War II," in E.A. Montigny, L. Chambers, eds., *Family Matters*; also D.O. Carrigan, *Juvenile Delinquency in Canada: A History* (Toronto 1998).

[53]T. Hareven, "Family Time and Industrial Time," in Hareven, ed., *Family and Kin in Urban Communities* (New York 1977), 35. American historical sociologist Glen Elder developed the life-cycle approach, precursor to life-course studies, in the early 1970s; see the essays in Hareven, *ed., Transitions: The Family and the Life Course in Historical Perspective* (New York 1978); also A. Rossi, "Life-Span Theories and Women's Lives," *Signs,* 6, 1 (Autumn 1980), 4-32.

bonds that have tied women to families in a manner that has never applied equally to men. They also recognize that, if families have constrained women on numerous counts, the familial role has also served women as a source — sometimes the unique source — of both private and public power. Despite their subordinate position, women have historically been the primary agents of family adaptation to the forces of change.[54]

In their path-breaking life-course studies, Veronica Strong-Boag and Andrée Lévesque traced the chronology of women's lives individually, in families, and against the wider backdrop of a newly "modern" Canada and Québec during the interwar years. With respect to ideas/ideals about womanhood and family, two cultures with divergent social and religious customs were more similar than not. The "new woman" enjoyed more options for education, employment, and political involvement than her predecessors, but, as they demonstrate, the traditional, biologically-defined roles and relationships premised on family remained her defining experience. Strong-Boag considers how the mass media, especially the "family magazines" that proliferated during these years, subsumed the interests of women within those of family, targeting the "home-maker" whose exhausting round of everyday labour literally made the happy home of middle-class ideal, and establishing her as the icon of a new consumer society. Lévesque's analysis shows how the maternalist ideals conveyed through intermeshing religious and national-istic discourses promoted a womanhood rendered near-divine by virtue of the familial role, all the while vehemently defending the rule of the father/provider. The Catholic Church may have dominated these discourses in Québec, but a flurry of secular experts across the land, especially (male) physicians, jockeyed for position as modern advisers to these ostensibly modern women. As Denise Lemieux and Lucie Mercier confirmed in their comprehensive life-course study of Québec women, even the structural changes and technological advances that marked the first half of the 20th century did not alter the fundamental ordering of women's lives, the day-to-day, morning, noon and night aspects of a domestic labour that upheld the family.[55]

[54]C. Hall, "Feminism and Feminist History," in Hall, *White, Male and Middle Class: Explorations in Feminism and History* (London 1992), 15. On maternal feminism in Canada, see L. Kealey, ed., *A Not Unreasonable Claim: Women and Reform in Canada, 1880s-1920s* (Toronto 1979); and Kealey, *Enlisting Women for the Cause: Women, Labour, and the Left in Canada, 1890-1920* (Toronto 1998). See also R. Rapp, E. Ross, R. Bridenthal, "Exam-ining Family History," in J. Newton, M. Ryan, J. Walkowitz, eds., *Sex and Class in Women's History* (London 1983).

[55]V. Strong-Boag, *The New Day Recalled: Lives of Girls and Women in English Canada, 1919-1939* (Toronto 1988); A. Lévesque, *La Norme et les déviantes: des femmes au Québec pendant l'entre-deux-guerres* (Montreal 1989), translated by Yvonne Klein, *Making and Breaking the Rules: Women in Quebec, 1919-1939* (Toronto 1994); D. Lemieux, L. Mercier, *Les Femmes au tournant du siècle, 1880-1940: Âges de la vie, maternité et quotidien*

By the mid-1970s, Canadian feminist sociologists were integral participants in the "domestic labour debates," which attempted to refine classical marxism in order to integrate the complexities of gender oppression with those of class oppression, to theorize the productive aspects of reproductive labour, and to incorporate into the evolving body of marxist thought an understanding of social reproduction as a necessary corollary to capitalist production. The outcome was a fresh appreciation of the centrality of domestic labour — historically the work of women — to capitalism, as the sociology of the family was "fundamentally transformed" by this understanding of the significance of gender in terms of the larger systems embodied in family, patriarchy and capitalism.[56] Social scientists who considered these interrelations in historical context, such as Meg Luxton (1980) and Marjorie Cohen (1985), turned attention to the false dichotomies represented in "separate spheres" notions of the gendered division of labour. Luxton discussed the class-bound, generationally transmitted values associated with women's domestic labour, which, in working-class homes, often made the difference between destitution and a measure of economic and familial security. Cohen revised the standard view of the family farm in relation to agricultural development and capitalist accumulation in 19th century Ontario, while revealing the importance of women's labour to this process, both in its reproductive sense – maintaining and sustaining the labouring population for farm work and occasional wage labour – and in active production in such areas as dairying.[57]

By reconceptualizing "women's work," these undertakings have had lasting effects on family and women's history. To untangle the threads binding women and family, feminist historians have reevaluated "separate spheres" and modified earlier views about the impact of factory production on women's roles and on the family economy. A newly-rigid division of labour within the home was replicated

(Québec 1992). See also A. Lévesque, "Réflexions sur l'histoire des femmes dans l'histoire du Québec," *Revue d'histoire de l'Amerique française,* 51, 2 (1997), 271-84; J. Parr, "Gender History and Historical Practice," in Parr and M. Rosenfeld, eds. , *Gender and History in Canada* (Toronto 1996).
[56]B. Fox, "The Feminist Challenge: A Reconsideration of Social Inequality and Economic Development," in Fox, Brym, *From Culture,* 120-23. The Canadian contributions to the domestic labour debates are extensive; some of the highlights are W. Seccombe, "The Housewife and Her Labour Under Capitalism," *New Left Review,* 83 (1974), 3-24; Smith, "Women, Class and Family," in Burstyn, Smith, *Women, Class, Family and the State,* 3-24; the essays in B. Fox, ed., *Hidden in the Household: Women's Domestic Labour Under Capitalism* (Toronto 1980); and the essays in R. Hamilton and M. Barrett, eds.,*The Politics of Diversity: Feminism, Marxism and Nationalism* (London 1986). For updates, see also S.J. Wilson, *Women, Families and Work,* 3rd ed (Toronto 1991), 47-62; P Armstrong and H. Armstrong, *Theorizing Women's Work* (Toronto 1990), 67-98.
[57]M. Luxton, *More Than A Labour of Love: Three Generations of Women's Work in the Home* (Toronto 1980); M. Cohen, *Women's Work, Markets and Economic Development in 19th Century Ontario* (Toronto 1988).

outside it, where women's work was also gender-defined, inferior to, and consequently not valued, in every sense, as much as that of men. Yet, if we simply accept that the separate spheres ideal was practised as much as preached, and that work and home were indeed "sundered" by industrialization, we falsify the domestic arrangements of many Canadian families. New research recognizes the permeability of boundaries between work and home, the overlap of domestic and productive labour, and the continued importance of a family economy of mutuality and reciprocity, often involving the exchange of services necessary to transform commodities into things that family members can use: hot lunches, clean clothes, mended shoes.

Whatever the prevailing views about where they belonged, then, women and children lived in networks of domestic and public, home and work, family and neighbourhood, just as did men, if not in precisely the same ways. Elizabeth Jane Errington has shown that the women who barely merit mention in the "official" pre-Confederation sources at the basis of much historical research were frequently the mainstays of their family's material well-being, as well as acting as principal caregivers. Sean Cadigan's discussion of the household economy of the 17th-century Newfoundland fishery reveals its near-total dependence on family labour, and the importance of women's labour in an ostensibly male-dominated enterprise. Marilyn Porter has traced the continuation of this family dynamic to the present day, indicating how women's work in the fishing family household, fiercely demanding and unrelenting, is vital to family and community reproduction. The persistently marginal economic position of Newfoundland fishing families ensured that individual self-interest had to be subsumed in the interests of the family. Gail Cuthbert Brandt and Naomi Black have compared the experiences of rural women in Québec and France to demonstrate the myriad interactions of gender, family, and work.[58]

What is striking is the continued importance of women's labour in both pre-industrial and industrial times, in rural and urban settings. In *The Gender of Breadwinners* (1990), the first Canadian study of gender, work and family to take advantage of the (then) new analytical tools offered by post-structuralist theory, Joy Parr sought to avoid the "binary opposites" grounding assumptions about what constitutes public/private, men's work/women's work, and to examine, instead, where they overlap and conjoin, and how they contradict. Parr's comparative case studies of the wage labour and private lives of female textile workers in Paris and male furniture workers in Hanover (Ontario), reveals how gendered understandings

[58] E.J. Errington, *Wives and Mothers, School Mistresses and Scullery Maids: Working Women in Upper Canada, 1790-1840* (Montréal 1995); S. Cadigan, *Hope and Deception in Conception Bay: Merchant-Settler Relations in Newfoundland, 1785-1855* (Toronto 1995); M. Porter, *Place and Persistence in the Lives of Newfoundland Women* (Brookfield, Vermont 1993); N. Black, G.Cuthbert Brandt, *Feminist Politics on the Farm: Rural Catholic Women in Southern Quebec and Southwestern France* (Montréal/Kingston 1999).

of work and family simultaneously supported and contradicted the roles of individual breadwinners, the existential gap being particularly wide for female breadwinners. Although many Paris families depended on the latter in the absence of steady local employment for men, women's strong position in the economies of both town and family did not translate into gender equality and familial authority. In Hanover, where both the local economy and family life were organized along traditional, male-dominant lines, providing for a family was inseparable from masculine identity; women, for the most part, did "women's work" in the home. Noteworthy about Parr's analysis, therefore, is the revelation that even the unusual work/family environment in Paris did not mitigate the socially sanctioned power relations defined by gender and class and reinforced in family. We see how, in countless ways, gender and family relations are influenced more by class and the dominant culture than by the family's own circumstances — how the quotidian can confute, and potentially conflict with, those values. What we need to figure out is *why*; what makes human beings committed to role ascriptions that differ from their actual roles? Even as historians challenge the binary opposites at the base of so much discussion about gender, the oppositional nature of the public self and the private self continues to perplex.[59]

Interpreting women's domestic labour solely as reproductive labour and management of consumption, and industrialization as a break in the historic relations of family and work, obscures the complexities of "getting by" and the different roles of family members in the process; it also oversimplifies the larger process of modernization. In more instances than we can know, supposedly dependent women and children were shoring up the family economy, often operating within a "hidden" or "informal" economy, outside the masculine marketplace, that was largely their own domain.[60] Recent work on the family economy, frequently conducted within a life-course framework and with a specific view to uncovering "family strategies," also emphasizes the blurred lines of productive/reproductive labour. Historians who focus on family strategies examine family decisions and actions as responses to external social, economic, and political pressures in light of the changing ages and roles of members. Their goal is to discern to what degree behaviour might correspond to external conditions, and to what degree it responds to the family's internal, traditional rhythms. Critics of this approach have questioned the viability of the concept of "strategies," with its implicit notions of choice and deliberation, when constraints both internal and

[59]J. Parr, *The Gender of Breadwinners: Women, Men and Change in Two Industrial Towns, 1880-1950* (Toronto 1990).

[60]J. Dickinson and B. Russell, "The Structure of Reproduction in Capitalist Society," in Dickinson, Russell, eds., *Family, Economy and State: The Social Reproduction Process under Capitalism* (New York 1986), 1-4; see also the discussion of social reproduction in S. Coontz, *The Social Origins of Private Life: A History of American Families, 1600-1900* (London 1988).

external may well have limited — even removed — the element of choice. Non-material and non-quantifiable factors out of the reach of known historical methods might hold the most explanatory force where household decisions are concerned, leaving historians to see as "strategies" only those whose outcomes are readily traced.[61]

The first Canadian study to look at family strategies within a life-course framework was Bettina Bradbury's examination of Montréal families between 1861 and 1891, a critical moment during which "the nature of the interaction between family and work [were] in the process of changing." As Herbert Ames detailed in his survey of the "city below the hill," these working-class families could not subsist on one wage. Their survival and reproduction, therefore, must be understood within the context of a family economy rooted in the labour of all family members. Age and gender determined the type and extent of individual contributions, which, in turn, defined the individual's familial status. No matter to what degree women and children facilitated the family's subsistence, as Bradbury shows, final authority rested with the male head of the household. Thus the family operated simultaneously as a unit of survival, solidarity, and support, and also as the setting, and source, of interpersonal tensions, gender inequality, and generational conflict. While she acknowledges the power struggles that took place between men and women, parents and children, Bradbury's emphasis on "strategies" perhaps exaggerates familial consensus, at times even in the face of contradictory evidence, such as that concerning alcohol abuse and domestic violence.[62]

The dynamics of class, age and gender still defined the roles and contributions of working-class family members a half-century later, in 1920s Halifax, as Suzanne Morton reveals in *Ideal Surroundings* (1995). Morton applies life-course analysis to a case study of Richmond Heights, a working-class Halifax neighbourhood reconstructed after the 1917 harbour explosion according to British "Garden City" standards. Attentive to class-based ideas about "respectable" domesticity, Morton echoes Bradbury's findings in revealing the continuities on the levels of ideas and material reality where working-class family life is concerned. Despite their modern

[61] Hareven, "Family Time and Industrial Time," 188-9. On family strategies, see the critical commentaries in "Family Strategy: A Dialogue," *Historical Methods*, 20, 3 (1987), 113-25.
[62] B. Bradbury, *Working Families: Age, Gender and Daily Survival in Industrializing Montreal* (Toronto 1993); S. Morton, *Ideal Surroundings: Domestic Life in a Working-Class Suburb in the 1920s* (Toronto 1995). Brian Clarke, *Piety and Nationalism: Lay Voluntary Associations and the Creation of an Irish-Catholic Community in Toronto, 1850-95* (Montréal/Kingston 1994), describes how "the parish and the hearth" were mutually supportive; Lévesque's study reveals that this ecclesiastical campaign continued to hold force in Québec during the interwar years. Similarly, Lynne Marks, *Revivals and Roller Rinks: Religion, Leisure, and Identity in Late-Nineteenth-Century Small-Town Ontario* (Toronto 1996), discusses how choices about religion and leisure were affected by gender and class, and vice versa, indicating how Protestant worship became increasingly feminized, while its most sustained challenge came from young single men of both classes.

"ideal surroundings" — as the housing project was billed — working-class women were still obliged to find "extra-market" ways to contribute to the family economy without detracting from the familial/social status of male breadwinners, just as the contributions of children remained important to the family's material welfare. The male-breadwinner-family ideal that was already well on its way to cross-class acceptance by the late 19th century was no closer to realization for the majority of the working class even during the so-called Roaring Twenties. Under-and unemployment were perennial threats to the security of Atlantic labourers and their families. Nor did the plight of single mothers improve; like Bradbury, Morton found that widowed, deserted and divorced women were fortunate if they could rely in some measure on the assistance of family and kin. Public provision for marginalized families remained ill-considered and largely ineffectual, as can be seen in the history of families set apart from the ideal due to "race" and cultural differences.

iv. *"Other" Families: "Race," Ethnicity, and Immigration*

The history of white settlement and immigration is in and of itself a family story. In order to facilitate this process in the name of nation-building, the existing population of the great Northwest — the vast clans of Aboriginal peoples for whom family and kinship were the central organizing principle of all life — had to be transferred to reserves under the wardship of the paternal state. We do not, as yet, have a study specifically about the culture and experience of family among the Native communities so painfully caught in this conjuncture of social and familial change. Twenty years ago, Sylvia Van Kirk and Jennifer Brown produced pioneering studies that effectively spanned several sub-fields of the "new social history," elucidating the largely-overlooked relations of race, gender, and family embedded in the structures of trade and governance of the Hudson's Bay and Northwest Companies. Van Kirk and Brown showed how disapproving missionaries, traders, government agents, and white settlers interfered with and disrupted the traditional family economies of Aboriginal societies, their understandings of gender roles and relations, and their kin-based economic, social and political networks. The emissaries of a "superior" civilization became increasingly hostile to "mixed" marriages, and more forceful in imposing their European notions about the patriarchal family.

By the 19th century's end, as J.R. Miller describes, Native childrearing culture had also met with misapprobation by Euro-Canadians, whose harsher brand of discipline was inimical to Aboriginal customs. Believing that their own ways were crucial to the development of morally-upright, productive modern "Christians," the government's Indian agents enforced a residential school system that broke up families, destroyed the generational process of cultural transmission, obliterated knowledge of language, customs and history, and exposed Native children to emotional, physical, and sexual abuse for the better part of a century. Sarah Carter's studies consider both the patriarchal and racist implications of Indian policy, indicating that strict regulations rendered Native women helpless to continue their time-honoured contributions to their family economies, making them scapegoats for the poor living and health conditions on reserves. Carter's *Capturing Women* (1998) explores the sexualized imagery that demonized Native women, the former helpmates of white traders and settlers. They were deliberately configured as brutish, predatory, morally degenerate, and slothful, in stark contrast to the pure, brave, selfless White Woman whose hard work and good housekeeping and mothering skills would transform the unruly West into the "cradle of the nation."[63]

The immigration vital to the national project was, from the original decision to leave the country of origin, a process motivated by family imperatives and sustained by family networks that functioned as cushions against alienation and destitution. In many cases, part of the family stayed behind, often sending out its youth, predominantly male, to improve the family's fortunes by means of temporary labour, or to prepare for its resettlement. One of the first Canadian histories of childhood, and still the only one that deals with child labour specifically, details the unique case of juvenile immigrants from the British Isles. Joy Parr's *Labouring Children* (1980) discusses a long-running campaign by British charitable organizations, eager to resolve their own problems with a growing urban under-class, to sponsor the immigration to Canada of disadvantaged British children. 80,000 children, mostly under the age of fourteen, were sent out under these circumstances. They were not necessarily orphaned; their fate was usually decided by family members, often their parents, who saw immigration as a way of bettering the young emigrants' prospects as well as those of the family left behind, if only by removing a mouth to feed. To their Canadian hosts, they were depicted as a replenishing wellspring for declining "Anglo-Saxon stocks." But even more important than these racial considerations was their function as a much-needed source of cheap labour, especially on farms. Cut off from kin, indifferently "supervised" by the Barnardo and other organizations involved, these children were often exploited and abused by the Canadian families who "adopted" them, not as true family members but as indentured servants. Their experiences show that, notwithstanding new ideas

[63]S. Van Kirk, *Many Tender Ties: Women in Fur-Trade Society in Western Canada, 1670-1870*; J.S.H. Brown, *Strangers in Blood: Fur Trade Company Families in Indian Country*; J.R. Miller, *Shingwauck's Vision: A History of Residential Schools in Canada* (Toronto 1996); S. Carter, *Lost Harvests: Prairie Indian Reserve Farmers and Government Policy* (Montreal 1990); Carter, *Capturing Women: The Manipulation of Cultural Imagery in Canada's Prairie West* (Montréal/Kingston 1997); see also the essays in J.S.H. Brown and E. Vibert, eds. *Reading Beyond Words : Contexts for Native History* (Peterborough, Ont. 1996); A. McGrath and W. Stevenson, "Gender, Race and Policy: Aboriginal Women and the State in Canada and Australia," *Labour/Le Travail*, 38 (1996), 37-53; J. Barman, "Taming Aboriginal Sexuality: Gender, Power and Race in British Columbia, 1850-1900," *BC Studies* (1997-98), 237-66.

about a protected childhood and its corollary legislation, labour remained the central fact of some children's experience well into the "Century of the Child."[64]

In the various historical instances of group and chain migration to and within Canada, the role of family in the community's reconstitution has been paramount, as has been the importance of the family's economic role. Bruno Ramirez (1991) compared the experiences of migrants in two agrarian societies, Québec's Berthier County, and Italy's Southern Appenines, to show how their pragmatic choices were essentially family ventures. In contrast to the Italian migration, largely a back-and-forth movement of men, the French-Canadian exodus to New England's factory towns was a collective undertaking. Economic betterment depended on the presence of an adequate number of children who could work for wages. Because fathers were less readily and consistently employed than their children, their roles as providers tended to become "if not subordinate at least complementary," though this interpretation may overdraw the distinctions between the farm family economy and the new family wage economy. There is no question, however, that family objectives were the motive force of immigration, as is also evident in the three generations of Mennonites studied by Royden Loewen in *Family, Church and Market* (1993). His comparison of two communities settled in Manitoba and Nebraska makes clear that the roots of a transplanted culture — what the Kleine Gemeinde Mennonites envisaged as "the essence of life"— were carefully tended through the preservation of family, religious, and community values. While modifying certain customs because of the new environment, they were remarkably successful in protecting the familial practices, immured in the economically self-sufficient nuclear family, that comprised their cultural heritage.[65]

The Ukrainians studied by Frances Swyripa (1993) share a similar story: they also arrived as family units, transplanting their communities in prairie bloc settlements that were grounded in mutually reinforcing cultural and family values,

[64]J. Parr, *Labouring Children: British Immigrant Apprentices to Canada, 1869-1924* (Toronto 1980; second edition, Toronto 1994). While child labour is recognized as playing a significant role in all industrializing societies, including Canada's, we have little historical analysis of its nature and magnitude, with the exception of various articles by the late John Bullen; see, for example, "Hidden Workers: Child Labour and the Family Economy in Late Nineteenth-Century Urban Ontario," in Bradbury, ed., *Canadian Family History*; J. Synge, "The Transition from School to Work: Growing Up Working Class in Early 20th Century Hamilton," in K. Ishwaren, ed., *Childhood and Adolescence in Canada* (Toronto 1979). J. Zucchi, *The Little Slaves of the Harp: Italian Child Street Musicians in Nineteenth-Century Paris, London and New York* (Montréal/Kingston 1992) suggests the possibilities for studies of immigrant children.
[65]B. Ramirez, *On the Move: French-Canadian and Italian Migrants in the North Atlantic Economy, 1816-1914* (Toronto 1991); R.K. Loewen, *Family, Church and Market: A Mennonite Community in the Old and the New Worlds, 1850-1930* (Toronto 1993). Also on out-migration, see G. Burrill, *Away: Maritimers in Massachusetts, Ontario and Alberta* (Montréal/Kingston 1992).

especially in regard to gender roles. While men mediated between their own and the host community, women were mostly confined to the family farm, where their labour as the mainstays of the family economy was much as it had been in Europe. The community's male leaders, dominated by clergy, made mothers the public representatives of its status and cultural identity. Such expectations, however, meant that women were often targeted for blame. Swyripa is very attentive to the culture clash that manifested itself in generational terms, as young people increasingly tried to be more "Canadian" than their families and community could sanction. This tension between old world and new, tradition and modernity, between parental authority and youthful autonomy, also had definite gender boundaries, in that boys were allowed more freedom than their sisters and received more rewards for their contributions to the family economy.[66] In immigrant families, individual adaptation to the adopted country could be impeded as well as facilitated by family and kin, with age and gender the crucial variables in the process.

Franca Iacovetta (1992) likewise highlights the traditions of mutuality and shared labour that infused the culture and family lives of her community of southern Italians in post-World War II Toronto.[67] Unlike the earlier wave of Italian immigration with its large cohort of lone male sojourners, the post-war immigration was primarily a process of family relocation. Iacovetta's examination of the family economy points to the continued interdependence of family members: even during the boom years of the 1950s and 1960s, male breadwinners could not consistently support families on their own. Although married women's wage work outside the home was no longer proscribed — Iacovetta finds that immigrant women were more likely to be employed after marriage and motherhood than those of the native-born working class — many women preferred to take in work, or to supplement income in time-honoured "feminine" ways without leaving the home. Like so many others of their class and circumstances, they carried an onerous double-load. Despite the limitations imposed by class, gender and ethnic customs, families were malleable enough, and the networks of kin and *paesani* secure enough, to allow adaptations that eased their transition from peasants to urban industrial labourers. Yet, as Swyripa found, the necessary sacrifices for the family's sake did not preclude resentment and possible conflict with the ultimate authority,

---

[66]F. Swyripa, *Wedded to the Cause: Ukrainian-Canadian Women and Ethnic Identity, 1891-1991* (Toronto 1993); not quite so family focused, but also useful, is L. Petroff, *Sojourners and Settlers: The Macedonian Community in Toronto to 1940* (Toronto 1995).

[67]F. Iacovetta, *Such Hardworking People: Italian Immigrants in Postwar Toronto* (Montréal/Kingston 1992); 55-65. On the first wave, see John Zucchi, *Italians in Toronto: Development of a National Identity, 1875-1935* (Montréal/Kingston 1988) and the essays in R. Perin, F. Sturino, eds. *Arrangiarsi : Italian Immigration Experience in Canada* (Montréal 1989). Recent work includes the essays in F. Iacovetta, P. Draper, R. Ventresca, eds., *A Nation of Immigrants: Women, Workers, and Communities in Canadian History, 1840s-1960s* (Toronto 1998).

as vested in fathers. It is highly likely that, finding themselves in a society bent on self-individuation, younger family members would have felt their subordination keenly. This aspect of immigrant family life, where the personal stakes, in some respects, were higher than for the Canadian-born, awaits further development. Also barely begun is the study of family life among people of colour in our nation's past. The preliminary work in this area strongly suggests that, for these families whose every move was "racialized" by the host society, and in regard to whom public policy was heavily weighted toward surveillance and regulation, we stand to learn a great deal about the familial structures supporting the formation of self and group identity.[68]

vi. *"Bringing the State Back In:" Family Policy and Politics*

As the history of immigration indicates, family formation is intrinsic to nation-building and state formation, not only in the crucial material sense of necessary bodies, but also because families forge the links between personal identity and public roles, effectively reproducing both the citizenry and the constellation of values concerning citizenship. In the past decade or so, historians' renewed commitment to "bringing the state back" might appear a concession to social history's critics that the field constitutes merely "history with the politics left out." The formidable politics of family are extremely difficult to ignore, however, much as generations of political historians have attempted to do. What "state studies" entail, within family history's parameters, is a recognition of the modern state's increasingly intimate ties to family. As more and more family-watchers theorized about modernization's negative repercussions, the state was compelled to step in with reinforcements for the beleaguered patriarchal family. Social policy developments such as mothers' allowances, old age pensions, unemployment insurance, and family allowances, comprised a political mediation of often-contradictory capitalist and reproductive imperatives, and a public commitment to a male-breadwinner familial ideal.[69]

[68]On African-Canadian families and those of other "visible minorities;" there is little apart from the collection by P. Bristow, D. Brand, L. Carty, A.P. Cooper, S. Hamilton and A. Shadd, *"We're Rooted Here and They Can't Pull Us Up": Essays in African Canadian Women's History* (Toronto 1994); see also S. Morton, "Separate Spheres in a Separate World; African-Nova Scotian Women in Late 19th-Century Halifax County," *Acadiensis,* 22, 2 (Spring 1992), 61-83; S. Yee, "Gender Ideology and Black Women as Community Builders in Ontario, 1850-20," *Canadian Historical Review,* 75, 1 (March 1994), 53-73. We need something along the lines of the essays in S. Coontz, M. Parson, G. Raley, eds., *American Families: A Multicultural Reader* (New York 1999).
[69]S. Coontz, *The Origins of Private Life,*10-12; for a survey of state measures on the provincial level, see J. Struthers, *The Limits of Affluence: Welfare in Ontario, 1920-1970* (Toronto 1994). Many of the works that I have discussed under other headings, especially those about child welfare, fit easily into this category of family/state relations.

Families were first identified as the sites of social problems potentially reme-
diable by state regulation during the last quarter of the 19th century, formative years
for organized reform and incipient welfare legislation in Western Europe and North
America, as the historical literature on "child-saving" suggests. Compulsory
schooling, temperance, protective legislation for working women and children, and
the instigation of family courts were the most noteworthy of an array of regulatory
policies exemplifying the new state intervention in this arena. The state was hardly
monolithic, however, and its measures coexisted, and were often supported by, the
voluntary and philanthropic efforts of community-based, frequently women-led,
organizations. The process inspired many interconnected reform campaigns and
much political rhetoric, shaping social policy as well as the contours of the modern
bureaucratic state and federal-provincial relations. Less discernible is how such
"external" forces were actualized in the family circle; how such developments as
the expansion of education, health and welfare systems, for example, actually
affected domestic arrangements and family strategies on the quotidian level that
most fascinates and yet eludes us.

The first survey of state regulation of reproduction, as seen through the politics
of contraception and abortion, was Angus McLaren and Arlene Tigar McLaren's
aptly titled *The Bedroom and the State* (1986). The ideological constancy behind
the restrictive legislation is not surprising, given how discussions on reproduction
were dominated by (male) politicians, lawyers, doctors, and clergy. The laws
necessarily reflected their hegemonic class-based patriarchal and racist views. The
ongoing decline in fertility, traceable to the mid-19th century, was thus "inextricably entangled in a web of social, sexual and cultural relationships" that made
discussions "more concerned by the broader issues of sexual, social and political
power than by the issue of family size." McLaren and McLaren uncovered working-class ambivalence about family limitation, construed as both a right and a
transparent attempt at bourgeois social control, but we need to know more about
the textures of sexual politics in their class setting. A close reading of the working-
class debates on fertility control would sharpen some of the amorphous ideas about
class, sex, and family currently circulating. What is ultimately disappointing about
this study probably cannot be helped. Despite the authors' stated interest "primarily
in private and public power struggles over the control of fertility," there is little
sense of the private struggles, of those that worked themselves out, or failed to do
so, in the family setting.[70]

In *Private Lives, Public Policy* (1993), sociologist Jane Ursel carefully syn-
thesized the key aspects of the social reproduction debates to examine state
intervention in the family in a manner both theorized and historicized. Her comparative case study of Manitoba and Ontario situates legislative initiatives within

[70] A. McLaren and A. Tigar McLaren, *The Bedroom and the State: The Changing Practices
and Politics of Contraception and Abortion in Canada, 1880-1997* (Toronto 1986; 2nd
edition, Toronto 1997).

the dynamics of industrial capitalism. Ursel employs a dual-systems model to explain the shift from "familial patriarchy" to "social patriarchy" during the 20th century: since patriarchy and capitalism are mutually supportive systems, state intervention in reproduction — the work of women — is required to sustain production, the work of men. From a similar perspective, sociologist Dorothy Chunn's examination of family courts in Ontario discussed how social patriarchy was enforced through special institutions that formalized state intervention on behalf of families. Chief among these were the new provincial family courts of the early 20th century, created to deal with the social menace of "disorganized families." Despite the obvious class angle, what is clear is that the material basis of many family problems was *not* made to be the key issue. As both authors show, reformers and state agencies chose to emphasize the perceived decline in parental — especially paternal — responsibility that, in their view, appeared the most serious outcome of historic shifts in social organization and the worst menace to society.[71]

This anxiety about family crisis and social anomie saw the community's interest in its young couples' choices made manifest in a developing body of legislation to regulate private relationships and personal behaviour for the national good. James Snell's *In the Shadow of the Law* (1993) traces 20th century changes in divorce legislation, revealing just as much about popular ideals concerning marriage and family as about legal objectives. Since divorce represented the irrefutable failure of these ideals, regulation of courtship and marriage was thought to be the key to its prevention. In this climate of middle-class consensus about the sanctity of family, the divorce law itself remained stringent, though the persistence of desertion — "the working-man's divorce" — and common-law unions indicates that "ordinary" Canadians were capable of subverting the moral/legal standards devised by the dominant class. In Lori Chambers' *Married Women and Property Law in Victorian Ontario* (1997), the life-stories that emerge from legal records and court files testify to the often-tragic outcome for women and children when legally sanctioned male/paternal authority is abused. Even expanded property rights and the courts' generally sympathetic response to women plaintiffs did not begin to address the conditions of subjection that kept women and children trapped in difficult, sometimes dangerous, domestic situations. In addition to explaining how legal structures scaffolded the social and familial subordination of women and children, both books underscore the need for a detailed study of domestic violence in Canada.[72]

---

[71]J. Ursel, *Private Lives, Public Policy: 100 Years of State Intervention in the Family* (Toronto 1992); D. Chunn, *From Punishment to Doing Good: Family Courts and Socialized Justice in Ontario, 1880-1940* (Toronto 1993).

[72]J. Snell, *In the Shadow of the Law: Divorce in Canada, 1900-1939* (Toronto 1993); L. Chambers, *Married Women and Property Law in Victorian Ontario* (Toronto 1997). On domestic violence, see K. Harvey, "To Love, Honour and Obey: Wife Battering in Working-Class Montreal," *Urban History Review*, 19, 2 (October 1990), 130-40; J. Fingard, "The

The relationship of the paternal state to the most problematic of all problem families, those that visibly deviated from the male-breadwinner-model, is the subject of Margaret Little's long-anticipated *No Car, No Radio, No Liquor Permit* (1998). Little lays bare the now-familiar racism and class bias of the maternal feminists leading the mothers' allowance campaign, also noting that organized labour supported this type of state provision because of its commitment to the male breadwinner family. She argues that the moral and the material were entwined in the requirements placed on recipients: eligibility rules were strict, funds supplied were minimal, and continued surveillance and judgement became part of the everyday lives of the families who finally qualified for assistance. If all single-mother families were suspect, none were more so than those also marked by "race," who faced the most rigorous eligibility criteria and the most intensive scrutiny. Once again, it is clear that public outcry against the employment of mothers and children somehow skirted these "problem families," whose members were expected to contribute substantially to their own upkeep. Little makes evocative, though frequently uncritical, use of mothers' voices as filtered through the Commission's records, allowing contemporary recipients to speak for themselves in interviews that expose the sad historic continuities in the lives of female-headed families. As well as the material deprivation and social stigma that have been their lot, it seems that privacy, too, is a class privilege not permitted to the poor.[73]

As historical trends have affected the life-course from one end to the other, the state has also played a major role in the lives of the elderly, whose story, so far, has been told within this specific framework. With expanding industry, the aged, like children, became superfluous to production. Re-ushered into the realm of age-defined dependency before many had attained that state mentally and bodily, their maintenance became another of the family duties that was gradually, but not smoothly, being relocated to the public sphere. Much of the debate about their situation revolved around the issue of responsibility for those who could not earn their keep: did their years of productive labour entitle men to state support, or should this be left to the families they had once worked to support? What should be done for women, whose labour was usually unwaged and whose socially subscribed dependence was much greater at all life-stages? Edgar-André Montigny examined the dilemma confronting families of the dependent elderly in late 19th century Ontario, as structural changes exacerbated the timeless challenges of their care. Governments used the rhetoric of family duty to justify their grudging measures, while family economies strained against the expenses and labour involved in elder

---

Prevention of Cruelty, Marriage Breakdown and the Rights of Wives in Nova Scotia, 1880-1900," *Acadiensis*, 22, 2 (Spring 1993), 84-101; A. Golz, "Uncovering and Reconstructing Family Violence: Ontario Criminal Case Files," in F. Iacovetta and W. Mitchinson, eds., *On the Case: Explorations in Social History* (Toronto 1998).
[73]M. Little, *No Car, No Radio, No Liquor Permit: The Moral Regulation of Single Mothers in Ontario, 1920-97* (Toronto 1998).

care. Deftly combining demographic data and institutional records, Montigny points to the contradictions between family realities and "the family" of ideal at the base of the state's efforts. Ultimately, the traditional supports of family, kin and community, though allegedly diminished in the wake of modernization, remained critical to the survival of the elderly. Taking up the story where Montigny concludes, James Snell confirms that, although fewer than 20 per cent of Canadians lived in an "extended family" arrangement during the first half of the 20th century, traditions of intergenerational reciprocity meant that the majority of the elderly, particularly in working-class and farm families, relied on children and grandchildren. This relationship did not decline with the passage of the federal Old Age Pensions Act in 1927. If it tended to lean more heavily on the younger generation, and especially on women, it was not one-sided. Some of the elderly had the resources, such as homes or perhaps savings, to help their children; at the least, many could offer useful services through domestic labour, household maintenance, and child care. While elderly women were unquestionably more financially needy than men, thanks to the sexual division of labour both within and outside the family, they were more likely to "fit" into extended-family households because of their predominantly maternal life-roles.[74]

Dominique Marshall's *Aux origines sociales de l'État-providence* (1997) investigates the modern accord negotiated between families and governments as it was arrived at in Québec during the foundational years of the post World War II welfare state. Marshall's painstaking case study of the development of social policy as shaped by a unique cultural heritage and political history is a necessary corrective to the anglo-Central-Canadian slant of much of the literature in this area.[75] As in every preceding instance of intervention, the state had to create a regulatory relationship with families — particularly those of the ever-benighted lower classes — so that parents could be educated about the "proper" form and function of domestic life. Institutionalizing prewar trends toward "expert" intervention, the emphasis on children's rights justified this surveillance, affixing parental cooperation to the receipt of family allowances. Yet the undermining of parental authority and domestic privacy was generally tolerable because the material benefits made the allowances, modest as they were, important to the welfare of many needy families. The outcome of these state initiatives was a cultural shift embodied in the new relationship between families and the state. The adoption of a language of citizens' rights, despite the province's profoundly anti-statist history, signified the adeptness of Québec parents at invoking state response to their families' needs,

[74]E.-A. Montigny, *Foisted Upon the Government? State Responsibilities, Family Obligations, and the Care of the Dependent Aged in Late Nineteenth-Century Ontario* (Montréal/Kingston 1997); J. Snell, *The Citizen's Wage: The State and the Elderly in Canada, 1900-1951* (Toronto 1996).
[75]D. Marshall, *Aux origines sociales de l'État-providence: Familles québécoises, obligation scolaire et allocations familiales 1940-1955* (Montréal 1998).

foreshadowing the vast reforms of the Quiet Revolution. In the end, as Marshall remarks, her culturally distinct Québec families appear to have reacted to family allowances much as did their anglo-Canadian counterparts. More regional and comparative studies will show how this assessment holds up in the face of other cultural variances.

vi. *The Material Culture of Family: Homes and Things*

Moving from the state back to the home, if the material basis of family has been a connective theme in the majority of works relating to Canadian family history, the family's material culture — the things that live with families in their homes, and are used by them for work, housekeeping, sustenance, and recreation, as well as the physical structure called "home" — is really only beginning to receive attention. Two just-released works, by Joy Parr and Peter Ward, suggest the richness of this vein of sociocultural history in relation to family history. Joy Parr's *Domestic Goods* (1999) is an innovative, complex, sometimes complicated, interpretation of the post World War II economy that interweaves political and economic history with a gendered analysis of the history of domestic technology and design. Her discussion suggests how often, and in how many ways, the state agents responsible for the postwar transition to peacetime production barely managed to control what little they could, notwithstanding any commitment to practical applications of Keynesian theory. The design and marketing of consumer goods for the "family home," and the issue of domestic (female) needs within this literally man-made frame of reference, speaks to the tenacity of the sexual division of labour in both marketplace and home. Parr contends that needs and luxuries were morally more than materially delimited: historic class-based notions about debt, thrift, "making do," the family economy, and the gendered nature of production and consumption, clashed with emergent views about buying, borrowing, and what constituted "the good life" in a time of prosperity new to many families after decades of restraint and want. There is much information about the material culture of everyday life in these years, with details drawn from the international scene regarding developments in modern design and their impact on Canadian consumer products, as well as the process involved in the actual "domestication" of such objects. The objects' history is fascinating, but at times overshadows that of their human owners. Nonetheless, this is a seminal study in what it demonstrates about the connections between a renewed domesticity and a burgeoning consumer economy, and how both hinged on updated, "modern," but still basically traditional, class-based ideas about gender, work, and domesticity.[76]

Another historiographical "first," Peter Ward's three-century survey, *A History of Domestic Space* (1999), attempts to transfer the architectural historians' focus on the aesthetic to one that regards houses as "the theatre[s] of our domestic

[76]J. Parr, *Domestic Goods: The Material, the Moral and the Economic in the Postwar Years* (Toronto 1999).

experience, both spatially confining action and permitting a wide range of possibilities." Ward follows the changing size and spatial configuration of Canadian homes admirably, and in a manner nicely illustrated with photographs, blueprints, floor plans and diagrams. He also considers how family and social relations have shaped, and have been shaped by, these changing spaces, a rather more abstruse undertaking that doesn't quite succeed. Although he considers how the small homes that typified urban working-class shelter became "problems" to early 20th century reformers intent on pathologizing much of their social inferiors' private lives, he does not take on the "intrinsic merit" of home ownership and the reasons why "the detached family house is deeply embedded in our archetypes of the home." In a nation where, historically, the majority of all classes have lived in detached housing that usually sheltered only the nuclear family, it would be interesting to know how this "family home" became a cross-class ideal. What about the growing power of advertising and real estate marketing and the kind of fetishizing of domestic goods that Parr details? Moreover, Ward's important assertion that "gender categories don't shed much light on the relations between privacy and domesticity," because "in Canada, men and women have always shared all parts of the house," is not remotely convincing. Perhaps a clearer view would result from asking who worked where. What explains the fact that women became so associated with "hearth and home," specifically with the kitchen, that it was configured as their own domain, even spoken of colloquially as "her indoors"?[77]

Getting On With It: The Dialectics of Family, Self and Society

My purpose was to survey the monograph literature that, even if not classified as "family history," has nonetheless touched upon the connections between family, class, work, and social change. I attempted to trace the field's development from the questions that attracted our early social scientists as they observed the familial impact of economic change in late 19th and early 20th century Canada. The structural-functionalist paradigm that dominated by mid-century accounts for the overarching narrative of family history that devolved, in which families were seen to recover from modernizing blows by means of a "transfer of functions" that entailed certain necessary losses. Within this interpretive framework, the family endured, but the costs in terms of "traditional" domestic relations were high: the loss of productive functions entailed in the separation of home and work, thus the

[77]P. Ward, *A History of Domestic Space: Privacy and the Canadian Home* (Vancouver 1999). On the gendered use of space, see Davidoff, *et. al.*, *The Family Story*, 83-7. The model for studies of gendered space is A. Adams, *Architecture in the Family Way: Doctors, Houses, and Women, 1870-1900* (Montréal/Kingston 1996). For an overview, see H. Kalman, *A History of Canadian Architecture*, 2 vols. (Don Mills, Ontario 1995). On material culture, see G. Pocius, *A Place to Belong: Community, Order and Everyday Space in Calvert, Newfoundland* (Athens, Georgia 1991), and Pocius, ed., *Living in a Material World: Canadian and American Approaches to Material Culture* (St. John's, Nfld. 1998).

family's key historic function, led directly to the decline of parental, especially paternal, authority, and the loosening of bonds between family, kin and community. For historians, their work — more prescriptive than analytical by far — is valuable for what it reveals about contemporary family ideals, but also for what shines through as the vitality of familial networks of labour and other forms of mutual assistance. When historians became interested in the question of modernization in relation to family, their research softened the story's sharper angles by disclosing the unevenness of modernizing processes and acknowledging the complexities of causality. In the socioeconomic order as in families, it was discovered, the demonstrably new or "modern" could coexist with the "traditional," which may have been recast but was only rarely obliterated.[78] Over the course of three decades since the inaugural publications in a field recognized as family history, successive phases of study in its interrelated subjects have succeeded in animating the passive, even hapless, historical family. No longer primarily recipients of change, families are depicted as active, shrewd participants, protecting their own interests, pursuing their goals both collectively and on behalf of individual members, though not necessarily consensually or to equal benefit. What is clear is that families make history at least as much as the inverse is true.[79]

Whatever the historic changes in families, their material basis, their form, functions and relations, "the family" serves as a kind of holy grail for unholy times. There is something of the search for the holy grail in the historical pursuit of families as well. Even if a treasure trove of sources were excavated, how much can historians generalize about social relations from family stories? Since family is just as culturally-delimited, value laden and subjectively understood now as ever, what about the ways in which our own "family values" and contemporary politics affect our approaches to families in the past? At the risk of resembling Stephen Leacock's infamous horseman, heading off in all directions at once, I offer a few rough ideas that presented themselves as I channelled through this archaeology of family history. No one should be surprised that they reflect my own interests and prejudices as much as the existing gaps in the literature.

First, whatever the focal point — gender, race, sexuality, life-stage, to name a few of the most important as these pertain to family — we can't get far without due consideration as to how class is embedded in family relations, in day-to-day family life, consequently in the formation of self-identity. In short, class matters where family matters are concerned. Without adopting a deterministic stance, it is possible to see just how critical class has been, and continues to be, in the gamut of social relations that can be linked to family: from courtship through sexuality, marriage

[78]Hareven, "The History of the Family and the Complexity of Social Change," 113-14; see also D. Scott Smith, "The Curious History of Theorizing About the History of the Western Nuclear Family," *Social Science History*, 17, 3 (Fall 1993), 325-53.
[79]Davidoff, *et. al.*, *The Family Story*, 21,157; I. Davey, "Rethinking the Origins of British Colonial School Systems," *Historical Studies in Education*, 1, 1 (Spring 1989), 149-60.

through parenting, gender roles through age relations, ethnic culture through "race" identification, any variety of work and any type of play, and all the choices, "constructions," and practices implicated in these.

The internal dynamics of family, consequently, beg more research, despite the advances in knowledge that have come about as a result of life-course and family economy studies. For example, we usually discuss marriage, parenting, and childhood separately, even though the first two were practically synonymous until very recently, and the interaction between parent and child is obviously key to their respective life-stages. We have little knowledge about how class and culture affect the familial transmission of gender roles and how this process operated. How, for example, might sons and daughters of employed mothers imbibe gender ideals differently —or not? What about the children of single-parent, especially single-mother, families, who worried so many experts due to the absence of a "father-figure?" All the gender studies mentioned here have made earnest attempts to give women and men equal time, but we still know far more about women's roles in families than we do about those of men. Although the article literature dealing with the historical/cultural specificity of manliness has expanded in size, scope, and sophistication, it is mostly concerned with the construction of masculine roles, or the enactment of those roles, outside of family and especially on the job. In a sense, the historiography itself has been built on a "separate spheres" foundation, perpetuating, even while gamely trying to avoid, the women/home, men/work dichotomies. We know about the conflict between middle-class separate spheres ideology and the exigencies of working-class life from women's perspective. What about that of the lauded male breadwinners who play such shadowy roles in the homes of the past, where their domestic labour, parenting, and recreation are as hidden as the productive labour of women has long been? We know little about real fathers and how they went about fathering as families become increasingly mother-centred, at least on the level of rhetoric. Even Parr's anti-binary study reveals more about men in the workplace than in the home.[80]

[80] J. Parr, "Gender and the Practice of History," 20-1, discusses the importance of considering "hegemonic masculinities." More than a decade ago, Steven Maynard also pointed to this void in the historiography; see "Rough Work and Rugged Men: The Social Construction of Masculinity in Working-Class History," *Labour/Le Travail,* 23 (1989), 159-69; also Maynard, "Queer Musings on Masculinity and History," *Labour/Le Travail,* 42 (Fall 1998), 183-97. The only monograph with masculinity as its specific subject is Thomas Dunk's historical-sociological case study of working-class culture in Thunder Bay, Ontario, *It's a Working Man's Town: Male Working-Class Culture in Northern Ontario* (Montreal/Kingston 1991). See also the oft-reprinted M. Rosenfeld, "It Was a Hard Life: Class and Gender in the Work and Family Rhythms of a Railway Town," in Bradbury, ed., *Canadian Family History.* See the special issue on Masculinities and Working-Class History, *Labour/Le Travail* , 42 (Fall 1998); and the contributions to K. McPherson, C. Morgan, N.M. Forestell, eds., *Gendered Pasts: Historical Essays in Femininity and Masculinity in Canada* (Toronto 1999). On fatherhood, see L. Chambers, "'You Have No Rights, Only Obligations:' Putative

It follows that we also need to know more about remarriage, about reconstituted, "blended" and step-families, a fairly common experience for many Canadians in times of high mortality, and, more recently, rising divorce rates. Then there are the roles and relations that strain against convention: singleness and celibacy, the experiences of widows, widowers, orphans, and unwed mothers, common law, and same-sex partnerships all deserve in-depth study.[81] Thanks to the Canadian reading public's fascination with biography and autobiography, we know a lot about some famous sibling relationships, next to nothing about ordinary sibling interaction.[82] As to the wider meanings of family, kinship is acknowledged for its continued importance, especially among working-class, rural, immigrant, and non-white families, but there is not much analysis as to how these networks operated and who maintained them. As well as being profoundly shaped by class and race, kinship is a gendered experience: men are socialized to focus on wives and children, while women's familial obligations include the sustenance of wider kin relations, even, perhaps especially, in regard to the husband's extended family — a duty that tends to persist beyond his death, beyond marital breakdown.[83] There

---

Fathers and the Children of Unmarried Parents Act"; C. Comacchio, "Bringing Up Father: Defining a Modern Canadian Fatherhood, 1900-40"; R. Rutherdale, "Fatherhood and Masculine Domesticity During the Baby Boom: Consumption and Leisure in Advertising and Life Stories"; all in E. Montigny, L. Chambers, eds., *Family Matters*. See Ralph LaRossa's American study, *The Modernization of Fatherhoodhood: A Social and Political History* (Chicago 1997).

[81]This is not to say that nothing at all is available: on bachelorhood, see C. Danysk, *Hired Hands: Labour and the Development of Prairie Agriculture, 1880-1930* (Toronto 1995); M. Danylewycz, *Taking the Veil: An Alternative to Marriage, Motherhood, and Spinsterhood in Quebec, 1840-1920* (Toronto 1987); Bradbury, Lévesque, and Morton discuss widows and single mothers in their respective studies. See also S. Maynard, "Horrible Temptations: Sex, Men and Working-Class Male Youth in Urban Ontario, 1890-1935," *Canadian Historical Review*, 78, 2 (June 1997), 191-235; P. Rusk, "Same-Sex Spousal Benefits and the Evolving Conception of Family," in Montigny, Chambers, eds., *Family Matters*; E. Setliff, "Sex Fiends or Swish Kids?: Gay Men in *Hush Free Press*, 1946-56," in McPherson, *et. al.*, eds., *Gendered Pasts*. On the historiography, see S. Maynard, "'In Search of Sodom North':The Writing of Lesbian and Gay History in English Canada," *Canadian Review of Comparative Literature*, 21 (March-June 1994); also C. Hood, "New Studies in Gay and Lesbian History," *Journal of Urban History*, 24, 6 (1998), 282-92; C. Jackson, "Against the Grain: Writing the History of Sexual Variance in America," *Borderlines: Studies in American Culture*, 3, 3 (1996), 278-86.

[82]On famous siblings, see C. Gray, *Sisters in the Wilderness: The Lives of Susanna Moodie and Catharine Parr Traill* (Toronto 1999). The importance of sibling relationships doesn't appear to have diminished over time; see the collection of letters to writer Edna Staebler from her sister (1950s) in E. Staebler, ed., *Haven't Any News: Ruby's Letters from the Fifties* (Waterloo 1995).

[83]M. di Leonardo, "The Female World of Cards and Holidays: Women, Families, and the Work of Kinship," *Signs*, 11 (1987), 440-53; see also A. Douglas, *The Feminization of*

is scarce written about extended family relations, including those involving grand-
parents, aunts, uncles, cousins, and in-laws, despite the evident material, personal
and cultural value ascribed to them in memoirs, diaries, and correspondence, in
legal documents, in literature, and art.[84]

In order to get at the meaning of family for different people in different times,
we need to step back from the collectivity that is family — the "unit" — to look
more intently at how our culture assigns meanings to the self. Despite the individualism pervading Western European-North American-capitalist societies, self-identity is formulated in the family setting, and always in relation to family. Many of
the studies reviewed here consider how men and women have profoundly different
involvements in family, as do young and old. Taken from another angle, how do
family obligations, so often upheld by class-defined conventions, religious and
cultural strictures, law and other forms of regulation and moral suasion, mould
self-identity? Some have described how ethnic, racial, and religious identities are
learned through generational transmission and kinship, but this area remains
underdeveloped, especially in regard to Native Canadians and those of non-white,
non-European origins. We know how those looking in at "other" families racialized
their domestic arrangements; how does race affect the sense of self and the meaning
of family? The interplay of family and religious ideals has been given some thought
in reference to Protestantism; Catholicism outside Québec is barely touched upon
as a formative element in self-identity, yet it has been fiercely imprinted through
family, separate schools, and an array of sociocultural institutions. Given the
tenacious nature of regional identities in Canada, it would be especially interesting
to know what distinctive meanings of self and family might be ascribed to, and
nurtured in regional cultures, or what comprises the social geography of family and
identity.[85]

The greatest hindrance where the history of sexuality is concerned is trying to
glean the degree of "fit" between what is represented and what was actually

---

American Culture (New York 1971); G. Neville, *Kinship and Pilgrimage: Rituals of Reunion
in American Protestant Culture* (New York 1987).

[84]Nor do we have to look to Jane Austen; the very popular early 20th century Canadian
series about Jalna is set at a family compound containing any number of shifting configurations of family related by blood and contract; see M. de la Roche, *Jalna* (Toronto 1927).

[85]Davidoff, *et. al.,The Family Story*, 53-5; 91. None of the following are specifically about
these issues, but Carter's two studies, cited previously, get at the racial aspects; on Protes-
tantism, we have Marks; Morgan; W. Westfall, *Two Worlds: The Protestant Culture of
Nineteenth-Century Ontario (*Montréal/Kingston 1989); S.A. Cook, *Through Sunshine and
Shadow: The Women's Christian Temperance Union, Evangelicalism and Reform in On-
tario, 1874-1930* (Montréal/Kingston 1995); N. Christie, M. Gauvreau, *A Full-Orbed
Christianity: The Protestant Churches and Social Welfare in Canada* (Toronto 1997). On
Catholicism, see the essays in G. Stortz ,T. Murphy, eds., *Creed and Culture: The Place of
English-Speaking Catholics in Canadian Society, 1750-1930* (Montréal 1993).

happening, or even how dominant the dominant discourses were. How different were class standards of sexual morality and commitment to monogamy and heterosexuality? Is there any substance to assumptions that premarital sex was a working-class proclivity, while extra-marital sex belonged to the social betters? This is an area where, as Gagnon's findings suggest, religion, culture, and ethnic background may matter as much as class. Respecting gender and sexuality, the emphasis again remains on women. Male heterosexuality seems to be much as it was described or prescribed. But the prescriptions themselves often exhibited internal contradictions, perhaps a sub-textual acknowledgement of a spectrum of male sexuality. Historians are careful to recognize oppression while avoiding wholesale delegation of victim status, but we lean toward assigning agency to those who may have had so little power on their own account as to render the concept of "choice" meaningless. Or we skirt the historical differences between present-day attitudes and experiences and those of our subjects, and call that difference "agency." Finally, within the context of sexuality, power and diversity, where are the historical forms of the erotic?[86]

The history of private lives has been greatly enhanced by cross-disciplinary borrowing, most recently in the field of cultural anthropology, especially where memory is a crucial source. It is likely that this particular method of data-gathering, though not uncomplicated, holds the key to many of the otherwise "dark corners" of family life. Critical theories borrowed from literature and psychoanalysis are also showing us how to reread memoirs, autobiographies, diaries — all forms of life-writing that have ever constituted important historical sources — to identify the narrative conventions, myths, silences, and tensions that are built into these accounts, to listen to *how* people recount their family stories as well as what they tell in them. Currently promising exciting research possibilities is a reconceptualization of "family time." John Gillis offers the provocative notion of family time as "time out of time," or ritualized time, and how it shapes what Gillis calls our "symbolic families:" those that exist in our family stories, myths, credos, customs, rituals, icons, and so on.[87] Many religious and secular holidays, ceremonies and

---

[86]See A. Giddens, *The Transformation of Intimacy: Sexuality, Love and Eroticism in Modern Societies* (London 1992). Some of the interesting work on sexuality/culture outside Canada includes K. White, *The First Sexual Revolution: The Emergence of Male Heterosexuality in Modern America* (New York 1993); S. Ullman, *Sex Seen: The Emergence of Modern Sexuality in America* (Berkeley 1997), and J.A. Boone, *Libidinal Currents: Sexuality and the Shaping of Modernism* (Chicago 1998).

[87]J. Gillis, "Making Time for Family: The Invention of Family Time(s) and the Reinvention of Family History," *Journal of Family History*, 21, 1 (January 1996), 4-21; further developed in Gillis, *A World of Their Own Making: Myth, Ritual and the Quest for Family Values* (Boston, Mass. 1996). See anthropologist E. Hall's study, *The Dance of Life: The Other Dimensions of Time* (New York 1983). Gillis's fascinating study establishes that many of the "eternal" family rituals are fairly recent. Most originated in Victorian times; some are literally "products" of the early 20th century, invented for middle-class consumers and sold

socially-recognized "passages," "special occasions" such as birthdays and anniversaries, even everyday "family dinner," are implicitly familial, intimate, and exclusive, but their creation and conduct are usually taken-for-granted as timeless and universal. What ideas and practices constitute "family traditions," and who decides these? How do they vary according to class, culture, region, race? Who participates? What roles are played by individual family members that are age and gender-defined — who is honoured, who is seated at the table, who is at the head of the table, who does the planning, who does the work? On a related note, we need to know more about how consumer culture, advertising, and technology have influenced family relations — radio, television, cars — all initially, and still, sold through family imagery, though simultaneously criticized as "things" that interfere in "real" family togetherness.

When it comes to self, symbol, and meaning, approaches derived from psychoanalytic and linguistic theory have compelled us to think about the often contradictory, near-chaotic but co-existing elements denoting the historical relationship between ideas and "things." Regarding discourse analysis, specifically social constructionism and Foucault-inspired textual readings, the benefits to the study of family history are apparent. "The family" is a multidimensional symbol system as well as a material, embodied set of social relations. Deconstruction has helped us to "unpack" terms and categories that we once failed to notice were "loaded." But constructions, plentiful and elemental though they be, are like the top of the table that makes us take its underside on faith, to borrow from the philosophers' store. Even while recognizing the fragmentary nature of historical reality, and accepting that we can only reconceive it imperfectly, indefinitely, and subjectively, it still seems worth trying to see what's underneath rather than contenting ourselves with what is publicly seen, acknowledged, constructed about family life in particular historical moments. There is a certain hint of determinism in over-focusing on what is constructed, perhaps taking away from the creativity of the subjects and that all-important agency to which social historians are so committed. A large part of actual roles and lives must necessarily be self-determined — self-constructed even — no matter who is saying what. We would do well to keep using these valuable tools of historical analysis — only not as one big Foucauldian hammer, applied as though everything were intrinsically meant to be hammered.

Let's turn to the concept of age, at the last. Age is an especially slippery category, all the while that it is a key signifier of personal identity, familial position, and social status. As long as we live, we are too young for some things, too old for others, or somehow "the right age" — and "age requirements" are determined by

---

through modern advertising, family magazines, cinema, and popular music. Whole new industries burgeoned as a result; think, for example, of the boon to greeting card and camera and film manufacturers, who have even lent their product names to these Hallmark occasions and Kodak moments as part of the popular lexicon.

fluctuating criteria as well. Age denotes transitory life stages, some more fleeting or more demarcated than others, but it is also about power, most of which belongs to those in the vast "middling" section who are "of age" but not yet "aged." The most subordinate of all humans in all social categories are the "under-aged." The same structural factors decide access to power and influence for children and young people as for other groups, but the former are also marginalized because authority, in all possible settings, belongs to adults.

We now have a good sense of how childhood was modernized, and, thanks to oral history and memory reconstitution, the hushed voices of children themselves are becoming more audible. We need to know more about those broadly classified as "youth," beginning with a time-specific notion of what this life-stage entailed, and for whom. Some youth were barely more than children, but compulsory schooling and factory laws designated their passage from childhood at age 12 or 14; unmarried men were often considered youth until well into their thirties, while unmarried women aged much faster in the public eye. Adolescence only came to be a distinct category in the early 20th century, part of the larger pattern of age systematization and rationalization that also distinguished and prolonged child-hood.[88] It is here, in this liminal stage of not-children/not-adults, that we stand to learn much about how power is negotiated in the absence of political rights — in the case of young people, through increasing recourse to cultural forms of resistance. Looking to the other end of the life course, we need to think about why political rights are not sufficient to ensure the power of those who are seen to lack cultural value. In both instances, economic power makes a significant difference: teenagers with money to spend are valued more than poor elderly people, while affluent seniors have more power than most teenagers dependent on parents and part-time income. This confirms economic advantage which is not necessarily correlated to class advantage; but it does not explain why the cultural value of youth has increased exponentially over the 20th century, while public respect for elders has declined. In sum, we have to work our way towards employing the concept of "age" analytically as we have done with the class-gender-race trinity, rather than just noting its presence in other kinds of power relations.

Although our purpose as historians is to look for common cultural, social and economic patterns in family life, we will always confront the simple truth that no two family stories are ever the same. However lyrical, Tolstoy's oft-cited theory about how "all happy families resemble each other, each unhappy family is unhappy in its own way" does not hold up in the face of the historical evidence. We might

[88]Among the recent non-Canadian studies, see Palladino, *Teenagers: An American History*; J. Austin and M. Nevin Willard, eds., *Generations of Youth: Youth Cultures and History in Twentieth-Century America* (New York 1998). On aging, see D. Kertzer and P. Laslett, *Aging in the Past: Demography, Society, and Old Age* (Berkeley, Calif. 1995).

do better to use G.K. Chesterton's metaphor: he declared families to exist as little kingdoms, "generally in a state of something resembling anarchy."[89]

[89]G.K. Chesteron, "The Institution of the Family" (1905), quoted in C. Hardyment, *The Future of the Family* (London 1998). The Tolstoy quote is the opening line of *Anna Karenina* (1886).

Bumping and Grinding On the Line: Making Nudity Pay

Becki L. Ross

It was always tricky explaining that I'd been a stripper once; it was startling to other sensibilities, as harsh a class distinction as one can make. People reacted with suspicion, pity or sometimes prurient fascination. They leaped into their assumptions, imagining me a whore, an idiot, a victim. I winced, not from my shame, because there really wasn't any, but from the shame people wanted to impose.[1]

Mining Erotic Exchange

THE ACT OF PAYING for sex as a customer is significantly different from selling it as a supplier. The act of having vacation sex on expensive sheets in a fancy, far-away hotel room is significantly different from laundering the same sheets for a living. The act of stripping in pasties and g-string on a nightclub stage is significantly different from watching striptease and guzzling beer from gynecology row. The act of running an early 20th century brothel or a 21st century escort service is significantly different from policing these businesses undercover and demanding sexual favours in exchange for silence. The act of posing as a centrefold for the inaugural issue of *Playboy* magazine in 1953 is significantly different from standing behind the camera, or banking the profits as publisher. The act of talking dirty on the telephone and getting paid per minute is significantly different from jerking off on the other end of the line. Indeed, the precise conditions organizing the sale and purchase of commercialized sex-related services have been contingent on a nexus of socio-economic factors: uppermost among them are the classed, gendered, and racialized relations between producers and consumers that constitute the nature of the exchange, at any given moment, in specific political economies.

[1]Lindalee Tracey, *Growing Up Naked: My Years in Bump and Grind* (Vancouver and Toronto 1997), 209. In her autobiography, Tracey criticizes the feminist film director, Bonnie Sherr Klein, who used and distorted her experience to tell an anti-stripper and anti-pornography salvationist parable in "*Not a Love Story*" (National Film Board 1982).

Becki L. Ross, "Bumping and Grinding On the Line: Making Nudity Pay," *Labour/Le Travail*, 46 (Fall 2000), 221-50.

Throughout the 20th century across North America, largely white, straight, monied men have had the means to define what they want sexually, how, and when they want it. Both married and unmarried, wealthy and working class, white and non-white, men have made payments for a variety of sex-related interactions with women.[2] Indeed, it has been working-class white women and women of colour who have enabled the carnal appetites and fantasies of men, or lubricated them, if you will, *through their paid labour*.[3] While the character of these women's labour has greatly varied, prostitution has been most vigorously singled out as a dire social problem in need of public, media, and state action.[4]

Beginning in the late 19th century, European sexologists, anatomists, physiologists, and physicians sought to territorialize the prostitute body as a working-class body — grotesque, diseased, and distinct from the bodies of bourgeois wives and chaste daughters. According to Shannon Bell, the prostitute was marked as dirty, repulsive, noisy, and contaminating, and was "produced as the negative identity of the bourgeois subject — the 'not-I'."[5] The medical discourse of nymphomania hailed working-class prostitutes, both white and black, as naturally and essentially hypersexual, prone to clitoral hypertrophy and sexual perversion of all sorts.[6] Assumptions about prostitutes as sinners, sex slaves, and unchaste vectors of disease have contributed to their vulnerability to violence, even murder: consider the mangled, sexually mutilated remains of five prostitutes at the hands of Jack the Ripper in 1888, in East London.[7] At the time, reporters for the *Pall Mall Gazette* and the *Daily Telegraph* blamed the women for their fate: "[These] drunken, vicious, miserable wretches whom it was almost a charity to relieve of the penalty of existence" were "not very particular about how they earned a living."[8] A hundred years later, between 1975 and 1999, an estimated sixty-seven street prostitutes in Vancouver's downtown eastside have either disappeared or turned up dead and

[2]The act of men paying men/male youth for sexual services has a long, compelling history, and is not a topic of consideration here.

[3]This is not to discount the uneven and complex sexual exchanges between young, largely working-class boys and older men. On this topic, see the superb essay by Steven Maynard, "'Horrible Temptations': Sex, Men, and Working Class Male Youth in Urban Ontario, 1890-1935," *Canadian Historical Review*, 78 (June 1997), 191-235.

[4]Deborah Brock, *Making Work, Making Trouble: Prostitution as a Social Problem* (Toronto 1998), 4.

[5]Shannon Bell, *Reading, Writing and Rewriting the Prostitute Body* (Bloomington, Indiana 1994), 43.

[6]Margaret Gibson, "Clitoral Corruption: Body Metaphors and American Doctors' Constructions of Female Homosexuality, 1870-1900," in Vernon Rosario, ed., *Science and Homosexualities* (New York 1997), 118-21.

[7]Judith Walkowitz, *City of Dreadful Delight: Narratives of Sexual Danger in Late-Victorian London* (Chicago 1992), 198.

[8]*Daily Telegraph,* 24 September 1888; *Pall Mall Gazette,* 10 September 1888, cited in Walkowitz, *City of Dreadful Delight,* 200.

dismembered, some in dumpsters.[9] Dehumanizing, anti-prostitute stereotypes have animated the campaigns of police officers, judges, lawyers, physicians, moral reformers, and civic politicians who have predicated their anti-vice agenda, in part, on the inadmissability of sex work as a labour relation.[10] In effect, century-old dismissals of sex work *as work* have afforded legions of medical, legal, and moral experts the licence to pathologize the working-class female supplier of erotic goods as nothing but a congenital type predisposed to sexual degeneracy, immorality, and innumerable societal transgressions.[11]

In spite of Foucault's astute observation that discourses about sex have multiplied and proliferated since the 17th century, and that discursive regimes have administered and regulated sexuality, the history of women's labour in the commercial sex industry has not much captured the imagination of Canadian scholars.[12] Historians of working-class labour in the 20th century have identified the injustices of structural unemployment, ugly conflicts between workers and management, the exploitation of non-Anglo immigrants, the consolidation of a gender-segmented labour force, declining rates of unionization, and deepening class schisms, as

[9]Daniel Wood, "Missing," *Elmstreet Magazine*, December 1999, 15-22.

[10]For selected reading on the topic of moral regulation by Canadian state and extra-state apparatuses, see Mariana Valverde, ed., *Radically Rethinking Regulation* (Toronto 1994); Carolyn Strange and Tina Loo, *Making Good: Law and Moral Regulation in Canada, 1867-1939* (Toronto 1997); Joan Sangster, "Incarcerating 'Bad Girls': The Regulation of Sexuality through the Female Refuges Act in Ontario, 1920-1945," *Journal of the History of Sexuality*, 7 (1996), 239-75; Becki Ross, "Destaining the (Tattooed) Delinquent Body: Moral Regulatory Practices at Toronto's Street Haven, 1965-1969," *Journal of the History of Sexuality*, 8 (April 1997), 561-95.

[11]See, for example, Alexander John Baptiste Parent-Duchatelet, *De La Prostitution dans la Ville de Paris, Volume I*, (1836), trans. by Jill Harsin, *Policing Prostitution in Nineteenth Century Paris* (Princeton 1985), 205-35; Havelock Ellis, *Sex in Relation to Society: Studies in the Psychology of Sex*, Volume VI (Philadelphia 1910), 277.

[12]For selected readings on the history of the sex trade, see Judith Walkowitz, *Prostitution in Victorian Society* (Cambridge 1980); Ruth Rosen, *The Lost Sisterhood: Prostitution in America, 1900-1918* (Baltimore 1982); Bell, *Reading, Writing, and Rewriting the Prostitute Body;* Nickie Roberts, *Whores in History: Prostitution in Western Society* (London 1992); Deborah Nilsen, "The 'Social Evil': Prostitution in Vancouver, 1900-1920," in Barbara Latham and Cathy Less, ed., *Selected Essays on Women's History in B.C.* (Victoria 1980), 205-28; Lori Rotenberg, "The Wayward Worker: Toronto's Prostitute at the Turn of the Century," in J. Acton, P. Goldsmith, B. Shephard, ed., *Women at Work 1850-1930* (Toronto 1974), 33-70; Bay Riley, *Gold Diggers of the Klondike: Prostitution in Dawson City, Yukon, 1898-1908* (Toronto 1997); Charlene Kish, "A Knee Joint is Not Entertainment: the Moral Regulation of Burlesque in Early Twentieth-Century Toronto," MA thesis, Department of History, York University, 1997; Brock, *Making Work, Making Trouble: Prostitution as a Social Problem.*

flagrant, wretched features of capitalist social formation.[13] Historians of sexuality have energetically explored the social inventions of homosexuality, bisexuality, and heterosexuality, as well as the formation of sexual communities, and the emergence of state and extra-state campaigns to police sexual fears, anxieties, and dangers.[14] New investigations include Karen Dubinksy's brilliant, cheeky meditation on Niagara Falls as a theme park for heterosexual honeymooners, Valerie Korinek's trenchant re-interpretation of *Chatelaine* magazine as a powerful (and at times contradictory) mid-century guide for "proper, modern womanhood," and Mona Gleason's impressive dissection of the role of postwar psychology in producing 'normal' male and female citizens at school.[15] However, the dual unfolding of sex-free labour studies alongside work-free sexuality studies within Canadian social history has meant that the rich registers of "sexuality" and "labour" have rarely been placed systematically in relation to, and in tension with, one another.

I suspect that myriad explanations account for the parallel-tracking that has hindered venturesome, fruitful intercourse between sex history and labour/working-class history. Among them is the lingering ambivalence, if not hostility, of some labour specialists toward the relevance and legitimacy of so-called private sexual matters. In addition, the initial focus of sex history specialists (whose numbers are quite low in Canada) was on recovering knowledge of queer sexual identities, communities, and *non-remunerated play*, in the context of an oppressive, heteronormative past. Sex historians have not, until recently, turned their attention to the participation of both queers and non-queers in the *remunerated work* of selling sexual arousal and activity which has itself, like homosexuality, been subject to punishing penalties, though for different reasons. And the proverbial dilemma of locating sources germane to the story one wants to tell — whether it's case files,

[13]For selected readings in Canadian labour history, see Bryan Palmer, *Working Class Experience: The Rise and Reconstitution of Canadian Labour, 1800-1980* (Toronto and Vancouver 1983); Craig Heron and Bob Storey, *On the Job: Confronting the Labour Process in Canada* (Montréal and Kingston 1986); Gregory S. Kealey, *Workers and Canadian History* (Montréal and Kingston 1995); David Bercuson and David Bright, eds., *Canadian Labour History: Selected Readings* (Toronto 1994), Franca Iacovetta, *Such Hard-Working People: Italian Immigrants in Postwar Toronto* (Montréal and Kingston 1992); Joy Parr, *The Gender of Breadwinners: Women, Men and Change in Two Industrial Towns* (Toronto 1990); Gillian Creese, *Contracting Masculinity: Gender, Class and Race in a White Collar Union* (Toronto 1999); Craig Heron, ed., *The Workers' Revolt in Canada, 1917-1925* (Toronto 1998).

[14]Carolyn Strange, "Bad Girls and Masked Men: Recent Works on Sexuality in U.S. History," *Labour/Le Travail*, 30 (Spring 1997), 261-75.

[15]Karen Dubinsky, *The Second Greatest Disappointment: Honeymooning and Tourism at Niagara Falls* (Toronto 1999); Valerie Korinek, *Roughing it in the Suburbs: Reading Chatelaine Magazine in the Fifties and Sixties* (Toronto 2000); Mona Gleason, *Normalizing the Ideal: Psychology, Schooling, and the Family in Postwar Canada* (Toronto 1999).

police records, personal scrapbooks, court transcripts, mayor's papers, diaries, or city directories — is especially acute for those of us who confront the legacy of sex work as "unspeakable," stigmatized and clandestine.[16] Absent from both Canada Census data and statistics that plot the contours of the formal labour force, sex trade workers have proved to be an elusive population.

It seems plausible to me that the discursive construction of the Sexual Other in 20th-century Canada most vigorously and unrelentingly targeted women who oiled the machinery of commercialized sex. This is certainly not to say, as some feminists do, that female sex trade workers, in every instance, have been coerced, degraded victims of patriarchal control.[17] While evidence of dangerous, violent working conditions exists, the complex agency of female sex workers throughout the 20th century remains under-explored — their challenges to grinding stereo-types, their efforts to combine migrant labouring with familial intimacy, their battles against the regulatory practices of police, politicians, and moral reformers, and their spirited bids to unionize, among other measures of resistance. Increas-ingly, activist female sex workers, primarily in the geo-political north, have found resources to write their own illuminating, bracing tales of exploitation *and* rebel-lion, resistance *and* accommodation.[18] However, unlike female cannery workers, fishers, bakers, stenographers, child-minders, and retail clerks, working-class women who marketed their sex-related skills found themselves at once desired *and* criminalized, or at the very least, scorned and marginalized, in unique and disturb-ing ways.[19]

In the absence of detailed empirical and theoretical studies, I have more questions than answers. When we consider Foucault's notion that the medicaliza-tion of sexuality "set about contacting bodies, caressing them with its eyes, intensifying areas, electrifying surfaces, dramatizing troubled moments," what

[16]See Rosen, *The Lost Sisterhood*, xi.

[17]Sara Wynter, "WHISPER: Women Hurt in Systems of Prostitution Engaged in Revolt," in Frederica Delacoste and Priscilla Alexander, ed., *Sex Work: Writings by Women in the Sex Industry* (Pittsburgh 1987), 66-70.

[18]For contemporary writings from the standpoint of sex trade workers, specifically prosti-tutes, see Valerie Scott, Peggy Miller, and Ryan Hotchkiss, "Realistic Feminists," in Laurie Bell, ed., *Good Girls, Bad Girls: Sex Trade Workers and Feminists Face to Face* (Toronto 1987), 204-17; Margo St. James, "The Reclamation of Whores," in *Good Girls, Bad Girls*, 81-87; Gail Pheterson, *A Vindication of the Rights of Whores* (Seattle 1989); Gail Pheterson, *The Prostitution Prism* (Amsterdam 1996); Alexandra Highcrest, *At Home on the Stroll: My Twenty Years as a Prostitute in Canada* (Toronto 1997); Jill Nagle, ed., *Whores and Other Feminists* (New York 1998); Frederique Delacoste and Priscilla Alexander, eds., *Sex Work: Writings by Women in the Sex Industry* (Pittsburgh 1987); Wendy Chapkis, *Live Sex Acts: Women Performing Erotic Labour* (New York 1997); Brock, *Making Work, Making Trouble*.

[19]In his book, *Vancouver: The Way it Was* (Vancouver 1984), Michael Kluckner comments: "Prostitutes followed the Canadian Pacific Railway workers across the country like a scruffy, pulchritudinous plague." (34).

might we learn about how sellers and buyers of erotic goods have been differently contacted and caressed?[20] How have the "promiscuous lower orders" — those presumed to be intrinsically lascivious — both consented to and resisted demands for sexual servicing from "the propertied and self-controlled?"[21] Specifically, what has been the nature of female-dominated job categories such as street prostitute, call-girl, stripteaser, peep show dancer, masseuse, and pin-up/porn model?[22] What occupational choices did sex workers confront prior to entering the business? How might we compare and contrast the occupational hazards and benefits faced by female sex workers in mid-century Canada with those encountered by textile workers, waitresses, domestics, and beauticians, or female journalists, nurses, and teachers? What differentiated professional stripteasers from the can-can and hula dancers employed to entertain workers at the Canadian Car and Foundry Company in Fort William before, during, and after World War II?[23] In decades past, female factory employees were subjected to forms of sexual harassment on the line, though Joan Sangster learned that former clerical staff at Quaker Oats in 1940s Ontario tended to accept this behaviour as "part of the job" in an era that predated feminist analysis of unwanted, intrusive male advances.[24] Did labouring to sell sex, or sexual arousal, expose female vendors to greater frequency and/or intensity of unsolicited male sexual attention and assault? To what extent did sex workers internalize the shame they were taught to feel for parading around skimpily-clad in public, for brazenly inciting men's lust (and getting paid for it), or for refusing the role of full-time wife and mother? Moreover, how did the stubbornly racist, sexist stereotypes of black women as oversexed jezebels,[25] Asian women as Dragon Ladies,[26] and First Nations women as sexually fast, loose squaws,[27] shape the experiences

[20] See Michel Foucault, *The History of Sexuality,* Volume I (New York 1978), 44.

[21] Angus McLaren, *Twentieth-Century Sexuality: A History* (Oxford 1999), 6.

[22] In the past twenty years, we might add telephone sex operator, internet sex operator, and professional s/m dominatrix.

[23] Helen Smith and Pamela Wakewich, "'Beauty and the Helldivers': Representing Women's Work and Identities in a Warplant Newspaper," *Labour/Le Travail*, 44 (Fall 1999), 93-5.

[24] Joan Sangster, *Earning Respect: The Lives of Working Women in Small-Town Ontario, 1920-1960* (Toronto 1995), 98, 112.

[25] See Patricia Hill Collins, "The Sexual Politics of Black Womanhood," in *Black Feminist Thought* (New York 1990), 163-180; Evelynn Hammonds, "Toward a Genealogy of Black Female Sexuality: the Problematic of Silence," in M. J. Alexander and C. Mohanty, eds., *Feminist Genealogies, Colonial Legacies, Democratic Futures* (New York 1997), 170-192.

[26] Linda Xiao Jia Chen, "Laundresses and Prostitutes: Deconstructing Stereotypes and Finding an Asian Feminist Voice," *Resources for Feminist Research*, 3/4, 20 (1992), 88-90.

[27] Sarah Carter, "First Nations Women of Prairie Canada in the Early Reserve Years, the 1870s to the 1920s: a preliminary inquiry," in Christine Miller and Patricia Churchryk, eds., *Women of the First Nations: Power, Wisdom, and Strength* (Winnipeg 1996), 51-76; Jean Barman, "Taming Aboriginal Sexuality: Gender, Power, and Race in British Columbia, 1850-1900," *BC Studies*, 115/116 (Fall/Winter 1997/98), 237-66.

of non-white female sex workers? In particular, how did stripteasers of colour use the stage to act out, and act against, the crushing colonial tropes of African primitivism, Indian savagery, and Orientalism?

"Ladies and Genitals...Let Us Tickle Your Pickle"[28]

In this paper, I ruminate on complicated entanglements of sexuality, labour, and social class in the history of 20th century erotic entertainment in North America. I utilize preliminary archival and ethnographic findings from my case study on burlesque and striptease culture in Vancouver, 1945-1980,[29] to explore the working conditions and artistic influences of former dancers, the racialized expectations of erotic spectacle, and the queer dimensions of strip culture.[30] Accepting "business insiders" as the expert practitioners of their own lives means discovering not only the identities of the women who performed striptease in postwar Vancouver, but the meanings that these entertainers attached to their craft.[31] And because men have been indispensable to the production and consumption of striptease as club owners/staff, musicians, choreographers, booking agents, costume designers, photographers, and patrons, their recollections must be solicited, and will be integrated in upcoming research reports.

Popular lore within striptease culture laments the decline of the glamorous, goldern era of the tasteful, lavish art of "the tease" in burlesque, and the gradual rise of the vulgar, anti-erotic, generic "cunt show" by the late 1970s.[32] Reflecting

---

[28]Tracey, *Growing Up Naked*, 5.

[29]There is an important sociological literature that focuses on the business of striptease or "exotic dancing" in the 1980s and 1990s, though much of the work is uncritically rooted in the tradition of the sociology of deviance. See Craig Forsyth and Tina Deshotels, "A Deviant Process: The Sojourn of the Stripper," *Sociological Spectrum*, 18 (1998), 77-92; Willliam Thompson and Jackie Harred, "Topless Dancers: Managing Stigma in a Deviant Occupation," *Deviant Behaviour* 13 (1992), 291-311; Scott Reid, Jonathon Epstein, and D.E. Benson, "Does Exotic Dancing Pay Well But Cost Dearly?," in A. Thio and T. Calhoun, eds., *Readings in Deviant Behaviour* (New York 1995), 284-88; and G.E. Enck and J.D. Preston, "Counterfeit Intimacy: A Dramaturgical Analysis of an Erotic Performance," *Deviant Behaviour,* 9 (1988), 360-81.

[30]My research assistants and I have much more archival material to consult, including Health Department records regarding forced veneral disease testing of dancers/prostitutes, records of booking agents, promotional photographs of dancers, dancers' autobiographies, Hollywood and independent film, records of the Pacific National Exhibition, RCMP and Vancouver Police, Attorney General's files on provincial liquor licensing, records of women's groups and clergy who lobbied for closure of nightclubs, among others. I also plan to travel to Hellendale, California to visit former stripper Dixie Evans' "Exotic World Museum" — a shrine in the desert that honours burlesque and striptease artists in the twentieth century.

[31]See Dorothy E. Smith, *The Everyday World As Problematic: Toward a Feminist Sociology* (Toronto 1987), 154.

[32]Lucinda Jarrett, *Stripping in Time: A History of Erotic Dancing* (London 1997), 192.

on her exit from the business in 1979, Montréal-based dancer Lindalee Tracey observes: "Striptease fell from grace because the world stopped dreaming."[33] In my larger project, I intend to subject this lore to careful sociological investigation of shifts within the business, and within the broader socio-economic context of B.C.'s lower mainland, over a forty-year period.[34] In what follows, my entrée into striptease history wedges open a window onto deep-seated cultural anxieties about gender and sexual norms, working-class amusements, and racial otherness. I conclude with some comments about the imbrication of sex and nation in the history of erotic entertainment.[35]

Nice Girls, Smart Girls, Good Girls Don't Disrobe in Public

Female burlesque, go-go, and striptease have been perceived by religious, civic, and moral reformers as commercialized sexual vice that inflame men's passions (already fuelled by alcohol), propel them to seek adulterous liaisons, abandon their families, and jeopardize their workplace productivity.[36] For almost a century, popular conflations of striptease with nymphomania, illiteracy, drug addiction, prostitution, and disease, have labelled female erotic performers dangerous to the social order, the family, and the nation.[37] In the 1920s and 1930s of the US and Canada, striptease within the broad rubric of burlesque was a unique combination of sexual humour and female sexual display, with a focus on sexual suggestiveness aided by the "tease" factor.[38] Historian Andrea Friedman notes: "The key to the striptease was not how much a woman stripped, but how much the people in the

[33]Tracey, *Growing Up Naked*, 210.
[34]Much has changed in the world of striptease since 1980, including the introduction of table dancing, lap dancing, in-house massage, merchandising, contests in Las Vegas, Internet transmission of live strip shows, and increasingly global movement of strippers within and across national borders. On the emergence of striptease clubs and the hiring of international dancers in the Caribbean, see Jacqueline Martis, "Tourism and the Sex Trade in St. Maarten and Curacao, the Netherlands Antilles," in Kamela Kempadoo, ed., *Sun, Sex and Gold: Tourism and Sex Work in the Caribbean* (Lanham, Maryland 1999), 207-8.
[35]For stunning insights into the place of sexuality in the process of Canadian state formation, see Steven Maynard, "The Maple Leaf (Gardens) Forever: Sex, Canadian Historians and National History," unpublished paper, Department of History, Queen's University, 1999.
[36]Ann Corio with Joseph DiMona, *This Was Burlesque* (New York 1968); Charles McCaghy and James Skipper, "Stripping: Anatomy of a Deviant Life Style," in Saul Feldman and Gerald Thielbar, eds., *Life Styles: Diversity in American Society* (Boston 1972); Jarrett, *Stripping in Time*.
[37]Cited in James Skipper and Charles McCaghy, "Stripteasing: A Sex-Oriented Occupation," in James Henslin, ed., *Studies in the Sociology of Sex* (New York 1971), 281-82. Also see James Skipper and Charles McCaghy, "Stripteasers: The Anatomy and Career Contingencies of a Deviant Occupation," *Social Problems,* 17 (1970), 391-404.
[38]Robert Allen, *Horrible Prettiness: Burlesque and American Culture* (Chapel Hill, North Carolina 1991), 244.

audience thought she stripped, as well as how successfully she encouraged their desire that she strip."[39] It was maintenance of the illusion of nudity that afforded the business some legal protection from obscenity laws. Italian American Ann Corio, a stripteaser throughout the 1930s, remembers incidences of state power over sexual representation, and the tricks employed to safeguard illicit shows:

[At the Howard Theatre in Boston], once the ticket-taker saw the censor coming up the stairs he pressed his foot on a pedal. On stage, the show might be in full production. A stripper might be giving her all for mankind, shimmying and grinding. Clothes might be flying in all directions. The crowd would be yelling, "Take it off," and the music might be crashing to a crescendo. Suddenly a red light would start blinking in the footlights. A censor had arrived... Imagine Mickey Mantle trying to stop in the middle of his swing. That's what those stormy strippers would have to do...Red light! Hold it! The hips would stop as if paralyzed. Those clothes would come flying back from the wings. The perspiring musicians would dissolve to a waltz. And by the time the censor reached the top of the stairs and looked down on the stage he would see — not a hip-swinging, hair-tossing, half-naked tigress — but a nun on a casual stroll through a most unlikely convent.[40]

Friedman shows how a decade-long campaign against burlesque waged in New York by religious, anti-vice, and municipal activists, including mayor LaGuardia, resulted in a city-wide ban on burlesque entertainment in 1937. Friedman's research also suggests that anxieties about the disorderliness and immorality of the male burlesque audience were at the heart of contests to eradicate sexual entertainment in New York in the 1930s.[41] By 1942, every burlesque theatre licence in the Big Apple was revoked, on the grounds that the shows promoted filth, vulgarity, immorality, and male sexual violence.[42] In effect, anti-burlesque initiatives were part of a larger set of strategies to regulate the sexual content of commercial culture, which included motion pictures, crime comics, and obscene or dirty magazines. Ironically, as Marilyn Hegarty notes, some mainstream American magazines during World War II featured "sizzling" female dancehall and canteen entertainers in g-strings as morale builders for the troops — for a brief moment, the nation, or the nation's solidiers, depended on public displays of feminine (hetero)sexiness. However, the entertainers' patriotism remained suspect due to their "potential promiscuity" and "descent into prostitution."[43]

[39]Andrea Friedman, "The Habitats of Sex-Crazed Perverts: Campaigns Against Burlesque in Depression-Era New York City," *Journal of the History of Sexuality*, 7 (1996), 204.
[40]Ann Corio and Joseph DiMona, *This Was Burlesque*, 175. Similar stories have been told about the use of red lights to warn lesbians and gay men engaged in illegal same-sex dancing in public bars and clubs in the 1940s and 1950s. See Joan Nestle, *A Restricted Country* (Ithaca, New York 1987), and *Persistent Desires: a femme/butch reader* (Boston 1992).
[41]Andrea Friedman, "The Habitats of Sex-Crazed Perverts," 237.
[42]Friedman, "The Habitats of Sex-Crazed Perverts,", 235, 238.
[43]Marilyn Hegarty, "Patriot or Prostitute: Sexual Discourses, Print Media, and American Women during World War II," *Journal of Women's History,* 10 (Summer 1998), 122.

Cameos of stripteasers in Hollywood film have worked to stabilize the age-old dichotomy between good, middle-class girls and wayward, working-class sex deviants. In the decorated blockbuster, "The Graduate" (1967), newly minted, aimless university graduate Benjamin Bradock (Dustin Hoffman) is pressured to escort Elaine Robinson (Katherine Ross), the daughter of his lover, Mrs. Robinson (Anne Bancroft), on a date. By insisting on accompanying Elaine to a downtown stripclub, Benjamin succeeds in sexually, publicly humiliating and punishing the white, upper-class, virgin by forcing her to witness the sullying, sickening debauchery of stripteasers who twirl ornamental tassels from jeweled pasties (double-dutch style) for a living. However, at the horrifying sight of Elaine's tears, Benjamin is jolted into class-conscious chivalry and proceeds to lunge angrily, violently at the dancer on stage. Pursuing a fleeing Elaine out of the club, he later comforts her with kisses and food in the safety and style of his red convertible sportscar.

In the post World War II era, burlesque and striptease flourished in Vancouver's blind pigs or afterhours booze cans, and a handful of nightclubs and mainstream theatres. Marketed as adult entertainment for both locals and tourists in the port city, erotic performance was "most legal" and "most respectable" in large, soft-seat nightclubs such as the Palomar and the Cave Supper Club that routinely staged swing bands, large-scale musicals, and big-name lounge acts.[44] In smaller nightclubs such as the Penthouse Cabaret, the Kobenhavn, and the Shangri-La, in poorer, working-class neighborhoods, including Chinatown, striptease acts that overlapped with "high art," though packaged to emphasize partial, and later, full nudity, faced multi-voiced opposition. Clergy, public officials, women's groups, and police argued for the careful scrutiny of "low class" venues associated (ideologically and spatially) with the "criminal classes," and at different times, mobilized a range of municipal by-laws, provincial liquor laws, and federal Criminal Code provisions, to turn up the heat on unscrupulous hoteliers, cabaret owners, and dancers.[45] Indeed, the flourishing of striptease, first on the stages of quasi-legal, unlicensed bottle clubs (which themselves traded in the forbidden), and later,

---

[44]Robert Campbell makes a similar argument when he distinguishes the sale of alcohol in first-class hotels from lower-end hotels with their overwhelmingly working-class clientele. See his article, "Managing the Marginal: Regulating and Managing Decency in Vancouver's Beer Parlours, 1925-1954," *Labour/Le Travail*, 44 (Fall 1999), 112.

[45]Robert Campbell, in *Demon Rum or Easy Money: Government Control of Liquor in British Columbia from Prohibition to Privatization* (Ottawa: Carleton University Press 1991), 50-55, argues that the BC Liquor Control Board enforced a "no food, no entertainment, no dancing" policy in Vancouver's beer parlours (in hotels), until 1954. In his article, "Managing the Marginal," Campbell points out that the Chief Inspector for the BC liquor board rejected applications for a liquor license from Chinese in Vancouver, as it "has been found that Chinese are not able to handle this type of business." (cited on p. 123)

post-1969, when "bottomless" strip acts were legalized, contributed to the city's reputation as home to the hottest nightclubs north of San Francisco.[46]

In Vancouver in 1941, a special Police Delegation of religious and temperance leaders toured and inspected the city's night spots: they were known as the "special constables," and were part of a long tradition of anthropological treatment of the city as, quoting Carolyn Strange, "a laboratory full of troubling specimens of urban life."[47] When they roamed city streets in search of flourishing vice both inside and adjacent to well-known red-light districts, they became social geographers, mapping the locations of moral evils. Upon visiting a local cabaret, Mrs. McKay of the Vancouver Local Council of Women, representing seventy-eight women's groups, told reporters for the *Vancouver News Herald*: "The floor show was objectionable, with girls naked except brassieres and loin clothes." Rev. Cook complained of "immoral conduct highly suggestive of Sodom and Gomorrah."[48] Years later, in 1965, Tom Hazlitt of the *Vancouver Daily Province* commented: "The city's cabarets are crowded with bottle-packing juveniles. Drunkenness and fights are commonplace. So is drug addiction, prostitution, and erotic dancing of a bizarre nature. Some places are frequented by men who dress up as women and women who dress up as men."[49] In 1966, reporter George Peloquin of the *Vancouver Sun* quoted the city's Chief Licence Inspector, Mitch Harrell: "Two carbarets were warned: the attire on their girls was too skimpy. One involved dancers with transparent, black chiffon blouses. The by-law forbids any person to produce in any building or place in the city any immoral or lewd theatrical performance of any kind."[50] Ten years later, in 1976, the Attorney General's office instructed the BC Liquor Control Board to enforce a ban on "bare-breasted waitresses" in Vancouver nightclubs.[51] A key paradox in the history of the nightclub scene in British Columbia and elsewhere, is the subjection of striptease to a concerted proliferation of speech and acts intended to prohibit it.[52]

The Penthouse Cabaret, which opened on Seymour Street in downtown Vancouver in 1947, was owned and run by the Filippone brothers — Joe, Ross,

[46]Chuck Davis, *The Greater Vancouver Book: An Urban Encyclopedia* (Surrey, British Columbia 1997).
[47]Carolyn Strange, *Toronto's Girl Problem* (Toronto1995), 106.
[48]"Drunken, Immoral Conduct in Cabarets: Church, Temperance Heads Related Visits to Night Spots," *Vancouver News Herald*, 13 December 1941; "Police Revert to One O'Clock Cabaret Closing," *Vancouver News Herald*, 13 December 1941.
[49]Tom Hazlitt, "Legal or Illegal: City's Night Spots Roar Wide Open," *Vancouver Daily Province*, 9 January 1965.
[50]George Peloquin, "Go-Go Cabarets Can't Go Topless, *Vancouver Sun*, 19 September 1966.
[51]"Cover Up, Says A-G," *Vancouver Sun*, 31 August 1976.
[52]Here, I am adapting insights of Judith Butler, *Excitable Speech* (New York 1997), 130-35.

Mickey, and Jimmy — and their sister Florence.[53] It started out as Joe's penthouse apartment where he "privately" entertained guests above the family's Diamond Cabs and Eagle Time Delivery service, and it was raided for liquor infractions the first night it opened. Still operating in 2000, and continuing to be run by members of the Filippone family, it is the longest-standing striptease venue in Canada. In 1968, reporter Alex MacGillivray wrote that The Penthouse was "a watering spot for bookies and brokers, doctors and dentists, guys and dolls, ladies and gentlemen, and just about anybody who could smell a good time."[54] Show business celebrities such as Tony Bennett, Sophie Tucker, Sammy Davis Jr., Liberace, and Ella Fitzgerald entertained at the Penthouse, as did headlining stripteasers such as Sally Rand (of the famous fan dance), Evelyn West, the "Hubba Hubba" girl (with breasts insured by Lloyds of London for $50,000), Lili St. Cyr, and Tempest Storm, beginning in the late 1950s, though the Filippone brothers prohibited full nudity until the mid-1970s. Extravagant Las Vegas-style revues full of scantily-clad, plumed, and spangled showgirls were imported, and the burlesque acts were accompanied by live jazz and swing bands.[55] By the early 1960s, the Penthouse had a reputation as the best place in the city to meet élite prostitutes who frequented the club, bought food and drinks, and charmed a loyal clientele of tourists and locals.[56]

For decades, the Penthouse was habitually raided and closed down. Between 1951 and 1968, nightspots like the Penthouse were strictly bottle clubs — patrons brought bottled liquor to the club or purchased drinks from the illegal stash behind the bar, as well as ice and mix. In so doing, they made themselves vulnerable to police busts. According to Ross Filippone, his brother Joe arranged for a lookout on the roof who buzzed a waiter downstairs when he spotted the "Dry Squad." The waiter then warned patrons to hide their booze on built-in ledges under the tables, and to deny any wrong-doing to the gun-and-holstered boys in blue. In 1968, after decades of lobbying by the West Coast Cabaret Owners Association, the Penthouse was finally awarded a liquor licence which legalized liquor sales years after hotel parlours in the city had been granted the right to sell beer (only, and by the glass). In December 1975, after a five-month-long undercover operation,[57] the Filippone brothers, a cashier and a doorman, were charged with living off the avails of

[53]Filippone is the anglicized version of the original Philliponi, invented by a racist immigration officer when Joe (the eldest) and his parents arrived in British Columbia from San Nicola, Italy, in 1929.
[54]Alex MacGillivray, "Column," *Vancouver Sun*, 20 December 1968, A2.
[55]Les Wiseman, "Not Your Average Joe," *Vancouver Magazine* (April 1982), 68.
[56]Daniel Wood, "The Naked and the Dead: Truth Isn't the Only Victim in the 50-year Penthouse Saga," *Vancouver Magazine* (December 1997), 104.
[57]According to a cover story in *Dick MacLean's Guide: the Fortnightly Restaurant Magazine,* 4-18 October, 1978, "the full operation, which involved 12 officers, included surveillance by means of electronic eavesdropping devices, hidden cameras, motor vehicle surveillance, and male officers entering the club to pose as protitutes' clients." (13)

prostitution and conspiring to corrupt public morals.[58] In his testimony, Joe Philliponi vowed that he never allowed total nudity on the stage at the Penthouse's Gold Room. All the dancers were cautioned to keep their g-strings firmly in place.[59] Finally, in 1978, after a forced, padlocked closure lasting two-and-a-half years, convictions, fines, appeals and $1.5 million in litigation fees, all of the accused were fully acquitted.[60] So, though Vancouver nightclubs were never closed down *en masse* à la New York City in 1942, hotspots like the Penthouse, as well as the Kobenhavn, Zanzibar, and Oil Can Harry's, were consistently under the gaze of moral and legal authorities, scapegoated as dens of immorality, obscenity, and indecency. Stripteasers, who were commonly assumed to moonlight as prostitutes, were never exempted from the scrutiny of those who damned nightclubs as the playgrounds of gangsters, bootleggers, bookies, pimps, hookers, and sex fiends.

Working The Stage: The Good, The Bad, The Ugly

Headliners Sally Rand, Gypsy Rose Lee, Lili St. Cyr, "Queen of the Strippers," and Tempest Storm, all of whom performed in Vancouver during the 1950s and 1960s, netted top salaries. Their price of upwards of $4,000 per weekend (even when they were over 40), meant they earned more than women in any other job category.[61] However, a handsome pay cheque did not necessarily translate into respect. In 1969, American sociologists Jesser and Donovan interviewed 155 university students and 122 parents of students, all of whom assigned stripteasers a lower occupational ranking than what were seen to be traditionally low status jobs: janitor, artist's model, and professional gambler.[62] Interviews with five former dancers suggest that female erotic dancers who performed in Vancouver clubs such as the Penthouse and the Cave, and later, the No. 5 Orange Hotel, the Drake Hotel, and the Cecil Hotel, negotiated salary and working conditions in a stigmatized, male-controlled profession.[63]

---

[58] *Dick MacLean's Guide*, 112-15.

[59] "The Penthouse Papers," *Dick MacLean's Guide*, 27.

[60] *Dick MacLean's Guide*, 113; and, see Pino Didon, "A Candid Interview: Philliponi Disapproves of Nudity," *L'Eco D'Italia*, 20 January 1978, 1-3, 8.

[61] Jarrett, *Stripping in Time*, 170.

[62] C. Jesser and L. Donovan, "Nudity in the Art Training Process," *Sociological Quarterly* 10 (1969), 355-71.

[63] For autobiographical writings on striptease from 1970 to 2000, see Misty, *Strip!* (Toronto 1973); Janet Feindel, *A Particular Class of Woman* (Vancouver 1988); Margaret Dragu and A.S.A Harrison, *Revelations: Essays on Striptease and Sexuality* (London 1988); Annie Ample, *The Bare Facts: My Life as a Stripper* (Toronto 1988); Lindalee Tracey, *Growing Up Naked*; Dianna Atkinson, *Highways and Dancehalls* (Toronto 1995); Shannon Bell, ed., *Whore Carnival* (New York 1995); Gwendolyn, "Nothing Butt: The Truth about the Sex Trade," *Toward the Slaughterhouse of History* (Toronto 1992), 16-23; Chris Bearchell, "No Apologies: Strippers as the Upfront Line in a Battle to Communicate," *The Body Politic,*

Commonly perceived as sex deviants (alongside unwed mothers, homosexuals, prostitutes, and unattached wage-earning women), female erotic dancers were subjected to surveillance, police arrest, detention, forced venereal disease testing, extortion, violence, and rejection by family and friends. One fifty-year old former dancer we interviewed has never told her twenty-something children about her years in burlesque. At the same time, a dancer like Val who was working-class and British-born, made more money, had more freedom, worked fewer hours, and had more control over her work than the waitresses, nurses, teachers, chambermaids, and secretaries she knew. Others like Michelle and Noelle, neither of whom had a high school education, told stories of long, twelve-hour days, split shifts "on an invisible leash," and six-day weeks cooped up in "ratty hotels with broken-down beds and cockroaches ... in small towns with people who had more keys to your room than you did."

Dancers were customarily paid in cash; they ear-marked a standard ten per cent of their earnings for their booking agent and, on occasion, paid fines to club owners for minor infractions such as showing up late or skipping a gig without adequate notice. Some like Val managed money wisely — saved it, got investment advice, and left the business after three years – and later secured a real estate licence. Others like Michelle had a tougher time: "I was raised Catholic, so it was like, you gotta have savings, but I had no money management skills whatsoever. When I retired, I pissed it all away on living for a year and a half, and on love. A dollar was like a penny to me. I could piss away money faster than anything ... that career did not set me up for being good with money."

The amount of pay, the quality of dressing room and performance space, lighting and music, food services, accommodation, promotion, and treatment by management and staff, depended on the nightclub. Headliners could clear $2000 a week, placing them in an economic position of superiority compared to women in any other occupation, but these were the privileged few. Stratified on a scale from high end to low end, Vancouver nightclubs varied greatly in the downtown core: booking agents in the late 1960s graded "their girls" as A, B, or C, and slotted them into the corresponding clubs. Upon retiring from the scene in Vancouver in 1975, Val, who often felt like a counselor and "the one bright thing" in her customers' lives, received a "solid silver tea service from the gentlemen, the skid row types" who were her regulars.

Some occupational hazards were unique to the business; others were common to female-dominated service work. Val and Michelle recall fears of carrying around wads of cash at the end of the night. Jack Card tells the story of Las Vegas show

123 (February 1986), 26-29; Kim Derko, "A High-Heeled Point of View," *Independent Eye*, 12 (Spring/Summer 1991), 1-8; Sasha, "Taking It Off is One Thing...," *Globe and Mail*, 22 January 2000, A15; Merri Lisa Johnson, "Pole Work: Autoethnography of a Strip Club," in Barry Dank and Roberto Refinetti, eds., *Sex Work and Sex Workers*, (New Brunswick, New Jersey 1999), 149-58.

girls in the 1950s running out at rehearsal breaks to get silicone injected directly into their breasts prior to the invention of implants. Diane Middlebrook, author of *Suits Me: The Double Life of Billy Tipton*, quotes a male nightclub goer who recalls that in the 1960s across the US, "guys would try to scrub out cigarettes or cigars on a stripper. Entice her over, use a cigarette to burn her leg, sometimes try to light their silken gowns on fire. I know one girl was burned to death when that happened, and many strippers carried burns on their bodies."[64] In future interviews with male patrons of Vancouver nightclubs, we will probe their reasons for attending strip shows, their perceptions of the business, and their relationships to the women on stage. Their very presence inside striptease venues was critical to the amount and quality of work available to erotic dancers. I suspect that the discourse "boys will be boys" offered male customers not only justification for a raunchy night out, but confirmation of their manliness, which was ratcheted up by "Hockey Night in Canada" broadcasts that began to fill TV screens inside stripclubs in the 1970s.

One male narrator who booked strippers for fraternity house parties on the campus of the University of British Columbia in the 1950s recalled that "college boys could be monsters." One evening, he escorted a dancer to a campus stag only to rescue her from "an ugly scene," and then "drove her home along back alleys, with the headlights out, in order to lose crazy kids who were following us."[65] Two dancers told stories about club owners offering cocaine to underage prospects as a recruitment ploy, and all of the dancers recalled the low-grade, lewd heckling from male customers. At the most extreme end of the spectrum, former booking agent Jeannie Reynolds was called to the Vancouver city morgue to identify the bodies of two strippers who had been murdered in downtown Vancouver nightclubs in the late 1960s.

Regardless of the venue, none of the former dancers had access to vacation pay, sick leave, disability leave, or pension plans. On the unionization front, in Vancouver in 1967, three "topless dancers" staged a two-night picket at a local nightclub.[66] They demanded higher wages, staff privileges, and a dressing room heater. They expressed the desire to organize dancers at six other nightclubs, though as far as we know, dancers never certified in Vancouver. In Toronto, the Canadian Association of Burlesque Entertainers (CABE) was a local of the Canadian Labour Congress in the 1970s, though it did not survive long, nor did the American Guild of Variety Artists, which represented sex performers in central Canada until the early 1970s.[67] Former dancer Barbara noted that waves of union agitation in

[64]Dianne Wood Middlebrook, *Suits Me: The Double Life of Billy Tipton (Boston 1998)*, 221.
[65]Interview with George P., 17 June 2000.
[66]"Picket Still On - Three Dancers," *Vancouver Sun*, 18 October 1967, "Dancers End Picket at Club: Deal Reached," *Vancouver Sun*, 19 October 1967.
[67]For more on efforts to unionize, see Amber Cooke, "Stripping: Who Calls the Tune?" and Mary Johnson, "CABE and Strippers: A Delicate Union," both in Laurie Bell, ed., *Good Girls/Bad Girls: Sex Trade Workers and Feminists Face to Face* (Toronto 1987), 92-9, 109-13.

Vancouver throughout the 1970s and 1980s often corresponded with times of economic affluence in the city, though club owners and booking agents consistently and fervently opposed the labour agitation. Additionally, Barbara recalled the competitive conditions under which dancers secured paying gigs, the lack of pro-union consciousness among the women, and the need for dancers to tour, all of which impeded worker solidarity and thwarted unionization. Stripteasers were migrant labourers whose travel and performance schedules were similar to those of employees of the Ice Capades, Barnam & Bailey's circus, and the National Hockey League. All of these "show biz folks" were contracted to move about from town to town, they had relatively short careers as entertainers, they typically rehearsed during the day and performed at night, and their vocations demanded top physical conditioning. However, unlike professional skaters, jugglers, and hockey players, stripteasers *explicitly* sold sexual allure and teetered on the edge of legality, which likely confounded efforts to attract union backing.

On occasion in postwar Vancouver, erotic dancers supplemented their night-club earnings by modeling, movie work, all-male stag events (which date back to the late 1800s), magazine work, and legitimate dance in chorus lines and with jazz troupes. In the 1960s, a number of Vancouver-based strippers were hired to perform a fifteen-minute act between porn reels on the stage of the Chinese-owned Venus movie house on Main Street, at the edge of Chinatown. I suspect that a small percentage of former strippers combined striptease with prostitution, though no one has disclosed their involvement in the exchange of sex for money. Instead, several dancers emphasized their careers as artists, and either implicitly or explicitly set themselves apart from 'no-talent' prostitutes, which is an important division to flesh out further.

(Un)dressing For Success

Under the rubric of striptease as production and consumption of spectacle, we turn our attention to the nature of the performances themselves — the artistic, cultural, aesthetic, and musical traditions that influenced dancers and choreographers. According to former stripper Margaret Dragu, "Burlesque queens of the 1920s through 1940s possessed trunkloads of vaudeville-style costumes replete with long gloves, stockings with garters, gowns with sequins, ostrich plumes, marabou trim, and rhinestone studded chiffon. They were the last purveyors of the classic bump and grind."[68] In the 1930s, recalls Italian American burlesque queen Ann Corio, some women disrobed on stage behind a screen or a white shadowgraph, while others alternately covered and "flashed" their flesh by manipulating artful props or peekaboo devices: a sheer body leotard (with strategically-placed sequins), the panel dress, feathers, parasols, fans, banana skirts, Spanish shawls, pasties, netting,

[68]Margaret Dragu, *Revelations: Essays on Striptease and Sexuality* (London, Ontario 1988), 24.

veils, smoke and bubble machines, body makeup, and g-strings.[69] The g-string, Corio observed, "was a tiny jewel-like bauble on a string around the waist covering up its specific subject."[70] In Vancouver, as elsewhere, the "A-class" feature dancers invested a considerable percentage of their earnings in costumes, props, expensive make-up, and, by the 1970s, taped music. They also combined elements of panto-mime, magic, puppetry, theatre, gymnastics, comedy, and dance training.

Jack Card, a well-known choreographer who was born in Vancouver, and worked the West Coast wheel, remembers that every dancer had a gimmick: at "Isy's Supper Club, strippers worked with live doves or did fire shows, Yvette Dare trained a parrot to pluck her clothes off, another stripper was a magician, Jane Jones had a tiger in her act, another dancer sat on an electric trapeze and stripped while swinging." Stage names were invented: some of the most popular headliners who performed for years in Vancouver included Miss Lovie, April Paris, Suzanne Vegas, Marilyn Marquis, Lilly Marlene, Bonnie Scott, and Lottie the Body.

Regardless of how much nudity was allowed, or required (by the early 1970s), female bodies were expected to conform to male-defined standards of female sexiness: pretty face, medium to large breasts, long, shapely legs, small waist, long hair. "Bombshells" like Annie Ample, Morganna, and Chesty Morgan had legen-dary breast sizes; Mitzi Dupré was a super-feature who sprayed ping pong balls and played a flute with her vagina.[71] According to Michelle, when Mitzi was on stage, she had people laughing in stitches while they played mock baseball games with the flying ping pong balls. For almost nine years, Bonnie Scott perfected her show-stopping extravaganza in Vancouver and across the country: on stage, under pink lights, she stripped off her super-deluxe, twelve-hundred dollar beaded gown (designed by Clyde), climbed a wrought-iron ladder, and once inside her five-foot tall, plexiglass champagne flute, she struck sexy poses amidst the bubbles.

Jack Card worked and travelled with headliner Gypsy Rose Lee who per-formed in Vancouver and, more regularly, in the extravagant Las Vegas revues where each of her costumes carried a $5,000 price tag. Underneath the sequined gowns and furs, in addition to jeweled pasties and g-strings (which were often worn layered over one another), rhinestone clips were popular in the 1950s and 1960s: v-shaped and glittery, they fitted over the pubic area, were made of sprung steel, and inserted into the vagina. In Montréal in 1951, Lili St. Cyr was arrested and subjected to a trial for "giving an obscene performance," and arrested again in 1967

[69]Corio with Joseph DiMona, *This Was Burlesque*, 71-6. Corio, who was believed to be in her eighties, died on 1 March 1999. See Lawrence Van Gelder, "Ann Corio, a Burlesque Queen on Broadway, Is Dead," *New York Times* , 9 March 1999, C27.

[70]Corio with Dimona, *This Was Burlesque*, 76.

[71]In a fascinating article, Kristina Zarlengo characterizes the "bombshell" as a "deeply desirable, unattainable woman with an inflated body and intense sexuality - a steadfast atomic age feminine ideal...who represented raw power of a kind frequently associated with the atom bomb." See Zarlengo, "Civilian Threat, the Suburban Citadel, and Atomic Age American Women," *Signs: Journal of Women in Culture and Society,* 25 (Fall 1999), 946.

before tourists arrived for Expo.[72] Perhaps because of St. Cyr's brush with the law, dancers in Montréal in the 1960s were known to wear "muckettes" — patches of artificial pubic hair glued to the pubic region in order to avoid arrest for indecency, all the while perpetuating the illusion of nudity.

The Colonial Carnivalesque Under Big Tents

Lured by the promise of a 20-week season and a steady pay cheque, many burlesque dancers packed their trunks and joined the traveling exhibition or carnival, often in the twilight of their career. Girl Shows had become staples of the touring carnival and circus across North America, beginning after the Chicago Columbia Exhibition in 1893.[73] Alongside the merry-go-rounds, arcades, shooting galleries, and side-shows spotlighting bearded ladies, alligator-skinned boys, and "midgits," strip-teasers were main features.[74] Borrowing from big revues like the Ziegfeld Follies, carnival showmen added "spice and less wardrobe" to give their tent-shows more edge than downtown cabaret acts.[75] While other show girls paraded their (hetero) femininity by baking cakes in competition, or strutting their stuff as beauty pageant contestants vying for the crown of Miss Pacific National Exhibition (PNE), strippers on carnival stages sang, danced, told jokes, and shed their elaborate costumes.[76]

In the 1950s in Vancouver, impresario Isy Walters, who owned the Cave Supper Club, and later, Isy's Supper Club, also booked strip acts at the PNE. Isy's Black Tent Show,[77] which was next door to his White Tent Show, invited patrons to pass between the legs of a 50-foot plywood cut-out of a black burlesque dancer at the tent's entrance on the fairgrounds. As Jack Card recalls, inside the neon-lit tent, the talker introduced: "'The African Queen, DIRECT from the jungles of

[72]Murray Campbell, "Memories of Montreal's Skin Queen," *Globe and Mail*, 3 February 1999, A3.
[73]According to A.W. Stencell, *Girl Show: Into the Canvas World of Bump and Grind* (Toronto 1999), in the 1860s it was said that in the various saloons and parlors, girls pretending to be can-can dancers, as practised in Parisian cabarets in Montmartre and Montparnasse, would do private dances without clothes for a dollar. (4)
[74]See Robert Bogdan, *Freak Show: Presenting Human Oddities for Amusement and Profit* (Chicago1988). For her inspiration, I am grateful to Helen Humphreys whose historical research for her prize-winning novel, *Leaving Earth* (Toronto 1997), 96 turned up evidence of women stripping underwater on the fairgrounds of the Canadian National Exhibition in Toronto in the 1930s.
[75]Stencell, *Girl Show*, 13.
[76]Candace Savage tackles the world of beauty pageants in *Beauty Queens: A Playful History* (New York 1998).
[77]In the US, the "black show" was typically referred to as the "Nig Show." See Carolyn Strange and Tina Loo, "Spectacular Justice: The Circus on Trial and the Trial as Circus, Picton, 1903," *Canadian Historical Review,* 77 (June 1996), 159-84.

Africa', and behind her there'd be Nubian slave girls in chains, a bumping and a thumping." Here, the colonial trope of African primitivism, bound up with the imperialist custom (and fantasy) of captivity, was remade as titillating foreignness at the same time, and in the same city, that African-American singer Lena Horne was refused hotel accommodation for "being a Negro." A decade later in Vancouver, Hogan's Alley — the city's working-class African-Canadian enclave —was bulldozed into the ground.[78] Significantly, the discourse of burlesque under the Big Tent was never about sex alone. It was tangled up with the economic, cultural and political privileges of a white body politic.[79]

The racist, colonial trappings of the business of striptease were no accident. In 1815, Saartjie Baartman, a west African woman was captured and displayed, fully nude, across England and Europe, as a wanton, orangatan-like, freak of nature.[80] In circuses and carnivals across North America throughout the 1900s, black performers who were paid consistently less than their white counterparts, were routinely consigned to the role of cannibals, "Zulu warriors," bushmen, and bear-women from the darkest Africa.[81] In addition, for more than a century, some white burlesque dancers disguised themselves as Algerian, Egyptian, Hawaiian, or Arabian in an effort to feed white appetites for the exotic, what Mary Douglas calls "radical strangeness."[82]

Gawking at dancers of colour and white women who impersonated the Other, white consumers were reassured of their own normality and cultural dominance; social boundaries between spectators and performers, the civilized and the uncivilized, were conserved, and the near homogeneity of Anglo, postwar Vancouver, affirmed. Pre-existing racial and gender stereotypes were animated in the interests of carnies or showmen smartly fluent in the common-sense, naturalized precepts of mass entertainment. The speech of the talker, the colourful images on the bally front, and the handbills advertising the event, were rooted in a racial, gender, and class grammar that distinguished native instinct from white self-discipline, and native lust from white civility.[83]

Josephine Baker (Figures 1 and 1a), (1906-1976), an African-American born poor in St. Louis, escaped in 1925 to work as a burlesque performer in France, and

---

[78] See "Hogan's Alley," directed by Andrea Fatona and Cornelia Wyngarten, 1994. Distributed by Video Out, Vancouver.
[79] See Ann Laura Stoler, *Race and the Education of Desire: Foucault's History of Sexuality and the Colonial Order of Things* (Durham and London 1997), 190.
[80] Sander Gilman, *Difference and Pathology: Stereotypes of Sexuality, Race and Madness* (Ithaca 1985), Anne Fausto-Sterling, "Gender, Race and Nation: The Comparative Anatomy of 'Hottentot' Women in Europe, 1815-1817," in Jennifer Terry and Jacqueline Urla, eds., *Deviant Bodies*, (Bloomington 1995), 19-48.
[81] Strange and Loo, "Spectacular Justice," 179-80.
[82] Mary Douglas, "My Circus Fieldwork," *Semiotica*, 85 (1985), 201-4.
[83] See Stoler, *Race and the Education of Desire,* 178-179.

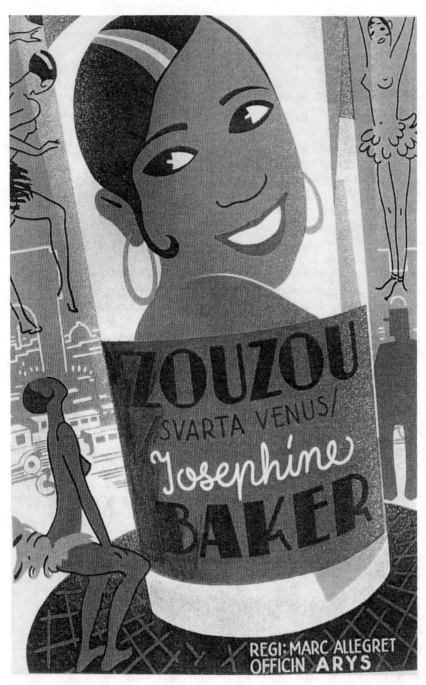

Figure 1: Josephine Baker

Figure 1a: Josephine Baker

later appeared in Vancouver in the 1950s. Cast in the show, "La Revue Negre" as a "tribal, uncivilized savage" from a prehistoric era, hence consigned to "anarchronistic space," Baker was rendered intelligible and digestible to white Parisian voyeurs.[84] Narrating the fantasy of the jungle bunny — the oversexed object of both white European fascination and repulsion — she danced in banana skirt and

---

[84]For an illuminating discussion of anachronistic space, see Anne McClintock, *Imperial Leather: Race, Gender and Sexuality in the Colonial Contest* (New York 1995), 40.

feathers. And in other shows, straight out of the racist ministrel tradition, "she was a ragamuffiin in black face wearing bright cotton smocks and clown shoes." Importantly, Baker also initiated desegregation in Las Vegas nightclubs in the 1950s by being the first dancer to refuse to perform for a white-only audience.[85]

Racism in burlesque and striptease played out in myriad ways. In the US in 1956, Princess Do May — "the Cherokee Half Breed" (figure 2) — was photographed in full feather headdress, beaded headband, and a (sacred) drum, freeze-framed in time and space anachronistically as an Indian artefact displaced from community and territory, and repositioned against an untouched, untamed wilderness ripe for conquest.[86] A picture of condensed and standardized symbols of Indianness, and of imperialism as commodity spectacle, she served to make invisible the multiple identities and multiple interests of diverse first nations.[87] All colonial histories of slaughter and subjugation are absented in this rendition of the myth of the noble savage. The Princess, and not her degenerate sister — "the drunken, broken-down, and diseased squaw" — was employed in burlesque to excite the sexual imagination of white men who engineered Euro-Canadian and Euro-American expansion, settlement, and industry on the frontier.[88]

Counterpose this image of Princess Do May against the seductive Lili St. Cyr (figure 3).[89] The American-born St. Cyr of Swedish/Dutch heritage, spent many famous years in Montréal, beginning in 1944, and was well-known for her on-stage bubble-baths, elaborate props, and her penchant for eccentric story-telling on stage.[90] The Nordic, voluptuous cowgirl, replete with ten-gallon hat, holster and guns, leather boots and lariat, is equally burdened by a condensation of symbols and metaphors — in this case, those of the conquerors of aboriginal peoples, and the keepers of Euro-Canadian myths of colonial rule. Here, St. Cyr stands in for the brave, heroic, pioneering men and women who have been memorialized as the founding ancestors of the contemporary nation, emblems of national identity, pride, and prosperity. St. Cyr embodies the colonial myth of the rough and tumble Wild West, the promise of abundant resources free for the taking, and the danger of encountering Indians who had never seen a white man or a white woman.[91] Decked

[85]Karen Dalton and Henry Louis Gates, Jr., "Josephine Baker and Paul Colin: African American Dance Seen through Parisian Eyes," *Critical Inquiry*, 24 (Summer 1998), 911.

[86]Len Rothe, *The Queens of Burlesque: Vintage Photographs from the 1940s and 1950s* (Atglen, Pennsylvania 1997), 29.

[87]McClintock, *Imperial Leather*, 56.

[88] Elizabeth Furniss, "Pioneers, Progress and the Myth of the Frontier: The Landscape of Public History in Rural BC," *BC Studies*, 115/116 (Fall/Winter 1997/98), 7-44; Jean Barman, "Taming Aboriginal Sexuality: Gender, Power, and Race in British Columbia, 1850-1900," *BC Studies*, 115/116 (Fall/Winter 1997/98), 237-66.

[89]Rothe, *The Queens of Burlesque*, 97.

[90]William Weintraub, "Show Business: Lili St.Cyr's Town - and Al's and Oscar's," in *City Unique: Montreal Days and Nights in the 1940s and '50s* (Toronto1996), 116-40.

[91]Furniss, "Pioneers, Progress and the Myth of the Frontier," 29.

Figure 2: Princess Do May

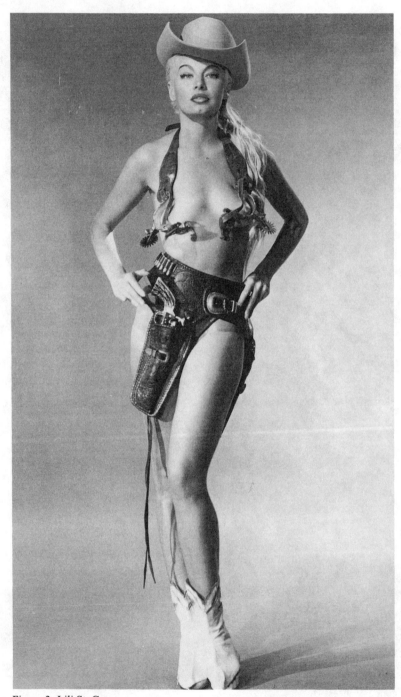

Figure 3: Lili St. Cyr

out in traditional cowboy garb, St. Cyr fetishized the triumph of European coloniz-
ers, and reminded white men in the audience that force was always at their disposal
if they needed or wanted it. At the same time, she sent up the machismo of the
Marlboro man.

Hoochie Coochie Queers?

In their 1965 study of women's prisons in the US, Ward and Kassebaum found that
a "disproportionate number" of strippers (and models) were likely to be homosexuals.[92] In 1969, American sociologists James Skipper and Charles McCaghy interviewed thirty-five "exotic dancers" who informed them that approximately 50 per
cent of their colleagues engaged in either prostitution or lesbian activities.[93] In
1971, Canadian journalist Marilyn Salutin stated that seventy-five per cent of
female strippers were gay.[94] In his book *Girl Show: Into the Canvas World of Bump
and Grind*, A.W. Stencell claims that, "Gays were often found in 10-in-1 side shows
doing the half-man/half-woman act and working in drag on carnival girl shows.
Many of the dancers who worked gay cabarets during the winter went with carnival
shows in the summer ... it was a safe world where you were judged only on the job
you did."[95]

In my "Striptease Project," I have learned that gay dancers and choreographers,
make-up artists, prop-makers, costume designers, wig-makers, and customers,
found a home in the business.[96] According to Jack Card, some of the most beautiful
showgirls he knew were gay, as were the dancing boys with their bare chests and
false eyelashes. Former erotic dancers Maud Allan, Josephine Baker, Gypsy Rose
Lee, and Tempest Storm are rumoured to have had women lovers. In 1958,
renowned lesbian historian Lillian Faderman began stripping in California clubs to
defray the costs of attending college. In 1998 at a queer history conference in
Tacoma, Washington, Faderman mused publicly about the shame that closeted her
bumping and grinding for forty years.

[92]David Ward and Gene Kassebaum, *Women's Prison: Sex and Social Structure* (Chicago
1965).
[93]James Skipper and Charles McCaghy, "Stripteasing: A Sex-Oriented Occupation," in
James Henslin, ed., *Studies in the Sociology of Sex* (New York 1971), 283.
[94]Marilyn Salutin, "Stripper Morality," *Transaction* 8 (1971), 12-22.
[95]Stencell, *Girl Show*, 95.
[96]African-American jazz singer, Teri Thornton, who died in May 2000 of cancer, found
work as the intermission pianist for strippers at the Red Garter nightclub in Chicago in the
1950s. She performed in Vancouver at Isy's Supper Club in January 1967, though it's not
clear whether or not she accompanied strippers at that gig. In Ben Ratliff's obituary in the
Globe and Mail, "Singer was a favourite of Ella Fitzgerald," there is no mention of
Thornton's sexuality, which suggests that she may have been gay. 8 May 2000, R6.

If stripteasers identified as gay women, what relationship (if any) did they develop to Vancouver's butch and femme bar culture?[97] Kennedy and Davis reveal that in the 1940s and 1950s, femmes in Buffalo, New York typically had steady paid employment while their butch lovers struggled with long stretches of unsteady, sporadic labour and financial uncertainty as car jockeys, elevator operators, and couriers.[98] What we don't yet know is: did the wages of femmes in g-strings subsidize the earnings of their butch lovers? Given the tendency of butches to bind their breasts, wear men's clothing, and spurn feminine artifice, was stripteaser a primarily femme occupational category?

Almost twenty years before the invention of "Xena: Warrior Princess" on prime-time TV, Klute — a butch lesbian in disguise — successfully reworked themes from "Conan the Barbarian" as an s/m dominatrix, and played with the fantasies of men who longed to be topped. As she recalled, she never fit the "high femme, mega-feature look." Instead, she played with gender ambiguity by adopting the personae of Michael Jackson and Grace Jones on stage until she was ostracized for being "too dykey." Notwithstanding Klute's impressive transgression, we suspect that butches were principally spectators who sought out striptease as exciting, titillating entertainment wherever it was staged; femme spectators likely balanced the opportunity to be mentored with pangs of envy. It is also probable that queer female customers in gay pubs that staged striptease — the Vanport and the New Fountain — were working-class gay girls who were less invested in the rigours of respectability than their middle-class, professional sisters.[99]

In 1962, American jazz musician Billy Tipton — a biological female who passed successfully as a man all his adult life — "married" Kitty Kelly, a well-known stripper.[100] Because striptease demanded public display of exaggerated hetero-femininity, Kitty's occupation surely enhanced Billy's masquerade as a red-blooded heterosexual male. And what about male-to-female transgenders who successfully passed on stage in the 1950s and 1960s as ultra-feminine, sexy girls in full view of adoring (straight?) male fans? Transsexual burlesque stripper, Hedy Jo Star not only performed her own striptease act, but she owned carnival girl shows where she employed female impersonators in the 1950s.[101] Jaydee Easton, a female

[97]On butch and femme culture in Vancouver in the 1950s and 1960s, see Vanessa Cosco, "Obviously Then I'm Not Hetersexual: Lesbian Identities, Discretion, and Communities," M.A. Thesis, Department of History, University of British Columbia, 1997; and "Forbidden Love: the Unashamed Stories of Lesbian Lives," dir. Aerlyn Weissman and Lynne Fernie, National Film Board of Canada, 1992.
[98]Elizabeth Lapovsky Kennedy and Madeline Davis, *Boots of Leather, Slippers of Gold: The History of a Lesbian Community* (New York 1993), 278-322.
[99]Katie Gilmartin, "'We Weren't Bar People': Middle-Class Lesbian Identities and Cultural Spaces," *GLQ: A Journal of Lesbian & Gay Studies*, 3 (1996), 1-51.
[100]Middlebrook, *Suits Me: The Double Life of Billy Tipton*, 220-32.
[101]Stencell, *Girl Show*, 92.

impersonator in the 1950s, flashed in drag by looping her penis with an elastic band, attaching it to a small rubber ball, and inserting it into her anus.[102] Other female impersonators such as Jackie Starr, most of whom were gay men, performed in straight nightclubs and in gay cabarets such as Seattle's famous Garden of Allah until the 1970s when full nudity in stripclubs made drag virtually impossible.[103] Jackie Starr replaced an ill Gypsy Rose Lee several times on music hall stages in New York in the 1940s, and was the top headliner at the Garden of Allah for ten years.

The presence of queers on and off striptease stages troubles the naturalized presumption that nightclubs and carnivals were indisputably straight milieux. Acting out moments of what Judith Butler calls "insurrectionary queerness"[104] inside cabarets, stripclubs, and under big tents, queer stripteasers, staff, and fans interrupted the heterosexual imperative. What is not yet apparent to us is the complexity of queer relationships to the closet, as well as to communities beyond the borders of the nightclub world. Given the criminalization of homosexuality prior to 1969, combined with the stigmatization of striptease, we suspect that most queers in the business prior to gay liberation in the 1970s sought the same subterfuge that sheltered Hollywood he-man Rock Hudson for so long.

The Imbrication of Sex and Nation

In the end, a fundamental paradox governed the business of erotic entertainment before 1980, and arguably still does today. On the one hand, stripteasers were, in the main, well-paid, glamorous entertainers who, as working-class women with limited employment options, stripped first for the money. The women we've interviewed took pride in putting on a good show, they loved the applause, and the challenge of developing new routines, costumes, and props. On the other hand, they were subjected to criminal and social sanctions that pressured them to be ashamed of their work, to pretend that they did something else for a living, or to abandon their careers as dancers altogether. Their skills and expertise, their dedication, flare, and originality as workers, were overshadowed, if not entirely discounted, by moral reformers, police, and civic officials who, at various times and for a variety of purposes, were in the business of scapegoating non-conformists. While professional female dancers in ballet, modern, and jazz increasingly inspired awe and veneration in the second half of the 20th century, stripteasers were consigned to the interstices between adoration and attention, and fear, resentment, and hostility.

It seems clear that female erotic dancers did not qualify as full-fledged citizens dedicated to the ideal family, the social order, and the health of the Canadian

[102]Stencell, *Girl Show*, 93.
[103]Don Paulson with Roger Simpson, *An Evening at the Garden of Allah: Seattle's Gay Cabaret* (New York 1996), 127-34.
[104]Judith Butler, *Excitable Speech*, 159.

nation.[105] Perceived by many as no better than disgraced whores who haunted the quasi-legal underworld in postwar Vancouver, dancers were positioned outside of discourses that elaborated what it meant to be a normal, moral, and patriotic citizen. As a result, they could never take for granted the fundamental constituents of substantive citizenship such as inclusion, belonging, equity, and justice.[106] Like prostitutes and other sex trade workers, in an era of suburbanized, privatized domesticity, and marital nuclearity, erotic dancers were presumed to be devoid of real jobs, families, and meaningful, intimate relationships.[107] No dancer raising children, especially if she was non-white, was ever honoured for her role as mother and moral guardian of "the race." Because strippers were commonly perceived as anti-family, they were presumed to possess no maternal honour worth protecting. Rather than being extended dignity, security, and safety, their family forms were stigmatized as a menace to the stability of the nation state.[108] Two retired dancers we interviewed who balanced child-rearing and their careers as strippers recall the painful judgment of other parents, day care workers, coaches, and teachers who disapproved of their chosen field of work. In her autobiography, *Growing Up Naked,* Lindalee Tracey describes her desire to donate the proceeds from a large-scale strip-a-thon ("Tits for Tots") in Montréal to a charity for disabled kids, and the rejections she faced from agencies which explained they had "reputations" to uphold.[109]

In 2000, all across North America, the paradox persists. More money is spent at stripclubs than at large-scale commercial threates, regional and non-profit theatres, the opera, the ballet, jazz, and classical music performances — combined.[110] In the US, the number of strip clubs has doubled in the past decade, with the fastest growth in upscale "Gentlemen's Clubs" which have reframed striptease as adult entertainment that upholds the highest standards of the hospitality industry. Over the past decade, Canada's Immigration Department has granted thousands of temporary six-month work permits to women from Romania, the Czech Republic, Hungary, and Poland, to serve Canada's burgeoning stripclub business as "bur-

[105]David Scott, *Behind the G-String* (Jefferson, North Carolina 1996), 12.
[106]See Jeffrey Weeks, "The Sexual Citizen," *Theory, Culture and Society,* 15 (August/November 1998), 35-9.
[107]On the post-World War II era, see Mary Louise Adams, *The Trouble with Normal: Postwar Youth and the Making of Heterosexuality* (Toronto 1997); Doug Owram, *Born at the Right Time: A History of the Baby Boom Generation* (Toronto 1996); Joan Sangster, "Doing Two Jobs: The Wage-Earner Mother, 1945-1970," in Joy Parr, ed., *Diversity of Women, Ontario 1945-1980* (Toronto 1995), 98-134; and Joanne Meyerowitz, ed., *Not June Cleaver: Women and Gender in Postwar America, 1945-1960* (Philadelphia 1994).
[108]Nora Räthzel, "Nationalism and Gender in West Europe: the German Case," in Helma Lutz et al., ed., *Crossfires: Nationalism, Racism and Gender in Europe* (London 1995), 168.
[109]Tracey, *Growing Up Naked,* 163.
[110]Eric Schlosser, "The Business of Pornography," *U.S. News and World Report,* 10 February 1997, 44.

lesque entertainers."[111] At the same time, striptease continues to be a lightning rod for cultural/legal and political conflicts all over North America.[112] Unresolved debates swirl around the legal and moral character of lap dancing, peep shows, live sex acts on stage, the physical location of "exotic dance," and nightclubs as venues for prostitution.

Community groups and politicians have staged protests to keep stripclubs out of their lives and neighbourhoods. Susan Marshall, Executive Director of Safe Neighborhoods, in Portland, Oregon, claims that, "Obscene speech, nude dancing, and hard core violent pornography serve no social purpose."[113] Residents all over North America have lobbied for stepped-up patrolling of stripping activities and surveillance. In a move that conjures up Foucault's panopticon, police in the US routinely install cameras in clubs and dressing rooms to record criminal activity — a move that engenders hyper self-consciousness and self-discipline among dancers.[114] At the same time, cameras positioned inside the performance space electronically transmit live strip shows to viewers via the Internet, a move that satisfies the needs of at-home consumers, blurs public and private boundaries, and deposits little or no extra cash in the hands of working women.

In 1996, New York mayor Rudy Guiliani called erotic dancing, "a dirty, vicious business ... [where one] finds the exploitation of sex that has lead to the deterioration of New York and places throughout the US." Defending his clean-up campaign, Guiliani argued: "If people express themselves in ways that destroy property values, increase crime, bring in organized crime and start to destroy a city, then you have to have the discretion to do something about it." Like Guiliani, Jerry Elsner, Executive Director of the Illinois Crime Centre, loathes the behaviour of strip club patons: "A certain element of people go night after night after night, buy porn when they leave, then go home and hide in the basement and watch dirty movies all night. They're a threat to everybody in our community; they tend to congregate at watering holes — this is where the action is, where their friends and peers are at. One degenerate in the neighbourhood is bad; two hundred is real bad."[115]

The combination of old-fashioned police pressure, residents' associations dedicated to protecting property and family values, media sensationalism, and the manipulation of zoning ordinances, has meant heated attacks on stripclub culture, with sobering results. Since 1993, striptease has been the number one topic of Free Speech litigation in the US.[116] According to anthropologist Judith Lynne Hanna,

[111] Estanislao Oziewicz, "Canada's Bare Essentials," *Globe and Mail,* 19 February 2000.

[112] Judith Lynne Hanna, "Undressing the First Amendment and Corsetting the Striptease Dancer," *The Drama Review,* 42 (Summer 1998), 62.

[113] "Gentlemen's Clubs," A & E Documentary, 1996.

[114] For more on techniques, practices and mentalities of self-governance see Nikolas Rose, *Governing the Soul: The Shaping of the Private Self* (London 1990).

[115] "Gentlemen's Clubs," A & E Documentary, 1996.

[116] Clyde DeWitt, "Legal Commentary," *Adult Video News* (1995), 112-127.

over sixty-two communities across North America have enacted laws to restrict striptease, including Seattle, Tacoma, Fort Lauderdale, Syracuse, and Phoenix. New laws continually resurface.[117] Only time will tell whether or not similiar, discriminatory prohibitions will be invoked to control (or obliterate) erotic dancing in Vancouver, or any other Canadian city. So long as stripper bodies conjure up popular associations of worthless, diseased, lazy, drug-addicted, oversexed, dangerous, and unCanadian bodies, the erotic labour performed by dancers, past and present, will never be appreciated *as labour*: it will be forever figured as something else.[118] And age-old struggles by dancers for improved working conditions, union certification, and destigmatization of their artform will continue in the absence of a titanic transformation in the cultural meanings attached to bump and grind.

This research is generously supported by a three-year SSHRC grant, 1999-2002. I am pleased to acknowledge the excellent research assistance of Kim Greenwell and Michelle Swann, both of whom have made a commitment to the "Striptease Project" well above and beyond the terms of their employment contract. My sincere thanks to all the women and men who we've interviewed so far, and whose plentiful stories impel us to keep going. I also thank Bryan Palmer for inviting me to contribute to Labour/Le Travail. *And I am grateful for the loving ways and incisor-sharp mind of Tracy Porteous.*

[117]Judith Lynne Hanna, "Undressing the First Amendment," 40-1.

[118]Recent articles in the *Vancouver Sun,* 10 June 2000, and *Globe and Mail*, 12 June 2000, that publicized my SSHRC grant, and my search for retired business insiders, catalyzed an international media feeding frenzy. The *Globe and Mail* article by Dene Moore at Canadian Press was printed in newspapers all across Canada, as well as in the *Bangkok Post* and *The Arab Times*. Radio, TV, and print journalists from England, Scotland, Australia, Germany, South Africa, the US, and Canada contacted me to justify my spending of "taxpayers' dollars" on "studying strippers." On several talk-radio shows in Toronto and Vancouver, I was attacked by successive callers incensed that the government would "waste their money" on such a "useless, disgusting project." Several male callers barked that a history of BC logging or mining was far more constructive. Though erotic dancers paid personal income tax and sales tax, and some bought Canada Savings Bonds, and later, RRSPs, they were automatically disqualified from national conversations about the allocation of state resources, which again underscores their lack of claim to substantive citizenship. Three weeks of media-heat confirmed my suspicion that, in the eyes of the majority, the impressive, century-long contribution of stripteasers to local economies and performance traditions is anything but deserving of state-supported study.

LAW, INDUSTRIAL RELATIONS, AND THE STATE

Pluralism or Fragmentation?: The Twentieth-Century Employment Law Regime in Canada

Judy Fudge and Eric Tucker

I. *Introduction: Employment Regimes and Fragmented Labour Markets*

ANY ATTEMPT AT A HISTORICAL overview inevitably involves contentious choices, including those of focus, the analytic lens to deploy, and the themes that structure the narrative. The first and most controversial choice that we have made is that of focus. Our topic is the legal regulation of employment in 20th-century Canada. Despite the fact that during the 20th century employment has come to be treated as a synonym for work, these terms are not equivalent. Employment is a mere subset of the broader domain of work; it emerged as a specific legal category in England in the 19th century to specify the rights and obligations that comprised a bilateral labour market contract. Work, by contrast, captures a much broader range of productive activity, including the labour of small independent producers and women in the household. The false equivalence of the terms "employment" and "work" in the 20th century is evidence of the hegemony of the neo-classical vision of the labour market in which employment dominates.[1]

[1]R.E. Pahl, *On Work: Historical, Comparative and Theoretical Approaches* (Oxford 1988). Also see Ann Forrest, "The Industrial Relations Significance of Unpaid Work," *Labour/ Le Travail*, 42 (1998), 199-225; Belinda Leach, "Industrial Homework, Economic Restructur-

Judy Fudge and Eric Tucker, "Pluralism or Fragmentation?: The Twentieth Century Employment Law Regime in Canada," *Labour/Le Travail*, 46 (Fall 2000), 251-306.

Our focus on employment reflects the separation of home and waged work that characterized the new industrial age. By the turn of the twentieth century, the once dominant form of family production was becoming a faint memory in most parts of Canada, replaced by a new sexual division of labour characterized by male employment and female domestic labour — an arrangement that deepened and expanded women's dependence on men's wages. One negative consequence of our focus on employment, then, is that it privileges the work experience of men over that of women.[2]

We also are aware that an exclusive focus on employment is becoming less defensible at the end of the 20th century as owners of capital seek ways of getting work done that does not entail entering into employment relations. Indeed, the coherence of the legal categories of employer and employee is being undermined by this inventiveness. We certainly doubt that it will be defensible for a history of the legal regulation of work in the 21st century to focus on the sub-category of employment.

Yet, despite its ideological baggage, gender-blindness, and partiality, a review of the 20th century focused on the legal regulation of employment is sensible both because employment has been the principal means through which productive relations were established and governed and because employment relations have been the primary subject of the legal regulation of work through most of this century. Other ways of organizing work have been subject to far less legal control, so that what is really notable in this regard are law's silences and exclusions, not its words and actions. Employment relations became a magnet for legal regulation precisely because it was through these relations that most families obtained access to the means necessary for their survival and reproduction and because, from time to time, their conflictual character threatened to disrupt the social order.

Our analytical lens is that of a regime of legal regulation by which we mean the constellation of laws, institutions, and ideologies through which employment relations are organized and legitimated. This heuristic allows us to capture both the continuities and dynamics of legal regulation as it developed over the 20th century. Central to the regime is the contract of employment within which the judiciary inscribed the legal subordination of the worker by implying duties of obedience and loyalty derived from older notions of status at the same time that it endorsed

ing and the Meaning of Work," *Labour/ Le Travail*, 41 (Spring), 97-115; Christopher Tomlins, "Why Wait for Industrialism? Work, Legal Culture, and the Example of Early America — An Historical Argument," *Labor History*, 40 (1999), 5-33; and Chris Tilly and Charles Tilly, *Work Under Capitalism* (Westview 1999).
[2]Pat Armstrong and Hugh Armstrong, *The Double Ghetto: Canadian Women & Their Segregated Work,* 3rd ed. (Toronto 1994), 83; Tannis Peikoff and Stephen Brickey, "Creating Precious Children and Glorified Mothers: A Theoretical Assessment of the Transformation of Childhood," in Elizabeth Comack and Stephen Brickey, eds., *The Social Basis of Law,* 2nd ed. (Halifax 1991), 71-94; Wally Seccombe, "The Housewife and her Labour under Capitalism," *New Left Review,* 83 (1973), 3-24, 6.

free exchange and exclusive private property rights. This juridical construction, however, could not resolve the inevitable conflicts over the employment relation and its governance fuelled by conflicting material interests and competing visions of justice.[3]

Three conceptions of justice have been invoked to deal with these conflicts. One relies upon market competition for labour to limit the abuses of property rights. Voluntary individual contracts, enforced by the courts, guarantee workers market freedom. In another conception of justice, workers' collective action to assert and enforce employment rights provides the crucial mechanism for the achievement of justice by offsetting the employers' superior bargaining power. Democratic freedoms, especially those of expression and association, provided the legitimacy for workers' collective institutions and actions. The third conception is rooted in democratic politics and involves direct state regulation of the terms of employment in accordance with politically determined norms of social and economic justice.[4]

These conceptions of justice were institutionalized in the employment law regime, albeit by no means in equal measure. By 1900, the regime consisted roughly of three parts: the common law contract of employment, the law of collective action, and statutory minimum standards. While it is tempting to associate each conception of justice with a component of the legal regime, reality defies such neat categorizations. Class struggle and ideological conflict were endemic throughout the entire regime and in each of its components, although the level of contestation ebbed and flowed and its location varied.

The third crucial choice we made is to emphasize the theme of fragmentation, and in particular, the role of law in supporting, constituting and challenging fragmented labour markets. This theme was selected because it allows us explicitly to take issue with industrial pluralism, the predominant approach to post-war Canadian employment relations.[5] According to it, after World War II, collective bargaining legislation administered by independent labour boards combined with a system of grievance arbitration to enforce collective agreements, to create a

[3] Daniel Jacoby, *Laboring for Freedom: A New Look at the History of Labor in America* (Armonk, NY 1998); Harry Glasbeek, "The Contract of Employment at Common Law," in John Anderson and Morley Gunderson, eds., *Union-Management Relations* (Toronto 1982), 47-77; Alan Fox, *Beyond Contract: Work, Power and Trust* (London 1974), 185; Margaret McCallum, "Labour and the Liberal State: Regulating the Employment Relationship, 1867-1920," *Manitoba Law Journal*, 23 (1995), 574-93.

[4] Jacoby, *Laboring for Freedom*, 8.

[5] Bora Laskin, first as a labour law professor and arbitrator and then as an Ontario Court of Appeal and Supreme Court of Canada judge, was one of the earliest and most prominent proponents of this view. See W. Laird Hunter, "Bora Laskin and Labour Law: The Formative Years," *Supreme Court Law Review*, 6 (1984), 431-66. More generally, see H.W. Arthurs, "Developing Industrial Citizenship: A Challenge for Canada's Second Century," *Canadian Bar Review*, 45 (1967), 786-830; Task Force on Labour Relations, *Canadian Industrial Relations: Final Report* (Ottawa 1968).

fundamentally different regime in which workers enjoyed the benefits of industrial citizenship. By contrast, we argue that collective bargaining expanded selectively and that most workers relied on individual contracts and minimum standards for the determination of their working conditions. Moreover, it was not simply the case that there was a plurality of institutions for the determination of conditions, but that the contours of labour market fragmentation significantly affected workers' access to the regime's various components.

Canada's highly regionalized political economy is one important source of fragmentation. Another is its complicated and decentralized political geography that divides state power between national, provincial, and local authorities. A third dimension of fragmentation is captured by labour market segmentation theory, which identifies primary and secondary labour markets and emphasizes ascribed characteristics such as gender and race, and institutional factors, such as state policies and union structures and practices, as determinants of where workers are likely to be located. Workers in primary labour markets are employed by large employers, partially shielded from competition, where collective bargaining has taken hold to produce conditions of employment that are comparatively good, while those in secondary markets are employed in more marginal and competitive sectors of the economy, where unionization rates are low, jobs lack security, and pay is poor.[6]

Although fragmented labour markets sometimes appear to be "natural" categories arising from "objective" differences, they are socially constructed. While these processes are complex, involving both structure and agency, we hope to show the salience of law as an instrument and an ideology through which fragmentation is institutionalized, reinforced, and contested by the actions of employers and workers. We hope also to demonstrate that an examination of the history of employment law as an instrument of fragmentation captures some of its most important features and dynamics in 20th-century Canada and illuminates the relations between its different components.

To capture the continuities and dynamics of the legal regime, we have divided the century into two periods that allow us to amplify and capture some of the most significant changes in the patterns of legal regime institutionalization. We have labelled the period from 1900 to 1948 as "industrial voluntarism" in order to capture its central characteristic: the overwhelming predominance of legal norms associated with market regulation, subject to a marginal role for state intervention through limited compulsory conciliation and direct regulation only for the most vulnerable. We have adopted the more conventional term "industrial pluralism" to identify the

[6]Peter B. Doeringer and Michael J. Piore, *Internal Labor Markets and Manpower Analysis*, 2nd ed. (Lexington 1985); David Gordon, Richard Edwards, and Michael Reich, *Segmented Work, Divided Workers: The Historical Transformation of Workers in the United States* (Cambridge 1982); Barbara L. Marshall, *Engendering Modernity: Feminism, Social Theory and Social Change* (Cambridge 1994).

second period, from 1948 to 2000 to recognize that the era following World War II signals the legal institutionalization of workers' collective institutions and the simultaneous growth of direct state regulation of the terms of the employment contract as a subordinate mechanism to collective bargaining. It also marks the development of an industrial jurisprudence and a conception of industrial democracy to replace the hegemony of contract law as the organizing principle of employment.

II. *Industrial Voluntarism, 1900-48*

Constructing the Regime of Industrial Voluntarism, 1900-1914

At the turn of the century, the transition from competitive to monopoly capitalism profoundly altered class relations. The National Policy promoted the expansion of manufacturing capacity and resource exploitation, both of which depended upon an infusion of foreign capital and immigrant workers. The benefits of this unprecedented economic growth, however, were not enjoyed equally. Between 1900 and the outbreak of World War I, productivity and prices soared, but wages lagged behind as working people struggled unsuccessfully to keep up with inflation.[7]

They were hampered in their efforts by increasing class fragmentation. The sexual division of labour both between and within the household and workplace was deeply entrenched, even as women's employment increased. In general, women's wages were roughly 40 to 60 per cent of men's. Ethnic and racial fragmentation grew in significance as different immigrant groups were recruited by employers to perform specific types of labour. The skilled crafts were composed almost exclusively of workers of Anglo-Saxon descent who, through their unions, pursued policies of ethnic and racial exclusion and advocated immigration restrictions. Craft unions exercised some control over the labour process in the early years of the century and extracted a share of the benefits of economic prosperity. Unskilled workers who made up the majority of the country's labour force, however, were not strategically placed in the production process and lacked the organizational resources to win improved wages and conditions.[8]

[7]Bryan D. Palmer, *Working-Class Experience,* 2nd ed., (Toronto 1992), ch. 4; Paul Craven, *"An Impartial Umpire": Industrial Relations and the Canadian State, 1900-1911* (Toronto 1980), ch. 4; Donald Avery, *Reluctant Host: Canada's Response to Immigrant Workers, 1869-1994* (Toronto 1995), ch. 1; Terry Copp, *The Anatomy of Poverty: The Condition of the Working Class in Montreal, 1879 - 1929* (Toronto 1974), ch. 2; Michael J. Piva, *The Condition of the Working Class in Toronto - 1900-1921* (Ottawa 1979), ch.2; Mary MacKinnon, "New Evidence on Canadian Wage Rates, 1900-1930," *Canadian Journal of Economics,* 39 (1996), 115-31.

[8]Wayne Roberts, *Honest Womanhood: Feminism, Femininity and Class Consciousness among Toronto Working Women, 1893-1914* (Toronto 1976); Marie Campbell, "Sexism in British Columbia Trade Unions, 1900-1920," in Barbara Latham and Cathy Kess, eds., *In Her Own Right: Selected Essays on Women's History in BC* (Victoria 1980), 167- 186;

The turn of the century was marked by a major strike wave in Canada, much of it led by skilled workers resisting their employers' efforts to carry through a second industrial revolution. But industrial action was not confined to this relatively privileged segment of the workforce; semi-and unskilled workers in the resource industries and on the public infrastructure frequently confronted their employers *en masse* to protest against their poor wages, dangerous working conditions and unsanitary habitation. Mass industrial unrest also erupted in Canadian cities, which grew at an astonishing rate during the first decade and a half of the century.

There were two prongs to the state's response to this strike wave. First, there was a refinement of the instruments of coercion. Some of this was accomplished in the courts where the judiciary held trade unionists civilly liable to employers for damages caused by various strike activities. Picketing was narrowly limited to protect employer property rights and the right of employers and non-striking workers to contract freely. This development in civil law was closely associated with the judicial interpretation of the criminal law of watching and besetting. Most judges were not prepared to hold that peaceful picketing *per se* was criminal, however, acts such as calling non-striking workers "scabs" attracted criminal sanction. Employers also used the law to limit broader manifestations of working-class solidarity. Secondary action such as organized consumer boycotts and refusals by workers to handle struck work were held to be civil conspiracies to injure.

Adequate remedies were needed to make these civil actions effective. Procedural rules expedited employer applications for injunctions that prohibited the unlawful conduct under threat of punishment. There was also much litigation over whether a union as an entity could be made financially responsible for the wrongful acts of its members. The situation was not always entirely clear, but the general view was that while a union could not be sued directly in its own name, its funds could be reached through a representative action against the union's officers.[9]

In sum, the courts further institutionalized a market-based conception of justice, which constructed workers and employers as juridically equal, rights-bearing subjects. The selection of rights, however, was far from neutral. Priority was given to rights of property and contract, rights that were quintessentially negative, aiming to protect the individual against interference. Their protection entailed the imposition of limitations on the positive freedom of workers to engage in collective action to advance their interests. Workers recognized the class bias of

---

Mercedes Steedman, *Angels of the Workplace: Women and the Construction of Gender Relations in the Canadian Clothing Industry, 1890 -1940* (Toronto 1993); Linda Kealey, *Enlisting Women for the Cause: Women, Labour and the Left in Canada, 1890 - 1920* (Toronto 1998).
[9]Eric Tucker and Judy Fudge, "Forging Responsible Unions: Metal Workers and the Rise of the Labour Injunction in Canada," *Labour/Le Travail*, 37 (Spring 1996), 81-120.

the courts but were unable to mobilize enough political support for legislation overriding these decisions, except in British Columbia.[10]

Although these legal principles applied to all labour market actors, craft workers were most subjected to them. Not only were their tactics more amenable to legal controls, but because these workers established permanent organizations, legal actions that threatened their assets could be particularly effective. While other workers did not experience directly the sting of judge-made law, it still affected them. Judicial pronouncements on the realm of permissible trade-union activity were important not only for their immediate legal consequences; they also aided in constructing a normative framework that legitimated other state actions, at least in the eyes of those who were inclined to believe law's words. The legal characterization of behaviour as wrongful or criminal provided a justification for government officials to deploy police or militia to restore the judicially endorsed view of public order.[11]

The deployment of direct state coercion was highly uneven in the pre-war period. Most craft unions could operate more or less successfully within the confines of the law and avoid confrontation with police authority. The situation of semi-skilled industrial workers was more difficult. They often confronted employers determined to resist unionization and frequently lacked the organizational strength to overcome that resistance. Faced with the threat of replacements, these workers resorted to more muscular tactics. In smaller communities, local police sometimes lacked the capacity or the will to defend employers' rights of property and contract to the extent employers demanded. In some regions, powerful employers could rely on economically dependent provincial governments for coercive assistance. Moreover, since many of the industrial unions espoused radical ideas and welcomed immigrant workers into their ranks, this made them dangerous in the eyes of employers and state officials, justifying close surveillance and, ultimately, direct coercion, including the deployment of the militia, police raids, prosecutions, and deportations. Dangerous foreigners and subversives, unlike respectful working men, could not count upon the strain of mercy in British justice.[12]

The second prong of the state's response aimed to promote conciliation and accommodation between employers and responsible unions as a strategy for

[10]For a fruitful application of the distinction between positive and negative freedoms in the labour context, see Jacoby, *Laboring for Freedom.* On the BC legislation, see A.W.R. Carrothers, "A Legislative History of the B.C. Trade-Unions Act: The Rossland Miners' Case," *U.B.C. Legal Notes,* 2 (1956), 339-46.

[11]Douglas Hay, "Time, Inequality, and Law's Violence," in Austin Sarat and Thomas R. Kearns, eds., *Law's Violence* (Ann Arbor 1992), 141-73.

[12]Greg Marquis, "Doing Justice to 'British Justice': Law, Ideology and Canadian Historiography," in W. Wesley Pue and Barry Wright, eds., *Canadian Perspectives on Law and Society: Issues in Law and History* (Ottawa 1988), 43-69; Mark Leier, *Where the Fraser River Flows: The Industrial Workers of the World in British Columbia* (Vancouver 1990).

reducing industrial conflict. To qualify for this treatment, unions had to demonstrate their support for the judicially constructed regime of industrial legality by not violating rights of property and contract or engaging in secondary actions such as sympathetic strikes or boycotts. To this end, the federal government began developing a legislative framework and an institutional infrastructure that enabled state officials to facilitate the settlement of disputes with a minimum of disruption. Industrial conflict that interfered with the success of its National Policy was particularly troubling and so the federal government's efforts focused on public utilities, defined to include mines, transportation, communications, and gas, electric, and power works. It claimed constitutional authority to legislate in these areas on the basis of its residual "peace, order and good government" powers.[13]

In 1900, the Laurier government established a Department of Labour which published the *Labour Gazette* (the official organ of labour relations information), and administered the newly enacted *Conciliation Act*. Mackenzie King was the department's chief bureaucrat and he shaped the government's labour policy over the coming years. The *Conciliation Act* (1900) provided the first general legal framework for federal intervention in labour disputes. It authorized the Minister to investigate a dispute and arrange a conference between the parties. As well, either party could request conciliation, however, there was no legal obligation to participate. The scheme's implementation tended to reflect King's personal predilections. His primary concern was to restore production on the basis of market conditions, rather than to advance some other idea of economic justice. Thus, the government's policies rested firmly within the realm of "voluntarism."

Federal conciliation proved to be ineffective in resolving railway and mining strikes where recognition issues often loomed large. But even the potentially serious consequences of railway strikes to the national economy could not persuade the federal government to compel recognition or impose compulsory arbitration. Instead, the *Railway Labour Disputes Act* (1903) provided that conciliation could be followed by non-binding arbitration by an *ad hoc* tripartite board authorized to conduct a quasi-judicial investigation (including the power to compel testimony and order the production of documents) and to issue a normative report recommending terms of settlement.

Although little used, this legislation was an important precedent when Mackenzie King decided, after a series of particularly bitter and hard-fought strikes involving intervention by the militia, that stronger legislation was required to contain industrial conflict. The 1907 *Industrial Dispute Investigation Act* (*IDIA*) not only incorporated the use of tripartite conciliation boards, but prohibited resort to industrial action prior to the completion of the board's work. Persons who

[13]Craven, *"An Impartial Umpire"*; Bob Russell, *Back to Work? Labour, State and Industrial Relations In Canada* (Scarborough 1990), ch. 3; Jeremy Webber, "Compelling Compromise: Canada Chooses Conciliation over Arbitration, 1900-1907," *Labour/Le Travail,* 28 (1991), 15-54.

violated the prohibition were liable to be prosecuted under the *Criminal Code*, although they rarely were. Conciliation was compulsory with respect to public utilities, but could be invoked by the mutual agreement of any disputants. It was hoped that delay and investigation would encourage the parties to accept the boards' recommendations which would be supported by enlightened public opinion. Government imposition of terms and conditions was still not accepted as a legitimate alternative to market voluntarism.[14]

The instrumental impact of the *IDIA* on those workers covered by its mandatory provisions was equivocal prior to World War I. Workers were most successful when they could force negotiations without state intervention; resort to *IDIA* conciliation was a second-best strategy. But it was also intended that the *IDIA* would have an ideological impact through the production by conciliation boards of a template of legitimate demands and acceptable conduct, publicized through the *Labour Gazette*. Boards generally accepted that workers should be entitled to a living wage, subject to the employer's ability to pay, and to be free to join a trade union without suffering discrimination, while employers should be free to manage their enterprises and maintain an open shop. On the issue of recognition, conciliation boards generally supported negotiation with employee committees when employers refused to deal with trade union representatives. This normative framework did not, however, gain widespread acceptance either among unions or employers. At best, there was pragmatic acceptance depending on the balance of power, but the practice of conciliation did not alter that balance.[15]

The simultaneous expansion of the state's power to coerce and to conciliate produced a regime of industrial legality that was both more powerful and more flexible than before. While the incremental increase in coercive power was more significant than the increase in conciliation, this dual development enabled the government more finely to calibrate the regime so that it could support the development of responsible trade unionism (understood to refer to unions that agreed to operate within the narrow confines of a market-based model of industrial legality) and impede more radical manifestations of working-class solidarity that challenged capitalist relations of production. The primary beneficiaries of this regime were craft unions which represented a small fragment of the labour market that was predominantly male and Anglo. Semi-skilled and especially ethnic and racialized workers were most likely to be the targets of the coercive side of state power.

---

[14]W. M. Baker, "The Miners and the Mediator: The 1906 Lethbridge Strike and Mackenzie King," *Labour/Le Travail*, 11 (1983), 89-117.

[15]Ben M. Selekman, *Postponing Strikes* (New York 1927); Jeremy Webber, "The Mediation of Ideology: How Conciliation Boards, Through the Mediation of Particular Disputes, Fashioned a Vision of Labour's Place within Canadian Society," *Law in Context,* 7, 2 (1989), 1-23.

State support for the centrality of market mechanisms in the determination of conditions of employment was also reflected in the modest changes to minimum standards legislation during this period. One apparent exception was hazardous working conditions which increasingly came to be regulated by provincial statutes. These laws also continued to limit hours of work for women and young adults and to prohibit the employment of children. As in the past though, the effect of these interventions was limited by weak enforcement and the predominant view that enlightened profit-seeking employers would discover that meeting the legislative requirements was in their economic self interest. In part, this was true because inspectors were loath to require employers to adopt measures that were uneconomical. As a result, divergence between state-established minimum standards and market outcomes was minimized. As well, household and agricultural workers were still denied any legislative protection, reflecting the continued unwillingness of the state to intervene in the domestic sphere, even when relationships within it were established and governed through contracts of employment.[16]

Compensation for work-related injuries, diseases, and fatalities was also contentious. Common law judges had constructed a legal presumption that workers voluntarily assumed the risk of being injured by hazards present in the workplace in exchange for their wages. This kind of market justice was unacceptable to workers and was legislatively modified in the 19th century, but these reforms still made the receipt of compensation dependent either on workers bargaining for disability insurance or proving in court that employer negligence caused their injuries. Workers continued to demand compensation for their injuries as a matter of justice and employers were unhappy with a system that required them to purchase private insurance, produced litigation conducted by insurance carriers to protect their own interests, and left employees disgruntled. A no-fault system of public insurance offered employers predictability and the de-politicization of work injuries by making them a routine cost of production for which no blame was assigned. For workers, it provided secure compensation. Despite serious disagreements about the terms on which compensation would be awarded and the administration of the scheme, there was enough common ground and political support to establish no-fault, state-administered workers' compensation systems in most provinces, beginning with Ontario in 1914.[17]

As with other minimum standards, though, workers' compensation was carefully tailored to minimize its interference with the market and the normative family. Compensation was set as a percentage of earnings (initially 55 per cent), without

[16]Eric Tucker, *Administering Danger in the Workplace* (Toronto 1990).
[17]R.C.B. Risk, "'This Nuisance of Litigation': The Origins of Workers' Compensation in Ontario," in D.H. Flaherty, ed., *Essays in the History of Canadian Law*, Vol. II (Toronto 1983), 418-91. Other provinces enacted legislation as follows: Nova Scotia (1915); British Columbia and Manitoba (1916); Alberta and New Brunswick (1918); Saskatchewan (1928); Québec (1931); P.E.I. (1949); and Newfoundland (1950).

any guarantee of a minimum payment that would keep low wage earners and their dependent families out of dire poverty. Widows, even those with dependent children, lost their pension if they re-married and widowers were only entitled to a pension if they were incapable of working. As well, domestic and agricultural workers were typically excluded.

There was little other protective legislation. Trade unions supported legislated limits on the length of the working day, but only in British Columbia, where labour-supported MLA's sometimes held the balance of power in a particularly fractious legislature, were eight-hour laws passed for underground miners, stationary engineers employed in metal mines, and smelter workers. Progress was aided by the health and safety dimension of the issue. The problem of low-wages for women, and more generally, for all workers who lacked bargaining power, was not addressed legislatively in any province, although some governments promulgated fair wage resolutions that secured workers on government contracts prevailing local wage levels.[18]

If special protection for women was a double-edged sword because it helped reproduce labour market discrimination by entrenching ideas about women's greater physical and moral vulnerability in the workplace, legislative restrictions aimed at Asian workers did not in any way purport to be for their benefit. Rather, these were motivated by a combination of white workers' fear about unfair wage competition and racist beliefs. Legislation restricting the employment of Asian workers was most common in British Columbia, the province with the greatest Asian population. Nineteenth-century statutes banned Chinese and Japanese from underground mining, but from 1899 onwards such laws were either struck down by the courts or disallowed by the Federal government because they interfered with the importation of Asian labour to build the railways and supply the CPR with coal and ran afoul of imperial British policy. A more widespread brand of anti-Asian legislation, ostensibly aimed to protect white women workers from the depredations of Asian employers, passed constitutional muster.[19]

In sum, the legal regulation of employment in this period tended to constitute and reinforce a market-based model of wage determination in which individual rights of property and contract took priority over the freedom of workers to act collectively. Responsible trade unions that agreed to operate within the narrow

[18]Harold Fabian Underhill, "Labor Legislation in British Columbia," PhD Thesis, University of California, 1935, 97-106; Linda Kealey, *Enlisting Women*, 29-37; Robert McIntosh, "Sweated Labour: Female Needleworkers in Industrializing Canada," *Labour/Le Travail*, 32 (1993), 105-38.

[19]Ross Lambertson, "After *Union Colliery*: Law, Race, and Class in the Coalmines of British Columbia," in Hamar Foster and John McLaren, eds., *Essays in the History of Canadian Law, Vol. VI, British Columbia and the Yukon* (Toronto 1995), 386-422; Constance Backhouse, "The White Women's Labor Law: Anti-Chinese Racism in Early Twentieth-Century Canada," *Law & History Review*, 14 (1996), 315-68.

confines of industrial legality could be accommodated within this regime, but not those who insisted on challenging the legally constituted rules of engagement. The male and largely Anglo craft fragment of the labour force was more likely to fall in the first category and the much larger industrial fragment into the second. It was only when market outcomes potentially outraged public standards of decency that the state evinced any willingness to impose minimum standards, particularly when paternalist values protecting honest womanhood and the normative family were at stake, or when racialized workers were constructed as the source of danger. But even then, protective legislation or, for that matter, legislation discriminating against racialized workers, was rarely allowed to impede important economic interests.

World War I Labour Policy, 1914-1918

World War I set in motion a chain of events that challenged the regime of industrial voluntarism, including its underlying gender order. Fuelled by tight labour markets, high inflation, and a growing sense of entitlement encouraged by political leaders' claim that this was a war for democracy, workers became increasingly radicalized and militant. The ensuing workers' revolt tested the limits of the legal framework and judges and politicians worked together to defend it. Some state officials, however, were convinced that a new regime was required to accommodate the legitimate demands of working men and women, and they took steps to better institutionalize collective bargaining and strengthen minimum standards (especially for women). Employers resisted these measures and were able to defeat or limit severely many of these initiatives. As a result, although the war and immediate post-war agitation left some imprint on the regime of industrial voluntarism, it survived largely intact for the remainder of the 1920s.[20]

The *War Measures Act* centralized power in the federal cabinet, allowing it to rule by order in council. Initially, the government's labour policy relied on the existing regime to maintain war production. It extended the *IDIA* to all war industries in 1916, despite the opposition of the dominant labour federation, the Trades and Labour Congress (TLC), which favoured the adoption of a fair wages policy. As the war progressed, however, these tools to contain rising labour militancy failed, and the Federal government experimented with a variety of increasingly interventionist responses.[21]

---

[20]See generally Craig Heron and Myer Siemiatycki, "The Great War, the State, and Working-Class Canada," in Craig Heron, ed., *The Workers' Revolt in Canada 1917-1925* (Toronto 1998), 11-42; Myer Siemiatycki, "Labour Contained: The Defeat of a Rank and File Workers' Movement in Canada 1914-1921," PhD Thesis, York University, 1986.

[21]Myer Siemiatycki, "Munitions and Labour Militancy: The 1916 Hamilton Machinists' Strike," *Labour/Le Travailleur*, 3 (1978), 131-151.

There were some attempts to accommodate the demands of responsible unions and better institutionalize collective bargaining with them. For example, state intervention prevented coal strikes in Nova Scotia by helping to secure an agreement that included union recognition and a dues check-off. On the railways, the government pressured the parties to establish a scheme of consensual, binding interest arbitration. As well, it actively sought a *rapprochement* with the TLC leadership in the hope that its more responsible leaders would help to contain the rising conflict. In January, 1917, Gideon Robertson, an officer with the railway telegraphers' union, was appointed to Senate and to Cabinet as a minister without portfolio with responsibility for labour matters. Trade union representatives were subsequently appointed to various government councils and commissions. Many provinces also took a slight corporatist turn, creating or expanding labour bureaux or departments.[22]

More militant unions and labour radicals faced a more coercive response, especially after the 1917 Bolshevik revolution. The state security apparatus was strengthened and it cracked-down on IWW agitators and other "undesirable," often foreign-born, radicals. In April 1918, the government issued PC 815 that made it an offence for an adult male not to be "regularly engaged in a useful occupation," and PC 915 that further restricted public expression of anti-war sentiment.[23]

Still, the government's primary response to labour unrest remained conciliatory. Indeed, that summer, the government issued PC 1743, a declaration of its war labour policy, which recognized the right of workers to join a union without employer interference or retaliation; supported the maintenance of union shops established by agreement; and endorsed the idea that all workers were entitled to a living wage sufficient to support themselves and their families in decency and comfort. In exchange, it called for no strikes or lockouts for the duration of the war and respect for the right of individual workers to refrain from joining a union. This order, however, was merely declaratory of the government's policy; no steps were taken to implement it.

Only in the very last days of the war did federal labour policy veer sharply towards coercion. In September 1918, the government issued orders banning enemy language publications and proscribing unlawful associations, and finally, in October, it banned strikes and lock-outs for the duration of the war. The signing of the armistice the following month, however, largely avoided the need for the govern-

[22]Paul MacEwan, *Miners and Steelworkers* (Toronto 1976), 39-53; David Frank, "The Cape Breton Coal Miners, 1917-1926," PhD Thesis, Dalhousie University, 1979, 297-301; Stephen G. Peitchinis, "Labour-Management Relations in the Railway Industry," Task Force on Labour Relations, Study No. 20, (Ottawa 1971), 101-12; Allen Seager, "'A new labour era?': Canadian National Railways and the railway worker, 1919-1929," *Journal of the Canadian Historical Association*, 3 (1992), 171-95; James Foy, "Gideon Robertson: Conservative Minister of Labour 1917-1921," MA Thesis, University of Ottawa, 1972.

[23]Gregory S. Kealey, "State Repression of Labour and the Left in Canada, 1914-20: The Impact of the First World War," *Canadian Historical Review,* 73 (1992), 281-314.

ment to resolve how it would enforce the ban, and, in general, left open the question of whether the government could successfully operate a dual labour policy which simultaneously promoted the institutionalization of responsible unionism and repressed labour radicalism.

The war also challenged the gender order of the second industrial revolution in which families' access to the means of survival was primarily through a male wage, and in which female wage earners were restricted to a limited number of lower paying jobs. Conscription deprived many families of their breadwinners and the ensuing labour shortage also drew some women into men's jobs. This situation raised in a particularly sharp manner the dual problem of low female wages; they were insufficient to support a household and undercut men's wages.

One means of minimizing downward pressure on male wages was to promote equal pay for women doing work ordinarily performed by men. The government formally embraced the principle in PC 1743, but most employers resisted the practice. The problem of low wages for the mass of women employed in women's jobs began to be addressed in 1917 by provincial female minimum wage legislation. Minimum wage boards were empowered to set female wages on an occupational basis, but instead of adopting an egalitarian approach, they took a protective one which, at best, provided working women with the bare minimum needed to reproduce their own labour. This idea of the minimum contrasted sharply with the "fair" or "living" wage principle that was embraced by *IDIA* boards and the federal and some provincial governments in their contracting practices. As a result, with the end of the war, fragmented labour markets reasserted themselves and women were once again confined to low wage work, even while the principle of state-established minimum standards for especially vulnerable labour force participants was further entrenched.[24]

The Defeat of the Post-War Workers' Revolt, 1918-1929

The end of the war did not bring labour peace but heightened conflict. Workers sought to obtain more democracy and prosperity at home, having sacrificed to protect it abroad, while employers sought to restore the *status quo ante,* having made concessions under the pressure of tight labour markets and government pressure to maintain war production. The Federal government stood between labour and capital, but was not a neutral umpire. Its primary objective was to maintain social order and economic growth within a capitalist framework. As before, this

[24]Bob Russell, "A Fair or a Minimum Wage? Women Workers, the State, and the Origins of Wage Regulation in Western Canada," *Labour/Le Travail*, 28 (1991), 59-88; Linda Kealey, "Women and Labour during World War I: Women Workers and the Minimum Wage in Manitoba," in Mary Kinnear ed., *First Days, Fighting Days* (Regina 1987), 76-99; Margaret McCallum, "Keeping Women in Their Place: The Minimum Wage in Canada, 1910-25," *Labour/Le Travail*, 17 (1986), 29-56; Ceta Ramkhalawansingh, "Women during the Great War," in *Women at Work* (Toronto 1974), 261-307.

required a mixture of conciliation and coercion, although disagreement emerged over the appropriate blend.[25]

In the immediate aftermath of the Armistice, the government continued both to construct an accord between responsible unions and employers and to contain manifestations of political and labour radicalism. Prime Minister Borden played an active role in drafting the labour sections of the Treaty of Versailles that established the International Labour Organization (ILO) and endorsed the principle of workers' freedom of association. The government also appointed the Royal Commission on Industrial Relations (RCIR) to inquire into means of improving relations between employers and workers. At the same time, however, it introduced amendments to the *Immigration Act* expanding its powers to prohibit radicals from entering the country and making it easier to deport them. It also embarked on the process of amending the *Criminal Code* to broaden the definition of sedition and ban unlawful associations.

Labour conflict reached unprecedented levels in the spring of 1919, much of it led by radicalized workers who split from the more conservative TLC to join the One Big Union (OBU). While the revolt was national in its dimensions, the centre of conflict was in Winnipeg where a general strike of some 30,000 workers began on 15 May and lasted until 26 June. The Federal government was determined that the strike must fail and it worked closely with the local bourgeoisie to achieve that result. After it became apparent that the strike would not collapse on its own accord, police arrested strike leaders. The British-born were charged with seditious conspiracy while the foreign-born were dealt with under the *Immigration Act* with the expectation that they would be deported. Following the arrests, strike supporters held a rally in defiance of a ban on public demonstrations and, after the crowd failed to disperse, police opened fire, killing two men and wounding many others.[26]

After the strike's defeat, the criminal trials of the British-born strike leaders became a *cause célèbre*. A judge sympathetic to the prosecution presided and most of the leaders were convicted and sentenced to terms of imprisonment that ranged from six months to two years. Ironically, the 'foreign'-born leaders fared better in

---

[25] See essays in Heron, *Workers' Revolt*.

[26] David J. Bercuson, *Fools and Wise Men* (Toronto 1978); A. Ross McCormack, *Reformers, Rebels and Revolutionaries* (Toronto 1997); Gregory S. Kealey, "1919: The Canadian Labour Revolt," *Labour/Le Travail*, 13 (1984), 11-44; David J. Bercuson, *Confrontation at Winnipeg*, rev. ed. (Montréal 1990); D.C. Masters, *The Winnipeg General Strike* (Toronto 1950); Norman Penner, ed., *Winnipeg 1919*, 2nd ed., (Toronto 1975); Tom Mitchell, "'To Reach the Leadership of this Revolutionary Movement': A.J. Andrews and the Suppression of the Winnipeg General Strike," *Prairie Forum*, 18 (1993), 239-55; Chad Reimer, "War, Nationhood and Working-Class Entitlement: The Counterhegemonic Challenge of the 1919 Winnipeg General Strike," *Prairie Forum*, 18 (1993), 219-37.

administrative proceedings: only one was ultimately deported and the rest were set free. Some of the less prominent aliens, however, were secretly deported.[27]

Significant outbursts of radicalism in other parts of the country also met with extraordinary assertions of state power. For example, in the Alberta coalfields, where there was an OBU breakaway from the more conservative United Mineworkers of America (UMWA), the state-appointed director of coal operations made a closed shop agreement between the UMWA and the coal operators legally enforceable. When the legality of the order was questioned, the federal government retroactively ratified it by statute. Meanwhile, in Nova Scotia, J.B. MacLachlan, leader of a radicalized local district of the UMWA, was convicted of seditious libel and sentenced to two years imprisonment.[28]

The exercise of coercive force to defeat the post-war labour revolt was not accompanied by an abandonment of the state's efforts to institutionalize an accord between responsible unions and employers. However, the overwhelming majority of employers had no interest in pursuing a partnership with organized labour, even if unions behaved responsibly. They preferred neo-paternalist employee representation schemes that excluded independent unions. Because the government was reluctant to compel unwilling employers to accept independent trade unions, its efforts at a *rapprochement* collapsed. The election of the Liberals in 1921, led by Mackenzie King, the architect of pre-war industrial voluntarism, ended the federal government's attempt to construct a new national labour relations policy.[29]

The institutional and ideological reconstruction of the labour market as local and consensual ultimately had constitutional significance. Under the constitution, provinces had jurisdiction over property and civil rights, while the federal govern-

[27]Tom Mitchell, "'Repressive Measures': A.J. Andrews, the Committee of 1000 and the Campaign Against Radicalism After the Winnipeg General Strike," *Left History*, 3, 2 and 4,1 (1996), 133-167; Desmond H. Brown, "The Craftsmanship of Bias: Sedition and the Winnipeg Strike Trial, 1919," *Manitoba Law Journal*, 14 (1984), 1-33; Leslie Katz, "Some Legal Consequences of the Winnipeg General Strike of 1919," *Manitoba Law Journal*, 4 (1970-71), 39-52.

[28]Charles Allen Seager, "A Proletariat in Wild Rose Country: The Alberta Coal Miners, 1905-1945," PhD Thesis, York University, 1981, 316-61; Bercuson, *Fools and Wise Men*, 136-43; Foy, "Gideon Robertson," 112-17; Frank, "The Cape Breton Coal Miners," and "The Trial of J.B. McLachlan," *CHA Historical Papers*, (1983), 208-25; John Manley, "Preaching the Red Stuff: J.B. McLachlan, Communism, and the Cape Breton Miners, 1922-1935," *Labour/Le Travail*, 30 (1992), 65-114; Barry Cahill, "*Howe* (1835), *Dixon* (1920) and *McLachlan* (1923): Comparative Perspectives on the Legal History of Sedition," *University of New Brunswick Law Journal*, 45 (1995), 281-307.

[29]Royal Commission on Industrial Relations, "Report of Commission" (Ottawa: Supplement to *Labour Gazette*, July 1919); Larry G. Gerber, "The United States and Canadian National Industrial Conferences of 1919: A Comparative Analysis," *Labor History*, 32 (1991), 42-65; Margaret McCallum, "Corporate Welfarism in Canada, 1919-39," *Canadian Historical Review*, 71 (1990), 46-79.

ment had authority over national trade and commerce, criminal law and peace, order, and good government. A challenge to the constitutionality of the *IDIA* in the midst of the 1913 strike wave failed when the court held that the act was "not legislation affecting private or civil rights" but rather protected the broad public interest in peace, order, and good government. When the *IDIA* was challenged after the war, most Canadian judges agreed with this view. However, the Privy Council of the House of Lords, the final court of appeal, disagreed. It held that labour relations was a matter of property and civil rights, thereby sharply curtailing federal jurisdiction. Although this was not the result that King's government desired, it was not radically inconsistent with the prevailing Liberal view about the limited role of the national government.[30]

The decentralization of labour law and policy allowed for more localized responses to particular conditions, but in practice little changed. The old coercive infrastructure of voluntarism (justified as the protection of individual rights of property and contract) remained in force and continued to be applied with particular vigour against the few militant unions that survived the immediate post-war defeats. In Nova Scotia, for example, local officials requisitioned troops during strikes by Cape Breton coal miners and steel workers in 1922, 1923, and 1925. Labour injunctions also became more common as many judges held that it was necessary to curb picketing in order to protect the rights of employers, individual employees, and members of the public. These limitations on picketing remained imprecise and different judges held competing views on the question. Still, the threat of liability was ever-present, even for responsible unions, and the TLC lobbied unsuccessfully for legislation that would unambiguously permit peaceful picketing and limit trade union liability for damages arising out of strike-related activity.[31]

Provinces did not enthusiastically embrace their new jurisdiction. Instead, most took advantage of federal legislation that enabled them to make the *IDIA* apply to mining, railway, and public utility disputes within their jurisdiction. The only legal innovations were in Nova Scotia and Québec, where concessions were made in order to promote more conservative unions and avoid incursions by less desirable ones. In Nova Scotia, where the UMWA was fighting off the communist-influenced Mine Workers Union of Canada (MWUC), the *Coal Mine Regulation Act* was amended in 1927 to make union dues deductions mandatory when requested in writing by an employee. This was subsequently used by the UMWA to enforce closed

[30]*Toronto Electric Commissioners* v. *Snider* [1925] A.C. 396.

[31]Don Macgillivray, "Military Aid to the Civil Power: The Cape Breton Experience in the 1920s," *Acadiensis*, 3, 2 (1974), 45-64; David Frank, "Class Conflict in the Coal Industry Cape Breton 1922," in Gregory S. Kealey and Peter Warrian, eds. *Essays in Canadian Working Class History* (Toronto 1976), 161-84; and Frank, "Cape Breton Coal Miners," 362-75; Craig Heron, *Working in Steel* (Toronto 1988), ch. 4; Steven Penfold, "'Have You No Manhood In You?': Gender and Class in the Cape Breton Coal Towns, 1920-1926," *Acadiensis*, 23, 2 (1994), 21-44; Seager, "Proletariat," 362-423.

shop agreements against MWUC members. In Québec, a Catholic trade union movement emerged that was committed to the church's social teachings which emphasized cooperative relations between workers and employers. The *Professional Syndicates Act* passed in 1924 permitted workers to form incorporated associations that were able to enforce collective agreements and shield their benefit funds from seizure by employers seeking to enforce damage awards. While the Act did not directly limit participation in the scheme to Catholic unions, it did so indirectly by requiring that to incorporate all directors had to be British subjects and that foreigners could only constitute up to one-third of the membership. This clearly disqualified international unions which were, in any event, ideologically opposed to incorporation, seeing it as a means of subjecting them to more extensive legal control. The provincial government's support for Catholic unions, however, only went so far. There was nothing in the scheme that compelled employers to recognize or bargain with incorporated unions.[32]

Overall, the coercive infrastructure of the post-war regime of industrial voluntarism applied to all workers, although its enforcement varied considerably. Conciliatory law was far more fragmented. The coverage of the *IDIA was* patchy, provincial trade dispute legislation was purely voluntary, and the frequency and effectiveness of *ad hoc* interventions by state officials varied enormously. Given this legal regime, the level of employer resistance, and the weakness of Canadian unions, collective bargaining in the 1920s was confined to a small segment of the labour market, benefiting a minority of mostly male, mostly Anglo workers.

For the majority, there were few minimum standards to protect against unfavourable labour market conditions and discriminatory practices. Provincial female minimum wage laws typically covered women employed in factories, shops and offices, but excluded those in rural areas and domestic service. The boards that administered these laws did not challenge labour market discrimination that denied most women access to "fair" or equal wages. Moreover, these laws also reinforced industrial and sectoral fragmentation. Instead of setting a flat rate, the boards set different rates for different industries, taking into account specific business conditions. In addition, further rate distinctions were based on age and experience. In sum, the boards' practices reinforced labour market fragmentation.[33]

[32]William Steward Arnold Martin, "A Study of Legislation Designed to Foster Industrial Peace in the Common Jurisdiction of Canada," PhD Thesis, University of Toronto, 1954, 263-72. Frank, "Cape Breton Coal," 376-82; Jacques Rouillard, *Histoire du Syndicalisme Quebécois* (Montréal 1989), 120-29, 169-70; *History of the Labour Movement in Quebec* (Montréal 1987), 90-94.
[33]J.W. Macmillan, *The Limits of Social Legislation* (Toronto 1933), 30; Kathleen Derry and Paul H. Douglas, "The Minimum Wage in Canada," *Journal of Political Economy*, 30 (1922), 155-88; Kealey, *Enlisting Women*, 169-175; McCallum, "Keeping Women," 42-56; Russell, "A Fair or Minimum," 80-88.

Wage inequality was not the only legally countenanced form of sex discrimination; governments also supported the re-entrenchment of labour market segregation in the post-war reconstruction period. For example, a veterans' preference clause was inserted into the federal government's *Civil Service Act* in 1918 and, in 1921, during a period of high unemployment, formal restrictions were placed on the employment of married women. In practice, these laws did not exclude women from the federal civil service, but they helped channel them into poorly paid occupational ghettoes.[34]

British Columbia was the only province that legislated maximum hours of work and minimum wages for men. Eight-hour laws had been passed in the pre-war era for underground miners and some related employees, but it was only in 1923, largely in response to fear of unfair wage competition from workers of Asian origin, that a law of more general application was enacted, covering mining, manufacturing, and construction. This was followed in 1925 by the passage of male minimum wage legislation that, again, was largely driven by anti-Asian sentiment. Employers challenged the law and convinced a court that it required wages be set job by job, not by occupation. This rendered the statute completely ineffective.[35]

The Final Crises of Industrial Voluntarism, 1929-45

The social and labour market disruptions resulting from the Great Depression and World War II undermined the foundation upon which industrial voluntarism was reconstructed in the post-World War I era. Several strike waves and political and ideological realignments produced a qualitatively different regime (commonly known as industrial pluralism), albeit one that bore the imprint of its predecessor and the struggles that marked its demise. Although these crises created the possibility of producing a less fragmented legal regime, in the end fragmentation increased, enhancing gaps between differently situated workers.

At the height of the Great Depression nearly one quarter of the labour force was unemployed and double-digit unemployment persisted for the remainder of the decade. Many of those lucky enough to be employed faced declining standards of living, as neither trade unions nor minimum standards laws were strong enough to protect workers from the downward pressure on wages. The state's response to the resulting human suffering, especially in the first and most critical years, was grossly inadequate. Federal relief failed to meet the needs of families, and single unemployed women and men were commonly denied relief altogether.[36]

[34]Judy Fudge, "Exclusion, Discrimination, Equality and Privatization: Law, The Canadian State and Women Public Servants, 1908-2000," (forthcoming), 7.
[35]The exception was a 1917 amendment to the Alberta *Factories Act* providing that all persons employed in factories, shops and offices were entitled to a $1.50 per shift. On the British Columbia legislation, see Underhill, "Labor Legislation," 133-67.
[36]John Herd Thompson with Allen Seager, *Canada 1922-1939* (Toronto 1985), 193-252; James Struthers, *No Fault of Their Own: Unemployment and the Canadian Welfare State*

In this climate, radicalism flourished among the employed, who resisted immiseration, and the unemployed, especially single men who were uprooted from their communities and later funnelled into relief camps established by the federal government. The Communist Party played a particularly active role in organizing both groups through the Workers' Unity League (WUL) and the Relief Camp Workers' Union (RCWU). The state responded with increased surveillance and repression. Leaders of the party were arrested in 1931 and convicted under the infamous section 98 for being members of an illegal organization. Strikes by WUL-affiliated unions in Anyox, British Columbia, Estevan, Saskatchewan, Flin Flon, Manitoba, Stratford, Ontario, and Rouyn, Québec were defeated by stiff employer resistance, bolstered by the armed force of the state and a sympathetic judiciary. The bloody police attack in Regina that terminated the 1935 On-to-Ottawa trek of unemployed workers represented the high point of this coercive turn.[37]

However much the federal government wanted to blame this unrest on a small band of radical agitators, it could not escape the reality of widespread human suffering and the sympathy this generated in the broader community. A last minute and poorly conceived attempt to launch a Canadian New Deal failed to save the federal Conservative government in 1935, but the election of King's Liberals did not produce a dramatic change in government policy.

The absence of a federal New Deal left the field open to the provincial governments which were being pressured on many fronts. Politically, the Co-operative Commonwealth Federation (CCF) attracted substantial working-class and farmer support, threatening established political parties. As well, unorganized industrial workers became increasingly militant and evinced a willingness to violate their employers' legal rights by, for example, occupying factories in support of their demands. Many provincial officials also were becoming convinced that low wages were part of a vicious cycle of weak demand and excess competition that depressed the economy and placed a heavy burden on state coffers. No longer was it a vulnerable minority (predominantly female) that needed protection from the vicissitudes of the market; the problem was endemic.

Provincial governments responded to these challenges in a variety of ways. On the one hand, governments made it clear that violations of the law would not be tolerated and the sit-down movement in Canada was short-lived. As in the past,

---

1914-1941 (Toronto 1983), ch. 2; Barry Broadfoot, *Ten Lost Years 1929-1939* (Markham 1975).

[37]Lorne Brown, *When Freedom Was Lost* (Montréal 1987); John Manley, "Communism and the Canadian Working Class During the Great Depression: The Workers' Unity League," PhD Thesis, Dalhousie University, 1984; Steve Hewitt, "September 1931: A Re-Interpretation of the Royal Canadian Mounted Police's Handling of the 1931 Estevan Strike and Riot," *Labour/Le Travail*, 39 (1997), 159-78; Jean-Michel Catta, *La grève des bûcherons de Rouyn, 1933* (Rouyn 1985).

threats to employers' property and contract rights evoked a strong state response, although the *Criminal Code* was unexpectedly amended in 1934 to restore the right to picket peacefully. On the other hand, governments felt pressured to address some of the underlying sources of labour discontent. The resulting initiatives varied from province to province, depending on local conjunctures of interests and ideologies, but essentially they extended trade union rights and minimum standards. This entailed departures from the norms of industrial voluntarism by limiting employers' freedom of contract and requiring the creation of a larger administrative apparatus.

Much of the post-1935 strike activity took place under the banner of the newly established, American-based, Congress of Industrial Organization (CIO). Trade-union organizing in the United States was given a shot in the arm by the *Wagner Act* (1935) which prohibited employer interference with trade union organization, required employers to recognize and bargain with trade unions that had majority support, and created an administrative body vested with the legal authority to enforce the scheme. In Canada, however, the craft unions that dominated the TLC were wary of that model, fearing that it would support industrial unions at their expense. Hence, the TLC refused to campaign for a Canadian version and instead, in 1936, drafted a model bill that prohibited various kinds of employer interference with the right of workers to join trade unions and bargain collectively.

In the following years, some version of the TLC bill was passed by nearly every province, except Ontario, where Premier Mitch Hepburn's fear and loathing of the CIO blocked any such move. This legislation limited employers' freedom of contract by, for example, making it a provincial offence, punishable by fine, for employers to require that workers agree not to join a trade union as a condition of their employment. By 1939, the federal government also became involved and made it a *crime* to refuse to employ a person for the sole reason that the person was a member of a lawful trade union formed for the purpose of advancing in a lawful manner their interests.

In some provinces, freedom of association was part of a larger package of reforms. For example, Manitoba and New Brunswick also enacted *IDIA*-type legislation that was applicable to provincial labour disputes, while Nova Scotia, Alberta, and British Columbia passed stripped-down versions of the *Wagner Act*. Only in Nova Scotia was the law used successfully. Elsewhere it had no impact, in part because enforcement was through prosecution in the courts, rather than through an administrative tribunal equipped with the remedial power to implement the law effectively and efficiently. As a result, prior to World War II collective bargaining spread slowly in the mass production industries.

The most interesting legislative innovation during this period was the enactment of industrial standards acts that conjoined collective bargaining with minimum standards to construct a framework for joint labour-management regulation of labour markets capable of resisting downward pressure in intensely competitive local markets. Inspired by Roosevelt's *National Industrial Recovery Act*, such schemes provided that an agreement reached between a group of workers and employers within a particular industrial sector and geographic region could become binding on all employers and workers in that sector and region even though they were not parties to the agreement. The law facilitated collective bargaining in highly competitive sectors by assuring employers who saw the benefit of cooperation, that they would not be disadvantaged by those who did not. Statutes along these lines were passed in Québec (1934), Ontario and Alberta (1935), Nova Scotia (1936), Saskatchewan (1937), Manitoba (1938), and New Brunswick (1939). Their major weakness was that there was no way to compel employers to participate and so industrial standards were only established in a few sectors, most notably construction and some branches of the garment industry, where employers saw a benefit from joint regulation. Another problem was that such schemes tended to reinforce fragmentation on a gendered basis; the wage schedule that was negotiated in the garment industry placed women at the bottom of an artificially constructed, gendered hierarchy of skill.[38]

The limited gains on the collective bargaining front left the vast majority of workers to fend for themselves through their individual contracts of employment. For many the result was unacceptably low wages, a consequence that provincial governments felt compelled to address not only for electoral reasons but to support macro-economic policies aimed at increasing demand, reducing industrial conflict, and relieving the strain on welfare budgets. The form of intervention was contested though and each province tended to follow a somewhat different path.

Since many women were already covered by minimum wage laws, in most provinces the issue was whether to extend minimum wages to men and, if so, on what basis. A few of the earliest Depression-era minimum standard laws were sector specific, including a number directed at the forestry industry. Between 1934 and 1937, all provinces except Nova Scotia enacted a general male minimum or fair wage law. Following the precedent of female minimum wage laws, they did not establish a flat rate, but rather empowered administrative bodies to establish industry- and geographic-specific minima. Typically, the statutes provided for conferences or consultations to be held in an effort to obtain voluntary agreement. Absent of an agreement, however, the schemes provided that a schedule of wages could be imposed by order. Most of these administrative bodies also were empowered to set maximum hours of work.

Beyond these basic similarities, the schemes varied considerably. Manitoba and Saskatchewan simply extended their female minimum wage laws to men, so that there were no differences between the minimum male and female wage rates. British Columbia and Alberta enacted separate male minimum wage laws and

[38]Steedman, *Angels of the Workplace*, ch. 7 and "Canada's New Deal in the Needle Trades," *Relations Industrielle*, 53 (1998), 535-61; Mark Cox, "The Limits of Reform: Industrial Regulation and Management Rights in Ontario, 1930-7," *Canadian Historical Review*, 68 (1987), 552-75.

issued separate orders that provided for a higher male minimum wage. Ontario enacted a consolidated minimum wage law in 1937, but the only order issued by the end of the decade set a lower wage rate for women than for men in the textile industry. Québec's fair wage law was the most extensively applied. A general order set wages for most categories of work in towns and municipalities, without a male/female differential. In rural areas, the earlier female women wage orders were adopted and extended to men performing the same duties as women.[39]

In sum, the regime of industrial voluntarism and its legitimating ideology began to unravel in the face of the social, economic, and political disorder caused by the Great Depression, leading to an expanded role for the state in regulating employment. This entailed restrictions on employers' freedom of contract to create a protected space for trade union activity and to guarantee that wages and some other conditions of employment did not fall below a socially acceptable level. These changes, however, had minimal impact. Collective bargaining spread slowly and little of its progress could be attributed to a more favourable legal climate. For the rest, a regime of individual contract prevailed, subject only to a few legislated standards. Minimum wage laws respected industrial and regional differences. In some provinces, differential male/female wage rates were directly enshrined in law, while in others, discrimination was indirectly inscribed by assigning lower wage rates to female-dominated occupational categories. These differences, however, were small — rarely more than ten per cent — because employers resisted paying higher wages to men, despite their breadwinner status. Finally, employment legislation of all kinds was poorly enforced.

World War II produced the second set of crises that ultimately brought about the demise of industrial voluntarism and its replacement by a new regime of industrial legality. As in the case of World War I, the federal government invoked its emergency powers to rule by order in council. Domestically, its primary objectives were to maximize war production and control inflation. To that end, it recruited leading industrialists into key government departments, kept organized labour frozen out of the inner circles, and adopted World War I precedents as war labour policy.[40]

The recruitment of women into the labour force was a priority for government, but concern about maintaining male breadwinner privilege shaped the pattern of

[39]William Parenteau, "Forest and Society in New Brunswick: The Political Economy of the Forest Industries, 1918-1939," PhD Thesis, University of New Brunswick, 1994, 386-425; Catta, *Grève des bûcherons*, 51-64; Ian Radforth, *Bushworkers and Bosses* (Toronto 1987), 130; A.E. Grauer, *Labour Legislation* (A Study Prepared for the Royal Commission on Dominion-Provincial Relations, Ottawa, 1937), 28-47, 94-102; Catherine Briggs, "Women, Men and the Minimum Wage in Ontario 1916-1940," MA Thesis, University of Guelph, 1992.

[40]Laurel Sefton MacDowell, "The Formation of the Canadian Industrial Relations System During World War Two," *Labour/Le Travailleur*, 3 (1978), 175-96.

their entry. The overwhelming majority of women were employed in traditional female occupations, but even those recruited into war industries were segregated into certain occupations and government policy enabled employers to re-classify jobs by creating lower-paid categories for less experienced women and youth. This segregation helped to keep women out of much of the industrial organization that occurred during the war.[41]

The federal government's industrial relations policy strengthened its capacity to coerce and conciliate. The Defence of Canada Regulations did not specifically target trade unionists, but officials used it to detain leading industrial unionists, often at key points in strikes. Indeed, by 1941 the government felt compelled to curb over-zealous officials by amending the Regulations to stipulate that peaceful picketing was not prohibited. Through the Regulations the government banned over thirty organizations including the Communists.[42]

In addition to coercion, the federal government's early war labour policy also promoted peaceful industrial relations through the extension of compulsory conciliation under the *IDIA* and by the adoption of a statement of principles. The first step brought nearly 85 per cent of Canadian industry under the federal *IDIA* by 1941, thereby assuring federal domination of the field. The statement of principles in PC 2685 expressed support for the right of workers to organize and bargain collectively, and for binding arbitration as a means of resolving disputes over the interpretation and application of collective agreements. These principles, however, were not enforceable.[43]

As the war progressed, the government's labour policy proved unable to accomplish its goal of maintaining industrial peace and restraining inflation. In the face of growing union militancy, government policy took a coercive turn in 1941. The hurdles that a union had to jump through before it could legally strike were increased, and a policy of prosecuting unlawful strikers was adopted. In December of that year, the government also introduced compulsory wage controls, but these actions did not produce labour peace. The increasing use of compulsion against workers, coupled with the absence of compulsion aimed at employers, made the government's proclaimed support for industrial voluntarism seem hypocritical. Not only did the policy fail to contain rank-and-file militancy, it also was becoming a

[41]Ruth Roach Pierson, *"They're Still Women After All": The Second World War and Canadian Womanhood* (Toronto 1986); Ellen Scheinberg, "The Tale of Tessie the Textile Worker: Female Textile Workers in Cornwall During World War II," *Labour/Le Travail*, 33 (1994), 153-86; Anne Forrest, "Securing the Male Breadwinner: A Feminist Interpretation of PC 1003," in Cy Gonick, Paul Phillips, and Jesse Vorst, eds., *Labour Gains, Labour Pains: Fifty Years of PC 1003*, (Winnipeg 1995), 139-62.
[42]Reg Whitaker, "Official Repression of Communism during World War II," *Labour/Le Travail*, 17 (1986), 135.
[43]Russell, *Back to Work?*, ch. 6.

political liability as the CCF was beginning to pose a serious electoral threat in a number of provinces.[44]

By the beginning of 1943 political support for compulsory collective bargaining was growing. Ontario, British Columbia, and Alberta enacted provincial laws in an effort to stave off the CCF threat, but it took another year of militant strike action to finally convince King, the architect of industrial voluntarism, that his creation was no longer viable. PC 1003 was unveiled on 17 February 1944 and it contained an amalgam of three distinct elements: compulsory bargaining, compulsory conciliation, and compulsory grievance arbitration. While the first aimed to satisfy union demands, the latter two emphasized the government's goal of limiting industrial conflict by narrowly circumscribing the timing and purpose of strike activity. Moreover, the move to compulsory bargaining was not accompanied by any measures that forced employers to conclude collective agreements. Disagreements were ultimately resolved by an economic contest of strength. As a result, a kernel of voluntarism resided at the core of industrial pluralism.[45]

Refining the Contours of Industrial Pluralism, 1945-48

PC 1003 brought the government what it wanted most, relative labour peace for the duration of the war. The shape of the post-war world, however, still needed to be resolved as federal jurisdiction began to wane. Industrial unions pressed to build upon their war-time gains by obtaining union security (both financial and membership), industry-wide bargaining, and significant wage increases. Employers opposed them at every turn and it was through these struggles that the parameters of the post-war settlement were defined.

The Windsor Ford strike in 1945 set a number of important precedents. First, it demonstrated that the state would not deploy massive force to help employers maintain production in the face of overwhelming public support for a strike that aimed to achieve "legitimate" collective bargaining objectives, even though unlawful mass-picketing violated employer rights of property and contract. Second, the Rand formula, which was used to settle the strike, established the normative principle that trade unions were entitled to financial security (but not necessarily membership security) in the form of a dues check-off for all workers in the bargaining unit whether or not they were members of the union. In return, however,

---

[44]Laurel Sefton MacDowell, *'Remember Kirkland Lake' The Goldminers' Strike of 1941-42* (Toronto 1983); Jeremy Webber, "The Malaise of Compulsory Conciliation: Strike Prevention in Canada during World War II," *Labour/Le Travail,* 15 (1985), 57-88.
[45]Judy Fudge and Harry Glasbeek, "The Legacy of PC 1003," *Canadian Labour and Employment Law Journal,* 3 (1995), 357-99; Aaron McCrorie, "PC 1003: Labour, Capital, and the State," in *Labour Gains, Labour Pains,* 15-38.

unions had to behave responsibly by repudiating illegal strikes and disciplining members who participated in them.[46]

While the Rand formula became the hegemonic form of union security, a further wave of strikes was fought to secure higher wages. In this regard, unions had to fight against employer recalcitrance and the federal government's declared policy of maintaining wage controls past the war's end. The CIO unions initiated a common wage plan that sought to overcome regional and industrial differentials. A series of strikes established industry-wide agreements in steel, rubber, electronics, and a few other major industries, but broader wage solidarity was not achieved. Moreover, these agreements were based on power rather than on right. Both under federal collective bargaining law and in the provincial statutes that were passed as industrial relations returned to provincial jurisdiction, bargaining rights predominantly were granted for a specific workplace and employer. The return to provincial jurisdiction also gave greater scope for the play of regional economic forces, leading to even greater fragmentation.

In sum, the new regime of industrial pluralism underwrote the gains made by industrial unions through the exercise of their economic power in the war and the post-war era, allowing for the spread of collective bargaining to core industrial sectors. Unions in these sectors obtained for their members improved wages and occupationally-based benefits, seniority rights, and protection against arbitrary discipline and discharge. The price was that unions were tightly wrapped up in a web of industrial legality that constrained militancy, recognized management rights, and favoured fragmented bargaining. Moreover, women did not share in the benefits of post-war industrial pluralism equally with men. Rather than seeing their war-time gains consolidated, women (especially married women) faced government policies that pushed them out of the labour market. Those who remained employed were segregated into a relatively small number of occupational categories, often in industries outside the industrial core, and even those who were in unions often were bargained into lower-paid female job classifications.[47]

III. Industrial Pluralism, 1948-2000

Introduction

Industrial citizenship, which comprised the freedom of association, the right to representation, and the rule of law, was the crowning achievement of industrial pluralism. By substituting legal right for industrial might in order for workers to insist that their employers recognize and bargain with their unions and abide by

[46]David Moulton, "Ford Windsor 1945," in Irving Abella, ed., *On Strike* (Toronto 1975), 129-61.

[47]Forrest, "Securing the Male Breadwinner"; Ann Porter, "Women and Income Security in the Post-War Period: The Case of Unemployment Insurance, 1945-1962," *Labour/Le Travail*, 31 (1993), 111-44; Gillian Creese, *Contracting Masculinity* (Toronto 1999), 60-70.

their collective agreements, collective bargaining legislation and grievance arbitration marked a rupture from the individualism of the common law and the absolutism of property rights. The post-war employment law regime also saw the imposition of liberal democratic constraints on freedom of contract and the rights of private property. These constraints took two forms: the enactment of anti-discrimination or human rights legislation and the extension of minimum standards of employment to a wider range of workers and conditions. Prior to World War II, employers were free to discriminate against individuals on the basis of ineluctable characteristics such as race and sex, since individual freedom from state compulsion was regarded as the paramount liberal value. After the Holocaust, this position was no longer tolerable. Moreover, unions endorsed a strategy of incremental legal reform regarding minimum conditions of employment and pushed for restrictions on hours of work, vacations with pay, minimum wages, and improvements to the workers' compensation regimes.

Thus, in many respects labour was no longer treated simply as a commodity; the employment law regime institutionalized decommodified conceptions of justice. Collective bargaining legislation enshrined the democratic commitment to freedom of association, human rights statutes embodied the liberal commitment to fairness and equality, and employment standards acts encapsulated a social understanding of public welfare. However, these competing conceptions of justice did not completely displace liberal voluntarism's commitment to freedom of contract and private property. A residual market voluntarism was the foundation upon which industrial pluralism was built. The operative assumption was that bargaining disputes should ultimately be settled by reference to the economic power of the parties themselves. The privilege to resort to industrial sanctions, the ultimate measure of bargaining power, continued to determine the contents of collective agreements. Moreover, employers could still call upon a sympathetic judiciary, predisposed to the common law's traditional emphasis on respect for individual property and contract rights, for assistance in labour disputes. Employment standards and human rights also operated within a fundamentally liberal voluntarist context. Minimum entitlement could not depart too markedly from market norms, and anti-discrimination law did not prevent employers from engaging in practices, which while facially neutral adversely affected protected groups. Occupational segregation, for example, replaced outright discrimination as the primary device for maintaining women's subordinate position within the labour market.

In short, the post-war employment law regime was pluralistic in that the three conceptions of justice were institutionalized within it, but it was still liberal voluntarist *at its core*. Moreover, it was also highly fragmented regionally and sectorally, and the norms of employment were gendered and racialized.

Stalemate or Beachhead: 1948 - 1964

After the reconversion period, regionalism once again became a defining element of state employment policies as primary jurisdiction over labour relations was transferred back to the provinces. While the federal collective bargaining legislation, the *Industrial Relations and Disputes Investigation Act (IRDI Act)*, which came into effect in September 1948, served as a model, its key features were filtered through each province's regional political economy. The most marked variations from the federal model were in Québec and Saskatchewan, which retained the collective bargaining legislation enacted during the war. For organized labour the most disturbing legal development was the willingness of conservative provincial governments to enact legal restrictions on the exercise of trade unions' collective power without imposing equivalent limitations upon employers.[48]

British Columbia saw the greatest amount of such legislative activity. While not as draconian as the anti-communist provisions of the *Taft-Hartley Act*, for which employers had lobbied, the predominant feature of the postwar amendments to the *Industrial Conciliation and Arbitration Act* was their anti-union tenor. The labour board was empowered to order a vote on any "bona fide" settlement offer from an employer during a strike or lockout; collective agreements were made actionable at common law; and the board was given the power to cancel the certification of any union striking illegally. These amendments wrapped unions in a straightjacket of legality; any violation of the multitude of restrictions on collective action not only threatened a union's legal status to insist upon recognition, it left it open to costly civil actions.[49]

The beauty of the BC legislation, from the provincial government's perspective, was that it both shifted the initiation of coercion away from itself and onto the parties, primarily employers, and shifted the locus of the debate about the legitimacy of coercion away from the political arena into the judicial one. It was up to the courts to decide whether the union was liable to the employer for any damages caused by the breach of the collective bargaining statute or collective agreement.

[48]Peter Stuart McInnis, "Harnessing Confrontation: The Growth and Consolidation of Industrial Legality in Canada, 1943-1950," PhD thesis, Queen's University, 1996; Russell, *Back to Work?*, 228; C.H. Curtis, *The Development and Enforcement of the Collective Agreement* (Kingston, Ont. 1966), 57-60; H.A. Logan, *State Intervention* (Toronto 1956); A.W. R. Carrothers, *Collective Bargaining Law in Canada* (Toronto 1965), 56-5, 61-4; Alvin Finkel, "The Cold War, Alberta Labour, and the Social Credit Regime," *Labour/Le Travail*, 21 (1988), 123-52, 134-6; A.C. Chrysler, *Labour Relations and Precedents in Canada* (Toronto 1949), 64.

[49]Stephen Gray, "Woodworkers and Legitimacy: the IWA in Canada, 1937-1957," PhD thesis, Simon Fraser University, 1989, 199, 265-71, 336; Paul Graham Knox, "The Passage of Bill 39: Reform and Repression in British Columbia Labour Policy," MA thesis, University of British Columbia, 1974, 120-33, 158-60; Carrothers, *Collective Bargaining Law in Canada*, 64.

This technique of restricting collective action stood in marked contrast to the Ontario approach embodied in the *Rights of Labour Act*, which provided a prophylactic for trade unions against attempts by employers to use compulsory collective bargaining legislation to impose civil liability on trade unions by making it clear that a trade union was not a legal entity for the purposes of civil litigation, and that a collective agreement was not legally enforceable in the ordinary courts. Initially, only Saskatchewan followed this legislative precedent. In most jurisdictions, the questions of a trade union's civil liability and the enforceablity of collective agreements in the ordinary courts remained as controversial and tricky as they were at the beginning of the century.[50]

At the war's end, the courts once again became the pre-eminent forum for dealing with picketing. The reconversion to peace ushered in the heyday of the labour injunction, which was used as a "sword of collective bargaining," rather than a "shield of legal rights." While the BC legislation created a strong impetus for the use of civil actions to tame trade unions, the existing common law and Criminal Code provisions continued to provide effective legal mechanisms for restricting traditional strike related tactics in other jurisdictions. Courts were just as likely in Ontario as they were in BC to find that mass picketing was an illegal form of watching and besetting.[51]

The transition to peace brought the role of the courts to the fore not only in restricting strike-related tactics, but also in determining the scope of powers that labour relations boards could exercise. In Saskatchewan, judges began to read down the labour-friendly legislation and overturn board decisions, prefiguring what would become a see-saw vendetta between the courts versus the legislature and the board over which legal entity had the final say over collective bargaining jurisprudence.[52]

Responsible unions were the only legitimate representatives of workers within the pluralist version of industrial democracy; communist-dominated or sympathetic unions were considered to be beyond the pale. By 1950, with a little assistance from the federal and provincial governments and some labour boards, both the TLC and CCL union leadership had either purged or side-lined their more radical counterparts. The TLC's expulsion of the Canadian Seamen's Union in 1949, followed by the Canadian Labour Relations Board's 1950 decision to revoke its certification on the ground that as a communist-controlled organization it did not fall within the meaning of a union as defined under the *IRDI Act*, was simply the most blatant

[50]Carrothers, *Collective Bargaining in Canada*, 50-1, 57, 59.
[51]Knox, "The Passage of Bill 39," 101-3; Phillips, *No Power Greater*, 145-6; A.W.R. Carrothers, *The Labour Injunction in British Columbia* (Toronto 1956), 108-10; 60 Carrothers, *Collective Bargaining Law in Canada*.
[52]Carrothers, *Collective Bargaining Law in Canada*, 57-8.

example of how labour boards and responsible unions colluded to exclude left-wing unions from the benefits of industrial legality.[53]

Despite the fairly rapid increase in trade union membership with the advent of industrial pluralism, the growth of unionization after World War II was extremely uneven. Workers in the resource, mass-production, and transportation industries joined their skilled craft brothers in the ranks of organized labour, so that in the mid-1950s "the typical union member was a relatively settled, semi-skilled male worker within a large industrial corporation." Except in Saskatchewan, collective bargaining legislation did not cover public sector employees, thereby excluding increasing numbers of workers from the right to bargain collectively through the union of their choice. Morever, even within the private sector, in which some form of collective bargaining legislation was very likely to apply, certain industries and workplaces were a better fit than others. Only the strongest trade unions obtained anything that approximated industry-wide bargaining and, even then in most cases, it was not legally enforceable. Bargaining unit determination policies adopted and administered by labour relations boards reflected and reinforced fragmentation. Plant-by-plant bargaining became the norm. In the secondary sector, which was highly competitive and labour intensive, the legislation tended to function more as an impediment, than an aid, to union representation and collective bargaining.[54]

The structural limitations of industrial pluralism were reinforced and overlaid by other features of the post-war compromise. At the macro level, the systemic segmentation of the labour market enabled leading firms to concede higher wages to some organized workers in the core sectors while at the same time a large category of unorganized workers would remain available, helping to lower aggregate labour costs. Workers in core firms shared a narrow economic self-interest in maintaining a segmented labour market, since it provided low-cost consumer goods. Moreover, the composition of the secondary workforce was sufficiently distinct from that of the primary sector such that different working conditions, wages, standards, and the absence of union representation were considered natural, or, at least, uncontroversial. As Ursel observed, "women constituted the largest pool of such labour in Canada and were, therefore, a key component in the segmentation

[53]E. Jean Nisbet, "'Free Enterprise at its Best': The State, National Sea, and the Defeat of the Nova Scotia Fishermen, 1946-47," in Michael Earle, ed., *Workers and the State in Twentieth Century Nova Scotia* (Fredericton 1989), 171-90; Craig Heron, *The Canadian Labour Movement* (Toronto 1989), 99-100; Palmer, *Working Class Experience*, 290-98; Desmond Morton with Terry Copp, *Working People* (Ottawa 1984), 201-13; William Kaplan, *Everything That Floats* (Toronto 1987); John Stanton, *Life and Death of the Canadian Seamen's Union* (Toronto 1978).

[54]Heron, *The Canadian Labour Movement*, 92; Jane Ursel, *Private Lives, Public Policy: 100 Years of State Intervention in the Family* (Toronto 1992), 249-50; Stuart Jamieson, *Times of Trouble* (Ottawa 1968), 348-9; Eileen Sufrin, *The Eaton's Drive; The Campaign to Organize Canada's Largest Department Store* (Toronto 1982); Forrest, "Securing the Male Breadwinner," 139-62.

strategy of capital." So, too, were immigrant workers. During the 1950s immigration played a central role in the growth of the labour force and as the decade wore on countries outside the British Isles provided an increasingly significant source of labour. A wage and occupational hierarchy, which divided British immigrants from their less affluent eastern and southern European counterparts, was firmly established.[55]

This racialized occupational and wage hierarchy persisted in the face of legislation that was designed to prohibit discrimination on the basis of invidious distinctions such as race, religion, and ethnicity. Human rights legislation became an important feature of the post-war public policy agenda, although the first piece of anti-discrimination legislation in Canada, Ontario's *Racial Discrimination Act*, was enacted in 1944. Inspired by the United Nations Declaration of Human Rights in 1948 and drawing upon US models, a series of "fair employment practices" laws were enacted, prohibiting employment discrimination on the grounds of race and religion. In the early 1960s, discrete fair practices statutes were consolidated into omnibus human rights codes under the authority of permanent human rights commissions, whose function was to administer a discrimination complaints process, to develop public education programs and to advise the government on future development of the code. Pioneered in Ontario, by 1965, laws dealing with discrimination in employment on the basis of race, creed, and colour were in force in eight Canadian jurisdictions.[56]

By contrast, most forms of employment discrimination on the basis of sex were permitted by law until the mid-1960s. The only illegal form of sex discrimination in employment was with respect to pay. In 1951, Ontario became the first jurisdiction in the Commonwealth to impose a legal obligation on employers to pay women workers the same wages as men who performed the same work when it enacted the *Female Employees Fair Remuneration Act*. This legislation was "rooted in the deployment of women's labour during the World War II and in the postwar human rights discourse" and its champions were organized labour, which wanted to ensure that women's low wages would not be used to undercut men's, and women's groups. However, the positive thrust of this legislation was undermined by its narrow commitment to requiring employers to pay women the same as men who performed the same work. Small differences in job descriptions were allowed to

[55]H.C. Pentland, *A Study of the Changing Social, Economic and Political Background of the Canadian System of Industrial Relations, Draft Study prepared for the Task Force on Industrial Relations* (Ottawa 1968), 170; H.D. Woods, *Labour Policy in Canada*, 2nd ed., (Toronto 1973), 25; Ursel, *Private Lives, Public Policy*, 239; Palmer, *Working-Class Experience*, 306-6; Avery, *A Reluctant Host*.

[56]R. Brian Howe and David Johnson, "A Study of Provincial Human Rights Funding," *Canadian Public Administration*, 38, 2 (Summer 1995), 244-45; Walter Tarnapolsky and William Pentney, *Discrimination and the Law* (Toronto 1985), Chapter 2; Paul Malles, *Canadian Labour Standards in Law, Agreement, and Practice* (Ottawa 1976), 12-13.

stand unchallenged as a basis for different wages and a union's consent to occupational segregation was considered to be a legitimate basis for wage discrimination. Employers learned that it was perfectly legal to avoid paying women the same as men through the practice of occupation segregation.[57]

Formal legal equality for women who sought employment was uneven and contradictory, revealing a "legislative bias towards access rather than equity." On the one hand, there was the extension of basic employment standards, such as minimum wages which were initially designed exclusively for women, to men, legislation providing for women's equal pay was enacted and the legislative barriers to the employment of women, especially married women, were dismantled. On the other hand, different wage rates for men and women workers under minimum wage legislation were the norm across the country until the late 1960s, unemployment insurance disqualified married women workers, and occupational segregation was legally acceptable.[58]

Even under propitious economic conditions industrial pluralism had a limited scope. By the mid-1950s, more than 65 per cent of Canadian workers were not union members. In fact, between 1955 and 1965 the percentage of the labour force unionized in Canada dropped from 33.7 per cent to 29.7. Union leaders focused their energies on defending their members' interests, not pursuing a broader agenda of social unionism. The type of reforms that organized labour most often demanded, minimum employment standards, and amendments to workers' compensation, were consistent with a segmentation strategy. In the late 1950s, provincial governments began to implement a series of changes to minimum standards, with the result that by the mid-1960s there were comprehensive minimum standards across the country. But these standards were significantly lower than those obtained by unionized workers since, by and large, they were devised for the unorganized sector. Employment standards legislation was treated as collective bargaining law's little sister. Thus, labour law, government policies and employer staffing practices, aided in part by union bargaining strategies, converged to help create and sustain a low wage sector, one which, in the long run, would have a drag-down effect on the conditions of all workers. The beauty of the segmentation strategy was that "the state could accommodate the demands of capital for a plentiful supply of cheap labour (women and immigrants) and contain the spread of unionization (through a

[57]Shirley Tillotsen, "Human Rights Law as a Prism: Women's Organizations, Unions and Ontario's Female Employees Fair Remuneration Act, 1951," *Canadian Historical Review*, 72, 1 (1991), 532-57; Robert Malarkey and John Hagan, "The Socio-Legal Impact of Equal Pay Legislation in Ontario, 1946-1972," *Osgoode Hall Law Journal*, 27, 2 (1989), 295-336.
[58]Ursel, *Private Lives, Public Policy*, 246-7; Ann Porter, "The Case of Unemployment Insurance," *Labour/Le Travail*, 36 (1993), 111-44.

cautious implementation of labour relations acts), without unduly provoking organized labour."[59]

Although the 1950s and early 1960s were principally a period of consolidation for industrial pluralism, there were clear signs that a crisis was brewing. Initially, it was expressed on a regional basis. Militancy in Québec, Newfoundland, and British Columbia was crushed by governments and employers who deployed legal techniques ranging from repressive legislation to court actions.[60]

The Golden Age of Industrial Citizenship: 1965-1980

By the mid-1960s, what had been regional outbreaks of labour unrest consolidated across the country to form a massive strike wave. In 1966, working days lost to strikes reached an unprecedented number, one-third of which was due to illegal or wild-cat strikes. It appeared that union leaders were either unwilling or unable to keep the contumacious rank and file within the bounds of industrial legality.[61]

Several factors drove workers' militancy. Heavy-handed legislation and judicial decisions that disproportionately restricted workers' collective action, combined with wage increases that lagged behind productivity gains, threatened the legitimacy of the industrial pluralist regime. Automation, especially on the railways and in the post office, not only challenged long-established work rules, but job security. Public sector workers were tired of being treated as civil servants whose freedom of association and right to engage in collective action was subordinated to antiquated notions of political sovereignty. Workers refused to obey the rule of law and struck to achieve their demands.

The strike wave triggered a typically Canadian response. The federal government appointed a Task Force, composed of industrial relations experts, to evaluate the existing federal labour relations law and policy. In British Columbia and Ontario, where employers' successful recourse to the courts had begun to tilt the balance away from industrial pluralism and back to individualism and voluntarism, the provincial governments appointed commissions to study the problems caused by labour injunctions. The expert commissions recommended variations on the same solution to the problem of labour unrest — strengthen the institutions of industrial pluralism. The idea was to minimize the vestiges of liberal voluntarism. In British Columbia, jurisdiction to regulate picketing in a labour dispute was transferred from the ordinary courts to labour tribunals, while in Ontario, restric-

[59]Palmer, *Working-Class Experience*, 299, 301, 305-7; Janine Brodie and Jane Jenson, *Crisis, Challenge and Change* (Ottawa 1988), 268; Heron, *The Canadian Labour Movement*, 88; Avery, *A Reluctant Host*, 198-218; Ursel, *Private Lives, Public Policy*, 239, 242, 245.
[60]Palmer, *Working-Class Experience*, 302; Carrothers *et al*, *Collective Bargaining Law in Canada*, 64-5.
[61]Gregory Albo, "The 'New Realism' and Canadian Workers," in Alain-G. Gagnon and James P. Bickerton, eds., *Canadian Politics* (Peterborough, Ont. 1990), 471, 478-9; Palmer, *Working-Class Experience,* 273, 315-6.

tions on the granting of injunctions in a labour dispute were tightened. The judiciary was also told to defer to the expertise of specialized tribunals.[62]

The militancy of the 1960s not only resulted in the strengthening of industrial pluralist institutions, it also led to their extension, albeit in a modified form, to the public sector. Starting in Québec and followed by postal workers across the country, public sector workers, who outside of Saskatchewan did not enjoy any legal right to bargain collectively or to be represented by a union, struck to press for their demands. Governments responded by introducing public sector collective bargaining legislation which, although modelled on private sector collective bargaining statutes, was inferior in several respects, including: restrictions on strikes and lockouts; criteria for arbitration; extensive cooling off measures; restrictions on who could strike; constraints on subjects of bargaining; rules regarding the choice of bargaining agent; and controls on partisan political activity. By 1973, every government in Canada had legislation providing for collective bargaining by public sector workers. The result, however, was a patchwork of measures ranging from the least restrictive model in Saskatchewan and Québec, which extended private sector collective bargaining legislation to the public sector with minimal modifications, to Ontario, which banned collective action outright for government workers. Moreover, with the advent of public sector collective bargaining there was an increase in *ad hoc* back-to-work legislation. Thus, the regime of industrial pluralism was modified to deal with the distinguishing feature of collective bargaining in the public sector — the absence of market competition as a discipline. Public sector collective bargaining legislation marked the third wave of unionization in Canada and the increased feminization of the labour movement. Between 1966 and 1976, there was a 106 per cent increase in unionization for women compared to a 40 per cent increase for men.[63]

Not only were the institutions of industrial pluralism strengthened and extended, so, too, were the other aspects of the employment law regime. The coverage

[62] *Canadian Labour Relations: Report of the Task Force on Labour Relations* (Ottawa 1968); A.W.R. Carrothers, *The Labour Injunction in British Columbia* (Toronto 1956) 108-10; 280; A.W.R. Carrothers and E.E. Palmer, *Report of a Study on the Labour Injunction in Ontario* (Toronto 1966); *Royal Commission of Inquiry into Labour Disputes*, Ontario (Rand) (Ottawa 1968); H.W. Arthurs, "'The Dullest Bill': Reflections on the Labour Code of British Columbia," *U.B.C. Law Review,* 9 (1974), 280-340.

[63] Gerard Hebert, "Public Sector Collective Bargaining in Quebec," in Gene Swimmer and Mark Thompson, eds., *Public Sector Collective Bargaining: The Beginning of the End or the End of the Beginning* (Kingston, Ont. 1995), 210-35; Joseph B. Rose, "The Evolution of Public Sector Unionism," in Swimmer and Thompson, eds., *Public Sector Collective Bargaining,* 20-52; John L. Fryer, "Provincial Public Sector Labour Relations," in Swimmer and Thompson, eds., *Public Sector Collective Bargaining,* 341-67; Morely Gunderson and Frank Reid, "Public Sector Strikes in Canada," in Swimmer and Thompson, eds., *Public Sector Collective Bargaining,* 135-63; Judy Fudge and Harry Glasbeek, "The Legacy of PC 1003," 384-5; Julie White, *Women and Unions* (Ottawa 1980), 22.

of human rights codes was expanded beyond groups identified in terms of ineluc-table characteristics to include marital status, disability and age, and specialized adjudicative tribunals began to develop a distinctive human rights jurisprudence. Moreover, Canada's international labour commitments and women's increased labour market participation, especially in the expanding public sector, combined with the increasingly vociferous political demands of the second wave of the women's movement to pressure federal and provincial governments to eradicate the last vestiges of protective and sex-discriminatory laws, and to enact legislation designed to remedy the legacy of sex discrimination in employment. Simultane-ously, new improved minimum employment standards proliferated and there was a wave of occupational health and safety legislative reform. Writing in 1967, H.W. Arthurs predicted a golden period of industrial citizenship:

Today the Canadian worker lives increasingly in a world of rights and duties created not by his individual contractual act, but by a process of public and private legislation. Members of the industrial community enjoy these rights and duties solely by virtue of their membership in the community. In effect there is emerging a new status — that of "industrial citizen" — whose juridical attributes may be analogized to those of citizenship generally.[64]

The next year, the Woods Task Force urged that the distinctive elements of industrial pluralism be strengthened at the expense of the common law notions of freedom of contract and private property. According to it, strikes and lockouts served both as a catalyst and catharsis to parties who had to learn to deal with inevitable distributional disputes while coming to an understanding of their sym-biotic relationship. Regulated disruptions served a valuable purpose in legitimating the "superior-subordinate nexus inherent in the employment relationship." Hence, responsible trade unionism had to be encouraged, and wages and conditions of work could be left to be determined by what were, basically, voluntarily reached agreements. Organizational activities should be given support by granting the distinctive institutions of industrial pluralism, the labour relations boards, more remedial powers and individual contract principles should be negated as much as possible.[65]

Governments across Canada opted for this approach to reducing labour conflict and, unlike the 1950s, by and large, the amendments to collective bargaining legislation in the 1970s imposed constraints upon employers. A range of labour-friendly changes were made: preambles declaring that public policy supported collective bargaining were added; the remedial powers of boards, especially with respect to unfair labour practices and breaches of the duty to bargain in good faith,

[64]Hucker, "Anti-Discrimination Laws in Canada," 567; Kathleen Archibald, *Sex and The Public Service* (Ottawa 1970), 19; H.W. Arthurs, "Developing Industrial Citizenship," 786.
[65]*Royal Commission of Inquiry into Labour Disputes*, Ontario (Rand) (Ottawa 1968); Ursel, *Private Lives Public Policy*, 243; *Canadian Labour Relations: Report of the Task Force on Labour Relations*; Fudge and Glasbeek, "The Legacy of PC 1003," 383.

were strengthened; provisions for the imposition of first collective agreements in specified circumstances were introduced; unions gained the right to compulsory dues check off; minimum reinstatement rights for workers who participated in economic strikes were enacted; and permanent replacement workers and professional strike breakers were prohibited. In 1977, organized labour achieved the acme of its demands when the Parti-Québécois government introduced legislation that severely limited the right of employers to use temporary replacement workers in a lawful strike or lockout. This step went farther than most industrial pluralist experts were prepared to tolerate.[66]

Just as the institutions of industrial pluralism flourished during the 1970s, so, too, did direct government intervention. The 1970s were a period of consolidation of women's participation in the labour market and the women's movement, which had pressured the federal government to establish the Royal Commission on the Status of Women in 1967, actively lobbied for legislation designed to promote sex equality in the workplace and allow women to combine child-bearing with employment. The Commission's 1970 report highlighted the pervasive nature of sex discrimination in the workplace and government legislation. By 1973 employment protection for pregnant employees was provided, in one form or another, in the federal jurisdiction as well as in six provinces, and in 1972 the *Unemployment Insurance Act* was revised to provide for maternity benefits. As well, human rights tribunals across the country made it illegal for employers to harass sexually female employees. In 1972, the federal government quietly ratified ILO Convention 100 on equal pay for work of equal value. By the end of the 1970s, the federal government, Québec, and the Yukon introduced legislation putting the principle of equal value into practice. Despite both the huge influx of women into the labour market and the legislative commitment to formal equality for women workers in employment in every jurisdiction in Canada, at the end of the 1970s the nature of women's paid work remained quite static. Legal prohibitions against discrimination on the basis of sex, while an important political victory, did not address the range of policies and practices that, while not explicitly discriminatory on the basis of sex, had a discriminatory impact on women workers. Women continued to be crowded into a small range of low-paid occupations. Moreover, the female norm of employment departed significantly from that of men; they were much more likely to work part time and on a temporary basis.[67]

[66]Palmer, *Working-Class Experience*, 276; Roy J. Adams,"A Pernicious Euphoria: 50 Years of Wagerism in Canada," *Canadian Labour & Employment Law Journal*, 3(3/4) (1995), 321-55, 328-29; George W. Adams, *Canadian Labour Law*, 2nd ed. (Aurora 1994); Jean Boivin and Ester Deom, "Labour Management Relations in Quebec," in Morely Gunderson and Allen Ponak, eds., *Union-Management Relations in Canada* (Don Mills, Ont. 1995), 455-93, 469-71.
[67]Pat Armstrong, *Labour Pains: Women's Work in Crisis* (Toronto 1984), 53; Ann Porter, "Gender, Class and the State: The Case of Unemployment Insurance in Canada," PhD thesis,

By 1970, minimum wages of general application, hours-of-work regulation, public holidays, paid vacations, and notice of termination of employment became the norm in many jurisdictions across Canada. Moreover, during the late 1970s, the model of occupational health and safety regulation that had prevailed since the turn of the century had run out of steam. Worker unrest and renewed concern about the social cost of work-induced disability led to a wave of regulatory reform. These reforms focused on two aspects of the regulatory system, in ways that made it more pluralistic. First, the internal responsibility system of the firm was reformed by giving workers some legal rights that were exercisable against their employers. The strength of these rights varied from jurisdiction, but they almost always included some kind of right to know about hazardous conditions, a right to participate in discussions about the identification and control of hazards, and a right to refuse unsafe work. The second target was to rationalize and strengthen the external responsibility system by: enacting omnibus health and safety statutes to replace a multiplicity of sector or hazard specific statutes; putting more emphasis on the control of health hazards; and centralizing administration and enforcement in ministries of labour. However, tensions were immanent within the emerging model. On the one hand, the ideology of common interest provided the foundation for mandated partial self-regulation while, on the other, it was recognized that *de facto* self-regulation (the result of chronic under-enforcement) had failed in the past. Some countervailing mechanisms were needed to spur employer health and safety activity. In practice, the new OHS regime relied primarily on the reformed internal responsibility system, but in the absence of consensus many workers found themselves powerless to force their employers to act. However, when workers demanded state enforcement, they were often put off by officials on the ground that they should be resolving OHS disputes directly with their employer. In this way, the new regime tried to preserve a core of voluntarism that was consistent with industrial plural-ism.[68]

Despite the fact that by the end of the 1970s contract was no longer the dominant principle in collective labour relations, the scope of freedom of associa-tion for workers was severely constrained under industrial pluralism. Unions of the responsible kind were predominantly wholesalers of labour power, not vehicles for

York University, 1998; Gillian Creese, "Sexual Equality and the Minimum Wage in B.C.," *Journal of Canadian Studies*, (1991) 26, 120-140, 133; Malles, *Canadian Labour Standards*, 13; Leah Vosko, "No Jobs, Lots of Work: The Gendered Rise of the Temporary Employment Relationship in Canada, 1867-1997," PhD thesis, York University, 1998; Julie White, *Sisters or Solidarity: Women and Unions in Canada* (Toronto 1993).

[68]Malles, *Canadian Labour Standards*, 12-13; Vivienne Walters, "Occupational Health and Safety Legislation in Ontario: An Analysis of its Origins and Content," *Canadian Review of Sociology and Anthropology,* 20 (1983) 413-34; Eric Tucker, "And Defeat Goes On: An Assessment of the Third Wave of Health and Safety Regulation," in Frank Pearce and Laureen Snider, eds., *Corporate Crime: Contemporary Debates* (Toronto 1995), 245-67.

the expression of class power. The separation between the economic and political was firmly policed when it came to workers' collective action. The 1972 common front strikes were met with old-style coercion and union leaders who defied court orders were convicted of contempt, receiving jail sentences of up to a year in duration. While the 1976 CLC-led Day of Protest against the federal Liberal government's Anti-Inflation legislation, which suspended collective bargaining and imposed wage controls for three years, was a much more orderly affair, it, too, received legal sanction. The Supreme Court subsequently affirmed the federal government's right to suspend free collective bargaining across the country on the ground that double-digit inflation constituted a national emergency. Moreover, when Jean-Claude Parrot, the leader of the postal clerks, had the temerity to refuse to obey the government's draconian back-to-work legislation, he was charged under the *Criminal Code*, prosecuted, and convicted. Union leaders who did not control members who defied legal restrictions on their freedom to strike faced incarceration. Collective withdrawal of labour power outside of a tightly restricted economic frame simply was not tolerable. However, the tradeoff was real gains for workers in terms of wages and economic security.[69]

This bargain was of limited value for workers employed in the secondary labour market, many of whom were women and members of visible minorities. Industrial pluralism did not provide collective bargaining to one-half of the Canadian workforce. Not only was it perfectly acceptable for employers to oppose unionization, the technical requirements for certification made it simply too risky and too costly for all but the most determined union to attempt to organize the private service sector or small workplaces. The unsuccessful attempt to organize bank workers combined with a series of first contract strikes in the late 1970s and early 1980s (many of which involved women workers), to demonstrate that collective bargaining legislation still operated as a barrier to unionization in certain contexts. Despite this, organized labour's confidence in industrial pluralism was not shaken and it maintained its commitment to incremental law reform.[70]

The legislative refinement of industrial pluralism in the private sector never overcame labour market segmentation. Similarly, the legal emphasis on equal rights, especially those for women, did not penetrate the deeper structural fragmentation embedded in the employment law regime. Moreover, the *Anti-Inflation Act* of 1975, which imposed wage and price controls across the country, presaged the

---

[69]Boivin and Deom, "Labour-Management Relations in Quebec," 213; Albo, "The 'New Realism' and Canadian Workers," 478-9; Palmer, *Working-Class Experience*, 344; Daniel Drache and H.J, Glasbeek, *The Changing Workplace* (Toronto 1991).

[70]Rosemary Warskett, "The Politics of Difference and Inclusiveness within the Canadian Labour Movement," *Economic and Industrial Democracy,* 17 (1996), 587-625, 595-98, 608; Adams, "A Pernicious Euphoria," 342; Rosemary Warskett, "Bank Worker Unionization and the Law," *Studies in Political Economy,* 25 (1988), 41-73.

era of coercive controls, or permanent exceptionalism, that undermined industrial pluralism in the public sector almost as soon as it was institutionalized.

Deepening Contradictions: 1980s

During the 1970s, the industrial pluralist regime of legality was subjected to contradictory pressures. Initially, the state responded to workers' militancy by strengthening its distinctive features, but, by mid-decade, the federal government's decision to suspend collective bargaining across the country signalled a broader realignment in the post-war entente. The contradiction between equality and monetarist economic policies that was latent in the late 1970s deepened, and by the mid-1980s the postwar employment regime was stretched to its breaking point.

Although the federal Liberal government started off the decade with what amounted to a new national policy, a centrepiece of which was a commitment to individual and equality rights embodied within the *Charter of Rights and Freedoms*, in the face of the severe recession of 1981-82 it soon targeted its own workers as a scapegoat for the country's economic woes. In 1982, it imposed wage controls on them and suspended collective bargaining rights for two years. This legislation, although not as comprehensive as the earlier controls, was significantly harsher. Moreover, the Treasury Board insisted that it had the right unilaterally to designate a government employee as essential and, thus, prohibit them from participating in an otherwise lawful strike.[71]

Most provincial governments quickly followed the federal government's lead, auguring an era of permanent exceptionalism for industrial pluralism in the public sector. By 1983, six provincial governments had imposed variations of the federal government's 6 and 5 legislation on their own workers. There was also a massive increase in the use of back-to-work legislation to end what were otherwise lawful public sector strikes. The decision to target public sector workers for coercive controls transcended the political orientation of the government. Not only did the Social Credit government in BC attack public sector unions, so too did the Parti-Québécois government, which historically had close ties with public sector unions.[72]

The wage control and back-to-work legislation of the early 1980s presaged a wholesale assault on public sector workers' collective bargaining rights as the decade progressed. The 1984 election of the Conservative Party as the federal government marked an ideological turning point in Canada as it initiated a round

[71]Palmer, *Working-Class Experience*, 346; Swimmer and Thompson, eds., *Public Sector Collective Bargaining in Canada*; L. Panitch and D. Swartz, *The Assault on Trade Union Freedoms: From Consent to Coercion* (Toronto 1993).
[72]Panitch and Swartz, *The Assault on Trade Union Freedoms*; Palmer, *Working-Class Experience*, 362; Hebert, "Public Sector Collective Bargaining in Quebec," 223; Boivin and Deom, "Labour-Management Relations in Quebec," 374.

of deregulation and privatization and attacked public spending and the deficit. The legitimacy of the Conservative government's economic policies was enhanced by the 1985 Report of the Royal Commission on Economic Union, which had been appointed by the Liberals to assess Canada's economic prospects and suggest how the government should retool the economy to meet the global challenges of the future. The Report strongly advocated the deregulation of the labour market and the dismantling of barriers to trade. According to it, "the presumption must be that in the great majority of cases, the market is the best available mechanism for resource allocation. The burden must be on those who propose intervention."[73]

In this political climate, public sector workers' collective bargaining rights had little legitimacy. Not only did the Tories' extend the wage controls on their own workers, they took a no-hold's-barred approach to bargaining, going so far as to authorize, for the very first time by the federal government, the use of replacement workers by a crown corporation. In the spring of 1987, the evening news displayed pitched battles between letter carriers, replacement workers, and police as Canada Post sought to keep the mail moving by using strikebreakers. That fall, the government put an end to the postal clerks' rotating strikes by back-to-work legislation which provided that any union official who defied it would be deposed from elected office.[74]

The continuing assault on public sector workers' collective bargaining rights was not confined to the federal government. Absolute prohibitions on the right to strike, increases in the proportion of workers designated as essential, limitations in the scope of bargaining, the imposition of ability to pay as a criterion to be considered by arbitrators when fashioning a settlement, and the increase in the power of the executive to end strikes and impose settlements were features common to many of the new provincial public sector collective bargaining regimes. Simultaneously, services were reduced and contracted out, and managers took a harder line at the bargaining table.[75]

Initially, it appeared as if governments would be able to suspend or repeal industrial pluralism in the public sector with impunity. In response to the suspension of collective bargaining and the imposition of wage controls, the Public Service Alliance of Canada lodged a complaint with the ILO, and filed a writ in a Canadian court alleging that its freedom of association had been violated. Unions that used their collective power to protest the infringements on their members' freedoms

[73]Duncan Cameron, "Selling the House to Pay the Mortgage: What is Behind Privatization?," *Studies in Political Economy*, 53 (1997), 11-36, 13.
[74]Palmer, *Working-Class Experience*, 349-59; Judy Fudge, "The Commercialization of Canada Post: Postal Policy, Business Strategy and Labour Relations," in Anil Verma and Rick Chaykowski, eds., *Contract and Commitment: Employment Relations in the New Economy* (Kingston, Ont. 1999), 293-337.
[75]Panitch and Swartz, *The Assault on Trade Union Freedoms*; Swimmer and Thompson, *Public Sector Collective Bargaining*.

were met with legal coercion as governments across Canada invoked the rule of law as a justification for restricting collective action. In the mid-1980s, the Newfoundland Association of Public Employees (NAPE) was subjected to huge fines for engaging in illegal strikes and dozens of picketers were arrested for violating a court injunction. Ultimately, Fraser March, the president of NAPE, was sentenced to four months in jail and placed on two years probation for contempt of court. In Alberta, the illegally striking nurses' union ignored the orders of the province's labour board that they return to work, only to be confronted with huge fines and court actions for criminal contempt.[76]

While the ILO had little difficulty in finding that governments across Canada repeatedly had violated international covenants designed to protect workers' rights to associate freely and bargain collectively, Canadian courts were not similarly inclined. In the infamous right-to-strike trilogy, the Supreme Court of Canada ruled that the freedom of association guaranteed by the Canadian *Charter of Rights and Freedoms* did not protect modern legislative rights such as collective bargaining. In fact, each time that unions argued before the Supreme Court of Canada that legal restrictions on the scope of collective bargaining, the right of workers to select a bargaining agent of their choice, and the right to strike or to engage in peaceful picketing constituted an unjustifiable infringement on fundamental rights and freedoms they were unsuccessful. The highest court made it clear that the Charter protected individual, not collective rights, and that it was not prepared to disturb basic common law principles of contract and private property. Not only did restrictions on public sector collective bargaining rights pass legal muster, so, too, did blanket injunctions and criminal contempt proceedings. However, in 1987 the Vander Zalm government in BC managed to overstep the bounds of acceptable legal coercion when it sought an injunction to stop the one-day general strike planned by the provincial federation of labour on the grounds the threatened action amounted to the use of force as a means of accomplishing governmental change, and thereby constituted criminal sedition. The BC Supreme Court endorsed the unions' request that the action be dismissed.[77]

By contrast with the legislative assault on public sector workers, in the private sector the industrial pluralist regime survived, albeit with increased regional differences. Restrictions on private sector collective bargaining rights depended not only upon the political ideology of the provincial government, but also upon the

[76]Palmer, *Working-Class Experience*, 359; Panitch and Swartz, *The Assault on Trade Union Freedoms*, 108, 122-3; Larry Haiven, "Industrial Relations in Health Care: Regulation, Conflict and the Transition to the 'Wellness Model,'" in Swimmer and Thompson, *Public Sector Collective Bargaining*, 236-71.

[77]Palmer, *Working-Class Experience*, 359, 393, 404; Panitch and Swartz, *The Assault on Trade Union Freedom*, 105, 148; Judy Fudge, "Labour, the New Constitution, and Old Style Liberalism," *Queen's Law Journal*, 13 (1988), 66-111; Harry Glasbeek, "Contempt for Workers," *Osgoode Hall Law School*, 28 (1990), 1-52.

nature of the regional economy. In the early 1980s, highly resource dependent economies were severely squeezed, and it was during this period that British Columbia, Alberta, and Saskatchewan introduced changes to their private sector labour relations legislation that made it harder for unions to organize, intervened in their internal affairs, and restricted their ability to resort to collective action. In many respects, these changes were reminiscent of the restrictive provisions enacted by the British Columbia and Alberta governments in the late 1940s and early 1950s.[78]

It was only in Manitoba and Ontario that industrial pluralism in the private sector was strengthened. In Manitoba, the NDP governed for most of the decade and it began its rule in the early 1980s, before the recession was entrenched, by enacting a series of amendments that labour had been calling for since the 1970s. In Ontario, manufacturing recovered in the mid-1980s, at the same time the Liberals, with the help of the NDP, deposed the long-ruling Tories. The result was some legislative tinkering to the collective bargaining legislation designed to assist unions.[79]

These minor legislative improvements, however, did little to protect workers from the ravages of work restructuring or make it easier for unions to organize the growing secondary labour market. The Gainers strike in Calgary in 1986 epitomized the extent to which a determined employer could call upon the courts for assistance in deploying replacement workers to defeat a strike in the absence of legislative restrictions on the use of temporary replacement workers. Faced with low wage competitors like Gainers, the big three meat packers refused the United Food and Commercial Workers' demand that they maintain industry-wide bargaining, and labour boards across the country ruled that it was unlawful for the union to resort to collective action to insist on anything other than bargaining at the level of the workplace. With the demise of broader-based bargaining in meat packing, wages dropped, unionization declined, and workplace injuries increased. Moreover, provisions such as first contract arbitration did little to shift the balance of power in favour of workers in the private service sector. Contracting out increased and collective bargaining legislation imposed few barriers on employers who were intent on restructuring in ways that had the effect of avoiding unionization.[80]

[78]Panitch and Swartz, *The Assault on Trade Union Freedoms*, Chapters 3 and 5; Palmer, *Working-Class Experience*, 348.

[79]Panitch and Swartz, *The Assault on Trade Union Freedoms*, 110, 119, 128-31; Errol Black and Jim Silver, eds., *Hard Bargains: The Manitoba Labour Movement Confronts the 1990s* (Winnipeg 1989).

[80]Palmer, *Working-Class Experience*, 394-5; Alain Noel and Keith Gardner, "The Gainers' Strike: Capitalist Offensive, Militancy and the Politics of Industrial Relations in Canada," *Studies in Political Economy*, 31 (1990), 31-72; Anne Forest, "The Rise and Fall of National Bargaining in the Canadian Meat-Packing Industry," *Relations Industrielles*, 44, 2 (1989), 393-407; Carl Cuneo, "Franchising Union Successor Rights," in Cy Gonick *et al*, eds., *Labour Gains, Labour Pains*, 307-40.

The recession initiated a fundamental restructuring of the Canadian economy. In 1982, union density peaked at 40 per cent, but it soon began to decline as manufacturing jobs were lost never to return. Unemployment was high and the private service sector outstripped the goods producing sector in creating jobs. The number of annual union certifications dropped from a per year average of 3500 in 1970s to 3000 in 1980s. Workers and their unions were unable to retain real wage levels, strike activity declined, master agreements were torn up, and two tiered contracts were implemented.[81]

At the same time as the collective power of workers was being undermined, substantive equality or equity was being institutionalized in law. The early 1980s marked the apogee of second-wave feminism's campaign for women's equality rights; the most prominent being the guarantee of sex equality in the Canadian constitution in 1982. The Liberal government appointed a Royal Commission to examine ways to achieve greater equality for groups historically discriminated against in the labour market. Across the country human rights codes were amended to prohibit indirect discrimination and impose on employers a duty to accommodate individuals who were discriminated against by workplace rules, practices, and policies. Sexual harassment was prohibited and, in several jurisdictions, so too was discrimination on the basis of sexual orientation. As the decade progressed, the highest court adopted a broader, substantive, less formal, approach to sex discrimination overturning outright or limiting a number of decisions from the 1970s that had restricted women's rights.[82]

In 1985, the equality rights in the *Charter of Rights and Freedoms* came into effect and Judge Abella issued her report on equality in employment, which coined the term "employment equity." In response, the Conservative government enacted the *Employment Equity Act*, which covered federally regulated undertakings, and the Federal Contractors Compliance program. This legislation monitored the attempts of federal enterprises to achieve proportional representation for target groups through a public reporting mechanism; it did not impose numerical targets or quotas. By the end of the decade, five provinces had enacted pay equity legislation which imposed a legal duty on employers to ensure that men's and women's jobs of the same value received the same pay, although only the Ontario legislation covered the private sector.[83]

[81] Albo, "'The New Realism' and Canadian Workers," 483, 487-9; Panitch and Swartz, *The Assault on Trade Union Freedoms*, 141-4; Palmer, *Working-Class Experience*, 347.

[82] Sylvia Bashevkin, *Women on the Defensive: Living Through Conservative Times* (Toronto 1998); W.A. Bogart, *Courts and Country: The Limits of Litigation and the Social and Political Life of Canada* (Toronto 1994), 147, 249; Shelagh Day and Gwen Brodsky, *Women and the Equality Deficit: The Impact of Restructuring Canada's Social Programs* (Ottawa 1998), 54-67.

[83] Rosemary Warskett, "The Politics of Difference," 613; Mary Cornish, "Employment and Pay Equity in Canada-Success Brings Both Attacks and New Initiatives," *Canada — U.S. Law Journal*, 22 (1996), 265-77; Panitch and Swartz, *The Assault on Trade Union Freedoms*,

But the problem was that neither pay nor employment equity legislation did anything to stop the underlying deterioration in terms and conditions of employment generally. The emphasis on substantive equality at a time when the labour market was polarizing and employment conditions for the majority of workers were deteriorating fuelled a backlash against equality which gained momentum in the 1990s.[84]

On the employment standards front, there was a flurry of legislative activity to improve maternity leave entitlements and provide parental leave. Québec went the farthest in requiring employers to accommodate the family and employment responsibilities of their workers. Ontario led the pack when it came to notice and severance pay. It also made extensive revisions to its *Occupational Health and Safety Act* in response to a number of plant occupations designed to force the state to ensure that employers met their legal obligations to provide a safe workplace. The main thrust of the amendments was to extend the bipartite structures for monitoring and regulating workplace health and safety down to the shop floor. This had the effect of absolving the government of responsibility in the setting and enforcing of health and safety standards and shifting it to the labour market parties. In the economic context of the 1980s, the effect of the legislation was to make occupational health and safety regulation even more market driven.[85]

The massive lay-offs of non-unionized, middle-level employees in the early 1980s resulted in an explosion of wrongful dismissal litigation. Employees argued that dismissal for economic reasons did not constitute just cause at law and that employers were required to pay them damages that amounted to reasonable notice. Courts accepted this argument; however, since reasonable notice was linked to the length of employment service, the employee's age and occupational status, wrongful dismissal litigation, and severance packages tended only to benefit a narrow band of employees relatively high up in the occupational hierarchy. The increasing numbers of contingent workers employed in part-time, temporary, and low status jobs derived little benefit from the common law.[86]

By the time the Conservative government won its second consecutive federal election in 1988, privatization had eclipsed equality as the dominant discourse in

132-6; Weiner, "Workplace Equity," in Swimmer and Thompson, eds., *Public Sector Collective Bargaining*, 78-102, 93-4.

[84]Judy Fudge, "Fragmentation and Feminization: The Challenge of Equity for Labour Relations Policy," in Jane Brodie, ed., *Women and Canadian Public Policy* (Toronto 1996), 57-87; Warskett, "The Politics of Difference," 617.

[85]Boivin and Deom, "Labour-Management Relations in Quebec," 482; Judy Fudge, *Labour Law's Little Sister: The Employment Standards Act and the Feminization of Labour* (Ottawa 1991); Panitch and Swartz, *The Assault on Trade Union Freedoms*, 129-30; Tucker, "And Defeat Goes On."

[86]Geoffrey England, Innis Christie, Merrit Christie, *Employment Law in Canada*, 3rd ed. (Toronto 1998).

Canadian politics. The Free Trade deal with the United States was the most profound step in the direction of economic continentalism and symbolized the hegemony of neo-liberalism. The emphasis on market-driven restructuring and the renewed legitimacy of individual ordering through contract and private property undermined the conditions upon which the industrial pluralist regime in the private sector had flourished without requiring a frontal assault on its central tenets. During the 1980s it was possible for governments simultaneously to exalt the superiority of market voluntarism, on the one hand, and substantive equality, on the other, when it came to the legal regulation of the labour market. The decade not only demonstrated the significance of broader macro-economic forces and political shifts on the law, it also demonstrated the flexibility in the regime of liberal legality. At the same time as courts and legislatures institutionalized the concept of substantive equality within the law, governments did not face any legal constraints in introducing labour market policies that heightened fragmentation and increased inequality.

The Hegemony of the Market: The1990s

During the 1990s, the federal government abandoned the last shreds of any commitment to full employment in its determination to fight the deficit and, together with provincial governments, substituted workfare for welfare as the guiding theme of social policy and embraced flexibility as the defining characteristic of a well functioning labour market. New technology and increased international trade were the drivers behind the economic revolution known as globalization, and nation states argued that it was necessary to submit any vestiges of political control over their national economies to the logic of the international market. In Canada, this economic wisdom was firmly institutionalized and it transcended traditional party politics; the 1988 Free Trade Agreement with the United States, negotiated by the Tory government, was extended to include Mexico by the Liberals in 1993. The need to adjust to international competition was used to justify the deteriorating standard of employment and the degradation of the social wage. Polarization and inequality in the Canadian labour market increased. Economic restructuring undermined the conditions for industrial pluralism to function in the private sector and simultaneously fuelled resentment against public sector workers and legal measures designed to achieve equality in employment. As legislatures across Canada asserted the primacy of market voluntarism and individual liberty, the courts increasingly became the defenders of equality; however, they were less willing to protect workers' rights to engage in collective action. Moreover, the very nature of the employment relationship was being transformed as capital has sought to shift the risks of production even further on to workers by avoiding all forms of political and legal regulation other than the individual liberty of the commercial contract.[87]

During the 1991-92 recession, the attack on the public sector deepened and the commitment to industrial pluralism was permanently undermined in favour of unilateral paternalism. No longer was the assault on the collective bargaining rights of public sector workers characterized as a temporary inflation fighting measure, but, rather, governments across Canada announced that they wanted to lead the way in wage restraint. Public sector unions were confronted with a choice between two evils: either accept wage freezes and reductions or endure massive lay-offs. In general, governments invoked three general types of measures: the first, legislated wage controls; the second, hard bargaining; and the third, unique to BC, the implementation of co-operative processes, reinforced by inducements, to engage public sector unions in cost reduction exercises. The first two measures provoked a wave of militancy as public sector workers across the country struck, following the precedent set in the 1980s by Québec and Newfoundland public sector workers and nurses.[88]

Once again, the federal government led the attack against public sector workers. In 1991, it announced that wage increases for its employees would be capped at 3 per cent and threatened to legislate the right to contract out public service work. In response, PSAC embarked on the largest strike by a single union in Canada's history as over 100,000 workers walked off the job. Although the government was found to have bargained in bad faith, it nonetheless legislated its employees back-to-work on terms virtually identical to what it had initially offered. Once elected, the Liberals simply extended the former Conservative government's wage controls until 1997. In its complaint to the ILO that the federal government was violating its members' right to bargain collectively, PSAC documented how the 1994 controls were but the latest installment in the campaign, first begun in 1981 by the Liberals, to retrench upon public sector workers' rights. The Freedom of Association Committee of the ILO expressed "its serious concern at the frequent recourse had by the [Canadian] Government to statutory limitations on collective bargaining."[89]

[87]Jim Stanford, "Discipline, Insecurity and Productivity: The Economics Between Labour Market 'Flexibility,'" in Jane Pulkingham and G. Ternowetsky, eds., *Remaking Canadian Social Policy* (Halifax 1996), 130-150; Greg Albo, "'Competitive Austerity' and the Impasse of Capitalist Employment Policy," in R. Miliband and L. Panitch, eds., *Socialist Register 1994: Beyond Globalism and Nationalism* (London 1994), 144-70.
[88]Fryer, "Provincial Public Service Labour Relations," 351.
[89]Gene Swimmer, "Collective Bargaining in the Federal Public Service of Canada: The Last Twenty Years," in Swimmer and Thompson, eds., *Public Sector Collective Bargaining,* 368-407; International Labour Office, 297th Report of the Committee on Freedom of Association," 282nd Session, Geneva, March-April, 1995, Case No. 1758, 53-65; Leo Panitch and Donald Swartz, "What happened to freedom of association?," *The Globe and Mail,* 7 April 1998.

While the federal government's attack on its workers may have been the most blatant, that by the NDP government in Ontario was the most duplicitous. It illustrated the extent to which economics trumped ideology; shortly after the social democratic party was elected, Ontario experienced the deepest recession since the Depressions. In 1993, the Rae government announced its Expenditure Control Plan, which would entail the loss of 11,000 jobs as part the $4 billion cut in expenditures, and its Social Contract, by which it hoped to induce public sector unions to participate in neo-corporatist arrangements in order to lend an aura of legitimacy to the imposition of a three year wage freeze on over 900,000 workers in the broader public sector. Although the government called its initiative a social contract, it used the threat of an additional 20,000 to 40,000 job cuts as a stick to prod labour. When the union-led Public Services Coalition rejected the government's terms and unveiled an alternative plan, the government went ahead and legislated *The Social Contract Act*, making a mockery out of the notion of a voluntary agreement. It imposed a three year wage freeze and empowered employers both to open unilaterally collective agreements in order to achieve the mandated cuts, allowing them to impose up to 12 days of unpaid leave, and to ignore provisions in the *Employment Standards Act*. As a gesture to equity, workers earning under $30,000 a year were exempted from the roll backs and the government guaranteed that the controls would not affect pay equity. As a sop to voluntarism, it gave unions and employers just over a month to reach agreements on compensation reductions, with the inducement that "voluntary" agreements would only have to meet 80 per cent of the imposed cut-back, and laid-off workers would be able to access a Job Security Fund. To add insult to injury, the same day that it imposed the Social Contract, the NDP government also amended the *Crown Employees Collective Bargaining Act*, which perfected industrial pluralism for government workers by extending the right to strike to them. Public sector unions' response was to withdraw their support from the NDP, which was soundly trounced by the Tories in the 1995 election, and file a formal complaint with the ILO.[90]

Public sector workers only enjoyed the institutions of industrial pluralism for a decade before they were suspended by the *Anti-Inflation Act* in 1975. Beginning in the 1980s, their collective rights were subject to legislative assault, with the result that their wages have declined both in real terms and relative to the private sector. Moreover, thousands of jobs were lost due to downsizing, privatization, and contracting out. The extraordinarily coercive measures deployed against public sector workers were justified on the ground that the market does not have control

[90]Fryer, "Provincial Public Service Labour Relations," 357-9; Panitch and Swartz, *The Assault on Trade Union Freedoms*, 169-175; Stephen McBride, "Coercion and Consent: the Recurring Corporatist Temptation," in Gonick *et. al.*, eds., *Labour Gains, Labour Pains*, 70-96, 88-90.

over the public sector. In the absence of competition, repression is necessary to discipline public sector workers. The Ontario Conservative government took this logic to an extreme when it revoked union successor rights, thereby ousting unions and abrogating collective agreements, when a public enterprise is sold to private interests.[91]

In the 1990s, changes to collective bargaining legislation in the private sector were increasingly ideologically driven. Although the basic structure of the post-war legal regime remained intact, provincial governments, depending upon their political persuasion, tinkered with it either to make it easier for unions to organize and obtain collective agreements or imposed additional requirements on union certification in the name of protecting individual freedom in the face of "big" labour. In the early 1990s, NDP governments, first in Ontario and then in BC, introduced a series of amendments to private sector collective bargaining legislation that gave unions much of what they had been asking for since the 1970s. The most significant changes included easier access to certification and first contract arbitration, expedited unfair labour practice procedures, and restrictions on the use of replacement workers. By contrast, Conservative governments in Alberta, Manitoba, and later, Ontario, introduced legislative reforms that revoked the traditional Canadian practice of certifying trade unions on the basis of membership evidence, and implemented the US model of requiring a representation vote in every instance. The breakdown of the post-war consensus on the benefits of union representation and collective bargaining was most sharply illustrated in Ontario, where the Conservative government repealed the previous NDP government's amendments without holding public hearings, calling its new legislation *An Act to Restore Fairness in Collective Bargaining.*[92]

Despite some modest attempts to update collective bargaining legislation to bring it in line with the labour market of the 1990s, the regime lost much of its purchase. Social democratic initiatives to refine industrial pluralism were too little, too late; the changes simply did not meet the challenges posed by the restructured labour market. Economic restructuring and corporate reorganization, especially vertical disintegration achieved via out-sourcing and contracting out, and the proliferation in the use of non-standard employment undermined the effectiveness of industrial pluralism in the private sector.

Union density in the private sector decreased across Canada, in part due to the changing composition of economic activity. From 1976 to 1992 union density in the goods sector declined from 43 to 38 per cent. This substantial decline is largely accounted for by the drop in employment and the consequent decline of unioniza-

[91]John Price, "Post-PC 1003: A Return to Coercion or New Directions for Labour?" in Gonick *et al.*, eds., *Labour Gains, Labour Pains*, 253-83, 266.
[92]Panitch and Swartz, *The Assault on Trade Union Freedoms*, 165-9,175-9; Russell, "Labour's Magna Carta?," 176; Boivin and Deom, "Labour-Management Relations in Quebec," 461.

tion in manufacturing: the share of paid workers in manufacturing dropped from 22 to 16 per cent and their unionization rate dropped from 43 to 33 per cent from 1976 to 1992. In contrast, the service sector saw major growth both in employment and unionization during the same period; however, the growth in unionization was largely confined to the public service sector, which was under attack.[93]

Not only was organized labour unable to unionize the private service sector, increasingly it was unable to defend what it had won. The informal bargaining structures, master agreements, and pattern-bargaining in particular, that large industrial unions developed to mediate and modify the fragmentation that resulted from the formal bargaining structure, were rejected by employers on the grounds that they faced increased competition and industrial restructuring. Beginning with meat-packing, employers in the steel, forest, and pulp and paper industries opted out of broader bargaining structures. Since unions do not have the legal right to use economic sanctions to compel employers to recognize a modified bargaining structure there was little they could do to halt the decentralization and fragmentation of bargaining.[94]

There has also been a downward trend in wage settlements and an upward trend in long-term collective agreements. In 1994, Québec amended its collective bargaining legislation to permit collective agreements of six years duration. Moreover, in the resource sector once powerful unions have agreed to accept wage reductions in the event that world prices for commodities fall. Throughout the 1990s, capital has been very successful in shifting more of the risks of production on to workers without sharing the profits.[95]

The contraction in unionization in the private sector has gone hand in hand with an erosion of standard employment — full time, indeterminate employment with one employer. The proliferation of non-standard employment arrangements has been the most significant recent labour market trend. In 1997, the growth of nonstandard employment was so extensive in the 1980s and 1990s that only 33 per cent of Canadian workers were said to hold "normal jobs." Moreover, its increase coincides with growing polarization in earnings amongst Canadians, which has deepened labour market poverty, especially among the young and the old. Young male workers — especially those that already had low earnings — bore the brunt

[93]Ernest B. Akyeampong, "A Statistical Portrait of the Trade Union Movement," *Perspectives in Labour and Income* (Winter 1997) 45-54.

[94]Fudge and Glasbeek, "The Legacy of PC 1003," 394; Ann C. Frost and Anil Verma, "Restructuring in Canadian Steel: The Case of Steelco Inc.," in Verma and Chaykowski, eds., *Contract and Commitment*, 82-112.

[95]Panitch and Swartz, *The Assault on Trade Union Freedoms*, 143; Peter Kennedy, "Miners' Union endorses Highland's wage offer," *The Globe and Mail*, 26 August 1999; Mark Mackinnon, "Inco lockout boosts world nickel price," *The Globe and Mail*, 17 Sept. 1999; Boivin and Deom, "Labour-Management Relations in Quebec," 461.

of this trend, as evidenced by the widening gap between the highest and the lowest earning men.[96]

The heightened polarization in men's wages has accompanied a convergence in men's and women's wages and employment profiles, and an increased wage and employment polarization among women workers. While fragmentation is still gendered, it is less so than it was prior to the mid-1980s and increasingly it has taken a generational form in light of the restructured labour market. The deterioration in the standard employment relationship, especially for young men, has fuelled a backlash against equity initiatives directed at women and members of visible minority groups. This was most evident in Ontario, where a centre-piece of the Conservative Party's campaign against the NDP government was its attack on the *Employment Equity Act* of 1993. The Tories' charge that the NDP legislation was a form of illegitimate reverse discrimination had a great deal of popular appeal. One of its first legislative moves was to enact the *Act to Repeal Job Quotas and Restore Merit.*[97]

Pay equity legislation, even in Ontario under the Tories, survived the backlash. However, it is not clear that governments will fund equal pay. Unless they do, employers in the broader public sector will be faced with the choice of laying off workers to make good on pay equity obligations. In the Atlantic provinces, pay equity has been sacrificed to public sector wage restraint. In 1999, the federal government reluctantly decided to ante up $3.8 billion owed to members of PSAC when the federal court upheld the Canadian Human Rights Tribunal's ruling. However, the PSAC decision became the focus of an equity backlash. It was portrayed in the press as unfair to taxpayers and a deviation from market norms.[98]

The response to employment equity also illustrates this process. Although the federal government strengthened its *Employment Equity Act* in 1995, the statute does not impose an obligation on the government to create new positions in order to achieve proportional representation in the occupational hierarchy. What it does is impose an obligation on employers to report on the composition of their workforce and make all reasonable efforts to eradicate systemic barriers to propor-

[96]B. Lipsett and M. Reesor, *Flexible Work Arrangements: Evidence from the 1991 and 1995 Survey of Work Arrangements* (Ottawa 1997); Michael Baker and Gary Solon, "Earning Dynamics and Inequality Among Canadian Men, 1976-1992: Evidence from Longitudinal Tax Records," Statistics Canada, Research Papers Series, 130, Analytic Studies Branch (Ottawa 1999); G. Picot, "What is Happening to Earnings Inequality and Wages in the 1990s?" Statistics Canada, Cat. 11F0019MPGE No. 116 (Ottawa 1998).

[97]Katherine Scott and Clarence Lochhead, "Are Women Catching up in the Earnings Race?," Canadian Council for Social Development, Paper No. 3 (1997), 2; Mark MacKinnon, "Women gaining ground in the workforce," *Globe and Mail,* 19 April 1999; Cornish, "Employment and Pay Equity," 273.

[98]Patricia Hughes, "A Model for Future Challenges to Government Action," *Canadian Labour and Employment Law Journal,* 6 (1998), 77-97; Fudge, "Exclusion, Discrimination, Equality and Privatization."

tional representation for equity groups. Despite the weakness of the equity provisions, the legislation is increasingly regarded as unfair. The attack against substantive equality initiatives such as those embodied in pay and employment equity legislation is fuelled both by a defence and celebration of the free market, on the one hand, and declining economic prospects for young men, on the other. These two elements are united by a shared commitment to an equal opportunities framework, one that sees the role of the state as limited to prohibiting overt discrimination and a return to formal conceptions of legal equality.[99]

During the 1990s, with a few social democratic exceptions, legislatures across Canada lost what little taste they had for measures designed to achieve substantive equality in employment. In this context, courts were regarded as the last bastion for preserving any public policy commitment to equity. The Supreme Court of Canada has issued a number of decisions that have strengthened employers' obligations to provide a discrimination-free workplace and to make accommodations for individuals who are adversely affected by workplace rules, policies, or practices. Moreover, the Court has also imposed corresponding duties on unions not to discriminate and to make workplace accommodations. It has also issued a number of decisions that have tempered the obvious harshness of the common law of employment and reinforced a remedial approach to the interpretation of employment standards legislation. However, although the Supreme Court of Canada has acknowledged the inequality in bargaining power in the labour market, it has refused to take any significant initiatives to ameliorate it on the ground that it is the appropriate responsibility of elected officials. Occasionally, this hands-off approach has redounded to the advantage of organized labour; in *Lavigne* the Court upheld the use of the compelled dues check off for political purposes. Moreover, in 1999, the Court made a slight detour from its position of deference to legislatures in the realm of collective bargaining when it held that legislative restrictions on peaceful consumer leafleting for informational purposes by unions amounted to an unjustifiable violation of the *Charter's* guarantee of freedom of expression. However, in permitting the practice of consumer leafletting in the labour context, the Court was careful to distinguish this informational activity from the coercive activity of a conventional labour picket.[100]

---

[99]Cornish, "Employment and Pay Equity," 271; Fudge, "Exclusion, Discrimination, Equality and Privatization."

[100]Both British Columbia and Québec introduced pay equity, although only Québec's took the form of legislation and extended to the private sector. Katherine Swinton, "Accommodating Equality in the Unionized Workplace," *Osgoode Hall Law Journal* 33, 4 (1996), 703-47; *BC (Public Service Employee Relations Commission)* v. *BCGSEU*, [1999] 3 S.C.R. 3; Judy Fudge, "New Wine into Old Bottles?: Updating Legal Forms to Reflect Changing Employment Norms," *U.B.C. Law Review,* 33,1 (1999),183-209; Panitch and Swartz, *The Assault on Trade Unions Freedom*, 185; *U.F.C.W., Local 1518* v. *KMart Canada Ltd.*, [1999] 2 S.C.R. 1083.

Like collective bargaining legislation, the fortune of employment standards statutes has depended upon the political persuasion of the government in power. Generally, however, improving minimum employment standards or revising them to meet the changed labour market has been portrayed as pricing Canadian workers out of jobs. More troubling is the fact that many standards are simply not enforced as governments across Canada have gutted the bureaucracies which had the authority to enforce the legislation.

Workers' compensation has also been reshaped by neo-liberalism. Under the guise that workers' compensation boards are running huge unfunded liabilities, caused by overly generous benefits, several provinces have changed their workers' compensation legislation. Some of the measures directly attack injured workers by reducing benefit levels, denying compensation for certain types of injuries, such as those caused by workplace stress, and limiting compensation for chronic pain. Other measures are more subtle, but equally harmful. For example, in some jurisdictions fixed pensions for permanent disability have been replaced by wage-loss systems that allow boards to reduce or eliminate payments to injured workers on the ground that there is theoretically a job in the labour market they are capable of performing, even though they are unemployed. Similarly, return to work obligations are often evaded or provide a pretext for hiding lost-time injuries. Finally, the increased reliance on experience rating in funding workers' compensation systems detrimentally effects injury reporting and more closely aligns occupational health and safety with market measures of value.[101]

IV. Conclusion

At the end of the millennium, individualism, competition, and the legal relations of contract and property vie with the official discourses of industrial pluralism and industrial citizenship for hegemony in the labour market. Ideologically, workers' collective action is increasingly portrayed as the self-serving and coercive privilege of big labour and, materially, it has less purchase in a world in which capital is less fettered by the political strictures of the nation state. While there has been no direct and sustained legal assault on private sector workers' freedom to associate and right to bargain collectively, the terrain on which these rights operate has narrowed. As an ever greater proportion of the labour force falls outside the scope of the institutions of industrial pluralism, political support for workers' collective rights is undermined, and the balance is likely to shift even farther towards individualism. Simultaneously, the legislative assault on public sector workers' collective rights illustrates the extent to which industrial pluralism is based upon a fundamental commitment to market voluntarism. It also evinces the degree to which fragmentation and competition between workers has been internalized; governments across

[101]Geoffrey C. Beckwith, "The Myth of Injury Incentives in Workers' Compensation Insurance," *New Solutions* (Winter 1992), 52-73; T.G. Ison, "The Significance of Experience Rating," *Osgoode Hall Law Journal*, 24 (1986), 723-42.

Canada have faced little opposition in dismantling industrial pluralism in the public sector.

The project of globalization and the accompanying logic of the race to the bottom have also made suspect legally enforceable minimum standards that constrain the exploitation of labour. Conservative and social democratic governments warn Canadian workers that legal standards which provide a living wage, a modicum of dignity at work and personal time outside of employment will price them out of the global labour market. At the same time, deep cutbacks to the public sector have undermined the capacity of the state to enforce employment legislation and the benefits of voluntary, co-operative bipartite arrangements are invoked to legitimate the devolution of standard setting and enforcement to the market parties. In the current economic context, this shift in responsibility favours capital at the expense of workers.

Unbridled capitalism has no respect for human rights.[102] While it is extremely difficult in a liberal democracy to revoke guarantees of formal legal equality after they have been won, such measures do not address the deeper, structural relations and institutions that generate and sustain substantive inequality. The partial legal institutionalization of substantive equality in Canadian law, itself the product of struggle, is under attack as people face tougher economic times. The "excessive" demands of feminists and "unfair" competition from poorly skilled immigrant labour are being blamed for the declining economic prospects of young white men. The unequal division of household labour, especially with respect to the care of children, will likely only deepen women's historical disadvantage in an increasingly competitive labour market. Human rights legislation which addresses discrimination on the basis of ineluctable characteristics, does not deal with inequality that is increasingly expressed on a generational, occupational, and educational basis.

Moreover, employment is no longer secure as the favoured means of organizing productive activity in a capitalist economy; unfree forms of labour — prison, indenture, and slave — and sweatshop conditions have increased internationally. In liberal societies, there has been a growth in the use of forms of labour that fall outside the traditional contract of employment, which, for all its inequality, was premised on a notion of mutuality. Nonstandard forms of employment, which includes a proliferation in independent contracting, may enhance individual freedom, but they also expose workers to greater risks.[103]

The official discourses and institutions of industrial pluralist legality and industrial citizenship may be losing their hegemonic status, but in Canada and Québec we have not yet reached a crisis of legitimacy. If such a crisis comes, it may initiate a more radical break than the transitions between the regimes examined here. These regimes were born of workers' engagement with the liberal democratic

[102]Jacoby, *Laboring for Freedom*, 149.
[103]Fudge, "New Wine into Old Bottles," 197-9.

state, which, despite its limitations, still preserved the idea that citizenship mattered and that the boundary between the political and the economic was permeable. The liberal state could be made to respond to social demands democratically expressed. It could impose limits on private property and freedom of contract.

The continuing political saliency of the liberal state can no longer be assumed. Democratic citizenship is being systematically narrowed by supra-national free trade regimes that require nation states to recognize the rights of property owners over the claims of their citizens. Such charters of corporate rights and international trade dispute resolution mechanisms have not been matched either by the guarantee of social rights or the creation of credible alternate institutions through which democratic demands can be effectively pursued. Instead of being a site for the mediation of class conflict, the liberal state is increasingly becoming a vehicle for imposing the discipline of the competitive market on its populations.[104] Much of this has been accomplished by convincing people that they have no choice since the forces of globalization are irresistible.

Increasingly, this ideological project is being contested. In the late 1990s, for example, the Days of Action campaign protested the Conservative government's attempt to institutionalize its slogan "Ontario: Open for Business."[105] Public and private sector unions, together with social movements representing women, visible minorities, disabled people, and the poor, marched in nine cities across the province, closing businesses and disrupting normal activities. In Toronto, there was an unprecedented display of solidarity as close to a million people took to the streets. However, the campaign foundered not so much because it pushed the limits of legality, but more because it ran aground on existing forms of fragmentation. Although workers' participation in the Days of Action was met by employers who sought injunctions and labour board orders to ban unlawful economic action, adjudicative officials refused to do the dirty business of repressing workers. In a liberal democracy, when public opinion supports workers' collective action the constraints of the law are loosened. The more difficult problem has been to forge solidarity in the face of historical lines of fragmentation. Private sector unions, in general, consider that their members provide the labour power fuelling the engine of economic activity and have a correspondingly low respect for public sector workers, although in certain sectors this is changing. Thus, it is difficult to persuade them to make sacrifices for workers who they consider to be a tax burden. Moreover, despite declining membership, unions still have a much stronger finan-

[104]Linda Weiss, "Globalization and the Myth of the Powerless State," *New Left Review*, 225(1997), 3-27; Joachim Hirsch, "Globalization of Capital, Nation-States and Democracy," *Studies in Political Economy*, 54 (1997), 39-58; Gary Teeple, *Globalization and the Decline of Social Reform* (Toronto 1995).

[105]Bryan Palmer, "Halloween in Harrisland," *Canadian Dimension*, 32, 1(January/February 1998), 29-32; Marcella Munro, "Comment on Ontario's Days of Action and Strategic Choices for the Left in Canada," *Studies in Political Economy*, 53 (1997), 125-40.

cial base and more firmly established institutional supports than do social movements, which tend to represent those people in the labour market who have only enjoyed a second class industrial citizenship. With social movements considered by organized labour to be little more than a junior partner, there is little pressure on unions to expand beyond narrow economism to a full-fledged support for social unionism. So far, despite repeated examples of its limits, especially in the context of a global competition for capital, the labour movements in Canada and Québec remain committed to a political program that consists of supporting the social democratic party, rather than providing an alternative vision of how society should be organized.

Economic restructuring and increased competition have exposed the limits of industrial pluralism. Although it is one of the highest mediations of the conflict between capital and labour, no legal regime can resolve the enduring problem of liberalism, the fundamental contradiction between labour as a commodity and the social solidarity necessary for the reproduction and sustenance of human life. All the regimes of industrial legality arise out of capitalist formations and the conflicts endemic to them. No regime has overcome or resolved finally the conflict that arises out of the commodification of labour power, although a central project of all of them has been to legitimate that commodification ideologically and materially, and to encourage existing organizations of workers to behave responsibly as wholesalers of the labour power of their members. Liberal voluntarism accommodated craft workers in this way at the beginning of the 20th century, just as industrial pluralism accommodated industrial workers in core sectors fifty years later.

But the material benefits that underwrite the ideological appeal of norms of voluntarism are only available to some workers for some of the time. Fragmentation and segmentation are inherent in the labour market, which, after all, is based upon competition between workers. "Given the fear induced by the basic insecurity of the labour market, workers tend to erect barriers against 'outsiders' in order to protect their 'privileged' position in relation to wages and the state."[106] Women workers and immigrants are regarded as a source of competition that puts downward pressure on men's wages, and a decent social wage and strong public sector are seen as diminishing the purchasing power of wages. Too often these views have been accepted as common sense within the labour movement. The political effect of such Malthusian notions is to displace social conflict from the profit/wage relation to an internal struggle within the working class.

There are indications, however, that some elements within organized labour have understood the limitations of strategies based upon the goal of narrow protectionism rather than that of social transformation. Campaigns that disclose the link between the imperatives of unbridled consumerism and sweated labour, especially in the international apparel and footwear industries, are gaining ground.

[106]Antonella Picchio, *The Social Reproduction of the Labour Market* (Cambridge 1992), 138.

Some public sector unions have been able to teach their counterparts in the private sector the significance of socially necessary labour. In some industries, such as auto, workers are located in a segment of the labour market that enables them to tackle historical forms of fragmentation around the sexual division of labour and across generations through collective bargaining.[107] The political challenge is to demonstrate how rapacious capitalism really is and to link the exploitation of working people with other forms of invidious discrimination. The distinction between the traditional working class, as represented by the labour movement, and social movements, comprising among others women, racialized groups, and social welfare recipients, must be abandoned because it reflects and reinforces, rather than challenges and minimizes, the social distinctions and political power that are part and parcel of labour market segmentation.

A concerted attempt by working people, broadly understood, to challenge market voluntarism would likely be met by old-style coercion. An assault on trade union rights may be the trajectory for the reconstruction of a new regime of industrial legality in the neo-liberal, global competitiveness state.[108] But such a regime would undermine what little basis that continues to exist for social cohesion and social stability. Historically, working people have not passively acceded to institutional and legal arrangements that fail to incorporate at least some of their demands. For legitimacy's sake, the nation state has leavened coercion with accommodation in responding to workers' collective action. It is unlikely that in the new millennium, despite the shift in power in its favour, capital can achieve on a global scale what it has been unable to achieve nationally.

---

[107]Kim Moody, *Workers in a Lean World: Unions in the International Economy* (London 1997).
[108]For some interesting reflections on these questions by a one-time active supporter of and participant in the industrial pluralist regime, see H.W. Arthurs, "Labour Law Without the State?," *University of Toronto Law Journal,* 46 (1996), 1-45.

La grève de l'amiante de 1949 et le projet de réforme de l'entreprise. Comment le patronat a défendu son droit de gérance

Jacques Rouillard

DANS LA MÉMOIRE collective des Québécois, la grève de l'amiante de 1949 représente certainement la grève la plus connue, largement perçue comme un grand moment de la lutte des travailleurs pour faire valoir leurs réclamations et souvent interprétée comme un événement capital dans l'évolution sociale du Québec. Cette vision triomphaliste a prévalu dans les médias et les films documentaires qui ont rappelé le cinquantième anniversaire du conflit en février 1999.[1] Un journaliste du *Devoir* en faisait "la grève la plus célèbre de l'histoire sociale québécoise" tandis que celui de *La Presse* y voyait "la pierre angulaire du mouvement de fond qui allait plus tard prendre le nom de Révolution tranquille."[2] Dans un long article, Michel Vastel du *Soleil* écrivait que "la plus grande victoire de ces modestes mineurs fut d'imposer le respect" face au pouvoir politique et au grand patronat: "Le Québec

[1]Outre des études et des analyses tant en français qu'en anglais, un roman, une pièce de théâtre et quelques documentaires lui sont consacrés. La pièce de théâtre de John T. McDonough est intitulée *Charbonneau et le Chef* (Toronto 1968) et le roman de Jean-Jules Richard, *Le Feu dans l'amiante* (Chezlauteur 1956). En 1996, la CSN a produit un vidéo : *'49. Un souffle de colère* (réalisé par Sophie Bissonnette), et deux documentaires ont été présentés à l'occasion du 50 ème anniversaire de la grève : l'un à Radio-Canada, *Asbestos, les grèvistes de 1949*, et un autre au réseau canadien History Television. Georges Massé a fait une analyse du video produit par la CSN et du documentaire présenté à Radio-Canada dans "Des images de la grève de l'amiante, 1949", *Bulletin du Regroupement des chercheurs-res en histoire des travailleurs et travailleuses québécois*, 25, 2 (automne 1999), 54-61.

[2]*Le Devoir*, 13 février 1999, A9; *La Presse*, 13 février 1999, A33.

Jacques Rouillard, "La grève de l'amiante de 1949 et le projet de réforme de l'entreprise. Comment le patronat a défendu son droit de gérance," *Labour/Le Travail*, 46 (Fall 2000), 307-42.

venait d'oser relever la tête."[3] C'est la même interprétation qu'on retrouve dans les deux documentaires diffusés en 1999 par les chaînes spécialisées de télévision, *History Television* et *Historia*, qui présente la grève, l'un pour le Canada et l'autre pour le Québec, comme un des moments privilégiés qui ont façonné leur histoire au 20e siècle.[4]

La grève a fait l'objet de nombreuses analyses et est même rappelée dans les manuels d'histoire destinés aux élèves québécois de niveau secondaire.[5] Elle est interprétée comme une étape importante dans l'histoire du syndicalisme québécois qui illustre l'antisyndicalisme du gouvernement Duplessis et son parti-pris patronal. En fait, on y reprend l'explication donnée traditionnellement par de nombreux travaux, qu'ils soient plus spécialisés sur l'histoire du syndicalisme ou d'un caractère général sur la société québécoise, dépeignant la grève des mineurs comme un grand moment de lutte des travailleurs et un tournant dans l'histoire sociale du Québec.[6] Cette interprétation est issue d'un volume consacré à la grève, publié en 1956 et dont Pierre Elliott Trudeau a assumé la direction. Comme son sous-titre l'indique: *La Grève de l'amiante. Une étape de la Révolution industrielle au Québec*, les auteurs y voient "un épisode-clé d'émancipation sociale,"[7] où, pour la première fois, la classe ouvrière s'affirme de façon autonome au Québec et se libère de la tutelle des forces sociales traditionnelles que sont l'Église, l'État et le patronat. Le conflit leur apparaît comme l'une des premières manifestations des transfor-

[3]*Le Soleil*, 13 février, A17.

[4]"Grève de l'amiante," *Tournants de l'histoire II, History Television*, Connections Productions, 1999; "La grève d'Asbestos," *Canal Historia*, émission du 3 avril 2000 de la série "Les 30 journées qui ont fait le Québec," (Eurêka 2000).

[5]J. Lacoursière, J. Provencher et D. Vaugeois, *Canada-Québec, Synthèse historique* (Montréal 1970), 539-540; Louise Charpentier, René Durocher, Christian Laville et Paul-André Linteau, *Nouvelle histoire du Québec et du Canada* (Montréal 1985), 352-353; Jean-François Cardin, Raymond Bédard et René Fortin, *Le Québec: héritage et projets* (Laval 1994), 401.

[6]Outre le volume dirigé par P.E. Trudeau, les principaux travaux sur la grève sont les suivants: Jacques Cousineau, *Réflexions en marge de la grève de l'amiante* (Montréal 1958); Hélène David, "La grève et le bon Dieu," *Sociologie et sociétés*, 1-2 (novembre 1969), 249-268; Gérard Dion, "La grève de l'amiante: trente ans après," *Mémoires de la Société royale du Canada*, tome XVII, 1979, 31-40; Alfred Charpentier, "La grève de l'amiante: version nouvelle," *Relations industrielles*, 19, 2 (avril 1964), 217-238; Alfred Charpentier, *Les Mémoires d'Alfred Charpentier* (Québec 1971), 328-359; Jacques Cousineau, *L'Église d'ici et le social 1940-1960* (Montréal 1982), 92-110; Fraser Isbester, "Asbestos 1949," dans Irving Abella (dir.), *On Strike* (Toronto 1974), 163-196; Jacques Gagnon "La grève d'Asbestos: comment transformer une défaite syndicale en succès médiatique," *Revue d'études des Cantons de l'Est*, 13 (automne-hiver 1998-1999), 83-89; Anonyme, "La grève d'Asbestos de 1949," *Centrale des syndicats démocratiques* (10 février 1999), 31.

[7]Pierre Elliott Trudeau (dir.), *La Grève de l'amiante. Une étape de la Révolution industrielle au Québec* (Montréal 1956), 401. La traduction en anglais a été faite en 1974 sous le titre: *The Asbestos Strike* (Toronto 1974), 382.

mations subies par la société francophone, soumise depuis la Guerre aux forces issues de l'industrialisation. La grève marquerait son passage de la société traditionnelle à la société urbaine et industrialisée.

Le volume, dont on entreprend la réalisation au début des années 1950, veut relater l'histoire d'un événement auquel le journal *Le Devoir* a accordé énormément d'importance en 1949, avant même que le conflit ne prenne de l'envergure. Malgré ses faibles moyens, il délègue à Asbestos un journaliste, Gérard Pelletier, présent dans la région pendant tout le conflit. Le quotidien lui consacre, selon les mots mêmes de Pelletier, "plus de reportages, de commentaires, d'éditoriaux et de dépêches ... qu'à n'importe quel autre sujet d'actualité."[8] Cette attention, qui tranche avec celle apportée par les autres quotidiens québécois,[9] se comprend à la lumière de la nouvelle orientation que veut lui donner son nouveau directeur, Gérard Filion, nommé en avril 1947. Désireux de rompre avec les orientations traditionnelles du journal, il explique, dans un de ses premiers éditoriaux, qu'il veut mettre le journal "au service de la classe des travailleurs", devenue la "classe dominante de la société", mais "ne disposant pas toujours des moyens de défense et d'attaque qu'il lui faudrait ... dans un monde livré aux excès de la concurrence."[10] Le quotidien s'applique alors, dans la nouvelle comme en éditorial, à défendre les travailleurs dans plusieurs conflits de travail entre 1947 et 1950.[11] Cependant, après la grève de l'amiante, il devient beaucoup plus circonspect et prend ses distances lors de débrayages. Néanmoins, l'attention apportée par le journal à la grève de l'amiante et l'ampleur prise par le conflit (durée du conflit, nombre de mineurs impliqués, violence, lecture de l'acte d'émeute, dure répression de la police

[8]Trudeau, *La Grève de l'amiante*, 282-283.

[9]*Le Devoir* s'est intéressé aux mineurs de l'amiante dès janvier 1949 en publiant une étude de M. B. Ledoux sur l'amiantose à East Broughton. En éditorial, il recommande au gouvernement de fermer les portes de cette mine (15 janvier). Son correspondant, Gérard Pelletier, se trouve à Asbestos une semaine avant le début de la grève et un premier article de sa plume est publié dans l'édition du 7 février, indiquant que la menace de grève pèse sur la région. Une fois la grève déclenchée, le journal y fait référence presque à chaque jour. Pour sa part, le journal *La Presse*, qui a une équipe de journalistes beaucoup plus importante, n'y porte attention qu'à la fin mars après avoir délégué un reporter à Asbestos (article du 21 mars) et ne revient sur le sujet que le 26 avril (*Index des articles de revues, des éditoriaux et autres reportages de journaux relatifs à la grève*), Grève de l'amiante (1949), Archives de la CSN, Présidence A9, 28-2-3-2.

[10]*Le Devoir*, 16 août 1947. Filion est probablement influencé par la "gauche catholique" française (courant personnaliste) qui voulait rejoindre les "masses prolétaires déchristianisées" pour les ramener à l'Église. Cependant, le prolétariat canadien-français était encore loin de la déchristianisation. Voir Jean-Philippe Warren, "Gérard Pelletier et Cité libre: la mystique personnaliste de la Révolution tranquille", *Société*, 20/21 (été 1999), 322.

[11]Nous avons fait une analyse de la position du journal à l'égard du syndicalisme depuis sa fondation dans Robert Lahaise (dir.), *Le Devoir. Reflet du Québec au 20e siècle* (Montréal 1994), 279-312.

provinciale, appui public des évêques, collecte pour les grévistes) demeurent gravées dans la mémoire des intellectuels critiques du gouvernement Duplessis et désireux de transformation sociale.

Certains d'entre eux s'emploient donc à fixer la grève dans la mémoire collective en publiant un volume qui, tout en reposant sur une recherche sérieuse, n'en présente pas moins une interprétation fort discutable sous de nombreux rapports. Certains chapitres sont plus neutres; d'autres dont ceux de Pierre Elliott Trudeau, Gilles Beausoleil, Réginald Boisvert et la préface de Jean-Charles Falardeau, abondent dans le sens d'un conflit qui a inauguré une ère nouvelle dans les rapports sociaux au Québec. Il n'est pas de notre intention ici de discuter de cette thèse (nous l'avons fait ailleurs[12]) qui a bien besoin d'être relativisée depuis qu'on connaît mieux l'histoire syndicale des décennies antérieures à 1949. Nous nous proposons plutôt de mettre en relief une réclamation faite par les syndicats au début de la négociation qui a braqué la partie patronale et qui serait à la source du conflit selon le président de la principale compagnie impliquée, la Canadian Johns-Manville. Elle touche la volonté du syndicat de jouer un rôle dans les promotions et l'organisation du travail dans les mines. Cette revendication, nouvelle à l'époque, émane directement de l'idée de réforme de l'entreprise, projet mis de l'avant par un groupe de jeunes clercs catholiques, et qui est reprise par des syndicats affiliés à la Confédération des travailleurs catholiques du Canada (CTCC). Assez curieusement, cette dimension de la grève a plutôt tendance à être minimisée par les collaborateurs du volume dirigé par Pierre Elliott Trudeau tout comme elle est mise en sourdine par les leaders de la grève pendant et après le conflit.[13] En nous appuyant notamment sur des archives patronales et syndicales, nous tenterons de saisir le sens de cette revendication, en évaluerons l'importance dans le conflit, analyserons l'appui dont elle jouit auprès de l'épiscopat et examinerons l'impact qu'elle a eu sur une organisation patronale d'inspiration catholique, l'Association professionnelle des industriels. Nous montrerons que cette réclamation a constitué un enjeu de taille opposant les syndicats, le patronat et l'épiscopat.

[12]Jacques Rouillard, "Vingt-cinq ans d'histoire du syndicalisme québécois. Quelques acquis de la recherche," dans Yves Roby et Nive Voisine (dir.), *Érudition, humanisme et savoir. Actes du colloque en l'honneur de Jean Hamelin* (Québec 1996), 171-194; "La grève de l'amiante, mythe et symbolique," *L'Action nationale*, 69, 7 (sept. 1999), 33-43. Jocelyn Létourneau fait aussi la critique de cette interprétation dans: "La mise en intrigue. Configuration historico-linguistique d'une grève célébrée: Asbestos, PQ, 1949," *Recherches sémiotiques/Semiotic Inquiry*, vol. 12, 1-2 (1992), 53-71, et dans "La grève de l'amiante entre ses mémoires et l'histoire," *Journal de la Société canadienne d'histoire orale"Canadian Oral History Association Journal*, 10 (1991), 8-16.

[13]Dans son histoire de la grève, Gilles Beausoleil reconnaît "l'anxiété" qu'a pu susciter une telle réclamation parmi les dirigeants de la compagnie. Mais il l'écarte rapidement de son analyse, reprochant à la compagnie de l'avoir pris trop au sérieux. Le projet serait trop radical pour être applicable et les Canadiens français aurait un penchant pour la "volubilité" et les "idéaux abstraits et parfois utopiques," Trudeau, *La Grève de l'amiante*, 173.

A- *Les enjeux du conflit*

Rappelons que la grève de l'amiante, qui s'étend sur plus de quatre mois, du milieu février à la fin de juillet 1949, touche plus de 5000 mineurs à Thetford Mines et Asbestos. Deux mille travaillent pour la Canadian Johns-Manville d'Asbestos (CJM), les autres étant à l'emploi des firmes Asbestos Corporation, Flintkote et Johnson de Thetford Mines. La partie syndicale est représentée par la Fédération nationale des employés de l'industrie minière affiliée à la CTCC qui cherche à uniformiser les conditions de travail dans l'ensemble des mines de l'amiante. Au centre des réclamations syndicales, il y a l'élimination de la poussière d'amiante, une augmentation générale de 15 cents l'heure, la retenue des cotisations syndicales à la source (déjà acquise pour les compagnies de Thetford) et la "consultation" ou "approbation" du syndicat dans tous les cas de promotion, de transfert et de congédiement. Au départ, le plus gros employeur, la Canadian Johns-Manville d'Asbestos, offre une augmentation générale de cinq cents l'heure et quelques autres améliorations, mais refuse de percevoir les cotisations syndicales de tous les travailleurs (formule Rand), une forme de sécurité qui commence à se répandre au Canada dans les grandes entreprises à la suite de la décision du juge Rand qui l'imposait dans un arbitrage à la compagnie Ford en 1945. En outre, la compagnie s'élève résolument contre la demande que les promotions, les mesures disciplinaires et certaines questions reliées aux méthodes de travail et aux taux de rémunération soient l'objet d'une "approbation" du syndicat. Nous reviendrons sur ce dernier point.

Comme la négociation piétine, le syndicat réclame un conciliateur qui, après quelques jours, se déclare impuissant à rapprocher les parties. Bien que la loi des relations ouvrières prévoie alors l'obligation d'un arbitrage, les mineurs, ayant perdu confiance envers les conseils d'arbitrage à cause de leur parti-pris et de leur retard à rendre leurs décisions,[14] décident de déclencher immédiatement la grève (le 13 février à Asbestos, le lendemain à Thetford).[15] Élément très important et sur lequel nous reviendrons plus bas, ils s'attendent à ce que le conflit soit de courte durée car, l'année précédente, une grève déclenchée illégalement contre les trois compagnies minières de Thetford s'est terminée trois jours plus tard avec des

---

[14]En octobre 1948, un arbitrage, qui fut particulièrement long (demande faite en février), rejetait la demande du syndicat d'Asbestos touchant la décision de la compagnie d'éliminer un homme sur une équipe de travail de quatre employés à extraire de l'amiante à l'aide d'une excavatrice électrique (Arbitrage du différend entre la CJM et le Syndicat national de l'amiante d'Asbestos, *Bulletin du service d'information du ministère du Travail*, 20 octobre 1948; Charpentier, "La grève de l'amiante: version nouvelle," 222-223).

[15]Une grève a déjà touché du 11 au 13 février 1949 la petite mine de la Nicolet-Asbestos à Saint-Rémi-de-Tinfwick à propos du congédiement d'un contremaître. Les mineurs retournent cependant au travail la veille du déclenchement de la grève à Asbestos. Ils abandonnent à nouveau le travail du 2 mars au 6 juin, Trudeau, *La Grève de l'amiante*, 171.

résultats très "fructueux" pour le syndicat.[16] Mais il n'en est pas ainsi en 1949. Devant l'illégalité de la grève, la Commission des relations ouvrières enlève au syndicat son accréditation le 21 février et la compagnie commence à recruter des briseurs de grève. Aux grévistes qui entendent faire respecter les piquets de grève, la compagnie réplique par une injonction et fait appel à la police provinciale pour protéger sa propriété. Le Premier ministre Duplessis et le ministre du Travail exigent, avant d'intervenir dans le conflit, que les grévistes retournent au travail et rentrent dans la légalité. Les compagnies refusent de négocier tant que les grévistes ne sont pas retournés au travail.

L'embauche de plus en plus nombreux de briseurs de grève suscite des altercations dans la municipalité d'Asbestos. Le 5 mai, des groupes de piqueteurs bloquent les entrées de la ville pour les empêcher de se rendre au travail et molestent des policiers provinciaux. Le lendemain, 200 policiers sont dépêchés à Asbestos et l'acte d'émeute est lu tôt le matin. De nombreuses arrestations (116) suivent où plusieurs grévistes sont brutalisés par les policiers.

Le conflit, qui a beaucoup de retentissements dans la province à mesure qu'il se prolonge, donne lieu à un vaste mouvement de solidarité et de générosité. Plus de 500 000$ en argent et 75 000$ de vivres sont recueillis parmi les syndiqués de toute allégeance et aux portes des églises, comme l'ont demandé plusieurs évêques. L'idée d'un appui aussi tangible de l'épiscopat, unanime dans ce dossier, provient de la Commission sacerdotale d'études sociales qui, comme nous le verrons, est à l'origine du projet de réforme de l'entreprise.[17] Cet appui est d'autant plus significatif que l'illégalité de la grève place l'épiscopat dans une situation très délicate tant au niveau des principes que dans ses rapports avec le gouvernement Duplessis. Si les évêques sont prêts à montrer un soutien public si tangible, c'est qu'ils craignent qu'un échec trop apparent dans un conflit aussi largement médiatisé ne mette en danger la survie même d'un mouvement que leurs prédécesseurs ont mis

[16]La grève est survenue du 7 au 9 janvier 1948 (Procès-verbal de la réunion du 18 janvier 1948 du Bureau de direction de la Fédération nationale des employés de l'industrie minière, *Cahiers des procès-verbaux du Bureau fédéral et de l'exécutif de la Fédération*, Fonds de la Fédération des syndicats des mines, de la métallurgie et des produits chimiques (CSN), POO5, I, 4, Société des archives historiques de la région de l'amiante (SAHRA), Thetford Mines).

[17]Cousineau, *L'Église d'ici...*, 104-106. La légende qu'a contribué à alimenter la pièce de théâtre de John T. McDonough (*Charbonneau et le Chef*) veut que Mgr Charbonneau, archevêque de Montréal, ait été démis de ses fonctions en 1950 à cause de son appui donné aux grévistes et à la suite d'intervention d'émissaires du premier ministre Duplessis auprès du Vatican. Cette interprétation est sans fondement, l'épiscopat étant unanime à l'appui des grévistes. Voir au sujet de sa "démission"; Jean Hamelin, *Histoire du catholicisme québécois, Le XXe siècle*, tome 2 (Montréal 1984) 110-116; Lionel Groulx, *Mes Mémoires*, tome IV (Montréal 1974), 269-278; Cousineau, *L'Église d'ici ...*, 94-106; Jacques Cousineau, "La grève de l'amiante, les évêques et le départ de Mgr Charbonneau, *Le Devoir*, 7 (mai 1974), 5.

sur pied.[18] Dans les lettres de remerciement qu'il fait parvenir à plusieurs évêques après le conflit, Jean Marchand, secrétaire général de la CTCC, est aussi d'avis que "la prise de position de l'Épiscopat a sauvé notre mouvement d'un échec qui aurait pu être désastreux."[19]

Dès la fin avril 1949, les grévistes sont prêts à rentrer au travail et à soumettre leur litige à la procédure d'arbitrage. Mais la négociation échoue car la compagnie CJM refuse de réembaucher tous les grévistes et tient à maintenir les procédures judiciaires intentées contre les organisations syndicales et les grévistes sur qui pèsent des accusations civiles ou criminelles. Ce n'est que deux mois plus tard, grâce à la médiation de Mgr Roy, archevêque de Québec, que les deux parties trouvent un terrain d'entente où la CJM retire les procédures intentées contre le syndicat et la fédération mais garde à son emploi les briseurs de grève et conserve la possibilité de sévir contre les grévistes qui pourraient être jugés criminellement responsables.[20] On s'entend aussi pour que les syndicats recouvrent leur accréditation et que la négociation puisse reprendre. Les grévistes commencent à retourner au travail à Thetford le 29 juin et à Asbestos le 6 juillet. La négociation aboutit rapidement à une impasse et le litige est soumis à un tribunal d'arbitrage pour les mineurs des deux principales compagnies de Thetford uniquement, l'Asbestos Corporation et la Flintkote Mines. La Canadian Johns-Manville attend la décision du tribunal avant de conclure une entente avec ses employés.

La sentence rendue le 10 décembre (l'arbitre syndical est dissident) accorde une augmentation de dix cents l'heure, cinq sous de plus que ce que les compagnies offraient avant la grève. Cependant, elle élimine des conventions la retenue obligatoire de la cotisation syndicale à la source (formule Rand) pour la remplacer par la

[18]Trudeau, *La Grève de l'amiante*, 255.

[19]Lettre de Jean Marchand, à son excellence Mgr Arthur Douville, évêque de Saint-Hyacinthe, 22 août 1949, Archives de la CSN, Fonds Secrétariat général (28-3-3-4), Correspondance avec les évêques (A5). Des lettres similaires sont aussi adressées à dix autres évêques dont Mgr Georges Courchesne de Rimouski (accusé parfois d'avoir été hostile aux grévistes) et à Mgr J.-C. Leclaire, président de la CSES, et Mgr Antoniutti, délégué apostolique à Ottawa. Les évêchés de Saint-Hyacinthe, Sherbrooke et Montréal ont prêté 50 000.00$ au syndicat pendant la grève (*Étude sur la grève de l'amiante* (juillet 1954), 24, Archives de la CSN, 28-2-3-2, Présidence A9). Jean Marchand dans son rapport au comité exécutif de la centrale admet là aussi que la grève "revêt présentement un caractère de lutte pour l'existence ou la mort du syndicalisme catholique" CTCC, *Procès-verbal de la réunion de l'exécutif de la CTCC*, 10 (juin 1949), 7.

[20]Lorsque les grévistes retournent au travail, la compagnie Johns-Manville refuse de reprendre à son service 19 d'entre eux accusés d'actes criminels graves. Trois semaines plus tard, elle se ravise cependant, acceptant d'embaucher neuf d'entre eux. Les dix autres sont repris graduellement un à un, le dernier ne retournant au travail qu'en janvier 1952 (Trudeau, *La grève de l'amiante*, 330-331). Jusqu'à leur retour au travail, les évêques de Québec, Montréal et Saint-Hyacinthe se sont cotisés pour leur verser une compensation équivalente à leur salaire (Cousineau, *L'Église d'ici....*, 108).

retenue volontaire des travailleurs. Il est prévu aussi que les nouvelles conventions aient une durée de deux ans alors que les syndicats s'attendaient à une seule année. Enfin, rien n'est prévu pour que les compagnies éliminent les poussières d'amiante, le tribunal se contentant de recommander qu'elles poursuivent l'effort déjà consenti. Les trois compagnies de Thetford acceptent le rapport tandis que les syndicats sont fort mécontents, jugeant qu'il donne raison aux compagnies sur presque tous les points.[21] On demande alors l'intervention d'un conciliateur au ministère du Travail. Une entente intervient finalement dans le bureau du Premier ministre Duplessis, le 29 décembre, qui ajoute une augmentation salariale additionnelle de cinq cents l'heure aux dix cents déjà accordés (formule d'indexation). La suggestion lui en a été faite par le président de la CTCC, Gérard Picard, qui tient à ce que les grévistes obtiennent une augmentation salariale supérieure à celle obtenue par les mineurs de la Bell Asbestos de Thetford en mars 1949.[22] Ces derniers, qui ne se sont pas mis en grève, font partie d'un syndicat qui n'est pas affilié à la CTCC.

À Thetford, les conventions collectives sont signées le 12 janvier 1950 tandis qu'à Asbestos, elle ne l'est que le 21 février. Au total, les contrats, qui sont assez similaires dans chacune des entreprises, n'apportent que de très minces avantages aux mineurs, la partie syndicale ayant graduellement reculé sur la plupart de ses positions à mesure que la grève se prolongeait. "On a réglé à plat-ventre, on a réglé pour sauver notre peau", racontera Rodolphe Hamel en 1974;[23] il a été l'un des principaux dirigeants de la grève en tant que président de la Fédération nationale des employés de l'industrie minière.

Dans l'entente de principe qui met fin à la grève, la compagnie CJM obtient que la fédération et le syndicat "reconnaissent le droit de propriété et le droit de la direction de diriger" et consentent à inclure dans la convention une clause dite des droits de la direction.[24] Et effectivement, la convention collective signée le 1er février 1950 contient un long article où est précisé que "la Compagnie doit avoir plein pouvoir, autorité et responsabilité dans l'exercice des fonctions habituelles de la Gérance" dont ceux "d'employer, transférer, accorder des promotions et congédier" et afin aussi d'adopter de nouvelles méthodes de production que le syndicat ne pourra pas refuser.[25] Ce souci découle d'un élément qui a joué un rôle important dans le raidissement des compagnies au tout début de la négociation. Voyons de plus près.

---

[21]Le Devoir, 23 décembre 1949, 12.
[22]Le Devoir, 2 mars 1974, 5.
[23]"Rodolphe Hamel raconte sa vie ouvrière", Dossiers "Vie ouvrière", 82 (février 1974), 75.
[24]La Tribune, 28 juillet 1949, 3.
[25] Convention entre la Canadian Johns-Manville Co., Limited, et le Syndicat national de l'amiante Inc. et la Fédération nationale des employés de l'industrie minière Inc., Asbestos, 1950, 7-8, 10-13.

B- *Approbation des promotions, transferts et congédiements*

Pendant le conflit, le 22 avril 1949, le président du conseil d'administration de la Canadian Johns-Manville, Lewis H. Brown, signe une pleine page d'annonce dans les quotidiens québécois reprochant aux dirigeants syndicaux de ne pas avoir comme but unique d'améliorer les conditions de travail des syndiqués. "Les vraies barrières qui empêchent un règlement amical n'ont, cette fois, qu'une relation éloignée avec le bien-être de nos employés. Le point crucial de la grève est l'insistance que les chefs du syndicats mettent à obtenir, pour eux-mêmes, une part d'autorité et de contrôle sur l'administration. C'est cette doctrine révolutionnaire voulant que le droit des propriétaires, jusqu'ici incontesté, de choisir leurs représentants pour administrer leur propriété, soit soumis au pouvoir de veto des chefs du syndicat." Ces derniers manifesteraient une "tendance croissante à prêcher une doctrine s'opposant au capitalisme et soutenant une philosophie plus apparente au communisme et au socialisme." C'est, selon lui, "le point crucial de la grève" qui empêche son règlement.[26]

Le président de l'Asbestos Corporation abonde dans le même sens lors de l'assemblée annuelle des actionnaires de sa compagnie le 21 avril 1949: "It was the moral and legal obligation of the company to stand for the principles that protect the proterty rights of the stockholders and the human rights of its employees." Il ajoute que les demandes syndicales sont excessives et que, s'il y cédait, elles dépasseraient l'ensemble des profits de la compagnie pour 1948.[27]

Dans la brochure qu'il rend publique en mai 1949, le président Brown élabore plus longuement sur ses accusations. Les demandes syndicales qui le hérissent particulièrement sont les suivantes :

a. Faire **approuver** les promotions par le Syndicat.
b. Faire **approuver** par le Syndicat les mesures disciplinaires prises par la Direction.
c. Ne fournir aucun encouragement à produire plus sans l'approbation du Syndicat.
d. Ne pas changer les méthodes de travail ou les taux de rémunération sans l'approbation du Syndicat.[28]

Le syndicat veut ainsi, selon lui, s'arroger les droits de la direction de l'usine, outrepassant les limites acceptables de la négociation collective. Citant à l'appui plusieurs passages de l'encyclique papale *Quadragesimo Anno* défendant le droit de propriété, il termine en évoquant celui où le pape dénonce ceux qui "s'appliquent à réduire tellement le caractère individuel du droit de propriété qu'ils en arrivent pratiquement à le lui enlever."[29] Comme président d'une compagnie qui détient des

---

[26]*La Presse*, 22 avril 1949, 7. Les mêmes commentaires sont repris par George Foster, vice-président de la CJM et gérant général de la mine *(Le Devoir*, 22 avril 1949, 12).

[27]*The Montreal Gazette*, 22 avril 1949, 3.

[28]Lewis H. Brown, *La grève d'Asbestos. Rapport sur le fond de la question et sur la position de la Canadian Johns-Manville Company*, 11 mai 1949, 8.

[29]Brown, *La grève d'Asbestos*, 16.

usines partout en Amérique du Nord, il juge n'avoir jamais eu à faire face à des demandes syndicales aussi extrêmes.

À l'assemblée annuelle des actionnaires de la compagnie en mai 1949, il fait émettre un communiqué expliquant que:

(...) the crus of the strike in the insistence B- the union leaders that the secoure for themselves certain controls over managerial policy. It is a revolutionary doctrine that the right to fix management policies has become the prerogative of union leaders...." "We are going to protect the right of Johns-Manville to have skilled engineers and local management operate our mine, mill and plant at Asbestos, Quebec, in accordance with the principles of free enterprise in a democracy (...) even thow to do so may require many more weeks or months of strike-bound inactivity.[30]

À la veille du règlement du conflit, il renouvelle ses reproches, accusant les syndicats de vouloir "s'immiscer dans la direction de son entreprise," ce qui lui apparaissait tout à fait intolérable.[31]

Mgr Maurice Roy, dont la médiation contribue au dénouement de la grève, corrobore que cette question a représenté une pierre d'achoppement à la négociation. Longtemps après la fin de la grève, dans une longue entrevue à un journaliste en 1972, il confirme que "le conflit d'Asbestos portait en grande partie sur un élément idéologique: la question de la participation" des travailleurs à la réforme de l'entreprise.[32] Pour sa part, dans le chapitre de ses *Mémoires* consacré à la grève, l'ex-président de la CTCC de 1935 à 1946, Alfred Charpentier, qui est devenu responsable du service de la recherche de la centrale en 1949, opine dans le même sens: l'idée de réforme de l'entreprise "heurte violemment toutes les grandes entreprises industrielles" de sorte que "pendant toute la durée de la grève, la résistance de la CJM aux revendications de syndicats et de la Fédération parut prendre figure de bouclier pour toutes les entreprises similaires dans l'Estrie."[33]

Suite à la parution des encarts dans les journaux en avril 1949, les dirigeants syndicaux repoussent les accusations de la CJM voulant qu'ils désirent s'arroger la direction de la compagnie. Pour Rodolphe Hamel, "les syndicats ne réclament pas de participation aux bénéfices" et le président Brown "répand de fausses rumeurs afin de faire perdre aux grévistes l'appui moral et matériel qui leur est si généreusement accordé par le grand public." Le secrétaire général de la CTCC, Jean Marchand, mêlé de près à la négociation, abonde dans le même sens: la déclaration du président "est semée de faussetés," la grève ne comportant pas de menace au droit de propriété ou à la liberté d'administration de la compagnie."[34] La semaine suivante, dans une assemblée syndicale, Hamel reconnaît cependant "qu'il y a quelque temps, alors

[30]*Asbestos*, vol. 30, 10 (mai 1949), 18-19.
[31]*La Tribune*, 26 juin 1949, 3.
[32]*L'Action*, 22 juillet 1972.
[33]Charpentier, *Les Mémoires d'Alfred Charpentier*, 332-333.
[34]*La Tribune*, 23 avril 1949, 1.

que nous étudions l'avenir des syndicats, il fut suggéré qu'un jour viendra où les ouvriers seront appelés à participer à la gérance et aux bénéfices des compagnies." Il conclut que la compagnie se sert de ce prétexte pour faire reculer les conditions de travail de 25 ans en arrière.[35]

Dans le numéro spécial consacré à la grève en mai 1949, le journal *Le Travail*, organe de la CTCC, fait état longuement des causes prochaines et éloignées de la grève. On élabore sur les différentes revendications des syndicats (surtout l'élimination des poussières) tout en dénonçant l'attitude antisyndicale du gouvernement Duplessis et les tactiques condamnables des compagnies dont en particulier celles de la CJM qui "vise à la destruction du syndicalisme catholique dans la Province de Québec."[36] Parmi les revendications syndicales, il est fait allusion vaguement à des "dispositions relatives aux transferts, congédiements et promotions," comprenant mal que le président Brown y voit une atteinte au droit de propriété. En conclusion, les compagnies d'amiante sont accusées d'avoir "une conception absolue du droit de propriété." Les syndicats ne chercheraient pas à vouloir affaiblir leur autorité mais à faire disparaître que ce qu'il y a "d'arbitraire" dans leurs comportements. La grève dans l'amiante serait l'effet d'un "choc violent entre la conception individualiste et la conception sociale des relations industrielles."[37] Le 22 juin, Jean Marchand revient sur le sujet dans un long historique de la grève. Il affirme que "jamais les syndicats de l'amiante n'ont formulé de demandes qui, de près ou de loin, pouvaient restreindre ou limiter les droits de direction de la compagnie. Au contraire, ils acceptèrent une clause incluse dans la convention collective les consacrant à tous." Les commentaires du président Brown me sont à son avis qu'une tactique pour expliquer devant l'opinion publique son refus de négocier la fin de la grève. La CJM n'aurait comme objectif que de détruire le syndicat.[38]

Tout au long du conflit, les dirigeants syndicaux ne cessent de répéter que leurs réclamations n'ont rien de révolutionnaire et que leurs principales demandes touchent l'élimination des poussières d'amiante, une hausse des salaires et le maintien de la formule Rand. Par contre, avant la grève, ils sont moins évasifs sur les exigences qui effraient tant la partie patronale. Voyons de plus près.

Le 21 novembre 1948, le Bureau fédéral de la Fédération nationale des employés de l'industrie minière, chargée de la négociation pour l'ensemble des syndicats de l'amiante, approuve un certain nombre d'amendements aux conventions alors en vigueur. Il faut se rappeler que la fédération tente d'uniformiser les conventions collectives de toutes les entreprises d'amiante où ses syndicats affiliés regroupent des travailleurs. Elle cherche également à étendre à la Canadian Johns-Manville plusieurs des clauses obtenues des compagnies de Thetford lors de la

[35] *La Tribune*, 2 mai 1949, 3.
[36] *Le Travail*, mai 1949, 4.
[37] *Le Travail*, mai 1949, 3.
[38] *Le Devoir*, 22 juin 1949, 12; *La Tribune*, 22 juin 1949, 5.

signature des conventions collectives précédentes, en février 1948. Les réclamations de la fédération pour 1949 sont les suivantes:[39]

1) Double temps le dimanche sans restriction
2) Toutes les fêtes chômées payées et en incluant le Vendredi Saint
3) Salaire: 15 cents l'heure générale, travail à la pièce 18%
4) Une prime pour le travail de nuit de 5 cents l'heure
5) Deux semaines de vacances consécutives après 2 ans de service et 3 semaines de vacances consécutives après 20 ans de service
6) Amendements à la clause 7 de la convention actuelle
7) 3% pour le fonds de sécurité sociale
8) Élimination des poussières
9) Biffer les paragraphes E et F de la clause 7

Les points six et neuf réfèrent à des amendements à apporter à la clause sept des conventions, dont on ne précise par la teneur, mais qui touchent les transferts et les promotions dans l'entreprise. Le procès-verbal du congrès de la fédération du 4 septembre 1949 fait référence aux mêmes exigences des syndicats tout en étant aussi peu précis sur la clause sept.[40]

Le 5 décembre 1948, une assemblée générale du syndicat de l'amiante d'Asbestos approuve un nouveau projet de convention qui comprend ces demandes. Le 14 décembre, le secrétaire de la fédération, Daniel Lessard, demande à rencontrer les représentants de la compagnie.[41] Une première séance de négociation a lieu le 23 décembre à laquelle assistent Rodolphe Hamel, président de la fédération, et Jean Marchand, secrétaire général de la CTCC, qui défend vigoureusement l'ajout d'une nouvelle clause à la convention touchant les promotions, transferts et congédiements. Il veut que la compagnie s'engage à "soumettre au syndicat tous les cas de promotions, transferts et congédiements."[42] Cette proposition est directement issue de l'idée de cogestion qui découle du projet de réforme de l'entreprise

[39]Procès-verbal de la réunion du 21 novembre 1948 du Bureau de direction de la Fédération nationale des employés de l'industrie minière (FNEIM), Société des archives historiques de la région de l'amiante (SAHRA), Thetford Mines, *Cahiers des procès-verbaux des réunions de la Fédération et du Bureau fédéral*, Fonds de la Fédération des syndicats des mines, de la métallurgie et des produits chimiques (CSN), POO5, II, 1, 4.

[40]*Procès-verbal du Congrès de la FNEIM tenu à Thetford Mines le 4 septembre 1949*, SAHRA, Fonds de la Fédération des syndicats des mines, de la métallurgie et des produits chimiques (CSN), POO5, III, 8.

[41]Lettre de Daniel Lessard à C. M. McGaw, 14 décembre 1948, SAHRA, "Correspondance reçue et envoyée," Fonds du syndicat des travailleurs de la Société Asbestos Limitée (CSN), POO3, II, 4,3. Des séances de négociation ont eu lieu avec les représentants patronaux de l'Asbestos Corporation et de la Johnson's Co. à Thetford les 10 et 11 décembre.

[42]Mémos à tous les employés, *Convention collective de travail*, J. E. Morrison et G. K. Foster, 27 décembre 1948, SAHRA, Fonds du Syndicat national de l'amiante d'Asbestos, PO90; *Le Travail*, mars 1949, 3; Charpentier, *Les Mémoires*, 333.

que défendent alors un certain nombre d'aumôniers catholiques et que nous analyserons plus bas. L'initiative est très mal reçue des représentants patronaux qui y voient un esprit radical et révolutionnaire.[43]

En réplique, la compagnie insiste alors pour inclure dans le nouveau contrat de travail une clause garantissant ses droits de gérance: "La Compagnie garde tous les droits, pouvoirs et autorités qui habituellement sont exercés par la "Gérance," excepté dans les cas où il est spécifiquement stipulé dans le contrat qu'un cas particulier a été concédé."[44] Elle décide aussi d'afficher des communiqués destinés aux employés pour les renseigner sur la marche des négociations. Le geste irrite la direction syndicale qui y voit un "indice de non-confiance" envers les négociateurs syndicaux. Le 11 janvier, le secrétaire Lessard de la fédération fait savoir qu'il mettra fin aux négociations si la compagnie poursuit son affichage.[45] Comme la compagnie persiste, le syndicat cesse de rencontrer ses représentants et demande, le 27 janvier, la présence d'un conciliateur au ministère du Travail. Lessard le presse aussi d'intervenir dans les négociations avec les compagnies de Thetford qui se trouvent également dans une impasse car la plupart des réclamations des syndicats ont été refusées.[46]

Une semaine plus tôt, le 16 janvier, a lieu à Asbestos une journée syndicale où Gérard Picard, président de la CTCC, et Jean Marchand, secrétaire, ont pris la parole. Marchand s'en prend à la CJM qui "se réserve trop de privilèges" en invoquant les droits de la direction. Il déclare que la CTCC "rend service à l'industrie et à la société en réclamant la participation aux bénéfices pour l'ouvrier." Picard revient sur le même sujet indiquant que la promotion de la classe ouvrière passe par "la participation ouvrière aux bénéfices de l'industrie."[47]

Le 31 janvier, le conciliateur nommé par le ministère du Travail évite *in extremis* la prise d'un vote de grève à Asbestos en obtenant de la compagnie de cesser l'affichage de communiqués sur la marche des négociations. Des rencontres de conciliation ont lieu du 7 au 10 février qui échouent sur plusieurs points importants: le syndicat réclame l'inclusion dans la juridiction du syndicat des ouvriers employés par les sous-contracteurs, l'élimination des poussières d'amiante, l'application de la formule Rand de même que des demandes monétaires; la compagnie, de son coté, cherche à déterminer les droits de la gérance et à établir une procédure pour l'étude des standards d'efficacité.[48] Les deux parties

[43]Charpentier, Les *Mémoires, 330-331.*
[44]Nouveau contrat de travail, Canadian Johns-Manville, 8 janvier 1949, SAHRA, Fonds du Syndicat des travailleurs de la Société Asbestos Limitée, POO3, II, 3.
[45] Lettre de Daniel Lessard à G. K. Foster, vice-président, Canadian Johns-Manville Limited, 11 janvier 1949, SAHRA, Fonds du Syndicat national de l'amiante d'Asbestos, PO90.
[46]Lettre de Daniel Lessard à Léo Massicotte, assistant secrétaire, Commission des relations ouvrières, Québec, SAHRA, Fonds du Syndicat national de l'amiante d'Asbestos, P003, 116,15.
[47]*L'Asbestos*, 21 janvier 1949, 1 et 6.
[48]Charpentier, "La grève de l'amiante," 224.

conviennent alors de soumettre leur différend à un tribunal d'arbitrage comme l'exige la loi. Mais, comme on le sait, à l'assemblée générale du 13 février, les mineurs de la CJM décident de débrayer immédiatement, convaincus que les délais d'arbitrage sont longs et qu'ils ne peuvent obtenir justice en suivant cette procédure. Le discours impétueux de Jean Marchand à cette assemblée, très critique du processus d'arbitrage, n'est rien pour calmer le penchant des mineurs pour l'action directe.[49] Le lendemain, les mineurs de Thetford se mettent aussi en grève.

À partir du moment où le conflit est déclenché, la partie syndicale met de l'avant que les points litigieux touchent l'élimination de la poussière, les hausses salariales, la retenue syndicale obligatoire et divers autres bénéfices sociaux. Il n'est plus question de soumettre au syndicat tous les cas de promotion, transferts et congédiements, mais uniquement de consulter le syndicat en ces occasions. C'est la formulation communiquée aux journaux et celle qu'ont retenu les collaborateurs du volume *La grève de l'amiante* dirigé par Pierre Elliott Trudeau.[50] Le choix d'une ou l'autre expression a son importance car elle n'a pas les mêmes conséquences. Le fait de soumettre consiste, selon la définition du *Petit Robert*, à "présenter, proposer au jugement, au choix"; le terme peut impliquer la nécessité d'une approbation tandis que la consultation représente uniquement la recherche d'un avis, sans obligation de s'y conformer.

Pendant l'arbitrage qui suit la grève (il ne concerne que les compagnies de la région de Thetford), le projet syndical de contrat de travail soumis aux arbitres contient une clause qui touche les promotions. Elle exige que les promotions, transferts permanents (excepté dans le cas des contremaîtres) et renvois soient soumis au syndicat avant d'être mise à exécution. Le syndicat peut alors faire des représentations par écrit à la compagnie qui garde cependant le droit d'effectuer sans délai ces changements. Cependant, il est loisible au syndicat de contester la décision de la compagnie en faisant un grief qui, si les parties ne s'entendent pas, pourrait être acheminé jusqu'à un comité d'arbitrage formé selon la loi des différends ouvriers.[51]

[49]*Le Travail* (mars 1949), 3. Alfred Charpentier soutient qu'à cette assemblée, Jean Marchand par sa fougue oratoire a accentué la prédisposition des syndiqués à déclencher la grève immédiatement (Charpentier, *Les Mémoires*, 334). Selon ses proches, Marchand ne s'est jamais relevé du traumatisme que lui a causé la grève de l'amiante; il est devenu par suite beaucoup plus prudent. Gérard Picard dira au début des années 1960: "Il a eu la peur de sa vie en 49 pendant la grève de l'amiante, devant l'ampleur du mouvement déclenché, et il ne s'en est jamais relevé" (Pierre Vadeboncoeur, *Souvenirs pour demain*, CSN, 1990, 5; Jacques Keable, *Le monde selon Marcel Pepin* (Montréal 1998) 134-138).
[50]Trudeau, *La Grève de l'amiante*, 214.
[51]Appendice "A" - *Projet syndical de convention collective de travail entre la Quebec Asbestos Corporation et le Syndicat national catholique de l'amiante de East-Broughton*, 1949, Archives nationales du Québec (ANQ), Centre de Québec, ministère du Travail E 24, Conciliation et arbitrage, 1948-1949, G8 (Asbestos Corporation), 19 et 24.

Il est important de noter que les syndicats n'innovent pas à ce chapitre car ils reprennent le texte de clauses de deux conventions collectives des compagnies de la région de Thetford, l'Asbestos Corporation et la Johnson's Company, pour l'année 1948, donc avant la grève. Elles exigent des employeurs qu'ils *soumettent* aux syndicats tous les cas de promotion, transfert et renvois avant de les mettre à exécution. En cas d'impasse, le syndicat peut formuler un grief qui ultimement pourrait être acheminé devant un comité d'arbitrage formé selon la loi des différends ouvriers.[52] Cet avancé tout comme la formule Rand constituent des gains significatifs suite à l'arrêt de travail à Thetford de trois jours du 7 au 9 janvier 1948.[53] Depuis l'automne de l'année précédente, ils faisaient partie des revendications de la Fédération nationale des employés de l'industrie minière pour le renouvellement des conventions collectives de tous les syndicats de la région. La demande en est faite aussi à la Canadian Johns-Manville, mais les travailleurs décident d'accepter l'offre de règlement de la compagnie, quatre mois avant la fin de la convention, soit des augmentations alléchantes de salaire en échange du statu quo sur presque toutes les clauses normatives. On sait que déjà à cette époque, la CJM considère comme des demandes radicales la formule Rand et l'exigence de soumettre les promotions, transferts et renvois au regard du syndicat.[54] Les compagnies de Thetford sont du même avis, mais devant le débrayage illégal de leurs employés le 7 janvier, elles acceptent la formation immédiate d'un tribunal d'arbitrage et de se conformer à la décision majoritaire. Le tribunal présidé par un conciliateur du gouvernement rend rapidement une décision favorable aux syndicats et les grévistes retournent aussitôt au travail "pleinement satisfaits" du règlement.[55] Les compagnies, par contre, sont plutôt déçues, escomptant probablement prendre leur revanche lors de la prochaine négociation.

[52]*Convention collective de travail entre l'Asbestos Corporation Limited et le Syndicat national des travailleurs de l'amiante de l'Asbestos Corporation Limited*, 1er avril 1948, 8, ANQ, E24, Conventions collectives, S 743, 45 (9972A); *Convention de travail entre la Johnson's Company Ltd et le Syndicat national des travailleurs de l'amiante de Johnson's Co.*, 1948, 12 et 17; *Procès-verbaux du tribunal institué pour régler le différend entre les compagnies minières et les syndicats de l'amiante,* vol. 12, séance du 6 octobre 1949, 102, SAHRA, Fonds P005.

[53]La convention collective de décembre 1946 de l'Asbestos Corporation laisse à la compagnie toute latitude (sans appel) touchant les promotions, transferts et renvois (*Convention collective de travail entre l'Asbestos Corporation Limited et le Syndicat national des employés salariés de l'Asbestos Corporation Limited*, 31 décembre 1946, ANQ, E24, Conventions collectives, S387, 40).

[54]En octobre 1947, les négociations de la Fédération avec la CJM sont interrompues précisément à propos de la réclamation touchant le droit de gérance (Assemblée de l'exécutif de la Fédération et des présidents de syndicats affiliés, le 18 octobre 1947, SAHRA, *Cahiers des procès-verbaux des réunions du Bureau fédéral et de l'exécutif de la FNSIM*, POO5, II 1, 4).

[55]Communiqué de Daniel Lessard, secrétaire de la Fédération, *L'Asbestos*, 23 janvier 1948, 1; *Le Soleil*, 9 janvier 1948, 1.

Après la grève de 1949, pendant les délibérations du tribunal d'arbitrage, il est peu question de la clause touchant les promotions. Il aurait peut-être pu en être autrement si la compagnie CJM avait été soumise elle aussi au processus d'arbitrage. Tout au plus, les avocats des compagnies de Thetford s'objectent-ils à ce que les compagnies doivent prendre en considération, outre la compétence et l'ancienneté, le statut syndical avant le statut familial lors de promotion, transfert ou renvois.[56] La sentence majoritaire du tribunal d'arbitrage (le juge Tremblay et l'arbitre patronal) s'est rendu à cette objection au nom des principes que la "famille est la cellule mère de la société" et que "dans notre société chrétienne et démocratique tout doit être centré autour de la famille."[57] Mais l'élément le plus important pour les syndicats à ce propos, c'est que le tribunal maintient et uniformise dans toutes les conventions des trois compagnies de Thetford la clause touchant les promotions, transferts ou renvois qui pourront faire l'objet d'un grief par le syndicat et par la suite être soumis à l'arbitrage.[58] Dans la négociation qui suit l'arbitrage, les deux parties acceptent que les conventions collectives signées pour 1949 et 1950 comprennent une clause d'ancienneté qui reprend textuellement le texte de la décision arbitrale.[59]

À Asbestos, la convention signée quelques semaines plus tard entre la CJM et le syndicat n'est pas de la même teneur. Comme on l'a vu, la compagnie tient à y insérer une clause précisant ses droits de gérance qui comprennent ceux "d'employer, transférer, accorder des promotions, congédier et renvoyer...." Comparativement à la convention précédente, elle accepte cependant, pour la première fois, la formation d'un comité des griefs et l'éventualité d'un arbitrage selon la loi des différends ouvriers.[60] Mais les questions qui peuvent être soumises à l'arbitrage sont très limitées. Elles ne peuvent concerner les standards d'efficacité et de production de même que les transferts, les rétrogradations et les promotions. Dans ces derniers cas, la compagnie peut "donner la préférence aux employés les mieux qualifiés pour remplir la tâche," l'ancienneté ne prévalant que si les employés ont

[56]*Procès-verbaux du tribunal...* , vol. 11, séance du 5 octobre 1949, 48; vol. 12, séance du 6 octobre 1949, 12 -18, SAHRA, Fonds P005.

[57]*Sentence arbitrale du tribunal d'arbitrage institué pour régler le différend entre Asbestos Corporation et le Syndicat national des travailleurs de l'amiante de l'Asbestos Corporation Limited* , 10 décembre 1949, 27, ANQ, E 24, ministère du Travail, Conciliation et arbitrage, 1949-1950, G44.

[58]Appendice "B", *Convention collective de travail entre la Quebec Asbestos Corporation Limited et le Syndicat national catholique de l'amiante de East-Broughton*, ANQ, E 24 ministère du Travail, Conciliation et arbitrage, 1948-1949, G8.

[59]*Convention de travail entre la Asbestos Corporation Limited et le Syndicat national des travailleurs de l'amiante de l'Asbestos Corporation Limited*, Thetford Mines, 1950, 15-16.

[60]*Convention collective de travail entre la Canadian Johns-Manville Co. Limited et le Syndicat national des employés de l'industrie minière Inc.*, Asbestos, 1948, 7-9.

des qualifications approximativement égales.[61] Dans l'éventualité de renvois temporaires et de transferts, il n'est pas question de tenir compte du statut syndical comme dans les conventions des compagnies de Thetford. En fait, les seuls cas où un litige peut être porté à la procédure de griefs et à l'arbitrage touchent les renvois et les suspensions pour avoir commis une infraction aux règlements de la compagnie. La CJM est donc beaucoup plus réticente que les compagnies de Thetford à ce que le syndicat limite l'autorité patronale tant dans l'organisation du travail que dans la gestion de la main-d'oeuvre.

Si lors des délibérations du tribunal d'arbitrage, la partie syndicale se satisfait du statu quo en ce qui touche les promotions, elle invoque par contre un principe issu de la réforme de l'entreprise pour justifier des augmentations supérieures de salaire. Ainsi, l'avocat des syndicats, Me L.P. Pigeon, fait valoir que le capitalisme est "un régime dans lequel tous ceux qui collaborent à la production doivent participer dans le produit de l'entreprise" et que "la participation du travailleur doit lui donner une part raisonnable du produit de l'entreprise." Selon lui, le travailleur dans les périodes de prospérité devrait "bénéficier au-delà de ce qu'exige la simple subsistance."[62] L'arbitre syndical, Me Théodore Lespérance, pousse plus avant l'argument dans son rapport minoritaire. Il rejette la conception du capitalisme voulant que l'employeur retire la totalité du profit d'une entreprise. La doctrine sociale catholique exige, selon lui, que les travailleurs, qui sont "le principal facteur de production," aient droit à une "part raisonnable du profit" des entreprises. Il s'en prend au rapport majoritaire du juge Tremblay et de l'avocat patronal qui s'inspire, à son avis, "d'un bout à l'autre, de la conception condamnable du capitalisme d'après laquelle le capital-argent a un droit exclusif à tous les profits de l'entreprise."[63] Son raisonnement s'inscrit pleinement dans le projet de réforme de l'entreprise que mettent de l'avant à l'époque les syndicats catholiques et des clercs membres de la Commission sacerdotale d'études sociales. Voyons de plus près l'enseignement de cette commission et l'influence qu'elle a pu avoir sur la CTCC.

C- La réforme de l'entreprise

Avant que de jeunes membres du clergé catholique ne fassent la promotion de la réforme de l'entreprise auprès des leaders de la CTCC, la centrale s'est laissée guider depuis sa fondation par un projet plus global de réforme du système de relations de

[61] *Convention entre la Canadian Johns-Manville Co., Limited, et le Syndicat national de l'amiante Inc. et la Fédération nationale des employés de l'industrie minière Inc.*, Asbestos, 1950, 24.

[62] *Procès-verbaux du tribunal*, vol. 10, séance du 4 octobre 1949, 82-83, SAHRA, Fonds P005.

[63] *Rapport minoritaire de l'arbitre syndical, Théodore Lespérance, au ministre du Travail, Antonio Barette, dans le conflit opposant l'Asbestos Corporation Limited et le Syndicat national des travailleurs de l'amiante de l'Asbestos Corporation Limited*, 10 décembre 1949, Centre de documentation de la CSN, Fonds de la grève de l'amiante, 123.1.1.

travail en mettant de l'avant l'établissement de la corporation professionnelle. Le projet corporatiste, une des composantes de ce qu'on appelle la doctrine sociale de l'Église, est propagé par le clergé pour faire échec au syndicalisme international et pacifier les relations de travail. Au rapport de force et aux tensions conflictuelles qui règnent entre patrons et ouvriers, on propose de substituer un esprit de collaboration et de bonne entente. La fraternité chrétienne, espère-t-on, remplacerait l'individualisme outrancier qui anime le système capitaliste. C'est précisément cet esprit que le syndicalisme catholique a pour objet de diffuser parmi les travailleurs et que les penseurs corporatistes souhaitent insuffler également parmi les patrons en les regroupant eux aussi dans des associations catholiques. À un second niveau d'organisation, les représentants des syndicats et des associations patronales catholiques forment la corporation professionnelle chargée des intérêts communs de la profession. C'est là que s'effectue la collaboration patronale-ouvrière, susceptible de ramener la paix sociale.[64] Cet objectif corporatiste est poursuivi par la CTCC de sa fondation en 1921 jusqu'à la Deuxième Guerre mondiale. Il faut dire cependant que cette visée influe relativement peu sur les pratiques des syndicats catholiques à partir des années vingt. Comme les syndicats internationaux, ils veulent négocier de bonnes conventions collectives de travail et s'organisent pour améliorer leur rapport de force lors de la négociation avec les employeurs.[65]

Mais la ferveur corporatiste, à la CTCC comme chez beaucoup d'intellectuels catholiques, commence à battre de l'aile pour être largement discréditée après la Deuxième Guerre. Le corporatisme est trop associé aux régimes fascistes qui se sont servis de la corporation en Europe pour dissoudre les syndicats libres, y inclus les syndicats chrétiens ou catholiques. Ainsi en est-il du pendant français de la CTCC, la Confédération française des travailleurs chrétiens, que le régime corporatiste de Vichy a interdit en 1940. Pour la jeune génération de leaders qui est portée à la tête de la CTCC tout juste après la guerre, la corporation professionnelle n'a plus rien d'attrayant. Elle fait figure d'idéal dépassé, fossoyeur du syndicalisme libre là où elle a été appliquée. Cet abandon se fait d'autant plus facilement que le leadership de la centrale s'est passablement renouvelé après la guerre. En 1949, plus de la moitié des directeurs du bureau confédéral ont moins de trois ans d'ancienneté à ce

---

[64]J. Rouillard, *Les syndicat nationaux au Québec de 1900 à 1930* (Québec 1979), 227-232; J. Rouillard, *Histoire du syndicalisme québécois* (Montréal 1989), 169-174.

[65]Les dirigeants justifient cette position en faisant valoir que le patronat est toujours imbu du même esprit de lucre et que les travailleurs ne doivent pas faire les frais de la formule. C'est pourquoi la centrale crée des fédérations professionnelles pour co-ordonner la négociation collective et revendique l'atelier syndical fermé. Ses syndicats n'hésitent pas non plus, à l'occasion, à déclencher des arrêts de travail. Nous avons compté 53 grèves auxquelles des syndicats catholiques sont mêlés entre 1920 à 1940 (Rouillard, *Les syndicats nationaux*, 240-250).

[66]Charpentier, *Les Mémoires*, 341.

poste.[66] Ces dirigeants ne font pratiquement plus allusion au corporatisme après la guerre, préférant lui substituer l'expression "organisation professionnelle" ou en traiter comme un jalon vers la "démocratie industrielle."[67]

C'est dans ce contexte qu'est apparu le projet de réforme de l'entreprise qui ne vise pas, comme le corporatisme, à transformer le système de relations de travail, mais propose d'élargir le rôle des travailleurs dans l'entreprise. Sa diffusion est l'oeuvre de prêtres membres de la Commission sacerdotale d'études sociales créée en 1948 par l'Assemblée des évêques du Québec en tant qu'organisme consultatif sur les problèmes sociaux du Québec. Sa fondation fait suite à des réunions de prêtres impliqués dans l'action sociale depuis 1945 qui désirent formuler un enseignement social commun touchant les associations patronales. L'objectif central de ces "journées sacerdotales," qui réunissent près d'une cinquantaine de prêtres venus d'un peu partout au Québec, est "d'appuyer la réforme de l'ordre social au Québec" en favorisant notamment l'organisation d'associations patronales catholiques.[68] Cette préoccupation se situe dans le sillage du projet corporatiste que les évêques ont placé, pendant la guerre, au troisième rang des facteurs de restauration sociale, après l'action de l'Église et de l'État.[69] Mais le projet ne peut s'actualiser que si les patrons se regroupent eux-aussi en association d'inspiration catholique. Et à ce niveau, le retard est considérable comparativement aux travailleurs salariés parmi lesquelles l'Église a fondé des syndicats catholiques depuis le début du siècle. La principale organisation d'obédience catholique, l'Association professionnelle des industriels née en 1943 et dont nous reparlerons plus bas, commence à peine à se développer.

Virage significatif, la délibération des prêtres impliqués dans l'action sociale en avril 1947 va se diriger du coté de la réforme de l'entreprise, un sujet qui est débattu parmi des intellectuels catholiques en Europe.[70] Le projet retient particulièrement l'attention des membres de la Commission sacerdotale d'études sociales formée l'année suivante, qui va en faire une promotion active, particulièrement à la CTCC. Des huit prêtres qui, à l'origine, font partie de la Commission, trois sont aumôniers de syndicats catholiques: Jacques Cousineau du Conseil central de Montréal, Omer Genest, des syndicats de la région Saguenay-Lac-Saint-Jean, et Henri Pichette, aumônier général de la CTCC. Un d'entre eux est uniquement professeur (Paul-Émile Bolté), un autre, aumônier d'une association patronale à Québec (Charles-Omer Garant) et deux autres à la fois professeurs et aumôniers d'associations patronales (Gérard Dion, Émile Bouvier). La présidence est assumée

[67]Jean Sexton, *La CTCC-CSN: du corporatisme à la réforme de l'entreprise*, mémoire de maîtrise, département de relations industrielles, Université Laval, 1969, 54.
[68]Cousineau, *L'Église d'ici, 48.*
[69]"Lettre pastorale collective des évêques et archevêques de la province de Québec," 11 mars 1940, dans *Mandements, lettres pastorales, circulaires et autres documents du diocèse de Montréal*, vol. 19, 75, 93.
[70]Cousineau, *L'Église d'ici*, 52-3.

par Mgr Jean-Charles Leclaire, vicaire général du diocèse de Sainte-Hyacinthe. Fondateur de l'École d'action ouvrière de ce diocèse, il a été aussi aumônier de syndicats catholiques. Comme nous le verrons, ils ont, jusqu'en 1951, une influence importante sur les évêques dont plusieurs sont sensibles à la cause ouvrière, notamment Mgrs Desranleau de Sherbrooke, Charbonneau de Montréal, Douville de Saint-Hyacinthe et Melancon de Chicoutimi. Tout en demeurant membre de la Commission, l'abbé Garant est promu à des fonctions importantes en 1948, en tant qu'évêque auxiliaire du diocèse de Québec et secrétaire de l'Assemblée des évêques du Québec.

Le compte rendu des délibérations des journées sacerdotales de 1947 est publié deux ans plus tard sous le titre *La participation des travailleurs à la vie de l'entreprise*. On peut y lire en avant-propos: "Le but de ces journées était de répondre à l'invitation des Souverains Pontifes qui demandent de travailler à l'assainissement du régime capitaliste, à une réforme du régime du salariat et, par conséquent, à une réforme de l'entreprise."[71] La Commission sacerdotale voit donc dans son projet de réformer l'entreprise rien de moins qu'une directive formelle des papes.

Les rédacteurs de la brochure s'inspirent, comme nous l'avons dit, de penseurs catholiques, surtout français, qui remettent à l'honneur une idée parfois évoquée chez des catholiques sociaux dans des travaux antérieurs à la Deuxième Guerre.[72] À l'appui de leur point de vue, ils citent souvent un passage de l'encyclique *Quadragesimo Anno* de 1931, où le pape Pie XI fait référence à cette notion: "Nous estimons cependant plus approprié aux conditions présentes de la vie sociale de tempérer quelque peu, dans la mesure du possible, le contrat de travail par des éléments empruntés au contrat de société. C'est ce que l'on a déjà commencé à faire sous des formes variées, non sans profit sensible pour les travailleurs, et pour les possesseurs de capital. Ainsi les ouvriers et employés ont été appelés à participer en quelque manière à la propriété de l'entreprise, à sa gestion ou aux profits qu'elle apporte."[73] Après la Guerre, comme l'idéal corporatiste est largement discrédité, des intellectuels s'appliquent à conserver une vision catholique de la question ouvrière à un moment où les thèses socialistes et communistes connaissent un regain de popularité en Europe. Délaissant l'idée de réformer l'ensemble du système économique, ils mettent l'accent sur une transformation des rapports entre employeurs et employés dans la cellule de base du système capitaliste, l'entreprise. Interprétant le passage de l'encyclique cité plus haut, ils conçoivent l'entreprise comme une association du capital et du travail (contrat de société) où les bénéfices et les responsabilités ne sont pas déterminés en vertu de leur apport respectif, mais

[71]Commission sacerdotale d'études sociales, *La participation des travailleurs à la vie de l'entreprise*, Compte rendu des journées sacerdotales d'études sociales de 1947, 4.
[72]Pierre Bigo, *La doctrine sociale de l'Église* (Paris 1965), 393-394.
[73]Pie XI, *Quadragesimo Anno*, no 72, dans CERAS, *Le discours social de l'Église catholique de Léon XIII à Jean-Paul II* (Paris 1985), 116.

comme le résultat de conventions mutuelles déterminant la bonne marche de l'entreprise.[74] Plus encore, certains y voient aussi une obligation morale des patrons de faire évoluer l'entreprise dans ce sens.

En 1945, les pères Gustave Desbuquois, directeur de l'Action populaire de Paris, et Pierre Bigo publient une brochure qui a beaucoup d'influence au Québec, *Les réformes de l'entreprise et la pensée chrétienne*.[75] La même année, les Semaines sociales de France consacrent des sessions à ce sujet sous le thème *Transformations sociales et libération de la personne*. La question fait aussi l'objet d'un numéro spécial de la *Chronique sociale de France* en 1946 et est traitée souvent de 1947 à 1949 dans des revues comme *Travaux de l'Action populaire* de Paris, *Les Dossiers de l'Action sociale catholique* de Bruxelles et le *Bulletin social des Industriels*, organe de l'Association des patrons et ingénieurs catholiques de Belgique.[76] Un volume influence également les penseurs sociaux québécois, celui de Alexandre Dubois, un membre du patronat français, dans *Structures nouvelles dans l'entreprise*.[77]

Ailleurs en Europe, le débat fait rage avec encore plus de force, notamment en Allemagne où le Congrès général des catholiques allemands, en septembre 1949, adopte une déclaration "affirmant que le droit de cogestion (dans les usines), pour ce qui regarde les questions sociales, économiques et du personnel, est un droit naturel dans l'ordre voulu de Dieu," et, conséquemment que ce droit soit reconnu légalement et qu'on l'introduise partout dans les entreprises.[78] Cette déclaration a des répercussions considérables qui, comme nous le verrons, détermine le pape à préciser sa pensée sur le sujet.

Au Québec, l'École sociale populaire consacre dès 1945 une brochure à la *Réforme de l'entreprise*, qui fait état de l'expérience de patrons chrétiens en Europe.[79] Mais c'est véritablement avec les journées sacerdotales organisées par la Commission sacerdotale en avril 1947 que l'idée se répand. Le *Bulletin des relations industrielles* lui consacre plusieurs articles à partir du numéro de novembre 1947 jusqu'à juin 1948; ils sont de la plume des abbés Paul-Émile Bolté, professeur à la Faculté de théologie de l'Université de Montréal et Marcel Clément, professeur à la Faculté de sciences sociales de l'université Laval. Le *Bulletin*, dirigé l'abbé Gérard Dion, est publié par le département de relations industrielles de

[74]Jean-Yves Calvez, *L'économie, l'homme, la société. L'enseignement social de l'Église* (Paris 1989), 160.

[75]Gustave Desbuquois et Pierre Bigo, *Les réformes de l'entreprise et la pensée chrétienne* (Paris 1945), 23.

[76]Voir la bibliographie sommaire de Paul-Émile Bolté et Gérard Dion dans *L'Actualité économique*, janvier-mars 1950, 728-736, 762-766, et Jean Sexton, *La CTCC-CSN: du corporatisme à la réforme de l'entreprise*, 1969, 97-9.

[77]Alexandre Dubois, *Structures nouvelles dans l'entreprise* (Paris 1946), 94.

[78]Calvez, *L'économie, l'homme, la société*, 158; *Le Pape et la cogestion*, brochure de l'Institut social populaire, no 440 (Montréal 1951) 13.

[79]*Réforme de l'entreprise*, brochure de l'École sociale populaire, 379 (Montréal 1945), 30.

l'université Laval dont il est le directeur. Ces textes traduits aussi en anglais sont réunis en une brochure bilingue diffusée en 1949, la même année où paraît *La participation des travailleurs à la vie de l'entreprise*. Enfin, un autre bulletin, *Ad Usum sacerdotum*, toujours dirigé par l'abbé Dion et destiné aux aumôniers syndicaux et patronaux, publie aussi plusieurs textes favorables à la cogestion dans les entreprises de 1948 à 1950.

L'influence de ces textes se fait rapidement sentir sur l'enseignement épiscopal. En 1948, Mgr Melancon, évêque de Chicoutimi, en reprend l'idée dans une lettre pastorale,

Les sociologues et les économistes constatent que le simple régime de salariat n'entretient pas assez chez l'ouvrier le souci du travail compétent et honnête, ne cultive pas une équitable distribution des profits de l'entreprise. Le Capital et le Travail trouveront grand avantage à faire évoluer leurs relations dans le sens de l'association, c'est-à-dire vers une participation plus effective des travailleurs à la vie de l'entreprise, à sa gestion et aux profits qui en résultent.[80]

Mais plus encore, deux ans plus tard, c'est l'ensemble de l'épiscopat qui approuve le projet dans sa lettre pastorale collective sur le travail et la doctrine sociale de l'Église, intitulée *Le problème ouvrier en regard de la doctrine sociale de l'Église*. La lettre en gestation depuis le début de 1949 (avant la grève de l'amiante) est issue de textes dont a confié la rédaction à des membres de la Commission sacerdotale d'études sociales. Ils vont évidemment y intégrer leur préoccupation pour la réforme de l'entreprise, présentée comme un moyen de favoriser la collaboration entre le capital et le travail en évitant la poursuite de profits abusifs pour l'entreprise et en favorisant le travail honnête et compétent de la part des travailleurs. La grande entreprise notamment est invitée à faire participer "les travailleurs organisés (...) à la gestion, aux profits et à la propriété de l'entreprise."

Cependant, des balises importantes sont fixées à ces réformes dans la dernière version de la lettre à laquelle les membres de la Commission n'ont pas participé.[81] On attache des bémols au projet qui doit "sauvegarder les droits légitimes des propriétaires des biens de production" et respecter le caractère d'ordre juridique privé de l'entreprise.[82] Le document accorde une place aussi importante à l'organisation corporative, "couronnement naturel" de l'économie nationale où les travailleurs par leurs syndicats "assumeront leur part de responsabilité dans la bonne ordonnance de la profession."[83] Pour ces deux réformes, la lettre appelle à des

[80]Mgr Melancon, évêque de Chicoutimi, *Le Sens Social* (1er mars 1948), dans Paul Paul-Émile Bolté et Gérard Dion, *L'Actualité économique*, janvier-mars 1950, 730.
[81]Cousineau, *L'Église d'ici*, 117.
[82]Lettre pastorale collective de Leurs Excellences Nosseigneurs les Archevêques et Évêques de la province civile de Québec, *Le problème ouvrier en regard de la doctrine sociale de l'Église* (Montréal 1950), 27.
[83]*Le problème ouvrier*, 28-9.

applications prudentes tout en mettant en garde les chefs d'entreprise qu'ils sont "dans l'erreur" si, au nom "d'une conception absolutiste de la propriété," ils ne veulent pas "partager certaines de leurs responsabilités avec les travailleurs."[84] La lettre, tout juste rendue publique après la grève de l'amiante, a des répercussions considérables et confirme, du moins pendant un certain temps, que le projet de réforme de l'entreprise bénéficie de l'aval de l'épiscopat.

En 1949, la Commission sacerdotale est impliquée dans deux autres dossiers qui ont eu de fortes incidences. Durant la grève de l'amiante, comme nous l'avons fait remarquer, c'est elle qui presse les évêques à appuyer l'organisation d'une collecte pour aider les familles des grévistes.[85] Trois de ses membres ont rédigé la déclaration rendue publique invitant les associations catholiques à collaborer avec les autorités religieuses pour en faire un succès. C'est deux jours après cette annonce que Mgr Charbonneau de Montréal fait sa célèbre déclaration jugeant qu'Il y a "complot pour détruire la classe ouvrière" et que l'Église se doit d'intervenir. Il ordonne alors des quêtes en faveur des grévistes aux portes des églises chaque dimanche jusqu'à la fin du conflit. La présence de la Commission s'était également fait sentir quelques mois plus tôt auprès du gouvernement et des députés lors de la présentation du projet de loi no 5, intitulé Code du travail, dénoncé en front commun par les centrales syndicales. Le mémoire de la Commission rendue publique "regrettait" que le projet de loi "ne rencontre pas toutes les exigences actuelles de la justice sociale."[86] Le journal Le Devoir titrait à la une que la Commission condamnait le projet de loi qui est retiré quelques jours plus tard. Dans ces deux dossiers, le gouvernement Duplessis est fortement outré de ces interventions publiques qui laissent croire que l'épiscopat désapprouve les politiques gouverne-mentales.

Attachons-nous maintenant à décrire plus précisément le sens et la portée donnés par ces clercs à la réforme de l'entreprise.[87] À la base de leur raisonnement, ils empruntent au corporatisme l'idée de communauté qu'ils attribuent non plus à la profession mais à l'entreprise. À leurs yeux, le droit de propriété des détenteurs des biens de production, notamment dans la grande entreprise capitaliste, n'est pas absolu: il comprend un aspect social qui impose des limites à l'exercice du droit individuel. On ne remet pas en question le régime de propriété privée, ni la recherche du profit, mais on estime que les travailleurs ont droit au partage des

---

[84]*Le problème ouvrier*, 29.

[85]Cousineau, *L'Église d'ici*, 101-8.

[86]Cousineau, *L'Église d'ici*, 83-8.

[87]Nous nous inspirons des brochures suivantes: Commission sacerdotale d'études sociales, *La participation des travailleurs*, 45; Paul-Émile Bolté, Marcel Clément et Gérard Dion, *Réformes de structure dans l'entreprise* (Québec 1949) 112; Paul-Émile Bolté et Gérard Dion, "La morale et la participation des travailleurs aux bénéfices," *L'Actualité économique* (janvier-mars 1950), 667-766; Émile Bouvier, *Patrons et ouvriers* (Université de Montréal 1951), 161-89.

fruits de l'entreprise. Tel qu'il fonctionne, le système capitaliste aurait trop tendance à mettre les personnes au service de l'argent et du profit et à devenir de simples facteurs de production assimilés aux marchandises et soumis aux lois de l'offre et de la demande. La conception chrétienne de la vie économique voudrait au contraire que l'entreprise soit au service de la communauté et des personnes qui y travaillent. Limiter la rémunération des travailleurs aux seuls salaires qu'ils retirent de leur labeur n'est pas la formule idéale car elle favorise l'injustice et l'antagonisme de classe tout en les rendant peu intéressés à la vie de l'entreprise et peu soucieux de leur compétence et de leur travail. Une conception de la vie industrielle plus conforme à la doctrine sociale de l'Église voudrait que les travailleurs aient droit à la participation aux bénéfices, à la gestion et à la propriété de l'entreprise. "Dans la mesure, écrit Marcel Clément, où le capital et le travail font partie d'une même communauté, il convient que les fruits de leur effort soient répartis entre les deux."[88]

Le droit de participation des travailleurs aux bénéfices de l'entreprise ne porte que sur les bénéfices résiduels de l'entreprise une fois que les salaires leur ont été versés et que les propriétaires de capitaux ont été rémunérés selon le risque couru. Les travailleurs ont alors le choix: ils peuvent se contenter de leur salaire forfaitaire ou réclamer qu'une partie de leur rémunération leur soit versée à titre de partage des bénéfices. Toujours parce que l'entreprise résulte d'une association entre le capital et le travail, on favorise aussi la cogestion, mais de manière prudente et progressive, soit sous une forme consultative ou délibérative. Pour mettre en place la formule, on réserve un rôle important aux syndicats qui apparaissent le meilleur agent pour représenter les travailleurs. Enfin, il est allégué que les travailleurs ont droit à une partie de propriété de l'entreprise qui ne s'applique pas cependant au capital initial de l'entreprise, mais à l'accroissement de son actif. Il faut alors qu'il y ait eu entente entre les parties à ce propos ou que les travailleurs n'aient pas reçu une juste rémunération ou une part légitime de la croissance de l'actif de l'entreprise. On invite donc les employeurs à se défaire d'une conception étroite de l'entreprise qui ne vise qu'au profit pour s'inspirer d'une conception chrétienne qui humanise son fonctionnement et respecte sa nature sociale.

Les abbés Bolté et Dion jugent même qu'il y a "obligation morale" pour les patrons comme pour les travailleurs de chercher à réaliser la réforme de l'entreprise et que ce sont normalement les syndicats qui devraient se charger d'en répandre l'idée parmi les travailleurs. Ils laissent aussi entendre que la négociation de convention collective serait un très bon moyen de réaliser cet objectif tout en précisant qu'il ne peut être imposé unilatéralement par l'employeur ou les travailleurs.[89] Ce discours va évidemment provoquer des remous tant du côté des syndicats que du patronat et même dans les rangs des membres de la Commission sacerdotale.

[88]Marcel Clément, "Les problèmes qui se posent," dans Bolté, Clément et Dion, *La morale et la participation*, 66.
[89]Bolté, Clément et Dion, *La morale et la participation*, 750-58.

D- *La réforme de l'entreprise dans la tourmente*

Les syndicats affiliés à la CTCC se sentent évidemment interpelés par le projet, eux qui tirent leur orientation de la doctrine sociale de l'Église. À l'été 1948, les congrès de deux fédérations, celles des travailleurs de la pulpe et du papier et des employés de l'industrie minière dont le président est Rodolphe Hamel, se donnent comme objectif de réclamer la participation aux bénéfices des employeurs.[90] Au congrès de la CTCC qui suit, en septembre, la Fédération de la pulpe et papier de même que le Conseil central de Shawinigan font adopter une résolution demandant à ce que la CTCC "prépare un programme pour assurer aux travailleurs une participation efficace à la gestion des entreprises et un partage équilibré des bénéfices." On invite de plus le Bureau de recherche de la centrale à recueillir tous les renseignements utiles sur le sujet.[91] Comme nous l'avons montré, quelques mois plus tôt, la Fédération des employés de l'industrie minière réussissait, après quelques jours de grève, à obtenir une clause dans les conventions collectives des compagnies de Thetford obligeant les employeurs à soumettre aux syndicats les cas de promotion, transfert et congédiement. En décembre 1948, Jean Marchand en défend l'idée lors de la première rencontre avec les négociateurs de la Canadian Johns-Manville qui y voient une réclamation révolutionnaire. En réponse, ils insistent alors pour faire ajouter à la convention une clause protégeant le droit de gérance de la compagnie.

Comme nous l'avons vu, les accusations de Lewis H. Brown pendant la grève voulant que le syndicat veuillent s'arroger le contrôle de son entreprise vont rendre les dirigeants de la fédération et de la CTCC beaucoup plus prudents lorsqu'il est question de réforme de l'entreprise. Rodolphe Hamel et Jean Marchand réfutent l'accusation que cette revendication soit importante pour les syndicats. Au congrès de la CTCC en septembre 1949, le président Gérard Picard dans son rapport annuel réserve plusieurs pages à critiquer la nouvelle tendance du patronat à "établir une nouvelle ligne de défense des droits de la direction."[92] Faisant allusion à l'ouvrage de Bolté, Clément et Dion sur la réforme de l'entreprise,[93] il ne va pas plus loin que de dire que le patronat doit faire des efforts pour mieux comprendre ce que sont les droits de direction dans l'entreprise moderne. Dans son rapport de 1951, il revient sur la question déplorant que la voie de la cogestion soit peu avancée au Québec contrairement à d'autres pays et que le patronat y soit violemment opposé.[94] À titre d'exemple, il rappelle la grève de l'amiante de 1949 et celles aussi du textile en

[90]CTCC, *Procès-verbal du congrès*, 1948, 299; *Le Travail* (septembre 1948), 12. Il est probable que des aumôniers en aient diffusé l'idée parmi les syndiqués. C'est le cas de l'abbé Pichette, membre de la CSES, dans une conférence prononcée devant une centaine de délégués syndicalistes à Sherbrooke au début de 1950, *Le Travail* (mars 1950), 9.

[91]CTCC, *Procès-verbal du congrès*, 1948, 226; *La Presse* (23 septembre 1948), 3.

[92]CTCC, *Procès-verbal du congrès*, 1949, 47-54.

[93]La lecture du volume est recommandée dans l'organe de la CTCC, *Le Travail* (novembre 1949), 3.

[94]CTCC, *Procès-verbal du congrès*, 1951, 36.

1947 et de l'aluminium en 1951 où les patrons ont fortement réagi à cette idée.[95] Cependant, l'aversion du patronat n'empêche pas la centrale d'inclure le projet de réforme de l'entreprise dans sa nouvelle déclaration de principes adoptée en préambule de sa constitution en 1951: "Dans l'entreprise, les travailleurs doivent être considérés comme des coopérateurs participant à une oeuvre commune. Ils doivent s'y sentir intégrés et participer à sa gestion et à ses bénéfices."[96] Mais c'est le chant du cygne du projet de réformer l'entreprise par la participation des travailleurs. La direction de la centrale n'y fait plus allusion par la suite et ses syndicats abandonnent l'idée d'en faire la réclamation lors de la négociation de conventions collectives.

Pendant la grève de l'amiante, l'opposition patronale au projet ne s'est pas manifestée que du coté des entreprises minières. L'Association professionnelle des industriels (API), organisation fondée en 1943 sous la gouverne du père Émile Bouvier et de l'industriel Eugène Gibeau, s'est sentie directement concernée par la résistance des compagnies minières à intégrer davantage les syndicats à la gestion de l'entreprise. En 1949, elle compte 345 membres avec des succursales à Montréal, Québec, en Mauricie, au Saguenay et dans la région des Bois-Francs.[97] Dès le début de 1948, la nouvelle interprétation que la Commission sacerdotale d'études sociales veut donner au rôle des travailleurs dans l'entreprise lui apparaisse particulièrement menaçante. Née pour diffuser chez les patrons la doctrine sociale de l'Église, l'API accepte très mal que des clercs veuillent leur faire obligation d'associer les travailleurs à la gestion et au bénéfice de leur entreprise. Cette question devient un sujet majeur d'appréhension de 1948 à 1950, années où elle s'inquiète aussi des grèves trop nombreuses et de la radicalisation de la CTCC.

Au printemps 1948, le directeur général de l'organisation, J.-G. Lamontagne, rencontre Mgr Leclaire, président de la Commission sacerdotales, quelques évêques et même le délégué apostolique à Ottawa pour faire valoir l'opposition de l'organisme.[98] On présente aussi à l'Assemblée des évêques du Québec un mémoire où on se dit d'accord pour accorder aux ouvriers une "collaboration active à l'entreprise", mais avec voix consultative uniquement. Quant à la participation aux bénéfices, on y est aussi favorable, mais sous "une sage et prudente formule d'intéressement par laquelle le patron accorde volontairement par équité à ses employés une certaine participation aux bénéfices." La lettre précise enfin que

[95]À Shawinigan, il semble bien que le syndicat cherche alors à obtenir l'arbitrage des griefs tel qu'obtenu par les syndicats de Thetford Mines en 1948 *Le Devoir*, 21 septembre 1951.
[96]CTCC, *Procès-verbal du congrès*, 1951, 217.
[97]On trouve un historique des premières années de l'API dans Yvan Senecal, *L'Association professionnelle des industriels ou une association patronale chrétienne dans l'industrie*, mémoire de maîtrise (relations industrielles), Université de Montréal, 1954, 222.
[98]*Réunions du Conseil d'administration* de l'API, 17 mars, 23 mai, 24 août 1948, Archives de l'Université du Québec à Montréal (AUQAM), Fonds du Centre des dirigeants des entreprises (CDE), no 43P-103A/001.

l'association rejette "les prétentions de l'École française avancée qui réclame pour les ouvriers un droit strict au partage des bénéfices, à la co-gestion délibérative et à la co-propriété des entreprises."[99] Toujours en 1948, une délégation qui participe au Congrès des associations patronales chrétiennes en profite pour remettre au pape un mémoire sur le sujet.[100]

Il est probable que le père Bouvier, qui est aumônier de l'API et membre de la Commission sacerdotale d'études sociales, ait participé à la rédaction de ces mémoires, dont les arguments rejoignent sa pensée. Ce dernier, qui aussi directeur-fondateur de la section des relations industrielles de l'Université de Montréal, prend donc ses distances envers l'interprétation que donne les autres membres de la Commission sacerdotale à la réforme de l'entreprise. Pour lui, comme le pape n'a pas encore formulé clairement ses directives, il peut se permettre d'interpréter son enseignement dans un sens plus favorable aux patrons. Les travailleurs n'auraient ainsi qu'une voix consultative et non délibérative dans la gestion de l'entreprise, ne disposant pas non plus d'un droit strict aux bénéfices car les salaires qu'ils reçoivent dégagent les employeurs de cette obligation.[101] Il n'y a donc pas obligation morale pour ces derniers à intégrer les travailleurs à la vie de l'entreprise. Dans un article de l'Actualité économique publié au début de 1949, il voit dans les prises de position de ceux qui défendent une intégration poussée des travailleurs à la vie de l'entreprise l'effet du socialisme chez les "catholiques de gauche" qui "transforment la nature de la propriété des instruments de production pour en faire un régime communautaire au service du prolétariat, plutôt qu'une institution qui, réformée, favorise une meilleure collaboration entre le capital et le travail."[102]

La grève de l'amiante en 1949 renforce encore davantage la détermination de la direction de l'API à combattre les principes de la réforme de l'entreprise d'autant plus qu'elle sait que les évêques préparent une lettre pastorale sur le problème ouvrier. C'est pourquoi elle convoque une réunion d'urgence à Montréal le 11 avril 1949 afin que les industriels du Québec "étudient ensemble les moyens de sauver l'entreprise privée et assurer la paix et l'ordre dans la société."[103] Plus de trois cents membres assistent à la réunion. Dans son discours d'introduction, Jean-Louis Héon,

[99]Mémoire confidentiel du Conseil d'administration de l'API à Leurs Excellences Nos Seigneurs les Archevêques et Évêques de la Province de Québec (non daté), dans Historique de l'API (sans nom d'auteur; il s'agit probablement d'Émile Bouvier), AUQAM, Fonds du CDE, Microfilm du Fonds Émile Bouvier en rapport avec l'API.
[100]Réunion du Conseil d'administration de l'API, 10 juin 1949, AUQM, Fonds du CDE, no 43P-103A/001.
[101]Émile Bouvier, "La co-gestion des entreprises," L'Actualité économique, octobre 1947, 403-420; Bouvier, Patrons et ouvriers, 161-76.
[102]Émile Bouvier, "Les méfaits du socialisme," L'Actualité économique (janvier-mars 1949) 627.
[103]Tirons Franc, (avril 1949), 9. Voir au sujet de cette rencontre Gérard Dion, "La grève de l'amiante: trente ans après," Mémoires de la Société royale du Canada, tome XVII, 1979, 36-7.

administrateur de l'organisme, s'inquiète des critiques dont l'entreprise privée est l'objet, critiques provenant notamment des syndicats qui s'enhardissent à réclamer la co-propriété des moyens de production et la participation à la gestion. Il appelle à la solidarité des employeurs pour se protéger "contre la vague montante et de plus en plus menaçante du socialisme communisant."[104] Des résolutions sont adoptées à l'unanimité par les congressistes qui, sans référer directement à la grève de l'amiante, visent, en fait, à soutenir le gouvernement et les compagnies dans le conflit. Elles demandent qu'aucune grève ne puisse être votée avant l'expiration des délais prévus par la loi, que les syndicats soient entièrement responsables de leurs actes en cas d'atteinte à la propriété, qu'ils perdent leur certificat de reconnaissance syndicale s'ils déclenchent une grève illégale, que la loi interdise les grèves qui ne respectent pas la liberté de travail, qu'il est inopportun d'accepter la clause d'atelier syndical fermé (formule Rand), etc.[105] La réunion se termine par une conférence de Thomas Lhoest, un patron belge, sur le respect dû à l'autorité du chef d'entreprise et sur le danger des "solutions de gauche" que représente la participation des travailleurs aux bénéfices et à la gestion des entreprises.[106] À nul moment pendant la réunion, du moins publiquement, il n'est question cependant de la Commission sacerdotale qui diffuse la théorie de la réforme de l'entreprise, ni des syndicats catholiques qui commencent à s'en imprégner.

Cette réunion a plusieurs conséquences importantes. C'est dix jours plus tard, le 21 avril, que le président Lewis H. Brown signe une pleine page d'annonce dans les quotidiens québécois reprochant aux dirigeants syndicaux impliqués dans la grève de l'amiante de propager une doctrine révolutionnaire en voulant s'approprier "une part d'autorité et de contrôle sur l'administration" de la compagnie. Depuis le déclenchement de la grève, la compagnie ne faisait plus référence à cet enjeu que ce soit dans le communiqué de la CJM remis aux lendemains du débrayage, dans la lettre du 2 mars expédiée aux ouvriers pour qu'ils retournent au travail, dans la publicité parue dans les journaux le 19 mars et dans le communiqué aux employés du 24 mars.[107] D'autre part, dans le document de mai 1949 où le président Brown met en relief les enjeux du conflit, il cite abondamment l'encyclique *Quadragesimo Anno*, lecture peu commune chez un président de compagnie américaine. On peut en déduire que des employeurs québécois (peut-être la direction de l'API) lui ont souligné le lien entre les revendications initiales du syndicat demandant qu'on lui soumette les promotions et le projet alors en vogue de réforme de l'entreprise. Il n'est pas exclu non plus que la réunion d'urgence de l'API l'ait sensibilisé, lui ou ses représentants au Québec, à mettre l'accent sur cette dimension du conflit.

---

[104]Voir le compte rendu de la réunion qu'en fait l'abbé Dion dans *Ad Usum Sacerdotum*, avril 1949, 76-7 (Archives de l'université Laval, P117/D1/12.1).

[105]*Tirons Franc* (avril 1949), 3; *Le Devoir* (12 avril 1949), 10.

[106]*Le Devoir* (12 avril 1949), 2; *Tirons Franc* (avril 1949), 4-5.

[107]*La Tribune* (17 février 1949), 3; (19 mars 1949), 5; *L'Asbestos* (4 mars, 1er avril 1949).

La réunion d'urgence du 11 avril a aussi une conséquence grave pour le père Bouvier qui conséquence grave pour le père Bouvier qui, pendant l'assemblée piénière à huis-clos, aurait présenté la grève de l'amiante comme un "cas-type" où la *Canadian Johns-Manville* ne devait pas céder et aurait "parlé du glissement à gauche des évêques qui le forcent à démissionner de ses fonctions d'aumônier de l'API.[108] La décision est prise le 3 mai par l'Assemblée des évêques du Québec qui lui reproche "ses indiscrétions et son manque de collaboration," refusant notamment "d'admettre la co-gérance et les co-bénéfices" comme le désirent les évêques du Québec.[109] L'auxiliaire du Provincial des Jésuites (Socius) a beau faire valoir que "la doctrine de la co-gérance n'est pas encore si claire dans l'Église,"[110] rien n'y fait, le père Bouvier est démis de ses fonctions, en même temps qu'il se retire de la Commission sacerdotale d'études sociales. Les évêques n'apprécient pas l'enseignement qu'il dispense auprès du patronat sur ce sujet et ils s'inquiètent de la tendance manifestée par la réunion du 11 avril, de transformer "un mouvement de formation patronale qu'elle était à l'origine" en "un syndicat de résistance en visant à opposer la force patronale à la force ouvrière."[111] Il est plausible que les autres membres de la Commission sacerdotale, Mgrs Leclaire et Garant, le père Cousineau et l'abbé Dion aient eu un rôle important à jouer dans cette décision grâce à leur influence sur les évêques. Dans sa lettre à Mgr Douville, le père Bouvier dit s'incliner "respectueusement et aveuglément devant cette volonté comme étant l'expression même de celle de Dieu," "sans comprendre toutefois les motifs de cette grave décision, sans connaître au juste les faits qui l'ont déterminée et sans avoir été au préalable averti de quoi que ce soit."[112] Victime d'une Église encore très autoritaire, le père Bouvier démissionne officiellement pour raison de santé.

---

[108]Selon l'abbé Gérard Dion, le père Bouvier était "conseiller de la *Canadian Johns-Manville*." Il aurait dit aux patrons, en parlant des grévistes "Écrasez-les!" (Entrevue donnée à Michel Sarra-Boumet en 1993, dans Michel Sarra-Bournet, *Entre le corporatisme et le libéralisme: les groupes d'affaires francophones et l'organisation socio-politique du Québec de 1943 à 1969*, thèse de Ph.D. en histoire, Universitè d'Ottawa, 1995, 125).

[109]Extrait du procès-verbal de l'Assemblée épiscopale de la province de Québec, 3 mai 1949; lettre de J. Iv. D'Orsonnens au révérend Père Léon Pouliot, provincial de la Compagnie de Jésus, 9 mai 1949; lettre du Père Pouliot à Mgr Arthur Douville, secrétaire de l'Assemblée des évêques, 22 mai 1949; dans *Historique de l'API*, AUQM, Fonds du CDE, Microfilm du Fonds Émile Bouvier en rapport avec l'API.

[110]Lettre de J. Iv. d'Orsonnens, s.j., Socius du Provincial, à Mgr Douville, évêque de Saint-Hyacinthe, 22 mai 1949, dans *Historique de l'API*, AUQM, Fonds du CDE, Microfilm du Fonds Émile Bouvier en rapport avec l'API.

[111]*Mémoire présenté au nom du Conseil d'administration de la régionale de Québec à la réunion spéciale du 15 décembre 1949, convoquée par le président général de l'Association*, 15 décembre 1949, AUQAM, Fonds du CDE, 43P-203h/2.

[112]Lettre de Émile Bouvier à Mgr Douville, 10 juin 1949, *Historique de l'API*, AUQM, Fonds du CDE, Microfilm du Fonds Émile Bouvier en rapport avec l'API.

La direction de l'API proteste énergiquement, ayant pleinement confiance dans son aumônier, et elle refuse son remplaçant, nul autre que l'abbé Paul-Émile Bolté, un membre de la Commission sacerdotale qui a des vues orthodoxes sur la réforme de l'entreprise.[113] La résistance de la direction de l'API ne fait pas l'affaire de la section de Québec, dont l'abbé Dion est aumônier. Au début de 1950, cette section quitte l'organisation pour fonder un groupe patronal dissident, le Centre des industriels chrétiens. Plusieurs raisons sont évoquées, dont la transformation de l'API en organisme antisyndical et sa décision de ne pas accepter le nouvel aumônier désigné par les évêques.[114] La décision de limoger l'aumônier cause beaucoup de mécontentement parmi les membres de l'API dont plusieurs abandonnent l'organisation. Finalement, en février 1950, le père Bouvier redevient aumônier, non pas de l'API dans son ensemble, mais de la section montréalaise uniquement. Mais pas pour longtemps.

Il se sent concerné par un autre conflit qui surgit entre la direction de l'API et le clergé de Québec en janvier 1950. On reproche au directeur général de l'API, J.-G. Lamontagne, de ne pas avoir fait état, dans l'organe de l'API, *Tirons Franc*, de la présence et du contenu de l'allocution de Mgr Roy, archevêque de Québec, lors du congrès de l'API à Québec en novembre 1949. L'archevêque y avait donné deux conseils aux patrons catholiques: "l'initiative sociale et la soumission aux directives de l'Église". En outre, une brochure publiée sous les auspices de l'API contenait un article de Thomas Lhoest "attaquant" Mgr Garant, évêque auxiliaire de Québec et membre de la Commission sacerdotale. Mgr Roy se serait senti "indigné".[115] Mgr Paul-Émile Léger, maintenant archevêque de Montréal en remplacement de Mgr Charbonneau, "démissionnaire", exige alors le limogeage de M. Lamontagne.[116] Le Conseil d'administration de l'API est divisé, mais la majorité s'y refuse, se contentant de modifier sa fonction de directeur général à secrétaire général.[117]

Cette seconde rebuffade de l'API envers les autorités religieuses place le père Bouvier dans une situation embarrassante. Il décide de démissionner comme

[113]Lettre de Eugène Gibeau, président de l'API, à Mgr Maurice Roy, archevêque de Québec, 10 décembre 1949, dans *Historique de l'API*, AUQM, Fonds du CDE, Microfilm du Fonds Émile Bouvier en rapport avec l'API.

[114]*Mémoire présenté au nom du Conseil d'administration de la régionale de Québec à la réunion spéciale du 15 décembre 1949, convoquée par le président général de l'Association*, 15 décembre 1949, AUQAM, Fonds du CDE, 43P-203h/2.

[115]*Bulletin des relations industrielles* (janvier 1949) 27; API, *Réformes de structure* (1949), 10; *Ad Usum Sacerdotum*, janvier 1950, 37-8, octobre 1951, 8; Téléphone de J,-M. Bureau à l'API, 13 janvier 1950, dans AUQM, Fonds du CDE, Microfilm du Fonds Émile Bouvier en rapport avec l'API.

[116]Entrevue du père Bouvier avec Eugène Gibeau, 13 novembre 1951, dans AUQAM, Fonds du CDE, Microfilm du Fonds Émile Bouvier en rapport avec l'API.

[117]*Réunion du Conseil d'administration de l'API*, 14 novembre 1951, AUQM, Fonds du CDE, no 43P-103A/002.

aumônier de la section montréalaise de l'API et de quitter aussi le poste de directeur et de professeur de la section des relations industrielles de l'Université de Montréal.[118] Pour éviter d'autres controverses, il obtient de son Supérieur un congé d'une année pour préparer un volume sur les relations industrielles. Pendant les années cinquante, il se tient éloigné du Québec, oeuvrant en Ontario et devenant en 1955 recteur de l'Université laurentienne de Sudbury. Le conflit entre l'API et l'épiscopat de 1948 à 1951 est révélateur de la forte influence exercée par les membres de la Commission sacerdotale sur les évêques et des tensions que la réforme de l'entreprise engendre dans la société québécoise.

Le débat va trouver un dénouement, non au Québec mais à Rome, car la lutte patronale contre le projet de réforme de l'entreprise ne se manifeste pas uniquement au niveau québécois. Outre l'API qui a fait parvenir un mémoire au pape au début de 1948, d'autres organisations patronales catholiques en Europe se sont élevées également contre l'interprétation voulant que le pape fasse de la cogestion de l'entreprise un droit naturel des travailleurs. Aussi, en mai 1949, au congrès international des patrons chrétiens, le pape Pie XII sent le besoin de préciser que "le propriétaire des moyens de production doit, toujours dans les limites du droit public de l'économie, rester maître de ses décisions économiques" et qu'on ne saurait concevoir l'entreprise selon les règles de la "justice distributive" où "tous les participants auraient droit à leur part de propriété ou tout au moins des bénéfices de l'entreprise". Il admet toutefois que l'entreprise "peut comporter" divers rapports personnels entre participants.[119] C'est un premier coup contre ceux qui voudraient que les employeurs aient une obligation morale à la cogestion. Ce texte inattendu du pape amène les évêques du Québec à nuancer davantage leur appui à la réforme de l'entreprise dans leur lettre pastorale sur le problème ouvrier de février 1950.[120]

En juin 1950, le pape précise à nouveau sa pensée en critiquant encore plus clairement la cogestion pour les salariés qui devient un "danger," un glissement vers une "mentalité socialiste," alors que "ni la nature du contrat de travail, ni la nature de l'entreprise ne comportent nécessairement par elles-mêmes un droit de

[118]*Entrevue chez M. Eugène Gibeau*, 14 novembre 1951, dans AUQM, Fonds du CDE, Microfilm du Fonds Émile Bouvier en rapport avec l'API. Le journal *Le Travail* de la CTCC allègue en 1951 que le père Bouvier est auteur d'un texte miméographié de 184 pages intitulé "*Recueil de documents - Sur la grève de l'amiante (1949) organisée par la Confédération des travailleurs chrétiens du Canada. À l'attention exclusive de MM. les membres du clergé*" (Rapport Custos). Cependant, rien n'est concluant sur l'identité de l'auteur. La thèse soutenue fait des dirigeants de la CTCC et des aumôniers compromis dans la grève des agents, conscients ou inconscients, du communisme. La thèse apparaît plutôt gauche *Le Travail*, 2 et 16 mars 1951; Trudeau, *La grève de l'amiante*, 259, 407-18.

[119]*Tirons Franc* (juin 1949), 2. Il semble que le débat au Québec ait influencé la décision de Pie XII de préciser sa pensée sur la réforme de l'entreprise lors de son allocution du 7 mai 1949. Bigo, *La doctrine sociale de l'Église*, 396.

[120]Cousineau, *L'Église d'ici*, 117.

cette sorte". Même s'il reconnaît l'utilité de différentes méthodes "pour ajuster le contrat de travail sur le contrat de société," il juge que "le droit de co-gestion économique, que l'on réclame, est hors du champ de ces possibles réalisations."[121] Il ferme donc presque complètement la porte ouverte par Pie XI dans *Quadragesimo Anno*. Non seulement la cogestion n'est-elle plus souhaitable, elle est même plus ou moins assimilée au socialisme. Revenant en 1952 sur le sujet, il confirme refuser "de déduire, soit directement ou indirectement, de la nature du contrat de travail, le droit de co-propriété de l'ouvrier au capital et partant son droit de co-gestion."[122] L'année suivante, l'évêque de Nicolet, Mgr Albertus Martin, décide de consulter le prosecrétaire du pape, Mgr J.B. Montini, sur le droit de cogestion, question qui est à nouveau soulevée à l'occasion des grèves chez Dupuis & Frères et parmi les tisserands de Louiseville. Ce dernier précise que "le syndicat n'a pas le droit de prétendre à s'intégrer d'une façon organique dans la marche même de l'entreprise en vue d'y réaliser la promotion ouvrière" et "qu'il ne peut être soutenu que les ouvriers ont un droit strict en raison de leur travail (...), en justice commutative, à une part du profit de l'entreprise, comme s'il fallait restituer à l'ouvrier une part de la 'plus value' que leur travail a produit."[123] Lévêque avise alors les membres de la Commission sacerdotale "qu'il verrait d'un très mauvais oeil" que ces derniers enseignent que les travailleurs ont un "droit strict à la plus-value" car cette notion n'est pas incluse dans l'enseignement pontifical. Il y voit l'utilisation de concepts dangereux empruntés au marxisme.[124]

Ces explications ont dû représenter une douche d'eau froide pour les membres de la Commission sacerdotale qui n'ont d'autre choix que d'abandonner la promotion de la réforme de l'entreprise. Le rôle de la Commission devient d'ailleurs plus discret à partir de 1951 et son influence sur les évêques beaucoup moins marquée. Avec l'arrivée de Mgr Paul-Émile Léger en 1950,[125] le conservatisme gagne l'Assemblée des évêques, moins intéressée à se mêler de conflits syndicaux, surtout après la commotion générée par la grève de l'amiante. Pour sa part, le directeur du journal *Le Devoir*, Gérard Filion, sympathique, en 1949, à une formule qui intègre le travailleur à l'entreprise comme voie entre le capitalisme et le communisme, devient plus réservé après l'allocution du pape de juin 1950.[126] Du coté de la CTCC,

[121]*Le Pape et la cogestion. Autour de l'allocution du 3 juin 1950*, brochure de l'Institut social populaire no 440, (Montréal195), 2.

[122]Message au Katholikentag autrichien, 14 septembre 1952, dans Calvez, *L'économie, l'homme, la société*, 161.

[123]Lettre de Mgr J.B. Montini, prosecrétaire du pape à Mgr Albertus Martin, 3 juillet 1953, AUL, Fonds Gérard Dion, P117/A5,7.

[124]Lettre de Mgr Albertus Martin aux membres de la Commission sacerdotale d'études sociales, 19 avril 1953, AUL, Fonds Gérard Dion, P117/A5, 11.

[125]Cousineau, *L'Église d'ici*, 35.

[126]*Le Devoir*, 7 et 14 mai 1949, 4;10 et 17 septembre 1949, 4; 15 octobre 1949, 4; 17 juin 1950, 4; 19 septembre 1950, 4; 23 juillet 1952, 4.

le projet de réforme de l'entreprise, après avoir été inscrit dans la constitution en 1951, ne constitue plus une revendication de la centrale ou de ses syndicats affiliés. Il faut attendre la fin des années soixante pour que la CTCC devenue CSN renoue avec l'objectif d'élargir le pouvoir des travailleurs dans l'entreprise. Bien que l'objectif s'apparente à la réforme de l'entreprise, l'inspiration intellectuelle vient alors d'une source bien différente de celle de la doctrine sociale de l'Église.

* * *

La grève de l'amiante est encore perçue dans la mémoire collective des Québécois comme le réveil de la classe ouvrière, une victoire syndicale et le début du Québec moderne. C'est un bon exemple de déformation historique où une interprétation mythique a transformé le sens d'un l'événement. Les instigateurs en sont les adversaires du régime Duplessis, artisans de la Révolution tranquille. Dans un premier temps, ils ont mis en relief le conflit dans les pages du journal *Le Devoir* qui y porte un intérêt considérable comparativement aux grèves antérieures et aux autres quotidiens. Il veut se porter à la défense de la classe ouvrière dont on prévoit qu'elle jouera un rôle social déterminant. Par la suite, en 1956, Pierre Elliott Trudeau et ses collaborateurs se chargent dans un volume d'en faire une représentation symbolisant l'entrée du Québec dans le monde moderne.

La grève ne marque pas l'éveil de la classe ouvrière au Québec car nombreux sont les conflits de travail avant 1949. Compte tenu des populations ouvrières respectives, la propension à la grève et la densité syndicale au Québec sont comparables à celles de l'Ontario depuis le début du siècle.[127] D'autre part, le conflit, loin de marquer une victoire des ouvriers, représente plutôt une défaite, le syndicat cédant sur la plupart de ses positions à mesure que la grève se prolonge. Le retour au travail s'effectue notamment sans que les briseurs de grève ne soient évincés et en soumettant le litige à un tribunal d'arbitrage, recours auquel les grévistes n'avaient pas confiance et qui a déterminé le déclenchement illégal de la grève. Finalement, le conflit n'annonce en rien le Québec moderne car l'Église catholique y joue un rôle de premier plan dans plusieurs phases du conflit. Le secours que les évêques, les associations catholiques et le clergé d'Asbestos apportent aux grévistes n'est pas négligeable et c'est l'intervention de Mgr Roy qui dénoue le conflit. "L'Épiscopat, écrit Jean Marchand, a sauvé notre mouvement d'un échec qui aurait pu être désastreux." Enfin, des clercs sont responsables des éléments touchant la réforme de l'entreprise parmi les réclamations syndicales.

Il est certain que la direction de la Canadian Johns-Manville lors de ses premières rencontres avec les négociateurs syndicaux en décembre 1948 est scan-

[127]Jacques Rouillard, "Vingt-cinq ans d'histoire du syndicalisme québécois. Quelques acquis de la recherche," dans *Érudition, humanisme et savoir. Actes du colloque en l'honneur de Jean Hamelin* (Québec 1996), 179-86. La recherche de Greg Kealey et Douglas Cruik-shank sur la propension à la grève au Canada arrive à la même conclusion ("Strikes in Canada, 1891-1950," *Labour/Le Travail*, 20 (automne 1987), 90-1, 120-2).

dalisée de la réclamation voulant que la compagnie soumette au syndicat les promotions, transferts et congédiements. Mais il ne semble pas que les négociateurs aient insisté car le conciliateur nommé par le gouvernement n'en fait pas mention dans son rapport de février 1949. Lorsque la grève est déclenchée, le syndicat fait passer au second plan cette revendication et se limite à réclamer seulement le droit de consultation. Durant les deux premiers mois de la grève, la partie patronale ne s'en offusque pas vraiment jusqu'à ce que le président Brown fasse paraître une pleine page dans les journaux accusant les dirigeants syndicaux de vouloir usurper les droits de la direction de sa compagnie. Il est fort probable que ce soit la publicité entourant la réunion organisée par l'API, le 11 avril 1949, qui le détermine à établir un lien entre les demandes syndicales et la réforme de l'entreprise. Il est possible que des membres de la direction de l'API lui ait mis la puce à l'oreille. Son insistance à réduire le conflit à la seule dimension de défense du droit de propriété vise à se gagner l'appui de l'opinion publique alors que le conflit s'enlise et que le syndicat marque des points en insistant sur les dangers de la poussière d'amiante. Pour plusieurs, la réclamation syndicale touchant les promotions peut apparaître excessive, d'autant plus qu'elle est nouvelle en contexte nord-américain. Pour le patronat québécois, les compagnies impliquées dans la grève (des multinationales) deviennent des boucliers qui protégeront les entreprises québécoises d'une usurpation syndicale du droit de gestion. Leur fermeté dans la grève sert également d'exemple: elle illustre le sort qui pourrait attendre d'autres syndicats tentés par de pareilles revendications.

Nous ne croyons pas que la réclamation syndicale visant à faire une plus grande place aux travailleurs dans la gestion de l'entreprise soit seule responsable de l'enlisement de la grève. D'autres enjeux sont également importants, notamment les augmentations salariales et la retenue syndicale obligatoire (formule Rand). En décembre1948, le salaire horaire moyen se situe à 1,00$ l'heure. La hausse demandée, 15 sous l'heure pour 1949, représente donc une augmentation de 15 % (l'inflation est de 14% en 1948, 3% en 1949).[128] Pour les compagnies, les hausses demandées ne sont pas négligeables quoiqu'elles soient en bonne posture financière, la demande d'amiante et la production étant en forte hausse au Canada depuis la Guerre (53% de 1945 à 1948).[129] Il est certain aussi que la formule Rand les inquiète car elle commence à peine à être réclamée au Canada dans les grandes entreprises manufacturières. Aux États-Unis, la loi Taft-Hartley la prohibe en 1947 et le gouvernement Duplessis s'applique à faire de même dans le projet de loi 5 qui est retiré au début de février 1949, tout juste avant la déclenchement de la grève des mineurs. Le contexte se prête donc éminemment à ce que les compagnies minières, des multinationales américaines, s'y opposent énergiquement.

[128]1949= 100.

[129]Ottawa, Bureau fédéral de la statistique, *The Asbestos Mining Industry* (26-205), 1953, 4. Voir Jean-Gérin Lajoie, "Histoire financière de l'industrie de l'amiante," dans Trudeau, *La Grève de l'amiante*, 115-121.

Comme on l'a vu, la Fédération nationale de l'industrie minière réclame dès l'automne 1947 un projet de convention identique pour toutes les entreprises minières qui comprend la formule Rand et un droit de regard du syndicat sur les promotions, transferts et renvois. Les compagnies sont réfractaires à ces demandes qu'elles trouvent radicales. Pour la CJM d'Asbestos, un règlement rapide lui permet d'éviter l'insertion de ces clauses dans la convention collective de 1948. La fédération a plus de succès à Thetford où un arrêt de travail de trois jours et un arbitrage rapide imposent aux compagnies les deux mesures. Selon le secrétaire de la fédération, Daniel Lessard, les conventions signées en 1948 représentent "une des plus avantageuses signées par les syndicats nationaux."[130]

À la veille des négociations pour le contrat de 1949, il est fort probable que les compagnies d'amiante se soient entendues pour se montrer fermes devant les demandes syndicales. Pour leur part, les syndiqués ont l'impression de pouvoir faire plier facilement les compagnies, quitte à déclencher une grève illégale comme cela leur a si bien réussi l'année précédente. Mais cette fois, les compagnies restent sur leur position après le débrayage illégal, laissant le soin au gouvernement du Québec de forcer les travailleurs à revenir au travail. L'embauche de briseurs de grève, des dommages causés aux biens des compagnies et des cadres molestés vont envenimer le conflit qui se prolonge parce que la CJM tient à conserver à son emploi les briseurs de grève et à ne pas réembaucher les grévistes sur qui pèsent des accusations civiles ou criminelles. Finalement, les syndicats de Thetford doivent se résoudre à l'arbitrage dont le rapport est plutôt désavantageux et à signer des conventions qui leur font perdre la formule Rand. L'entente finale avec la CJM est encore moins reluisante, la compagnie imposant un rôle encore plus limité du syndicat qu'à Thetford dans l'organisation du travail et la gestion de la main-d'oeuvre. Elle fait même ajouter à la convention un long paragraphe sur son droit de gérance. L'échec de la grève a aussi pour effet de faire perdre les illusions des dirigeants de la CTCC sur la possibilité d'appliquer des éléments de la réforme de l'entreprise au Québec.

Au niveau des principes, le coup de grâce donné à ce projet est venu de Rome en 1950, victime des représentations des organisations patronales catholiques, dont l'API au Québec. Le pape en juin 1950 ferme définitivement la porte ouverte par son prédécesseur en 1931 voulant que la participation à la gestion et aux profits soit des formules souhaitables de fonctionnement des entreprises. Dans l'année qui précède, il est remarquable de constater que les évêques du Québec se sont ralliés à tel point au projet qu'ils font grief à l'API et à son aumônier de le critiquer. Leur prise de position pendant la grève de l'amiante montre également qu'ils ont développé un penchant prosyndical assez marqué sous l'influence de la Commission sacerdotale d'études sociales. Mais Rome a le dernier mot et l'épiscopat se soumet. Le patronat québécois peut alors dormir sur ses deux oreilles. Dans une causerie en 1951, Jules-A. Brillant, conseiller législatif et homme d'affaires bien connu, rappelle que "seuls, les épargnants ont le droit de participer aux bénéfices

[130]CTCC, *Procès-verbal du congrès*, 1948, 303.

d'une entreprise" et que c'est "dilapider notre main d'oeuvre en lui faisant croire qu'elle a droit de participer aux bénéfices des entreprises sans effort et sans sacrifice de sa part, uniquement pour satisfaire à des plaisirs matériels."[131]

Je remercie Mélanie Ouellette et Maude Beausoleil pour l'aide apportée à cette recherche.

[131]*Le Devoir* (11 juin 1951), 10; (12 juin 1951), 3.

After Seattle:
A New Internationalism?

The protests against the World Trade Organization (WTO) in Seattle in November and December 1999 surprised people across the globe. Massive, militant actions took place in the United States, the stronghold of global capitalism, for the first time in decades. New alliances were built between labor and environmentalists, young and old, radicals and reformers. This special double issue of *Monthly Review* examines several facets of the movement that has seized the spotlight since Seattle and asks what is required for it to become truly internationalist. Articles cover a range of topics, including globalization; labor's role in the Seattle protests; a historical understanding of internationalism; and voices from the global South calling for unified strategies against capitalism.

Readers familiar with recent protests against international financial institutions and transnational corporations, including the ones against the International Monetary Fund (IMF) and the World Bank in April 2000, will find fresh analysis here and those who are new to the issues will discover clear, accessible approaches to some of the burning questions of our time. Written for a wide audience, this special issue of *Monthly Review* promises to be an invaluable resource for scholars as well as activists.

CONTENTS

Toward a New Internationalism
by the Editors

Marx and Internationalism
by John Bellamy Foster

The Language of Globalization
by Peter Marcuse

Turtles, Teamsters, and Capital's Designs by William K. Tabb

"Workers of All Countries, Unite"
by Michael Yates

The Future of the Labor Left
by Khalil Hassan

World Labor Needs Independence and Solidarity by David Bacon

Strategic Thinking About Movement Building by Martin Hart-Landsberg

Defunding the Fund, Running on the Bank by Patrick Bond

Where Was the Color in Seattle?
by Elizabeth (Betita) Martinez

Address to the South Summit
by Fidel Castro

TO ORDER
1-4 copies: $10 each / 5-24 copies-$8 each / postage: add $3 for 1-4 copies, $7 for 5-24 copies

MONTHLY REVIEW 122 West 27th Street, 10th floor, New York, NY 10001
www.monthlyreview.org/ toll-free 1-800-670-9499

THE NATIONAL QUESTION

Political Economy and the Canadian Working Class: Marxism or Nationalist Reformism?

Murray E.G. Smith

In our epoch, which is the epoch of imperialism, i.e., of *world* economy and *world* politics under the hegemony of finance capital, not a single communist party can establish its program by proceeding solely or mainly from conditions and tendencies of development in its own country. – Leon Trotsky, 1928[1]

Introduction

AS CANADIAN WORKING PEOPLE face the new millennium, anxiety about the future of the economy is pervasive, notwithstanding the economic buoyancy of the late 1990s. A counter-revolution of declining expectations amongst workers over the past two decades, in Canada as elsewhere, has coincided with a wide-ranging assault on working-class living standards and an erosion of economic security.[2] Since the mid-1970s, Canadian capitalism has weathered a malaise involving three severe recessions, historically slow growth rates, persistently high rates of unemployment, declining real wages, and wildly fluctuating rates of return on capital

[1] L. Trotsky, *The Third International After Lenin* (New York 1970), 3-4.

[2] The working class, on my definition, includes wage-labourers and some salary-earners who derive their income primarily through the sale of their labour-power either to private capital or the capitalist state. It includes skilled and unskilled as well as productive and unproductive wage earners. See M. Smith, *Invisible Leviathan: The Marxist Critique of Market Despotism beyond Postmodernism* (Toronto 1994), 195-200.

Murray E.G. Smith, "Political Economy and the Canadian Working Class: Marxism or Nationalist Reformism?," *Labour/Le Travail*, 46 (Fall 2000), 343-68.

investment. The response of Canadian big business and the state has been to demand that labour markets be made more "flexible," that social programs be sacrificed on the altar of deficit and debt reduction, that trade union rights be curtailed, that capital and trade be freed from "undue" regulation, and that the tax system be made more regressive. The upshot has been that the rate of exploitation of labour has been jacked up dramatically in order to restore the profitability and enhance the international competitive position of Canadian capital under the allegedly "new" conditions of economic and political "globalization."

Despite the palpable failure of Canadian capitalism to sustain the rising prosperity enjoyed by the working class in the 1950s and 1960s, and despite the recurring demands of capital and the state since the mid-1970s that workers tighten their belts in the interests of restoring economic stability, the "official" leadership of the Canadian working class — the trade union officialdom and the New Democratic Party — has maintained a steadfastly pro-capitalist outlook and policy. A decade after the demise of Soviet-bloc "actually existing socialism," the leadership of the Canadian labour movement, in both English Canada and Québec, is more remote than ever from advocating anti-capitalist social change. Indeed, its refusal to resist the capitalist ideological triumphalism of the last decade has contributed in no small measure to the popular perception that "there is no alternative" to actually existing capitalism or to the neo-liberal policies that have strengthened capital's hand against labour throughout the world. Debate within the mainstream of working-class politics has regressed to the question of how labour can preserve the gains of past struggles (many of which were inspired by an explicitly anti-capitalist world-view and strategic project) while at the same time submitting "responsibly" to the fundamental rules, values, and boundaries of liberal democratic capitalism.

The point of departure of this article is that a fundamental condition for the emergence in the next century of a labour movement capable of both defending and advancing the interests of the working class is the diffusion of an authentically Marxist account of the political economy and recurrent crisis tendencies of advanced capitalism.[3] Certainly, such a Marxist political economy must become a central part of the "conventional wisdom" of Canadian labour if its practice is to be fundamentally reoriented toward a struggle for workers' power and a socialist society. To be sure, the influence of an ostensibly *socialist* political economy, originating in left-academic circles in the 1960s, has long been felt within the organizations of Canadian labour. Its dominant form — associated with what has

---

[3]This article does not seek to provide an introduction to Marxist political economy or to elaborate at length on its applicability to Canada. A basic knowledge of Marxist economic theory on the part of the reader is assumed. My own interpretations of Marx's theories of value and capitalist crisis may be found in Smith, *Invisible Leviathan*, and M. Smith, "Productivity, Valorization and Crisis: Socially Necessary Unproductive Labor in Contemporary Capitalism," *Science & Society*, 57, 3 (Fall 1993), 262-93.

become known as the "New Canadian Political Economy" (NCPE) — is remote from the key ideas and concerns of Marx's *critique* of classical political economy and has served to divert attention from the class-struggle program of Marxist socialism in the direction of labour-reformism, "left-nationalism," and class-collaboration.[4] Far from arming labour with the theoretical tools required to advance the struggle for socialism and social justice, the NCPE has helped lead the labour movement into its current impasse.

My purpose here will not be to disparage the scholarly contributions of the NCPE or to deny that it has advanced our understanding of the historical development of capitalism in Canada; but it will be to suggest that the NCPE's major preoccupations constitute an obstacle to the elaboration of a class struggle socialist program for Canadian labour, and the need for a Marxist alternative to it. For just as there is an "internal" connection between the theoretical shibboleths of the NCPE and the "nationalist reformism" that has been its perennial programmatic upshot, so too is there an internal relationship between Marx's analysis of the fatal contradictions of capitalist production and the Marxist insistence upon working-class political independence, an internationalist perspective and a class-struggle program.

The Condition of the Working Class in Canada

At the end of the 20th century, the Canadian working class still occupies, in many ways, an enviable position within the structure of the world capitalist economy. Indeed, compared to the rapidly growing army of wage labourers in the semi-colonial world, Canadian workers enjoy what many would consider to be a *privileged* position. In comparison to workers in the United States, Canadian working people are substantially better organized at the trade union level and better able to project their power into the political arena. They enjoy an array of social programs that are superior to those found in the United States and comparable to those won by better-organized and more-powerful labour movements in Western Europe. Moreover, in comparison to the working class of other "late-developing" industrial capitalist countries, the Canadian working class has a high standard of living and a relatively low official unemployment rate.

Like working people in other regions of the advanced capitalist world, Canadian workers have not been immune to important changes in the capitalist mode of production or to the deteriorating performance of the world capitalist economy over

---

[4]The best-known of Marx's "economic" works all bore the title or subtitle "critique of political economy." See K. Marx, *Capital: A Critique of Political Economy, Volume One* (New York 1977); *A Contribution to the Critique of Political Economy* (Moscow 1970); *Grundrisse: Foundations of the Critique of Political Economy (Rough Draft)* (Harmondsworth, Middlesex 1973). See also footnote 43.

the past thirty years.[5] Within the industrialized core of the world economy (Japan excepted), a general shift of waged employment from manufacturing to the service sectors has occurred, and this has contributed to a slowdown in productivity growth as well as to the rapid expansion of a secondary labour market characterized by low wages and meagre benefits. In North America, waged employment in manufacturing declined by 3.18 per cent from 1974 to 1984 and by a further 7.04 per cent from 1984-93, while in Western Europe it fell by 19.6 per cent in the former period and by 6.3 per cent in the latter.[6] In Canada, the service producing segment of the labour force increased from 62 per cent of the total in 1971 to 73 per cent in 1997.[7]

On average, the growth of the real (inflation-adjusted) hourly wage in Canadian manufacturing was about 1.0 per cent per year from 1973 to 1993, slightly higher than the near 0 per cent registered in the United States.[8] The overall shift in employment from full-time manufacturing jobs to service sector jobs (both full-time and part-time) cancelled out any gains for the labour force as a whole. Reliable disaggregated data for hourly wage-earners in Canada are not available, but the average real compensation of waged (as distinct from salaried) employees almost certainly declined over this twenty-year period. (In the United States, real hourly wages in the private business economy as a whole fell by at least 12 per cent between 1973 and 1990 and saw no growth between 1990 and 1997.[9]) When one takes into consideration the cumulative effects of the shift of the tax burden away from corporations and towards workers (through regressive changes to the income tax as well as the proliferation of sales taxes), it is clear that the average *after-tax real wage* declined even more dramatically than did the nominal real wage.

There are many other indicators that Canadian working people have been working harder in return for less compensation since the 1970s. Average inflation-adjusted incomes for families and unattached individuals have been virtually stagnant for the past twenty years, while most working-class households have been contributing more labour to the economy.[10] The labour-force participation rate of

[5]For general surveys, see R. Brenner, "Uneven Development and the Long Downturn: The Advanced Capitalist Economies from Boom to Stagnation, 1950-1998," *New Left Review*, 229 (1998),1-264; and M. Webber and D. Rigby, *The Golden Age Illusion: Rethinking Postwar Capitalism* (New York 1996).

[6]Massimo De Angelis, "The Autonomy of the Economy and Globalization," unpublished manuscript, Winter 1996, 7, drawing on P. Knox and J. Agnew, *The Geography of the World Economy* (Harlow 1992).

[7]H. Dickinson, "Work and Unemployment as Social Issues," in B. Bolaria, ed., *Social Issues and Contradictions in Canadian Society* (Toronto 2000), 25.

[8]D. Gordon, *Fat and Mean: The Corporate Squeeze of Working Americans and the Myth of Managerial "Downsizing"* (New York 1996), 27-8.

[9]Brenner, "Uneven Development," 3.

[10]P. Urmetzer and N. Guppy, "Changing Income Inequality in Canada" in J. Curtis, E. Grabb and N. Guppy, eds., *Social Inequality in Canada,* 3rd Edition (Scarborough1999), 58.

women has increased substantially at least partially in response to the loss by many men of "family-wage" manufacturing jobs. As the number of households with two or even three bread-winners has increased, so too has the number of individuals who have been obliged to work at two or more part-time jobs in order to make ends meet. Moreover, as average household income has stagnated, the share of before-tax income going to the bottom 80 per cent of families and unattached individuals has declined from 58.2 per cent in 1981 to 55.6 per cent in 1996.[11] This suggests that most working-class and even many "middle-class" families have actually seen a decline in their before-tax incomes over the same period in which they have been compelled to increase the total number of hours they work, to give up a greater share of their nominal income in taxes, and to accept cutbacks in social programs like health care, unemployment insurance, education and social assistance.

Unemployment and underemployment have also been persistent features of the economic malaise that has confronted the Canadian working class. In every decade since the end of World War II, the average annual (official) unemployment rate has tended to increase. From 1945 to 1954, it stood at 2.9 per cent; from 1955 to 1964 at 5.5 per cent; from 1965 to 1974 at 5.5 per cent; from 1975 to 1984 at 8.7 per cent; and from 1985 to 1994 at close to 10 per cent.[12] Even in the closing years of the 1990s, during a phase of relatively rapid expansion of the Canadian economy, the official unemployment rate remained persistently within the 7.2 per cent to 9 per cent range. Bleak as this picture is, it tells only part of the story. Official unemployment statistics mask the true unemployment rate by ignoring those "discouraged workers" who are no longer counted as part of the labour force, as well as many "self-employed" workers who have been driven into non-lucrative sales and consulting activities after being laid off from waged or salaried employment. Adjusting for the falling labour force participation rate in the 1990s, the Canadian Auto Workers union estimated that Canada's true unemployment rate exceeded 13 per cent in every year between 1992 and 1997. In the same study the CAW documented a decline in the employment rate (the per centage of working-age Canadians actually employed at any given time) from 62.4 per cent in 1989 to 58.5 per cent in 1997, with the *full-time* employment rate falling below 50 per cent in 1997.[13]

Underemployment refers to a situation in which a worker seeking a permanent or full-time job is forced to settle for temporary or part-time employment. In 1994 only 58 per cent of Canada's workers held permanent, full-time jobs, while 42 per cent worked part-time or on a seasonal or temporary basis. Not all of the latter were "underemployed" as defined above, since many wanted part-time or temporary employment. Still, the number of full-time jobs has declined relative to the number

[11]Urmetzer and Guppy, "Changing Income Inequality," 59.

[12]Averages calculated from data provided by Statistics Canada.

[13]CAW, "The Jobs Crisis Continues," *Economic & Social Action*, 3,1 (Sept.1997), 2-3.

of people desiring full-time employment. Part time employment accounted for only 15 per cent of all jobs in the early 1980s, but increased to 20 per cent by 1997.

Self-employment is also an index of underemployment. Between 1991 and 1997 fully 60 per cent of all new jobs created in Canada were self-employed.[14] Not at all coincidentally, as the ranks of the self-employed were swelling, public-sector employment fell from 10.3 per cent of the labour force in 1989 to 8.8 per cent in 1997.

The over-all conclusion is unmistakable: *in the last quarter of the 20th century, the Canadian working class experienced a declining standard of living and an increasing measure of economic insecurity.* While this all too obvious fact is seldom acknowledged by "mainstream" economists, the declining fortunes of the Canadian working class is a fact of singular importance to the labour movement and to those broadly associated with the intellectual traditions of left-wing political economy. Yet in seeking to explain this erosion of "popular prosperity," both the labour officialdom and most Canadian political economists have tended to highlight issues that deflect attention away from the responsibility of *capitalism,* as a determinate economic system and "mode of production," for the declining fortunes of Canadian workers. Instead, they have drawn attention to a "corporate agenda," which has undermined Canadian economic sovereignty and compromised the capacity of the existing state apparatuses (both federal and provincial) to safeguard the interests of "Canadians." This way of understanding the economic problems facing the working class in advanced capitalist economies is characteristic of the nationalist and pro-capitalist bureaucratic leaderships of labour throughout the world, including the United States. What is perhaps unusual about the Canadian situation, however, is the degree to which many avowedly radical political economists speak the same language as the trade union bureaucracy: *the language of nationalist economic retrenchment.*

This has certainly been true for the NCPE, a school of thought that has rarely addressed the *crisis tendencies* of modern capitalism or the *class imperatives* animating Canadian capital's offensive against working-class living standards. The NCPE has rather concentrated its attention upon such issues as Canada's status within the world system, Canada-US relations, foreign ownership of Canadian industry, the "structure" of the Canadian capitalist class, "free trade," regional underdevelopment and inter-regional exchange imbalances, as well as other issues that lend themselves to a preoccupation with "national sovereignty," "state policy," or "corporate agendas." Even those political economists who have resisted the left nationalism that has characterized the NCPE have often felt obliged to address themselves to many of these same issues, with the result that the elaboration of a Marxist analysis of the real history of Canadian capitalism since World War II has been neglected.

[14]CAW, "The Jobs Crisis," 3.

In what follows, I shall review two very different ways of accounting for the erosion of popular prosperity that has occurred in Canada since the 1970s, one suggested by the proponents of the NCPE and another informed by Marx's law of the falling tendency of the average rate of profit. The NCPE, in keeping with its traditional theme of the victimization of Canada by stronger imperial powers, essentially views the economic malaise of the past twenty-five years as a product of US economic domination and the "continentalist" orientation of the leading fractions of the Canadian capitalist class. A Marxist analysis, to the contrary, sees this malaise as the result of an objective "law of motion" of capitalist production, one that is characteristic of advanced capitalism in general but which different national capitalist economies "manage" with different degrees of success. It is precisely the fact that tendencies toward capitalist crisis manifest themselves *unevenly* across the world economy that creates an opening for "nationalist" explanations of economic downturn. Viewed in this light, left-nationalist accounts of Canada's economic "victimization" by the United States are qualitatively no different than the arguments of the protectionist "Left" in the US (centred in the AFL-CIO bureaucracy), which depicts the American economy as a victim of the "unfair trading practices" of the Japanese and that deplores the relocation of manufacturing enterprises from "American soil" to low-wage regions in Mexico. Whether espoused by "America-first" demagogues or "socialist" political economists, however, such economic nationalism produces a substantially similar political agenda: one leading to class-collaboration and the erosion of international labour solidarity.

"Canadian" Political Economy versus Marxist Political Economy

Despite its occasionally Marxist verbiage, the New Canadian Political Economy has always been more indebted to the Canadian political economy tradition associated with Harold Innis and to "dependency theory" than to Karl Marx, just as it has always been far more interested in debates surrounding imperialism and more recently "globalization" than to the debates over Marxist *crisis theory* that characterized the revival of political economy in other advanced capitalist countries after the onset of the New Left radicalization of the 1960s. It is symptomatic that the comprehensive bibliography for a 1989 collection of articles on the NCPE contained only two references to Marx and none to V.I. Lenin, Paul Sweezy, Ernest Mandel, Paul Mattick, Joseph Gillman, Shane Mage, David Yaffe, Ben Fine, John Weeks, Anwar Shaikh, Michel Aglietta, Alain Lipietz, Makoto Itoh, or many other influential Marxist political economists writing on the dynamics and crisis tendencies of advanced capitalist societies.[15] Moreover, the narrow national parochialism of the volume is evidenced by the fact that even the leading exponents of the dependency school, to which the NCPE was heavily indebted, received only occa-

[15]See W. Clement and G. Williams, eds., *The New Canadian Political Economy* (Kingston, Montréal, London 1989).

sional mention: the bibliography contains only one reference each to Samir Amin, Arghiri Emmanuel, and Andre Gunder Frank. While a later collection consisting largely of articles from the journal *Studies in Political Economy — A Socialist Review* displayed a wider theoretical purview and sought explicitly to offer "a new way of thinking about the long-standing concerns of the NCPE," it is noteworthy that it too lacked a single contribution devoted to the crisis tendencies of capitalism in Canada from a Marxist perspective.[16] In view of this, it is hardly surprising that NCPE intellectuals have tended to attribute the erosion of popular prosperity in Canada over the past twenty-five years variously to foreign ownership of Canadian industry, to a "deindustrialization" process stemming from the weakness of indigenous Canadian industrial capital, to policies imposed by a Canadian state overly obeisant to American corporate power, or to plant closures occasioned by "free trade" with the United States and Mexico, but *not* to the "normal" dynamics, contradictions, and crisis tendencies of capital accumulation characteristic of a mature, advanced capitalist economy. The upshot has been that NCPE diagnoses have lent themselves not to Marxist-socialist programmatic conclusions, but to national-reformist ones.

As a distinct current within Canadian intellectual and political life the NCPE is most appropriately seen as the product of an historical intersection, beginning in the mid-1960s, of a rising tide of (English-Canadian) nationalism and an international radicalization inspired in large part by anti-imperialist struggles in the colonial and semi-colonial "Third World." As Canada celebrated the centennial of its confederation in 1967, there was growing alarm, extending across the political spectrum, concerning the increasing level of foreign (primarily US) ownership of the Canadian economy. At the same time that Liberal politicians like Walter Gordon and social-democratic academics like Mel Watkins were calling attention to the US "take-over" of Canadian industry, a growing number of young people were identifying with an international New Left that saw the struggle for human emancipation as being spear-headed by national liberation movements and social revolutions in Asia, Africa, and Latin America. Throughout the Third World, the struggle for national self-determination and against imperialist domination was seen as inextricably bound up with the struggle for socialism. To many, the Chinese, Cuban, and Vietnamese revolutions were inspiring examples of how national-democratic goals could be — and indeed needed to be — combined with a communist program of eradicating class division. Yet even where national liberation struggles being led by forces that eschewed "Marxist-Leninist" aims, socialism was almost always invoked as both the goal of the struggle and as the means to safeguarding and consolidating national sovereignty. Thus, an "Arab socialism" was espoused by Egypt's Nasser, Algeria's Ben-Bella, and Libya's Qadhafi; a made-in-India social-

[16]J. Jenson, R. Mahon and M. Bienefeld, eds., *Production, Space, Identity: Political Economy Faces the 21st Century* (Toronto 1993). Quoted line is from Rianne Mahon's introductory essay, 6.

ism was the avowed goal of Nehru's Congress government as its foreign policy tilted toward the Soviet Union; and in sub-Saharan Africa, Julius Nyerere and Kwame Nkruhma, as well as South Africa's African National Congress and the independence movements of Rhodesia/Zimbabwe, Angola, and Mozambique, all spoke the language of "African socialism."

Thirty to forty years on, we know that the term socialism had a great many different meanings in different national contexts, and that for many Third World nationalists "socialism" was at best a subordinate goal of the national liberation struggle and at worst an empty promise made to elicit working-class support (both domestically and internationally) for a "popular alliance" against foreign domination or, as in the case of Rhodesia and South Africa, white-settler colonialism. However, for most New Left activists of the 1960s and early 1970s, the *class* content of the various Third World "socialisms" was of little concern. Indeed, the prevailing assumption within the New Left was that the working class was no longer the most prominent agent of anti-capitalist social change, and that socialism was much more likely to be championed by peasants, intellectuals, students, oppressed nationalities or even the lumpenproletariat.

The proponents of the NCPE were undoubtedly influenced by this spirit of the times — and specifically by the association of national liberation and socialism as congruent and mutually reinforcing goals. The most important political movement associated with the NCPE was the left-nationalist Waffle current within the New Democratic Party, which later became the short-lived Movement for an Independent Socialist Canada after the Waffle's departure from the NDP in 1972. Following the demise of the MISC, the NCPE was kept alive by a diverse group of left-leaning academics, most of whom lacked any well-defined political affiliations or commitments but who associated themselves episodically with the NDP, the Council of Canadians, the Canadian Centre for Policy Alternatives, the Action Canada Network, and the Liberal Party.

Although the ultimate political destinations of most NCPE intellectuals suggests that the preponderant political thrust of the NCPE was nationalist rather than socialist, it should be stressed that many people associated with the Waffle and the MISC saw Canadian nationalism as simply a convenient *means* for making the case for a socialist transformation of Canadian society. They saw themselves as socialists first and foremost, and nationalism as a "strategy" for advancing the popular appeal of the socialist project. If capitalism meant growing ownership of the Canadian economy by US-based multinational corporations and a resulting cultural colonization of Canada by the United States, they reasoned, then perhaps those committed to an "independent Canada" could be persuaded of the need for "public ownership" of the commanding heights of the economy. Many Canadian leftists were also convinced that the struggle for socialism in Canada had to proceed through two distinct stages: a stage of repatriating Canadian industry (with the assistance of "progressive," nationalist elements of the Canadian bourgeoisie) and a later stage in which the working-class would struggle for socialism.

The NCPE furnished what many saw as a compelling and rigorous theoretical rationale for linking the theme of national liberation to socialism in the Canadian context. Rehearsing the ideas of an earlier generation of Canadian political economists, while also drawing upon the analytical perspectives of dependency and world-systems theories, the NCPE depicted Canada as a case of arrested economic development that had evinced a colonial or semi-colonial relationship successively to France, Britain, and the United States.[17] The key to understanding Canada's perennial victimization by larger, imperial powers was to be found in Harold Innis' understanding of Canada as a "staples economy" — an extractor and exporter of primary resource products (like fish, timber, minerals, and grain) which had failed to make a full transition to industrialism. Canada's class structure reflected its status as a dependency within the world economy and as a victim of the "imperialism of trade." The indigenous Canadian bourgeoisie, it was argued, was located primarily in the commercial and financial sectors of the economy and displayed little interest in developing the country's manufacturing capacity; at the same time, industrial production was dominated by US-based multinational corporations and consequently by capital that also exhibited little long-term commitment to the industrialization of Canada and still less to "nation-building." Furthermore, the increasingly fragmented and decentralized character of the Canadian state/confederation was viewed as a product of the weakness of Canadian industrial capital. As foreign ownership of the Canadian economy reached an all-time high in the early 1970s, the proponents of the NCPE warned that Canada was falling ever deeper into a neo-colonial relationship with the United States and that, with the faltering of American economic dynamism, US-owned branch-plant operations in Canadian manufacturing were imperilled. In the absence of a concerted struggle by Canadians to win economic sovereignty, Canada was at risk of being "deindustrialized" and relegated to the role of a "hewer of wood and a drawer of water."

To be sure, the NCPE was far from homogeneous, and as the dire predictions of the imminent deindustrialization and colonization of Canada lost their lustre in the late 1970s and 1980s and a younger cohort of Marxist theorists committed to class analysis appeared on the scene, new post-"dependency school" currents began to assert themselves as "internal" critics of the NCPE. In a survey of the literature, Glen Williams identifies two influential "non-dependency" positions that nevertheless remained within the orbit of at least some of the nationalist themes of the NCPE: a position according to which Canada combines features of a dependent

[17]The key early texts of the NCPE were K. Levitt, *Silent Surrender: the Multinational Corporation in Canada* (Toronto 1970); I. Lumsden, ed., *Close the 49th Parallel etc.: The Americanization of Canada* (Toronto 1970); G. Teeple, ed., *Capitalism and the National Question in Canada* (Toronto 1972); R. Laxer, ed., *(Canada) Ltd.: The Political Economy of Dependency* (Toronto 1973).

socio-economic formation and an advanced imperialist country, and a position which holds that Canada constitutes "a lesser region within the centre of the international political economy."[18] The first position describes Canada as occupying an "intermediate" status within the global hierarchy — as a "sub-imperial" power, a "white-settler dominion capitalism," and/or a "semi-industrial" country. Proponents of this view insist that while Canada is in a position to victimize the truly "dependent" regions of the world economy (the real "periphery" of the world-system) and possesses an indigenous, albeit non-cohesive, capitalist class in control of the state apparatus, it remains in a subordinate position in relation to the most advanced industrialized imperialist states, particularly the United States. In the vernacular of "world-system theory," Canada is "rich but semi-peripheral" — a social formation in which the tasks of industrial modernization and nation-building remain incomplete, and where their achievement is impeded by the economic and political influence of the US behemoth.[19]

The position that treats Canada as a region within the centre (or "core") of the world capitalist system is similar but distinguished by its focus on "the decisive role played by cultural and political variables in determining the structure and content of Canada's socioeconomic formation," rather than on "Canada's place in the inter-imperialist struggle of national capitals."[20] Williams' own treatment of Canada as a "white-settler dominion," Leo Panitch's analysis of the historic impact of Canada's "high-wage proletariat" on Canadian economic development, and Gordon Laxer's exploration of the significance of the political weakness and disunity of the agrarian classes for the consolidation of a commercial capitalist ruling class in Canada are all variants of this approach.[21] While differing on what should be emphasized in defining the historical roots of the subsumption of the Canadian economy by the American, the proponents of this position are united in seeing Canada as fully integrated with the US economy ("as a geographically large zone" within it) and the Canadian bourgeoisie as a "junior partner" of its US counterpart. At the same time, however, they argue that the formal autonomy and democratic character of the Canadian state makes possible nationalist initiatives that pose a threat to the "continentalist *status quo*," even if nationalist programs are usually defeated by the "continentalist definitions" of the Canadian national interest that are hegemonic within civil society and Canada's "state élites."[22] The political

---

[18]G. Williams, "Canada in the International Political Economy," in W. Clement and G. Williams, eds., *The New Canadian Political Economy*, 130.

[19]See D. Glenday, "Rich But Semiperipheral: Canada's Ambiguous Position in the World-Economy," *Review of the Fernand Braudel Center,* 12 (Spring 1989), 209-61.

[20]Williams, "Canada," 130.

[21]See G. Williams, *Not for Export: Toward a Political Economy of Canada's Arrested Industrialization* (Toronto 1986); L. Panitch, "Dependency and Class in Canadian Political Economy," *Studies in Political Economy,* 6 (Autumn 1981), 7-33; G. Laxer, *Open for Business: The Roots of Foreign Ownership in Canada* (Toronto 1989).

[22]Williams, "Canada," 132.

upshot of this analysis is to see English Canadian nationalism as a thorn in the side of a continentalist project to which the Canadian capitalist class is unequivocally committed; and to this extent left nationalism remains an important weapon in the arsenal of those who would seek to disrupt the capitalist *status quo*. In arguing for the "Canada within the centre" approach, Williams suggests that its great virtue is that it permits the incorporation of perspectives derived from both the "dependency and neo-Marxist approaches." It is crucial to note that it does so on a programmatic basis, which sanctifies the "progressive" potential of English Canadian nationalism — which is precisely the unifying political theme of the New Canadian Political Economy taken as a whole.

Writing in 1993, Rianne Mahon provided the following retrospective on the NCPE, in which she reaffirmed the fundamental soundness of its analysis:

While the NCPE was certainly enlivened by internal debate, most practitioners accepted the core problematic — Canada as a "rich dependency" — and the politico-strategic horizons which followed therefrom — struggle for an independent, socialist Canada.

In many respects, the serious challenges that Canada faces today seem to bear out the Waffle-NCPE analysis of the accelerating tendency toward the subordinate integration of Canada into a structure of continental corporate power and the balkanization of the Canadian state. The Canada-US Free Trade Agreement (FTA) and its successor, the North American Free Trade Agreement (NAFTA), can thus be seen as merely hastening the deindustrialization process that had already begun in the seventies ....

NCPE thus still seems to make sense of contemporary reality: the web of dependency and uneven development, woven by a continental bourgeoisie, is becoming more visible as the various parts of Canada are differentially incorporated into the North American economic bloc, while the Canadian state fragments as a result of centrifugal forces ....[23]

In the same article, Mahon argued that three concepts — dependency, class, and state — were "central to the NCPE's problematic." But, curiously, her characterization neglected the overarching significance of the concept of "Canadian nationhood" to the NCPE project. Indeed, the concepts of dependency, class, and state acquired their significance within the NCPE by virtue of their relationship to NCPE's central commitment to identifying the principal obstacles to an "independent Canada" and to informing the struggle for Canadian sovereignty with an appropriate theory (one centred on the weakness of the Canadian capitalist class and Canada's victimization by imperial powers) and an adequate program (one centred on rolling back foreign ownership, strengthening the Canadian state as a bulwark against "Americanization," and promoting "public ownership" of key industries as a means to achieving these goals). Certainly, in arguing for "an independent socialist Canada" the NCPE avoided defining socialism in terms of the

[23]R. Mahon, "The 'New' Canadian Political Economy Revisited: Production, Space, Identity," in J. Jenson, R. Mahon and M. Bienefeld, eds., *Production, Space, Identity: Political Economy Faces the 21st Century*, 2-3.

transcendence of capitalism, the elimination of class exploitation, or workers' power. Rather socialism was usually understood in left-social-democratic terms: as an expansion of "public ownership" and a strengthening and democratizing of the role of *the existing state* in the allocation of economic resources and the regulation of markets. From a Marxist standpoint, however, such a "socialism" amounted to little more than "nationalist reformism" — an attempt to achieve a capitalism with a "progressive," and distinctly Canadian, face. It is a "socialism" in the service of "nation-building" — but in a political context where English Canada (an entity with at best a weak claim to distinct nationhood) had long played an oppressive role in relation to the Québécois and aboriginal peoples.

A consequence of this made-in-Canada nationalist "socialism" was that it became a factor of some importance in the fragmentation of the North American labour movement along national lines. Although the Waffle and most proponents of the NCPE formally supported the right of Québec to self-determination, the political logic of their analysis and program was to resist the decentralization of the Canadian state and to promote the existing (capitalist) federal state as the principal vehicle of economic repatriation and social progress. As "socialists" in both English Canada and Québec identified themselves with the rising nationalist tides in their respective societies, they were to become increasingly estranged from one another, and less and less able to define a common program of struggle for the labour movement on a pan-Canadian scale. At the same time, English-Canadian left-nationalism sanctioned and encouraged the movement toward the disaffiliation of Canadian unions from their "international" (US-based) parent organizations. Persuaded that the international unions were an obstacle to the development of the fighting capacity of Canadian workers in the struggle for their "national" as well as their class interests, the left-nationalists rejected the task of campaigning for a class-struggle, socialist program within the North American labour movement as a whole. US labour was largely "written off," and the notion was promulgated that Canadian working people could and even should go it alone in the struggle for progressive social change and "socialism."

From a Marxist perspective, the idea that either English Canada or Québec could achieve a socialism worthy of the name in the absence of a struggle for workers power on a continental scale is simply absurd. Moreover, many English-Canadian and Québec leftists who saw socialism as a qualitative transcendence of the capitalist mode of production — as a rationally planned and democratically administered economy and society in which political and economic power is wrested from the bourgeoisie by the working class and in which the means of production, distribution, and exchange are collectively owned — were rightly skeptical of left-nationalist calls for an independent socialist Canada (or Québec). The rejection of social-democratic conceptions of the socialist project found a theoretical expression in a variety of challenges to the NCPE. By the mid-1970s, most Canadian Trotskyist groups (the League for Socialist Action, the Revolutionary Marxist Group and the Trotskyist League) as well as the Canadian Party of Labour and the left-Maoist In Struggle/En Lutte group were firmly opposed to English-Canadian left-nationalism, and this "far-left" political milieu provided the soil for the germination of an *anti-nationalist* political economy.[24]

One of the earliest and most influential of the "far-left" challenges to the NCPE was made by Steve Moore and Debi Wells in their book *Imperialism and the National Question in Canada*, published in 1975. Moore and Wells empirically disputed the "deindustrialization" thesis promulgated by the proponents of the NCPE and made the case that Canada was a minor imperialist country in which the major tasks associated with "national-democratic revolution" had been completed. In the years to come, the idea that Canada was a full member of the club of advanced imperialist countries, albeit one exhibiting some distinctive features, was taken up by a number of academic leftists, most notably William Carroll, Michael Ornstein, and John Fox.[25] At the same time, labour historians associated with this journal, *Labour/Le Travail*, were also making contributions to a Marxist analysis of Canadian social and economic development that were in many respects at odds with the nationalist tropes of the NCPE.[26]

The emergence of a strongly anti-nationalist Marxist political economy was a salutary development, one that provided a much-needed "reality check" to an analysis of Canadian history and society that had been skewed by the nationalist programmatic appetites of the NCPE. Although inconclusive, the ensuing debates

[24]The Canadian "far left" also included a number of "Marxist-Leninist" and Trotskyist organizations that adapted themselves politically to left-nationalism to varying degrees. The most consistently "patriotic" were the Communist Party of Canada (Marxist-Leninist), the Canadian Liberation Movement, and the Communist Party. The support of the Canadian Communist League (Marxist-Leninist) for an "independent Canada" — including a strong Canadian military — was in line with their support for the Maoist position of promoting "unity against the superpowers." Amongst ostensible Trotskyists, the Socialist League argued that English Canadian nationalism expressed an elementary "anti-imperialist senti-ment." The early International Socialists equivocated by declaring themselves opposed to "American imperialism in Canada and Canadian imperialism in the Third World" before moving toward an anti-nationalist stance in late 1976.

[25]See in particular: W. Carroll, J. Fox, and M. Ornstein, "The Network of Directorate Interlocks among the Largest Canadian Corporations," *Canadian Review of Sociology and Anthropology* 19 (1982), 44-69; W. Carroll, *Corporate Power and Canadian Capitalism* (Vancouver 1986); M. Ornstein, "The Social Organization of the Canadian Capitalist Class in Comparative Perspective," *CRSA*, 26 (1989), 151-77; and W. Carroll, "Neoliberalism and the Recomposition of Finance Capital in Canada," *Capital & Class*, 38 (1989), 81-112.

[26]See in particular: B. Palmer, *A Culture in Conflict: Skilled Workers and Industrial Capitalism in Hamilton, Ontario, 1860-1914* (Montréal 1979); Gregory S. Kealey, *Toronto Workers Respond to Industrial Capitalism, 1867-1892* (Toronto 1980); B. Palmer, *Working Class-Experience: The Rise and Reconstitution of Canadian Labour, 1800-1980* (Toronto 1983).

on the precise status of Canada within the world economy and the structure and peculiarities of the Canadian capitalist class enriched and extended left-wing scholarship on these issues in significant ways. Yet in certain respects many anti-nationalist Marxist political economists seemed tacitly to accept a key presup position of the NCPE: the notion that *if* Canada's capitalist class could be shown to be "dependent" on the US bourgeoisie or that *if* Canada's deteriorating economic performance could be linked to its subordinate status within the North American political economy, then a nationalist orientation on the part of the socialist left in Canada could be warranted.

Moore and Wells had set the tone for the anti-nationalist challenge to the NCPE by observing that:

left-nationalism leads to alliances with the bourgeoisie and the dropping of the socialist program in the first stage of the two-stage revolution. Even the Waffle leadership has fallen into line on this point. Nationalism in an imperialist country, like Canada, is the root cause of this reformism. Clearly, the fight against reformism (two-stage revolution; alliances with the bourgeoisie) is linked to the struggle against Canadian nationalism.[27]

Yet, Moore and Wells also implied that a "two-stage revolution" involving collabo-ration and alliances between the working class and "progressive" elements of the national bourgeoisie might be an appropriate strategy for socialists in colonial or semi-colonial countries. Key to their polemic was an appeal to the authority of the program adopted by the Sixth Congress of the Third (Communist) International in 1928, a program which *inter alia* committed the International to the anti-Marxist doctrine of building "socialism in one country" in the USSR. Moore and Wells noted that the program called for "two-stage revolution" only in clearly colonial or semi-colonial countries (like China), while advocating "one-stage revolution" in "highly developed capitalist countries, with powerful productive forces, a high degree of centralization of production, relatively insignificant small-scale enter-prise, and an old and well-established bourgeois-democratic political regime."[28] Moore and Wells made a compelling case that Canada conformed to this latter description, and therefore that a "left-nationalist strategy" was out of place in the Canadian context. By lending credence to the idea of two-stage revolution in more backward countries (an idea rejected by Leon Trotsky in his "The Draft Program of the Communist International — A Criticism of Fundamentals"), they appeared to make their programmatic position *contingent* on the accuracy of their analysis of Canada's status as a secondary imperialist power. The political stakes in the debate surrounding Canadian political economy were thereby raised, but at the expense of a clear understanding that "two-stage revolution" was a non-viable

[27]S. Moore and D.Wells, *Imperialism and the National Question in Canada* (Toronto 1975), 116.
[28]Cited by Moore and Wells from J. Degras, ed., *The Communist International 1919-1943* (documents) Volume 2, (London 1960), 505-7.

strategy for the working class in *all* countries in what Lenin and Trotsky had called "the imperialist epoch."

In his critique of the Stalin/Bukharin draft program for the Sixth Comintern congress Trotsky wrote: "On August 4, 1914, the death knell sounded for national programs for all time. The revolutionary party of the proletariat can base itself only upon an international program corresponding to the character of the present epoch, the epoch of the highest development and collapse of capitalism."[29] Trotsky was not suggesting that working-class socialists should no longer champion the right of oppressed nations to self-determination (that is, the right to formal political independence); but he was arguing that the task of the working class in all countries was to seek power in its own name with the aim of over-turning the global rule of capital. A "progressive" national capitalist development was no longer possible anywhere in an era marked by the consolidation of a capitalist *world* market, an exacerbation of capitalism's structural crisis tendencies, and a consequent intensification of imperialist rivalries between the most developed capitalist countries. Trotsky's theory and strategic perspective of *permanent revolution* flowed inexorably from these considerations:

Marxism takes its point of departure from world economy, not as a sum of national parts but as a mighty and independent reality which has been created by the international division of labour and the world market, and which in our epoch imperiously dominates the national markets ....

[In backward countries] the proletariat which has risen to power as the leader of the democratic revolution is inevitably and very quickly confronted with tasks, the fulfilment of which is bound up with deep inroads into the rights of bourgeois property. The democratic revolution grows over directly into the socialist revolution and thereby becomes a *permanent* revolution ....

The completion of the socialist revolution within national limits is unthinkable. One of the basic reasons for the crisis in bourgeois society is the fact that the productive forces created by it can no longer be reconciled with the framework of the national state ....

The socialist revolution begins on the national arena, it unfolds on the international arena, and is completed on the world arena. Thus, the socialist revolution becomes a permanent revolution in a newer and broader sense of the word; it attains completion only in the final victory of the new society on our entire planet ....

Insofar as capitalism has created a world market, a world division of labour and world productive forces, it has also prepared world economy as a whole for socialist transformation. Different countries will go through this process at different tempos. Backward countries may, under certain conditions, arrive at the dictatorship of the proletariat sooner than advanced countries, but they will come later than the latter to socialism.[30]

[29]Trotsky, 4.
[30]L. Trotsky, *The Permanent Revolution* (New York 1969), 146, 278-9.

Proceeding from these general theoretical considerations, Canadian Trotsky-ists, as already noted, have usually been opposed to left-nationalism politically, and skeptical of the NCPE theoretically. For them, the starting-point for both analysis and program is *the world economy,* "not as a sum of national parts but as a mighty and independent reality which has been created by the international division of labour and the world market, and which in our epoch imperiously dominates the national markets."

Methodologically, such an approach is anathema to those primarily interested in achieving "socialism" — or even "capitalism with a human face" — within the borders of their "own" country. For such national reformists the truly important question is not whether capitalism has exhausted its potential to promote human progress on a global scale, but whether any "wiggle room" can be found that might permit an improvement in the relative status of their country within the existing world system. Such an outlook fundamentally aligns Canadian left-nationalism with the interests of the bourgeoisie — even if the left nationalists are inclined to use different measures than the capitalists in determining what constitutes "pro-gress" on the national terrain. This points to the *operational* significance of many of the otherwise arid debates on Canada's precise status within the international political economy. What does it *matter* if Canada is considered a member of the imperialist "core" or a "rich but semi-peripheral" country? Clearly, it matters only insofar as the latter characterization may brain-trust and justify a *nationalist* perspective, while the former characterization serves to undermine the "progres-sive" claims of Canadian left-nationalism.

Given these political stakes, such debates can lead to a focus on truly "mar-ginal" differences between Canada and other advanced capitalist countries. A telling example is provided by Daniel Glenday, who, in defending the charac-terization of Canada as "rich but semi-peripheral," has made much of Canada's balance of trade in machinery and transportation equipment over the period from 1976-86. Comparing Canada's export/import ratio in this area with eight other countries, Glenday argues that this economic indicator "places Canada somewhere near the developed capitalist core, but still not a member of that select group." In other words, on this criterion of dependency/independence, Canada ranks some-where between "the profile of Australia or Greece" (a fellow "white settler dominion" and a clearly "semi-peripheral" member of the European community, respectively) and that of the USA, Japan, France, West Germany, the United Kingdom, and Italy (that is, Canada's fellow members of the "G7" group of countries).[31] But Glenday neglects to comment on the fact that his data also show that, with respect to this same export/import index ratio, the United States and Britain lag behind Italy to almost the same extent that Canada falls behind the US and Britain. Moreover, over the same period that the export/import ratio rose for

[31]Glenday, "Rich But Semiperipheral," 250, 251, 255-6.

Canada, it fell rather dramatically for the United States.[32] Does this suggest that while Canada was moving closer to the core, the United States was moving toward the semi-periphery? The absurdity of this question underlines the problems with making too much of the marginal differences that exist between advanced capitalist countries in relation to a single economic indicator.

Even so, the implication and political upshot of Glenday's comparative analysis is that, so long as Canada lags behind its partners in the G7 club of nations with respect to indicators like the balance of trade in machinery, it remains semi-peripheral and in dire need of "economic nationalist" policies. Indeed Glenday suggests that the Trudeau government's pursuit of just such policies may have enabled Canada to "move from the semiperiphery into the 'perimeter of the core' during the 1970s and the first half of the 1980s."[33] A further implication of his analysis, however, is that Canada's rising status may be imperilled by the reversal of such nationalist policies resulting from "free trade" with the United States, and that organized labour is right to be worried about a possible "hemorrhaging" of "our national economic and cultural identity." Thus, Glenday's discourse reflects a concern that is actually quite common, yet often understated, within the NCPE and Canadian "left-nationalism" in general: a preoccupation with "protecting" Canada's momentum toward full membership in the "capitalist core," that is, toward a fully *imperialist* status in the world economy. Such a concern is obviously very remote from Marxism both theoretically and politically. In fairness to Glenday, however, it should be acknowledged that, unlike many of his co-thinkers on the nationalist left, he at least refrains from associating the national-capitalist one-upmanship implicit in his analysis with rhetoric about an "independent socialist Canada."

The left-nationalists' preoccupation with the "free trade" agreements of 1989 and 1994 is also indicative of their continuing attachment to the notion that Canada as a "nation" — and not working people as a class — is the proper "unit of analysis" for understanding the depredations produced by the economic malaise of the 1980s and 1990s. The deep and long-lasting recession of the early 1990s was almost universally depicted by the left nationalists as the bitter fruit of the Canada-US Free Trade Agreement (as well as the related "high-interest rate policies" of the federal government and the Bank of Canada). The fact that the recession in Canada was more severe than that in the United States bolstered their argument that Canada's weak economic performance was attributable, once again, to Canada's "victimization" by its trade-bloc partner to the south. Yet there are substantial grounds for doubting that the Canadian recession of the early 1990s would have been less severe had the FTA not been in place. Increased access to the US market was, after all, critical to the strategy of Canadian corporations trying to expand their global market share and with it their output. While it is true that many Canadian businesses

[32]Glenday, "Rich But Semiperipheral," 251-2.
[33]Glenday, "Rich But Semiperipheral," 255.

historically dependent upon protectionist trade policies fell victim to the heightened competition unleashed by the FTA, it is possible that many more Canadian firms would have been adversely affected by a renewed American protectionism that was the most likely alternative to the FTA. Either way workers would have lost ground, and for this reason Canadian workers, arguably, had no clear stake in the "great Canadian debate" over the Canada-US Free Trade Agreement.[34] What is clear, however, is that the fundamental cause of the recession of the early 1990s was not "free trade" but the normal *cyclical operations* and *maturing crisis tendencies* of an advanced capitalist economy. By laying the blame for the recession on "free trade," the left-nationalists were true to form in absolving *capitalism* of the responsibility for the hardships that the recession visited upon Canadian working people.

The Global Capitalist Malaise: Outline of A Marxist View

As previously indicated, a Marxist analysis of the economic malaise and declining living standards that have characterized Canada over the past quarter century must begin with an appreciation of what is transpiring across the world economy. Viewed from this angle, the "crisis tendencies" exhibited by the Canadian economy in recent decades may be seen to be *qualitatively* similar to those experienced by other advanced capitalist countries.

For the G-7 core of the advanced capitalist world, a systematic comparison of key economic indicators for the periods 1950-73 and 1973-93 respectively suggest that, beginning in the early 1970s, the United States, Britain, France, West Germany, Italy, Japan, and Canada entered collectively into a period of protracted economic downturn. Output in the private business sectors of the G-7 countries declined from an average annual growth rate of 4.5 per cent in the former period to 2.2 per cent in the latter. Over the same periods, the growth of labour productivity fell from an annual average rate of 3.6 per cent to 1.3 per cent, and the average annual unemployment rate rose from 3.1 per cent to 6.2 per cent. In the United States, still the undisputed leader of the advanced capitalist world, the growth of GDP per hour worked averaged 0.9 per cent annually over the period from 1973 to 1996 — *well under half the average for the preceding century*; and from 1990 to 1996 it fell to just 0.7 per cent. By the mid-1990s, unemployment levels throughout most of the advanced capitalist countries of the OECD (the United States and Japan excepted) had reached heights comparable to the Great Depression of the 1930s. In 1996, the unemployment rate in the 11 countries of the European Union averaged 11.3 per cent; for the 28 OECD countries including the US and Japan, 7.3 per cent; and in the US, just 5 per cent. These figures compare to an average annual rate of

[34]From a Marxist standpoint, the Canadian working class had an internationalist responsibility to oppose the North American Free Trade Agreement of 1994, however, since the latter agreement further entrenched Mexico in a clearly semi-colonial relationship with American and Canadian imperialism.

unemployment of 10.3 per cent for the sixteen leading capitalist economies for the years 1930-38.[35]

The downturn that beset the world capitalist economy beginning in the early 1970s was the result of a long-term decline in the average rate of profit, and in particular a crisis of profitability in the manufacturing sectors of the leading capitalist economies.[36] Comparing official data sets on G-7 profitability for the periods 1950-70 and 1970-90, Robert Brenner reports that the net profit rate in manufacturing declined from an average annual rate of 26.2 per cent to 15.7 per cent over the two periods, while the average annual net profit rate for private business as a whole declined from 17.6 per cent to 13.3 per cent.[37] Following Duménil and Lévy's analysis of the centrality of the average rate of profit to capitalist economic performance,[38] Brenner argues convincingly that falling profitability was the root cause of the global economic downturn rather than simply a consequence of it. He writes:

The radical decline in the profit rate has been the basic cause of the parallel, major decline in the rate of growth of investment, and with it the growth of output, especially in manufacturing, over the same period. The sharp decline in the rate of growth of investment — along with that of output itself — is ... the primary source of the decline in the rate of growth of productivity, as well as a major determinant of the increase of unemployment. The reductions in the rate of profit and of the growth of productivity are at the root of the sharp slowdown in the growth of real wages.[39]

Although particular economic crises may be triggered by a variety of unpredictable events, the average rate of return on invested capital is the central regulator of capital accumulation and growth, and its decline therefore "sets the stage" for capitalist stagnation and slump.

Brenner argues that the profitability crisis was the result of "overcapacity and over-production" stemming from "intensified, horizontal inter-capitalist competi-

---

[35]Brenner, "Uneven Development," 3, note 5, citing OECD, *Economic Outlook*, 62, (December 1997), A24, Table 21, and A. Maddison, *Dynamic Forces in Capitalist Development* (Oxford 1991),170-1, Table 6.2. All other data in this paragraph are cited from Brenner, "Uneven Development," 5, Table 1. Of course, the absolute levels of hardship associated with high unemployment were greater during the 1930s depression owing to the absence or weakness of unemployment insurance and other social welfare programs in many of these countries.

[36]The following discussion borrows heavily from my article "The Necessity of Value Theory: Brenner's Analysis of the Long Downturn and Marx's Theory of Crisis," *Historical Materialism*, 4 (Summer 1999), 149-69.

[37]Brenner, "Uneven Development," 5, Table 1.

[38]G. Duménil and D. Lévy, *The Economics of the Profit Rate. Competition, Crises and Historical Tendencies of Capitalism* (Aldershot 1993).

[39]Brenner, "Uneven Development," 7-8.

tion." This competition is itself a manifestation of "the introduction of lower-cost, lower price goods into the world market, especially in manufacturing, at the expense of already existing higher cost, higher price producers, and their profitability and their productive capacity."[40] As suggestive as his account of inter-capitalist competition is in explaining the longevity of high-cost fixed capital assets and the debilitating effect of the resulting "over-capacity" and "over-production"on prices, Brenner fails to explain why the sale of manufactured commodities at unprofitable prices would fail to free up demand for other commodities enjoying higher than average profit margins, and why productive capital would not move massively enough into the production of such commodities to prevent a fall in the economy-wide rate of profit. To pose the question slightly differently, Brenner is unable to account for the *aggregate* fall in "purchasing power" (in relation to the total capital invested) that prevents *aggregate prices* from remaining at levels compatible with a stable average rate of profit.

In contrast to Brenner's analysis, Marx's theories of value and of the falling rate of profit allow for the resolution of just this problem — a problem that must be addressed in any account of the long downturn which, like Brenner's, traces its source and intractability to a *generalized crisis* of profitability across the advanced capitalist world, and not simply to a particular *distribution* of profits amongst competing capitals and capitalist economies. At the same time, Marx's theories also provide an indispensable foundation for an analysis of capitalist crisis on a *world* scale and a compelling framework for resisting the efforts of economic nationalists everywhere to seek the source of capitalist crisis in the sphere of commodity exchange and trade rather than in *the sphere of production*.

Marx's theory of labour-value involves the defence of two fundamental propositions. The first is that living labour is the sole source of all *new value,* including the value embodied in profits and in the wages of productive workers. The second, is that total value ("previously-existing" as well as "new") constitutes a definite quantitative magnitude at the level of the capitalist macro-economy — a parametric determinant that *limits* profits, wages, and prices.[41] Marx's theory of the falling rate of profit is crucially predicated on the truth of these propositions. Indeed, they can be regarded as necessary, if not entirely sufficient, presuppositions of his argument that capital's displacement of living labour from production will produce a crisis of valorization (surplus-value production) and a downward pressure on the average rate of profit, whether or not this displacement involves an elevated level of labour productivity.[42]

[40]Brenner, "Uneven Development," 8-9.
[41]Smith, *Invisible Leviathan*; M. Smith, "Alienation, Exploitation and Abstract Labour: A Humanist Defense of Marx's Theory of Value," *Review of Radical Political Economics*, 26 (March 1994), 110-33.
[42]See Smith, *Invisible Leviathan,* Ch.7, for a discussion of the falling tendency of the average rate of profit and its relationship to productivity growth.

If the two propositions central to Marx's theory of value are true, then the contradiction between capital's continuous success in increasing productivity at the *micro-level* of the individual firm and the tendency of the capitalist macro-economy to descend into periodic crises of profitability and "deficient effective demand" can be adequately specified. For contrary to conventional economic theories that assume a monotonic relationship between rising labour productivity and economic prosperity, Marx's value-theoretic analysis of capitalism recognizes that the "life-blood" of the capitalist economy is not physical output but rather *surplus-value,* that is, the value newly created by living labour in excess of the value embodied in the wages of productive workers.

Productivity growth is, of course, a matter of central concern to capitalists, for it is precisely by enhancing productivity that individual capitalist firms try to reduce their costs per unit of output and thereby enlarge their market share and mass of profits. But it is only because individual firms can "capture" and "realize" the surplus-value produced by workers employed elsewhere in the economy (as a result of competitive processes of surplus-value redistribution in circulation) that labour-displacing productivity enhancements are an effective "micro-level" profit-maxi-mizing tactic of individual capitals. What is "rational" from the point of view of the individual firm in the short term, however, is inimical to the interests of "capital-in-general" in the medium to long term. For the labour-displacing innova-tions used by firms to enhance labour productivity diminish the role played by living labour in production, increase the "organic composition of capital," and thereby depress the average rate of profit. In other words, the unintended and unanticipated consequence of efforts by individual capitals to reduce their reliance on living labour in production, in order to increase their share of social surplus value, is a proportionally reduced role in total production for the living labour that is the sole "input" capable of producing surplus value. Capitalists compete to increase their share (profit of enterprise) of a pie (social surplus value) that is expanding at a rate slower than the expansion of their combined investments — and this is the necessary consequence of a shift away from the employment of variable capital (the productive living labour that directly produces surplus value) toward ever-greater investments in constant capital (the elements of the process of capitalist production and reproduction that play only an *indirect* role in the produc-tion of surplus value).

The logic of capitalist development, defined by the exploitative and antago-nistic relation between capital and labour as well as by the competitive relations between capitals, is to reduce continuously the socially necessary labour time required to produce a given quantity of material output. This means that as the magnitude of physical or material output expands, the quantity of value it represents may well decrease. Accordingly, it is quite possible for material productivity to grow as the production of surplus value declines. Indeed, the ever-sharpening contradiction between humanity's command over nature in production (expressed in the growth of productive forces embodying *labour-saving* technology) and the social-structural imperatives of capitalism to exploit wage-labour and therefore to measure "wealth" and economic performance in terms of *abstract labour time* (the phenomenal form of which is money) is central to Marx's understanding of the historical limits of the capitalist mode of production.

For Marx, an *unresolvable contradiction* exists under capitalism between progress in overcoming the (technical-natural) obstacles to increased material productivity and the (class-appropriative) requirements of valorization — that is, between the "natural" and the "social" dimensions of capitalist production.[43] Accordingly, the labour-saving technological innovation that enhances productivity must also, at the macro level, reduce the magnitude of aggregate values that are the basis of aggregate prices. This phenomenon is at the root of the problem that Brenner, among many others, emphasises, but fails to theorize: the problem of "realization." Once this phenomenon is understood it becomes clear that *aggregate prices must fall as the values sustaining them recede,* and it is precisely this that accounts for the inability of capitalists to command prices for their commodities, in the aggregate, that can sustain the average rate of profit.

I have elsewhere reported on the results of an attempt to empirically evaluate the relevance of Marx's law of the falling tendency of the rate of profit in the Canadian context.[44] Briefly, these results indicate that the performance of the Canadian economy over the period from 1947 to 1991 was consistent with Marx's understanding of the "laws of motion" of an advanced capitalist economy:

In general, the data support Marx's expectations of a long-term rise in the rate of surplus value and in the organic composition of capital. Furthermore, the data suggest that a long-term decline in the average rate of profit occurred over the period 1947 to 1975. The falling trend in the profit rate was arrested over the period 1976-89, only to reassert itself with the onset of the recession [of the early 1990s] ....

[43]The confusion of the "natural" and the "social" is at the heart of Marx's theory of "commodity fetishism" — a concept that figured prominently in David McNally's interesting critique of the NCPE. See his "Staple Theory as Commodity Fetishism: Marx, Innis and Canadian Political Economy," *Studies in Political Economy*, 6 (Autumn 1981), 35-63. The fact that McNally's critique was met with such incomprehension and even derision by many proponents of the NCPE attested to their lack of interest in Marxian value theory, which in turn reflected their rejection of Marx's larger practical project of overcoming capitalism. Indeed, the *relevance* of Marx's *critique* of classical political economy on the basis of his theory of value is that it establishes the historical limits of the value form, dispels the mystifying influences of commodity fetishism, and suggests the possibility — and indeed the necessity — of other, "higher" forms of social production. See my discussion in Smith, *Invisible Leviathan*, 58-62.

[44]Smith, *Invisible Leviathan*, ch. 8; M. Smith and K. Taylor, "Profitability Crisis and the Erosion of Popular Prosperity: The Canadian Economy, 1947-1991," *Studies in Political Economy*, 49 (Spring1996), 101-30.

Clearly, the average rate of profit, and with it "capitalist prosperity," made something of a recovery in the 1980s. Nevertheless, the recovery did not restore an average annual rate of profit to the level of the immediate post-war period (1950 to 1969). From 1947 to approximately 1976, the average rate of profit experienced a secular decline that was significantly correlated to a rise in the organic composition of capital [OCC]. This was accompanied by a rising rate of surplus value which was apparently compatible with long-term gains in working-class living standards. However, from the mid to late 1970s on, the data indicate a dramatically ascendant rate of surplus value, which apparently had less to do with a rising accumulation rate and associated productivity gains (for which the OCC is something of an index) than with stagnant or declining real wages.[45]

In observing the consistency of political-economic trends in the Canadian context with Marx's theoretical expectations, it is important to note that Marxist political economists have pointed to broadly similar trends for the US economy over the same period.[46] In both countries, the profitability crisis and associated economic malaise may be seen as resulting from two main factors: a rising organic composition of capital, stemming from labour-saving and labour-displacing technical innovation; and rising systemic "overhead costs" associated with the expansion of "socially necessary but unproductive labour." In their own ways, each of these trends point to a growing conflict between the "forces of production" and the "social relations of production" of advanced capitalism — a conflict which finds expression in long-term profitability problems. At the same time, however, these trends are also related to the shift from manufacturing employment to service-sector employment that economic nationalists on both sides of the Canada-US border have pointed to as evidence of a "deindustrialization" process. Far from signifying the movement of either Canada or the United States toward a "deindustrialized" or "semi-peripheral" status in the world economy, however, this shift reflects, to a very great extent, the growing investments within the "industrial" sectors of the two economies in increasingly sophisticated fixed capital assets that require less and less living labour to be set in motion. From the Marxist standpoint, the "solution" to this problem is not a beggar-my-neighbour conflict over the geographical distribution of manufacturing jobs, but the socialization of the means of production and their deployment in such a way as to permit rising living standards and declining hours of work for the mass of the working population.

The Road Ahead for Canadian Labour: Nationalism or Class Struggle?

The tendency of the average rate of profit to fall can be counter-acted in a number of ways, and the social capital of the advanced capitalist countries can be expected to bend every effort to "mobilize" these counter-tendencies as profits decline and

---

[45]Smith and Taylor, "The Profitability Crisis," 118.
[46]See A. Shaikh and E. Tonak, *Measuring the Wealth of Nations* (Cambridge1994); F. Moseley, *The Falling Rate of Profit in the Postwar United States Economy* (New York 1991).

economic growth slows. Broadly speaking, the social capital seeks to arrest and reverse the falling rate of profit by 1) increasing the rate of exploitation (or rate of surplus value) of workers in ways that stabilize or lower the organic composition of capital, and 2) resolving "the internal contradiction" by "extending the external field of production."[47] The first of these strategic measures involves efforts to drive down the real wage, increase the average number of hours worked, curtail the strength of labour in the workplace, and reallocate revenue from state-sponsored (non-profit) social programs toward the consumption of commodities produced for profit. The second involves laying claim to a larger share of the world market and seeking out new arenas for profitable capitalist investment abroad. Both of these strategies have been pursued by the Canadian capitalist class over the past quarter century in order to restore the average rate of profit to "acceptable" levels. But each is problematic. The strategy of dramatically jacking up the rate of exploitation carries with it the very real risk of increasing the level of class antagonism on the domestic front and unleashing higher levels of class struggle. The second, "international" strategy, on the other hand, involves heightened levels of competition with the social capital of other countries, and raises the spectre of trade wars that might eventually turn into shooting wars. Foreign trade and investment is also a two-edged sword. To the degree that it fails, a retreat to nationalist protectionism may become unavoidable, while its success may be predicated on raising the rate of exploitation to levels incompatible with maintaining domestic "class peace."

In trying to combine and balance the two strategies available to it, social capital in Canada has so far met with a weak response from Canadian labour and the Left. Its efforts to increase the rate of exploitation through an assault on working-class living standards have met with considerable success as the labour movement has refrained from any serious fight-back. At the same time, the dominant fractions of Canadian capital have sought to consolidate a North American economic bloc with US capital, beginning with the "free trade" agreement of 1989. The response of Canadian labour and the reformist Left has been to oppose this project on a *nationalist* basis, essentially projecting a policy of national economic retrenchment as an alternative to further continental economic integration. By concentrating their fire at the political level on "free trade," the leadership of the Canadian labour movement has sought to blame the depredations associated with the rising rate of exploitation upon the "policies" of big business and the state. In doing so they not only deflect attention from the maturing, structurally rooted crisis tendencies of advanced capitalism, they also conceal the inadequacy of their own fundamentally pro-capitalist policies in the face of a renewed offensive by capital against labour. Meanwhile, the nationalist Left, while giving occasional lip service to a watered-down "socialism," abets the labour officialdom by continuing to depict Canada as a victim of the US behemoth and arguing that a significant improvement in working-class living standards is possible through nationalist economic policies

[47]K. Marx, *Capital, Volume Three* (New York 1981), 353.

(including "alternative budgets," Tobin-tax capital controls, *etc.*) that accept the framework of the capitalist order.

Canadian labour will remain effectively disarmed in the face of capital's continuing offensive so long as it accepts the national-reformist political framework that the trade union bureaucracy and the nationalist Left have sought assiduously to maintain. The road forward for Canadian labour can only be through a renewed commitment to *class struggle* — to a program which is informed by Marx's critique of political economy, and which anticipates the social, economic, and political content of a future Socialist Federation of North America.

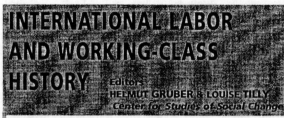

"Rapprocher les lieux du pouvoir": The Québec Labour Movement and Québec Sovereigntism, 1960-2000

Ralph P. Güntzel

IN RECENT YEARS the Québec labour movement has undertaken great efforts to advocate the idea of a sovereign Québec nation state. Having made the promotion of sovereignty a keystone in their respective political action programs in 1990, the province's three major labour union centrals, the Fédération des travailleurs et travailleuses du Québec (FTQ), the Confédération des syndicats nationaux (CSN), and the Centrale des syndicats du Québec (CSQ), actively campaigned for a "yes" in the 1995 referendum on sovereignty. Even after the sovereigntist option had been defeated in the referendum, the three centrals reiterated their commitment to propagating sovereignty. However, Québec labour's recent policy stands in stark contrast to its initial reaction to the rise of sovereigntism. During the first half of the 1960s, when modern sovereigntism first emerged, the three centrals defended Canadian unity. During the second half of the 1960s and the 1970s this position gave way to an increasingly pro-sovereigntist orientation. It will be the purpose of this essay to trace and explain Québec labour's sovereigntist turn.

The Three Federations and the Emergence of Sovereigntism, 1960-1967

Since the mid-1960s unionization rates in Québec have oscillated between 35 and 40 per cent, thus making Québec the most densely unionized society in all of North America, except for Newfoundland.[1] During the period from 1960 to the present, the vast majority of Québec's unionized labour force belonged to affiliates of either

[1] Jacques Rouillard, *Histoire du syndicalisme au Québec: Des origines à nos jours* (Montréal 1989), 289; Bernard Dionne, *Le syndicalisme au Québec* (Montréal 1991), 63-4; Luc Allaire and Nicole de Sève, "La CEQ deviendra-t-elle la Centrale syndicale du Québec? " www.ceq.qc.ca/nouvelle/mars00/congres.htm

Ralph P. Güntzel, "'Rapprocher les lieux du pouvoir': The Québec Labour Movement and Québec Sovereigntism, 1960-2000," *Labour/Le Travail*, 46 (Fall 2000), 369-95.

the FTQ, the CSN, or the CSQ. Of the three centrals, the FTQ was —and continues to be — the largest. At present, almost half a million workers, or nearly 45 per cent of unionized workers in the province, hold FTQ membership cards. The CSN has about a quarter of a million members, while about 140,000 workers belong to the CSQ. While the FTQ membership has traditionally been dominated by private- and secondary-sector workers, currently about one third of its members work in the public sector. The CSN underwent a transformation from a central, dominated by private- and secondary-sector workers, to one dominated by public- and tertiary-sector workers during the 1960s and early 1970s. Having originally served as the corporate body of Québec's francophone primary- and secondary-school teachers, the CSQ added other public-sector workers since the late 1960s and, thus, became a veritable public-sector central.[2]

During the last four decades, the three centrals devoted considerable energies to political action. During much of the 1960s, the three centrals subscribed to social-democratic reformism, which aimed at "civilizing" rather than destroying capitalism. The centrals' social-democratic vision entailed state interventionism, economic planning aimed at providing for full employment, extended welfare-state services, the democratization of the workplace, redistributive taxation policies, and the abolition of poverty. During the late 1960s and early 1970s, the centrals espoused an increasingly radical discourse, largely in response to a series of public-sector conflicts with the provincial government. While the FTQ radicalized its rhetoric, but continued to adhere to social-democratic reformism, the CSN and CSQ espoused anti-capitalist positions inspired by a Marxist analysis of capitalism and the role of the state. In 1972, the CSQ adopted a manifesto which defined capitalism as, "une société d'exploitation où les classes dominantes et leur valet servil, l'Etat, exploitent le travail des hommes ... pour accroître leurs profits et leur puissance." The manifesto also called for a workers' struggle to produce, "[une] société égalitaire, sans classe." In the same year, the CSN went on record, "en faveur du socialisme, en tant que système réalisant la démocratie économique, politique, industrielle, culturelle et sociale." The two centrals continued to promote socialism until the early 1980s. Not having made much headway in raising an anti-capitalist consciousness among their members, the CSN and the CSQ discontinued their socialist discourse and began to undergo a deradicalization process. By the mid-1980s, they once again adopted social-democratic positions.[3]

[2]Dionne, *Le syndicalisme au Québec*, 66-78; FTQ, "Membres affiliés," www.ftq.qc.ca/html/membres.html; CSN, "La CSN au Québec," www.csn.qc.ca/Pageshtml/MvntCSNque.html; CEQ, "Profile of the CEQ" www.ceq.qc.ca/ceq/proa3.htm
[3]Rouillard, *Histoire du syndicalisme au Québec*, 287-370; Louis Fournier, *Histoire de la FTQ: 1965-1992: La plus grande centrale syndicale au Québec* (Montréal 1994). For CEQ quotations: CEQ, *L'Ecole au service de la classe dominante* (Sainte Foy, Québec 1972), 12, 32. For CSN quotation: CSN, *Procès-verbal, Congrès, 1972* (Québec 1972), 176.

Québec labour was first confronted with the idea of a sovereign Québec nation-state in the early 1960s when the Rassemblement pour l'indépendance nationale (RIN) and several other small sovereigntist organizations sprang up. Most of these organizations were influenced by anti-colonial struggles in Africa and Asia. "A l'époque actuelle," the RIN declared in its 1960 manifesto, "où dans le monde entier les peuples s'affranchissent du joug colonial et les nations revendiquent leur pleine indépendance le Canada français ne peut plus accepter de demeurer sous la tutelle économique et politique de l'étranger. L'idéal de l'indépendance nationale ... est valable au Canada français comme partout ailleurs." The RIN further stressed that Québec was the political embodiment of the French-Canadian nation and that nations must strive for sovereign nation-state status. The RIN also argued that Québec must separate from Canada in order to provide an effective framework for the cultural survival and economic development of the French-Canadian nation.[4]

Most parts of Québec labour rejected the RIN's arguments. Many unionists regarded nationalism as an inherently conservative ideology.[5] Some unionists also rejected sovereignty because they approved of Canadian federalism. "Le régime fédéral ... doit être maintenu," the FTQ's Montréal regional council resolved in 1961. "Il a été un des instruments qui ont permis à la nation canadienne-française de se développer, d'affirmer son charactère et de maintenir et repandre sa culture et sa langue."[6] Other unionists took a more critical attitude toward Canadian federalism, but feared that an independent Québec would jeopardize, rather than improve, the condition of the French-Canadian nation. They were particularly concerned that sovereignty might entail economic turbulence, rising unemployment, and declining standards of living.[7] Thus, during the early and mid-1960s, both the FTQ and the CSN flatly opposed the notion of a sovereign Québec.[8]

By the mid-1960s, however, more and more members of the FTQ and the CSN became attracted to Québec nationalism. Nationalist attitudes were particularly strong among the mine workers who belonged to the FTQ-affiliated Québec section of the United Steelworkers of America (QcUSWA). The mine workers had a long

[4]Marcel Chaput, *Pourquoi je suis séparatiste* (Montréal 1961); Pierre Bourgeault, *Ecrits polémiques* (Montréal 1982), I. For quotation: "Manifeste du rassemblement pour l'indépendance nationale (1960)," in Daniel Latouche and Diane Poliquin-Bourassa, eds., *Le Manuel de la parole: Manifestes québécois: Tome 3: 1960-1976* (Montréal 1979), 26.

[5]"Les deux solitudes se rencontrent ...," *Monde ouvrier* (January-February 1966), 6; Jacques Keable, *Le monde selon Marcel Pepin* (Outremont, Québec 1998), 223.

[6]Conseil des travaileuses et travailleurs du Montréal métropolitain, *Cent ans de solidarité: Histoire du CTM 1886-1986* (Montréal 1987), 106.

[7]"Sixth Annual Convention of the Quebec Federation of Labour (CLC)," *Labour Gazette*, February 1962, 136-7.

[8]François Cyr and Rémi Roy, *Eléments d'histoire de la FTQ: La FTQ et la question nationale* (Montréal 1981), 61-62; Ralph P. Güntzel, "The Confédération des syndicats nationaux (CSN), the Idea of Independence, and the Sovereigntist Movement, 1960-1980," *Labour/Le Travail*, 31 (Spring 1993), 157-8.

history of acrimonious conflict with their English-Canadian or American employers. Having created the mining towns of northern Québec, English-Canadian
companies such as Noranda Mines Ltd. or American companies such as the
Iron-Ore Co., dominated life in the small communities and exercised a tremendous
hold on the miners' lives even outside the workplace. The economic division in the
mining towns was accentuated by a cultural division of labour. As one high-ranking
civil servant in the Québec Ministry of Natural Resources noted in 1965,

Allez à Rouyn-Noranda. Là-bas, vous allez voir deux économies qui vivent une côté à l'autre.
La petite économie, celle qui est le lot des Canadiens français: les garages, les postes
d'essence, les épiceries, les mineurs bien entendu. Tout ce monde-là c'est en grande majorité
des Canadiens français. A côté d'eux, ou plutôt en marge d'eux, vous avez la Noranda, la
grande économie de la place. A partir d'un certain niveau dans l'echelle de cette économie,
on vit en anglais, on travaille en anglais, on habite un quartier qui n'est pas celui du pompiste
ou de l'épicier, d'ailleurs — ce n'est pas par hasard — on est entre Canadiens anglais
surtout.[9]

French-speaking workers were disgruntled with this ethnic hierarchy. An
anecdote told by a QcUSWA staff member illustrates the proto-nationalist nature of
this unhappiness. During the summer, members of the wealthy English-speaking
minority and the much poorer French-speaking majority of his hometown would
go to a nearby lake. "Je me souviens," he relates," qu'il y avait des Anglais qui nous
lançaient des '5 cennes,' ils trouvaient ça ... drôle de voir nous écraser les doigts
pour ramasser les sous dans le sable .... Avec des cents, ils faisaient nous battre
entre nous et même nous blesser; ils trouvaient cela 'wonderfull [sic]:' 'it looks like
a football game.' J'ai commencé par avoir honte; mais le lendemain, quand j'ai
pensé à tout cela, je suis devenu enragé noir. C'était un sursaut de nationalisme
causé par doigts déchirés."[10]
    The anguish of French-speaking miners in the company towns of northern
Québec was further aggravated by the companies' opposition to the workers'
attempts to unionize. Even if they managed to establish local union sections, the
miners were forced to negotiate in English and continuously faced staunchly
anti-union policies aimed at crushing local union sections.[11] In this situation the
miners enthusiastically welcomed the reform of the Québec labour code in 1964,
which increased union security and stipulated that the workers could choose the
language of the collective agreement.[12] The revision of the labour code was one of
the reforms the Québec Liberal government undertook under the instigation of René

[9]James Bamber, "Lévesque contre la Noranda," *Magazine Maclean* (November 1965), 69.
[10][Emile Boudreau,] "Les Anglais nous lançaient des 5 sous ...," *Monde ouvrier* (May 1980),
7.
[11]Jean Gérin-Lajoie, *Les Métallos 1936-1980* (Montréal 1982), 76-87; Rouillard, *Histoire
du syndicalisme québécois*, 282-5.
[12]Gérin-Lajoie, *Les Métallos*, 125-8, 142.

Lévesque, its Minister of Natural Resources. Lévesque shared the miners' dislike of Noranda, whom he accused of displaying, "the supreme arrogance of the colonizer," and of cultivating, "[a] Rhodesian climate" in the mining industry.[13] As minister he actively helped the QcUSWA to organize Noranda employees.[14] The influx of mine workers tipped the scales within the QcUSWA in favour of its nationalist wing. In 1965, Jean Gérin-Lajoie, candidate of the nationalist wing, was elected QcUSWA director.[15] Following Gérin-Lajoie's election victory the QcUSWA began to advocate special status for Québec within Canada.[16]

The CSQ opted for a similar constitutional solution. As teachers using the French language as a medium of instruction, CSQ members reproduced an essential part of French Canada's distinctive culture. Hence, cultural survival played a crucial role in their outlook on the question of Québec's constitutional status. This vantage point led many CSQ members to a critical assessment of Canadian federalism's ability to safeguard the French language and French-Canadian culture.[17] In a memorandum adopted in 1964, the CSQ charged that Canadian federalism promoted English Canada's culture to the detriment of French Canada's culture. "L'Etat canadien," the brief noted, "s'est montré incapable de sauvegarder suffisamment le bien commun spécifique de la nation canadienne-française."[18] For the protection of their national interests, French Canadians had to rely solely on the Québec state. Thus, the brief continued, it was imperative that the Québec state possess all the powers necessary to protect the French-Canadian nation. These powers were to include, but not be limited to, the right to withdraw from federal-provincial shared cost programs, conduct immigration policies tailored to the needs of Québec, and negotiate treaties and agreements with other countries.[19] The original draft of the document had even advocated, "la souveraineté politique et économique du Québec" in combination with, "une structure pan-canadienne composé à part égale des représants des Etats nationaux."[20] The central's enlarged executive, however, eschewed the associated-states model as not reflective of the opinion held by the majority of the membership and replaced it with a call for an ill-defined, but less controversial, special status for Québec.[21]

[13] René Lévesque, *Memoirs* (Toronto 1986), 187.
[14] Gérin-Lajoie, *Les Métallos*, 128-30.
[15] Gérin-Lajoie, *Les Métallos*, 159-66.
[16] Gérin-Lajoie, *Les Métallos*, 174.
[17] Albert Gervais, "Repenser la Confédération à neuf ou l'envisager ... à 9," *Enseignement* (November 1961), 2.
[18] "La relation Nation-Etat," *Enseignement* (December 1965/January 1966), 18.
[19] "La C.I.C. a présenté un mémoire à la commission Laurendeau-Dunton," *Enseignement* (November 1965), 14.
[20] Archives de la CEQ, Sainte-Foy, Québec (henceforth: ACEQ), CIC, Procès-verbal, conseil provincial, 24-25 October 1964, 18.
[21] ACEQ, CIC, Procès-verbal, conseil provincial, 17-9, 22-3.

For both the QcUSWA and the CSQ espousal of the special status formula constituted but a temporary step on their way to an endorsement of sovereignty. For the time being, however, they were held back by two concerns: first, the economic risks involved in sovereignty; and second, their distrust of pro-sovereignty politicians and parties. Soon the sovereigntist movement began to evolve in a way that greatly diminished both concerns.

The FTQ and the Ascendancy of Social-Democratic Sovereigntism, 1967-1976

Having broken with the Liberal Party over the issue of Québec's constitutional status, in 1967 Lévesque founded the Mouvement Souveraineté-Association (MSA). In 1968 the MSA merged with another sovereigntist party to form the Parti québécois (PQ), with Lévesque at its helm. The PQ significantly changed the outlook of sovereigntism in two respects. First, it discontinued the use of the term "French-Canadian nation" and instead used the term "Québec nation." Second, it departed from the pure separatism of the RIN and other earlier sovereigntist organizations and espoused sovereignty-association, a constitutional formula, which advocated political sovereignty for Québec alongside continued economic association with Canada. Only a few months after the creation of the PQ, the RIN dissolved itself and recommended that its members join Lévesque's party. Thus, within a short period of time the PQ became the almost exclusive political agent of Québec sovereignty. Drawing on Lévesque's political clout, the PQ developed a social-democratic programme and soon became the province's most important left-of-centre political party.[22]

The arrival of the PQ had a profound impact on Québec labour, since after 1968 support for sovereignty increased significantly among union activists. While the PQ's sovereignty-association formula failed to entirely eliminate fears about the potential risks involved in severing Québec's political ties with Canada, it did reduce them. Indeed, growth of pro-sovereignty sentiment was not limited to public-sector workers, who enjoyed a certain safety valve due to relatively high employment security. It also spread to private-sector unions including, most noticeably, the QcUSWA. When Lévesque left the Liberal Party, his popularity with QcUSWA members was such that many of them spontaneously adopted a more sympathetic attitude toward sovereignty. As FTQ president Louis Laberge remarked, "Lévesque leur avait souvent donné des preuves de son progressisme et, pour eux, il était presque comme un bon Dieu!"[23] In January 1970, less than two years after the creation of the PQ, Gérin-Lajoie informed USWA president I.W. Abel that there were PQ supporters in all QcUSWA sections. According to Gérin-Lajoie,

[22]Vera Murray, *Le Parti québécois: de la fondation à la prise du pouvoir* (Montréal 1976); Kenneth McRoberts, *Quebec: Social Change and Political Crisis* (3rd ed., Toronto 1988), 218-9, 238-62.
[23]Louis Fournier, *Louis Laberge: Le syndicalisme c'est ma vie* (Montréal 1992), 187.

they were particularly numerous among the iron-ore and hard-rock miners.[24] The head of the QcUSWA also estimated that the PQ garnered the votes of 50 per cent of the union's members in the 1970 provincial elections, the first ones in which the party participated.[25]

Political events during the late 1960s and early 1970s further increased the appeal of the PQ among organized labour. In 1969 the provincial government passed Bill 63 which provided for English-language education wherever it was demanded. Many French-speaking Québecers feared that the bill might accelerate the integration of newly arrived immigrants into the English-speaking community and, thus, adversely affect their own upward social mobility and even threaten the survival of the French language in Québec. In this situation, the three federations joined the PQ in calling for French unilingualism. Meanwhile, the federal government headed by Pierre Elliott Trudeau pursued centralist policies based on the premise that Québec was a province like all others. These policies collided with many Québecers' hopes for the devolution of federal powers to the Québec government. Frustration with Trudeau's policies reached a peak in 1970, when the federal government invoked the War Measures Act in response to activities of the terrorist Front de libération du Québec (FLQ). Under the Act, several hundred sovereigntists, including many labour activists, were arrested. While some saw the military intervention as justified, others, including the PQ and the three centrals, opposed it as an undue infringement on civil liberties and human rights. The language debates, Trudeau's centralism, and the October Crisis, polarized Québec society, but also increased the size of the sovereigntist camp.[26]

In the 1973 provincial elections the PQ won one third of the popular vote.[27] In the elections several union members ran as PQ candidates. One of them was QcUSWA staff member Clément Godbout. Like other unionists, Godbout saw sovereignty as a means to end the cultural division of labour which he had experienced in his formative years as a mine worker in Abitibi-Témiscamingue. "Je tiens à bâtir un véritable pays pour mes enfants," Godbout declared. "Je ne veux pas qu'ils aient à vivre ce que j'ai vécu."[28] According to Godbout, sovereignty and social democracy were interconnected. "Nous sommes tous d'accord," he noted,

[24]Archives nationales du Québec, Montréal (henceforth: ANQ), USWA Collection, P 144, 1A, 1, 42, J. Gérin-Lajoie to I.W. Abel, 22 January 1970, 2.

[25]Jean Gérin-Lajoie, "Je me rejouis de la liberté de parole ...," *Métallo* (June 1972), 7.

[26]On the language debate: Richard Jones, "Politics and the Reinforcement of the French Language in Canada and Quebec, 1960-1986," in Michael Behiels, ed. *Quebec Since 1945: Selected Readings* (Toronto 1987), 228-230. On Trudeau's centralism: Kenneth McRoberts, *Misconceiving Canada: The Struggle for National Unity* (Toronto 1997), 55-148. On the October Crisis: Jean-François Cardin, *Comprendre Octobre 1970: la FLQ, la crise et le syndicalisme* (Montréal 1990).

[27]Graham Fraser, *PQ: René Lévesque and the PQ in Power* (Toronto 1984), 59.

[28]Pierre Richard, "Le syndicat des métallos opte pour l'indépendance," *Devoir*, 14 January 1972, 3.

"que le capital est essentiel au développement et à l'évolution d'un peuple. Cependant, sur ce capital, un contrôle doit être excercé, de façon à organiser une planification nécessaire à tout peuple, et cette planification économique se fait par des dirigeants gouvernementaux compétents et forts." The federal government was unwilling, however, and the Québec government unable to provide competent economic leadership. In this situation, Godbout concluded, only sovereignty would enable the Québec government to pursue the economic development policies so desperately needed.[29]

Godbout professed not to fear the possible economic repercussions of sovereignty. When members of a QcUSWA local at International Harvester aired their concern that the company might transfer production outside Québec in case of a PQ election victory, Godbout replied that companies made decisons about production transfers solely on the basis of business considerations. Companies would stay or move out of Québec if doing so would increase their profit margin, regardless of the constitutional status of Québec.[30] Antonio Bruno, another QcUSWA staff member and former mine worker who ran for the PQ in 1973, put it more bluntly: "Tant aux investissements étrangers," he said, "il y en aura aussi longtemps qu'il y aura des profits à faire au Québec et Dieu sait combien les resources sont énormes, et ça peu importe que le Québec soit indépendant ou non. Les Américains investissent en Espagne fasciste, en Yougoslavie communiste et au Canada capitaliste. Les investisseurs se foutent éperdument du genre de régime dont un peuple se veut doter. Ça leur est complètement égal le genre de régime que nous installons au Québec." [31]

While Bruno's line of argumentation seemed to reflect an opinion widely held among the more politicized QcUSWA unionists, it appeared to be at odds with the outlook of many less politicized rank-and-file members. At the 1972 convention of the QcUSWA the overwhelming majority of delegates adopted a pro-sovereignty resolution, thus making QcUSWA the first FTQ affiliate to go on record in favour of sovereignty. The same delegates who had backed the resolution, also indicated that only about 43 per cent of the workers whom they personally knew supported sovereignty.[32] Internal QcUSWA estimates made after the 1973 provincial elections revealed that in the urban centres of the St. Lawrence valley the PQ was only slightly

[29]ANQ, USWA Collection, P 144, 1A, 2, 754, Clément Godbout, "Option Québec, 14 June 1973," 4.

[30]Pierre Richard, "Le syndicat des métallos opte pour l'indépendance," *Devoir,* 14 January 1972, 3.

[31]ANQ, USWA Collection, P 144, 1A, 1, 83, A. Bruno to PQ members in Abitibi-est, June 1973.

[32]"L'Assemblée annuelle des syndicats locaux," *Métallo* (December 1972), 13-14; ANQ, USWA Collection, P 144, 1A, 2, 263, untitled collation of votes taken, 3.

more popular than the Liberal Party. Only in the mining towns did the PQ enjoy support levels that put it clearly ahead of the Liberals.[33]

In the absence of any polls or internal estimates, it is difficult to assess the degree of popularity which sovereignty attained within the FTQ as a whole during the early and mid-1970s. Given the QcUSWA estimates, it is unlikely that rank-and-file support for sovereignty across the FTQ exceeded forty per cent. The majority of the central's executive, including president Laberge, still opposed sovereignty for economic reasons.[34] Support for the PQ, however, was more widespread than support for sovereignty, because even federalist FTQ unionists were attracted to the PQ's social-democratic program.[35] In 1975, the FTQ convention adopted a resolution endorsing the PQ. The resolution noted that the PQ did not constitute a workers' party, but emphasized that it was the party closest to organized labour.[36] Most convention delegates agreed. About 80 per cent of the delegates polled indicated their preference for the PQ over other parties.[37] The 1975 FTQ convention sealed a rapprochement with the PQ that had been in the making since 1968.

The CSN, the CSQ, and the Rise of Socialist Sovereigntism, 1970-1976

While the PQ's social-democratic programme elicited favourable reponses among some unionists, in particular in the private sector, it met with suspicion among others, in particular in the public sector. By the early 1970s, the CSN and the CSQ underwent a radicalization process whereby both centrals adopted anti-capitalist positions which became increasingly incompatible with social-democratic reformism. As a result of the radicalization process, by 1972-1973, the leadership of both centrals became dominated by socialists. Most of these socialists opted for sovereignty. They did so because they saw it as an essential component of national liberation and because they believed that pan-Canadian solidarity did not constitute a viable option to achieve socialism. As the CSN's Montréal regional council argued in a 1972 position paper, progressive movements born in English-speaking Canada were doomed to fail in Québec, while progressive movements born in Québec were consigned to the same fate in the rest of Canada. "Dans un pays comme le Canada," the paper stated, "l'impérialisme et le capitalisme n'ont pas à diviser pour régner, vu que les divisions sont déjà inscrites dans la géographie, les cultures, l'histoire, les traditions, les mentalités et les intérêts particuliers entre le Québec d'une part

[33] ANQ, USWA Collection, P 144, 1A, 1, 83, 48 sheets with USWA staff member's estimates of QcUSWA members' voting behaviour in 1973 provincial elections.
[34] Fournier, *Louis Laberge*, 238.
[35] ANQ, USWA Collection, P 144, 1A, 2, 200, R. Lemoine to J.M. Carle, 25 September 1972, 3; Louis Fournier,"'Changer le régime ... avec le PQ!' – Louis Laberge," *Québec-Presse* 27 May 1973, 11; Rob Bull, "New steel union chief defends his PQ ties," *Toronto Star* , 26 February 1977, B4; Cyr and Roy, *Eléments d'histoire de la FTQ*, 134, 138.
[36] Fournier, *Histoire de la FTQ*, 119-22.
[37] "Les délégués au congrès de la FTQ: Qui sont-ils?" *Monde ouvrier* (January 1976), 3.

et les provinces anglophones d'autre part."[38] In short, national liberation and social emancipation were two sides of the same coin.

The CSN's and CSQ's socialist sovereigntists took their cue not from the PQ, but from ideas that had been diffused during the mid-1960s in left-wing journals such as *Parti pris* and *Révolution québécoise*. The left-wing contributors to these journals had claimed that national liberation was meaningless without social emancipation and called for the creation of an independent and socialist Québec. While one group of writers affirmed that independence constituted a first step toward the creation of a socialist society in Québec,[39] another group declared that independence and socialism must come about simultaneously.[40] Adherents of the two-step model argued that Québec's working class lacked political consciousness and, thus, was incapable of leading the struggle for national liberation. Partisans of the one-step model retorted that neither the petty bourgeoisie nor the bourgeoisie, but only the working class, could be counted upon to bring about national liberation. Despite lengthy debates, the two groups did not arrive at a consensus. Although their discourse had led a marginal existence in the shadows of mainstream sovereigntism, as propagated by the RIN and the PQ, it attracted a sizeable following among young intellectuals. During the second half of the 1960s many of them joined public-sector unions or began to work for CSN and CSQ suborganizations.

By the early 1970s, several CSN and CSQ subgroups and decision-making bodies adopted positions inspired by anti-capitalist sovereigntism. Some espoused the two-step model. In 1971, for instance, the convention of the CSN's federation of salaried professionals endorsed a position paper which stated: "La CSN et le PQ sont des outils de politisation. A l'heure actuelle, la libération nationale prime; mais elle doit être suivie de la libération sociale."[41] Others, however, followed the one-step model. The 1972 CSQ convention, for example, rejected a motion, which called for independence and instead adopted one in favour of, "l'indépendance du Québec réalisée avec la participation active et critique de la classe laborieuse, pour autant qu'elle se réalise au bénéfice de la classe laborieuse." (The resolution did not constitute official CSQ policy, however, because the convention had not been mandated to take a stand in the matter.)[42] In 1973, the CSN's Montréal regional council also embraced the notion that independence and socialism must come about simultaneously. In a position paper entitled *L'indépendance est plus sorcier qu'on pense*, the council argued that the PQ only defended the interests of Québec's bourgeoisie and petty bourgeoisie. Québec's working class needed a political party

[38]CCSNM, "Résolution pour l'indépendance du Québec, 14e congrès du CCSNM, avril 1972," in Louis LeBorgne, *La CSN et la question nationale depuis 1960* (Montréal 1975), 197.

[39]"Manifeste 64-65," *Parti pris* (September 1964), 14.

[40]Gilles Bourque and Gilles Dostaler, *Socialisme et Indépendance* (Montréal 1980).

[41]Archives de la CSN, Montréal (henceforth: ACSN), Fonds S-44, FPPSCQ, Procès-verbal du congrès fédéral de 1971, 13.

[42]ACEQ, Procès-verbal du congrès de 1972, 140-1.

of its own, which would advocate both independence and socialism. This new party should aim at eclipsing the PQ as the major pro-sovereignty force in the province and thereby weaken, "l'hégémonie politique de la petite et moyenne bourgeoisie dans la lutte nationale."[43] Like the intellectuals of the 1960s, labour's socialist sovereigntists did not arrive at a consensus on the strategy to be chosen. For the next few years, they engaged in heated debates over the respective virtues of the one-step and two-step models.

Although socialist sovereigntists dominated the CSN and CSQ executives by the mid-1970s, they remained a minority in their respective organizations. An internal CSQ poll conducted in 1973 suggests that about 42 per cent of the central's members supported sovereignty-association. About twelve per cent opted for independence without economic association. Without doubt, the level of support for sovereignty in the CSQ exceeded that in the CSN. CSQ members possessed higher employment security then many CSN members, and thus tended to be less moved by considerations of sovereignty's potentially adverse economic repercussions. Moreover, as noted previously, CSQ members had a direct stake in the status of French as the dominant language. As the poll revealed, almost all of those in favour of sovereignty-association or independence were convinced that sovereignty would be beneficial for the maintenance and development of Québec's distinct cultural identity centered around the French language. Only a minority of them were persuaded that sovereignty would ameliorate the situation of the working class. In short, most CSQ unionists were swayed by mainstream sovereignty ideas as propagated by the PQ rather than by socialist sovereigntists.[44]

CSN and CSQ leaders staunchly believed in the need to create a workers' party to the left of the PQ. Since there was little support for such a project among the rank-and-file, the leaders of the two centrals decided to stick to their organizations' traditional neutrality regarding party politics. Unable to nudge along the process of creating a workers' party, they were caught in a vicious circle. Although they resented the PQ, for the time being they had nowhere else to go. Among the major parties in the province only the PQ advocated a progressive program and stood a chance of toppling the Liberal government, which the CSN and CSQ leaders loathed. "S'il est important de donner une leçon au Parti libéral," the CSN executive stated prior to the 1976 provincial elections, "il faut être bien conscient qu'au lendemain de l'élection, même si le PQ prenait le pouvoir, nous serions placés devant une autre gouvernement qui, de gré ou de force, serait asservi à la classe dominante."

[43]CCSNM/Centre de formation populaire, L'Indépendance c'est plus sorcier qu'on pense (Montréal 1973), 4.
[44]Ralph P. Güntzel, "The Centrale de l'Enseignement du Québec and Quebec Separatist Nationalism, 1960-80," Canadian Historical Review 80:1 (March 1999), 73-4.

Paradoxically, on the eve of the 1976 provincial elections, the CSN and CSQ both hoped for and feared a PQ victory.[45]

The FTQ and the First Referendum on Sovereignty, 1976-1980

In 1976 the Lévesque-led PQ won the provincial elections with about 40 per cent of the popular vote and, thus, came to power a mere eight years after its creation. Having promised to hold a referendum on sovereignty-association, preparing the referendum constituted one of the priorities of the Lévesque administration. In the meantime, the new government also implemented various reforms in areas of direct concern to organized labour. In 1977, the government adopted Bill 101, which strengthened the status of French in Québec. The bill contained a stipulation, which gave workers the right to work in French in all enterprises, with at least 50 employees. In the same year, the PQ government also revamped key aspects of the provincial labour code. The new labour code simplified certification procedures, increased union security, and limited employers' rights to hire strike breakers. In 1979, the government passed an industrial health and safety bill, which introduced improved health and safety standards in the workplace and set up a system by which employers and employees became jointly responsible for putting the new standards into practice. Although the reforms addressed long-held union grievances, they did not meet with uniform approval among the three centrals.[46]

The FTQ warmly applauded the government's reforms and maintained a cordial relationship with the Lévesque adminsitration. As FTQ president Laberge said in retrospect, "Le PQ a formé un bon gouvernement, le meilleur qu'on ait jamais eu. Un gouvernment fort, travaillant, qui a respecté ses promesses durant son premier mandat. On n'avait jamais vu des politiciens faire de la belle ouvrage comme ça."[47] Reactions were more lukewarm on the part of the CSN and the CSQ. Both centrals welcomed Bill 101, but rejected the reform of the labour code and the health and safety bill as too sympathetic to the interests of business. Unlike the FTQ, both the CSN and the CSQ eschewed a cooperative type of relationship with the Lévesque administration. Two reasons accounted for this approach. First, the socialists who dominated the federations wished for the emergence of a socialist workers' party. Such a party, however, could get off the ground only if a sufficient number of PQ sympathizers would switch allegiances. Thus, criticizing the PQ government was

[45]Louis Fournier, "La CSN: du PQ à un 'socialisme d'ici,'" *Jour*, 27 May 1977, 15-16; Pierre Vennat, "La base répond NON à l'éxécutif de la CSN," *Presse*, 3 June 1978, A9; Vincent Price, "Pas de parti des travailleurs," *Presse*, 6 June 1978, A4; Rouillard, *Histoire du syndicalisme au Québec*, 424-425; Güntzel, "The Centrale de l'Enseignement du Québec," 71. For quotation: ACSN, CSN, Procès-verbal, bureau confédéral, 31 October 1976, 34.
[46]On Bill 101: McRoberts, *Quebec*, 277-280. On the reform of the labour code and the health and safety bill: Rouillard, *Histoire du syndicalisme au Québec*, 424-5.
[47]Fournier, *Louis Laberge*, 281.

the first step toward the creation of a political alternative to its left. Second, since most CSN and CSQ members worked in the public sector, both federations perceived the Lévesque administration not only as the provincial government but also — and perhaps most importantly — as the employer and, hence, antagonist. To cooperate with the employer might well have meant to weaken one's bargaining position. An attack on the PQ government's shortcomings, in contrast, constituted a promising build-up for the 1979 public-sector negotiations.[48]

The same attitudes that guided the three centrals' policies in relation to the PQ government's reformism, also coloured the positions they adopted in view of the impending referendum on sovereignty-association. At the November 1979 FTQ convention the executive presented a working paper which noted that, "ni Ottawa, ni Québec ne possèdent aujourd'hui les pouvoirs suffisants pour adopter une politique économique collective, s'ils en avaient envie. Cette division des pouvoirs incite à la démission des pouvoirs face à l'entreprise privée, domestique ou étrangère." The parallel jurisdiction of the governments in Ottawa and Québec City in economic matters translated into a waste of resources and the absence of an effective economic development policy in Québec, the working paper argued. Thus, a concentration of powers either in Ottawa or in Québec City was necessary. The federal government could not be trusted to make the right decisions for Québec, the paper claimed, since it had traditionally given priority to the industrial development of southern Ontario and the agricultural development of the Prairie provinces. Having thereby ruled Ottawa out, the paper concluded that Québec needed complete jurisdiction over economic policies and manpower training.[49] Since the working paper stopped short of endorsing sovereigntism without, however, rejecting sovereignty, it met with approval among both sovereigntists and federalists.[50]

In December 1979, the PQ government announced that the referendum question would ask for a mandate to negotiate sovereignty-association. Given the content of the referendum question, consensus-building for an official FTQ position in view of the referendum became an easy task. Obviously, partisans of sovereignty were only too willing to recommend a "yes " vote in the referendum. Federalists, too, rallied around a recommendation to vote "yes. " To endorse a "yes " vote meant to avoid alienating FTQ sovereigntists and the Lévesque administration without actually having to endorse sovereignty. Moreover, given their penchant for a special status for and a massive transfer of powers to Québec, FTQ federalists had reason to see negotiations *d'égal à égal* as the most promising means to bring about the change which they aspired to. The FTQ organ *Monde ouvrier* explained this reasoning in the following terms:

[48]Güntzel, "Le Confédération des syndicats nationaux," 166-167; Güntzel, "Le Centrale de l'Enseignement du Québec," 75.
[49]Archives de la FTQ, Montréal (henceforth: AFTQ), FTQ, *La FTQ et la question nationale: Congrès tenu à Québec du 26 au 30 novembre 1979* (Montréal 1979). Quotation, 16.
[50]AFTQ, FTQ, Procès-verbal, congrès, 1979, 34-5.

Les Québécois sont sur le point de négocier 'leur convention collective' avec Ottawa et le reste du Canada. Nous avons déjà un syndicat dûment accrédité et un comité de négociation élu: le gouvernment actuel du Québec. Il s'agit maintenant de lui donner un mandat de négocier une nouvelle convention; le [jour du référendum], nous devons nous prononcer sur notre projet de convention collective. Ce n'est pas parce que nous voterons ce projet, qu'il s'appliquera automatiquement; il faut d'abord le négocier. Et, comme tout comité de négociation, le gouvernement québécois reviendra devant les membres, tous les Québécois, pour rendre compte des résultats des négociations. Ce sera alors le temps d'accepter l'entente de principe s'il y an a une, de re-mandater notre comité de négociation ou bien de voter la grève.[51]

At a special convention held in April 1980, the FTQ officially went on record in favour of a "yes " vote in the referendum, which was to take place on May 20, 1980.[52] In his convention speech, Laberge stressed that Québec workers had all the more reason to vote "yes, " because capital was solidly behind a "no" vote. "Il suffit de regarder qui se retrouvent dans le camp du 'non'," Laberge said,

pour nous apercevoir qu'il s'agit là d'un regroupement sans précédent dans l'histoire du Québec des 'forces de la réaction' .... Il est significatif de retrouver côte à côte le Parti libéral du Québec, le Parti libéral du Canada, le Parti conservateur, le Conseil du patronat du Québec, les principaux porte-parole des milieux financiers, les représentants de Power Corporation, de Bell Canada, de ITT, de l'Alcan, de l'Iron Ore .... Il est évident que le principal intérêt de ces forces réactionnaires est de maintenir le Québec dans un état de dépendance qui leur a largement profité et d'étouffer tout mouvement vers un changement quel qu'il soit. Il aurait été pour le moins indécent pour le mouvement syndical de penser s'aligner avec ce 'club des exploiteurs.'[53]

The FTQ, though, was not content to merely recommend a "yes " vote. Rather, the federation undertook great efforts to convince as many of its members as possible to vote "yes." At the end of the special convention Laberge called on his troops to give their best. "D'ici le 20 mai vous n'avez plus le droit d'être fatigués ou malades, tout le monde à l'ouvrage." Following the convention, the FTQ embarked on a full-fledged internal propaganda campaign. Numerous union meetings were devoted to convincing the undecided; FTQ officers toured the province; *Monde ouvrier*

---

[51]"Le Québec veut négocier une nouvelle convention collective," *Monde ouvrier* (May 1980), 8.

[52] "Le congrès extraordinaire de la FTQ se prononce à 90% en favuer du OUI," *Devoir*, 21 April 1980, 6; "Un mandat clair pour le 'oui,'" *Monde ouvrier* (May 1980), 2.

[53]AFTQ, Louis Laberge, *Discours inaugural de Louis Laberge, Président de la FTQ, Question nationale – Réponse syndicale, 2e congrès extraordinaire de la FTQ, Québec, le samedi 19 avril 1980* (Montréal 1980), 7.

devoted its pages to the referendum; and FTQ affiliates set up a "Regroupements des travailleurs pour le oui" and urged workers to sign lists in support of a "yes ."[54]

The CSN, the CSQ, and the First Referendum on Sovereignty, 1976-1980

Referendum-related debates in the CSN and the CSQ differed markedly from those in the FTQ. At the CSN's special convention in 1979, the central's enlarged executive presented a working paper on the national question, which was largely devoted to designing a socialist vision of society. The position paper charged that the federal government was responsible for Québec's economic underdevelopment relative to Ontario, because it had favoured southern Ontario to the detriment of Québec. The paper also accused the federalists of wanting to perpetuate Québec's national oppression and dismissed sovereignty-association as insufficient, since it did not envisage complete liberation from the federal stranglehold. In order to end Québec's national oppression, the paper argued, the people of Québec needed to create a regime, that would wrestle the strategic sectors of the economy from the hands of foreign capitalists. All essential industries must be nationalized and savings be centralized in a public capital fund, which would then become the centre-piece of a new industrial development policy. Publicly owned enterprises and the central capital fund would have to be controlled and administered "[par] la classe ouvrière en fonction des intérêts des travailleurs."[55]

Subsequent to the reading of the working paper, the convention debated whether or not to go on record in favour of independence. The motion to endorse independence failed to get the support of CSN president Norbert Rodrigue and most other high-ranking CSN officers. Despite being favourable to independence, Rodrigue and his associates feared that such a stand might lead to internal divisions. Many CSN members remained opposed to sovereignty. Sovereigntists were divided between PQ sympathizers and socialist sovereigntists, who were split between moderates advocating the two-stage model and radicals promoting the one-step model. Fear of internal strife was not the only reason that motivated Rodrigue and his lieutenants. Like many public-sector unionists they felt that an endorsement of independence might strengthen the hand of the government in the approaching public-sector negotiations. In the absence of support from the central's most prominent leaders, the motion in favour of independence failed.[56] Instead, the convention resolved to endorse the following position: "Pour lutter efficacement contre l'oppression nationale et ses diverses manifestations, la CSN s'inscrit dans

[54]"Créer un 'regroupement pour le oui" dans chaque milieu de travail, *Monde ouvrier* (May 1980), 3; "Selon la direction de la FTQ, 70% des membres de cette centrale diront Oui," *Devoir*, 15 May 8. For quotation: "Le congrès extraordinaire de la FTQ se prononce à 90% en faveur du OUI," *Devoir*, 21 April 1980, 6.
[55]CSN, *Procès-verbal, congrès spécial, 1979* (Montréal 1979), 74-5.
[56]Güntzel, "The Confédération des syndicats nationaux," 167-9.

une démarche d'appropriation par le peuple québécois des pouvoirs et institutions politiques, économiques et culturels."[57]

After further intenal debates, the confederal council, the CSN's highest decision-making body between conventions, met in April 1980 to decide whether or not to recommend a "yes" in the referendum. This time, all high-ranking CSN officers were in agreement. As Rodrigue told the council members, a victory of the 'yes' side would improve the chances of success in the struggle for a socialist society. Since the CSN had sufficiently established its critical distance to the Lévesque administration, a CSN recommendation to vote "yes " could not be interpretated as an endorsement of either the PQ or its vision of society.[58] After some debate, the CSN confederal council adopted the following resolution:

Le project de souveraineté-association ... tend à rapprocher les lieux du pouvoir .... Un oui au référendum créerait de meilleures conditions pour la lutte démocratique visant à accroître l'emprise des travailleurs et classes populaires sur toutes les dimensions de leur vie .... La CSN, dans le respect de l'opinion de chacun de ses membres, et tout en conservant son autonomie, considère qu'il est dans l'intérêt des travailleurs et des couches populaires de voter oui au référendum.[59]

Unlike the FTQ, the CSN did not try to mobilize its members for a victory of the "yes" forces. As the referendum campaign unfolded, the CSN looked on from the sidelines. The CSQ remained similarly aloof, albeit for different reasons.

At the 1978 CSQ convention, the executive presented a position paper, which argued that the Québec government needed to obtain more powers to redress Québec's weak economic structure and to defend and promote the French language. The CSQ executive also recommended that the central "se prononce en faveur de l'indépendance du Québec et considère que la lutte pour l'indépendance est indissociable de la lutte pour une société que les travailleurs québécois ont à définir et à bâtir sur les plans économique, social, culturel et politique, en fonction de leurs intérêts."[60] The convention resolved that the CSQ take a stand only after an internal referendum on Québec's constitutional status. There was severe disagreement, however, over the question to be asked in the internal referendum. PQ sympathizers wanted a question which offered a choice between independence as defined by the CSQ executive, sovereignty-association, and federalism. The socialists insisted that the question be limited to either accepting or rejecting the recommendation of the CSQ executive. After acrimonious debate, the socialists' proposal carried the day.[61]

[57]CSN, *Procès-verbal, congrès special, 1979*, 147.
[58]Güntzel, "The Confédération des syndicats nationaux," 169.
[59]Conseil confédéral de la CSN, "Résolution générale," *Travail* (April 1980), supplément sur la question nationale, 7-8; Laval LeBorgne, "Le conseil confédéral de la CSN vote OUI," *Presse*, 12 April 1980, A2.
[60]ACEQ, CEQ, Procès-verbal, congrès, 1978, annexe, 80.
[61]Güntzel, "The Centrale de l'Enseignement du Québec," 77-78.

In March 1979, all CSQ members received a questionnaire which asked them whether the central should participate in Québec's referendum debate and promote independence as a means of building a workers' society.[62] Many CSQ social democrats were irate. They supported sovereignty but opposed socialism. Their wish to be able to choose the former without having to endorse the latter had been repeatedly ignored. In this situation, the leaders of several CSQ affiliates decided to strike back against the CSQ's socialist executive. "Nous n'acceptons pas," they stated in a joint declaration to the media, "que le débat [interne] soit mené de telle façon que le oui à l'indépendance soit assoçie automatiquement à un oui inconscient à une vision marxiste de la société québécoise." Thus, they decided to oppose any participation of the CSQ in Québec's referendum debate.[63] During the following weeks the front of rejection broadened. In the end, almost two thirds of those who returned the questionnaire rejected a participation of the CSQ in Québec's referendum debate. Only 17.4 per cent had followed the CSQ executive and endorsed independence and socialism. In accordance with these results, the CSQ's special convention in June 1979 resolved non-intervention of the central in the referendum debate.[64]

The May 1980 referendum dealt the sovereigntist movement a severe blow as almost 60 per cent of the voters voted "no." There are no data indicating the voting behaviour of unionized workers in the referendum. Laberge subsequently estimated that about two thirds of the FTQ membership voted "yes."[65] While this may be a somewhat exaggerated estimate, it is probable that more than half of the members of the three centrals voted "yes." Most likely, support for the "yes " option was highest among QcUSWA miners and CSQ members. Irrespective of the voting pattern among unionized workers, the referendum outcome ended debates on sovereignty in all three centrals as well as within Québec society in general. Québec sovereigntism went into a prolonged decline.

The Three Centrals and the Decline of Sovereigntism, 1980-1985

Soon after the defeat of sovereigtism, the Trudeau-led federal government instigated negotiations on constitutional reform. After much acrimony, in November 1981 these talks resulted in agreement between the federal government and all provincial governments except Québec. The Québec government judged the constitutional revisions as unacceptable for Québec and refused to endorse them. Thus, when the British North America Act was officially replaced by the Constitution Act in July 1982, Québec remained outside the Canadian constitutional family (although the revised constitution did apply to Québec). Rather than having made

[62]Güntzel, "The Centrale de l'Enseigntism du Québec," 79.
[63]Paule des Rivières, "Trois syndicats d'enseignants contestent l'analyse marxiste de la CEQ," Devoir, 12 April 1979, 9.
[64]Güntzel, "The Centrale de l'Enseigntism du Québec," 79-80.
[65]Fournier, Louis Laberge, 300.

Canadian federalism more attractive to Québec, the reform of 1981-82 enlarged the gulf between Québec and the rest of the country. The imposition of the Constitution Act further disillusioned Québecers who had been frustrated by the referendum defeat.[66]

The decline of sovereigntism and the imposition of constitutional reform coincided with other developments, which left Québec labour morose. Against the backdrop of a severe economic crisis, both the CSQ and the CSN began to undergo a political-ideological de-radicalization. The economic and political developments of the mid- and late-1980s further forced labour on the defensive. Like unions elsewhere, Québec labour found it difficult to come to terms with new issues such as privatization, deregulation, globalization, and free trade. Moreover, despite all consciousness-raising efforts during the 1970s, the creation of a socialist society remained as utopian and remote as ever. In this context, the CSN discontinued its socialist discourse by the mid-1980s. The CSQ had already ended its anti-capitalist rhetoric a few years earlier, as a direct result of the stalemate between reformists and radicals, which ensued from the referendum debate. By the end of the decade, both centrals had watered down their visions of social change and joined the FTQ in promoting social-democratic reformism. Since the mid-1980s, factional strife within the CSN and the CSQ no longer focused on ideological issues, but rather on questions of leadership personnel and militancy in relation to the employers. To a certain extent, the militant factions in both centrals derived their motivation from the anguish and bitterness of the confrontation with the PQ government in 1982-83.[67]

The crisis of the early 1980s increased unemployment and put increasing pressures on the provincial budget. In this situation the PQ government, which had been reelected in 1981, decided to cut expenses in the public sector. In April 1982, the government asked the public-sector unions to give up wage increases, which had been negotiated in 1979, for the period from August to December 1982. After the unions' refusal, in June 1982 the government legislated severe wage cuts for the first three months of 1983. In the fall of 1983 the government and the public-sector unions began negotiations for a new collective agreement. As the negotiations dragged on and a consensus remained elusive, the government legislated wages and working conditions in the public sector for the period from 1982 to 1985. The unions retaliated by going on strike in January 1983. The government passed back-to-work legislation and succeeded in splitting the common front of public-sector workers. By February 1983, the epic struggle came to an end when the CSQ, which had been the last part of the common front to hold out, agreed to a

[66]Fraser, *PQ*, 279-301.

[67]Roch Denis and Serge Denis, *Les syndicats face au pouvoir: Syndicalisme et politique au Québec de 1960 à 1992* (Ottawa 1992), 86-89, 150-156; Pierre Vennat, *Une révolution non tranquille: Le syndicalisme au Québec de 1960 à l'an 2000* (Montréal 1992), 37-129; Fournier, *Histoire de la FTQ*, 179-261.

conciliation process. The conciliation verdict improved the government's terms only marginally.[68]

After the events of 1982-1983, relations between the PQ and organized labour reached a low point. The government's treatment of public-sector workers left so much bitterness that even the FTQ, which had long been the PQ's ally in the labour movement and which was dominated by private-sector workers, did not endorse the PQ in the 1985 provincial elections.[69] The elections resulted in a return to power of the Liberal Party under Robert Bourassa. In an ironic twist of fate, the Liberal reign during the second half of the 1980s and the first half of the 1990s resulted not only in a rapprochement between the PQ and the three centrals but also a resurgence of sovereigntism.

The Three Centrals and the Resurgence of Sovereigntism, 1985-1995

During the mid-1980s, the PQ undertook little to recuperate the social-democratic credentials it had lost in 1982-83. Under the leadership of Pierre-Marc Johnson, who had taken over from Lévesque as PQ president in 1985, it even shelved sovereignty in favour of autonomist nationalism, which it referred to as "national affirmation." In 1988, however, Jacques Parizeau, one of Lévesque's former lieutenants, succeeded Johnson as PQ leader. Under Parizeau the PQ once again stressed its social-democratic aspirations and reintroduced sovereignty as the centre-piece of its program. Prior to the 1989 provincial elections, Parizeau expressed his regret and apologies for the imposition of the wage and salary cuts in 1983. Shortly thereafter the FTQ returned to its tradition of recommending to vote for the PQ. As Laberge noted, "malgré les graves erreurs du Parti québécois dans le passé, il faut reconnaître que c'est le programme de cette formation qui se rapproche le plus du projet de société que met de l'avant la FTQ .... Le programme que le PQ propose à l'électorat rejoint la plupart des grands objectifs de la centrale. C'est le cas, notamment, de la politique de plein emploi, du rôle accordé à l'Etat dans la conduite de l'économie, de l'autodétermination du Québec, de la francisation, de la législation syndicale et de la protection de l'environnement." Although it lost the 1989 provincial elections, the PQ managed to recuperate some of the labour vote that had deserted the party in 1985.[70]

The resurgence of sovereigntism was intimately tied to the demise of the Meech Lake Accord. Signed by the first ministers in 1987, the accord was meant to make the constitution acceptable to Québec by adding several amendments including, most notably, a clause which recognized Québec as a "distinct society." The recognition of Québec's distinctiveness initially appeared as a significant

[68]Rouillard, *Histoire du syndicalisme au Québec*, 388-93.
[69]Fournier, *Louis Laberge*, 328-30.
[70]Graham Fraser, "PQ elated over wins in semi-final," *Globe and Mail*, 27 September 1989, A7; Fournier, *Louis Laberge*, 348-349. Quotation in: Martin Pelchat, "FTQ: la direction recommande un 'soutien critique' au PQ," *Devoir*, 23 August 1989, 2.

victory for Bourassa, who had been one of the prime movers in the negotiations which had led to the accord. By 1989-1990, however, the ratification process of the amendment got bogged down. At the same time, public opinion polls revealed that more and more English-speaking Canadians opposed the notion that Québec constituted a distinct society. In the months before the expiration of the ratification deadline in June 1990, controversy intensified. When the deadline finally arrived, not all provinces had ratified the amendment and the accord became defunct. At that point, English-Canadian unwillingness to recognize Québec as a distinct society had risen to a groundswell. In several instances, well covered by the media, this unwillingness translated into anti-Québec demonstrations and desecrations of the Québec flag. As a result, Québecers were left with the impression that English Canada rejected Québec's distinctiveness.[71]

In Québec, the demise of the Meech Lake Accord revived old fears about cultural survival and increased skepticism about the capacity of the Canadian federal system to accommodate Québec. More importantly, it imbued many francophone Québécers with a strong urge to reassert their sense of group worth in the face of massive disparagement and rejection. In this situation, support for sovereignty quickly soared to the 60 per cent mark.[72] Economic considerations no longer acted as an effective counterweight, since Québec's economy had made great strides in the course of the 1980s. "The economic arguments used by the business community in 1980 don't hold true anymore," Ghislain Dufour, a staunch federalist and head of the Conseil du Patronat, told the Globe and Mail in October 1989. "The Quebec economy is strong; our entrepreneurs are successful."[73] In the spring of 1990 even corporate institutions such as Merrill Lynch, a US investment firm, and the Bank of Montreal, predicted that sovereignty would not entail economic turbulence.[74] By the summer of 1990, more Québecers than ever jumped on the sovereigntist bandwagon.

The developments convinced labour leaders that the time had come to commit their organizations to the promotion of sovereignty. Many leading unionists, such as CSN president Gérald Larose, had already supported sovereignty in the debates of the 1970s and 1980. Others, such as FTQ president Laberge, had joined the sovereigntist camp subsequent to the 1980 referendum.[75] For some time the leaders of the three centrals had regarded sovereignty as an important strategic goal which

[71]Andrew Cohen, A Deal Undone: The Making and Breaking of the Meech Lake Accord (Vancouver 1990); Patrick Monahan, Meech Lake: The Inside Story (Toronto 1991).
[72]Edouard Cloutier, Jean H. Guay, and Daniel Latouche, Le Virage: l'évolution de l'opinion politique au Québec depuis 1960 (Montréal 1992), 45.
[73]Barrie McKenna, "Quebec's powerful Caisse driving force behind nationalist economy," Globe and Mail, 31 October 1989, A3.
[74]Robert Winters, "Bank plays down Quebec independence," (Montréal) Gazette, 13 March 1990, A1.
[75]Fournier, Louis Laberge, 338, 362-3.

remained beyond reach. Yet, by 1990, sovereignty no longer appeared as elusive as it had during the 1980s. Unlike in the late 1970s and 1980, in 1990 there were no major internal obstacles that made it difficult or undesirable for the centrals to endorse sovereignty. A decade earlier, some leaders and many rank-and-file members had opposed sovereignty. In contrast, by 1990, re-alcitrant leaders and rank-and-file members had either espoused sovereignty in the course of the 1980s or became infected with the sovereigntist spirit that spread like wildfire through Québec society in 1990. Moreover, the differences between the sovereigntist factions, which had shaken the CSN and temporarily paralysed the CSQ a decade earlier, faded as a result of the two centrals' de-radicalization. Thus, the fear of internal factionism no longer prevented the centrals from taking the next step in their sovereigntist evolution.

At its convention in early May1990, the CSN became the first of the three centrals to endorse independence and commit itself to promoting sovereigntism.[76] In mid-May, Laberge informed the media that the FTQ would begin to actively promote sovereignty on 24 June, Québec's national holiday.[77] A few weeks later, the CSQ followed suit. In the wake of an internal poll revealing that 74 per cent of the central's members supported sovereignty, the CSQ convention adopted a resolution which committed the CSQ to struggle for Québec independence.[78] The sovereigntist pamphlets and memoranda, which the centrals produced in the summer and fall of 1990, stressed four points; First, Québec must attain sovereign nation-state status, because it is natural for nations to do so. "We want Québec to be a country rather than a province," the FTQ stated, "because it is normal for a people to have a country and Canada will always be the country of others"; Second, a sovereign Québec would be in a better position to safeguard the distinct character of Québec society; Third, Canadian federalism constituted a burden without which Québec could conduct more efficient economic development policies; Fourth, sovereignty would democratize Québec society. Sovereignty, the CSN declared, "will strengthen the people's capacity to influence those who make the decisions. It will help democracy to grow and function." Hence, the CSN concluded, "sovereignty will bring about more favorable conditions for fulfilling many demands of the unions and mass organizations."[79]

[76]François Berger, "La CSN s'engage à promouvoir l'indépendance," *Presse*, 9 May 1990, A4; Josée Boileau, "Vote massif des délégués de la CSN pour le principe de l'indépendance du Québec," *Devoir,* 9 May 1990, 3.

[77]Marie-Claude Lortie, "Plus souverainiste que jamais, la FTQ promet de mobiliser dès le 24 juin," *Presse*, 19 May 1990, G3.

[78]François Berger, "La CEQ en faveur de l'indépendance du Québec," *Presse*, 26 May 1990, A20; Lia Lévesque, "Le congrès de la CEQ appelé à se prononcer en faveur de l'indépendance," *Devoir*, 26 May 1990, A12; Lia Lévesque, "Les trois grandes centrales syndicales s'engagent à promouvoir la souveraineté," *Devoir*, 3 July 1990, 2.

[79]Richard Fiedler, *Canada, Adieu? Quebec Debates its Future* (Lantzville, British Columbia 1991),122-150. For FTQ quotation, 123. For CSN quotations, 134.

In order to back up their sovereigntist discourse, the centrals became involved in several important political battles fought in Québec during the first half of the 1990s. After a renewed round of constitutional negotiations with first ministers from the rest of Canada, the Bourassa administration agreed to the Charlottetown Accord of August 1992. The accord included a watered-down version of the distinct-society clause which had played such a prominent role in the Meech Lake Accord.[80] On 26 October 1992, the Charlottetown Accord was put to a referendum vote in all parts of Canada. During the referendum campaign, the three centrals vociferously opposed the accord.[81] Their efforts were rewarded as more than 55 per cent of voters in Québec voted " no." Having met with rejection in most other parts of Canada as well, the Charlottetown Accord became defunct.[82] The FTQ also supported the Bloc québécois (BQ) which had been created in 1990 by a group of independent members of the House of Commons previously belonging to the Progressive Conservative Party. Led by Lucien Bouchard, a former Tory cabinet minister, the BQ espoused sovereignty and, thus, become the federal wing of the sovereigntist movement. In the 1993 federal elections, the FTQ urged its members to vote BQ. Bound by their traditional neutrality regarding party politics, the CSN and the CSQ refrained from following the example of the FTQ. They both, however, supported individual BQ candidates. Again, the centrals' efforts were rewarded as the BQ won the vast majority of Québec ridings.[83]

The centrals also became involved in the 1994 provincial elections. Once again, the FTQ supported the PQ, while the CSN and the CSQ stopped short of officially endorsing the PQ. Their formal neutrality barely veiled their sympathies for the PQ. "Du côté de la CSN et de la CSQ," one observer commented, "on s'en tient à une vieille tradition de 'neutralité', mais cette abstention officielle ne fait guère illusion: les directions des deux centrales souhaitent ardemment le victoire du PQ."[84] CSN and CSQ leaders severely criticized the Liberals and categorically

[80]André Picard, "Deal will bring era of security, Bourassa says," *Globe and Mail*, 23 September 1992, A5; Graham Fraser, "Parizeau says deal ensures decline," *Globe and Mail*, 26 September 1992, A5.

[81]"Pour bien des raisons la CEQ invite ses membres à voter NON," *Devoir*, 9 September1992, A2; Clément Trudel, "Congrès extraordinaire de la FTQ pour préciser son NON à l'entente," *Devoir*, 17 September 1992, A2; Carole Montpetit, "Les centrales louent la lucidité des Québécois," *Devoir*, 27 October 1992, A6.

[82]J.M. Bumsted, *A History of the Canadian Peoples* (Toronto 1998), 387.

[83]Josée Boileau, "La CSN travaillera à l'élection du souverainiste Gilles Duceppe dans Laurier/Sainte-Marie," *Devoir*, 14 July 1990, 2; Josée Boileau, "Les syndicats investissent le Bloc québécois," *Devoir*, 11 April 1993, A1, A12; Serge Truffaut, "Le Bloc québécois plutôt que le NPD," *Devoir*, 20 September 1993, A1, A8; Pierre O'Neill, "Une première: la CEQ se mouille," *Devoir*, 24 September 1993, A5.

[84]Louis Fournier, "Les camarades et les candidats," *Devoir*, 18 August 1994, A7.

declared that the Liberal government must not be re-elected.[85] It was thus with great satisfaction that the three centrals greeted the PQ election victory in 1994.[86] The coming to power of the PQ headed by Parizeau also set the stage for the second referendum on sovereignty. The referendum took place on 30 October 1995, and asked Québecers to agree that Québec become sovereign after having made a formal offer to Canada for a new economic and political partnership.[87]

During the months preceding the referendum, the three centrals once again engaged in a major propaganda effort. Besides reiterating earlier arguments in favour of sovereignty, they contrasted the social and collective nature of Québec's political culture with the liberal values of English-speaking Canada. "Ici, nous sommes davantage syndicalisés que partout ailleurs en Amérique du Nord," CSN president Larose remarked. "Ici, l'intervention de l'Etat a toujours été plus importante que partout ailleurs en Amérique du Nord. Pourquoi? Essentiellement parce que pour vivre, pour survivre, le peuple québécois a été obligé de compter sur ses forces collectives."[88] To strengthen Québec, the argument implied, meant to strengthen a political culture incompatible with the cold-blooded, neo-liberalism that had become popular in English-speaking Canada. The centrals also attacked the federalists' negative propaganda. Larose, for instance, dismissed statements by federal finance minister Paul Martin, who declared that the federal government would not negotiate a new partnership with Québec following a sovereigntist referendum victory. The rest of Canada would undoubtedly negotiate a new partnership with Québec, Larose said, "parce que de l'autre côté, il y a autant de capitalistes que de ce côté-ci. Et on les connaît. Ni foi, ni loi, l'argent n'a pas d'odeur; s'il y a une piastre à faire, on va venir le faire."[89]

Labour's finely tuned propaganda machine temporarily sputtered when the CSN's federation of health and social service workers went on record against sovereignty to protest against planned cuts in public health services. At its convention in May 1995, the federation, which had traditionally been one of the more

[85]Paul Cauchon, "Johnson est un démolisseur, estime Lorraine Pagé," *Devoir*, 28 June 1994, A2; Stéphane Baillargeon, "Le dilemme CSN," *Devoir*, 3 May 1994, A1, A10; Suzanne Colpron, "Larose tire à bulets rouges sur le gouvernement Johnson," *Presse*, 10 May 1994, A5; Suzanne Colpron, "Trois des quatre présidents de centrales syndicales appuient le PQ," *Presse*, 20 August 1994, F15; CSN Executive Committee, "Un constat d'échec," *Devoir*, 8 September 1994, A7.

[86]Clément Godbout and Henri Massé, "FTQ-PQ en neuf engagements," *Devoir*, 10 October 1994, A11; Lia Lévesque, "Les syndicats sont emballés, le patronat reste sur sa faim," *Devoir*, 30 November 1994, A4; Paul Cauchon, "Une rupture avec le discours néolibéral," *Devoir*, 2 December 1994, A2.

[87]Bumsted, *A History of the Canadian Peoples*, 421-2.

[88]Gérald Larose, "Le Québec qu'il nous faut," *Devoir*, 16 October 1995, A9.

[89]Mario Fontaine, "'Je n'ai jamais vu de peuple se libérer parla force de ses hommes d'affaires' – Gérald Larose," *Presse*, 28 September 1995 B7. For quotation: Michel Venne, "Larose parlera franc," *Devoir*, 14 September 1995, A4.

militant segments of the CSN, resolved to take a stand "contre le projet souverainiste du Parti québécois, et ce tant et aussi longtemps que ses politiques sociles actuelles et sa façon d'agir concernant les services publics et parapublics du Québec seront maintenus."[90] Somewhat embarassed, Larose was quick to note that the federation's resolution constituted a tactic to force the government to rethink planned hospital closures, rather than a rejection of sovereignty. Even the federation's president Louis Roy conceded, "[c]'est un retrait temporaire du projet péquiste. Nos membres demeurent souverainistes ...."[91] Still, the incident pointed to a neuralgic spot in the relationship between the Québec labour movement and the PQ. Whenever the PQ won political power, the two sides immediately became opponents in the struggle for wages and working conditions in the public sector. In this struggle the temptation to strike-out against sovereignty was high, since an attack against sovereignty would hit the PQ government at its most vulnerable point and, thus, potentially constituted a major bargaining chip. At the same time, such an attack carried enormous risks as it jeopardized labour's political strategy and credibility. While the CSN stopped short of disavowing the federation's resolution, both the FTQ and the CSQ declared that their sovereigntist position constituted a strategic choice, which was not contingent on public-sector negotiations or specific government policies. "[L]a FTQ ne mêlerait pas la souveraineté et les négociations du secteur public," FTQ secretary general Henri Massé declared. "La souveraineté est trop importante."[92]

Despite the propaganda efforts of the three centrals and their allies, the referendum campaign got off to a poor start. For the first few weeks of the campaign, the sovereigntist camp trailed by a large margin in public opinion polls. The momentum shifted though, a few weeks before the referendum, when Parizeau stepped to the side to make room for Bouchard. Once he had taken the helm of the sovereigntist campaign effort, Bouchard infused his troops with new energy and optimism. Drawing on his tremendous popularity with Québecers and stressing the need for self-respect and reparation for the humiliations of the past, Bouchard almost succeeded in turning a disastrous campaign into a triumph. When millions of Québecers and Canadians turned on their television sets, on the evening of 30 October 1995, the outcome of the vote remained very much in doubt. In the end, the sovereigntists garnered 49.4 per cent of the vote. Some 50.6 of the voters voted "no." The difference between the two camps was less than 55 000 votes out of a total of almost 4.7 million voters.[93] Like their sovereigntist allies, the three centrals shrugged off the narrow defeat and renewed their commitment to promoting sovereignty.[94]

[90]Mario Fontaine, "La FAS rejette le projet de souveraineté," *Presse*, 24 May1995, B1.

[91]Mario Fontaine, "Souveraineté: la FAS se défend de faire du chantage," *Presse*, 25 May 1995, B5.

[92]Denis Lessard, "Quoi qu'il advienne, les centrales diront Oui," *Presse*, 26 May 1995, B1.

[93]Bumsted, *A History of the Canadian Peoples*, 422-3.

[94]www.cam.org/_poursouv/presentation.html

Recent Developments and Prospects for the Future

As was the case after the first referendum on sovereignty, the 1995 referendum ushered in a period of public disinterest in the sovereignty option. Despite their efforts to the contrary, Québec sovereigntists have so far failed to recreate the enthusiasm for sovereignty that preceded the second referendum. While Québec's constitutional status has been relegated to the backburner, organized labour and the PQ government have focused on fiscal policies and their impact on the public sector.

In February 1996, Bouchard took over from Parizeau as Québec Premier. In this function, Bouchard promised to work toward building the conditions under which the sovereigntists could win the next referendum on sovereignty. Bouchard saw elimination of the deficit as one of the winning conditions. Soon after his inauguration, the new Premier declared that eradicating the deficit was unavoidable if Québec did not want to run the risk of losing potential investors to Ontario or New Brunswick, where governments pursued pro-business fiscal policies. According to Bouchard, the drastic treatment he envisaged was inspired by pragmatism, not neo-liberalism. As one observer summarized Bouchard's position: "Pour le premier ministre, pas question de mettre de côté les principes sociaux-démocrates du PQ, la compassion nécessaire du gouvernement, mais ils devront pour l'instant s'accommoder des choix imposés par l'état inquétant des finances publiques."[95] Not surprisingly, the government's austere policies met with disapproval among organized labour.

While labour leaders had initially welcomed Bouchard's arrival at the helm of the PQ government,[96] they lost much of their enthusiasm when confronted with Bouchard's deficit-elimination plan. By 1997-98, relations between organized labour and the government deteriorated, as the centrals tried in vain to shield the public sector from government cuts. Frustrated by the cuts, CSN and CSQ leaders accused the PQ government of pursuing neo-liberal policies. Yet, while labour's anti-government discourse became increasingly accusatory, it did not reach the hostility reserved for the oppositional Liberal Party, which the centrals' denounced for wanting to return to the savage capitalism of the 19th century.[97] Relations between the Bouchard administration and the three centrals improved somewhat

[95]Denis Lessard, "L'option sociale-démocrate péquiste mise en veilleuse," *Presse*, 26 February 1996, A1, A2; quotation on A2.

[96]Philippe Cantin, "'Nous sommes en danger d'opération dévastatrice,' selon Gérald Larose," *Presse*, 30 November 1995, B1.

[97]Mario Cloutier, "Larose s'oppose à Bouchard," *Devoir*, 22 February 1997; Denis Lessard, "Les négociations ont refroidi l'ardeur syndicale pour le Bloc," *Presse*, 23 April 1997, B5; Mario Fontaine, "Le Bloc paie pour le pots cassés par le PQ: la FTQ ne l'appuiera pas," *Presse*, 10 May 1997, B10; François Normand, "La CEQ adopte la ligne dure," *Devoir*, 30 June 1997, A1, A8; Marie-Andrée Chouinard, "La CEQ promet un vent de changement," *Devoir*, 2 July 1997, A3; Claude-V. Marsolais, "La CSN s'éloigne du PQ," *Presse*, 31 March 1998, A7; Marie-Claude Ducas, "La CSN exerce de la pression sur les partis," *Devoir*, 30

after the government balanced Québec's budget in 1998. The 1999 budget met with muted criticism rather than vociferous denunciation. The FTQ and the CSN admonished the government for injecting insufficient resources into the health and education sectors. CSQ president Lorraine Pagé, however, declared that she found the budget satisfactory, because it favoured public services. She also commended the PQ government for having resisted the neo-liberal temptation of reducing taxes.[98] In December 1999, after a year and a half of negotiations, the presidents of the three centrals and the government concluded a collective agreement for Québec's public-sector workers, which satisfied both sides. The agreement diminished the tensions that had accompanied the long, drawn-out negotiations.[99]

Despite the temporary return to a certain degree of cordiality between organized labour and the government, both sides remain apart on social and economic issues. Organized labour continues to adhere to social democracy, while the PQ government combines pro-business policies with social-democratic elements. In all likelihood, there will be more conflicts over resource allocation between labour and the PQ government. Still, as long as the PQ will remain somewhere to the left of the Liberals, these conflicts will not cause labour to turn its back on sovereignty. Although not entirely unconnected to the PQ's degree of progressivism, labour's support for sovereignty rests on more fundamental arguments. As Larose pointed out in May 2000, labour sees Québec society as more community oriented and Québec political culture as more social than the society and political culture of English-speaking Canada. Thus, sovereignty would diminish the influence English-speaking Canada's individualist social values and liberal, political-culture exercise on Québec via the federal government. In short, Québec sovereignty would create better conditions for implementing social-democratic policies. Political realignment in a sovereign Québec might even entail the creation of a workers' party, which would be a more faithful ally of organized labour than the PQ has been.[100]

As long as labour continues to be inspired by its analysis of the fundamental differences between Québec and English-speaking Canada, it will pursue its sovereigntist orientation. Only a fundamental change in Québec's political culture may put this analysis into question. The PQ's recent cutbacks did not constitute such a change, especially if viewed in the context of the austere policies pursued by

October 1998, A2; Paule des Rivières, "La CSN égratigne tous les partis," *Devoir*, 11 November 1998, A2; Claude-V. Marsolais, "La CSN adopte un plan de campagne timoré," *Presse*, 10 November 1998, B4.
[98]François Normand, "Les syndicats donnent une note de passage avec réserve," *Devoir*, electronic edition [www.ledevoir.com], 10 March 1999.
[99]Norman Deslisle, "Les négociations 1999 dans le secteur public: un example à suivre," http://pressecan.infinit.net/Nationales/991230/N123001U.html [30 December 1999].
[100]Pierre O'Neill, "Gérald Larose au Devoir: l'heure n'est pas venue pour la gauche," *Devoir*, electronic edition [www.ledevoir.com], 27 May 2000.

various governments in English-speaking Canada. Yet, even if Québec's social values and political culture, as well as the PQ's programme, were to take a turn to the right, Québec labour might hesitate to embrace federalism. After all, the political influence of the three centrals is limited to Québec. Since extension of this influence to Ottawa does not constitute a viable option, it is a much more rational strategy to demand increased powers for the government that Québec labour *can* influence. Thus, there are good reasons to expect that Québec labour will continue to support sovereigntism for some time to come.

REVIEW

FERNAND BRAUDEL CENTER

**A Journal of the
Fernand Braudel Center for the Study of
Economies, Historical Systems, and Civilizations**

Vol. XXIII (2000) contains:

Marjolein 't Hart — **Warfare and Capitalism**
Christopher McAuley — **Oliver Cromwell Cox's World-System**

and special issues on
**Commodity Chains in the World-Economy, 1590–1790
Development Revisited**

Previous Special Issues and Sections still available include:

A brochure containing the Table of Contents of past issues
is available on request.

Institutions $90/yr.
Individuals $28/yr.
Non-U.S. addresses,
postage $8/yr.
Special rate for low gnp
per capita countries $10/yr.

Managing Editor, *Review*
Fernand Braudel Center
Binghamton University
State University of New York
PO Box 6000
Binghamton, NY 13902–6000

Libraries & Culture

EDITOR: Donald G. Davis, Jr., University of Texas at Austin

Libraries & Culture is an interdisciplinary journal that explores the significance of collections of recorded knowledge — their creation, organization, preservation, and utilization — in the context of cultural and social history, unlimited as to time and place. Many articles deal with North American topics, but **L & C** also publishes articles on library history in other countries, as well as topics dealing with ancient and medieval libraries.

"Topics are diverse...Book reviews are detailed, evaluative, and scholarly in approach. This is a delightful journal, beautifully illustrated."
— **Magazines for Libraries 1995**

RECENT CONTENTS FOR 2000

James Alfred Pearce and the Question of a National Library
in Antebellum America
Carl Ostrowski

Museums, Management, Media, and Memory: Lessons
from the *Enola Gay* Exhibit
Elizabeth Yakel

Failure or Future of American Archival History: A Somewhat Unorthodox View
Richard J. Cox

American Library History, 1947-1997: Theoretical Perspectives
Wayne A. Wiegand

Library Feminism and Library Women's History:
Activism and Scholarship, Equity and Culture
Suzanne Hildenbrand

Single copy rates: Individual $14, Institution $22,
Canada/Mexico, add $2.50; other foreign, add $5 (airmail).
Yearly subscription rates: Individual $30, Institution $59,
Student/Retired $18,
Canada/Mexico, add $10; other foreign, add $20 (airmail).
Refunds available only on unshipped quantities of current subscriptions.

University of Texas Press Journals
Box 7819, Austin, Texas 78713-7819
Phone # 512-471-4531, Fax # 512-320-0668, journals@uts.cc.utexas.edu

Labour/Left Memorabilia, 1880-1980: A Photographic Representation

Karl Beveridge

Advocates of One Big Union, 1880-1925
Button and enamel pins of the One Big Union (c.1919-1927), the Industrial
Workers of the World (c. 1905-1920), and the Knights of Labor (c. 1880s).
In the Knights of Labor pin SOMA refers to Secrecy, Obedience, and Mutual
Assisance.

Karl Beveridge, "Labour/Left Memorabilia, 1880-1980: A Photographic
Representation," *Labour/Le Travail*, 46 (Fall 2000), 397-416.

Brotherhood of Locomotive Firemen &
Engineers, Charity Lodge, St. Thomas,
Ontario
Ribbon, the reverse of which was in black,
'In Memorium,' for use at funeral services
of lodge members. In use from 1870s to
World War I.

25th Session of the Order of Railroad Telegraphers, May 1927

International Brotherhood of Paper Makers,
Beaver Local 192, Thorold, Ontario
The mill where workers wearing this
ribbon would have worked still exists today,
and in 1999 workers occupied the factory to
save it from being closed.

Longshoremen's Union, 1878 & Marine Trades and Labour Federation,
Great Lakes, St. Lawrence River & Atlantic Coast, July, August, September 1919

International Union of the United Brewery Workers of America (c. 1890s)
United Mine Workers of America, 8 Hours (c. 1890s)

Boot & Shoe Workers Union, Factory No. (c. 1890s on)
Cigar Makers International Union of America, with blue union label (c. 1890s on)
Brotherhood of Locomotive Firemen, Ottawa meeting (c. 1930s-1950s)

Labour Day

Amalgamated Association of Street Electric Railway and Motor Coach Employees of America, Division 113 and Toronto Railway Employees, Division 113, Labour Month, September 1919

Toronto Waiters Club, Hotel and Restaurant Employees International Alliance, September 1913 & Civic Employees Union, Toronto Local 43, January 1921

Early Congress of Industrial Organization [CIO] Union buttons
Dues and agitational buttons from the mass production unions of the
1930s and 1940s.

Political Action
Labour support for James Simpson in Toronto mayoralty bid, 1930s, and
1940s Political Action Committee of the CIO.

United Automobile Worker pins, October 1941
Pins reflect a jurisdictional battle between the American Federation of Labor
[AFL] and the CIO, between 1939-1941, when Homer Martin attempted to
affiliate a faction of the union to the AFL.

Left Causes: May Day (Canadian-Soviet Trade and Friendship League) and the Spanish Civil War (Mackenzie-Papineau Battalion)

Internationalism: May Day and Bethune

Socialism: Socialist Party of Canada (c. 1905-1915) & New Party (transitional name adopted between demise of the Co-operative Commonwealth Federation [CCF] and the founding of the New Democratic Party [NDP] in 1961)

Socialist Party of Canada Penant

Strike/Dues Pins
The shovel pin was issued during the United Steel Workers of America, Local 6500, strike against Inco, in Sudbury, 1979.

Race & Class: United Packinghouse Workers of America
The black and white hands of the handshake supposedly represent
the integration of separate Locals for black and white workers
which took place in 1947.

Union Support
A reflector for the back bumper of a car, dating from the 1920s or 1930s.

Short Takes:
The Canadian Worker on Film

David Frank

Take One

LONG EXTERIOR: It is snowing. The wind is blowing. There is a large building at the top of the hill. The professor is walking up the hill to this building. As we look over his shoulder we see that it is a research library. But will it be useful in researching the history of film? And what if the professor wants to know about the history of Canadian films, by which in this case we mean films that tell stories about Canada and Canadians? And what if the subject is the appearance of the Canadian worker in such films? In short, is there a Canadian labour film? Roll titles.

Take Two: Titles

Close Up, Interior: It is a library book shelf. Not a long one, for there are not many standard titles on the history of Canadian film, and they can be squeezed in between books such as *The Australian Film Reader* and *Cinema and Politics in the Third World*. The standard Canadian titles stand out — *Embattled Shadows*, *John Grierson and the National Film Board*, *Hollywood's Canada*, *Canada's Hollywood*.[1] Film studies in Canada seem to have been largely nationalistic in spirit, rather like the older studies of broadcast history. There is room here for a more critical perspective, and it is starting to arrive in the newer titles. Cut to Michael Dorland, *So Close to the State/s*, with its useful reminder of the prominence of governmentality in the construction of the field of film studies in Canada. Pan along

[1]Peter Morris, *Embattled Shadows: A History of Canadian Cinema, 1895-1939* (Montréal 1978); Gary Evans, *John Grierson and the National Film Board: The Politics of Wartime Propaganda* (Toronto 1984); Pierre Berton, *Hollywood's Canada: The Americanization of our National Image* (Toronto 1975); Ted Magder, *Canada's Hollywood: The Canadian State and Feature Films* (Toronto 1993).

David Frank, "Short Takes: The Canadian Worker on Film," *Labour/Le Travail*, 46 (Fall 2000), 417-37.

to a feminist reading of Canadian film under the title *Gendering the Nation*.[2] A wide-angle view also gives us the nearby shelves, with periodicals such as *Cinéaction* and the *Canadian Journal of Film Studies*; both interpret their mandate as global in scope, even while devoting substantial space to Canadian subjects.

There are at least two recent reference works on the library shelves, but on first inspection the labour film seems relatively invisible in these pages. A filmography of Canadian features for the period 1928-1990 includes 1,341 entries. The subject index has no references to "labour," "work" or "workers"; there is one entry under "strikers and strikes" and there are two additional entries under "unions." The three titles in question include *Les 90 Jours* (1959), a film written by Gérard Pelletier about a strike in a single-industry town in Québec during the Duplessis era; *Canada's Sweetheart: The Saga of Hal C. Banks* (1985), Donald Brittain's docudrama about crime and corruption on the waterfront after the removal of the Canadian Seamen's Union; and *Labour of Love* (1985), a more lighthearted television movie about a union organizer who comes down from Ottawa to the Miramichi to support five strikers at a local garage. There are more entries under general headings for themes such as "Business and Industry," "Mines and Mining," and "Clerical Workers." And turning through the short plot summaries, it is possible to detect recurring signs that the working-class experience has not been entirely overlooked in Canadian feature films even if it has rarely been the main focus of productions. In the first few pages we encounter plot summaries such as these: "Lumberjack O'Brien works in a lumber camp in the Canadian Northwest. Chandley is the romantic interest" (*Rough Romance*, 1930); and "Mercer, a Scottish cleaning woman, claims that Cooper, a Canadian in the Black Watch Regiment, is her son" (*Seven Days' Leave*, 1930). Or, among more recent productions, here is the plot summary for *Les Tisserands du Pouvoir 2: La Révolte* (1988): "Gélinas is the patriarch of a French-Canadian family that had gone to Rhode Island to work in the textile mills. His memories include labour disputes and a fight to maintain use of their language in the parochial schools."[3]

Meanwhile, a major two-volume bibliography on Canadian film and video also seems discouraging on first inspection. There are no entries in the subject index for "labour," "unions" or "workers," and only two very specific items under Trades and Labour Congress and Trade Union Circuit. There is, however, an interesting group of more than 30 entries under the genre title "Industrial Films/Cinéma industriel." This consists mainly of references to periodicals such as *Canadian Business* and *Industrial Canada* and, in smaller numbers, the old *Canadian Congress Journal* and *Canadian Labour*. The annotations describe the use of film

[2]Michael Dorland, *So Close to the State/s: The Emergence of Canadian Feature Film Policy* (Toronto 1998), and Kay Armatage, Kass Banning, Brenda Longfellow, and Janine Marchessault, eds., *Gendering the Nation: Canadian Women's Cinema* (Toronto 1999).
[3]Ian K. Easterbrook and Susan Waterman MacLean, comps., *Canada and Canadians in Feature Films: A Filmography, 1928-1990* (Guelph 1996), 5, 216-7.

for promotion, publicity, training and education purposes on the part of business and labour, with most of the references dating from the 1940s and 1950s. Despite the lack of appropriate subject references, this large two-volume reference work contains numerous entries for individual films and film-makers. In the search for the labour film, this source will be useful in developing supplementary documentation.[4]

From the library shelves we track our way to a display terminal. *Film/Video Canadiana*, a bibliography produced by the National Film Board in collaboration with the National Library, National Archives, and Cinémathèque Québécoise, is available to us in a 1994 edition on CD-ROM. This database contains some 30,000 Canadian film and video productions, about 18,000 in English and 12,000 in French. In the English-language database there are 5,800 NFB titles and 12,500 by other producers; among the French-language productions there are 4,000 NFB titles and 8,000 from other Canadian producers. The coverage dates from 1939 in the case of the NFB titles and from 1980 for other titles. Using a list of 12 search terms, we scan the English database for uses of these keywords in both subject and synopsis fields, with the following results:

Search Word	Subject	Synopsis
labour	11	41
labour history	0	4
labour organization	0	4
strike	3	61
strikes	29	26
trade unions	1	12
union	100	155
unions	38	44
work	42	1227
worker	2	105
working class	11	31
working-class	6	15

In each case it is possible to call up the full text for the entry. After allowing for the deletion of inappropriate references and limitations in coverage, this is still an enormous archive of references to visual evidence concerning workers and their

[4]Loren Lerner, ed., *Canadian Film and Video: A Bibliography and Guide to the Literature*, 2 vols. (Toronto 1997), 84-88 et passim.

place in Canadian life. Indeed it can be overwhelming, as occasional television interviews sit side by side with major productions.[5]

In this quest, we may also pass through the screen into the world wide web. One standard bookmark is the Internet Movie Data Base [www.imdb.com], one of the largest and most frequently used film sites. In response to keyword queries with various combinations of the words labour/union/worker/work and Canada/Canadian, this popular site was capable of producing only one palpable hit, in the form of *Canada's Sweetheart*. Meanwhile a visit to the National Film Board site [www.nfb.ca] yielded 342 individual entries under the category "Work and Labour Relations" (one of 87 subject categories). The earliest entry in this list was also the NFB's first production, *The Case of Charlie Gordon* (1939), a film addressing issues of youth unemployment and commissioned by the Dominion Youth Training Programme. Clearly, the NFB had counted the labour film within its mandate from the very beginning, and even as the NFB seems to be in retreat from active film production it continues to distribute selected independent productions that fall within this scope.

Keep in mind that the Canadian worker also shows up in unexpected places. The surly handyman played by Humphrey Bogart in *The African Queen* (1951) claimed to be a Canadian, an effect no doubt of the notorious Canadian Cooperation Project of the time that promoted gratuitous mentions of Canada in Hollywood films, but still within the meaning of our inquiry as an identifiable appearance of the Canadian worker on film. Similarly, when k.d. lang bundles herself onto a company airplane departing for a remote work site in the north in the opening scenes of *Salmonberries* (1991), surely she too can be counted as a Canadian worker (although some plot summaries describe her as an "Alaskan pipeline worker"). But there is no need to be exhaustive at this stage in the search. It is clear that, as the librarians say, there are weak bibliographic controls in this field. Our survey will remain preliminary, and the search will remain far from comprehensive.

Unfortunately there is nothing in Canada that is the equivalent of Tom Zaniello's book about labour films, *Working Stiffs, Union Maids, Reds, and Riffraff*. It is a wonderfully useful reference work, a selective, critical guide to films about workers and unions, mainly in the American context. He identifies the films, discusses the contents, proposes supplementary reading, organizes them by occupational groups and social themes. There are only a few Canadian entries in the volume, but Tom promises more Canadian content in a revised edition.[6]

[5]*Film/Video Canadiana 1994* (Montréal 1994) [CD-ROM]. Unfortunately, the coverage is increasingly incomplete, as this publication was suspended after the 1995 edition. The CD-ROM was issued only in PC-compatible formats; in my own search it was not possible to install the Windows version, nor was it possible to print entries. These suggest some of the reasons to prefer internet websites as research tools.
[6]Tom Zaniello, *Working Stiffs, Union Maids, Reds, and Riffraff: An Organized Guide to Films about Labour* (Ithaca 1996). For my review, which includes suggestions for additional Canadian entries, see *Labour/Le Travail*, 41 (Spring 1998), 292-5.

Take Three: Flashback

Now the action moves from bibliothèque to cinémathèque, from the realm of the printed and electronic word to the world of visual documents. The importance of such a distinction was pointed out as early as 1898, at the very dawn of the age of film, by a pioneer cinematographer who called for the establishment of public institutions to collect — and preserve — this new form of cultural production. That advice was largely ignored, until it was too late and much of the unstable nitrate-based film stock in use prior to the 1950s had dissolved into brown dust or gone up in smoke. With apologies to Walter Benjamin, we may wish to pass a comment on this particular irony of cultural production in the age of mechanical reproduction! As a result, in this kind of retrospective survey of perishable evidence we will have to use our imagination.[7]

The first films made in Canada were at once novelty items and travelogues. They appealed to curiosity but also supplied information about the country. Many of the early films focused on natural wonders such as Niagara Falls and various exotic winter activities such as skating and snowshoeing, but there was also a significant amount of attention to the economic life of the country and the consequent opportunities for employment. The appearance of this theme was not an accident, as film was rapidly recognized as an effective means to attract interest in immigration. The earliest example is that of a British immigrant from Bristol, who settled on a farm near Brandon, Manitoba in the 1880s. A former printer and publisher, James Freer started making movies of farm life as early as 1897, only a year after the first public exhibitions of motion pictures on theatre screens in Canada. Freer's early films, none of which have survived, included such apparent pioneering epics of Canadian social realism as: *Six Binders at Work in Hundred Acre Wheatfield, Typical Stooking Scene, Harvesting Scene with Trains Passing By*, and *Cyclone Thresher at Work*. A year later, Freer was conducting a lecture tour in Britain under the sponsorship of the Canadian Pacific Railway; a second tour was later supported by the Department of the Interior.

The CPR proved especially enthusiastic about using film to promote immigration to "the last best west," and the company contracted with both British and American film companies to make films about Canada. For instance, the *Living Canada* series of 1903 and 1904 consisted of some 35 short films — including views of immigrants arriving at Québec City, and scenes of lumbering, harvesting, and ranching activities. Interestingly, film historian Peter Morris has pointed out that the Bioscope Company of Canada, set up by the British film producer Charles Urban, did not always follow the CPR's instructions "not to take any winter scenes under any conditions;" this independent-mindedness on the part of the film-makers may also account for the inclusion in this series of scenes from a Labour Day Parade in Vancouver, for the CPR was not known to encourage the recruitment of workers

[7]Sam Kula, "Film Archives and the Centenary of Film," *Archivaria*, 40 (Fall 1995), 210-25.

with union ideas. In addition to these short documentaries, there were also story-films with more substantial plot-lines. In 1910 the CPR commissioned a series of ten-minute romantic melodramas presenting Canada as the land of opportunity for the ambitious young worker, in this case with special attention to recruitment from the American labour market. Surviving examples from this series include *An Unselfish Love* and *The Song that Reached His Heart*, each featuring a male working-class hero whose hard work on the resource frontier brings not only economic rewards but also reunion with his lost love. One intriguing title from this series was a Romeo-and-Juliet of the Alberta coal mines, released under the title *A Daughter of the Mines*. And *The Little Station Agent* was the story of a capable young woman who operated a railway depot in the Rockies, where she fended off unwanted lovers and prevented train wrecks.[8]

These early productions remind us of a time when Hollywood did not exist, at least not in the way it did after Hollywood came to dominate film production and distribution after the end of the silent era. Before that happened, a certain amount of diversity in North American film culture was possible. Given the low survival rates of early film stock, it is difficult to be certain of the numbers or to discuss the content in any depth, but it is clear that several interesting Canadian films were produced during this era. Moreover, there can be no doubt that the early movies were patronized by working-class audiences. As Steven Ross has pointed out in his study of this era, this context helps explain the positive images of workers, and sometimes unions, that are visible in pre-Hollywood films, notably in the work of D.W. Griffith and, from the point of view of a comic anti-authoritarian, that of Charlie Chaplin. It is part of Ross's argument that the movies helped workers to "visualize" class in the silent era, but that this became less possible as the structure of production and consumption changed.[9] Although no study of the theme has yet been undertaken in the Canadian context, the movies were occasionally the subject of comment in the labour press. Chaplin, for instance, received a favourable review in the pages of the *Maritime Labour Herald* in 1922: "The only fault with Chaplin comedies is that they end," noted a contributor, "One could sit and watch 'The Idle Class' until Europe pays the United States her war debts."[10]

While it is easy to lose sight of much of the early film production, we are grateful for the visual evidence that does remain available for scrutiny. None is more famous than Robert Flaherty's *Nanook of the North* (1922). Although originally rejected by most distributors, following its release the film was acclaimed as a masterpiece of social observation and the art of storytelling. In John Grierson's

---

[8]The discussion in this and the previous paragraph is based on the evidence in Morris, *Embattled Shadows*, 30-44.

[9]See Steven J. Ross, *Working-Class Hollywood: Silent Film and the Shaping of Class in America* (Princeton 1998). For a review, including suggestions for the Canadian research agenda, see *Labour/Le Travail*, 44 (Fall 1999), 259-62.

[10] *Maritime Labour Herald*, 25 February 1922.

words, *Nanook* was "a record of everyday life so selective in its detail and sequence, so intimate in its shots, and so appreciative of the nuances of common feeling, that it was a drama in many ways more telling than anything that had come out of the manufactured sets of Hollywood."[11] The film can also be described more prosaically as the record of one man on the northern shores of Hudson Bay going about his daily chores of hunting, fishing, travelling, and building, or at least acting out these routines for the benefit of the camera that follows him. At this level, *Nanook* may be considered a story about a man and his work, invested with significance by the realist aesthetic of the film-maker. Many subsequent NFB films produced by "the children of Grierson" — such as the profile of tobacco pickers in *The Back-Breaking Leaf* (1959) to take one influential example — have also aimed to invest similar meaning in the working lives of their subjects.

A neglected but interesting film of the 1920s was *Carry On, Sergeant* (1928).[12] The film was planned as a tribute to the long-suffering heroes of the Canadian lower ranks in World War I. Directed by the British writer and cartoonist Bruce Bairnsfeather, the film was launched with great expectations (including support from investors such as Arthur Meighen and R.B. Bennett) and, despite the disappointment of its financial failure (and lack of an American distributor), it remains an interesting example of Canadian attempts to come to grips with the wartime experience. For the purposes of this discussion, what interests us is that the film features a working-class hero. In the early scenes prior to the war in 1914, Bob MacKay and his buddy Syd Small are presented as industrial workers employed at the Atlas Locomotive Works (soon to be converted to wartime munitions production). MacKay is what labour historians will recognize as an "honest workingman," a self-respecting, dependable, productive worker who takes his work and responsibilities seriously; his chief ambition is to wed his sweetheart, who works at the local 5 and 10 store. By contrast, Small is the comic relief, an idler who cannot be taken seriously by the foreman and must be protected from his own follies. Their world of pipes and boilers and smoke is far different from the handsome country lodge where the company president entertains visitors. But when the war comes, there is no question how these workers will behave: "It didn't much matter whose war it was, or what about," says the silent title, "MacKay and others just had to go." The war turns out to be more than a "great adventure;" it is instead "the championship disaster of the world." MacKay struggles his way through the trenches, gas attacks and enemy fire of the front lines, and his travails justify the film's final dedication to "all those unsung heroes who silently make history by just 'carrying on'."

[11] Quoted by Dorothy Harley Eber, "True North," *Horizon Canada*, Vol. 5 (1987), 1416.
[12] This film was unfortunately named, at least for the purposes of film history. "Canada Carries On" was later the NFB's premier domestic wartime series. And then there were the "Carry On Gang" British comedies of the 1950s and 1960s. For the background to this film, see Morris, *Embattled Shadows*, 71-80.

Finally, may we comment on one Hollywood film, on the grounds that it includes one near-Canadian scene? The director King Vidor originally thought of this film as a portrait of the struggles of an "average fellow" caught up in the hopes and dreams of the white-collar working class. The original working title was "One of the Mob," but the M-G-M producer Irving Thalberg thought that "Mob" made it sound "too much like a capital-labour conflict" [sic]. They settled instead on "The Crowd." The Canadian scene, or what we may choose to view as a Canadian scene, takes place on a hillside overlooking Niagara Falls. Our hero believes he has escaped from the drudgery and anonymity of his office job. He is about to be married and start a family. Niagara roars silently, and there are no disappointments of any kind in sight. As the story unfolds, however, his expectations are betrayed, and the American Dream resolves itself into a series of setbacks and frustrations. Although the film is placed in the so-called Roaring Twenties, it conveys a mood of uncertainty and malaise that seems to anticipate the Great Depression. As such this remarkable film strikes a dissonant note within the emerging Hollywood consensus of the 1920s on the satisfactions of North American civilization.[13]

Take Four: Documentary

The documentary tradition looms large in any discussion of Canadian film. The founder of the National Film Board in 1939, John Grierson, had been a promoter of the documentary film —some observers claim he invented the word, at least in its English-language translation from the French "documentaire" — as early as the 1920s. Grierson always distinguished his work from what he considered mere travelogues or lecture films and staked out his territory in his famous description of the documentary as "the creative treatment of actuality." He regarded the documentary as the greatest achievement of the film culture of his time; Hollywood productions were in his view mere "movies" designed for the purposes of escapism and entertainment, and he specifically discouraged the idea that the NFB, or Canadian film-makers generally, should become involved in making feature films.[14] While Grierson's film aesthetic may have been limited by his preoccupation with the documentary, it is notable that much of the Canadian feature film tradition as it later developed contains significant traces of the documentary legacy.

The wartime NFB films are a familiar reference point for film historians, but they are also important for labour historians. Under the direction of Grierson, the NFB saw itself as a branch of the state dedicated to the mobilization of citizens for public purposes connected to the war itself and the construction of a post-war liberal democracy. During the war this meant, among other things, the making of films that promoted the enlistment of women in the armed forces as well as into the civilian labour force in unprecedented numbers. Some 50,000 women enlisted in

[13]King Vidor, *A Tree is a Tree* ([1952] New York 1977), Chapter XIV.
[14]John Grierson, "A Film Policy for Canada" [1944], in Doug Fetherling, ed., *Documents in Canadian Film* (Peterborough n.d.), 51-67.

the several women's services, and at the height of wartime demand about one million Canadian women had entered the full-time labour market, many of them in non-traditional sectors directly related to war work. Several of these films have received close scrutiny in recent years, and the NFB has released a series of these, mainly related to enlistment, on a compilation videocassette that allows for easy access for study purposes.[15]

Films such as, *Wings on Her Shoulder* (1943) and *Proudly She Marches* (1943) portrayed the participation of women in the armed forces in positive terms but also depicted the situation in not-so-subtle ways that identified women's roles as abnormal, secondary, and temporary. No one voiced this limitation more succinctly than Lorne Greene, in one of his voice-over narrations, when he stated that the "girls" employed in industrial establishments were finding factory work "no more difficult than house work." It was even more clear in post-war films such as *Careers and Cradles* (1947) that the promises of women's equality implied in wartime films were not central to Canada's plans for reconstruction. In one of her influential studies of the mobilization of women for the war effort, Ruth Roach Pierson has concluded that little permanent change in the status of women resulted from the wartime experience, and that by the end of the war "Traditional attitudes about women's role held sway once more and the contribution that women had made to the war effort was allowed to fade quietly from public memory."[16]

Part of an effort to recover those memories, *Rosies of the North* (1999) is a new NFB film that takes us to Fort William (now part of Thunder Bay) where Canadian Car and Foundry operated Canada's largest World War II aircraft plant. While the majority of the work force were male workers, about 40 per cent of the workers were women. The film uses round numbers of about 7,000 workers, of whom 3,000 were women.[17] The film treatment cuts back and forth between present and past, as the women review the evidence of their experience and share personal observations. As such it seems very much an exercise in a visual form of oral history. From these women we learn that they hired on at the plant because they needed work. Their mothers were widowed or incapacitated, and at the end of the Depression their families were much in need of the money. Where domestic labour paid $10 a month, factory work could bring in $20 a week. They tell us also that the women were dedicated to their work. They never missed a shift. They followed the progress of the war and took pride in their contribution to the war effort. They were better welders than the men, but the men got better wages, even those who were trained by women. At quitting time men insisted on punching out first. There were

[15]Yvonne Mathews-Klein, "How They Saw Us: Images of Women in National Film Board films of the 1940s and 1950s," *Atlantis*, 4:2 (Spring 1979), 20-33.

[16]Ruth Roach Pierson, *Canadian Women and the Second World War* (Ottawa 1983), 27.

[17]A recent article gives a peak work force of 6,760, of whom 2,707 were women. See Helen Smith and Pamela Wakewich, "'Beauty and the Helldivers': Representing Women's Work and Identities in a Warplant Newspaper," *Labour/Le Travail*, 44 (Fall 1999), 72.

romances, but you lost your job if you got married — or you kept it quiet. Unlike the men, the women were under the supervision of matrons who served as nurses, nannies, and cops. The women interviewed, who all appear to have been local residents, expressed considerable sympathy for the young women recruited from across the Prairies and housed in barracks at the plant site. One of the most memorable documents in the film is a still photograph showing several of these women holding up a "We Want Work" sign at the end of the war. It was not to be. By August 1945 there were only three women on the shop floor, all that remained of a work force of almost 3,000. Were unions relevant in any way to this experience? There is no indication in the film as to whether workers at Canadian Car and Foundry were, at any time during the war, represented by a union, and what contribution to the advancement of women's concerns that union made or might have made.

The story of Elsie MacGill runs like a refrain throughout this film. The first woman to graduate with an engineering degree in Canada, MacGill went on to study aeronautical engineering in the United States and then worked in the industry in Montréal; she was hired by Canadian Car and Foundry as chief aeronautical engineer and at Fort William supervised plans for production of Hurricane fighters for the RAF and subsequently for the Helldivers for the USAF. The daughter of a first-generation feminist (Helen Gregory MacGill), Elsie MacGill herself later served on the Royal Commission on the Status of Women (where she was likely responsible for ensuring that so many of the recommendations were directed towards issues of educational opportunity and economic citizenship). During her time at the plant (she was dismissed in 1943 for what is shown as a combination of professional and personal reasons), MacGill was respected by the women workers for her achievements but it is also clear that there was no special relationship between this formidable woman professional and the workers on the shop floor. There was even some resentment of the recognition she was receiving, for MacGill was celebrated in the media — and even in a comic book — as "Queen of the Hurricanes." As one of the women notes, reporters "couldn't see anybody but Elsie." The film would obviously be different without MacGill, but the tensions are solved by keeping the working-class women at the centre of the story.

Does this story confirm the pessimistic conclusion that the participation of women was ideologically constructed as an exceptional wartime experience and had little later impact? Did the war "do wonders for women's liberation," as some contemporaries and writers assumed? Or was the war at the very least a "window on the future" that helps explain the long-run increase in women's employment in subsequent decades? Although the documentary tradition as practised by Grierson in wartime left few open questions at the end of a film, in *Rosies of the North* the answers seem less certain. In the end, the film provides a good deal of evidence and leaves it up to the viewers to formulate their own questions about the significance of the story. In the context of a classroom discussion, this is not a difficulty.

Take Five: 1919 and All That

The year 1919 is the most famous year in Canadian labour history, and the Winnipeg General Strike is the one event in Canadian labour history that might be considered part of the general knowledge of educated Canadians. Was Winnipeg unique? Probably, in the sense that all historical events are unique. But the recent historiography has drawn attention to the larger pattern of events, pointing out that in 1919 there were more workers on strike in Ontario and Québec than there were in Western Canada. From the historical point of view the events of that one year can be seen as part of a longer cycle of labour unrest that occurred across the country, running from the middle of World War I to the middle of the 1920s and resulting in a series of significant defeats and a variety of adjustments to the apparent stability of the capitalist system.[18]

In Canadian film history, 1919 was also notable as the year of *The Great Shadow*, a film supported by the CPR and other major employers as part of an effort to combat the influence of "Bolshevism" on organized labour. With British actor Tyrone Power in the starring role, the film was shot principally at studios in Trenton, Ontario; and when scenes were shot at the Vickers factory in Montréal union members were recruited to serve as unpaid extras. *The Great Shadow* reached the movie screens in late 1919 and 1920. It received a favourable response from the daily press; in *Saturday Night* Hector Charlesworth compared it to *Birth of a Nation* and *Intolerance*.[19] No copies of this film have survived, but another "red scare" film released a few months earlier, *Dangerous Hours*, seems to be a close cousin and tells much the same cautionary tale. The all-American university graduate John King has a natural instinct for interfering in social conflicts on behalf of the underdog. As a result he is rapidly seduced into the cause of class struggle and violent revolution, characterized by a "New Woman" by the name of Sophia Guerni and a Bolshevik agitator by the name of Boris Blotchi. Their intentions are conveyed in flashbacks to scenes of the Russian Revolution that include the destruction of churches and the "nationalization of women." There are also a couple of unsavoury labour agitators and disreputable labour bureaucrats in evidence, who use the opportunity of a national steel strike to engage in blackmail and extortion. Soon enough, John sees the light. The outcome is not in doubt. After all, the proprietor of the shipyard turns out to be a young woman who is John's childhood sweetheart.

Winnipeg does remain controversial, as indicated in the responses, published in this journal, to a recent History Television documentary on the strike.[20] Written

[18]Craig Heron, ed., *The Workers' Revolt in Canada, 1917-1925* (Toronto 1998).
[19]Morris, *Embattled Shadows*, 67-70.
[20]"History Television and the General Strike: Three Views," *Labour/Le Travail*, 45 (Spring 2000), 255-70. This includes comments by David Bercuson, Kurt Korneski, and James Naylor and Tom Mitchell.

and directed by film-maker Audrey Mehler (based on an idea presented to her by historian David Bercuson), *Prairie Fire: The Winnipeg General Strike of 1919* featured a strong narrative line identifying the principal stages in the strike story and a good mix of sources, including photographic images and interviews with eyewitnesses and historians. The voice-over narrative may have been marred by a certain amount of hyperbole ("never again in the 20th century would Canadian workers stand so steadfast for their beliefs") and one major gaffe ("The *Canadian Cooperative Federation*"). The main criticism of the film voiced by the specialist critics was that the film gave little indication of the relatively rich and diverse body of historical writing on the strike. Of course, films have no footnote references, and this lack of interest in historiography seems to be one of the characteristics of history on film as it has been practised. Because documentary films like to rely on the authority effect of "History," historians themselves are rarely shown disagreeing with what is in the film or with each other. In his own comments on *Prairie Fire*, Bercuson (author of one of the standard treatments of the strike and credited as "creative consultant" for the film) agrees that a film of this kind cannot be expected to do full justice to the subject: "What those viewers saw was, no doubt, much more superficial a treatment of the strike than what they may read in *Confrontation at Winnipeg*, or in the dozen or so serious treatments of the strike written by others of different ideological perspectives. But so what? At least the 100,000 plus viewers now know something about the strike and if their curiosity is aroused, they can easily seek out more substantial reading matter on the subject."[21] In the right context, of course, a television film series under a title such as "History on Film" could be followed with on-air discussions of the historical and intellectual context of the film treatment. Better still, there could be more and different kinds of films based on this and other strikes. It is interesting that there are at least half a dozen plays and novels placed in and around the events of the Winnipeg General Strike, but none of these has yet made its way onto the screen.

A second famous episode in Canadian labour history is attractively presented in *On to Ottawa* (1992), directed by Sara Diamond.[22] This film originated in a different kind of cultural production, a lively historical stage performance featuring song and story presented by veterans of the Great Depression as well as contempo-

---

[21]Bercuson, "Prairie Fire: A Personal View," *Labour/Le Travail*, 45 (Spring 2000), 257.

[22]Sara Diamond has also produced several films on the history of working women in British Columbia. These include *Keeping the Home Fires Burning* (1988), *Ten Dollars or Nothing!* (1989), and *The Lull Before the Storm* (1990). The latter is an ambitious four-part film consisting of two short documentaries and two full-length dramas. According to the catalogue for a National Gallery of Canada exhibition devoted to Diamond's work as a visual artist, the dramas, entitled *The Forties* and *The Fifties*, follow the fortunes of a working-class family through the decades of war and reconstruction and "centre on the changing definitions of femininity and how these changes affect family and working life," Jean Gagnon and Karen Knights, *Sara Diamond: Memories Revisited, History Retold* (Ottawa 1992), 74.

rary musicians. Besides relying on this theatrical setting, those who made the film combed the film archives with care in order to produce a detailed visual context for the film. In addition, several re-enactments introduce themes or tell stories not otherwise available in the visual archives. It is also notable that there is original historical detail in this film, not previously presented in print, on such themes as the treatment of Chinese and Japanese workers and aboriginal people who were denied relief in British Columbia. In due course, episodes of community mobilization and agitation among the relief camp workers lead on to the mobilization that produced the trek itself, but not until we are half-way through this one-hour film. The film reaches its predictable climax with the arrival of the trekkers in Regina, their uncertainty about whether to advance on to Ottawa and the police riot that ended the Trek. The mix of approaches in this film is invigorating, as the film regularly cuts away to the band and, to introduce the themes and maintain a narrative focus, the group of three veterans, Robert Jackson, Ray Wainwright, and Jean Sheils (the daughter of trek organizer Arthur 'Slim' Evans). What message do they deliver? Says Robert Jackson, addressing himself to a younger generation: "There's no shame in being unemployed, but if you don't fight back and organize —that would be a shame." In all, this is a most appealing film treatment that benefits greatly from the numerous forms of collaboration that went into its creation.

Another key moment in Canadian labour history, the unrest at the end of World War II, is presented in *Defying the Law* (1997), an account of the 1946 strike at the Steel Company of Canada plant in Hamilton, Ontario. This was a crucial time in post-war reconstruction, as Canadians remained uncertain whether wartime concessions to workers would translate into permanent rights in peacetime. If there was no general strike similar to that in Winnipeg, it was largely because strikes such as the Hamilton one were successful in meeting their objectives. The specific issues at stake — wage increases, paid vacations, union security — were less important than what the strike represented in terms of the changing balance of power in industrial Canada. The strike wave that engulfed the country in 1946 and 1947 was about staking out workers' claims to an enhanced status in the post-war world. The fact that the Hamilton strike was actually illegal when it started in July 1946 (the government had placed the plant under government control only days earlier and strikers were threatened with fines and jail terms) did not seem to be of great importance to the strikers, although in retrospect we can see that the strike revolved around the issue of industrial legality as the formula for post-war labour peace. The work force at Stelco was divided over support for the union, and one prominent theme in this film treatment is the role of the strikebreakers who remained inside the plant, where they earned triple pay for their 24-hour shifts. Access to the plant became a key issue in the strike, and the strength of the picket line enabled workers to prevent shipments or supplies from entering or leaving. Another issue was the role of the municipal government, headed by the labour mayor Sam Lawrence, who refused to call in the provincial police or the RCMP to maintain their version of law and order at the plant gates. The solidarity of workers at other industrial plants is also important to the story, and it appears that if Canada was going to have a general strike in 1946, Hamilton was likely to be the centre of it. The film is strong on visual evidence drawn from photographic and film collections — including early colour footage of the strikebreakers playing ball and running races inside the plant. It also rests on substantial background research from the archives, which include extracts from the Prime Minister's diary in which he meditates on his strategy for ending the strike and correspondence from a subdued C.D. Howe warning that the political fallout from the Winnipeg General Strike had produced too many unnecessary labour Members of Parliament. Unfortunately, the only filmed interview is with the film producer Richard Nielsen, who in 1946 was a returned veteran and striking steelworker, and we do not meet other workers and their families telling their own stories firsthand; the voice-over statements read by actors seem pale by comparison. In the end the strike was won, and all workers, scabs and strikers alike, benefited from the gains. Moreover, according to a statement by union leader Charlie Millard (apparently from an older film or television interview), the corporation was assured that the steel industry was not an immediate target for a socialistic takeover under any potential CCF government. Every strike takes its own shape, and this film conveys the particular drama of Hamilton in vivid ways. At the same time it never fails to remind viewers of the larger issues of union security at stake. The same message might be presented in accounts of a dozen other local struggles of the time, but there is no denying the significance of the Hamilton strike.[23]

Take Six: Cinéma Québécois

In Québec the observer may have the impression that the labour film has a long history. This is probably a misapprehension. It is certainly true that the unique evolution of cinema in Québec has favoured a "refusal of Hollywood" and has privileged the documentary approach, even in the making of feature films. Language has provided a natural form of protectionism. So did the legislative exclusion of children from the movie theatres during the golden age of Hollywood (due to a disastrous moviehouse fire in Montréal in 1927). A distinct Québec film culture did emerge in the years prior to the Quiet Revolution, but the labour film itself is probably best regarded as part of the rebellion against the prevailing cultural and ideological limitations of that era. One contributing factor was the relocation of the National Film Board from Ottawa to Montréal in the 1950s, which provided creative opportunities for a generation of talented film-makers. At the same time,

[23] A similar moment in the battle for union rights, in this case in the public sector, is presented in the film *Memory and Muscle: The Postal Strike of 1965* (1995), a lively presentation relying on newsreel footage and retrospective interviews with the local rank and file leaders who led that struggle. A hopeful sign of the interest of organized labour in documenting its own history, this film was produced and directed by Michael Ostroff for the Canadian Union of Postal Workers.

the use of portable sound equipment stimulated the growth of the cinéma direct techniques that captured the language as well as the images of modern Québec during a time of social change and cultural reorientation.[24]

Among the most important documentaries of the Quiet Revolution were portraits of working-class life in films such as Clément Perron's *Jour après Jour* (1962) and Arthur Lamothe's *Bucherons de la Manouane* (1962). The most controversial was Denys Arcand's *On est au coton* (1970), which ran into official disapproval at the NFB and contributed to Arcand's transition from the documentary to the fictional film. In the making of feature films, traces of the documentary tradition remain visible. Claude Jutra's *Mon Oncle Antoine* (1971) provides a social portrait of the asbestos mining country on the eve of the Quiet Revolution, making it not only a study of adolescence but also a portrait of the awakening of a society. A viewing of Jean Beaudin's *J.A. Martin Photographe* (1977), which focuses primarily on the relationship between a rural photographer and his long-suffering wife, is also rewarded along the way with glimpses of working-class life in 19th-century rural Québec, such as a visit to a small sawmill employing numerous children. Similarly, the feature film *La Sarrasine* (1992), based on the true story of a crime that occurred in Montréal, recreates the world of Italian working-class immigrants in the early 20th-century city.

Most recently, in 1999 there was the popular téléroman broadcast by Radio-Canada under the title *Chartrand et Simonne*. This is a well-scripted, well-acted dramatic series based on the life of Michel Chartrand and Simonne Monet as they battled their way through the personal and political struggles of the 1950s and the Quiet Revolution. We watch them move back and forth between the tensions of family life in a labour organizer's household and famous moments in Québec labour history such as the strikes at Dupuis Frères and Murdochville. From this evidence, it appears that the labour film may be alive and well in Québec. Will audiences beyond French Canada ever see this series in subtitled or dubbed versions, or is it assumed that this kind of labour-oriented family saga has a limited appeal?

Meanwhile, the documentary tradition has also continued to produce contributions to the genre of the labour film. One fascinating example is the feature-length documentary by Richard Boutet and Pascal Gélinas, *La Turlutte des années dures* (1983). Like *On to Ottawa*, this film also attempts to break with conventional structures of documentary film-making. This wide-ranging, episodic treatment of the Great Depression has been described as a "documentary musical tragedy." In the tradition of the cinéma direct, the film gives voice to a working-class narrative, and it displays a rich visual portrait of the decade, all of which is energized by the

---

[24]For some background, see Paul Warren, "The French-Canadian Cinema: A Hyphen Between Documentary and Fiction" and Philip Reines, "The Emergence of Quebec Cinema: A Historical Overview," in Joseph. I. Donohoe, Jr., ed., *Essays on Quebec Cinema* (East Lansing 1991). A dramatic feature by Bernard Develin, *Alfred J.* (1956) is identified by Donohoe as a film that "describes the union movement in a working-class setting." (174)

songs known as "turluttes." The technical achievements of the film in creating a visual archive and capturing the unique folk music of the streets earned this film a major award. At the same time the political engagement of the film makers is also obvious, as the film does not pretend to treat the era with the authority of retrospective objectivity and insists on making direct links between the past of the 1930s and the present of the 1980s.[25]

Another remarkable feature-length documentary is Sophie Bissonnette's treatment of the life and times of Léa Roback, *A Vision in the Darkness* (1991). This is an exceptional visual document of a labour activist, anti-fascist, and feminist who grew up with the 20th century. Born in 1903 at Beauport, Québec, the daughter of Jewish Eastern European immigrants, she moved easily in both francophone and anglophone *milieus*, learning first hand about the shape of anti-semitism in Québec and the exploitation of workers, especially young women. A sense of adventure and possibility brought her to urban Montréal in 1919, where she was soon immersed in new worlds, including detours to New York and Berlin, that led her to become a union organizer in the garment and munitions industries and, politically, a Communist. With the participation of Roback herself and her friends young and old, the story is told in all its visual and emotional complexity. One comes away from this film with an understanding of the spirited sense of social responsibility that animated activists such as Roback and the unfailing humour and "gros bon sens" that made her so effective as an organizer. Equally impressive are the preparation and care that have gone into this production. We are reminded that documentary films need not be simple translations of well-established historical material but that they have the capacity to seek out new sources and new information, most notably in the areas of oral testimony and visual evidence. Most recently, Bissonnette has applied her skills to a film about the best known labour struggle in Québec, the Asbestos Strike of 1949.[26]

Take Seven: More Features

The long hiatus in feature film production in English Canada lasted with little significant interruption from the end of the 1920s to the beginning of the 1970s, when the cultural nationalism of the times established tax incentives and funding opportunities to encourage film-making in Canada. Much of the new activity failed to address Canadian themes at all and amounted to little more than an effort to emulate Hollywood standards. But among those film-makers who did focus on

[25]"La Turlute[sic] des années dures," *Cinema Canada* (May 1984), 18-20.

[26]Bissonnette's earlier work includes *A Wives' Tale* (1981) and *"Quel numéro? What number?" Or the Electronic Workshop* (1985), both of which were made as contemporary social and political statements but can now be viewed as historical treatments as well. See Himani Bannerji, "Sophie Bissonnette and Her Films," *Fuse* (February-March 1986), 25-7. For a discussion of films on the Asbestos Strike, see Georges Massé, "Des images de la grève de l'amiante," *Bulletin du RCHTQ*, 70 (automne 1999), 54-61.

Canadian stories, the documentary tradition remained a strong influence on the selection of themes and on the treatment of subjects.

The classic example is Don Shebib's *Goin' Down the Road* (1970), a film that is more tragic than comic in its account of the misadventures of two likeable Maritimers who set out to seek their fortune in the big city at the end of the 1960s. They leave behind a broken landscape of abandoned mines and boats and arrive ready to work and prosper in the office towers of Toronto. It does not take long for them to discover that working-class life in the big city presents its own challenges and they make their troubled adjustments to these reduced expectations. The best work they can locate is in the warehouse of a bottling plant, which has its own thresholds of frustration and alienation — as we learn when Pete sits Joey down to calculate and discuss the number of bottles they have moved through the plant in the course of their work. It is a moment of revelation for both characters. Peter Harcourt has captured the sensibility of the film thoughtfully in a comment originally published in *Cinema Canada* in 1976: "Pete and Joey are pals, real comrades in the way that Shebib believes in; but they are also very different guys. While they are both typical members of the 'lumpenproletariat' — unskilled workers with no sense of the political implications of the role society has assigned them — Pete has a more reflective nature. He tries to think about things. Clumsy though his articulations may be (for language, among other things, is the property of the middle-classes), he is doubly aware that life for other people offers something more, something which he wants access to."[27] A generation later, the most memorable scenes in this film still ring true, and this classic film can be expected to receive renewed attention now that it is available on video.

There are more glimpses of working-class life in dozens of feature films produced in this period. A viewing of a popular film such as *The Apprenticeship of Duddy Kravitz* (1974) shows passing scenes of neighbourhood and workplace life in Montréal in the 1940s, although, like the novel on which it was based, the film is primarily about characters who wanted to get out of the working class. By contrast, *John and the Missus* (1987), based on a novel by Gordon Pinsent and starring the actor as a hardrock miner, was about a character who embraced his class identity and resisted attempts to restructure his social environment through a state-sponsored resettlement programme in Newfoundland in the 1960s. Similarly, *Bye Bye Blues* (1989) is not only the entertaining story of a female singer and piano player but also a perceptive account of the opportunities and frustrations available to a single woman who is seeking to make a living in the rural west during World War II. *Why Shoot the Teacher?* (1977) is an appealing memory film about a young man from Toronto teaching in Saskatchewan during the Great Depression and learning something about the place and the people. And while *My American Cousin* (1986) is mainly about growing up young and female in rural British Columbia in

---

[27]Peter Harcourt, "Men of Vision: Some Comments on the Work of Don Shebib," in Seth Feldman and Joyce Nelson, eds., *Canadian Film Reader* (Toronto 1977), 211.

the 1950s, it is also possible in watching this film to reflect on the shape of the household economy in the Okanagan fruit orchards and, for a few moments, the role of itinerant pickers who help bring in the harvest.

More recently, several features, made primarily for non-theatrical audiences, have addressed themes closer to the traditional focus of labour history. One of the most effective of these is *Canada's Sweetheart*, the treatment of the degradation of labour relations on the waterfront from the time of the CSU strike in 1949 to the investigations of the Norris Commission in 1962. At the centre of the story is the unlovely Hal Banks, memorably acted by Maury Chaykin, and the supporting cast is equally strong. While Banks comes across as a pathological villain, the film does not shrink from identifying the complicity of employers and governments in plotting the downfall of the CSU and accepting Banks and his notorious "Do Not Ship" list. Even the labour establishment is slow to respond and is unwilling to curtail Banks until he finally goes too far in challenging existing union jurisdictions. Similarly, *Net Worth* (1995) presents another unsavoury episode in the history of labour relations in the 1950s, in this case in the context of the National Hockey League. The action revolves around the talent-laden Canadian staff of the Detroit Red Wings of the mid-1950s as the hockey players make their first feeble efforts to stand up to the NHL owners. The film shows how the hockey heroes of the time were treated as shabbily as any low-paid blue collar employee, perhaps worse, as they were repeatedly reminded how lucky they were to be paid for something that was "just a game." Especially in the characters of the young Gordie Howe and the veteran Ted Lindsay, one gets a feeling for the complexity of emotions among these workers as they struggle with issues of deference, resistance, and solidarity.[28]

Take Eight: Germinal?

And what of the coal miners, who do figure prominently in labour films in advanced industrial states such as Britain and the United States, where the coal industry sits close to the cultural imagination and political economy of the country? In Britain a group of remarkable dramatic films in the late 1930s brought images of the coal

[28]Not all efforts at historical drama based on the workplace experience have been equally successful. One instructive failure was the well-acted and thoughtful film *Lyddie* (1996), based on an excellent juvenile novel of the same title by Katherine Patterson. While the novel was situated in the cotton mills of Lowell, Massachusetts, in the 1850s and explored the relationships between young women workers in that setting, for the purposes of the film the story was improbably transposed to Cornwall, Ontario — a generation before the textile industry reached the town. Meanwhile, one of the women finishes the film by deciding to go to university — another premature option at the time. Another short effort to portray the early industrial experience in dramatic terms was the NFB production *Chandler's Mill* (1991), which also introduced historical anomalies and anachronistic expectations. I have discussed this film briefly in "One Hundred Years After: Film and History in Atlantic Canada," *Acadiensis*, xxvi, 2 (Spring 1997), 122-3.

industry and class conflict to national attention — *The Citadel, The Stars Look Down, Proud Valley.* These were films that could be broadly defined as social problem films, and to a greater or lesser degree they implied solutions based on class solidarity and socialist politics. Even in Hollywood there were coal mining films, notably *Black Fury* and *How Green Was My Valley*, although the messages were somewhat less positive as far as labour unions were concerned.[29] More recently, productions such as Barbara Kopple's *Harlan County, U.S.A.* and John Sayles's *Matewan* have set a much different standard. In the Canadian case, setting aside for the time being the matter of documentaries such as the wartime mobilization film *Coal Face Canada* (1943) and the attempt at local labour history in *12,000 Men* (1978), the coal miners have remained largely in the shadows.

In the case of *The Bay Boy* (1984), a well-received coming-of-age film set in the coal town of Glace Bay in 1937, the predominant working-class population is almost invisible. This is in part explained by the class position of the family at the centre of the story. The father is a local soft-drink manufacturer who is trying to rebuild his failed business in the basement of their home; the mother, an immigrant war bride, keeps the family economy going by baking for local restaurants and taking in boarders. In one of the few references to coal miners, the mother (Liv Ullman) comments briefly on the status of the coal miners, who are perceived as the least fortunate members of the community: "I am glad your father isn't a miner. The worst job for the poorest wages. Having to live in those company houses, shop at the company store." The conversation, misleadingly, goes on to lament the influence of the company stores — which had closed permanently a dozen years earlier at the time of the 1925 strike. For Donald Campbell (played by Kiefer Sutherland) this is a time in his life when he must reach decisions about his future, and in the course of the action in the film it becomes clear to him that the surrounding environment is a negative one and that the only option for him is to effect his escape from "this mining town at the edge of the earth." From such a film it would be difficult to know that Glace Bay was coming out of the Great Depression with one of the country's strongest local unions and social reform movements and about to elect the first CCF MP east of Manitoba. In dramatic terms, *The Bay Boy* works well and addresses several difficult themes, but although it is based on director Daniel Petrie's personal memories of growing up in the Bay, it is too narrowly focused to serve as a portrait of the life of the coal country in the 1930s.[30]

Some similar reservations apply to *Margaret's Museum* (1995), a very successful feature film whose action also takes place in Glace Bay, in this case a decade

[29]See Peter Stead, *Film and the Working Class: The Feature Film in British and American Society* (London 1989), Chapter 5; Francis R. Walsh, "The Films We Never Saw: American Movies View Organized Labour, 1934-1954," *Labor History*, 27 (1986), 564-80.

[30]My thanks to Mark Van Horn for sharing insights from his research on this film. See Mark Van Horn, "A Tale of Two Films: A Reading of *Johnny Belinda* (1948) and *The Bay Boy* (1984)," MA Report, University of New Brunswick, 2000.

later. Here the coal miners and their families appear to be much closer to the centre of the story, as the main character is a young woman (Margaret, played by Helena Bonham Carter) who has already lost her father to the coal mines and is watching her grandfather waste away; she is determined to do what she can to protect her brother Jimmy and her husband Neil from the same fate. In Sheldon Currie's original stories, which provided the basis for the film, Margaret's brother Jimmy is an articulate advocate of labour organization and political action. However, the labour theme virtually disappears in the translation from the page to the screen, thus providing a misleading impression of the balance of class forces in the mining community and the choices available to the local population. Again, in this film there recurs the persistent illusion of the company store, that powerful symbol of company domination, long after its actual historical demise. The explanation appears to be that the film subscribes to a view of mining communities as unchanging places exempt from history. Accordingly, the sensibilities of the 1990s can be applied to the social relations of the 1890s and the physical landscape of the 1940s without interrupting the static essentialism of local history. *Margaret's Museum* is in many respects a well-crafted and moving production, but it is essentially a romantic tragedy rather than an historical film.[31]

Take Nine: Final Cut

In the end, it should come as no surprise that the Great Canadian Labour Film does not exist. There are only short takes, many of them arising from incidental processes of documentation and fictionalization. There is also a more purposeful body of work, but its promise has remained contingent on circumstances of patronage and funding and the contending priorities of other projects. The virtual absence of labour history from the sample version of Canadian history contained in the *Heritage Minutes*, for instance, suggests the difficulties in gaining access to the cultural apparatus that governs the Canadian discourse. And it still remains to be seen how labour and working-class history themes will be integrated into the CBC/Radio-Canada production of the ambitious multi-part visual history, *Canada: A People's History*, to be released on television during the 2000 and 2001 seasons. Will it be possible to reconcile the traditional narratives of state-formation with the history of the working-class experience in this country? Or is it more likely that labour films will arise out of different kinds of sponsorships and partnerships? Do the imperatives of film and television production lead naturally towards reduction-ist, homogenized treatments of history? Are more creative approaches possible in

[31]For my earlier critique, see "The Social Landscape of Margaret's Museum," *Canadian Dimension* (July-August 1998), 41-3 and comments in "One Hundred Years After," 132-5. For additional commentaries on the film, see Noreen Golfman, "Mining: Margaret's Museum," *Canadian Forum* (April 1996), 28-31 and Peter Urquhart, "The Glace Bay Miners' Museum/Margaret's Museum: Adaptation and Resistance," *Cinéaction*, 49 (1999), 12-18.

making history films? Readers of this journal are likely to recognize the relevance of these challenges, as a concern with public history has been a regular feature in these pages. Whether there is a master narrative or a multiple one to be told, there certainly are stories. After all, there is an enormous accumulation of cultural energy stored in the back volumes of our publications and the recesses of our imaginations over the quarter-century since the emergence of labour and working-class history as a field of research. Sooner or later it will be time for these stories to be shown on film.

It is a Sunday morning. The sun is streaming in through the windows. The professor is ironing shirts and listening to the radio and thinking about his overdue assignment for *Labour/Le Travail*. Meanwhile, Natalie Zemon Davis is explaining to the radio host Michael Enright how historians look at films. She is explaining that history is about getting things right, and by this she means not just the materiality of the situation but also the meaning of the times. History is not just about the collection of information, she explains, much as generations of history teachers have patiently instructed their students; it is also about the patterns of meaning in human experience. The same applies to films, or should apply. But we must always keep reminding ourselves that films are not just like books. They speak a different language, and here Natalie is agreeing with Robert Rosenstone, who says that historians who want to think about films need to learn how to think in pictures. At the same time, he adds, film-makers have something to learn about thinking historically.[32] It is hard to avoid concluding that visual history will benefit from greater collaboration between historians and film-makers. We do need to learn from each other. As in all stories, there is a need for dialogue.

[32]Davis was summarizing the themes of her Barbara Frum Lecture at the University of Toronto, published as Natalie Zemon Davis, *Slaves on Screen: Film and Historical Vision* (Toronto 2000). See also Robert Rosenstone, *Visions of the Past: The Challenge of Film to Our Idea of History* (Cambridge 1995).

Canadian Journal of Political Science
Revue canadienne de science politique

The *Canadian Journal of Political Science* is an international quarterly review which publishes articles, research notes, review articles and book reviews in English or in French. / La *Revue canadienne de science politique* est une publication trimestrielle internationale qui publie des articles, des notes de recherche, des synthèses bibliographiques et des recensions en français ou en anglais.

Recent articles published include:
Des articles publiés récemment comprennent :

""Welcome In, But Check Your Rights at the Door": The James Bay and Nisga'a Agreements in Canada", Paul Rynard

"Public Brokerage: Constitutional Reform and the Accommodation of Mass Publics", Matthew Mendelsohn

"Persuasion, Domination and Exchange: Adam Smith on the Political Consequences of Markets", Thomas J. Lewis

"British Imperial Politics and Judicial Independence: The Judicial Committee's Decision in the Canadian Case Nadan v. The King", Jacqueline D. Krikorian

"La mesure de la science et la construction statistique d'un territoire : la Région de la capitale nationale du Canada", Benoît Godin

"Regional Perspectives on Canada's Charter of Rights and Freedoms: A Re-examination of Democratic Elitism", Richard Vengroff and F.L. Morton

Editorial correspondence in English should be directed to:

Sandra Burt
Department of Political Science
University of Waterloo
Waterloo, ON   N2L 3G1

Business correspondence, including requests for information about subscriptions, should be sent to:

Canadian Journal of Political Science
#204 - 260 Dalhousie Street
Ottawa, Ontario   K1N 7E4
Fax: (613) 241-0019
http://info.wlu.ca/~wwwpress/cjps.html

Veuillez adresser toute communication en français au sujet de la rédaction à :

Diane Éthier
Département de science politique
Université de Montréal
C.P. 6128, succursale Centre-ville
Montréal (Québec)   H3C 3J7

Veuillez adresser toute communication de caractère commerciale, y compris toutes demandes pour renseignements au sujet d'abonnements, à :

Revue canadienne de science politique
#204 - 260 rue Dalhousie
Ottawa (Ontario)   K1N 7E4
Télécopieur : (613) 241-0019
http://info.wlu.ca/~wwwpress/cjps.html

Canadian Universities, Academic Freedom, Labour, and the Left

Michiel Horn

IN 1934 THE UNIVERSITY OF ALBERTA classicist William Hardy Alexander used the pages of a recently established left-wing periodical to pose the question: "Will radical leadership emerge from our Canadian universities?" He answered in the negative. "The 'successful' way of life in our universities may be equated with the life of conformity both to doctrine and authority."[1] Five years later, Alexander wrote in a *Canadian Forum* article that there was an agreeable future in academe for the acquiescent, those willing to fit in, but not for those of a critical disposition. Addressing himself to a fictional "young man contemplating an academic career," Alexander noted that capitalism sanctioned "a most painfully unbalanced distribution of the satisfactions and opportunities of life, to say nothin of the bare necessities." But it was dangerous for academics to point this out, he added, for in a state university it was "invariably described as Bolshevism," and in a privately endowed institution the situation was even worse. "An unflinching examination of the defeat sustained by the 'good life' in modern capitalistic conditions is regarded as a personal criticism of the benevolent persons who have established the academic foundation."[2]

Most professors wisely did not challenge the economic *status quo*, Alexander continued: they were easily replaced, and the principle of academic freedom offered them little protection. If such freedom had ever existed in the past, and he did not think it ever did "in things deemed by the ruling powers to be essential to the preservation of their power," it was now in decline. "We affect to shudder at the fate of the German universities without quite realizing the tendency of our own to

[1]W.H. Alexander, "Will Radical Leadership Emerge from Canadian Universities," *CCF Research*, 1 (July 1934), 15.
[2]W.H. Alexander, "'Noli Episcopari': Letter to a Young Man Contemplating an Academic Career," *Canadian Forum*, 19 (October 1939), 220-3.

Michiel Horn, "Canadian Universities, Academic Freedom, Labour, and the Left," *Labour/Le Travail*, 46 (Fall 2000), 439-68.

move towards ... the same silence on 'essentials' accompanied by loud mouthings about inconsequentials." *Noli episcopari*, do not join the professoriate, Alexander concluded, for the universities "are far too respectable either to fight or to tolerate within themselves a fighter."[3]

Alexander was overstating the case, for his "letter" was partly a parody. In spite of an occasional brush with notoriety, he himself had become dean of arts and science by the time he went to the University of California, Berkeley, in 1938. Still, his remarks were rooted in his experiences in Alberta, where he taught for almost three decades. More important, his message has had relevance in other places and at other times. By and large, Canadian universities have not welcomed adherents of the left on their faculties. They have, however, come gradually to tolerate them.

* * *

The Canadian universities with which W.H. Alexander was familiar mostly served the needs and interests of Canada's middle classes. They were very largely staffed by men and women (mostly the former) who had been born into professional, business, and well-to-do farming families, and who taught young people very largely drawn from backgrounds similar to their own. Paul Axelrod gave his monograph on student life in English Canada during the 1930s the title *Making a Middle Class.*[4] This aptly describes the function of Canadian universities throughout their history.

Even during the last thirty to forty years, when student bodies have become rather more socially and ethnically diverse and when young women have become much more heavily represented, especially in the professional faculties, than ever before, the role of the university in "making a middle class" has remained essentially unchanged. The great majority of students have hoped to become teachers, lawyers, engineers, physicians, clergymen, social workers, and the like, or to find management positions in the private- as well as public-sector economy. Although universities may seem like élite institutions, most of those attending them have not expected to join the Canadian social or economic élites.

All the same, members of these élites play a key function in Canadian higher education. Universities and colleges have been supervised by lay governing boards on which wealthy and socially-prominent Canadians have usually been more than willing to serve. Wealth and success in business or the learned professions (especially the law) have always been welcome attributes for members of governing boards.

These lay boards have been (and still are) the employers of all those who work in the institution, with the right to appoint and dismiss. The boards' authority, although generally modified by a presidential right to recommend appointments

[3]Alexander, "'Noli Episcopari'," 223.
[4]Paul Axelrod, *Making a Middle Class: Student Life in English Canada During the Thirties* (Montréal and Kingston 1990).

and dismissals, long influenced faculty staffing. Until faculty members came to be involved in recruitment during the 1960s, presidents, deans of faculties, and eventually department heads did the actual work of selecting candidates, but they tended to recommend men (and occasionally women) who were unlikely to encounter governing-board disapproval. "Safe and sound" candidates have usually been preferred. A.B. McKillop writes of mid-19th century hiring practices in Canada West: "Careful attention was paid ... to the academic pedigrees, social backgrounds, and personal connections of professors at Ontario universities in order to assure that no heretical views issued from the lectern. Family ties and letters of recommendation by scholarly acquaintances ... dominated academic hiring at the time."[5] Since a central part of the purpose of higher education well into the 20th century was to build character and good deportment in students, those who taught them had to be sound themselves, had to hold unexceptionable ideas and to have proper relations. "Nothing is more important than to profess Correct Opinions, unless to possess a correct Acquaintance."[6] Expressed by John Graves Simcoe, first lieutenant-governor of Upper Canada, the sentiment has effectively served many administrators (and not a few professors) as a guiding principle.

In 1914 President Frank F. Wesbrook of the University of British Columbia described one candidate as "a large, upstanding, athletic, manly fellow ... with very wholesome views, [and] with seemingly a very charming wife, who appears to be a good house-keeper."[7] In recommending the young Harold Adams Innis for appointment in 1923, McMaster University's Humfrey Michell referred to him as "a very nice fellow in every way and one likely to be an agreeable colleague, a consideration which is an important one."[8] That same year, McGill University Principal Sir Arthur Currie received a letter describing a candidate as having "a pleasant personality and good manners," and being someone who enjoyed participating in sports, "especially tennis and boxing."[9] Academic achievement mattered, but the emphasis was on soundness and all-roundness, on "the whole man."

Men identified (on whatever grounds) as "radicals" usually got short shrift in the hiring process. The attitude of Sidney Smith, president of the University of Manitoba and later of the University of Toronto, was probably not atypical. Seeking to appoint an economist, he wrote of Robert McQueen in 1935: "I have been told that McQueen is a radical in his economic thinking and if this is the case I would

[5] A.B. McKillop, *Matters of Mind: The University in Ontario 1791-1951* (Toronto 1994), 88.

[6] John Graves Simcoe, quoted in S.R. Mealing, "The Enthusiasms of John Graves Simcoe," *Canadian Historical Association: Historical Papers* (1958), 61.

[7] University of British Columbia Archives, President's Office, microfilm reel 6, F.F. Wesbrook to S.D. Scott, 12 January 1914, copy.

[8] University of Western Ontario, Regional Collection, University Archives, Dean of Arts, box 25, Humfrey Michell to W. Sherwood Fox, 14 February 1923.

[9] McGill University Archives (MUA), RG2, Principal's Office (PO), c.61/1001, R. du Roure to A.W. Currie, 7 April 1923.

rule him out." Only after J.W. Dafoe, the editor of the *Winnipeg Free Press*, assured Smith that rumours of McQueen's radicalism were "groundless" did Smith recommend him for appointment.[10]

Escott Reid was less fortunate. In 1932 the political scientist and recently-returned Rhodes Scholar passed up an opportunity to teach at Harvard University in order to become the national secretary of the Canadian Institute of International Affairs (CIIA). Active in the League for Social Reconstruction (LSR), regarded as the "brain trust" of the Cooperative Commonwealth Federation (CCF),[11] Reid shared the neutralist views current in LSR and CCF circles. This troubled influential members of the CIIA governing board, and by 1937 Reid was actively looking for academic work.

In 1937-38 he had a replacement appointment at Dalhousie University, and from that vantage point he applied for a position at the University of Saskatchewan. Its president, James S. Thomson, asked Dalhousie's President Carleton Stanley for a reference. "They say he is somewhat radical in his outlook," Thomson wrote, "but probably he is none the worse for that." He went on to say that he was all in favour of free speech, but "at the same time, there is a wisdom and a discretion in all things and, particularly, in a chair of Political Science."[12]

"Mr. R. has something of a reputation for indiscretion in the matter of urging Canadian nationalism, and for radicalism generally," Carleton Stanley replied. "I was well aware of this when I engaged Mr. R., and heard, as I expected to hear, some rumblings about the appointment, even though it was known that he was here only temporarily."[13] Did this frighten Thomson? We do not know; we do know he did not offer Reid a job.

Neither did Manitoba's Sidney Smith. Soliciting suggestions for an associate professorship in political science, he was told by an acquaintance, W.Y. Elliott, that "Escott Reid is knocking around loose." However, "his politics may not please you."[14] Reid did not get an offer. In early 1939 he joined the Department of External Affairs — Under-Secretary O.D. Skelton was evidently unworried by his reputation — and had a distinguished career in the public service before becoming the first principal of York University's Glendon College in 1965.

A more recent and better-known example of an individual, thought to be radical, who was kept out of a teaching position for which he was well-qualified was Pierre Elliott Trudeau. In his youth a supporter of the Québec labour movement, editor of a 1956 study of the 1949 Asbestos strike, the future prime minister paid

[10]University of Manitoba Archives (UMA), UA20, President's Papers (PP), vol. 2, S.E. Smith to A.K. Dysart, 11 January 1935, copy; J.W. Dafoe to Smith, 2 February 1935.

[11]Michiel Horn, *The League for Social Reconstruction: Intellectual Origins of the Democratic Left in Canada 1930-1942* (Toronto 1980), 46-7.

[12]Dalhousie University Archives (DUA), MS 1-3, 299, R.A. MacKay Personal, J.S. Thomson to Carleton Stanley, 17 December 1937.

[13]DUA, MS 1-3, 299, Stanley to Thomson, 23 December 1937, copy.

[14]UMA, UA20, PP, vol. 21, W.Y. Elliot to Sidney E. Smith, 29 January 1938.

a price. His biographers write that he "was denied the teaching job he wanted in the Université de Montréal, where the government controlled appointments though the church hierarchy."[15]

If radicals of various kinds were not exactly welcome on university teaching staffs, some nevertheless managed to gain appointment, either because they came well recommended or because they had managed to hide their views. Others became "radical" some time after appointment. Professorial radicalism has usually been of the left-wing variety, critical of capital and supportive of labour. Since presidents and board members (and many academics) tended strongly to support the established capitalist order and to believe that overt criticism of it by academics was inappropriate (if not worse), conflict ensued from time to time.

By contrast, positions one might characterize as right wing have rarely brought trouble to those espousing them. Something of an exception occurred in 1916, when the University of Toronto political economist James Mavor attacked the forerunner of Ontario Hydro in the *Financial Post*, his perspective being that of a *laissez-faire* liberal critical of a government-sponsored monopoly. Upon reading several of Mavor's articles, Premier Sir William Hearst complained to President Sir Robert Falconer. The government of Hearst's predecessor and sometime colleague, Sir James Pliny Whitney, had created the Ontario Hydro-Electric Power Commission in order to meet the needs and wishes of a large segment of Ontario's manufacturing industry. Hearst did not appreciate an attack from someone he associated with Toronto interests that opposed the Power Commission. Noting that Mavor had also criticized the Workmen's Compensation Act (presumably as an unwarranted intervention in the labour market), Hearst claimed that Mavor's writings brought "condemnation upon the University" and undermined the government's efforts to support it.[16]

Falconer passed Hearst's letter on to Mavor for a response. Little cowed, the economist wrote a long letter that controverted every point the premier had made and which Falconer passed on almost verbatim. Contrary to what one might have expected, Hearst backed off and did no more than send Falconer a face-saving letter. There the incident ended. Both Hearst and Falconer must have known that Mavor had powerful friends in the Toronto business establishment, among them bank president and chairman of the board of governors Sir Edmund Walker, board vice-chairman Zebulon Lash, and the utility and railway magnate Sir William Mackenzie. There was probably little point in taking Hearst's complaint further, since the board of governors was unlikely to take action against Mavor.

This did not mean Falconer simply passed over what had happened and forgot it. More than likely he was irritated with Hearst for seeming to threaten the

---

[15]Stephen Clarkson and Christina McCall, *Trudeau and Our Times*, vol. 1, *The Magnificent Obsession* (Toronto 1990), 66.

[16]University of Toronto Archives (UTA), President's Office (PO) (Falconer), A67-0007/42, William Hearst to Robert Falconer, 2 November 1916.

university and with Mavor for providing Hearst with a reason to complain. Threats to the university's financial support had to be taken seriously, so that the incident unquestionably gave Falconer food for thought.

A few years later the writings of another political economist, Robert M. MacIver, led to a disagreement between Falconer and a wealthy member of the board of governors, Reuben Wells Leonard. A recent arrival from Scotland, MacIver in 1919 published *Labour and the New Social Order*, which supported workers in their efforts to organize. Leonard was hostile to anything that smacked of unionism. He also believed that professors should refrain from subverting an economic order in which he could discern no serious fault. After he got hold of MacIver's book in early 1921, he complained to Sir Edmund Walker about the Scot's "ultra-socialistic teachings."[17]

Walker's reply sounded a note of mild concern, but he added: "Nothing would seem more dangerous than to restrain a free expression of opinion by a professor short of almost anything but treason."[18] Having received copies of this letter and Leonard's, Falconer evidently wanted to add his voice to Walker's. It would be "extremely injurious were the Board of Governors to attempt to restrain the expression of views on economic subjects which were different from their own," he wrote to Leonard. That was not the British way. Besides, "the most treasured privilege of the University is freedom of thought."[19]

Such freedom should not extend to the promulgation of "extreme, unusual or dangerous doctrine" such as the championing of labour unions, Leonard responded.[20] Falconer then restated his belief that academic free speech was beneficial and that Canada had nothing to fear from "the thoughtful, earnest man, who is endeavouring to arrive at principles that will stabilize the country."[21] He did not persuade Leonard, who wrote later that year that, if MacIver were to be permitted to teach his ideas, "we should ... establish a Chair of Political Anarchy and Social Chaos, so that the people of Ontario, who pay for the University, and the students who take the courses, will know what is being taught under its proper name."[22]

Leonard's hostility to unionization was extreme, and his criticism of MacIver seems to have lacked support among other board members. Nevertheless Falconer thought it advisable to call the political economist into his office in January 1921 for a chat about the latter's ideas. MacIver subsequently sent Falconer a statement of his views, commenting that this was not to be construed "in any way" as a defence of them: "To offer a 'defence' would ... be contrary, not only to the dignity of a University teacher but also to the idea of the University."[23] Should he be asked to

[17]UTA, PO, A67-0007/67, R.W. Leonard to Sir Edmund Walker, 14 January 1921, copy.
[18]UTA, PO, Walker to Leonard, 17 January 1921, copy.
[19]UTA, PO, A67/0007/65, Robert Falconer to Leonard, 18 January 1921, copy.
[20]UTA, PO, Leonard to Falconer, 21 January 1921.
[21]UTA, PO, Falconer to Leonard, 22 January 1921, copy.
[22]UTA, PO, A67/0007/72, Leonard to Falconer, 9 December 1921.
[23]UTA, PO, A67/0007/65, R.M. MacIver to Falconer, 27 January 1921.

CANADIAN UNIVERSITIES 445

defend his views, MacIver added, he would feel his integrity as a teacher so threatened that he would feel compelled to look for another position.

Falconer had no intention of allowing matters to go that far. Having studied at the universities of Berlin and Marburg before the war, he was well-acquainted with the 19th-century German idea of *Lehrfreiheit* — the freedom of the professor to teach and publish — and the role of research as the basis of that freedom.[24] He valued MacIver's contribution to the university, moreover. Indeed, in 1923 he recommended that the Scot succeed Mavor as head of political economy. The board of governors accepted the recommendation, with Leonard registering a dissenting vote. MacIver served as head until 1927, when he resigned in order to join the faculty of Columbia University.

Interesting in their own right, the Mavor and MacIver incidents gained wider significance because of the speech (later published) on academic freedom that Falconer gave to the alumni association on 14 February 1922. He referred to neither incident but did address the issues they raised. The academic freedom enjoyed by professors was "one of the most sacred privileges of a university," Falconer said, but it was subject to limits. Like judges and civil servants, professors were not free to do as ordinary citizens did. "It is ... expedient that a professor in a State University should take no active share in party-politics" whether by running for office or engaging in partisan debate. Any discussion of "burning political questions" might harm his institution. "A government might well without giving any reason easily show its displeasure in such a way as to affect adversely the fortunes of the institution and the financial position of many guiltless and wiser colleagues." If, as seems likely, this was aimed at Mavor, Falconer concluded with some words meant for Leonard. "The best possible persons available for the professorial office" might well hold views that members of governing boards found uncongenial, Falconer said, but they would be unwise either to challenge a professor's competence or to deny "that there is no place in the university for his type of thought." It was better "to tolerate an erratic or even provocative teacher" than to disturb the normal functioning of the university.[25]

Leonard stuck to his guns: "The inference I would draw from your Paper is the necessity for exercising extreme caution in the selection of professors."[26] Caution was, in fact, already the policy used in selecting professors. Falconer's speech was notice to any politically engaged or radically minded professors at the University of Toronto that they should think twice before expressing unconventional or controversial views on religion, politics, economics, or labour relations. At the five other provincial universities in existence at that time — New Brunswick, Manitoba,

[24]Walter P. Metzger, "The Age of the University," in Richard Hofstadter and Walter P. Metzger, *The Development of Academic Freedom in the United States* (New York and London 1955), 387.
[25]Robert Falconer, *Academic Freedom* (Toronto 1922).
[26]UTA, PO (Falconer), A67-0007/72, Leonard to Falconer, 24 April 1922.

Saskatchewan, Alberta, and British Columbia — circumstances were much the same.

The state of affairs in the private institutions was somewhat different. By and large the denominational institutions received no public financial support, and few of the non-sectarian institutions did. This meant that the displeasure of a provincial government need not concern professors or the institutions employing them.

It did not mean that professors were free from restraint in discussing public affairs. Their institutions relied heavily on tuition fees and gifts, and both might be endangered by a controversial or indiscreet professor. When such professors got into trouble, the inference that their opinions or activities must be the reason lay readily to hand. That was the case when Wesley College, Winnipeg, dismissed the church historian Salem Bland in 1917.[27] For years he had been an outspoken champion of the Social Gospel, critical of capitalism, and favouring a new order in which farmers and labour would get a larger share of the economic pie. His supporters believed that the financial crisis facing the college was being used to purge a man whose views offended powerful people on the college board of regents, a belief reiterated in 1977 by the political scientist Norman Penner.[28] There is no evidence for this, however.

In 1923 the University of Western Ontario economic historian Louis A. Wood wrote to the Progressive Member of Parliament W.C. Good that his (Wood's) support for the United Farmers of Ontario (UFO), his interest in labour issues, and his being "offered a labor-progressive nomination for the [1921] federal election," had resulted in a demand for his resignation.[29] The available documents do not substantiate this claim. They indicate, rather, that the acting president, Sherwood Fox, had become persuaded that Western needed a business-oriented economist to head the department and that Wood did not meet this need. We can only guess why Wood resigned. His support for the UFO and the labour movement may have been at issue, but there is no evidence for this or for Norman Penner's claim that Wood was fired for his "radical views."[30]

That professorial "radicalism" was generally unwelcome became abundantly clear during the Depression of the 1930s. Economic catastrophe had the effect of pushing a small minority of academics (perhaps thirty among a professoriate totaling some 3000) leftward. A few joined or sympathized with the Communist Party of Canada (CPC), and at least one, the poet and English professor Earle Birney, became a Trotskyist. Most were active in or hovered on the fringes of the CCF, the

---

[27]Michiel Horn, *Academic Freedom in Canada: A History* (Toronto 1999), 50-1.
[28]Norman Penner, *The Canadian Left: A Critical Analysis* (Scarborough, Ont. 1977), 178.
[29]National Archives of Canada (NAC), MG 27 III, C1, W.C. Good Papers, vol. 6, 5023-4, L.A. Wood to W.C. Good, 16 May 1923; also, vol. 8, 6250-1, Wood to Good, 5 July 1924. See also: Horn, *Academic Freedom in Canada*, 76-8.
[30]Penner, *The Canadian Left*, 178.

new "farmer-labour-socialist" party that took shape in 1932, or in the organization unofficially linked to it, the League for Social Reconstruction.

Since even the LSR and CCF, firmly committed to achieving change by constitutional and democratic means, struck not a few Canadians as extreme, obvious involvement by academics in anything further left was imprudent. The historian Stanley B. Ryerson, who joined the CPC in his early twenties but kept this a secret, lost his position at Montréal's Sir George Williams College in 1937 after the principal learned that he had written some Communist party pamphlets under an assumed name. He did not teach in a university again until the 1960s. In a 1990 interview Ryerson spoke about several academics he knew in the 1930s who might have been philosophical Marxists, but he doubted any of them ever belonged to the CPC. Indeed, the party discouraged academics from joining, he claimed, because of the fear that they would be dismissed if their membership became known.[31]

No university seems to have barred professors from being active in the LSR and taking executive positions in it, though some presidents might have objected had the League been officially associated with the CCF. Involvement in that party was a different story. Membership in it was generally tolerated, but in late 1932 President Henry J. Cody of the University of Toronto instructed the historian Frank H. Underhill to resign from the executive of the Ontario CCF Clubs. Underhill gathered data about American and British academics who were active in politics, some, like the political scientist Harold Laski, in the British Labour party. This cut no ice with Cody. Much like Falconer, he believed that professors in provincial universities should eschew partisan activity, in any case of the left-wing variety.[32]

Although W.H. Alexander's membership in the CCF must have been well-known at the University of Alberta, this caused no reaction. What did was an engagement to speak in Calgary late in 1932 on behalf of a CCF candidate in a provincial by-election. President Robert C. Wallace asked him not to, a 1930 resolution of the board of governors having banned political activity by professors. Alexander complied. This led a government backbencher, Fred White, to complain to Premier John Brownlee — the province was governed by the CCF-affiliated United Farmers of Alberta — who conveyed White's complaint to Wallace. He replied directly to White. "Professors are free to express their points of view at any time in whatever method they desire," Wallace wrote, but they should not take part in provincial elections. This was bound to drag the university into provincial politics, Wallace asserted, adding that he did not doubt "that the university would inevitably suffer."[33]

---

[31]Interview with Stanley B. Ryerson, Montréal, January 1990.
[32]Horn, *Academic Freedom in Canada*, 93-5.
[33]University of Alberta Archives (UAA), RG 19, W.H. Alexander Personal, 81-37-9, R.C. Wallace to Fred White, 3 January 1933, copy. See also: UAA, Board of Governors (BoG), Executive committee, Minutes, 25 June 1930.

In late 1934 Alexander expressed a wish to seek the CCF nomination in a federal constituency in Edmonton. Wallace was unhappy, and in early January he asked the board of governors to consider a document he had drafted. It argued that federal politics were not so sensitive from the point of view of a provincial university that professors should be barred from commenting on them. But "a member of the staff cannot serve as a member of the House of Commons and carry on his duties to the University." He therefore "should not ... offer himself as a candidate without first resigning his university position."[34]

Given an advance copy of this document and asked whether he wanted to appear before the board of governors in order to discuss it, Alexander declined. He did, however, identify the *non sequitur* in Wallace's argument. It might make sense to ask a professor who had won a seat to resign, but why make resignation a prerequisite for candidacy? Running was one thing, winning another.[35] A board member who belonged to the CCF made the same point, without success. Only two board members voted against the Wallace proposal. The ruling was "ridiculous," Alexander wrote to his friend Frank Underhill, not least because he would not have had a shadow of a chance of winning his seat. However, given a choice between political candidacy and his professorship, he preferred the latter.[36]

Whether or not Wallace's objective was to discourage political candidacy in general or a CCF candidacy in particular must remain an open question. He must have known that in 1933 the University of British Columbia had granted — reluctantly, it must be said — a leave of absence to George M. Weir, head of the university's department of education, to run for election and take office as Provincial Secretary and Minister of Education. Weir was respectably Liberal, however, and the relations between the British Columbia government and its university were closer than those between the Alberta government and *its* university, so that when Premier T.D. Pattullo indicated that he wanted Weir to be given leave, board members thought they had no real choice but to grant the request.[37] At the time, no other provincial university permitted its faculty to run for office without resigning, although only the University of Saskatchewan had a clearly stated policy on candidacy.[38]

At that institution only one professor was clearly identified with the CCF in the 1930s, the English literature scholar Carlyle King. He did get into trouble in 1938, but not because of his work in the CCF. It was, rather, his comments on Canada's foreign policy and the country's relations with Great Britain that caused offence. The British government "would go to war for only two purposes," he told a March

[34]UAA, BoG, Minutes, 4 January 1935.
[35]UAA, RG 19, W.H. Alexander Personal, Alexander to Wallace, 31 December 1934.
[36]National Archives of Canada (NA), MG 30, D204, Frank H. Underhill Papers, vol. 2, Alexander to Underhill, 26 January 1935.
[37]Horn, *Academic Freedom in Canada*, 101-04.
[38]"Regulations of the Board," *Statutes of the University of Saskatchewan* (Saskatoon 1912), 53.

1938 meeting of the Young Communist League in Saskatoon, "to maintain the British Empire or to prevent the spread of Socialism in Europe."[39] Neither was in his view worth fighting for. When complaints reached President James S. Thomson, he deprecated King's comments but defended his right to make them. Half a year later, King stated his opposition to Canadian participation in the war that threatened to break out between Britain and Germany over the latter's claim to the Czech Sudetenland. Thomson met demands for King's dismissal with a public defence of academic freedom, but then undermined that freedom in a private meeting with King. Having gained the impression from Thomson "that another offence of the kind would bring a demand from the board for my dismissal," King told a friend, he had cancelled an undertaking to address another anti-war meeting.[40]

At the University of Toronto, awareness that President Cody disapproved of the CCF led the social scientist Harry M. Cassidy to resign his membership. "I think that I can, for the present at least, be more useful if I am free of connection with a political party," he wrote to the St Paul's CCF Club in October 1933.[41] At the same time he asked the secretary of the Ontario CCF Clubs to remove his name from the provincial speakers' list: "It would be easier for me to meet criticisms if my name did not appear."[42] Two years later the economist Joseph Parkinson declined an invitation from CCF leader J.S. Woodsworth to join a committee formed to put the party's financial policies in simple language. "I have refrained from becoming an official of the CCF," he wrote, because "this step would put a weapon in the hands of opponents who take different views from ourselves as to the rights of a professor in a state university."[43] He offered informal help instead. We may infer he believed the LSR to be less open to criticism than the CCF, for the LSR's book *Social Planning for Canada* had appeared some weeks earlier with Parkinson listed as one of its seven authors. (The others were Eugene A. Forsey, Leonard C. Marsh, and Frank R. Scott of McGill, J. King Gordon, a travelling lecturer for the United Church of Canada and the Fellowship for a Christian Social Order, the journalist and political organizer Graham Spry, and Underhill.)

The presidents and governing boards of the private universities were not, we may assume, particularly pleased when a professor became active in the CCF, but they generally put up with it. Academics at private institutions who were active in the CCF from the 1930s into the 1950s included Eric A. Havelock and John Line at

[39]University of Saskatchewan Archives, President's Papers II B22(1), unidentified newspaper clipping, 30 March 1938.
[40]NA, Underhill Papers, vol. 5, Carlyle King to Underhill, 6 October 1938. See: Horn, *Academic Freedom in Canada*, 104-05.
[41]UTA, H.M. Cassidy Papers, B72-0022/17(01), Cassidy to L. Eckhardt, 18 October 1933, copy.
[42]UTA, HM Cassidy Papers, Cassidy to D.M. LeBourdais, 18 October 1933, copy.
[43]NA, MG 28 IV I, CCF Records, vol. 109, J.F. Parkinson to J.S. Woodsworth, 20 December 1935.

Victoria University, George M.A. Grube at Trinity College, R.E.K. Pemberton at the University of Western Ontario, Martyn Estall, Glen Shortliffe, and Gregory Vlastos at Queen's, J. Stanley Allen at Sir George Williams College, King Gordon and R.B.Y. Scott at United Theological College, Montréal, and Forsey, Marsh, and Scott at McGill. (Havelock, Grube, Allen, and Pemberton ran as CCF candidates in federal and provincial elections.) Almost all also belonged to the LSR, and several were members of the Fellowship for a Christian Social Order, a movement of Christian socialists founded in 1934. Most faced few or no institutional barriers to their political involvement, but almost all experienced criticism. Moreover, four of them — Gordon, Forsey, Marsh, and Allen — lost their positions from 1933 to 1944 amidst suspicions of varying strength that their left-wing views had been at issue.

Among the four dismissals, the one that attracted most attention was King Gordon's. Appointed to teach Christian Ethics at United Theological College (UTC) in 1931, he lost his chair in 1933 when the college abolished it on budgetary grounds. (He left academe and did not return to it until he joined the department of political science of the University of Alberta in 1962.) Since there had been hostile reaction to the Montréal-based Social and Economic Research Council, in which Gordon was active, and to his rose-coloured account of the Soviet Union, which he and Forsey had visited in 1932, it was not surprising that some observers believed Gordon's opinions, more than UTC's financial crisis, to be the explanation of what had happened.

With enrolments and endowment income both falling, the financial crisis was genuine.[44] In 1932 the General Council of the United Church instructed UTC to reduce the number of professors from five to four within two years. UTC's board responded by abolishing the chair of one of the two members of the faculty who had joined the college most recently. The other was R.B.Y. Scott, an Old Testament scholar who was, like Gordon, active in the CCF and LSR, and who would later co-edit the book written by members of the FCSO, *Towards the Christian Revolution* (1936). The key difference between the two was that Scott was married while Gordon was not.

Upon hearing that Gordon's chair was to be abolished, some of his friends undertook to raise a salary for him. When Gordon declared himself to be willing to teach for the $1,500 they were able to get together, the UTC board accepted the arrangement. In 1934, however, the board would not accept an extension of the arrangement, the board chairman stating that, since no one had approached the board, they had assumed that the support would end. He denied that disapproval of Gordon's socialism explained the board's decision: "Prof. Gordon is going because he is the latest comer and his chair can most easily be vacated."[45] Backing up this

[44]Horn, *Academic Freedom in Canada*, 114-15.
[45]NA, MG 30, D211, Frank R. Scott Papers, "Charge J. King Gordon 'Sacrificed' for Stand on Economic Questions," unidentified, undated newspaper clipping.

claim, W.D. Lighthall, a board member acquainted with Gordon, assured him: "The decision of the Governors was not influenced by any hostility to yourself or your work. That was a very minority attitude & was dropped."[46] The issues, wrote Lighthall, were the budgetary crisis and how to put into effect the instructions of the church council with least pain.

Gordon may have been tempted to believe this, but a number of friends and acquaintances encouraged him to be skeptical. Commenting in the weekly newspaper of the Ontario CCF, Graham Spry charged that the board's action resulted from "a deliberate and determined effort on the part of reactionary members of the board" to rid themselves of Gordon.[47] Recalling the matter in 1972, however, Gordon seemed unsure. "I doubt if you will be able to get 'proof' that the elimination of the chair of Christian Ethics was on account of the political views of the occupant," he wrote.[48] But he added that the board did seem curiously unwilling "to explore other methods of economizing" or to accept outside funding of his position for a second year. Indeed, were it not for the board's unwillingness to renew the 1933-4 arrangement, we could safely conclude that Gordon's views, however much some board members may have objected to them, were not at issue. Economies on the scale necessary to match the dismissal of one professor would have been impossible without a major cut in salaries that were none too generous to begin with. However, the board's failure to solicit continued outside funding gave grounds for suspicion that lingers to this day.

Research into the cases of Forsey, Marsh, and Allen offers evidence that, in apparent contrast to Gordon's experience, their non-renewals were related to their left-wing opinions and activity. All three were handled discreetly, however, and aroused little controversy.

Forsey was eased out of McGill on a pretext apparently scripted by Principal Lewis H. Douglas and executed by his successor F. Cyril James.[49] Forsey had been under a cloud since the early 1930s, when he drew criticism for his vocal attacks on capitalism and his favourable assessment of the Soviet Union. There had also been questions about the quality of his teaching and research.[50] But no principal wanted it to be thought that Forsey was being let go because of his opinions. In 1933 Sir Arthur Currie explained to Premier Louis-Alexandre Taschereau that for two years he had been trying to shed Forsey without creating an uproar and hoped to be able to do so yet, but that it would not be easy. Noting "the great importance" which professors attached "to what they are pleased to call 'academic freedom'," Currie explained that if he were to dismiss Forsey "it will be heralded from one end

[46]NA, MG 30, C241, J. King Gordon Papers, W.D. Lighthall to Gordon, 18 April 1934.
[47]Graham Spry, "The Case of King Gordon," *New Commonwealth*, 27 October 1934.
[48]J. King Gordon to the author, 2 October 1972.
[49]Horn, *Academic Freedom in Canada*, 142-4.
[50]Horn, *Academic Freedom in Canada*, 129-32.

of Canada to the other that McGill dismisses its professors because of their political views."[51]

When Forsey was given notice in 1940 that his contract would not be renewed in 1941 — he had been a sessional lecturer in political economy since 1929 — Cyril James referred to an understanding that the successful defence of Forsey's doctoral dissertation in the year just ended would be required for reappointment. Forsey and his department head, J.C. Hemmeon, denied that such an understanding existed: in vain. Forsey thought of putting up a struggle but thought better of it when he became aware that few of his colleagues — "rabbits" he called them in a letter to Frank Underhill[52] — would support him. He left in triumph, having won a Guggenheim Fellowship, and upon returning to Canada from a year spent in the United States he became research director for the Canadian Congress of Labour. (In 1970 he was appointed to the Senate, serving until 1980.)

Marsh's removal was much easier. Almost from his arrival at McGill in 1930 he had taught only one course, the remainder of his time being devoted to directing the Rockefeller Foundation-funded McGill Social Science Research project. The grant, renewed once, was due to end in 1940. This provided the occasion for Principal Lewis Douglas, who had a low opinion of socialism and of the "collectivist" bias he perceived in the publications of the research project,[53] to give Marsh notice. Believing (mistakenly) that his salary was paid from the grant, Marsh went quietly.[54] During the war he worked in Ottawa and wrote the *Report on Social Security for Canada* (1943), one of the blueprints for the Canadian welfare state. After some years with the United Nations after the war, he joined the UBC faculty of social work in 1950.

The chemist J. Stanley Allen began teaching at Sir George Williams College in 1932. A member of the FCSO and LSR, he ran as a CCF candidate in Montréal's Mount Royal constituency in the 1940 federal election. He came in a very distant third but had greater success in local politics, serving during the war years as a member of the Montréal City Council and the Protestant School Board. Allen's Christian socialism, his work in the CCF, and his opposition to the limits imposed on the number of Jewish students in the college irritated more than one board member. In the late winter of 1944 Principal Kenneth Norris asked for Allen's resignation, stating as the grounds that his public life encroached on his teaching and his service to the college. A board member, D. Prescott Mowry, informed Allen some days later that his socialist activities constituted the real reason. The issue remains obscure, however: the historian Richard Allen has found that the board's

[51]MUA, RG2, PO, c.43/301, A.W. Currie to L.-A. Taschereau, 21 October 1933, copy.
[52]NA, Underhill Papers, vol. 4, Forsey to Underhill, 2 May 1941.
[53]MUA, RG2, PO, c.54/730, Lewis Douglas to E.W. Beatty, 3 February 1939, copy.
[54]Horn, *Academic Freedom in Canada*, 141-2.

minutes contain no discussion of the case.[55] In any case, Stanley Allen believed that fighting his dismissal would damage both him and the college and resigned. Soon afterwards he moved to Ontario; he never taught in a university again.

A few private-university professors active in the CCF or other left-wing groups — R.E.K. Pemberton, Martyn Estall, Gregory Vlastos, R.B.Y. Scott — reported when asked in the 1960s that they felt no constraint and heard little or no criticism from within their universities. Others did run into trouble, probably none more spectacularly than the Victoria College classicist Eric A. Havelock. In the early 1930s, speeches made by him and his friend and colleague John Line, a professor of divinity in Emmanuel College, more than once aroused the ire of Premier George Henry. A member of the United Church, Henry thought it inappropriate that members of Victoria's faculty should engage in "wild tirades"[56] or belong to "an organization [the LSR] ... which is definitely affiliating itself with ... the CCF," a party Henry linked to "the Communism and Despotism of Russia."[57] President E.W. Wallace gently countered such complaints with references to the importance of academic freedom and "our British tradition of open discussion."[58]

Line and Havelock were aware that some important Ontarians disliked their views, but so long as Victoria tolerated them they had scant cause for worry. Certainly Havelock felt few inhibitions when, speaking as a representative of the FCSO, he addressed the striking General Motors workers in Oshawa on 14 April 1937. Recalling the incident thirty years later, he said he was carried away by the "mood of defiance" he sensed in his listeners.[59] At one point he asked rhetorically whether the solicitousness for General Motors shown by Premier Mitchell Hepburn and his cabinet was a sign that they had a pecuniary interest in the company. No reporter was present, and the account that appeared in the *Globe and Mail* on 17 April was second-hand: "Professor Havelock is alleged to have suggested that the Government's backing of General Motors ... possibly had been influenced by the shares of stock which the Prime Minister and members of his Cabinet held in the Motor Company."[60]

Premier Hepburn denied the suggestion, and Provincial Secretary Harry Nixon said that Havelock's remarks would be referred to the governing board of Victoria College. President Wallace called Havelock into his office and in the course of "a long and unpleasant conversation" — Havelock's words — charged him with

[55]I owe much of my information about the case to Dr. Richard Allen of Hamilton, Ont., who has written about his uncle in a history of the Allen family, publication forthcoming. See also Horn, *Academic Freedom in Canada*, 169-70.

[56]United Church/Victoria University Archives (UC/VUA), President's Papers (PP), 89-130V, vol. 53-4, George S. Henry to E.W. Wallace, 28 October 1932.

[57]UC/VUA, PP, Henry to Wallace, 13 February 1933.

[58]UC/VUA, Wallace to Henry, 8 February 1933, copy.

[59]Interview with Eric A. Havelock, New Haven, Conn., April 1967.

[60]*Globe and Mail* (*GM*), 17 April 1937.

harming Victoria, ordered him not do so again, and instructed him to apologize to Hepburn. Havelock did so; he also promised Wallace that he would "abstain from any platform discussions concerning controversial issues ... for at least a year" and even longer.[61]

Another classicist had accompanied Havelock to Oshawa, G.M.A. Grube of Trinity College. His name did not appear in 1937, but he did get into hot water for comments made during the Ontario CCF convention on 7 April 1939. The *Globe and Mail*, identifying him (mistakenly) as a "U. of T. Professor," quoted him as saying "that any war that would come in Europe at the present time would 'have nothing to do with democracy'." Grube made the comment in speaking to a motion that described the Canadian defence budget as "a waste of public funds in the interests of British imperialism."[62] When some Ontario MPPs put the text of the motion in Grube's mouth and attacked him for it, they unleashed a storm that threatened briefly to blow away not only him but also his friend Frank Underhill.

Liberal and Conservative MPPs unanimously deplored Grube's supposed remarks. Several suggested that the University of Toronto should take him to task. Contacted by the press, President Cody pointed out that Grube was employed by Trinity College and therefore not the U of T's responsibility. When Premier Hepburn was told of this, he said that either Trinity should discipline "this foreigner" (a naturalized British subject, Grube was born in Belgium) or its link with the university might be adjusted in some way harmful to the college — perhaps be revoked.[63]

At this point the Leader of the Opposition, George Drew, shifted the focus from Grube to the more familiar figure of Frank Underhill. The historian was notoriously a critic of the British connection and its potential for drawing Canada into a European war, and Drew's quoting of a provocative passage written more than three years earlier — it included the words "the poppies blooming in Flanders fields have no further interest for us"[64] — reinforced the hostility that many people, including several members of the university's board of governors, already entertained towards him. The difficulties created for Underhill by Drew's intervention were considerable. Cody berated him; he also had to explain himself to the board. "This is the worst business I've been through yet," he wrote to the journalist George Ferguson.[65] To another friend, the United College (Winnipeg) historian Arthur Lower, he wrote: "This trouble has been so extreme that we [he and Grube] pretty well have to keep quiet for a time .... I think the only effective protection that

[61]UC/VUA, PP, 89-130V, vol. 53-4, Havelock to Wallace, 1 and 2 May 1937.

[62]*GM*, 8 April 1939.

[63]*GM*, 13 and 14 April 1939.

[64]Originating in a private document written for the Canadian Institute of International Affairs, the passage had appeared, without Underhill's knowledge, in a book by R.A. MacKay and E.B. Rogers, *Canada Looks Abroad* (Toronto 1938), 269.

[65]NA, Underhill Papers, vol. 4, Underhill to George Ferguson, 21 April 1939, copy.

professors will have in a society like ours is to form a trade union of their own and affiliate with one of the American bodies."[66] (No faculty association existed at the University of Toronto before 1942; the Canadian Association of University Teachers (CAUT) was not founded until 1951.)

Underhill would face even more serious trouble in 1940-41, when he came close to losing his position.[67] Grube escaped such jeopardy. All the same, the Trinity authorities did not appreciate the attention he had drawn to himself and the college. Particularly unwelcome was Premier Hepburn's threat to alter Trinity's federation with the University of Toronto. The college board responded by sending Grube a statement that began ominously: "We believe that the issue in this case is not one of Freedom of Speech" but of responsibility. Professors should speak only when they were sure that their words would not harm those with whom they worked. Someone who spoke or acted "in a way that outrages the feelings of many of his fellow-citizens" ought to resign so as to save the college authorities from having to choose between restricting a professor's freedom or suffering the consequences of his irresponsible use of that freedom.[68]

Grube had already written twice to Provost Frederick H. Cosgrave, expressing his regrets for the negative publicity his remarks had caused but also pointing out he had been misquoted and asserting his right to address issues of public policy. His response to the memorandum he received granted "that one has a loyalty to the institution with which one is connected" and that adverse publicity should be avoided whenever possible. Although he had until the recent events managed to avoid such publicity, he realized he needed to be "even more careful in the future" and undertook to try not to associate his name "with statements so construed that they are likely to give rise to the kind of emotional outburst which is regrettable from every point of view."[69] This seems to have satisfied the Trinity authorities, and in 1940 they acquiesced in his request to be allowed to run for the CCF in a federal constituency, on the understanding that he would resign if elected. (He finished third in Toronto-Broadview.) He also ran for municipal office during the war years. In June 1943, Provost Cosgrave mentioned to Grube "certain difficulties" that had arisen out of the character of some of Grube's "activities and utterances."[70] The record of the interview does not contain specifics, but six months later a report in the *Toronto Star* led Cosgrave to complain that the classicist was

---

[66]Queen's University Archives (QUA), coll. 5072, A.R.M. Lower Papers, vol. 1, file A13, Underhill to Lower, 1 May 1939.
[67]R. Douglas Francis, *Frank H. Underhill: Intellectual Provocateur* (Toronto 1986), 114-27; see also Horn, *Academic Freedom in Canada*, 154-65.
[68]Trinity College Archives (TCA), Grube Provostial file, 987-0003, Memorandum to Professor Grube as Approved by Executive Committee, April 1939.
[69]TCA, Grube Provostial File, G.M.A. Grube to Provost Cosgrave, 27 April 1939.
[70]TCA, Grube Provostial File, Memorandum re Interview between the Provost and Professor Grube, 1 June 1943.

breaking the promise made in 1939 not to comment provocatively on current events. Trinity might "suffer severely," presumably through the loss of donations or even enrolments, if this sort of thing continued.[71]

Grube replied that he had been misquoted. The *Star* had reported him as urging the CCF, once in office, to act "quickly and ruthlessly" against its enemies. What he had actually said was "that a CCF government would have to use its power 'quickly, legally and democratically, but firmly and even ruthlessly' to put into effect its mandate." Grube assured Cosgrave that he had "never advocated anything but democratic processes, both in achieving power and in exercising it."[72] This explanation seemed to be sufficient.

Of the academics who were active in the CCF in the 1930s and 1940s, none was more prominent than the McGill law professor Frank Scott. From time to time he came under attack, especially by businessmen and newspaper editors, for activities which included the national chairmanship of the party from 1942 to 1950, and for his views. Within the university, however, criticism was muted. Unlike Forsey and Marsh, Scott was tenured. He was also well-connected and well-known. In early 1943 Principal James's secretary, the influential Dorothy McMurray, suggested to her boss that the board should try to frighten Scott into silence. "Nothing much has been heard from Underhill ... since the Board of Governors there at least scared him," she wrote: "He hasn't published a controversial statement since, has he?"[73]

This went too far for James and, we may assume, the board. We may also assume that they continued to look askance on his work in the CCF. When the deanship of law became vacant in 1948, Scott was next in line, but the board wanted none of him. As Principal James explained to the outgoing dean, C.S. LeMesurier, the position required full-time attention. For this reason "the Board has unanimously adopted a resolution providing that no individual who is ... an executive officer of a political party can be considered eligible for a deanship." James continued: "Quite frankly, I would be very doubtful, if I may judge the sentiment of the Board of Governors, whether [Scott] would be considered a desirable candidate even if he were to resign from executive office in the party to which he belongs."[74]

LeMesurier gave a copy of this letter to Scott, who was sufficiently irritated that he considered challenging the board, using the offices of the American Association of University Professors. He thought better of this, but soon had new reason to be angry when the board adopted a new policy on political activity which

[71]TCA, Grube Provostial File, Memorandum, 14 December 1943. See: *Toronto Star (TS)*, 9 December 1943.
[72]TCA, Grube Provostial file, 987-0003, Grube to Cosgrave, 22 December 1943.
[73]MUA, RG2, PO, c.85/2202, [Dorothy McMurray], comments on [F. Cyril James], "Academic Freedom of Speech," n.d. [1943].
[74]NA, Scott Papers, vol. 1, Academic Freedom file, F. Cyril James to C.S. LeMesurier, 10 October 1947, copy.

stated, among other things, that "the Board ... considers it adversely affects the interests of the University for members of the staff to hold positions on the principal executive body of any political party."[75] Although this was not to be applied retroactively, Scott took it as direct criticism of his own involvement and lobbied to have this part of the policy repealed. In March 1948 the board did so.

In 1961 Scott did become dean and spent three conflict-ridden years that he did not much enjoy. A few years afterwards he wrote about his earlier exclusion from the deanship: "Actually the situation suited me admirably. No one in his right senses wants to be dean, but he certainly wants even less to belong to a university which discriminates against its staff for political reasons."[76] His failure to gain promotion enhanced his reputation as a constitutional lawyer, enabling him to act as counsel in two high-profile cases, *Roncarelli v. Duplessis* and *Switzman v. Elbling*, the latter better known as the Padlock case.[77] Premier Maurice Duplessis, who was also Québec's Attorney General, was implicated in both, which led many law firms to back off. Scott took note of this and came in time to express appreciation for the academic freedom he had enjoyed. "I never at any time felt my position as teacher and writer was threatened," he wrote in the preface of his last book, "and while my behaviour was under close scrutiny and doubtless constrained in consequence, I owed the university my freedom from the much more inhibiting restraints imposed by the practice of law in which I was first engaged. A group of law partners can be even more repressive than a Board of Governors, as I was eventually to learn in the Padlock Act and Roncarelli cases."[78]

One more person should be mentioned, chiefly because his experience does not fit the mould. Watson Kirkconnell was a professor of literature at McMaster University, a polyglot who had mastered more than twenty languages, and a committed but liberal-minded Baptist. Deeply suspicious of dictatorships of all kinds, he feared communists quite as much as fascists and served Ottawa during the war by monitoring the ethnic press for possible subversion. Cooperation between countries with conflicting ideologies was "necessary for the political equilibrium of the world," he wrote in 1944, but our view of the Soviet Union should be clear-eyed and "not based on sentiment and illusion."[79] Stalin was no greater friend of freedom than Hitler.

[75]MUA, BoG, Minutes, 14 January 1948; NA, Scott Papers, vol. 1, William Bentley to distribution, 21 January 1948.
[76]Frank Scott to the author, 11 September 1968.
[77]The 1937 Padlock Act, officially known as "An Act Respecting Communistic Propaganda," allowed the authorities to padlock (and thereby deny use of) premises which the Attorney General or his designates believed were being used for the dissemination of communistic (not defined in the act) propaganda. See: Sandra Djwa, *The Politics of the Imagination: A Life of F.R. Scott* (Toronto 1987), 297-317.
[78]Frank R. Scott, "Author's Preface," in Michiel Horn, ed., *A New Endeavour: Selected Political Essays, Letters, and Addresses* (Toronto 1986), x.
[79]Watson Kirkconnell, *Seven Pillars of Freedom* (Toronto 1944), ix.

Criticism of the Soviet Union was unfashionable in 1944: for three years Canadians had been propagandized to see the Soviets as gallant allies in the war against Nazi Germany. Kirkconnell came under attack, especially after he wrote a series of articles critical of Soviet foreign and domestic policy that appeared in the Toronto *Telegram* in the spring of 1945. Kirkconnell writes in his memoirs that Albert Matthews, chairman of McMaster's board of governors, told him in mid-May 1945 "that he had been waited on by Joe Atkinson, proprietor of the *Toronto Daily Star*, and a lady member of his editorial staff," who had urged that Kirkconnell be dismissed because of his articles in the *Telegram*.[80]

There is no corroborating evidence for this story, but the *Star*'s hostility to Kirkconnell is a matter of record. On 29 May 1945, an editorial charged that "those who stir up hostility to the Soviet Union, who try to weaken the bonds between the Allied Nations, are ... carrying on [Joseph] Goebbels's work now that his printing presses have been stopped."[81] Two weeks later the *Star* accused Kirkconnell of misrepresenting the Soviet treatment of the Jews and claimed he had thereby "revealed his intention to arouse hatred toward Russia."[82] Still, it seems less than likely that Atkinson sought Kirkconnell's dismissal. The *Toronto Star* supported academic freedom and free speech more consistently than almost any other Canadian newspaper of the time. In any case, Kirkconnell's chair was not in danger. When he left McMaster in 1948 it was to become president of Acadia University.

* * *

The Cold War that characterized international relations for many years after 1945 modified the pattern so far described. Communism appeared as the great threat, while the CCF gradually gained a degree of respectability. The party supported the North Atlantic Treaty Organization (NATO), formed in 1949, as well as the United Nations "police action" in Korea from 1950 to 1953, and came to be seen as anti-communist by all but fevered reactionaries. Nevertheless, many of its policies continued to meet the hostility of business. The party that succeeded it, the New Democratic Party (NDP) — it took shape in 1960-61 — seemed even less threatening. Nevertheless, stating views that could be characterized as communist or "fellow-travelling" could get those who expressed them in trouble, especially in the immediate post-war years. One thing remained constant: those who got into difficulties belonged somewhere on the political left.

The University of Alberta biochemist George Hunter provides an interesting example. Radicalized during the Depression, both Hunter and his wife were by the end of the 1930s sympathetic to communism though not, it seems, members of the CPC. Their involvement in aiding veterans of the Spanish Civil War (1936-39) drew

---

[80]Watson Kirkconnell, *A Slice of Canada: Memoirs* (Toronto 1967), 321.

[81]"The Nazi Line," *TS*, 29 May 1945.

[82]"Soviet Russia and the Jews," *TS*, 14 June 1945. On Joseph Atkinson's attitude to the Soviet Union, see: Ross Harkness, *J.E. Atkinson of the Star* (Toronto 1963), 325.

them to the attention of the Royal Canadian Mounted Police (RCMP), which placed an undercover agent in Hunter's introductory course in 1939-40. In April this agent wrote a report, subsequently made available to President W.A.R. Kerr, stating that Hunter had used his last class of term to make some remarks whose "general trend ...was anti-Christian and pro-Marxism."[83] In time this resulted in a directive to Hunter to cease his custom of using the last class of term to link the course and his research interest in nutrition to wider social, economic, and political issues. In the process a cloud gathered over him. Both the president and members of the board came to think of him as a communist.[84] This served him ill nine years later.

Sometime after the war, Hunter resumed his custom of delivering a "last lecture" in which he discussed national and world events. In early April 1949 this prompted an inquiry by a newspaper reporter and a complaint from seventeen of the 257 students in his course.[85] Some of his comments had been provocative — he had denounced the 1945 US decision to drop atomic bombs on Hiroshima and Nagasaki and had predicted that the recently signed North Atlantic Treaty was more likely to bring about war than to prevent it. The complaint started a process that culminated in Hunter's dismissal, with 24 hours notice, on 29 June 1949. (He received about twenty weeks' pay in lieu of notice.) He returned to Great Britain, whence he had come thirty years earlier, and never taught in a university again.

Outside the university the dismissal was widely seen as an attack on academic freedom, with Hunter's last lecture and his support for the peace movement and other left-wing causes identified as the reasons for the board's action against him. The truth is more complicated and may never be fully known. The university did not give Hunter a reason for dismissal, and it declined to make any reason public, but President Robert Newton stated that Hunter's political views were *not* the reason. That is also too simple. Some board members had, in fact, wanted to fire Hunter in the fall of 1947 for his alleged communism, and this motive cannot have been absent from their minds two years later. Newton, however, had argued against doing so, and since the board could not dismiss Hunter without a presidential recommendation, Hunter had stayed on.

It does seem that Newton had by 1946 come to the view that Hunter was dishonest, disloyal, and disagreeably combative, and regarded him as an intolerable nuisance. But two letters he received in September 1947 apparently persuaded him that dismissing Hunter because of his political views would be a mistake. "Have you any avowed Communists on your academic staff and, if so, what is your attitude towards them?"[86] Newton had asked McGill's Cyril James and University of

[83] UAA, RG19, Personnel files, 73-112, George Hunter file (GHF), "Re: Prof. G. Hunter, University of Alberta, Edmonton, Alta," 12 April 1940.
[84] Horn, *Academic Freedom in Canada*, 150-2.
[85] Horn, *Academic Freedom in Canada*, 195-203.
[86] MUA, RG2, PO, c.118/3209, Robert Newton to F. Cyril James, 3 September 1947; UTA, PO (Smith), A68-0007/30(01), Newton to Sidney E. Smith, 3 September 1947.

Toronto president Sidney E. Smith. James replied that he would be disinclined to pay attention to whether a faculty member was a communist or not, "provided that his political beliefs did not interfere with the efficiency of his teaching and his general cooperation in the work of the university."[87] Smith replied that he knew of "only two avowed communists" among the faculty — he did not name them — and "to date" they had been "very discreet." To act openly against them would be a mistake, he continued, for they would thrive on persecution. "Of course, if any member of the staff participates in activities which would carry the disapproval of his colleagues, one would be on good ground for tough treatment."[88]

Newton already knew that Hunter, able and accomplished as a scientist but prone to biting sarcasm, was disliked by many of his colleagues. What Newton needed was an opportunity to mete out the tough treatment Smith had mentioned. Hunter's classroom comments in 1949 provided that opportunity. If journalists writing in the newspapers as well as in *Time*, *Saturday Night*, and the *Canadian Forum* assumed that Hunter's political views were the reason for his dismissal, Newton was willing to let them think so. He was secure in the knowledge that he enjoyed the support of most of the faculty in dealing harshly with the biochemist. Alberta's dean of law, W.F. Bowker, assured Frank Scott (who had written to obtain more information than was contained in media reports) that Hunter's alleged communism had not been at issue, so "academic freedom was not involved." Bowker added that Hunter had been "quarrelsome and obstinate and disaffected," and although individually his actions had been no more than "pin-pricks," together they had been intolerable.[89]

Another Edmonton friend whom Scott wrote, a CCF member of the legislature named Elmer Roper, offered a different reason for Hunter's dismissal. As far as he could determine, Roper wrote, Hunter was "a communist or a very rabid fellow traveller" who had been indiscreet in expressing his opinions in class and outside. This, presumably, was the reason for his dismissal.[90] (It was relevant to Roper's assessment and Scott's reaction to it that there was no love lost between the CCF and the communists.) Scott ignored the contradictions between the two reports he had received in informing Arthur Lower that Hunter seemed to be "an impossible fellow to represent because he insisted on filling his lectures full of political propaganda."[91] There was broad agreement at the time that politics should be left out of the classroom.

The post-war fear of "reds" affected several other academic careers. At Queen's University the mathematician Israel Halperin was implicated in a possible

[87]MUA, RG2, PO, c.118/3209, James to Newton, 10 September 1947, copy.
[88]UTA, PO, A68-0007/30(01), Smith to Newton, 5 September 1947, copy.
[89]NA, Scott Papers, vol. 1, Academic Freedom Correspondence 1938-1950, W.F. Bowker to Scott, 18 October 1949.
[90]NA, Scott Papers, Elmer E. Roper to Scott, 24 October 1949.
[91]NA, Scott Papers, Scott to A.R.M. Lower, 27 October 1949, copy.

breach of the Official Secrets Act during the inquiry made into the disclosures by Igor Gouzenko, a cipher clerk in the Soviet embassy who defected in September 1945. Halperin was put on trial, but the charges against him were dismissed. Nevertheless a member of the board of trustees, D.A. Gillies, stated "that Halperin's record as a Communist fellow traveller indicates that he is not the type of individual who should be teaching in a Canadian university."[92] Principal Robert C. Wallace thought this unwise, but Gillies had some support from other board members. In the end Chancellor Charles A. Dunning saved the day for Halperin, arguing that it would seriously damage the reputation of Queen's if it dismissed a man who had been cleared by the courts.

Halperin's colleague Glen Shortliffe became a Cold-War casualty in an unusual way.[93] A scholar of 19th-century French literature and history, to whose study he brought a perspective in which the concept of class conflict took a significant place, Shortliffe was also interested in current French politics. In 1945 he began to contribute talks on this subject to the CBC radio program *Midweek Review*. These received a generally favourable response, leading to an invitation to share the political commentary on another CBC program, *Weekend Review*, starting in the fall of 1948. Speaking more regularly than in the past, Shortliffe had to inform himself about areas other (and more controversial) than his beloved France. Soon he was at odds with the editors of the *Kingston Whig-Standard* and the Montréal *Gazette*, both of whom thought he was too friendly to communism. By the end of 1948 written attacks on Shortliffe's alleged communist sympathies, joined to criticism of Queen's for failing to silence him, had been forwarded to Principal Wallace by at least three members of the board of trustees.

In February 1949 Shortliffe spoke about the trial of Cardinal Jozsef Mindszenty and the conflict between church and state in Hungary, comparing that country's experiences with anti-clericalism with those of late 19th-century France. This prompted another strongly-worded letter attacking Shortliffe, one Wallace decided to pass on to him. It was not the only letter of its kind that had reached him, Wallace told Shortliffe. Criticism had also come from people close to the university. This was a problem, for a fund-raising campaign was about to begin, and Shortliffe's views were unpopular with the very people from whom large sums were expected.

The historian of Queen's University, Frederick W. Gibson, writes that Wallace, while believing in academic freedom, "unfortunately" gave more weight to his university's need for money, hoping that a word to the wise would lead

[92]QUA, coll. 1125, F.W. Gibson Papers, vol. 4, Israel Halperin file, D.A. Gillies to R.C. Wallace, 30 May 1947. All documents in the Gibson Papers are photocopies of documents in other collections, almost all of them in the Queen's University Archives and chiefly the records of the Principal's Office.

[93]Horn, *Academic Freedom in Canada*, 186-90.

Shortliffe to "tone down his comments and be more prudent and discreet."[94] Having learned to his shocked surprise that his broadcasts might do damage to Queen's, Shortliffe decided simply to drop them. "I do not believe my own views on freedom ... to be sufficient justification to bring opprobrium upon my colleagues," he wrote to Wallace.[95] A few days later Shortliffe added that he had "contempt" for "the motives of those who choose to attack the University because of their disagreement with the view of one member of its staff." So long as influential people did so, however, universities and their faculty members were put in "an almost impossible situation." Since he had "no desire whatever ... to become the centre of a *cause célèbre* which could harm only myself and the University," his decision to end the broadcasts stood.[96]

The story did not end there. Shortliffe's failure later in 1949 to gain admission to the United States after he had accepted an offer from George Washington University in St Louis may have been a consequence of his broadcasts. (In October, when the US attorney general said he was admissible after all, he no longer wanted to go.) In 1954 a further incident occurred. Invited to teach French to subalterns in the summer school of the Royal Military College, Shortliffe was relieved of his duties on 8 June, just as the course was about to begin. His efforts to obtain an explanation were for several months unsuccessful. Not until December 1954 did he get a letter from the minister of national defence, Ralph Campney, who explained that "active participation in public controversy on the part of ... officers is naturally viewed with disfavour and the Armed Forces are inclined to regard those with an established tendency in this direction as somewhat unsuited for the task of instructing junior officers."[97]

Questioned in 1961 by a CBC writer gathering information for a program on security screenings in Canada, Shortliffe stated that his experiences in 1949 and 1954 had undermined his scholarship. Shaken by what had happened, he had decided "not to write at all on any subject which might have social significance for our thought police." This had ruled out a subject that had been of great interest to him, namely the impact of the Revolution of 1871, the class war evident in it, and the murderous reaction to it, on certain French writers. Instead he had begun to work on language laboratory techniques, which being apolitical were eminently safe. "In other words I think I have voluntarily blown my own brains out."[98]

The Cold War also affected the careers of the economic historian Henry S. Ferns and the theoretical physicist Leopold Infeld. Ferns's left-wing associations — he had been a Marxist while at Cambridge in the 1930s — contributed to the

[94]Frederick W. Gibson, *Queen's University*, vol. 2, *1917-1961: To Serve and Yet Be Free*, (Kingston and Montréal 1983), 291, 292.
[95]QUA, Gibson Papers, vol. 4, Glen Shortliffe to Robert C. Wallace, 15 February 1949.
[96]QUA, Gibson Papers, vol. 4, Shortliffe to Wallace, 23 Feb. 1949.
[97]QUA, Gibson Papers, vol. 4, Ralph Campney to Shortliffe, 13 December 1954.
[98]QUA, Gibson Papers, vol. 4, Shortliffe to Monroe Scott, 18 February 1961.

nonrenewal of his teaching contract at United College in 1947 but did not keep him from being appointed at the University of Manitoba.[99] After being offered an associate professorship in history and economics at Royal Roads Military College near Victoria, BC, in the spring of 1949, he received a Civil Service Commission letter in August, just before he was to begin teaching, informing him that the Department of National Defence had judged him to be unacceptable. No explanation was offered, and Ferns never got one. Instead he settled for close to half a year's pay and moved to England, where he had a distinguished academic career.[100]

A member of the department of applied mathematics at the University of Toronto, Leopold Infeld also left Canada, though under different circumstances from Ferns's.[101] Associated with several left-wing causes after his arrival in Toronto in 1938, the Polish-born Infeld nevertheless experienced little or no criticism before the late winter of 1950. At that time his sabbatical plans became embroiled in politics. A journalist, upon interviewing him, formed the impression that Infeld was politically unreliable and asked in print why a man who had access to atomic secrets was being permitted to spend part of his sabbatical in Poland, a country embedded in the Soviet bloc. This led George Drew, who had become Leader of the Opposition in Ottawa in 1949, to ask the same question in the House of Commons.[102] Infeld had no access to atomic secrets, as the government (no doubt briefed by the RCMP) knew. However, with the sabbatical having become controversial, President Sidney Smith, who had some months earlier approved Infeld's plans, now tried to get him to change his mind and, when Infeld would not, refused to recommend his sabbatical to the board of governors.

Infeld, already in England by this time, was reluctant to abort his sabbatical plans and resigned at the end of the summer, much to Smith's relief. As he explained to the chairman of the board of governors, Eric Phillips, he had been readying himself to recommend Infeld's dismissal but had not relished doing so because he anticipated a storm of protest from faculty and students.[103] Infeld's resignation prevented this.

Infeld settled down at the University of Warsaw and made a significant contribution to the development of theoretical physics in his native country. He remained active in the international campaing for peace and nuclear arms control, and in 1955 he was one of eleven signatories (two others being Albert Einstein and Bertrand Russell) of the manifesto against nuclear weapons that led the industrialist Cyrus Eaton to establish the Pugwash conferences. In 1995 the sole surviving

[99]Horn, *Academic Freedom in Canada*, 190-1.
[100]H.S. Ferns, *Reading from Left to Right: One Man's Political History* (Toronto 1988), 284-96.
[101]Horn, *Academic Freedom in Canada*, 203-11.
[102]Canada, House of Commons, *Debates*, 16 March 1950, 793.
[103]UTA, PO (Smith), A68-0007/062(18), S.E. Smith to W.E. Phillips, 22 September 1950, copy.

signatory, Joseph Rotblat, won the Nobel Prize for Peace.[104] In 1995, too, the University of Toronto posthumously made him a professor emeritus. The Cold War having ended, it had become possible to see Infeld clearly at last.

During the 1950s there were no high-profile cases of the kind that marked the 1930s and 1940s. The best-known dismissal in Canadian university history, that of the historian Harry S. Crowe from United College, had little if anything to do with his left-wing views or activities.[105] Crowe was a member of the CCF, to be sure, and after he left United College in 1959 he became research director for the Canadian Brotherhood of Railway, Transport, and General Workers. But there is no real evidence that his politics affected the decision of the board of regents to give him notice. However, labour relations were at issue, for Crowe's vigorous defence of what he believed to be his rights led to his first dismissal. The board clearly thought him to be an employee who did not know his place.

A sign of the changing times was that, starting in the 1940s, a growing number of universities adopted policies that allowed professors to run for political office and to take a leave of absence if they succeeded in gaining election. In his study of class and power in Canada, *The Vertical Mosaic* (1965), the sociologist John Porter stated: "It would probably be difficult to find another modern political system with such a paucity of participation for scholars."[106] All the same, when the national secretary of the CAUT, Stewart Reid, polled a handful of academics who had been nominated for House of Commons seats in the 1963 federal election, he learned that most reported having had no difficulty getting leave to run.[107] Something of an exception was the Dalhousie political scientist James Aitchison, whose offer of an NDP nomination in a Halifax constituency in 1962 met with objection from the board of governors. The opposition, it seems, was less to his candidacy than to the party. After Reid supplied information about the state of affairs in other Canadian universities, however, the board relented.[108]

A shortage of qualified academics that became noticeable by 1962 and grew steadily more serious from that year into the very early 1970s created the conditions for increased faculty involvement in university decision making, while also making academic tenure more secure. As well, it made left-wing political affiliation seem less important than in an earlier age. In this more permissive climate, even the occasional Communist was able to survive, something that would have been difficult to imagine during the Depression or World War II. *A Place of Liberty* was the title chosen for a book of essays about university government that appeared in

[104]Leopold Infeld, *Why I Left Canada: Reflections on Science and Politics*, trans. Helen Infeld, ed. Lewis Pyenson (Montréal and London 1978), 67-9; *GM*, 14 October 1995.
[105]Horn, *Academic Freedom in Canada*, 220-45.
[106]John Porter, *The Vertical Mosaic: An Analysis of Social Class and Power in Canada* (Toronto 1965), 503.
[107]NA, RG 28, I 208, CAUT Papers, vol. 2, file AF & T.
[108]NA, RG 28, I 208, J.H. Aitchison to J.H.S. Reid, 1 May 1962.

print under CAUT auspices in 1964.[109] For some academics, access to the freedom celebrated in the book was a recent concession, indeed.

Conditions changed dramatically in the late 1960s. The student movement is beyond the scope of this essay, but it provided the occasion for a new kind of faculty radical — "new left" was a term soon widely in use — to challenge universities they believed to be too closely tied to corporate capitalism. The McGill political scientist Stanley Gray was an example of the type. In February 1969 he joined several students in disrupting meetings of the university senate and board of governors, chiefly in protest against the establishment of the Faculty of Management. If this had the force of novelty, so did the university's response. Seeking to determine whether cause existed to dismiss Gray, Principal H. Rocke Robertson offered him arbitration by a committee to be named by the CAUT. Gray accepted the offer. A committee headed by Walter Tarnopolsky, dean of law at the University of Windsor, ruled in August 1969 that "the manner and the circumstances in which Mr. Gray acted constituted gross misconduct," justifying his dismissal.[110] He left university life and became active in the labour movement.

A more spectacular instance of conflict involving a university administration on one hand and some of its students and faculty on the other occurred in 1969 at Simon Fraser University (SFU).[111] Opening in 1965, SFU attracted a good many students and teachers who wanted to break with academic tradition. Some were vocally critical of capitalist society. This was especially the case in the department of Political Science, Sociology and Anthropology (PSA), whose founding chairman, T.B. Bottomore, recruited men and women with a wide range of political views, among them several "new leftists." Since SFU was one of the hotbeds of the student movement in 1968-69 — a student sit-in led to more than a hundred arrests — the resulting mixture proved highly volatile. Several faculty members cooperated with students to develop a set of procedures for governing the department that diverged widely from those drafted earlier by the Simon Fraser University Faculty Association and adopted by the university's senate and board of governors. When the department insisted on using its own procedures to select a new chairman, it was put under trusteeship. The anger this generated was intensified when the university's tenure committee overturned several positive recommendations made for PSA members by the dean's committee. Since the negative decisions mainly affected the more radical members of PSA, they claimed that this was a purge — a claim made credible by the strong academic record of several of those affected.

In September 1969, eight members of the department voted to support a student-sponsored strike intended to secure the approval of President Kenneth B.

[109]George Whalley, ed., *A Place of Liberty: Essays on the Government of Canadian Universities* (Toronto and Vancouver 1964).

[110]Ronald Lebel, "Board Dismisses McGill Lecturer, Recommends Year's Compensation," *GM*, 19 August 1969.

[111]Horn, *Academic Freedom in Canada*, 313-15.

Strand and SFU's governing bodies for PSA's procedures. Strand suspended the university's statement on academic freedom and tenure to fire all eight — Kathleen Gough Aberle, Saghir Ahmad, Mordecai Briemberg, Louis Feldhammer, John Leggett, Nathan Popkin, David Potter, and Prudence Wheeldon (two, Popkin and Wheeldon, were eventually reinstated). Not only did this step and its aftermath seriously divide the university, but in 1971 it prompted the CAUT to censure SFU, which remained under this sanction until 1977.

The 1960s sellers' market in academic employment abruptly became a buyers' market in 1972. As a consequence, young scholars identified as radicals once again faced growing difficulties in being appointed, gaining renewal of their contracts, or getting tenure. The chairman of the CAUT's Academic Freedom and Tenure committee, A.E. Malloch, reported in 1972 that some professors were using budgetary cutbacks to undermine intellectual diversity: "The time has come ... when departments, by a delicate mixture of non-renewals and new appointments, can insure that no one teaches in the department unless he shares a particular orientation toward the discipline — defined by the voting majority of the department." This had implications beyond disciplinary orientation, of course. "To repeat the blunt question put to me last autumn by a departmental chairman: 'Yes, but how do I recognize a good radical sociologist when I see one?'" The CAUT believed that professors should have the major role in personnel decisions, Malloch continued. However, "if the procedures of the Policy Statement [on Appointments and Tenure (1967)] come to be used as a kind of formal orchestration of our ... intolerance or prejudices, then they will appear infinitely more mischievous than the naked authoritarianism of bad old deans and department heads."[112] Like Walt Kelly's Pogo, Malloch had "met the enemy, and he is us."

Three high-profile cases involving the alleged purging of political radicals occurred in the early and mid-1970s.[113] Two involved McGill. At the centre of one was the political scientist Pauline Vaillancourt, a Marxist, feminist, and Québec nationalist. Denied a renewal of her contract in 1972, she appealed the decision. A committee headed by the University of Toronto law professor David L. Johnston (later principal of McGill) identified several irregularities and inconsistencies in the department's handling of her file and recommended that she be given a further three-year contract. The board of governors accepted this recommendation, but Vaillancourt took a tenured appointment at the Université du Québec à Montréal instead.

The sociologist Marlene Dixon was also a Marxist. From the moment she joined the faculty of McGill she experienced heavy weather. Believing that most of her colleagues did not want to her to be tenured, she resigned in October 1974. Two years later she published *Things Which Are Done in Secret*, a book that

[112]A.E. Malloch, "Committee on Academic Freedom and Tenure: Annual Report," *CAUT Bulletin (CAUTB)* 21, 1 (October 1972), 7.
[113]Horn, *Academic Freedom in Canada*, 317-18.

expresses disdain for "value-free social science" and argues that the "liberal university" will not protect the academic freedom of radicals such as herself.[114]

At the centre of yet another controversy was a teacher of social work, Marlene Webber. A member of the Communist Party of Canada (Marxist-Leninist), she resigned from Renison College, an Anglican institution affiliated with the University of Waterloo, during her final year of a three-year contract, charging that its principal and board would not reappoint her because of her politics. Moving to the Memorial University of Newfoundland in 1976, she learned within three months of arriving there that her contract would not be renewed for 1977-78. A CAUT committee of inquiry chaired by the University of Toronto political theorist C.B. Macpherson found "that there had been a serious breach of academic freedom in that the university had based its non-renewal on the political activities of Professor Webber ... without providing admissible and cogent evidence that these ... constituted professional wrongdoing."[115] When Memorial would not agree to binding arbitration of the dispute, the CAUT in 1978 censured the president and board of regents. The censure remained in place for a decade.

* * *

In the early 1970s the situation changed because academic jobs suddenly ceased to be plentiful. With academic recruitment entering a slump from which it has not yet recovered, many candidates have sought to make themselves acceptable to hiring committees in a variety of ways. This has usually meant adopting current academic fashions and publishing articles and books intended to demonstrate that candidates are at "the cutting edge" of their disciplines. It has usually also meant avoiding social and political causes that have the potential of offending members of hiring committees. As a result political radicals have once again found it difficult to obtain appointments

Historically, the opinions of professors — overt and covert — have tended to cluster near the social and political centre. This seems to have changed little during the last 25 years. It is true that most of the academics who contribute conspicuously to public debate — David Bercuson, Michael Bliss, Barry Cooper, Tom Flanagan, to name a few — are identified with the political right. But that may say more about the preferences of the print media than about the political convictions of academics as a group. Those same media preferences make it hard for left-wing or pro-labour academics to get much exposure. Melville Watkins, as a left-wing economist a rare bird indeed, has retired. James Laxer, a political scientist who once ran for the NDP leadership, appeared regularly in the *Toronto Star* for several years, but his byline now is rarely seen. The *Star*, it should be added, is the only major newspaper in Canada not clearly identified with the right.

[114]Marlene Dixon, *Things which Are Done in Secret* (Montréal 1976), 273-81.
[115]Helen Baxter, "CAUT Board Votes to Censure Memorial," *CAUTB*, 25, 11 (December 1978), 1.

It does seems likely, however, that professors as a group (with many individual exceptions) have become somewhat more sympathetic to the claims of organized labour since the mid-1970s. The reason is that, starting in Québec in the early 1970s, Canadian academics have increasingly reorganized themselves into faculty unions, certified as bargaining units under the terms of provincial labour relations stat-utes.[116] In this respect they have a good deal in common with the experience of other public-sector employees since the 1960s. Except in Québec, however, faculty unions have been reluctant to affiliate with over-arching labour bodies, signalling a continuing ambivalence towards unionization or "blue collar" workers or both. Furthermore, at a few universities a majority of faculty members resist unionization, and minorities at unionized universities continue to oppose the step taken by their colleagues. All the same, even critics of unionization might agree that the proce-dures worked out by faculty unions to deal with tenure, promotion, and dismissal have made it impossible to discipline or dismiss anyone without showing cause. They have also made it difficult as never before for administrators or professors to expel "radicals" and other mavericks.

For many years universities were inhospitable places for people on the left, and professors by and large took little notice of organized labour. It would be going too far to say that, at the beginning of the 21st century, we have entered a golden age of academic tolerance for radicals, or that the labour movement enjoys much support in the groves of academe. Yet it is true that the academic environment is more tolerant of leftists than in the past, and the word "unionization" does not arouse the hostility it once did.

Might W.H. Alexander's advice to a young man contemplating an academic career today be more encouraging than in 1939? A bit more, perhaps, but surely not much. It may be easier for leftists to survive in academe, but they seem to have little impact within the university or beyond it. One looks in vain for today's equivalents of those professors who tested the limits of academic free speech in the inter-war years, advocating social democracy and labour's right to organize. Even academics who locate themselves on the left seem to be saying little in an age in which neoliberalism is close to being the dominant ideology. Perhaps they seek to have no influence beyond that which is achieved by their scholarship. If so, it has been all too easy for the media to trivialize or ignore them. The universities and, indeed, Canadian society, face huge challenges from those for whom the mantra "private is good, public is bad" has the force of revealed truth, who exalt the "free market," who glorify the pursuit of self-interest. Those who do not share the neo-liberal dogma, and that must include everybody on the left, would do well to speak out in defence of what they value.

[116]Michiel Horn, "Unionization and the Canadian University: Historical and Personal Observations," *Interchange*, 25, 1 (1994), 39-48.

ABSTRACTS / RÉSUMÉS

Some Millennial Reflections on the State of Canadian Labour History

Desmond Morton

THE SURPRISE of being invited to comment on the state of Canadian labour history was exceeded by the honour. The explosive early growth of the field in the 1970s, and its domination by the team that created *Labour/Le Travail*, has concealed stasis and even a decline in the past decade, as a harsh economic climate sent the paths of the labour movement and of younger historians in unexpected directions. Historians who believed they got closer to the present by understanding the past might reflect on misjudgments as well as successes.

LA SURPRISE d'être invité à donner des commentaires sur l'histoire de la classe ouvrière canadienne été dépassée par l'honneur. Le domaine était en pleine crois-sance au début des années 1970, et sa domination par l'équipe qui a créé *Labour/Le Travail*, a caché la stase et même un déclin au cours de la dernière décennie, en même temps qu'un climat économique féroce envoyait les chemins du mouvement syndical et des jeunes historiens dans des directions imprévues. Les historiens qui croyaient se rapprocher du présent en comprenant le passé pourraient réfléchir sur les jugements mal fondés ainsi que sur les oeuvres réussies.

Industrial Relations at the Millennium: Beyond Employment?

Anthony Giles

THIS ESSAY EXPLORES the current state of the field of Industrial Relations. The first part of the essay traces the emergence of IR out of the general concern with the "labour question" to form a distinct field of study and research in the Anglo-American countries. The second part argues that the field has been plagued by a profound crisis of relevance in the 1980s and 1990s, registered by a decline in its importance within universities, a shrinking of its academic associations, a loss of interest on the part of its traditional audience, increased isolation from other disciplines, and a theoretical incapacity to come to grips with the sweeping changes that have occurred in labour markets, the workplace, and the wider political economy. This situation is leading to a redefinition of the field as "Employment Relations." In the third part of the essay, this drift towards Employment Relations is criticized for moving the field more squarely into the area of managerial science, for leaving it incapable of analyzing future waves of collective mobilization, and for its continued adherence to a geographically and historically constricted conceptual foundation. A better strategy, it is suggested, would be to go beyond employment by reconceptualizing the field in terms of "work relations."

CET ARTICLE PERMET D'EXPLORER la situation actuelle des relations industrielles. La première partie de l'article trace l'émergence des relations industrielles à partir du problème général de la « question du travail » pour former un domaine distinct des études et de la recherche dans les pays anglo-américains. La deuxième partie présente l'argument selon lequel le domaine a été touché par une crise profonde de pertinence dans les années 1980 et 1990, caractérisé par un déclin de son importance au sein des universités, une réduction des associations académiques, une perte d'intérêt de la part de son auditoire traditionnel, un isolement accru des autres disciplines et une incapacité théorique de confronter les changements importants qui se sont produits sur le marché du travail, en milieu de travail et dans l'économie politique en général. Cette situation mène à une nouvelle définition du domaine des « relations de l'emploi ». Dans la troisième partie de l'article, cette tendance vers les relations de l'emploi est critiquée pour avoir déplacé le domaine vers celui de la science de la gestion, pour avoir donné lieu à l'incapacité d'analyser les prochaines vagues de mobilisation collective et pour avoir continué à respecter une fondation conceptuelle géographiquement et historiquement restreinte. Une meilleure stratégie, serait d'aller au-delà de l'emploi en reconceptualisant le domaine en termes de « relations du travail ».

For a New Kind of History: A Reconnaissance of 100 Years of Canadian Socialism

Ian McKay

THE TURN OF THE MILLENNIUM also marks the centenary of Canadian socialism, dated from 1901 (the first free-standing country-wide organization) or 1905 (the formation of the first electorally successful socialist party). By probing the logic and rhetoric of key texts from the Canadian socialist movement, we can discern four distinct formations — evolutionary science, revolutionary praxis, national state management, and revolutionary humanism and national liberation — in a history marked throughout by a hegemonic liberal order. These strategies are worth careful, sympathetic, and critical study as socialist movements regroup in the 21st century.

LE NOUVEAU MILLÉNAIRE marque aussi le centenaire du socialisme canadien, daté de 1901 (le premier organisme national indépendant) ou 1905 (la formation du premier parti socialiste qui a réussi au scrutin). En explorant la logique et la rhétorique des textes principaux du mouvement socialiste canadien, nous pouvons faire la distinction entre quatre formations différentes — la science évolutionnaire, la praxis révolutionnaire, la gestion de l'État, et l'humanisme révolutionnaire et la libération nationale — dans une histoire marquée partout par un ordre libéral hégémonique. Ces stratégies méritent d'être étudiées de façon soigneuse, sympathique et critique à mesure que les mouvements socialistes se regroupent au cours du vingt et unième siècle.

Feminism and the Making of Canadian Working-Class History: Exploring the Past, Present and Future

Joan Sangster

THIS PAPER EXPLORES the writing of women's labour history in Canada over the last thirty years. Three interconnected forces have shaped the contours of this intellectual production: the course of feminist, Left, and labour organizing; trends in international social theory; and directions in Canadian historiography. Feminist challenges to the initially 'masculinist' shape of working-class history, along with more recent calls to integrate race and ethnicity as categories of analysis, have produced important shifts in the overall narrative of Canadian working-class history and in the dominant paradigms used to examine labour. As a result, gender has been more effectively, though certainly not completely, integrated into our analysis of class formation. More recent post-structuralist theoretical trends, along with the decline of the Left and labour militancy, have called into question some fundamental suppositions of women's and working-class history, creating an unsettled and uncertain future for a feminist and materialist exposition of class formation in Canada.

CET ARTICLE PERMET D'EXPLORER l'histoire de la femme au travail au Canada au cours des trente dernières années. Trois forces interconnectées ont façonné les contours de cette production intellectuelle : le dévelopement du féminisme, l'organisation de la classe ouvrière; les tendances dans la théorie sociale internationale; ainsi que les directions dans l'historiographie canadienne. Les contestations féministes à la structuration initialement « masculine » de l'histoire de la classe ouvrière, accompagnée des appels récents en faveur d'intégrer la race et l'ethnie comme catégories d'analyse, ont produit des changements importants dans la rédaction générale de l'histoire de la classe ouvrière canadienne et dans les paradigmes dominants utilisés pour examiner la classe ouvrière. En conséquence, le genre a été intégré de façon plus efficace dans notre analyse de la formation de la classe, bien que cette intégration ne soit ni certaine ni complète. Les tendances théoriques poststructuralistes les plus récentes, accompagnées du déclin de l'état militant de la classe ouvrière, mettent en question quelques suppositions fondamentales de l'histoire de la femme et de la classe ouvrière, donnant un avenir incertain de l'exposition féministe et matérialiste de la formation de la classe ouvrière au Canada.

"The History of Us": Social Science, History, and the Relations of Family in Canada

Cynthia Comacchio

THIS ESSAY PROVIDES a selective overview of the Canadian historiography on family. The roots of family history not only extend backwards much further than the "new social history" born of the tumultuous 1960s, they are buried deep in several other disciplines, most notably sociology, anthropology, and demography, whose practitioners were concerned as much with the historical process of family change as with the state of families contemporary to their times. I consider how pioneering social scientists, by grappling with the family's relationship to structural change, historicized early 20th century family studies and offered up many of the questions, concepts, theories, and methods that continue to inform historical scholarship on families. Turning to the body of historical publications that followed in the wake of, and were often inspired by, the "new social history," I highlight the monograph studies that served as signposts in the field's development, especially for what they have revealed about the critical nexus of family, work, and class. The historiography mirrors the family's history: "family" consists of so many intricately plaited strands that separating them out is frustrating and often futile. I have attempted to classify this material both topically and chronologically within broad categories, but the boundaries blur so that most of these works could fit as comfortably in several others. Many of them, in fact, will be recognized as important contributions to fields such as labour, ethnic, women's, or gender history rather than as works of family history *per se*.

CET ARTICLE DONNE un aperçu de l'historiographie canadienne sur la famille. Les racines de l'histoire de la famille non seulement reviennent en arrière beaucoup plus que la « nouvelle histoire sociale » née des années 1960, elles sont enterrées en profondeur dans plusieurs autres disciplines, notamment la sociologie, l'anthro- pologie et la démographie, dont les praticiens se préoccupaient du processus historique des changements de la famille ainsi que de la situation actuelle des familles contemporaines. Je considère comment les scientistes sociaux avant- gardistes, en étudiant les relations de la famille avec les changements structuraux, ont inclus dans notre histoire les études de la famille du 20e siècle et présenté de nombreux concepts, questions, théories et méthodes qui continuent à renseigner les chercheurs historiens sur les familles. En ce qui concerne les publications historiques qui ont suivi, la plupart étaient souvent inspirées par la « nouvelle histoire sociale ». Je tiens à souligner les études monographiques qui ont servi de points de repère dans le domaine du développement du champ, en particulier en ce qui a trait aux critiques essentielles de la famille, du travail et de la classe. L'historiographie reflète l'histoire de la famille dont la notion consiste en nombreuses subtilités qui séparent les unes des autres est souvent frustrante et inutile. J'ai essayé de classifier ce matériel à la fois topique et chronologique dans des catégories plus grandes, mais les limites se chevauchent et la plupart des oeuvres peuvent s'intégrer dans plusieurs catégories en même temps. En réalité, beaucoup de ces oeuvres seront reconnues comme des contributions importantes aux domaines divers tels que le travail, l'ethnie, la femme ou l'histoire du genre plutôt que comme des oeuvres de l'histoire de la famille uniquement.

Bumping and Grinding On the Line: Making Nudity Pay

THIS PAPER INVITES labour and queer historians and sociologists to reconsider frameworks that have excluded attention to experiences of female workers who, throughout the 20th century, supplied sexual services to (largely) male consumers. Specifically, Vancouver, BC, 1945-1980, acts as a case study for the exploration of postwar erotic entertainment — burlesque, go-go dancing, and striptease. Preliminary archival and ethnographic findings reveal the working conditions and artistic influences of former dancers, the racialized expectations of erotic spectacle, and the queer dimensions of strip culture. Adored and celebrated by fans, stripteasers also laboured under the 'whore stigma' circulated by moral reformers, the popular press, and the police. It is this tension between the reverence and the hostility aroused by erotic dancers that forms a central theme of the paper.

CET ARTICLE INVITE les historiens et les sociologues qui s'intéressent à la classe ouvrière et à la communauté homosexuelle à prendre en considération les structures qui ont exclu l'attention portée aux expériences des travailleur(se)s qui, au cours du vingtième siècle, ont fourni des services sexuels aux consommateurs, hommes dans la plupart des cas. Plus précisément, Vancouver, C.B., 1945-1980, est un cas d'étude pour l'exploration du spectacle érotique après la guerre — le burlesque, la danse à-go-go et le strip-tease. Les archives préliminaires et les résultats ethnographiques révèlent les conditions de travail et les influences artistiques des ancien(ne)s danseur(se)s, les attentes de nature raciale du spectacle érotique et les dimensions homosexuelles de la culture du strip-tease. Adorés et célébrés par les admirateur(ice)s, les strip-teaseur(se)s ont aussi travaillé sous le stigmate de la prostitution signalé par les réformateurs moralistes, la presse populaire et la police. C'est sur cette tension qui existe entre la révérence et l'hostilité engendrée par les danseur(se)s érotiques sur que se base le thème principal de cet article.

Pluralism or Fragmentation?: The Twentieth-Century Employment Law Regime in Canada

Judy Fudge and Eric Tucker

IN 1947, BORA LASKIN, the doyen of Canadian collective bargaining law, remarked that "Labour relations as a matter for legal study ... has outgrown any confinement to a section of the law of torts or to a corner of the criminal law. Similarly, and from another standpoint, it has burst the narrow bounds of master and servant." That standpoint was liberal pluralism, which comprises collective bargaining legislation administered by independent labour boards and a system of grievance arbitration to enforce collective agreements. After World War II, it came to dominate our understanding of labour relations law such that, according to Laskin, reference to "pre-collective bargaining standards is an attempt to re-enter a world that has ceased to exist." But this picture is only partially true. Instead of replacing earlier regimes of industrial legality, industrial pluralism was grafted on to them. Moreover, it only encompassed a narrow, albeit crucial, segment of workers; in the mid-1950s "the typical union member was a relatively settled, semi-skilled male worker within a large industrial corporation." More than 65 per cent of Canadian workers at that time, a large proportion of whom were women and recent immigrants, fell outside the regime. This paper broadens the focus from collective bargaining law to include other forms of the legal regulation of employment relations, such as the common law, minimum standards, and equity legislation. In doing so, it examines the extent to which liberal pluralism regime was implicated in constructing and reinforcing a deeply segmented labour market in Canada. It also probes whether the recent assault on trade union rights may be the trajectory for the reconstruction of a new regime of employment relations.

EN 1947, BORA LASKIN, le doyen de la Loi canadienne sur la négociation collective, a remarqué que « les relations de travail en tant qu'étude juridique ... ont dépassé toute contrainte d'une section de la loi ou du droit criminel. D'une manière similaire, mais d'un autre point de vue, elles ont aussi dépassé les rôles traditionnels que jouent le maître et le serviteur. » Ce point de vue fait partie du pluralisme libéral, qui comprend la législation de la négociation collective administrée par des conseils du travail indépendants et un système de règlement des griefs par voie d'arbitrage pour faire valoir les conventions collectives. Après la Deuxième Guerre Mondiale, notre compréhension de la loi sur les relations de travail a été dominée, selon Laskin, par la référence aux « normes de négociation collective préalable comme un essai de rentrer dans un monde qui a cessé d'exister. » Mais cette représentation ne montre que partiellement la vérité. Au lieu de remplacer les anciens régimes de la loi industrielle, le pluralisme industriel s'y est imposé. De plus, il ne comprend qu'un segment étroit et crucial de travailleurs; dans les années 1950 « le membre du syndicat typique était un travailleur de sexe masculin ayant des compétences relativement médiocres dans une corporation industrielle relativement grande. » Plus de 65 p. 100 des travailleurs canadiens à ce moment-là, dont une grande proportion des femmes et des immigrants récents, tombent en dehors du régime. Cet article met davantage l'accent sur la loi de la négociation collective pour inclure d'autres règlements relatifs aux relations de travail, tels que le droit commun, les normes minimales et la législation relative à l'équité en matière d'emploi. De ce fait, il examine jusqu'à quel point le régime du pluralisme libéral était impliqué dans la construction et le renforcement d'un marché du travail profondément segmenté au Canada. Il met aussi en question le faitque l'assaut récent aux droits des syndicats peut être la trajectoire pour la reconstruction d'un nouveau régime de relations en matière d'emploi.

La grève de l'amiante de 1949 et le projet de réforme de l'entreprise. Comment le patronat a défendu son droit de gérance

Jacques Rouillard

LA GRÈVE DE L'AMIANTE de 1949 est certes le conflit qui a le plus marqué la conscience historique des Québécois. Depuis la publication en 1956 du volume sur la grève dirigé par Pierre Elliott Trudeau, le conflit est interprété comme un événement capital dans l'histoire sociale du Québec. À partir d'une recherche neuve dans divers fonds d'archives, nous en avons revu l'interprétation en faisant ressortir que le conflit représente une défaite assez cuisante des syndicats, qui aurait pu encore être plus désastreuse n'eut été l'aide du clergé. En outre, notre recherche nous a permis de mettre en relief un enjeu négligé de la grève, le projet de réforme de l'entreprise (cogestion, copropriété, participation aux bénéfices) mis de l'avant par de jeunes clercs qui reprennent des idées alors en vogue chez des intellectuels catholiques en Europe et qui trouvent une oreille sympathique chez certains évêques québécois. Cette revendication est reprise par des syndicats catholiques au Québec dont ceux de l'amiante en 1948 et 1949. Les compagnies minières y sont fermement opposées accusant les syndicats de vouloir s'arroger les droits de la direction et la Canadian Johns Manville insiste pour ajouter à la convention collective de 1950 un long paragraphe sur son droit de gérance. La question intéresse aussi vivement un organisme patronal, l'Association professionnelle des industriels fondée en 1943 pour regrouper les patrons catholiques. L'organisme combat vivement l'idée de cogestion auprès des autorités religieuses. Mais le dernier mot appartient au pape qui, en 1950, y voit un danger et un glissement vers une mentalité socialiste. La promotion de la réforme de l'entreprise est alors abandonnée par les clercs et mis en veilleuse par les syndicats catholiques.

THE ASBESTOS STRIKE of 1949 is without a doubt the labour conflict which has most deeply marked Québec's historical consciousness. Since the 1956 publication of a volume on the strike, edited by Pierre Elliott Trudeau, the conflict has been interpreted as a success and a signal event in the social history of Québec. New research in various archival collections, however, leads us to revise this interpretation and to argue that the conflict was a serious defeat for the unions, and could have been even worse had it not been for the help of the clergy. In addition, our research highlights a neglected aspect of the strike — the project of enterprise reform (co-management, co-ownership, profit-sharing) brought forward by young clerics enamoured of ideas popular among Catholic intellectuals in Europe and who had found a sympathetic ear with certain Quebec bishops. These demands were taken up in turn by Catholic unions in Quebec, including the asbestos unions in 1948 and 1949. The mining companies were strongly opposed, and accused the unions of attempting to infringe on management rights. The Canadian Johns Manville Company insisted on adding a long paragraph on management rights to the collective bargaining agreement of 1950. The question was of interest as well to l'Association professionnelle des industriels, an employers' organisation founded in 1943 to bring together Catholic employers. This organisation fought strongly against the idea of co-management, complaining to religious authorities. But the final word belonged to the Pope who, in 1950, saw a danger of a slide toward socialist ideas. The promotion of enterprise reform was then abandoned by the clergy and back-burnered by the Catholic unions.

Political Economy and the Canadian Working Class: Marxism or Nationalist Reformism?

Murray E.G. Smith

THE DOMINANT, NATIONALIST TRADITION of left-wing political economy in Canada has always stood as an obstacle to the articulation of a Marxist political economy of Canada capable of contributing to the development of a class-struggle, socialist politics. The evolution of the "New Canadian Political Economy" that emerged in the 1960s is traced and its main schools of thought are delineated. Against the nationalist preoccupations of the NCPE, the argument is made that the economic troubles of Canada in the past quarter century are attributable to the "normal" crisis tendencies of an advanced capitalist economy (as analyzed by Marx) and should not be seen as the product of "foreign domination" of the Canadian economy.

LA TRADITION NATIONALISTE DOMINANTE de l'économie politique de gauche au Canada a toujours été un obstacle à l'articulation d'une économie politique marxiste du Canada capable de contribuer au développement de la politique socialiste de la luttre des classes. L'évolution de la « nouvelle économie politique canadienne » qui a émergé dans les années 1960 est tracée et les principales écoles de pensée sont exposées. Contre les préoccupations nationalistes de la nouvelle économie politique canadienne, on présente l'argument que les problèmes économiques du Canada dans les vingt-cinq dernières années peuvent être attribués aux tendances de crise « normales » d'une économie capitaliste avancée (telle qu'elle est analysée par Marx) et ne devraient pas être vus comme le produit de la « domination étrangère » de l'économie canadienne.

"Rapprocher les lieux du pouvoir": The Québec Labour Movement and Québec Sovereigntism, 1960-2000

Ralph P. Güntzel

THE ARTICLE EXAMINES the evolution of the positions Québec's three major trade union centrals — the Fédération des travailleurs et travilleuses du Québec (FTQ), the Centrale des syndicats nationaux (CSN), and the Centrale des syndicats du Québec (CSQ) — have taken on the question of Québec sovereignty since 1960. In the course of the four decades since the emergence of the modern sovereigntist movement, the three centrals adopted increasingly sympathetic attitudes toward sovereigntism and eventually became stalwarts of the sovereigntist coalition. In the process Québec labour activists shed their fears about the economic repercussions of sovereignty and espoused the notion of a sovereign Québec nation-state mainly because they came to perceive it as a tool to improve conditions for implementing social-democratic and labour-oriented policies.

CET ARTICLE EXAMINE l'évolution des positions des trois principaux syndicats du Québec — la Fédération des travailleurs et travailleuses du Québec (FTQ), la Centrale des syndicats nationaux (CSN) et la Centrale des syndicats du Québec (CSQ) — par rapport à la question de la souveraineté du Québec depuis 1960. Au cours des quatre décennies, depuis le début du mouvement souverainiste moderne, les trois syndicats ont adopté graduellement des attitudes sympathiques vis-à-vis de la cause souverainiste et sont devenus éventuellement les piliers de la coalition souverainiste. En même temps, les syndicalistes québécois se sont débarrassés de leur peur des répercussions économiques de la souveraineté pour défendre la cause d'un pays indépendant du Québec principalement parce qu'ils le voient comme un outil pour améliorer les les conditions de la mise en oeuvre des politiques socio-démocratiques axées sur la classe ouvrière.

Short Takes:
The Canadian Worker on Film

David Frank

IS THERE A CANADIAN LABOUR FILM? After a century of film production in Canada, the answer is uncertain. Canadian workers do appear in a variety of documentary and feature film productions, but their presence often arises from the incidental processes of documentation and fictionalization. There is also a more purposeful body of work focused on the concerns of labour history, but its promise remains relatively underdeveloped. Although film has become one of the dominant languages of communications at the end of the 20th century, the practice of visual history stands to benefit from closer collaboration between historians and filmmakers.

Y-A-T'IL UN FILM SUR LA CLASSE OUVRIÈRE CANADIENNE? Après un siècle de réalisation de films au Canada, la réponse est incertaine. Les travailleurs canadiens figurent en effet dans une variété de documentaires et de grands films, mais leur présence fait souvent partie d'un processus annexe ou secondaire de documentation et de fiction. Il existe aussi des oeuvres dont l'objectif est de se concentrer sur l'histoire de la classe ouvrière, mais la mise en valeur de ces films reste relativement insuffisante. Alors que le film est devenu l'un des langages de communication les plus importants à la fin du 20e siècle, l'histoire visuelle pourra certainement bénéficier de la collaboration étroite entre les historiens et les cinéastes.

Canadian Universities, Academic Freedom, Labour, and the Left

Michiel Horn

DURING MOST OF THEIR HISTORY, Canadian universities, institutions staffed by and serving largely middle class people, have not been hospitable to organized labour or the political left. Professors who expressed support for such causes generally found that doing so often strained the limits of academic freedom as it was understood by governing boards, administrators, a good many academics, and many people outside the institutions. If the situation has improved during the last three decades, one reason is that faculty unions have become commonplace. More important, however, may be that the outside world has come to pay less attention to what professors say, on almost any subject, than used to be the case.

DEPUIS LE DÉBUT DE LEUR HISTOIRE, la plupart des universités, établissements académiques canadiens dotés du personnel de la classe moyenne qui s'occupe des gens de la même classe, ne sont pas accueillants vis-à-vis de la syndicalisation ou de la gauche. Les professeurs qui se sont prononcés sur ces causes ont trouvé qu'en général, en le faisant, ils risquent de mettre en danger la liberté académique telle qu'elle est comprise par les conseils de gestion, les administrateurs, un bon nombre d'universitaires et beaucoup d'autres en dehors des établissements scolaires. Si la situation s'est améliorée au cours des trois dernières décennies, c'est parce que la syndicalisation du personnel académique est devenue plus courante. Ce qui est plus important, toutefois, c'est que peut-être le monde extérieur prête moins d'attention à ce que disent les professeurs, sur n'importe quel sujet, comme c'était le cas dans le passé.

Eugene A. Forsey Prize in Canadian Labour and Working-Class History

Thanks to an anonymous donor, the Canadian Committee on Labour History (CCLH) is pleased to announce the fourth Eugene A. Forsey Prize competition. The CCLH, with the consent of the late Dr. Forsey's family, chose to name it in his honour because of his pioneering work in the field of Canadian labour history. Dr. Forsey, Research Director of the Canadian Congress of Labour and later the Canadian Labour Congress, also served on the committee which founded *Labour/Le Travail*.

The CCLH invites submissions for the fourth Forsey prize competition for graduate and undergraduate work on Canadian labour and working class history.

Three prizes are awarded annually: two prizes of $250 each for the best undergraduate essays, or their equivalents, written in the academic year 1999-2000, and one prize of $500 for the best graduate thesis completed in the past three years. Separate committees, established by the executive of the CCLH, will award the prizes.

The committees, like *Labour/Le Travail* itself, intend to interpret widely the definition of Canadian labour and working-class history. Undergraduate essays may be nominated by course instructors, but nominators are limited to one essay per competition. Additionally, authors may submit their own work. Essays not written at a university or college may be considered for the undergraduate awards.

For the graduate prize, supervisors may nominate one thesis per competition or an author of a thesis may submit a copy. Submissions of both MA and PhD theses are welcome. Theses defended on or after 1 May 1998 are eligible for consideration in the initial competition.

The deadline for submissions is 1 June 2001. Prizes will be announced in the Fall 2000 issue of *Labour/Le Travail*. Four copies of essays and one copy of a thesis must be submitted for consideration to Forsey Prize, Canadian Committee on Labour History, Department of History, Memorial University of Newfoundland, St. John's, NF A1C 5S7.

2000 Forsey Prize Winners

Graduate

Marcus Klee, "Between the Scylla and Charybdis of Anarchy and Depotism: The State, Capital and the Working Class in the Great Depression, Toronto, 1929-1940," Ph.D., Queen's University, (Sept.) 1998.

Undergraduate

Juanita Nolan, "Vancouver Trade and Industrial Unionists in Conflict: Baking Bread and Battling Capitalism in 1903 British Columbia," Simon Fraser University.

Allison Howell, "Retail Unionisation: A Historical Approach to the Suzy Shier Case," Trent University.

CANADIAN COMMITTEE ON LABOUR HISTORY

JOURNAL

Labour/Le Travail is the official publication of the Canadian Committee on Labour History. Since it began publishing in 1976, it has carried many important articles in the field of working-class history, industrial sociology, labour economics, and labour relations. Although primarily interested in a historical perspective on Canadian workers, the journal features documents, conference reports, an annual bibliography of materials in Canadian labour studies, review essays, and reviews. While the main focus of the journal's articles is Canada, the review essays and reviews consider international work of interest to Canadian labour studies. Many of *Labour/Le Travail*'s articles are illustrated and each issue is book length, averaging 350+ pages.

SUBSCRIPTION RATES: Canada *(Foreign)*
Individual—1 Year $25 *($30 US)*; 2 Years $45 *($55 US)*; 3 Years $60 *($75 US)*
Institutional—1 Year $35 *($50 US)*; 2 Years $60 *($90 US)*
Student/Retired/Unemployed—1 Year $15 *($25 US)*; 4 Years $50 *($90 US)*

PRESENT SPECIAL ISSUE: "Labour Confronts The Millennium"

As Canadian workers, the labour movement, and scholars confront a new millennium, new opportunities and new challenges loom large. *Labour/Le Travail* has commissioned a number of articles addressing themes that will be of consequence as we enter the 21st century. The articles that will appear in our Fall 2000 issue are authored by some of the more prominent social scientists working in the field of labour-related studies, among them Desmond Morton, Ian McKay, Joan Sangster, Cynthia Comacchio, David Frank, and Jacques Rouillard. Their writing appears in our special Millennium issue, grouped in a series of thematic sections: institutions and ideas; gender, sexuality, and family; Quebec and the national question; culture; and workers and the state. Topics such as Canadian socialism, pivotal events such as the 1949 Asbestos strike, and important cultural undertakings, such as working-class representations on film and video, are addressed. Historiographical controversies and debates associated with the relations of women's and working-class histories or different generational styles associated with the presentation of labour's past are surveyed. This is an issue all interested in Canadian society and its development will not want to miss.

Send orders with payments to **Labour/Le Travail**,
c/o Faculty of Arts Publications, FM 2005, Memorial University,
St. John's, Newfoundland, CANADA, A1C 5S7 (All foreign orders, please remit in US dollars.)
Telephone: (709) 737-2144, Facsimile: (709) 737-4342
For more information, visit our web site: http//www.mun.ca/cclh/

AGMV Marquis

MEMBER OF THE SCABRINI GROUP

Quebec, Canada
2001